WHITMAN COLLEGE LIBRARY

A HISTORY OF
INDIA

Withdrawn by
Whitman Colle~~

D0789442

The Blackwell History of the World

General Editor: **R. I. Moore**

Published

A History of Latin America
Peter Bakewell

A History of India
Burton Stein

In Preparation

Elements of World History
R. I. Moore

The Beginnings of Civilization
Robert Wenke

A History of the Middle East
David Morgan

A History of the Mediterranean
World
David Abulafia

A History of China
Morris Rossabi

A History of Australia, New Zealand
and the Pacific
Donald Denoon

The Birth of the Modern World
C. A. Bayly

The Origins of Human Society
Peter Bogucki

A History of Africa
Paul Lovejoy

A History of the Classical West
Ian Morris

A History of Russia and Central Asia
David Christian

A History of South-East Asia
Anthony Reid

A History of Japan
Conrad Totman

The Early Modern World
Sanjay Subrahmanyam

WHITMAN COLLEGE LIBRARY

A HISTORY OF
INDIA

BURTON STEIN

DS
407
.S82
1998

Copyright © the estate of Burton Stein, 1998

The right of Burton Stein to be identified as author of this work has been asserted in accordance with the Copyright, Designs and Patents Act 1988.

First published 1998

2 4 6 8 10 9 7 5 3 1

Blackwell Publishers Ltd
108 Cowley Road
Oxford OX4 1JF
UK

Blackwell Publishers Inc.
350 Main Street
Malden, Massachusetts 02148
USA

All rights reserved. Except for the quotation of short passages for the purposes of criticism and review, no part of this publication may be reproduced, stored in a retrieval system, or transmitted, in any form or by any means, electronic, mechanical, photocopying, recording or otherwise, without the prior permission of the publisher.

Except in the United States of America, this book is sold subject to the condition that it shall not, by way of trade or otherwise, be lent, resold, hired out, or otherwise circulated without the publisher's prior consent in any form of binding or cover other than that in which it is published and without a similar condition including this condition being imposed on the subsequent purchaser.

Library of Congress Cataloging-in-Publication Data

Stein, Burton, 1926–
    A history of India / Burton Stein.
        p.   cm. — (Blackwell History of the world)
    Includes bibliographical references and index.
    ISBN 0-631-17899-6. — ISBN 0-631-20546-2
    1. India–History. I. Title. II. Series.
DS407.S82   1998
954—dc21   97-37370
                                                                                        CIP

Commissioning Editor: Tessa Harvey
Desk Editor: John Taylor
Production Controller: Emma Gotch

British Library Cataloguing in Publication Data
A CIP catalogue record for this book is available from the British Library.

Typeset in 10 on 12 pt Plantin
by Best-set Typesetter Ltd., Hong Kong
Printed in Great Britain by TJ Press International, Padstow, Cornwall.
This book is printed on acid-free paper

CONTENTS

Whitman College
Library

AUG 1 1 '98

99-1099

Acquisitions Dept.

AUG 1 4 1998

PENROSE MEMORIAL LIBRARY
WHITMAN COLLEGE
WALLA WALLA, WASHINGTON 99362

ILLUSTRATIONS

MAPS

SERIES EDITOR'S PREFACE

THERE is nothing new in the attempt to understand history as a whole. To know how humanity began and how it has come to its present condition is one of the oldest and most universal of human needs, expressed in the religious and philosophical systems of every civilization. But only in the last few decades has it begun to appear both necessary and possible to meet that need by means of a rational and systematic appraisal of current knowledge. History claimed its independence as a field of scholarship with its own subject matter and its own rules and methods, not simply a branch of literature, rhetoric, law, philosophy or religion, in the second half of the nineteenth century. World history has begun to do so only in the second half of the twentieth. Its emergence has been delayed on the one hand by simple ignorance – for the history of enormous stretches of space and time has been known not at all, or so patchily and superficially as not to be worth revisiting – and on the other by the lack of a widely acceptable basis upon which to organize and discuss what is nevertheless the enormous and enormously diverse knowledge that we have.

Both obstacles are now being rapidly overcome. There is almost no part of the world or period of its history that is not the subject of vigorous and sophisticated investigation by archaeologists and historians. It is truer than it has ever been that knowledge is growing and perspectives changing and multiplying more quickly than it is possible to assimilate and record them in synthetic form. Nevertheless the attempt to grasp the human past as a whole can and must be made. Facing a common future of headlong and potentially catastrophic transformation, the world needs its common history. Since we no longer believe that a complete or definitive account is ultimately attainable by the mere accumulation of knowledge we are free to offer the best we can manage at the moment. Since we no longer suppose that it is our business as historians to detect or proclaim 'The End of History' in the fruition of any grand design, human or divine, there is no single path to trace, or golden key to turn. There is also a growing wealth of ways in which world history can be written. The oldest and simplest view, that world history is best understood as the history of contacts between peoples previously isolated from one another, from which (some think) all change arises, is now seen to be capable of application since the earliest times. An influential alternative focuses upon the tendency of economic exchanges to create self-sufficient but ever expanding 'worlds' which sustain successive systems of power and culture. Others seek to understand the differences between societies and cultures, and therefore the particular character of each, by comparing the ways in which they have developed their values, social relationships and structures of power. The rapidly developing field of ecological history returns to a very ancient tradition of seeing interaction with the physical environment, and with other animals, at the centre of the human predicament, while insisting that its understanding demands an approach which is culturally, chronologically and geographically comprehensive.

The *Blackwell History of the World* does not seek to embody any of these approaches, but to support them all, as it will use them all, by providing a modern, comprehensive and accessible account of the entire human past. Its plan is that of a barrel, in which the indispensable narratives of very long term regional development are bound together by global surveys of the interaction between regions at particular times, and of the great transformations which they have experienced in common, or visited upon one another. Each volume, of course, reflects the idiosyncrasies of its sources and its subjects, as well as the judgement and experience of its author, but in combination they offer a framework in which the history of every part of the world can be viewed, and a basis upon which most aspects of human activity can be compared. A frame imparts perspective. Comparison implies respect for difference. That is the beginning of what the past has to offer the future.

A History of India lacks an author's introduction. Burton Stein died in April 1996, leaving a manuscript that was almost, but not quite, finished. The Series Editor and publisher are deeply grateful to Dorothy Stein, David Washbrook and Sanjay Subrahmanyam for completing and checking Stein's manuscript and seeing it through the press. This is therefore the last book, as well as the only comprehensive synthesis, of one of India's most original and influential historians in modern times. Burton Stein was born in Chicago in 1926 and, after service in the Second World War, studied at the University of Illinois (Chicago) and the University of Chicago, where he completed his PhD in 1957. He taught at the Universities of Minnesota (1957–65) and Hawaii (1966–83) and retired to London, where he was a Professorial Research Associate of the School of Oriental and African Studies. An appraisal of Burton Stein's methods as an historian and his unique contribution to Indian history will be found in the epitaph to this volume.

R. I. Moore

SERIES EDITOR'S ACKNOWLEDGEMENTS

The Editor is grateful to all of the contributors to the *Blackwell History of the World* for advice and assistance on the design and contents of the series as a whole as well as on individual volumes. Both Editor and Contributors wish to place on record their immense debt, individually and collectively, to John Davey, formerly of Blackwell Publishers. The series would not have been initiated without his vision and enthusiasm, and could not have been realised without his energy, skill and diplomacy.

ACKNOWLEDGEMENTS

WHEN the author of a book has died before completing his work, those to whom this task has fallen are doubly indebted to the many scholars and experts who so generously contribute their time, labour and knowledge to assist them. In addition to the unknown colleagues and students who, over the years, read the early drafts and discussed his ideas with the author, in this instance, therefore, heartfelt thanks and appreciation must go to Champakka Lakshmi, Indrani Chatterjee, Sumit Guha, David Kellogg, R. I. Moore, Harbans Mukhia, Joseph E. Schwartzberg and Romila Thapar, who answered questions, read the text, in part or in whole, and/or made detailed comments and suggestions as to both style and contents.

For assistance with the illustrations, we are indebted to Vivek Nanda, Richard Blurton, K. Gajendran, Rod Hamilton, Harald Lechenperg, George Michell, Divia Patel, N. Ram and Deborah Swallow. Joseph Schwartzberg designed the maps, which were executed by Philip A. Schwartzberg of Meridian Mapping. For contributions to the suggestions for further reading we are indebted to Sumit Guha, Barbara Harriss-White, David Ludden, George Michell and Harbans Mukhia and Frits Staal. And, finally, an unusual debt of gratitude is owed the staff of Blackwell Publishers, who commissioned this work, provided unstinting and sympathetic guidance, and patiently bore with the unavoidable delays: John Davey, Emma Gotch, Tessa Harvey, Leanda Shrimpton, John Taylor and no doubt others whose identity we do not know. At this point, it is customary to remind the reader that responsibility for any remaining errors and infelicities belongs to the author, but in this case it must inevitably be divided with the editors.

Dorothy Stein
Sanjay Subrahmanyam
David A. Washbrook
London, 1997

NOTE ON THE MAPS AND SPELLING

THE maps in this book are intended both to complement and to supplement the text. The reader will find virtually all the names of dynasties, states, regions, cities and physical features mentioned in the text plotted on at least one of the maps. As a rule, the spellings used are those of the text; but, in that the pronunciation and spelling of many locations and other geographic names have changed – often repeatedly – over time, some of the features are indicated by different spellings on different maps, and occasionally by two spellings on a single map (e.g. Bombay/Mumbai). Following the convention used by the author, diacritical marks have been omitted. Instead, within the constraints of the twenty-six letters of the English alphabet, we have used spellings that seemed to express the closest possible phonetic resemblance to the pronunciation in vogue at the time to which the map relates. A few exceptions to this rule occur in cases where the name is commonly known in a particular form – e.g. Sri Lanka rather than Shri Lanka, or Ganges rather than Ganga.

But, in addition to the states and other mappable features indicated in the text, others appear on the maps that are not mentioned. We have also provided on many maps a background tint to differentiate rugged from smooth terrain. Such supplementary information is intended to provide the reader with a fuller sense of the spatial context, both physical and geopolitical, in which the history of India has unfolded. (The interested student will find more detailed information in: Joseph E Schwartzberg (ed.), *A Historical Atlas of South Asia.* Chicago: University of Chicago Press, 1978; or New York: Oxford University Press, 2nd impression (updated and expanded), 1992.)

Until very recently, states in India did not have fixed or clearly demarcated boundaries. Rather, the area under the control of a particular ruler or dynasty continually grew and shrank, and control over its periphery tended, more often than not, to be tenuous and incomplete. Hence, we have shown the outer boundaries of only a few particularly important states and caution the reader that the areas depicted as lying within such boundaries were not all ruled simultaneously by the state in question. A great many states, however, did control certain core areas, usually fertile lands of relatively smooth terrain, for protracted periods, often extending over several centuries. We have been at pains to indicate these core areas and to provide notes on the periods when they were under the sway of particular dynasties. We have also indicated on some maps the periods when certain states were at their territorial apogee and/or extended well beyond their core areas. Finally, we have indicated the capital and other cities that figured prominently in the histories of the states depicted, even when they are not given in the text itself.

Joseph E Schwartzberg
Philip A Schwartzberg
Meridian Mapping
Minneapolis, MN, USA

PART I

EXTENDED READING FOR PART I

Joseph E. Schwartzberg (ed.), *Historical Atlas of South Asia*. Chicago: University of Chicago Press, 1978. Many interesting maps and extended discussions of topics in the subcontinent's prehistorical and historical past.

Richard H. Grove, *Green Imperialism: Colonial Expansion, Tropical Island Edens and the Origins of Environmentalism, 1600–1860*. Cambridge: Cambridge University Press, 1995. Discusses conflict of interests (in both senses) between early British commercial purposes and the scientifically and philosophically influenced officers and civil servants who were sent to India.

Madhav Gadgil and Ramachandra Guha, *This Fissured Land: an Ecological History of India*. Delhi: Oxford University Press, 1992. A sort of dirge about the misuse of India's natural resources. Deals almost exclusively with forests. More sympathetic to 'tribal' people than to peasants who use the forests.

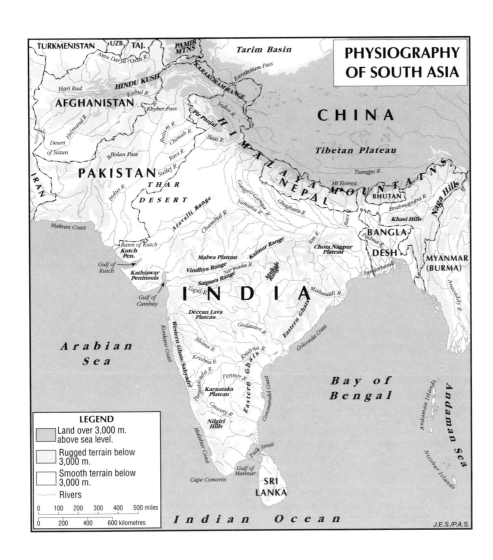

PHYSIOGRAPHY OF SOUTH ASIA

TURKMENISTAN   UZB.   TAJ.   PAMIR MTNS   Tarim Basin

Amu Darya (Oxus R.)

KARAKORAM RANGE

Karakoram Pass

Hari Rud   HINDU KUSH   Kabul R.   Indus R.

AFGHANISTAN   Khyber Pass   Pir Panjal   CHINA

Desert of Sistan   Helmand R.   Jhelum R.   Chenab R.   Beas R.   Tibetan Plateau

IRAN   Bolan Pass   Ravi R.   Tsangpo R.

PAKISTAN   Sutlej R.   HIMALAYA   Mt Everest   MOUNTAINS   Naga Hills

Indus R.   THAR   DESERT   Aravalli Range   Ganges/Ganga R.   NEPAL   BHUTAN

Yamuna R.   Ghaghara R.   Ravi R.   Brahmaputra R.   Khasi Hills

Makran Coast   Chambal R.   Son R.   BANGLA-   DESH

Rann of Kutch   Kutch Pen.   Malwa Plateau   Kaimur Range   Chota Nagpur Plateau   MYANMAR (BURMA)

Gulf of Kutch   Kathiawar Peninsula   Vindhya Range   Narmada R.   Rajmahal Hills   Sunderbands   Padma R.

Satpura Range   INDIA   Mahanadi R.   Irrawaddy R.

Gulf of Cambay   Tapti R.

Deccan Lava Plateau   Godavari R.   Eastern Ghats   Golconda Coast

Arabian Sea   Konkani Coast   Western Ghats/Sahyadri   Bhima R.   Krishna R.

Krishna R.   Eastern Ghats

Penner R.   Coromandel Coast   Bay of Bengal   Andaman Islands   Andaman Sea

Tungabhadra R.   Karnataka Plateau   Cauvery R.   Nicobar Islands

Nilgiri Hills

Malabar Coast   Palk Strait

LEGEND
Land over 3,000 m. above sea level.
Rugged terrain below 3,000 m.
Smooth terrain below 3,000 m.
Rivers

0   100   200   300   400   500 miles
0   200   400   600 kilometres

Cape Comorin   Gulf of Mannar   SRI LANKA

Indian   Ocean   J.E.S./P.A.S.

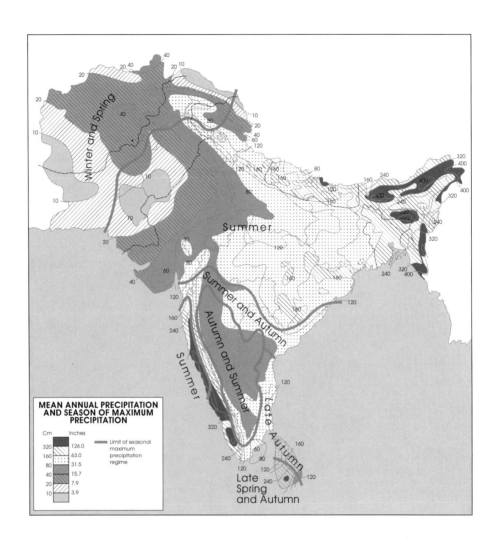

MEAN ANNUAL PRECIPITATION AND SEASON OF MAXIMUM PRECIPITATION

Cm	Inches
320	126.0
160	63.0
80	31.5
40	15.7
20	7.9
10	3.9

Limit of seasonal maximum precipitation regime

Winter and Spring

Summer

Summer and Autumn

Autumn and Summer

Summer

Late Autumn

Late Spring and Autumn

[1] *INTRODUCTION*

Writing history involves the selective compression of time; recency has a decided priority. Only a fraction of the number of pages given to the contemporary period of less than two centuries are devoted here to tracing the formation of Indian civilization, from about 7000 BCE to 500 CE. This is often the case for general histories and the practice may be justified on the grounds that for writer and reader alike the more recent is often more familiar as well as better documented. In addition, the historian of the present necessarily applies the tools and methods peculiar to his or her own time. All of this suggests that books of history could be read from the present backwards to the past, in the way they are implicitly framed if not actually written.

In addition to distortion in time resulting from uneven proportions of the extant historical evidence, a selective factor is at work which has much to do with the interests and knowledge of historians within each time period, with their ideas of what at each point in time is significant for developments that subsequently took place. And, finally, it must be admitted that a selection is made of that material which seems to the historian most curious and engaging. Thus a book of history is something like a building where the historian and reader stand outside and peer into the windows, one after another, and find each sometimes murky, sometimes curtained, sometimes giving on to dramatic scenes, and sometimes on to settings of the most humdrum sort. We can only make a few inferences about what lies within the walls between, and the historian chooses which windows to linger over. This, then, is a personal 'take'.

Although historians may view and even create their histories back-to-front, the results of this view are presented here, for readability, as a kind of narrative, perhaps even as an epic drama nine thousand years long, with a monumental setting, cast of characters and even a denouement: the present. By way of prologue, this chapter will first introduce the setting by discussing India as a physical landform. We shall then consider the characters by looking, not at individuals, but at the roles they play when organized into communities and states and the ways in which community and state exclude, coexist with and modify each other. It must be borne in mind that the discussion of community and state is not a synopsis of the history to follow; it is intended merely as a description of the political contexts in which that action will take place.

THE PHYSICAL SETTING

In addition to the distortion of time, writing history also invites a distortion of familiar shapes. In the case of the Indian subcontinent, the familiar shape at first glance resembles a triangle or diamond hanging with its apex to the south. Much of it, however, is pressed up against the Asian landmass. The area that is modern Pakistan faces the northwest, from which numerous invaders and settlers penetrated the territory. It is bounded to the north by the Himalaya Mountains, the highest in the world, and by progressively lower flanking ranges which reach to the sea to the east and west. To the east, it nestles up against Myanmar (Burma) in the form of Assam and the recently created Bangladesh. The southern tip of the triangle or diamond terminates at Kanyakumari (Cape Comorin). To the east and to the west of this peninsula are the Arabian Sea and the Bay of Bengal, gulfs of the Indian Ocean. Beyond the Bay of Bengal lie the islands and peninsulas that constitute Southeast Asia, which historically has had close commercial and cultural links with the Indian mainland.

As a landform, the Indian subcontinent has not changed over the course of human history, but as a concept what we will call India did not always appear as it does on modern maps. The mountain ranges separating the landmass defined by the Indo-Gangetic river systems have never impeded the passage of people and their products, material and intellectual; from the era before there were datable documents we have inherited an orally preserved body of literature and archaeological evidence of continuous relations between the people of the Indus region and those of western and central Asia. Artefacts found on scattered sites connect the early cities of western India with those of Mesopotamia in southwestern Asia from about 3000 BCE. Shared hymns connect Aryan settlers south of the Himalayas with Indo-European speakers of the Iranian plateau from whom they separated around 2000 BCE. Thus an accurate depiction of early 'India' would extend well into central Asia and Iran (while attenuating the links between those living in the Indus region and the peninsula). Moreover, the extension of India to the northwest, and a mental map to reflect this, persisted well into medieval times. India shared with the Iranian world to the west a common hazard from and reaction to Mongols and Afghans, to whom must be attributed significant influence upon both Indians and Iranians.

If the conjectural map of India can be altered to encompass western Asia and Iran, a similar reshaping of the familiar inverted triangle of the subcontinent occurs to the southeast. Historical contacts with Southeast Asia date from the time of the Mauryan king Ashoka, when Buddhist missionaries were sent to Sri Lanka and beyond. By the early years of the common era our mental map of India must take in many places to the south and include kingdoms on the mainland and in the islands to the southeast which were the beneficiaries of a transfer of Indic cultural elements and a rich trade with the Pallavas and Cholas of the southern peninsula. Accordingly, the Pallavan capital of Kanchipuram and the Chola capitals at Tanjavur or Gangaikondacholapuram, in their respective times, might be considered centres of an extended Indian polity that reached well beyond the shores of the subcontinent. It was from these shores and those across the peninsula in Malabar that Islam, too, was carried to the Malaysian peninsula and the Indonesian archipelago in later times. All of this points to relations as dense, significant and enduring as those between regions within the subcontinent as conventionally viewed, and the historical imagination must be taught to adjust the mind's map to register these interactions.

If we look at the familiar diamond in geological cross-section, however, the subcontinent is rather like a wedge, the broad end plunging under the Asian supercontinent, and pushing up the central Asian plateau. The separation of the subcontinent from the rest of Asia is also evident geologically. A broad band of recent unconsolidated sediments separates the bedrock of older deposits to the north and to the south. This and the still increasing height of the Himalayas are evidence of the continuing northward tectonic drift of a land mass which aeons ago was a completely detached island continent, and is now undergoing progressive (though slow) subduction under the Asian mainland.

Historically and prehistorically, west Asian peoples have drifted or thundered into the Indian subcontinent from what is now Iran and Central Asia, whose rulers have even occasionally, as in the case of the Persian Achaemenids (sixth to fourth centuries BCE), tried to assimilate parts of the subcontinent. The mountainous isolation from Tibet, however, was so much sharper that only once, early in the twentieth century, was it successfully invaded from India.

CLIMATE

The climate of the Indian subcontinent is exceedingly variegated, ranging from the snow-capped Himalayas to the baking plains of the north and the hot humid coastal plains of the south, from the Thal and Thar deserts in the northwest to the abundantly watered regions of the northeast and the southwest. South of the Himalayas runs the broad continuous band of the Indus and Ganges river plains, whose connectedness played such a large role in enabling the rise of early empires. Further south, ranges of mountains and plateaus run down the peninsula to the southern tip and tend to compartmentalize the terrain of the whole of peninsular India. These features made for the greater historical isolation and smaller political units of the south compared to the north. Thus, as will be seen, physiography shaped the political as well as the economic and social history of the people.

India is monsoonal, swept by the rain-bearing clouds that move seasonally across Asia, so that most of its rainfall occurs within a period of only a few months. The natural maximum precipitation of the subcontinent occurs in winter in the northwest, in summer across the broad centre and on the west coast, and in October and November on the eastern peninsula and Sri Lanka.

Every Indian crop season was and remains shaped by the monsoon, its timing and amplitude. Even with the construction of modern irrigation works, their supplies of water depended on monsoons and the melting of the snow cover of the Himalayan Range. Monsoonal rains renewed ground water that supplied wells, or filled the small reservoirs formed by reinforcing natural drainage ponds with earthen embankments. Proverbs in all Indian languages preserve the lore associated with anticipating the monsoon and with defensive cultivation practices in the event of delays. Thus do economic and cultural activities combine to avert the terrors of 'great hungers'. The concentration of rainfall, and its failure in some years, has frequently crippled agricultural production; man-made attempts to counteract this unreliability, mostly through irrigation schemes, have had political and environmental effects of their own.

In tropical climates it is available moisture, in both amount and distribution over the year, more than seasonal variations of temperature, that determines agricultural productivity, and, in the past, the population densities thereby sustained. Ancient and medieval cities depended on their local water supplies and the fruitfulness of their hinterlands. This condition applied even to those whose *raison d'être* seemed primarily to function as trading posts, or as religious or political centres. When water or wood failed, cities declined or were abandoned. An example of this was the sudden evacuation of the royal city of Fatehpur Sikri, built by the great Akbar during the sixteenth century and deserted after only fourteen years of use when the water situation became intolerable.

EVIDENCE OF PHYSICAL CHANGE

The huge South Asian population comprises one-fifth of that of the world, and that of India alone will exceed that of China in the mid-twenty-first century. Its sustenance still depends to an extent not yet sufficiently appreciated on the forests and supplies of water. Hence, evidence of changes in river courses, of the advance of deserts and of the destruction of woodlands, as well as soil erosion and sedimentary deposits, in the course of the human prehistory and history of the subcontinent is of enduring interest and significance.

Evidence of climate change in prehistory can now be obtained from such sources as radiocarbon dating, tree rings and pollen counts. This evidence indicates a period of greater rainfall in northwestern India and Baluchistan (in modern Pakistan) commencing about ten thousand years ago and reaching a peak about 3000 BCE, shortly prior to the period of the growth of the early Harappan settlements. Thereafter, precipitation gradually declined. The current rejection of conquest by Aryan invaders as an explanation of the mysterious end of the great Harappan cities, with their elaborate urban planning and sophisticated sanitary engineering, together with the apparent diffusion eastward and southward of patterns of concentrated settlement, has stimulated a variety of environmental hypotheses. These include climate change, floods, changes in the course of the Indus river and its tributaries and/or the exhaustion of local wood supplies, caused in part at least by the profligate consumption of fuel for the baking of bricks, the smelting of copper and other human uses.

It is generally conceded that deforestation contributes to soil erosion, the silting of rivers and the loss of underground water. Forests have always had a spiritual meaning for Indians. They figure prominently in their sacred texts and epics, and in Indian conceptions of the proper conduct of the human life cycle. The final, ideal and culminating stages were to be spent in contemplation in the forest, and mountain dwellers have often had, for both religious and economic reasons, traditions of strict forest conservation or replenishment.

Deforestation often occurs as an unintended outcome of human activities, yet there is literary evidence that deliberate deforestation took place as early as the vedic period. When Aryan settlers turned from nomadism to sedentary agriculture, forests that were found inconvenient for farming were wilfully torched; as usual, responsibility for human action was attributed to a god, in this case Agni, the god of fire:

> Mathava, the Videgha [a clan or tribe], was at that time on [or in] the [river] Sarasvati. He [Agni] thence went burning along this earth towards the east; and Gotama Rahugana and the Videgha Mathava followed after him as he was burning along. He burnt over [dried up?] all these rivers. Now that [river], which is called 'Sadanira', flows from the northern [Himalaya] mountains: that one he did not burn over. That one the Brahmans did not cross in former times, thinking, 'it has not been burnt over by Agni Vaisvanara' . . . At that time [the land east of the Sadanira] was very uncultivated, very marshy, because it had not been tasted by Agni Vaisvanara.[1]

The connectedness and fertility of the Indo-Gangetic plain meant it could support a very large and dense population – today 40 per cent of the whole of India – amenable to unified rule and the development of steep social hierarchies.

In the north, copper objects were found at Mehrgarh, a site dated as far back as the fifth millennium BCE, and there are hymns in the *Rigveda*, thought to have been composed before 1000 BCE, which mention the use of iron in arrows and axes used as weapons. (Their use for forest clearance seems to have occurred only several centuries later.) South of the Gangetic plain, population was dense in the smaller alluvial tracts, but sparser elsewhere. Less connectedness meant a slower pace of cultural diffusion, and a later passage from the stone age to the use of iron, which was not accomplished until the end of the first millennium BCE (apparently without an intermediate copper or bronze age).

THE SOUTHERN PENINSULA

In addition to the smaller expanses and greater variety of environments, the southern peninsula was also influenced by the greater proximity to the sea. While inland localities tended to be more isolated from each other, the coasts

Plate 1 Santhal scroll painting of the Baha festival, honouring the Lady of the Grove. Bihar/Bengal border, 1920/1930s. The Santhals dance and process to the sacred grove, where a cockerel is sacrificed. The artists, once only Kheroals but now sometimes caste Hindus, take the scrolls to the home where a death has recently taken place and recite the story illustrated by the scroll. The story recited changes slightly according to the religion of the mourning family. For example, the divine trinity of Marangburu (the Great Mountain God), Singbonga (the Sun God) and Jaher Era (the Grove Goddess) is equated with the Hindu divinities Jagannatha (Krishna or Rama), Balarama (his brother) and Durga (or Sita). One of their songs goes: 'We are not happy where there is no forest' (BM OA. 1988. 7-3. 02. (second register), Courtesy of the Trustees of the British Museum).

were in contact with the outside world at an early date. It is even possible that immigrants of Mediterranean stock came by sea to settle in remote antiquity, and certainly cultural as well as economic goods flowed in both directions before the common era. The enduring impact of the Tamil kings who dominated the eastern part of the peninsula in the early first millennium BCE is attested in the remains of the much later Cambodian kingdom of Angkor and in Sri Lanka and the Malay peninsula. Chinese records mention Kanchipuram as an important trade centre in the second century BCE, and Roman sources mention other entrepôts of the Coromandel coast.

Trade on the Malabar, or western, coast was of even greater antiquity than in the east. Before the middle of the fifth millennium BCE, cedars were exported to pharaonic Egypt and Mesopotamia, and hardwoods appear to have been transported to ancient Ur in the third millennium. At least one Harappan site in Gujarat suggests a sea connection with west Asia 4000 years ago. By the beginning of the common era, traders were depositing goods in western ports to be carried over land routes – which can still be traced by the finding of Roman coin hoards – to the east. Jewish traders from the Middle East settled in Cochin, on the Malabar coast, and the remnant of their rapidly disappearing descendants (most of whom have migrated) are still to be found there.

By the thirteenth century CE, however, this sea trade on the part of Indians had largely ended. By then Muslim traders dominated the Indian Ocean trade routes, while the internal trade in the peninsula had become better organized and more important. From around the ninth century, associations of wealthy merchants, linked together in 'guilds', merged into the local merchant groups which were already integrated into advanced agrarian communities, and these were increasingly connected with each other. The importance of external trade to south India diminished and was not to be regenerated until the advent of European dominance. Indeed, by the thirteenth century, Indians appeared to consider seagoing a sort of folly that could be prompted only by greed; a royal inscription of that period speaks of 'those [foreigners] who have incurred the great risk of a sea-voyage with the thought that wealth is more valuable than even life'.[2]

In any case, the peninsular environment, with its separated river basins and dry upland interior, gave rise to historically persistent forms of social and economic organization. Indians themselves recognized the overwhelming influence of variations in the environment in which they lived; the Tamils identified five 'landscapes' in their early poetry, each associated with particular aspects of the usual poetic subject matter, sex and violence. The seacoast was connected with low-caste fishermen, their frequent separation from their wives and pitched battles; the hills were the setting of pre-nuptial courtship and cattle raids. The dry lands, the forest and the cultivated plains, too, had their own associations with love and war.

By the thirteenth century, within the agrarian setting, three basic environmental types, each with variant forms, were identified; these correlated strongly (though less romantically) with the economic and social patterns of the inhabitants: those which were based on highly controlled and reliable irrigation from wells or tanks; those based on rainfall alone; and those which combined the two. Only on the west coast did reliable, heavy monsoons assure sufficient moisture for wet-rice cultivation by individual household-based estates, without the need for supra-local cooperation or regulation. At the other extreme, the poor soils and sparse rainfall of the dry lands could support only scattered populations who grew millet and relied to a large extent on animal husbandry for their livelihood.

Where moisture was reliable, the land supported large populations of religious and military specialists (brahmans and warrior-kings); here the division of labour and the status hierarchy were most elaborate. In the arid zones, by contrast, the division of labour was at its simplest, there was little differentiation of status and rank, and few brahmans or temples were to be found: a state of affairs often termed 'tribal', where everyone was poor. In both of these contrasting environments, ironically, the actual productive processes were highly routinized, with little opportunity for skill or initiative on the part of the cultivators. The semi-dry, or mixed, ecotype, however, did provide opportunities for a mobile, independent and skilful peasantry (who were called 'sat', i.e. clean, shudras); there merchants and artisans also enjoyed relatively high status and were linked to the dominant landed peasants. These three general regimes, and their associated social patterns, often endured well into the nineteenth century.

With the coming of Europeans in the seventeenth century, the Indian landscape came to be viewed from a new perspective. For Europeans, the tropics represented both paradise and peril. From late antiquity at least, earthly Edens had often been situated by western imagination in the valley of the Ganges (which was considered one of the rivers of paradise) or at Kanyakumari in the south. But the climate of the tropics was fraught with danger to northerners, physical and moral, as well as promise of voluptuous ease. Diseases of all kinds flourished in the energy-sapping temperatures. Moreover, the monsoonal distribution of the rainfall meant the regular loss of water and the soil needed for maximum productivity. Floods, earthquakes, droughts and famines were frequent.

The Europeans, who were at first traders and then colonists, had an interest in extracting the maximum amount of profitable agricultural produce, and also in assuring that the labour force did not starve, but reproduced itself reliably. The extent to which these interests conflicted depended upon how secure they considered their tenure as traders, loggers, planters or revenue collectors. To protect the health and interests of the European settlers, many of the officials and employees who were sent out to survey and administer the distant tropical Edens that promised to yield so much wealth were medically and hence scientifically trained. They were also steeped in Enlightenment and Romantic philosophies, and often became fascinated by the beautiful and exotic flora and fauna, to the extent that they sometimes took positions contrary to the aims of their commercial employers. Eventually, once the colonial government felt itself securely established, they were actually able to exert considerable influence on the state in favour of 'protection' of the forests and wildlife, as they saw it. Thus the commercial and political purposes of the imperialists were sometimes at variance, the latter requiring stability and long-term power and revenue, the former quick and maximum profit.

The general result was that the idea of 'protection' was often twisted to mean protection against the local inhabitants and their traditional rights to use the forests; that such use was often environmentally beneficial was not recognized. Instead, 'protection' was made an excuse for the state to seize control of what had been held in common and to use it arbitrarily in service of the policy of the moment – a practice that persisted into independence and still endures. Hence, on the whole, perhaps, the early botanists and conservationists were more successful in developing the roots of western environmentalism, which is struggling once more to influence the policies of dominant western countries, than in affording any real protection to the forests, soils and water supplies of the tropics; during the British colonial period, in both the north and the south, some areas of forest were laid waste in favour of tea, coffee and rubber plantations, and, under the pressure of the growing populations of peasant agriculturalists, even larger areas were cleared of their wild vegetative cover. Many of these policies and attitudes survived Independence and contributed to the environmental problems of today.

THE SOCIAL SETTING

We have seen that the physical setting has played a very important role in shaping the social groups which arise within that setting. Yet it is not possible to reduce India's history to the study of the influence of nature on culture; the culture of the subcontinent assumes forms which take on a life of their own. In the pages that follow, two of these forms in particular are emphasized. It will be seen that these forms – communities and states – play principal roles in the epic which follows. This introduction will merely sketch them and suggest a rather schematic overview of how one arose from, coexisted alongside and eventually annihilated the other.

Two aspects of the idea of 'community' in India should be noted. The first is that from an early time communities were in some sort of relationship with states. The relations could be mutual and symbiotically nurturing, such as those between ruling lineages of clans and the generality of clansmen which long endured in Rajasthan. Alternatively, relations between communities and states could be confrontational, as they were in some instances between Muslim rulers and the communities they designated 'Hindu'.

The second is that of 'communalism', which has been a well-recognized feature of the politics of the subcontinent from the 1920s on, whenever diverse political constituencies were mobilized for parliamentary and extra-parliamentary activities by appeals to religious, linguistic and ethnic affiliations and loyalties. Whether as 'vote-banks' or as instant mobs, the success of communal appeals has recently raised questions about the purported 'secularism' of the Congress movement and party. But consciousness of community or 'communalism' is, arguably, an older phenomenon, and appears to be a consequence of perceived threats from other communities or from states. In short, a sort of community-for-itself has a long history in India.

The earliest communities of which we have some knowledge were those that existed before there were states. These were neolithic settlements scattered over much of the subcontinent. The oldest of which we have record is the site of Mehrgarh, recently excavated by French archaeologists in northern Baluchistan, modern Pakistan. Human occupation there dates from 7000 to 3500 BCE. What we know of Mehrgarh and other early communities is limited, of course: something of its food (cultivated grains such as wheat and hunted animals such as the swamp deer), its domestic architecture, tools, the layout of its settlements and burial grounds. About the community consciousness of neolithic society we can only speculate, but we can trace the development of later settlements. One settlement of the medieval age, the city of Vijayanagara, grew from a small locality sacred to Jainas and to Shiva worshippers to become the capital of a kingdom ruling a substantial part of peninsular India, and one of the great cities of the world from 1336 CE to 1565. Then it was sacked and subsequently reduced to a tiny hamlet of cultivators visited today by a handful of tourists.

Recent settlements have been created and developed in other ways, too. A forested tract used by slash-and-burn cultivators became the Tata Iron and Steel Works in 1907 and, as the city of Jamshedpur in Bihar, remains a major industrial centre. Among the latest communities to be founded is Auroville, at the other end of the subcontinent in the Indian state of Tamil Nadu; this was set up with financial aid from the United Nations to foster the humanistic and religious movement inspired by Aurobindo Ghosh, a charismatic teacher-politician. Thus, community formation and change do not characterize only the earliest period of the history with which we are concerned.

Three interlinked aspects of social organization form a framework for examining the themes of community and state formations in India. These are: structures of productive organization extant in the various periods examined; politics; and the dominant ideologies, often religious, evolved by the states and social collectivities that supported and were supported by them.

ECONOMY AND SOCIETY

With respect to the first of these aspects, I assume that all social relations and institutions are shaped, though not completely determined, by the extant systems of production and the places of particular groups within productive systems. In the period before social classes as we know them became clearly identifiable, about 300 years ago, entitlements to the use of productive resources such as arable and pasture lands, mines, fisheries and labour supposedly arose from kinship or co-residence in a locality; but even in very early times, in India as elsewhere, resources and access to them were often within the gift of powerful men, who thereby imposed individual, heritable claims upon collective ownership, which has declined precipitately in the recent past.

Commerce was another source of wealth as well as a persistent link with the larger world. To a modern world that makes India a synonym for massive poverty, it may be surprising to learn that for almost the whole of its past, India was regarded as a place of fabulous wealth and exquisite artefacts. Hegel spoke for generations of Europeans when he told his Heidelberg history students during the 1820s:

> India as a *Land of Desire* forms an essential element in General History. From the most ancient times downwards, all nations have directed their wishes and longings to gaining access to the treasures of this land of marvels, the most costly which the Earth presents; treasures of Nature – pearls, diamonds, perfumes, rose-essences, elephants, lions, etc. – as also the treasure of wisdom. The way by which these treasures have passed to the West, has at all times been a matter of World-historical importance, bound up with the fate of nations.[3]

The Romans had sought the 'treasures of nature' and those created by Indian craftsmen so assiduously that their emperor, Hadrian, banned the export of precious metals to pay for Indian products lest Rome's gold and silver be drained away.

THE ANTIQUITY OF STATES

Politically, the consideration of Indian state formation must reach back very far in time, since Indian states are nearly as old as any in the world. Impressively large polities, dating from 2500 BCE, seemed to be implied by the ruins of vast cities in the northwestern subcontinent. Yet little is known about the governments of the Indus cities of Mohenjo-Daro and Harappa, how they were organized or by whom they were ruled. Nor are we able to form such judgements about any polities older than those observed and recorded by the conquering army of Alexander the Great, around 325 BCE. Around 270 BCE, the first Indian documentary records, issued by the Buddhist king Ashoka, were added to the Greek source. Though Ashoka's inscriptions were deciphered in the nineteenth century, we still cannot be sure about the political formation that existed under this Mauryan king, much less under the kingdom's founder, Ashoka's grandfather Chandragupta, who was possibly a contemporary of Alexander. Evidence in the form of a Sanskrit treatise called the *Arthashastra* – depicting a centralized, tyrannical, spy-ridden and compulsively controlling regime – probably does not pertain to Mauryan times. If its political world was not pure theory, it could only have been achieved within a small city-state, not a realm as vast as that defined by the distribution of Ashoka's inscriptions, over some 1500 miles from Afghanistan to southern India. What local political institutions might have been, far from the radiance of kings, remains unsettled historiographically, as the discussion below will make clear; and, since that is the case, the interface between community and state is frequently a matter of historiographical contention, and likely to remain so.

IDEOLOGY

Ideology is the third and final dimension to be given importance in this book. Ideology consists of expressed ideas, not hidden motives, and concerns the ways in which Indians explained their world to each other, beginning with the composition of the Sanskrit hymns that comprise the *Rigveda*, the earliest Indian religious texts. Although the means for understanding ideological forms are usually preserved in writing, the vedic hymns were for centuries transmitted orally, and also elaborated by other orally transmitted 'texts', the Brahmanas and Upanishads, whose philosophical contributions have excited the admiration and high appreciation implied by the label 'civilization' in the estimation of both ancient and contemporary peoples. Moreover, the religious and philosophical achievements of Indian civilization did not mark only the early phases of Indian history, but continued through the later ancient and medieval periods, bolstered by 'law books' and codes that were intended to cover proper or advantageous behaviour in all aspects of life.

'Civilization', with its connotation of a high level of cultural development, is marked conventionally by such attributes as the adoption of writing and the construction of monumental urban environments, yet when and in what manner such markers occurred in India remains controversial. The limited number of samples of an as yet undeciphered script found on small clay seals in the settlements of the Indus basin has created doubt about the appropriateness of the term 'Indus Civilization' and encouraged the more modest appellation of 'Harappan Culture'. Ironically, when the temporal focus shifts to the Gupta age, and a great literature flourished which informs us about all aspects of Gupta life, we find few cities like the ancient Indus urban settlements. Instead there were settlements not much larger than modern villages.

THE MYTH OF COLONIZATION

Until recently, little was known of the prehistory of India, and it was widely thought that the first urban settlements in the subcontinent – Mohenjo-Daro and Harappa – were colonies of Mesopotamia, planted around the third millennium BCE. This diffusionist explanation for India's ancient cities has now been rejected, and centres of civil organization are believed to be an indigenous part of India's earliest past.

On the other hand, it is tempting to treat the development of a civilization as ancient and as rich as that of India in isolation from the larger world, as if it were a world unto itself. The same sort of distortion arises in the quest for understanding China. Assuredly, in both of these ancient and culturally diverse societies, the determining forces for historical development and change were generated from within – at least until the epoch of European imperialism, which, in both cases, occupied brief moments of long historical trajectories. Nevertheless, well before Europeans appeared on the scene, external influences intruded at numerous strategic moments to shift the direction of development, to quicken or slow the pace of it and, above all, to alter the structure of movement – the underlying dynamic elements comprising the whole of the civilization and the place and significance of its parts in relation to that whole.

The early centuries of the present era, which saw the rise of the Guptas, were also a period of intensive interactions between the peoples of India and those of Rome and the eastern Mediterranean. Far from developing in isolation, from the earliest times of their history, Indians were a part of the larger world with respect to which their communities, cultures and states were partly shaped. A continuing theme in the historical evolution of India pertains to the connections with the world beyond, and, of course, to the reciprocal process of the influence of India on the wider world.

RELIGIOUS AND COMMERCIAL CULTURAL INFLUENCES

The subcontinent shelters one of the largest Muslim populations of any modern state; most Indian Muslims are descendants not of colonists but of converts to that faith during the seven centuries when it was the religion of the northern Indian political elite. On the other hand, the distinctively Indian religion of Buddhism, which commands the faithful adherence of major populations in Asia, is almost absent in India itself, despite modern attempts to revive it.

The influence of Buddhism abroad in ancient and medieval times was enhanced by India's numerous centres of learning, which offered hospitality and instruction to monks from China and Southeast Asia for many centuries. At the same time, intensive commercial relations with Southeast Asian communities led to the establishment there of religious practices and styles of kingships drawn from Sanskrit texts. This required the learning of the Sanskrit language by Southeast Asians, first in India, then later in schools set up in their own lands in one of the first deliberate 'modernizations'.

The traces of India's commercial interactions with the larger world reach back to prehistoric times and are found in archaeological deposits of Indian products scattered to the west and to the east, as well as in signs of the reciprocal import into the subcontinent of Chinese ceramics, aromatic woods from Java and precious stones and inscribed seals from the fertile crescent. It was not only Indian ideas of religion or statecraft, but wealth and goods, that lured first Arabs, then Turkic Muslims and later Europeans, first to loot, then to conquer.

Other traces of interaction are found in the bone structures and skin colours of the faces encountered in the streets of contemporary Bangladesh, India, Pakistan and Sri Lanka. All of these manifestations of openness on the part of the peoples of the Indian subcontinent to others belie the popular tendency to suppose that India was ever isolated from the forces and influences of the world beyond, and hence not amenable to explanation in any terms but 'its own', whatever those are considered to be. From the first, the making of India involved what was beyond the subcontinent.

STATES AND COMMUNITIES IN INDIAN HISTORY

'Indian exceptionalism', the belief that India is *sui generis*, and can be understood only in its own special terms, has long existed in western social science, and especially when considering civil society. A related question is whether the Indian people can be said to have had the institutional base upon which modern states and societies can be formed; that is, whether modern Indians are capable of progressing towards the secular, pluralistic and modern society that supposedly characterizes the 'First World', or whether theirs is a separate destiny, shared with other 'Third World' peoples, of distorted particularisms and intolerance. Since the explosion at Ayodhya in December 1992, doubts will surely have resurfaced on this point.

Ayodhya and the extension of its violence into Bombay and elsewhere was the clearest sign that we have had about the present strength of forces that will determine whether secularism or sustained communal violence prevails in India. Doubts were inevitably raised about whether India, even with its post-independence history of free elections and democratic institutions and its advanced scientific and industrial institutions, had escaped its legacy of inter-community competition, which had already produced partitions of the subcontinent. Is India to be judged by the general terms of those purportedly Enlightenment values of modernity or according to its new solipsisms? Will Indian violence in the name of communities and their alleged pasts of glory and shame continue to justify the exclusion of India as a suitable object for modernity?

Here I intend to sketch the relationship between communities and states over the millennia for which we possess any evidence, no matter how speculative, to attempt to put these questions into perspective. During these millennia local and small societies of considerable complexity constituted 'civil society' before there were formal states; later they coexisted with states for over a millennium, until subordinated by the twin influences of the modern state and capitalism. During this latest period, communities in India have been transmuted from functioning societies cohabiting particular places into metaphors, synecdochic emblems, usually of a religious sort and at the service of political groupings and their interests. If one of the consequences of this reduction of communities from genuine and comprehensive social institutions to mere signs is the violence waged by majority Hindus against minority Muslims and *dalits* (oppressed castes), can the transformation be understood, if not reversed? And what are the intellectual implications in comparative social scientific and in political terms, if these are applied?

The notion of 'community' occupied an important place in the Enlightenment project of seventeenth-century Europeans upon which the modernization theories of 'normal' social science are based. 'Natural rights', it was thought, stemmed from 'natural communities' and protected the autonomy of towns, social estates and individuals from absolutist monarchs. This theory found its fullest expression in the writings of Locke and Montesquieu, who agreed about the connection of rights and communities, but configured the relationship between kings and their subjects differently. Locke posited that 'natural communities' existed prior to states, with whose rulers they engaged on a conditional contractual basis, while Montesquieu understood community and state to arise simultaneously, with a contractual relationship between them to limit the oppression of the state. Both of these formulations attribute first importance to subjective rights, and these rights are seen to lodge in the community.

From such formulations, it was but a short step to Hegel's assertion that community rather than contract was the source of statehood and that the foundation of the state was 'love'. Affective binding was thus at once the foundation of the family and the foundation of 'civil society', as 'universal family', itself. Hegel united the ideas of Locke and Montesquieu at the time that such radical understandings about civil society and the state as those of Thomas Paine, and a 'public' and 'public opinion', emerged in Europe capable of formulating and publicizing nationalist doctrines. At the same time, too, capitalism was laying a new foundation for both states and societies.

Non-European societies, of whatever antiquity and however much admired, were long thought to be largely outside these developments. As the subjects of oriental despots and later as colonized subjects, they were denied the rich medieval European tradition of rights as free citizens; as colonized subjects, they were even deprived of the benefits of capitalism while serving and even financing part of European capitalist development, in the manner that India helped to fund British industrial development for a century. Still, the notion of community continued to loom large within the entire post-Lockean narrative, and eventually it was accepted that 'community' and 'state' have as much conceptual validity for India as for Europe.

While there have been doubts about whether pre-modern Asians could be thought to possess 'civil society', there have been fewer doubts about the state: Asia has known states as general political formations as early as Europe, if not earlier. But these were deemed to be states of another sort and were denied the developmental potential of pre-modern European states, in particular of the absolutist centralized monarchies of France, Spain and England. These kingdoms, as Perry Anderson observed, shattered the 'parcelized' sovereignty of medieval social formations and opened the way for the modern state: unified territorially, centralized administratively and possessed of all coercive means. The modern state was considered *the* state; all other political forms merely approached this universal type. Some peoples – notably Europeans – were destined to attain that sort of state in accordance with an evolutionary logic that cast other peoples – such as Indians – on to history's wayside, to be subjugated to the rule of others.

THE SEGMENTARY STATE

I disagree with this Eurocentric political formulation. Colonial subjugation during the eighteenth century altered and may have distorted the trajectory of state formation in India, but even before the imposition of British dominance, and very likely as a precondition of that dominance, relations between states and historic urban and rural communities had changed irreversibly. During the eighteenth century there is clear evidence of class-divided societies in many of the advanced parts of the subcontinent and, along with that, a radically different enstructuration of civil institutions.

In place of the conventional view of the pre-modern state in south India, in my previous work I adopted the notion of the 'segmentary state' from its use by the African anthropologist, Aidan Southall. The segmentary state differs both from the unitary state with its fixed territory, its centralized administration and coercive power, and from the 'feudal' polity, by which is meant a variety of political relationships, but most usually – as in the Anglo-French species – a form of prebendalism. In positive terms, the segmentary state is a political order in which:

1   There are numerous centres, or political domains.
2   Political power (in Indian classical reference, *kshatra*) and sovereignty (*rajadharma*) are differentiated in such a way as to permit some power to be wielded by many notables, but full, royal sovereignty only by an anointed king.
3   All the numerous centres, or domains, have autonomous administrative capabilities and coercive means.
4   There is recognition by lesser political centres, often through ritual forms, of a single ritual centre and an anointed king.

In medieval south India, hundreds of local societies, called *nadu* in the inscriptions and literature of Chola times, constituted a communitarian structure, and were the fundamental components of society. The relationship between these hundreds of communities and the medieval Chola kings seemed crucial to me for an understanding of these, and perhaps other pre-industrial, societies. At the most general level, in this view a state is that political formation comprising several or many communities, which, through their community political leaders (typically 'chiefs'), acknowledge and often serve kings and accept and even participate in the anointed status of the latter.

'Community' in this usage is to be understood in its usual English meaning as simultaneously a people and a place, rather than in its limited sense of subcaste or religious group. In this sense, community pertains to shared sentiments and values; however, it is also about shared rights or entitlements over human and material resources, and thus, in particular, pertains to small, local spatial entities under conditions of pre-modern technology. It is because very localized affinities, sentiments and, especially, entitlements, as well as the cultural, social, and political means for defending them, continued to persist in India until well into contemporary times, that I have been encouraged to see segmentary political forms as extending into the nineteenth century, a perception that gives the concept considerable historiographical reach.

The earliest documentary sources from the subcontinent – those related to the career of the Buddha and the evolution of the *sangha* (congregation of monks) which transmitted his teachings – exemplify this type of community. The context is sectarian: the elaboration of doctrine. Later, medieval historical accounts of states and communities were embedded in inscriptions recording religious endowments by the devotees of Siva or Vishnu, kings and their more affluent and respectable subjects. Again, the context is religious, not as an accident of documentary survivals, but as a reflection of the dominance of a discourse about worship and worshipping communities in relation to states and societies. Again, it was not an artefact of documentary survival that inscriptions virtually cease to record great events and their main actors by the year 1700. This was an era of state creation and of very much more powerful and grasping political authorities who notably failed to find an alternative language for expressing the totalities previously expressed through religion. Indeed, even as the twentieth century opened and communities, weakened by increasingly successful mercantilist regimes both prior to and during British hegemony, were assaulted by class divisions from within and by penetration by state powers from above, religious expressionism was still employed by the most vulnerable groups, those we now speak of as *dalits*.

Resituating Communities and States

In the evolution of political forms in India, environmental factors, economic complexity and religious ideology all played important and interlinked roles. As a first step in delineating the long conjoined history of states and communities in the subcontinent, I propose the following chronological scheme:

1   Communities without states from BCE 7000 to 800.
2   Communities *as* states ('great communities') from BCE 800 to 300 CE, when the Gupta monarchy was founded.
3   Communities *and* states, 300 CE to 1700.
4   States without communities, from 1700 to the present, when the historic conception of 'community' had been reduced from what had been historically vital and changing community formations to decorticated shells of ideology.

Communities without states

The idea of complex communities persisting over an extended period of time and space forced itself upon me some years ago when, in Paris, I visited the superb exhibition devoted to the microlithic site of Mehrgarh, near the Bolan Pass. This site had completely overturned previous beliefs about the pre- and proto-history of the subcontinent. It had long been held that the urban phase in the northwest was preceded by so shallow a pre-urban era that the cities of the Indus – Mohenjo-Daro and Harappa – must have been colonies of Mesopotamian city-states of the third millennium BCE. Civilization was thought then to have been introduced into the subcontinent in these western Asian colonies. But Mehrgarh's carbon-dated evidence of occupation shows that stone-using farmers and pastoralists lived in communities with large mud-brick storage buildings and other public structures, and sustained a variety of ceramic, metallic and textile industries between about 7000 and possibly 2000 BCE.

This back-projection of sophisticated community forms discredited and even reversed fundamental beliefs about colonization from Mesopotamia; it was rather the long delay in the development of urban forms that now required explanation. Moreover, Mehrgarh seemed to have been linked to other pre-urban sites in the northwest through pottery types and the signs of extensive trade networks and contact between Central Asia and Baluchistan, which suggested a wholly new sequencing of prehistory.

Among the newer views of scholars of Harappan culture is that complex chieftaincies rather than unified states were the prevailing political form, and that some of the urban places – simultaneously and successively – were actually independently governed 'gateways' to agrarian and pastoral hinterlands, trading centres rather than imperial capitals. Furthermore, the Harappan phase is now thought to have initiated a dispersal, beginning around 2000 BCE, in which urban centres moved south and west into the farming cultures of the Gangetic Plain, Rajasthan and central and peninsular India. These later urban places were agrarian and iron-using chiefdoms that eventually attained quite extensive form in the *janapada* (clan territories) datable certainly from around 800 BCE and possibly earlier.

COMMUNITIES *AS* STATES

Since the turn of the twentieth century, Indology and Indian history has recognized a type of polity, dubiously and always within inverted commas denoted 'republic'. These so-called 'republics', or janapadas, are far better viewed as 'communities *as* states'. In some reckonings, they existed from about 800 BCE to the time of Kautilya's *Arthashastra*, conventionally ascribed to the fourth century BCE. As clan-based polities, janapadas have been identified from the Pali sources of early Buddhism and from Jaina texts; other sources, such as the *Mahabharata*, the *Arthashastra* and Panini's *Ashtadhyayi*, add to this evidence and also shift the ground of investigation from north-western to northeastern India during the sixth to fourth centuries BCE.

Janapadas and mahajanapadas ('great communities') were seldom monarchical. According to R. S. Sharma and some other historians of ancient India, the social key to these regimes was *gana*, glossed by the term 'tribe'. Sharma sought to avoid reducing gana to simple blood affinity, choosing instead to take it to mean an association of people living in the same area. For others, the key term designating this form is *sangha*, or the combined *gana-sangha*, but there seems to be no significant difference in meaning among these terms, nor less general agreement about its being a distinctive form of political organization that may have came into existence around 800 BCE. This form was characterized by collegiate government; its leading members were recruited in part through birth in a particular place. Accordingly, eligibility derived partly from clan affiliation and corporate entitlements to status and property; the rest derived from individual achievement. In such polities there might or might not be one man bearing the title *raja* (king), but if there was, his authority would be circumscribed by a council.

There are models of non-monarchical governance dating from the later-vedic institutions called *sabha* and *samiti*, and these are assumed to be models for the 'Sixteen Mahajanapadas' known from later vedic as well as from Jaina texts. 'Mahajanapada' is translated, variously, as: realm, state, domain and political region. However, taking a somewhat more literal gloss and mindful of R. S. Sharma's distinctions, I prefer 'great community'; that is, a conjoint sense of people and place, the governance of which was often carried out by sophisticated and religiously legitimated collegial institutions. For this reason, I identify a long era – lasting from 800 BCE to 300 CE – as one during which communities *were* states. To hold that communities *as* states continued to exist in much of the subcontinent until the founding of the Gupta regime, and only then did a different style of monarchy take hold, one in which communities *and* monarchies simultaneously formed the basis of state regimes, contradicts much old and some new wisdom to be sure.

But I do not imply some sort of communal stasis; a picture of unchanging social forms might constitute yet another sort of 'orientalist' distortion. The work of Romila Thapar, for example, is rich in references to multiple modes of production, divisions of labour, social stratification and considerable urbanization as well. These endured well beyond the onset of monarchical polities on the order of Mauryan grandeur, as we are reminded by the work on early Rajputs by B. D. Chattopadhyaya; according to his argument, royal lineages among Rajputs were still emerging in the ninth century CE!

Was the Mauryan empire a monarchical form fundamentally different from mahajanapada communities *as* states? In one sense the answer must certainly be yes: there was a profound difference in the ideological content of the hegemonic expressions of Ashoka. His inscriptions were long held to delineate a rule over a gigantic territory. The Mauryans, and before them the Magadha kings, did stimulate the development of state societies in south India. Yet the Mauryan kingdom did not become a model for later states; this was to be the accomplishment of the Guptas, who provided a template for a millennium of states by which, in part, we are able to define a medieval epoch in India.

STATES IN THE SOUTH

The appearance of states in the south was initiated by the founding of the Pallava kingdom during the sixth century CE and owes much to the influence of external trade from the Gangetic basin and from the eastern Mediterranean. Beginning in the megalithic period of south India's Iron Age, and markedly during the last half of the first millennium BCE, an important shift of domination from the pastoral upland to the riverine plains occurred. Associated with this was the decline of an older elite of chiefly families in various parts, which were supplanted by a new elite formation. Among the Tamils the old chiefs were superseded by three new chiefly lines called *muventar*, who adopted the names of Chola, Chera and Pandya and founded kingdoms; the term *ventar* is used in the texts of the Tamil sangam to mean 'crowned king'. These kingships cannot have been much removed from the lineage structure from which they emerged when they were previously noticed in the Ashokan inscriptions, but they must have been based on complex sedentarized farming communities with some degree of commodity production in a number of riverine plains of the southern peninsula, even if they retained elements of an earlier pastoral society and economy.

The differences between the northern kingdoms that succeeded the lineage-based janapadas, described by Thapar, and the southern kingdoms which appeared later sprang from the different environmental and social substructures of the two regions. The core communities that formed the heartland of the Mauryans and their successors in the north were the farming villages of the Ganges basin. Between the border of Bengal and the intersection of the Ganges and the Yamuna a single extended riverine environment supported a homogeneous structure of communities. By contrast, most of the southern communities, except in some parts of the river valleys, retained a balance of the sedentary and pastoral activities consistent with the ecotypic cores and peripheries of the particular locality; hence, settlement units were accordingly more varied. Another important difference was the sea, and the advanced maritime commerce that, together with the intrusive commerce of the Mauryans into Karnataka, acted as a catalyst for the development of the southern kingdoms of Tamil Nadu and Karnataka.

While the reassertion of Brahmanical religious authority and Puranic Hinduism was a shared element between north and south, the fate of Jainism and Buddhism differed in interesting ways between the two regions. The accounts of the Gupta age emphasize the continued presence of Jaina and Buddhist institutions and the continuation of important writings in both beliefs. Buddhism flourished in Bengal along with Jainism for many centuries thereafter, whereas Buddhism began its long decline elsewhere partly as a result of the destruction wrought by the Hunic invasions in the northwest and partly as a result of the incorporation of the Buddha as an avatar in a revived worship of Vishnu. The practice of intermarriage among Buddhist and Vaishnava and Saiva devotees in some of the great families of the time, including royalty, also contributed to the decline of Buddhism.

The peaceful displacement of Jainism and Buddhism in the north contrasts starkly with the violent suppression of both by devotees of the new devotional (*bhakti*) worship of Siva in the South: the proudest boast of the new kings of the Pallava and Pandyan kingdoms was that they had slaughtered Jainas. Such claims have embarrassed modern historians but not moved them to offer explanations. One possible explanation for the violence could focus on the different ways in which commerce and communities were structured in the southern peninsula. Jainism, along with Buddhism, may be characterized as an ideology of transactionalism, a religious tradition whose core teachings are atheistic and ethical and whose social practices of moderation and conservancy appealed to merchants. They found pragmatic interactions governed by codes of decency more congenial to their commercial interests than the profligate norms of social interaction and ritual associated with the behaviour of even the most devout practitioners of bhakti worship.

In Karnataka, Jainism enjoyed a very long prominence as a major religion and attracted considerable royal patronage as a legacy of early Magadhan and Mauryan trade via the famous Dakshinapatha route from the Gangetic plain.

This commercial connection continued during and after medieval times, and Gangetic products continued to find their way into the south. Jainas found niches in Karnatak culture that were denied to them among Tamils after the sixth century CE.

The adoption, indeed, the invention, of devotional practice and theology in the worship of Shiva and Vishnu among Tamils was conterminous with the establishment of the new kingdom of the Pallavas and the resurgence of one of the old *muventar*, the Pandyans. Bhakti Hinduism was made a central ideological element in both of these kingdoms. Not only were its kings devotees of the Puranic gods and generous benefactors of them and their Brahman priests through construction of temples and grants of land, they also claimed to have defeated kings who had been devoted to Buddhism. Such royal claims and their connection with state formation suggest the importance of revived Hinduism as an ideology of place. If it is appropriate to speak of Jainism and Buddhism as ideologies of transactionalism, as suggested above, it is equally fitting to see place/territoriality as the salient political element of bhakti worship. There is a persuasive fit between the structuring of communities among Tamils and the form of religion that Tamils made their own after the sixth century CE.

The composition of landed communities between that time and the much later period of the Vijayanagara kingdom is noteworthy. Beginning in the pre-state era, localities consisted of combinations of various ecotypic zones, from a simple upland/pastoral with plains/agricultural to more complex combinations of substantial wet zones, fed by rivers or tanks, with zones of mixed wet and dry cultivation and pasturage with herdsmen at the peripheries. In a few areas, such as segments of the Kaveri (Cauvery), Vaigai and Tambraparni basins, extended zones of irrigated cultivation made for considerable uniformity and the possibility of replications of localities resembling the practice of numerical clustering in the Gangetic basin; but that was exceptional. For the most part, community identity was culturally constructed by religious affiliation through temples housing the gods of particular places. The gods were patronized by specific landed groups, including their chiefs, who might be organized into discrete territorial hierarchies under great chiefly houses. Temple worship and patronage, and related processes involving communities, commerce and the formation of state regimes, set the foundations of early medieval society, in which new configurations of community and state emerged.

COMMUNITIES *AND* STATES

Characterizing the politics of the medieval age remains difficult. Most of us who argue about the issue agree that it is essential to take into account both formal state structures – however we designate them – and a civil society that was still localized, or, as I would say, 'communalized', in the manner of the political regimes that seem to have become general around Gupta times, which I refer to as 'communities *and* states'.

Of the early medieval state, B. D. Chattopadhyaya observes that the technological basis for something like a single subcontinental state was plainly non-existent. He notes that as late as the eleventh century there were about forty ruling houses in the subcontinent. The work of Brahmans was the propagation of a theory of 'state society': the idea that the state was in and part of society as well as outside and regulative of it. They did this as cult leaders, ritual experts and priestly custodians of the numerous sacred centres that had begun to exist in early medieval times. Brahmans were also involved in yet another of the set of social transformations that, with the religious ones, mark the age: expanding caste institutions and agrarian settlement and production.

Communities existed in balanced relationships with states. Sometimes, as in the case of the Rajputs and the Orissan kinglets, states emerged directly from previous clan/communal formations; and sometimes, as in the case of the Cholas, imperial-like states emerged from local chiefdoms and endured without eliminating the stratum from which they emerged. This is a form I see dominating Indian politics until the eighteenth century, when the differentiated modern state comes into being in the subcontinent and, with that, the gradual decline of communities into mere shells of an ideological sort.

It was a gradual development. During the Mughal age, localized community institutions of clan, sect and caste were numerous and often embraced tens of thousands of people who were stratified in various ways, reflecting the ideologies of divine and royal honour, of caste and blood ties; local communities were also multiple, intersecting and cutting across one another to give multiple identities to family and individual sharers of collective property; extensive exchange relations traced a logic of redistribution according to differential 'honour' and 'status'; and localized communities performed the juridical and political functions deemed to be appropriately theirs.

South Indian medieval polities could not be centralized and transformed from above, even by the powerful Mughals, not least because they failed to develop a bureaucratic structure to encompass and subdue the patrimonial formation of their base. On the contrary, the Mughal regime was itself transformed by developments from below, where local and regional institutions and rulers came into conflict with and undermined imperial authority. In southern, western and, to a degree, eastern India, a noticeable feature, perhaps dating back to the late medieval period but becoming clearer by the seventeenth century, was the rise of local 'lordships' or 'little kingships' out of community institutions.

In the north, where the Mughal Empire came to rest upon and to utilize prior kingships based upon the clan structures of predatory Rajput warriors, the case was rather different. Because they were never expunged by Mughal authority, the re-emergence of the community-based polities that ultimately transformed the Mughal polity is not surprising. I say 'ultimately' because political developments took a long and twisting path beset by countless contingencies. The tendencies towards lordship existed at several different levels of the system, creating tension and conflict between regional and local would-be kings: resultant tensions and conflicts worked themselves out in different patterns in different places.

From the later seventeenth century, large numbers of lightly armed, fast-moving Central Asian cavalrymen drifted into the South Asian plains, looking for military work or to found kingdoms of their own. They were widely available for hire by would-be overlords (whom they sometimes subsequently displaced). Their military techniques partially transformed the nature of warfare, undermining the supremacy previously attached to the heavy cavalry and siege equipment of the central Mughal armies. The new military cutting edge supplied by the tribal influx made it possible for often communally founded lordships to emancipate themselves further from the final sanctions of Mughal domination.

What emerged from these processes by the eighteenth century, in terms of authority and property rights, was a very different kind of state for all that it sometimes tried to hark back to the Mughal past. Perhaps the strongest consolidation of state authority occurred where regional cultures and political traditions were rooted in former Mughal provincial governorships or surviving medieval Hindu kingships. Rulers there sought to deepen and extend their claims to rights and resources over and within community institutions and over the local magnates sustained by those institutions. Effective demands for tax and tribute escalated and royal institutions sought to dominate and extract resources from commerce on a new scale, not least to pay for the mercenary armies on which rulers now depended.

By the middle of the eighteenth century, the effects of all this on concepts of property and the state were considerable. States sought to centralize their authority and control of resources as never before, confiscating or claiming power over much that previously had been held under community tenure. Yet two problems stood in the way of the realization of the 'dream of despotism' (dreamt most fully, perhaps, by Tipu Sultan of Mysore, who proposed nothing less than a total state economy). The first problem was, once more, the lack of a bureaucratic apparatus. Consequently, the administration of 'royal power' tended to be farmed out, usually for cash, to merchants, bankers and local notables within community institutions, a sort of 'commercialization of royal power'. There were rarely difficulties in finding willing financial agents: the new and expanding claims of royal power, besides providing lucrative perquisites, could be used by money men to wrest control of rights and resources from community institutions and to divert the resulting cash flows away from redistributional pathways and into their own pockets. Maharashtra, in the seventeenth century, witnessed the rise of 'great households' of administrators, including the Bhonsle house of Shahji and Shivaji, who bundled together collections of rights drawn both from 'the king' and from community institutions. The entitlements gained were administered promiscuously within the individual household economies. Recent research on Bengal, the south and Punjab has identified similar developments in these places.

The seventeenth- and eighteenth-century worlds of Shivaji and of Tipu Sultan mark the final stage in the proposed dialectic between communities and states over the long duration of Indian history. It is here that 'community' is divested of all purpose and meaning save the ideological; for that, a contextualizing of social and political relations within a class frame is required, a task that can be sketched here only in the briefest of terms.

DECORTICATED COMMUNITIES

Rural communities of eighteenth-century India were partly unified, but always stratified. Moreover, they were increasingly connected with and dependent upon, but also opposed to, the larger political, social and cultural world. That connection and dependency dated from the early medieval age when polities were constituted of state regimes *and* communities, and communities continued to have means of resistance. When entitlements were threatened from without, opposition was first articulated through assemblies of protest against what were considered unjust state demands. Dissent then proceeded to such measures as the withholding of taxes or labour services to state officials, and finally to armed opposition. The mobilization of resistance was facilitated (and even made possible) because rural communities retained the vestiges of belief that local entitlements of all sorts were shared (however unevenly) among the members of various groupings according to generally agreed rules of local origin.

By the eighteenth century, however, new conditions affecting the relationship between states and communities were in place. Communities had become increasingly divided and internally stratified according to wealth and the consequent ability of some individuals and households to buy the office of headman or accountant, to deploy freely their domestic resources of land and stock, to hire the labour of others and to enter into more or less advantageous share-cropping agreements. Entitlements were also affected by the perceived status of the claimant, whether individual or group, as resident in or foreign to the community. The inequality of access to benefits further intensified during the colonial period and encouraged the generation of ideological surrogates for the weakening capacity for unified community action.

Wealthy members of communities, the holders of landed privilege during the eighteenth century and later, constituted a part of the emergent middle class of the nineteenth century. Its members became major commodity-producers, linked to urban markets and periodic rural markets, and thus ultimately to export production. Landlords hired labourers and specialists to irrigate and cultivate the fields they owned, and to transport the commodities produced. These agricultural capitalists were often drawn from ancient landed and chiefly families and clans; they constituted a small rural elite. More numerous were middle peasant households, of lower social standing and less wealth. Middling households in the countryside held small properties whose productivity was based upon family labour; they constituted part of a rapidly growing 'lower-middle class'. Included in the same category were households that lacked the means to exploit their often large holdings, and were therefore dependent upon the wealthier cultivators to lease their holdings at rates below the usual land tax. The bulk of these households were those who had acquired land on privileged revenue terms, priests or mullahs, temple and mosque officials, pensioned soldiers and village servants; the rental of their land to cultivators of independent means amounted to a disguised form of share-cropping.

It is easier to define classes of proprietors, holders of large and small properties, than it is to define something that would qualify as a 'proletariat'; indeed, the latter task even in today's India is a fraught exercise. During the eighteenth century a large underclass existed whose subsistence and very survival depended on money wages or on the consumption and production loans which they were, as coerced labourers, compelled to make. Estimating the size of this section of the agrarian population is obviously difficult, and little better than a broad range can be suggested. In highly commercialized, late eighteenth-century Bengal, an estimated 70 to 80 per cent of rural families had too little land, tools and stock to sustain themselves without wage labour for even a single season. However, in the dry Deccan districts of the Madras Presidency, at about the same time, the proportion of similarly impoverished and wage dependent cultivating families was about 35 per cent. The per capita consumption of this lowest stratum was about one-half that of the highest stratum, which suggests a flatter income distribution than in Bengal.

The underclass in eighteenth-century towns and cities is, if anything, more difficult to estimate, since the urban poor were less likely to be found in the records of revenue collections than the rural poor. A large urban pauper population – 'a sub-proletariat' of carters and casual labourers, and street vendors and artisans with paltry stocks and tools – must be assumed. In eighteenth-century towns like Madras, they could be a volatile and riotous presence.

In numerous rural and urban locales were formed important elements of the modern classes of India, including the petty bourgeoisies of the time. The pre-eminent non-agrarian capitalists of the eighteenth century were the mon-eyed revenue contractors. As fiscal agents of contemporary Indian mercantilist regimes, they were able to extend the reach of the commercial and banking operations that initially made them eligible to farm taxes. Unquestionably, tax farming involved others as well. The petty tax contractors were village head-men, who acted as an important hinge between direct producers and the commodity networks of which they also formed a part. Direct investments in agrarian production were made by both large and small revenue contractors as suppliers of credit to producers with whom they had long-term share-cropping arrangements; all such investments and engagements were made more secure for the small or large capitalists by the police powers that accompanied revenue responsibilities. In addition, moneyed men, both great and small, enjoyed monopolistic powers over military contracting and immunities from ordinary business liabilities, as a result of the efforts of minor lords to foster mini-mercantilism in their small jurisdictions.

The building of mini-states during the eighteenth century carried forward earlier practices of major and minor rulers, which included establishing towns and markets, investing in roads, warehousing and forgoing the collection of trade taxes – for a time at least. By these means, the burden of paying the usual revenue was shifted to smaller merchants and artisan-traders.

The viability of small-holding landlords was delicately balanced. They required a certain prevailing level of capitalist development to entice rich peasants into leasing their low-rent holdings (an arrangement that enabled them to avoid higher, fixed, land revenue payments), and a political regime that permitted their petty privileges while maintaining tax demands on the smaller direct producers who provided a modest stream of rental income for those with landed privilege. Too much capitalism or too strong political regimes could and eventually did threaten the interests of this large rural middle stratum and thrust many former beneficiaries into a land market where they were relatively weak participants.

New towns were another kind of hinge between mercantilist and community structures, although town growth had long been fostered by religious developments as well. In south India, towns were the centres of temple and sect organization, contributing a diffuse ideological element to the political and economic functions of urban centres. Towns became the district and locality headquarters of the nineteenth-century Company and Imperial Raj. Militarily, they were the fortified garrisons of state regimes, the places where soldiers were provisioned and housed between forays to maintain order and to assist in the collection of the revenue by a tax contractor. Economically, they were the nodal points for bulking and distributing commodities that flowed to and from the coastal ports of high, international commerce. In cultural and ideological terms, towns harboured temples and mosques, sect and cultic centres, with their linkages to surrounding villages.

The rural hinterlands of small eighteenth-century towns anticipated the emergent modern classes as well. In addition to merchants, money-lenders, artisan-traders and others directly linked by economic activities with urban markets of all sorts, there were peasant-cultivators, who must also be placed on a class continuum along with the landless agrarian workers who formed a large underclass of wage-dependent labourers. Along with these groups, who were rooted in the ancient community structures of India but possessed branches in the proliferating towns, the new lower-middle classes provided the major support for local cultural/ideological forms: religious institutions and practices, 'proper' caste relationships, and the entitlements they fought to preserve.

THE ROLE OF RELIGION AND IDEOLOGY

Hinduism and caste relations must be situated within some general social context to provide them with useful ideological content rather than an undefined and vague global explanatory privilege. Caste, religion and values were defined by and to a degree fell under the custodianship of India's massive petty bourgeoisie, and caste and Hinduism were adopted by the colonial regime as a useful sociological analysis to support their subjugation of India. Eventually this handy structure of meaning was passed intact to the successor regime of independent India as well as to the normal social science of our own era.

State ideology during the eighteenth century was in most cases not very different from what it had been in medieval times. In the states ruled by Hindus, the state was the monarch, and his duty (*rajadharma*) was to maintain something called *varnashramadharma*; that is, the proper order of castes and the protection of the places in which Vishnu and Shiva were worshipped. Hindu rulers continued to celebrate their sovereignty with rituals dating from earlier times, such as the *mahanavami* in south India and *dasara* elsewhere. On the other hand, the militarized rule of Muslims, which was founded on patrimonial forms of sultanism developed in northern India from the fourteenth century, proliferated over most the subcontinent. Muslim rulers bothered less than Hindus about locating the source of their legitimacy; they did not even seek any sort of legitimating installation from whoever stood as Caliph in the Islamic world. The ideological poverty of eighteenth-century Indian states partly accounts for their fragility before the modest military threat of Europeans, including the English East India Company.

However, ideology flourished below the state level. In both Muslim and Hindu communities of the time, there were vigorous cultural movements of reform, synthesis and ideological reconstitution, and the main purveyors and foci of these movements were priests and mullahs, the intellectual guides of bazaar men, middle peasants and other refined and less-refined sections of both urban and rural society. The cultural politics in which they engaged was reflected in the urban disorder fomented in south India by the dual division of left and right castes and the proliferation of goddess shrines representing the tutelary deities of countrymen and townsmen in southern India, and it seems not to have been otherwise in the north as well.

Transformation and competition in localistic, communitarian groups during the colonial period continue to await investigation, especially the link between eighteenth-century communitarian self-consciousness, or 'communalism', and what are seen as 'communalist' mobilizations of later times. From the early decades of the nineteenth century, the colonial regime was determined to displace all foci of political loyalty that might endanger or merely limit the Raj; many institutions and individuals within community structures that refused subordination by the East India Company were laid waste. This included most of the 'poligars' in southern India and numerous 'recalcitrant' chiefs and rajas elsewhere. During the early nineteenth century, colonial 'founders' such as John Malcolm and Thomas Munro attended with care the way in which regional Indian authorities based their rule upon a variety of local authorities and hierarchies whose legitimacy, in turn, arose from linkages with dominant landed castes and important cultural institutions like temples, mosques, schools and seminaries.

STATES WITHOUT COMMUNITIES;
COMMUNITIES AS COMMUNALISM

By the later nineteenth century, after the great Mutiny of 1857, British policy was set to undermine the territorial basis of communities. This was accomplished partly by converting erstwhile locality chieftains into dependent landlords, breaking any that resisted the change; partly by atomizing previous territorial unities; partly by legal changes to individuate what had previously been group entitlements; and partly by favouring some groups and individuals over others. The scribal castes, especially the Brahmans, flourished; Muslims, long held to be responsible for the Mutiny, suffered; most landlords benefited, while most tenants and landless labourers lost out.

Nevertheless, the idea of community as a local manifestation of some generalized morality continued, and in time new ways were devised for advancing the interests of certain groups through communalism. *Community* historically and at present is something into which Indians consider themselves to be born, socialized and ultimately bound to perpetuate. They are born in particular places with languages, social and caste groupings, political and cultural attachments. Territoriality and temporality, or history, have been and remain the critical dimensions of community. 'Communalism' is the means of mobilization, the symbols that stir people into action, often mass and violent action. There are well known examples of this, beginning with the formation of caste associations in response to the caste categories used in censuses by the British. The goals of these associations were to contest the rankings presumed by the colonizers and to challenge the denigration of lower-ranking castes by higher castes. Later in the nineteenth century, the 'cow protection' and 'script reform' movements – the latter being the demand for the replacement of Urdu, written in Persian script, by Hindi written in Devanagari – proved to be effective means of mobilizing Hindus against Muslims, often to protest against one or another local irritant or to achieve some local advantage.

To these revival and reform movements were added the politically focusing incentive of separate electorates. The Morley–Minto council reform of 1909 altered the way in which the seats that were opened to local electorates in the 1860s were now to be filled; Muslims were granted the power to elect their co-religionists to a set number of seats. This modest concession to popular political participation was seen by officials as promising simply to divide Hindus from Muslims, but the inevitable concomitant of mass elections of the sort that India has known since independence is the minting of evocative, mobilizing symbols and slogans, which have served to emphasize social divisions of many sorts. Social revivalism and separate electorates acted together to redefine community once again through a process in which ethnic, linguistic and religious elements were taken to be constitutive of bounded, legal/administrative categories. This redefinition in the early twentieth century was to mark and mar Indian political life and to create the conditions – though not the necessity – for partition, a tragedy for Indian nationalism, but not the only one.

Nationalism intensified communalist activities in a number of ways. First came the manipulative reaction of the British to demands from educated Indians for participation in administrative roles and consultation in policy determination, as well as for government support of the Indian economy. The communal electorates of 1909 represented a shift in imperial policy from hostility to support for Muslims; henceforward, they, along with landlords, were to constitute a bulwark against Indian middle-class professional critics of the Raj.

But nationalists contributed yet more to communalist forms of organization and agitation. In 1925, the Rashtriya Swayamsevak Sangh (RSS) was founded as a cultural organization to make Hindu-ness ('*Hindutva*') the ideological core of Indian political life and nationalist strivings, and it succeeded over the decades in winning the support of many within the Congress movement, including some of its leaders. In addition to the appeal to primordial religious sentiment, the religious component in nationalist politics reflected the weak and confused alternative ideological bases of Indian nationalism. Other organizations sprang from the RSS, among them the Vishva Hindu Parishad, the Bajrang Dal and the Bharatiya Janata Party. All were dedicated to the defeat of the secular programme of the National Congress.

During M. K. Gandhi's stewardship over the Congress, a mass movement was created to carry the freedom struggle forward after the First World War. At its Nagpur session of 1920, the Indian National Congress met jointly with the Muslim League, and this represented the high point of unity between Hindus and Muslims, and the apparent healing of embittered inter-religious feelings. However, a new type of ideological saliency emerged, this time linguistic, which would establish the basis for other kinds of communalist foci to trouble Indian politics into an indefinite future.

The reforms of the Indian National Congress constitution urged by Gandhi at the Nagpur Congress made linguistic regions, rather than the British provinces, the basis for Congress organization and mobilization. Making language the foundation for political action and constitutional viability opened the Congress, as intended by Gandhi, to participation and even eventual leadership by those who had been excluded by elite dominance up to that time. Not only was there a class shift from higher professional, western-educated, urban men to lower-middle-class members of the humbler professions, such as teachers, but it also opened the possibility for peasant and other lower-middle-caste groups to advance their prospects against those with better educations and professional credentials, who had long ruled the party. At the same time, the popular religiosity of the respectable castes, the urban and rural lower-middle class, gained a new prominence, which was the most general public discourse of the twentieth century. Finally, the decision to eschew class demands within Congress programmes, upon which Gandhi had insisted, meant that other forms of mobilization took precedence – most persistently and dangerously, religious – while the demands for justice of India's poor were consistently denied. Gandhi wanted only a unified mass movement capable of freeing India from British rule, one without internal divisions and one that he could charismatically control.

The failure to free Indians from bigotry, poverty and oppression, after all the high hopes, ideals and claims, can make a half century of freedom from foreign rule appear ignoble. Community rhetoric, whether in linguistic or subnationalist, caste or Hindu-ness terms, has only increasingly served the classes that were formed by capitalism under colonial subjugation. The reasons for the failure to destroy communalism can be found in the use that was made of the 'community' idea by the colonial regime and its nationalist opponents alike. 'Community' was divested of its historic political, social, economic and cultural attributes in the course of the twentieth century; it remains a decorticated monstrosity, a husk of meaning, open to manipulation by conflicting groups and classes, most especially the godmen/politicians of the Indian petty bourgeoisie. The Indian nationalist movement chose not to contest class oppression; hence the ideal of 'community', recast as 'communalism', has become merely a rhetorical shell, though a flourishing one.

Full circle: the oppressed appeal to religion

Unnoticed until quite recently have been other voices who have also resorted to a religious idiom to press their appeals for justice. These groups were subordinate to, and victims of, that petty bourgeoisie which had succeeded in making religious communalism their ideology, just as the professional bourgeoisie made secularism theirs. In an era when there no longer exist whole and viable communities to extol or preserve, religion continues to provide a language for claims even when these are but the wistful and in the end ineffectual pleas of the oppressed who hope their oppressors can be blackmailed by tradition, shamed by old values into honourable conduct. Nevertheless, the effort on the part of dalits (oppressed) to use religious argumentation to advance their justice claims deserves brief notice at least.

Why should the very sections of Indian society whose ascriptive pollution has always barred them from ordinary religious participation now cast their appeals in religious terms? Historically, claims to social and religious justice were heard by kings and by agents of the gods, the priests and sect leaders who pronounced on behalf of the gods in their temples. The establishment of colonial authority during the late eighteenth century expunged most of the royal authority in the subcontinent in all but the princely states. In place of royal adjudication, Company courts were instituted whose remit was to administer a version of 'traditional' law according to British understandings of the ancient moral texts (*dharmashastra*). But courts could not fill the void left by the previous norms of consensual decision-making according to community usage and custom. Thus religion alone remained as the basis of social adjudication, and Company policy was quite willing to leave to panchayats and mahants the settlement of disputes in which the colonial authority had no interest, such matters as who might or might not worship and have respectable status. It was to such bodies and in such terms that the most direct victims of petty bourgeois religious oppression were forced to appeal.

Communalist politics in India, like fundamentalist politics in the Middle East and the United States, reflect the interests and the fears of the large segment of national populations of the lower-middle class whose economic and social security is ever at hazard and is so perceived. From one quarter come the dangers of a modern capitalism which readily sunder forms of protection and petty privilege long enjoyed by small property holders and by members of humble professions. And from another quarter come the demands for social justice for the poorest in all societies, including India. During the twentieth century the poor have been encouraged to want and expect better opportunities and resources by the promises of politicians. In India, with its robust democratic and electoral participation, these expectations were kept alive through frequent electoral campaigns. But the masses stand to gain, if they gain at all, from those only slightly better-off; the wealth of the very rich is never at risk. The lower-middle classes in India, as everywhere else it seems, wrapped the vulnerability of their economic position in religion symbols – saffron here, black there. In India, in Iran and in Texas, these symbols signify conventional righteousness and the preservation of things as they are. The very rich and powerful, associated in India with secularism, remind them of the better state to which they aspire, but also teach them how unlikely they are to achieve it. The very poor threaten a frightening alternative. Religion provides a surrogate discourse for the maintenance of the barely adequate in the face of dangerous kinds of change.

HISTORIAN'S CHOICE

As already implied by the notion that a book like this could and perhaps should be written or read from the present to the past, it should be taken not as a recording of events as they sequentially unfolded in real time but rather as an accounting. In the first instance, it is an account of how that part of mankind that has inhabited the Indian subcontinent devised ways of coping with the variable habitats of its landform, of the ideas and institutions they invented to give shape and continuity to their societies, and of how they exploited opportunities and coped with threats from beyond their land, often by incorporating threatening outsiders.

But there is another accounting to be made as well: my own view of that long, complex history. That is the outcome of a complex of knowledge, experience and sentiments that have shaped my present attitudes and understanding of the history of the Indian subcontinent and influenced my evaluation of older historical views of events and processes as well as the newer interpretations that have not yet received much attention.

An historian must be counted fortunate if important evidence comes to light such as to alter fundamental understandings. That happens only rarely when an historiography has existed for as long as that of India, about two centuries. More probable than new evidence are changes in methodology and theory requiring the re-evaluation of old evidence or the consideration of what had not previously been included as evidence. The past two decades have witnessed such new interpretations, and these, more than new evidence, have recast the framework for the understanding and appreciation of the Indian history presented here, and pointed to certain major themes in examining that history. One example is the rise of subaltern studies: writing history from below rather than concentrating so heavily upon the rulers and elite who have determined the written record, the artefacts and the archaeological remains of the past. Another is the rapidly proliferating field of gender studies: the consideration of the previously neglected (sinisterly less than) half of Indian humanity whose regulation nevertheless takes up so much time and space in the ideologies and thoughts of the historically and currently more powerful half. A third is the rise of environmental movements, in which India has played a pioneering role, both in the inspiration of Gandhian principles and in the world's first government-sponsored birth control programmes. Teasing out meaningful interpretations of events and conditions as they affected the relatively inarticulate and illiterate but numerous subordinate social groupings requires new attitudes, understandings and sensitivities to the vestiges of the past, which I am still struggling to attain.

PART II

Ancient India

CHRONOLOGY OF PART II

Before 100,000 BCE Scattered stone age sites.

40,000–10,000 BCE Middle stone age.

10,000–7000 BCE Microlithic tool users.

7000–4000 BCE Evidence of domesticated plants and animals; Mehrgarh.

4000–2500 BCE Copper and bronze; basketry and pottery.

c.3000 BCE Speculative date of the Mahabharata War.

c.2500 BCE Beginnings of Harappan culture, urban sites.

c.1500 BCE Decline or overthrow of Harappan cities.

c.1300 BCE Aryan infiltration of North India.

c.1200 BCE Composition of early vedas.

c.1000 BCE Use of iron.

1000–500 BCE Later vedas and Brahmanas.

c.900 BCE Possible actual date of Mahabharata War.

8th century BCE Period of formation of the sixteen 'mahajanapadas'.

7th to 6th centuries BCE Rise of large states: Kuru, Panchala, Koshala, Magadha.

Late 6th century BCE Persian king Darius I occupies Gandhara and Sind.

c.550 BCE Birth of Mahavira.

c.480 BCE Birth of the Buddha; death of Mahavira.

c.400 BCE Composition of the *Ramayana* and *Mahabharata*; death of the Buddha.

c.360 BCE Founding of Nanda kingdom at Pataliputra; decline of mahajanapadas.

327 BCE Invasion of Alexander the Great.

Late 4th century BCE Chandragupta establishes the Mauryan kingdom. Composition of Panini's Sanskrit grammar. Possible composition of the *Arthashastra*.

268–233 BCE Reign of Ashoka Maurya.

185 BCE Overthrow of last Mauryan ruler and founding of the Shunga dynasty.

Mid 2nd century BCE Reign of Indo-Greek king Menander.

c.100 BCE Conquests and establishment of the Shakas. Jaina cleavage into Digambaras and Shvetambaras. Composition of Manu's *Dharmashastra*.

c.100 CE Composition of the *Bhagavad Gita*. Rise of importance of Vishnu and Shiva worship.

1st century CE Emergence of kingdoms in central and east India. Tamil poetry and Pandyas, Cheras and Cholas in the South.

Early 4th century CE Establishment of the Pallava kingdom.

320 CE Chandragputa founds Gupta dynasty; marriage alliance with Licchavis.

4th to 5th centuries CE Composition of early Puranas. Gupta golden age.

4th century CE Narada's *Dharmashastra*.

401–410 CE Fa Hsien seeks Buddhist texts and visits the Gupta court.

5th century CE Huna [Hun] invasion.

EXTENDED READING FOR PART II

B. B. Lal and S. P. Gupta (eds), *Frontiers of the Indus Civilization*. New Delhi: Books and Books, 1984. A survey, in both time and space, of the archaeology of the many sites of the earliest South Asian civilization, written by scientists who are or were actively engaged in making new discoveries. Many issues, including the often overlooked one of terminology, are thoughtfully addressed.

A. L. Basham, *The Wonder that Was India*. London: Sidgwick & Jackson, 1963. Classical cultural history of South Asia before the coming of the Muslims. Lavishly illustrated with both extracts and pictures.

J. A. B. van Buitenen (ed. and trans.), *The Mahabharata*. Chicago: The University of Chicago Press, 1973–80. Like most attempts to create a definitive edition and translation of India's founding national epic, uncompleted, in this case because of the translator's death. Particularly interesting introductory essay, arguing that the basic epic and its accretions reveal the change from warrior to priestly control of 'Hindu' ideology.

Robert P. Goldman et al. (eds and trans.), *The Ramayana of Valmiki*. Princeton, NJ: Princeton University Press, 1984–91. Still uncompleted edition of India's other (and, in the versions surviving, even older) great epic. Again, interesting introductory essay arguing evidence of the takeover of a warrior epic by, in this case, Vaishnava devotional ideology. (In both cases, as in the Homeric epics, the editors' view is that the deification of mortals ruins a good story.)

T. W. Rhys Davids (trans.), *Buddhist Birth Stories, or Jataka Tales*. London: Trubner and Company, 1880. Based on the Pali edition of V. Fausboll, these stories of the Buddha's previous lives stand to Buddhists as Hadith does to Muslims. The translator draws attention to the parallels with folklore in other traditions, such as the Bible and Aesop's fables, arguing the priority of the Jatakas.

Wendy Doniger (O'Flaherty) (ed. and trans.), *Hindu Myths: a Sourcebook*. A set of traditional stories about the principal Hindu gods from a variety of classical sources; selected by the translator.

Romila Thapar, *From Lineage to State: Social Formations in the Mid-first Millennium BC in the Ganga Valley*. Bombay: Oxford University Press, 1984. The transition from a society of rights and decisions made collectively to one of territories, kings and taxes told as an updated and scholarly version of the Kaliyuga: population density and increased competition rather than sin created the need for centralized authority.

Romila Thapar, *Asoka and the Decline of the Mauryas*. Oxford: Oxford University Press, 1961, 2nd edn. 1997. Thorough descriptions of the extant primary sources, and the author's translation of all Ashoka's surviving edicts.

J. Frits Staal, *Universals: Studies in Indian Logic and Linguistics*. Chicago: University of Chicago Press, 1988. Refreshingly hardheaded view of the ancient Indian cognitive sciences, which were based on classification. Very deep.

Debiprasad Chattopadhyaya, *Science and Society in Ancient India*. Calcutta: Research India Publications, 1977. Determinedly materialist, if naively positivist, argument that the later vedas were a sinister conspiracy on the part of brahmans and kshatriyas to dominate and mulct the rest of the populace, creating thereby an early anti-intellectual tradition. Very readable, but guaranteed to put one off aryurvedic remedies.

George Woodcock, *The Greeks in India*. London: Faber, 1966. Highly entertaining account of the adventures of the first Europeans who came to trade and invade, stayed and faded into the rich Indian population mix. Reads like a novel.

Xinru Liu, *Ancient India and Ancient China: Trade and Religious Exchanges*. Delhi: Oxford University Press, 1994. A study of the connections between religious transmission and the growth of commercial links.

Jeannine Auboyer, *Daily Life in Ancient India, from Approximately 200 BC to 700 AD* (Simon Watson Taylor, trans.), New York: Macmillan, 1968. Structurally oriented descriptions of elite and non-elite social structure, politics and administration, trade and production, individual and collective existence, and royal and aristocratic life styles.

Diana Eck, *Banaras: City of Light*. Princeton, NJ: Princeton University Press, 1982. For denizens of the crassly materialistic west in search of the spiritual east. About one-quarter history, the rest more travel guide.

R. E. Frykenberg (ed.), *Delhi through the Ages*. Delhi: Oxford University Press, 1986. A set of essays by various authors that includes not only the history of Delhi but history that happened to take place there.

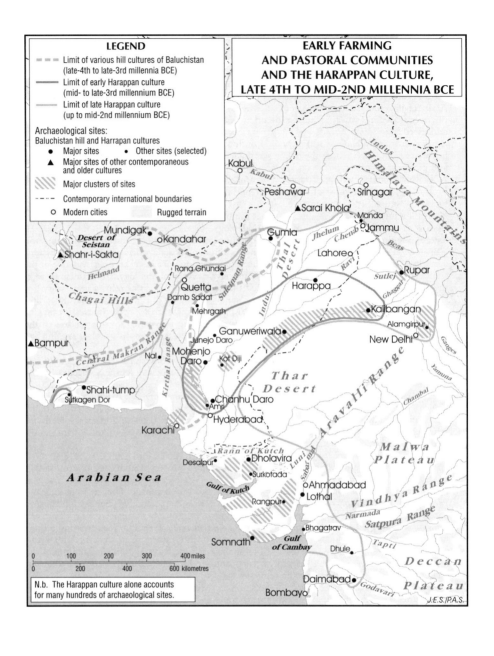

LEGEND

- – – – Limit of various hill cultures of Baluchistan (late-4th to late-3rd millennia BCE)
- ——— Limit of early Harappan culture (mid- to late-3rd millennium BCE)
- ——— Limit of late Harappan culture (up to mid-2nd millennium BCE)

Archaeological sites:
Baluchistan hill and Harrapan cultures
- ● Major sites
- ● Other sites (selected)
- ▲ Major sites of other contemporaneous and older cultures
- ▨ Major clusters of sites
- – ·· – Contemporary international boundaries
- ○ Modern cities   Rugged terrain

EARLY FARMING AND PASTORAL COMMUNITIES AND THE HARAPPAN CULTURE, LATE 4TH TO MID-2ND MILLENNIA BCE

Kabul
Kabul
Peshawar
▲Sarai Khola
Srinagar
Manda
○Jammu
Himalaya Mountains
Indus
Gumla
Jhelum
Chenab
Thal Desert
Lahore○
Ravi
Sutlej
Beas
Rupar
Mundigak
Desert of Seistan
○Kandahar
▲Shahr-i-Sakta
Helmand
Rana Ghundai
Quetta
Damb Sadat
Mehrgarh
Sulaiman Range
Indus
Harappa
Ghaggar
●Kalibangan
Alamgirpur
Ganweriwala
New Delhi○
Ganges
Chagai Hills
Junejo Daro
Kirthal Range
Nal
Mohenjo Daro
Kot Diji
Thar Desert
Aravalli Range
Yamuna
Chambal
Malwa Plateau
▲Bampur
Central Makran Range
Shahi-tump
Sutkagen Dor
Chanhu Daro
Amri
Hyderabad
Karachi○
Arabian Sea
Rann of Kutch
Desalpur
●Dholavira
Surkotada
Gulf of Kutch
Rangpur
○Ahmadabad
●Lothal
Luni
Sabarmati
Vindhya Range
Narmada
Satpura Range
Bhagatrav
Somnath●
Gulf of Cambay
Dhule
Tapti
Deccan Plateau
Daimabad●
Godavari
Bombay○

```
0      100     200     300    400 miles
├───┼───┼───┼───┼───┼───┼───┼───┤
0        200       400      600 kilometres
```

N.b. The Harappan culture alone accounts for many hundreds of archaeological sites.

J.E.S./P.A.S.

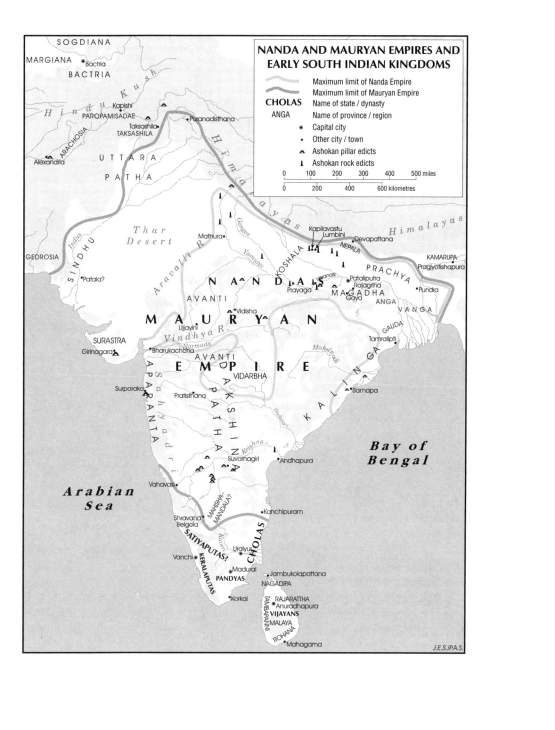

NANDA AND MAURYAN EMPIRES AND EARLY SOUTH INDIAN KINGDOMS

〰️〰️ Maximum limit of Nanda Empire
〰️〰️ Maximum limit of Mauryan Empire
CHOLAS Name of state / dynasty
ANGA Name of province / region
● Capital city
· Other city / town
▲ Ashokan pillar edicts
⌐ Ashokan rock edicts

0 100 200 300 400 500 miles
0   200   400   600 kilometres

SOGDIANA
MARGIANA ·Bactria
BACTRIA
Hindu Kush
·Kapishi
PAROPAMISADAE
·Puranadisthana
ARACHOSIA
Taksashila·
TAKSASHILA
·Alexandria
UTTARA
PATHA
Sindhu
GEDROSIA
·Patala?
Thar Desert
Aravalli R.
Mathura·
Ganges
Himalayas
Kapilavastu
Lumbini
Devapattana
NEPALA
Himalayas
KAMARUPA
·Pragjyotishapura
KOSHALA
Varanasi·
·Pataliputra
Rajagriha
·Prayaga
MAGADHA
Gaya
ANGA
·Pundra
VANGA
PRACHYA
N A N D A S
AVANTI
·Vidisha
M A U R Y A N
Ujjayini·
GAUDA
·Tamralipti
Vindhya R.
Narmada
Mahanadi
SURASTRA
Girinagara▲
·Bharukachcha
AVANTI
E M P I R E
VIDARBHA
APARANTA
Surparaka▲
Pratisthana·
Godavari
K A L I N G A
·Samapa
DAKSHINA
PATHA
Krishna
Suvarnagiri·
·Andhapura
Vahavasi·
MAHISHA-
MANDALA?
Shravana-
Belgola
·Kanchipuram
SATIYAPUTAS?
Kaveri
Vanchi·
Uraiyur·
CHOLAS
·Madurai
·Jambukolapattana
PANDYAS
NAGADIPA
KERALAPUTAS
·Korkai
RAJARATHA
·Anuradhapura
VIJAYANS
TAMBAPANNI
MALAYA
ROHANA
·Mahagama

Arabian Sea

Bay of Bengal

J.E.S./P.A.S.

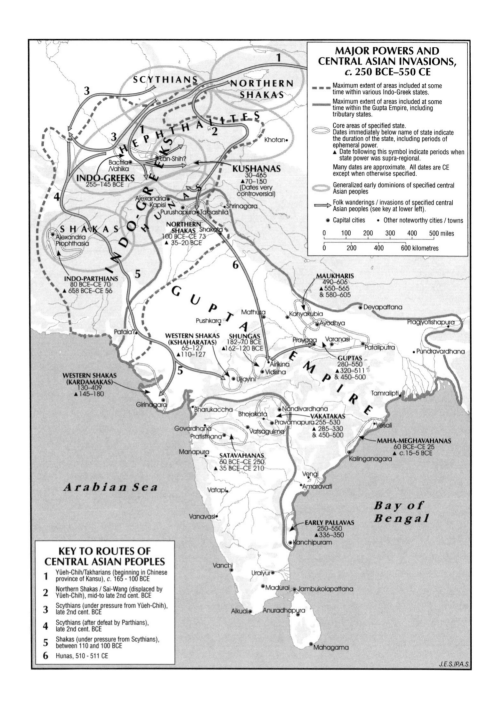

MAJOR POWERS AND
CENTRAL ASIAN INVASIONS,
c. 250 BCE–550 CE

- – – Maximum extent of areas included at some time within various Indo-Greek states.

——— Maximum extent of areas included at some time within the Gupta Empire, including tributary states.

⬭ Core areas of specified state.
Dates immediately below name of state indicate the duration of the state, including periods of ephemeral power.
▲ Date following this symbol indicate periods when state power was supra-regional.
Many dates are approximate. All dates are CE except when otherwise specified.

⬭ Generalized early dominions of specified central Asian peoples

⟶ Folk wanderings / invasions of specified central Asian peoples (see key at lower left).

● Capital cities   ● Other noteworthy cities / towns

| 0 | 100 | 200 | 300 | 400 | 500 miles |
| 0 | 200 | 400 | | 600 kilometres |

SCYTHIANS

NORTHERN SHAKAS

HEPHTHALITES

Khotan●

Bactria /Vahika
Lan-Shih?
INDO-GREEKS
255–145 BCE

KUSHANAS
30–465
▲70–150
(Dates very controversial)

Alexandria Kapisi
Purushapura●Taksashila
Shrinagara●

SHAKAS
Alexandria Prophthasia

NORTHERN SHAKAS
100 BCE–CE 73
▲ 35–20 BCE
Shakala

INDO-HUNA

INDO-PARTHIANS
80 BCE–CE 70
▲ 658 BCE–CE 56

Patala?●

MAUKHARIS
490–606
▲ 550–565
& 580–605

Devapattana●

Mathura●
Pushkara●
Kanyakubja●
Ayodhya●
Pragjyotishapura●

WESTERN SHAKAS
(KSHAHARATAS)
65–127
▲ 110–127

SHUNGAS
182–70 BCE
▲ 162–120 BCE

Prayaga●
Varanasi●
Pataliputra●
Pundravardhana●

GUPTAS
280–550
▲ 320–511
& 450–500

WESTERN SHAKAS
(KARDAMAKAS)
130–409
▲ 145–180

Airikina
Vidisha
Ujjayini

G U P T A   E M P I R E

Girinagara

Tamralipti●

Bharukaccha●
Bhojakata●
Nandivardhana●
Pravarapura 255–530
VAKATAKAS
▲ 285–330
& 450–500
Vesali●

Govardhana●
Pratisthana●
Vatsagulma

Manapura●

SATAVAHANAS
60 BCE–CE 250
▲ 35 BCE–CE 210

Vengi●
Amaravati●

Kalinganagara●

MAHA-MEGHAVAHANAS
60 BCE–CE 25
▲ c.15–5 BCE

Arabian Sea

Vatapi●

Vanavasi●

Bay of Bengal

EARLY PALLAVAS
250–550
▲ 336–350
Kanchipuram●

Vanchi●
Uraiyur●

Madurai●
Jambukolapattana●

Aikudi●
Anuradhapura●

Mahagama●

J.E.S./P.A.S.

KEY TO ROUTES OF
CENTRAL ASIAN PEOPLES

1 Yüeh-Chih/Takharians (beginning in Chinese province of Kansu), c. 165 - 100 BCE

2 Northern Shakas / Sai-Wang (displaced by Yüeh-Chih), mid-to late 2nd cent. BCE

3 Scythians (under pressure from Yüeh-Chih), late 2nd cent. BCE

4 Scythians (after defeat by Parthians), late 2nd cent. BCE

5 Shakas (under pressure from Scythians), between 110 and 100 BCE

6 Hunas, 510 - 511 CE

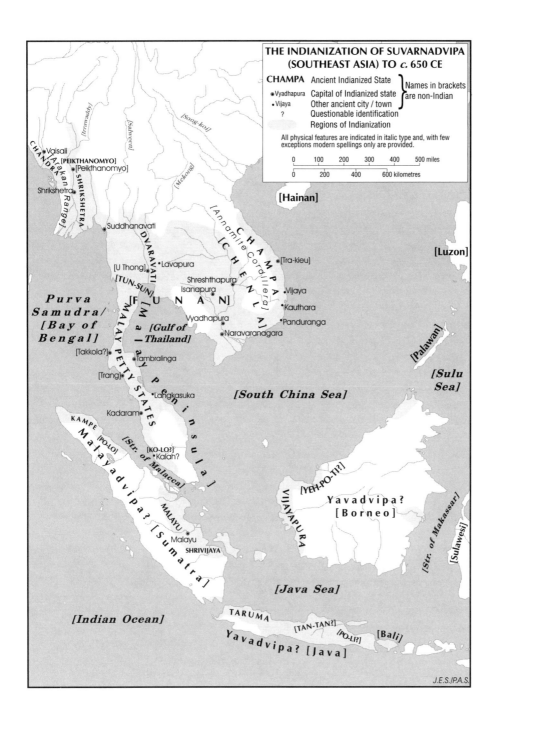

THE INDIANIZATION OF SUVARNADVIPA
(SOUTHEAST ASIA) TO *c.* 650 CE

CHAMPA — Ancient Indianized State
●Vyadhapura — Capital of Indianized state
• Vijaya — Other ancient city / town
? — Questionable identification
— Regions of Indianization

Names in brackets
are non-Indian

All physical features are indicated in italic type and, with few
exceptions modern spellings only are provided.

0   100   200   300   400   500 miles
0   200   400   600 kilometres

[Hainan]

[Luzon]

[Irrawaddy]

[Salween]

[Song-koi]

[Mekong]

Vaisali
CHANDRA
[Arakan Range]
[PEIKTHANOMYO]
●[Peikthanomyo]
Shrikshetra
SHRIKSHETRA

Suddhanavati
DVARAVATI
[U Thong]● ●Lavapura
[TUN-SUN]
Shreshthapura
Isanapura
[F U N A N]
M a l a y
Vyadhapura●
[Gulf of
— Thailand]
●Naravaranagara

C H A M P A
[Annamite Cordillera]
I C H E N L A

●[Tra-kieu]

●Vijaya
●Kauthara
●Panduranga

P u r v a
S a m u d r a /
[B a y o f
B e n g a l]

[Takkola?]●
P E T T Y S T A T E S
●Tambralinga
[Trang]●
●Langkasuka
Kadaram●

[South China Sea]

KAMPE
[PO-LO]
[Str. of Malacca]
[KO-LO?]
●Kalah?

VIJAYAPURA

[YEH-PO-TI?]

Y a v a d v i p a ?
[B o r n e o]

[Palawan]

[Sulu
Sea]

[Str. of Makassar]
[Sulawesi]

M a l a y a d v i p a ? [S u m a t r a]
MALAYU
●Malayu
SHRIVIJAYA

[Java Sea]

[Indian Ocean]

TARUMA
[TAN-TAN?]
[PO-LI?]
[Bali]

Y a v a d v i p a ? [J a v a]

J.E.S./P.A.S.

[2]   ANCIENT DAYS

THE PRE-FORMATION OF INDIAN CIVILIZATION

Human communities are thought to have inhabited the Indian subcontinent for 500,000 years, according to stone age sites found scattered between the far south of Kerala and Tamil Nadu and the Soan and Beas river valleys in northern Punjab, and from one coast to the other; estimates of dates for some of these range between 400,000 to 150,000 years ago.

So-called 'middle stone age' societies appeared between 40,000 and 10,000 years ago, followed by those using microlithic tools, first found around 15,000 years ago. Some microlithic communities overlap the first neolithic communities by around 7000 BCE, and both types of culture continue to be found in most parts of the subcontinent along with hunting-gathering and nomadic pastoral economies; often their activities have been caught in rock art, such as the examples found at Bhimbetka, in Madhya Pradesh, a middle stone age as well as a microlithic site, and occupied in later times as well. Other late stone age sites have also been identified, half of them scattered around the continental portions of the subcontinent and the rest found in various parts of the peninsula, or southern extension.

Around 7000 BCE neolithic communities began to be founded in the valleys draining the mountains which separated the Indian subcontinent from Afghanistan and continental Asia. Before 4000 BCE, hunter-gatherers had merged into more complex and advanced communities of farmers and artisanal specialists in settlements of circular mud-covered bamboo huts. The earliest known of these are found in Baluchistan, with similar communities appearing shortly after in the Gangetic plain and on the Deccan plateau. There, archaeologists have discovered neolithic assemblages: domesticated cattle, sheep, goats and plants, including rice. These stone age cultures merged into iron age communities by 1000 BCE, again divided between northern and southern India.

THE 'MESOPOTAMIAN CONNECTION'

The microlithic tool-makers who settled at a place now called Mehrgarh, in the Bolan river basin in Baluchistan, initiated a new phase of human organization in India which has shattered all previous beliefs about early society there. From the first forays by European scholars into Indian prehistory during the late nineteenth century a single general paradigm held sway. It consisted of the following propositions about civilization in northwestern India:

1 An urban culture, or civilization, emerged suddenly in the middle of the third millennium BCE, rather late in comparison with other areas of the Old World and therefore thought to be a plantation of colonists from Mesopotamia or elsewhere in western Asia.
2 This urban culture remained static and uniform over much of the Indus River basin.
3 It then collapsed suddenly and uniformly.
4 The collapse came in the face of the onslaught of Indo-Aryans from the central Asia steppe.

This formulation held sway until the 1950s and was based on a thin store of field data, lacking both substantial stratigraphic and quantitative analysis. Moreover, little heed was paid to ecological variations among known sites in Sind and the Punjab, and little attention given to human occupation before the advent of cities.

It could scarcely have been otherwise given what was known and not known during the first century of modern Indian scholarship. European scholars had not had the slightest intimation of the existence of the cities of the Indus basin before they were found. The discovery of ancient urban ruins of Mohenjo-Daro was made wholly by chance, for what had concerned Sanskrit and philological scholarship of the late eighteenth and nineteenth centuries was the antiquity of Indo-European languages, to which Germanic ones were linked. From the outset what was intellectually valuable to them about India were the vedic hymns of the 'Aryan invaders' of India. The hymns inspired esteem for and interest in Sanskrit, but also made it clear that Sanskrit came from elsewhere; it was not considered originally Indian.

Our understanding of what was called 'the Indus civilization' has undergone considerable modification over the past three decades. What persuaded many to give up the older view was the growing evidence of farming communities in the northwest long before the emergence of cities in about 2500 BCE, and the evidence of continuous evolution of these agricultural communities into urban configurations. Mehrgarh is the earliest of such communities and one on which a fine assemblage of physical evidence has been amassed. The neolithic communities initiated an epoch which culminated around 500 BCE, when the pre-formation of something to be called Indian civilization was completed. The excavation of Mehrgarh in the 1970s has shown this epoch to be longer than standard historical accounts had hitherto reckoned.

Received wisdom had long held that the process which transformed India from its prehistoric origins through a protohistory into history proper was decisively shaped by forces outside the subcontinent. Thus, it is not surprising that when the ruins of immense Indus cities were uncovered during the 1920s they were assumed to be outliers of the cities of ancient Mesopotamia, not products of indigenous invention. It not until later that many pre-urban archaeological sites were uncovered in northwestern India. That, together with the philological bias toward imported culture, explains several erroneous notions that persisted even after colonial control ended in the aftermath of the Second World War.

The governments of the post-colonial states of their subcontinent – the republics of India and Pakistan – were determined to extend the limited knowledge of prehistoric times upon which the prevailing view was based. Launching ambitious programmes of field archaeology and often guided by new theories, they succeeded in revising our views of the protohistoric cultures of the subcontinent, for which there was a wide array of material evidence, but no written documentation. Where previously virtually nothing had been known of the pre-urban phases of occupation and it was assumed that urban culture had been imported around 3500 BCE, there were now grounds for believing that a very long, indigenous, pre-urban phase, dating to 7000 BCE, was followed by a swift transition to a full-blown urban phase beginning about 3500 BCE. The urban phase might have been stimulated by external contacts, including trade; however, the length of gestation suggests that it was home-grown.

FROM AGRICULTURAL COMMUNITIES TO URBAN CONFIGURATIONS

Mehrgarh's seventh millennium BCE occupants made buildings of several rooms for habitation and storage out of mud-brick; they made stone tools for harvesting the barley and wheat they cultivated and for shaping ornaments out of local as well as imported substances; they buried their dead and interred tools and ornaments with them, and sacrificed domesticated goats. The layers above the earliest occupation levels reveal other developments occurring by 5000 BCE. Buildings had become larger and some were used exclusively for storage, presumably serving all in the settlement. The number of crafts had increased to an extent that suggested the settlement had begun to specialize in such commodities as basketwork, wool and cotton textiles, handmade pottery and copper ware. None of these changes appears to have been imposed from distant, external sources, but rather they constituted indigenous elaborations that continued to the middle of the fourth millennium BCE, when yet more new forms of production appeared: wheel-thrown pottery to replace the handbuilt ware; the use of larger copper ingots, with new technologies of mining and smelting; and a consumption of domesticated cattle higher than anywhere else in the contemporary ancient world.

By 3500 BCE Mehrgarh covered 75 hectares – a third of a mile square – and served other communities in the Quetta valley that have since become the subjects of archaeological study. In them, Mehrgarh pottery and other products are found, as well as the stamp-seals and female figurines characteristic of the Harappan material culture. By this time too – that is, around 3000 BCE – similar evolutionary developments can be documented in neighbouring valleys of Baluchistan and the Indus basin, showing variation around a coherent set of cultural elements which provided the foundation for the emergence of what is now known as Harappan culture.

THE HARAPPAN STATE AND SOCIETY

It is this culture to which the now rejected paradigm outlined above pertains. Much has been learned about Harappan settlements in recent years. The number of known sites is now over 400 in a 1000 square mile triangle of the northwest. While few if any scholars currently support the idea that these hundreds of settlements were transplanted from western Asia, the older notion has been replaced by several different conceptions of how a few great cities and numerous smaller satellite communities dated between 3500 and 2500 BCE continued a smooth evolutionary trajectory stemming from neolithic settlements like Mehrgarh. In addition, some scholars have considered the possibility that there might have been a sudden and rapid series of external stimuli that jolted an old evolutionary process into the new urban forms typified by the large cities of Mohenjo-Daro and Harappa on the lower and upper Indus. None of the known Harappan sites contains stratigraphic sequences capable of falsifying one or the other of these hypotheses, so the Indus urbanization remains unresolved, as do other aspects of Harappan culture.

One area of persistent mystery pertains to the nature of the state that might have existed from around 2500 BCE. Under the supposition that the cities of northwestern India were colonies of Mesopotamia, it was assumed that the mode of government was the same. A theocratic polity was posited, with a degree of centralized control that exceeded anything known in western Asia, because the area governed by Indian cities was far greater. It was believed that this unified state managed a vast and homogeneous culture area from its inception in 3500 BCE until it was destroyed around 1500 BCE.

Now that postulated homogeneity is considered to have been vastly exaggerated, especially considering that the region defined by the distribution of Harappan cultural elements covers 158,000 square miles; hence, the distances over which an administrative grid supposedly extended would have had to link the city of Harappa with the cluster of recently uncovered Harappan sites in northern Afghanistan called Shortugai. This was a distance of 300 miles and very unlikely, given the terrain and the transportation available at the time.

Each subregion of these sites contained one or more clusters of dense population in a river valley or coastal area, demarcated from neighbouring subregions by ecological differences. It was in these several settings that the cities emerged, each becoming a commercial gateway for a hinterland of agricultural villages and each, it is now thought, the seat of local government in the form of complex chieftaincies, with a hierarchy of rank and multiplicity of sources of legitimacy, function and power. Beyond that the extant evidence does not permit us to proceed, except to stress that this civilization was essentially an indigenous development that evolved in relation to other civilizations from which it differed in its political forms and in other ways.

No documentation exists to explain the very high degree of civic control implied by the massive 'citadels' and other monumental structures of Mohenjo-Daro and Harappa, but it was assumed that the 'state' implied by these structures would have been impressive, even if the cities were not simultaneous, but successive, political capitals of a single changing political order. Such a state, or states, would have had government as powerful as any in the world at that time, including the Egyptian Old Kingdom of the third to sixth dynasties or Minoan Crete. Yet there was and is not a shred of corroborating documentary evidence about this state, or any other Indian 'state', until much later.

Whatever their government, sustaining such a network of major urban sites would have required advanced levels of surplus production, commerce and elaborate divisions of labour; all of these are substantiated in archaeological remains of foreign trade goods, workshops and grain storage facilities. Wood was prodigiously consumed in construction, especially for firing the bricks that were used in the splendid buildings and drainage works. In fact, deforestation and eventual erosion may have forced the evacuation of the Indus cities and migration to new lands to the east and to the south, where the characteristic Harappan goods and architecture are found in smaller urban places and farming settlements.

Nevertheless, the unlikelihood of the existence of a strong, unified political system is reinforced by the absence of any building that can be identified as a temple or a palace that housed the state's autocrats and of fortified walls, which might have protected them from attack. Nor have the excavations of numerous cemeteries of the time yielded the sort of grave goods that would support the presence of a ruling elite, and there are few signs of the treasure from western Asia that might have been expected of a colonial elite, notwithstanding the substantial evidence of intensive trade relations between northwestern India and central Asia, southern Iran, Mesopotamia and the Gulf region.

HARAPPAN COMMERCE

If the notion of a centralized autocracy has been rejected, the degree of commercial activity involving cities and towns of the northwest is only now beginning to be adequately appreciated. Evidence from the cities of the Indus basin that have been extensively excavated indicates large populations of craftsmen producing commodities that were placed in public storehouses and identified by the use of clay seals. Regulated weights are also found. All of this testifies to a degree of urbanization comparing favourably to that of Mesopotamia in size and sophistication, since Mohenjo-Daro, Harappa and several newly discovered sites in Punjab and Gujarat exceed 400 acres, about 2.5 square miles. Exchanges between the two Eurasian zones of bronze age civilization involved exports of grain and animal products from the high agriculture and pastoralism of Mesopotamia, as well as tin. From the Indian side came an array of timber products originating in a zone of western India extending from the Himalayan foothills to the Deccan plateau, some copper and precious stones, red pigments for cloth dyeing (supporting other evidence

Plate 2 Impression from an Indus Valley seal, depicting a humped bull (*Bos indicus*). From Mohenjo-Daro (2500–2000 BCE). The writing has still not been satisfactorily deciphered (BM OA. 1947. 4-16. 1, Courtesy of the Trustees of the British Museum).

of precocious textile production), gold, ivory and pearls. These were produced and sold from six different subregions of the large Harappan cultural area.

THE DECLINE OF HARAPPAN CULTURE

As to what became of the Harappans, much uncertainty remains about everything except that their culture did not come to an abrupt end. Rather, from around 2000 BCE, a series of retreats from high civilization can be traced. Many settlements of the Indus basin seem to have been abandoned around that time, but not destroyed as had been presumed in the old view. Simultaneously, moreover, new settlements arose in eastern Punjab and Gujarat displaying many Harappan cultural elements. Most were smaller than the earlier Indus

Plate 2a General view of the (much reconstructed) ruins of Mohenjo-Daro. The Buddhist stupa on the mound is of course of a much later date (Courtesy of George Michell).

sites, the largest of which were by then abandoned. Some Harappan features seem also to have vanished, including the remarkable clay seals with their exquisitely sculpted figures and undeciphered graffiti.

Archaeologists now often label this changed 'Indus' society as 'Late Harappan', and examples of it extend beyond eastern Punjab and Gujarat into the Ganges–Yamuna basin east of Delhi. There, links have been seen between the stone- and bronze-using communities of the third millennium BCE and the iron-using people of the Gangetic plain and the Deccan of around 1000 BCE. In terms of the prehistoriography of the subcontinent, the continuity of the Harappan cultural phase with a new phase of urbanization in the Gangetic basin suggested a continuous movement of urbanization from Harappa and other older Indus cites to the urban site of Kaushambi near modern Allahabad in the central Gangetic plain. Its stratigraphy indicates a period from about 1000 BCE to 1300 CE but includes features suggesting a close association with the classic *Ramayana* story formulated around 500 BCE. Nevertheless, still more recent discussion of this question has revived in some scholars a preference for a fresh process of urbanization in the Ganges valley, based on crop patterns and other features that differed from the earlier process observed in the Indus valley. It may be some time before the questions of continuity and discontinuity are finally resolved.

VEDIC CULTURE

The vedic age has carried several different labels: 'iron age India', 'the second urbanization', and 'Gangetic culture'; each can be justified, though the designation 'vedic culture' points to the main trajectory of historical development.

It is now widely accepted that the subcontinent began to be infiltrated well before the middle of the first millennium BCE by people speaking an Indo-European language, later to be called Sanskrit and closely associated with the ancient language of people of the Iranian plateau, as evidenced from the ancient Zoroastrian text *Avesta*. Historical linguists find this a plausible chronological basis for the later developments of languages like Marathi, which possess a strong element of ancient Dravidian linguistic features, and also for Panini's grammar (written around 400 BCE), which may have been intended to standardize Sanskrit usage against strong tendencies to incorporate other and older languages of the subcontinent. (Indeed, some scholars find evidence of Dravidian linguistic influences in the language of the *Rigveda* itself.) Such conjectures clearly do not refute the older hypothesis that Indo-Aryans destroyed the Indus cities in a series of invasions, much as the later Turkic Muslims conquered northern India, but that notion is now dismissed on other grounds.

THE INDUS AND THE ARYANS

The notion that the ancient Indian cities of the Indus were overwhelmed and destroyed by Aryan invaders has lost credibility, notwithstanding the apparent simultaneity of urban decline and migrations into the subcontinent by people from around the Caspian Sea who called themselves Arya. Their hymns do not speak of finding cities, but of a more primitive society. Even the later Sanskrit compositions are similarly unmoved by whatever urban legacy remained. In effect, therefore, the high, urban culture spread over the northwest of the subcontinent for a millennium disappeared as mysteriously as (but far more rapidly than) it seems to have been imposed over the scattered stone- and bronze-using farmers in their village communities. If we assume that the Indus cities were a genuinely autochthonous development, and not implants from the urban cultures of western Asia, then that urban impulse was, if not entirely lost, submerged by the prevailing life of the farming and pastoral communities found throughout the vast subcontinent by 1000 BCE.

THE VEDAS

The 1028 hymns preserved as the *Rigveda* were composed between about 1500 and 1200 BCE by a horse-using, and possibly iron-using, people, but it is the language particularly that sets 'Aryans' apart from other peoples, not race, as long assumed. The hymns were preserved in oral tradition by means of a poetic canon devised by Aryan priests to praise their gods during the ritual of sacrifice. In one of the earliest, the hymnist offers a paean to the god Agni:

I extol Agni, the household priest, the divine minister of the sacrifice, the chief priest, the bestower of blessings.[1]

Another hymn, 'The Hymn of Creation', may be one of the earliest recorded expressions of doubt about the nature of knowledge and the process of creation:

Darkness was hidden by darkness in the beginning; with no distinguishing signs, all this was water. The life-force that was covered in emptiness . . . arose through the power of heat.
Who really knows? Who will here proclaim it? Whence was it produced? Whence was this creation? The gods came afterwards, with the creation of this universe. Who then really knows whence it has arisen?
Whence this creation has arisen – perhaps it formed itself, or perhaps it did not – the one who looks down on it, in the highest heaven, only he knows – or perhaps he does not know.[2]

Here, without the monotheistic certainty, is the formless void of the opening of the book of Genesis. The vedic hymns praise a variety of gods to whom sacrifices were offered. Chief among these was Indra, a warrior god whose thunderbolt and whose troops of charioteers dazzled and defeated many a non-Aryan chief, called *dasa* (which later became a pejorative term). Others who were praised were: Surya and Savitir, chariot-driving sun gods, and another minor sun deity called Vishnu; Agni (cognate with the Latin *ignis*), at once keeper of the sacred flame of the mystical sacrifice and the practical agency for destroying the forests that harboured enemies of the Aryan hordes and opening new ground for cultivation; and Varuna, a king among gods and utterly unlike the boisterous Indra, who was also a brawler and easily manipulated by adroit ritual. Varuna was an ethical and judging god, unswayed by the blandishments of sacrifices and not confused by the drug or drink *soma* that other gods imbibed.

At the core of the Aryan religion was the sacrificial act performed punctiliously by expert brahman priests. A hymn attached to the *Rigveda*, though composed in later vedic times, the 'The Hymn of the Primeval Man' (*Purushasukta*), asserts the centrality of the sacrifice. All of creation resulted from the sacrifice by the gods of the 'Lord of Beings', Prajapati, or the first man (*purusha*). All things and creatures having been made, men were created by a dismemberment of Prajapati (who nevertheless appears to have survived his sacrifice):

When the gods made a sacrifice with the Man [Prajapati] as their victim, Spring was the melted butter, Summer the fuel and Autumn the oblation . . . The brahman was his [Prajapati's] mouth, of his arms were made the warrior [*rajanya* or kshatriya]; his thighs became the vaishya [free farmer and merchant], of his feet the shudra [servant] was born.[3]

This stunning image of ritual power reflected the great prestige and privilege enjoyed by priests as ritual principals. But all was not poker-faced austerity and ritual sacrifice, at least not for the gods, seers and rulers depicted in these hymns. Sex, sport, gambling and drinking also figured, and even charitable works. The Asvins, twin horsegods (or horse guards), cured a female seer, Ghosa, of a skin disease that had long rendered her unmarriageable, and went on to provide the son she and her husband could not produce on their own, owing to the advanced age and impotence of the latter. They rescued ship-wrecked sailors and provided a woman warrior with an iron leg when she lost her own in battle. (With compassion surprising in an ancient warrior liter-ature, the Rigvedas deal with handicap sympathetically; for example, blind-ness does not seem to disqualify a woman from marriage, but is a reason for both father and husband to behave with special forbearance.[4] More serious was a lack of wealth and talent, but even that could be remedied.[5])

THE UPANISHADS

Along with the sacred, domestic and philosophical hymns, an ancillary canon came into existence as a comment upon them. There were three later Vedas: the Sama, Yajur and Atharva Vedas, dealing respectively with liturgical verses to be sung, with magical incantations to be pronounced, and with sacrificial formulae to guide the ritualists. Manuals of ritual (called Brahmanas), of which the Satapatha Brahmana was an important example, specified practices to be carried out in the homes of the elite, as well as in public at specially constructed altars. Two further commentaries speak of the mystical meanings of certain Rigvedic hymns. These are called Aranyakas, or forest texts (con-taining knowledge so secret it should be learned only in the seclusion of the forest), and the Upanishads, which are now considered to contain secret knowledge of salvation and the nature of deity, and to have been a major influence on the later Buddhist theology. In one of the Upanishads, the 'he' of the creation hymn cited above is a more abstract, cosmic quality rather than a person:

> He encircled all, bright, incorporeal, scatheless, sinewless, pure, untouched by evil; a seer, wise and omnipresent, self-existent, he dispensed all things well for ever and ever.[6]

In another, somewhat later, Upanishad, divine agency is personal and theistic. Shiva is identified with Rudra, and later devotional conceptions of deity are adumbrated:

> There is one Rudra only, they do not allow a second, who rules all the worlds by his might. He stands behind all things, he made all of the worlds, and protects them, and rolls them up at the end of time.
> The Lord lives in the faces of all beings . . . He lives in the inmost heart of all, the all-pervading, all-present Shiva.[7]

The Indic world of the *Rigveda* was restricted to a region defined by the Saraswati and Indus rivers, together with the tributaries of the latter; that is, principally to the Punjab and the mountains of the northwest, with but little of the Ganges basin. Later Vedas, however, do speak of the Ganges and a fire-marked course to the Sadanira, or modern Gandak river, that demarcated an early Indo-Aryan frontier.

CLEARING THE FORESTS

Between 1000 and 500 BCE iron tools and weapons provided the technological foundations for the expansion of agricultural communities over the entire basin of the Ganges. One important consequence of the replacement of copper and bronze implements by stronger iron weapons and tools was the greater ease in removing the forest cover from the banks of the Ganges, so that these fertile lands could be planted. That much of the tree cover was also removed by burning is inferred from the ritual manual called the *Satapatha Brahmana*, thought to have been composed between 800 and 600 BCE. In it, the god of fire, Agni, sets a path of sacrificial flames from the western valley of the Ganges to the east, thereby consecrating certain areas for occupation by Aryans. Reaching modern Bihar, Agni commanded the Aryan chief Videgha Mathava, who had followed his fiery trail, to carry him over the river Gandak (then called the Sadanira) in order to sanctify the far bank for Aryan occupation as well; the newly consecrated land east of the Gandak was thereafter ruled by Videgha Mathava, now called Videha, and constituted one of the sixteen great chieftaincies (mahajanapada) of the age.

The supersession of bronze by iron and pastoralism by sedentary agriculture laid the foundation for a new period of political consolidation beginning around 1000 BCE. Numerous small cities in the Gangetic valley reflect the twin processes of agricultural development and state formation. Out of these processes came a set of monarchies around the eighth to sixth centuries BCE, and the first imperial regime, the Mauryans, around 320 BCE. The opening of the vast, fertile Gangetic plain to agrarian exploitation can be glimpsed in the post-Harappan archaeological record, to which has been added the rich documentation of the Sanskrit vedic corpus. From both come details of settlements by horsemen with iron weapons imposing their rule over other peoples, first in the Punjab and the western Gangetic plain and later over the whole of the plain to the Gangetic delta in Bengal. It has to have been a gradual change rather than the cataclysm implied by the oft-used term 'Aryan invasion'. Archaeology and the vedic documents permit two simultaneous changes to be traced, one to a fully settled agrarian economy and the other from clans with a lineage-based society to the more complex social and political forms that have marked all subsequent developments in India and made it distinctive.

ARYAN SOCIAL DIFFERENTIATION

By later vedic times – that is, between 1000 and 500 BCE, when the sacrificial cult of Indo-Aryan brahmans had attained a prestigious place – the main locus of Aryan society had shifted from the river valleys of the Punjab and the plains of northern Rajasthan into the western parts of the plain (*doab*) formed by the

Ganges and Yamuna rivers. In this fertile middle Ganges–Yamuna region agriculture soon overtook pastoralism as the dominant mode of production, and sedentary villages with planted and irrigated fields replaced the wandering life of Aryan herdsmen. Cattle-keeping and cattle-wealth still marked the highest ranking and ruling clans of Aryans, called *rajanya*, but all the Aryan clans, as well as non-Aryans (*vis*) among whom they settled in the Gangetic plain, increasingly looked upon land as wealth. The successful cattle raids that had marked earlier Aryan life ceased to be the most desirable attribute of Aryan chiefs, and more esteem attached to skilfully managing the incorporation of Aryan clans into larger political groupings. For example, the highest Aryan clans of the later vedic age were the Panchalas, formed of five previously independent clans, and the Kurus, formed of earlier clans known as Porus and Bharatas.

In addition to the aggregation of weaker clans into larger, stronger ones, there were other changes revealed in later vedic texts and contemporary Buddhist stories (*jatakas*), which traced the multiple lives and divine mission of the Buddha. Aryans of the early *Rigveda* were organized into tribes (*jana*), and further divided into ruling lineages (*rajanya*), and commoner clans (*vis*). By degrees, some of the ruling clansmen took another title, 'kshatriya', from the word *kshatra*, or power, and they along with the most adept of the priestly ritualists (*brahmans*) constituted the elite of society, each group contributing to the welfare and interests of the other. Brahmans conferred legitimacy by carrying out powerful sacrifices that ritually converted warriors into kings, and kings reciprocated with fees and gifts to brahmans. To others were left the mundane tasks of providing the sustenance for the elite. *Praja*, which emerged as a term for these subaltern sections of the society and still means 'children' (i.e. subject people), consisted of lower Aryan groups as well as non-Aryans, probably descendants of the farmers of late Harappan times.

Ritual knowledge in the Brahmanas, like other vedic lore, was transmitted orally and not as written texts until much later. The Brahmanas of the later vedic age refer to certain regions associated with clusters of particular Aryan clansmen, as *janapada*, tracts where particular clans were dominant; that is, where they placed their feet (*pada*). Janapadas took their names from the ruling kshatriya lineage and each had a ruler (*raja*), often chosen by an assembly of chiefly members of the ruling clan as a great fighter capable of protecting the land of his lineage (*rashtra*).

Subjects of the raja of later vedic times and servants of the elite for whose protection he was selected, praja, were divided into 'shudras' and 'dasas'. Dasas are described as unattractive and uncultured, with broad, flat noses and black skin, speaking a strange language and practising 'crude magic' in contrast to the prestigious vedic ritual of the Aryans. However, many dasas were said to have been captured in wars among Aryan clans as well as between Aryans and non-Aryans, so it may have been only defeat that set them apart in reality, and the negative descriptions are simply the victors' insults. Dasas were set to working the lands and tending the herds of lower Aryan clansmen and other vis. Another designation for a people despised by Aryans was *mleccha*, a term meaning 'one who speaks indistinctly', in later times connoting a barbarian whose origins were not in the subcontinent.

Those called vis adopted the title of vaishya, which at first designated the leading households of farmers, herdsmen or merchants. The heads of such households were called *grihapati* in some later vedic sources and *gahapati* in Buddhist texts; they were sources of tribute to Aryan rajas and fees to brahman priests. Thus by the later vedic times of 1000 to 500 BCE, the structural elements of the caste system were in place, summarized as well as canonically accounted for in the 'Hymn of the Primeval Man': the four *varnas* (colours or castes) of brahmans, kshatriyas, vaishyas and shudras. These categories were ranked according to the amount of pollution attached to being born into one or another of them. The least polluted were the brahmans, the most were the shudras; the term varna reinforced these ranked differences: brahmans were supposed to wear white, kshatriyas yellow, vaishyas red and shudras black. Another invidious distinction made manifest by Buddhist times was that between the three highest varnas, who were considered twice-born (*dvija*), and the shudras. The former participated in a ritual 'second' birth (*upanayana*, initiation) while the latter did not.

In addition, there were groups ranked even lower than shudras; to them was attached the stigma of untouchability, supposedly because their occupations were deeply polluting. These included leather workers, who disposed of sacred cattle when they died. The reason for the low rank of artisans such as blacksmiths and other metal workers is less obvious, but may be attributed, as it is in modern Tibet, to their occupational handling of the leather bellows.

Intermarriage and eating together were determined by the smaller units into which all the varnas were divided; these were called *jati* (literally 'birth group', but also translated as caste); jati is in fact what Indians usually mean when they speak of caste today. The jati was often originally an occupational group, one into which each individual was in theory immutably born. Later writers denounced intermarriage between jatis, and consigned the offspring of such unions to low-status castes of their own, but in practice there continued to be a certain amount of caste mobility, both of individuals between castes (as when slaves were occasionally adopted into the jatis of their masters), and of whole jatis, as will be discussed below.

THE STATUS OF WOMEN

In the early vedic period, caste development was apparently weak enough for marriage between groups to be common. Much in the Rigvedic corpus, too, suggests that the status of women was higher than it was to be in later centuries. For example, daughters as well as sons were given the education of the time; both memorized the hymns and were instructed in their meanings. One text says: 'An unmarried young learned daughter should be married to a bridegroom who like her is learned.'[8] In the hymns, female as well as male seers (*rishis*) appear, and are equal or better in ascetic exercises. The texts are often cast in the form of dialogues in which females as well as males have speaking roles, which has led to the speculation that some hymns were actually composed by women. Nor were women even barred from public speaking, as shown by the hymn that exhorts the newly married wife: 'You should address the assembly [*vidatha*, a type of popular meeting] as a commander.'[9]

Girls were permitted to move about freely in public, attend the festive gatherings called *samanas* in search of husbands or lovers and sometimes spend the night abroad. Marriage, although expected to be universal (as occasionally it was not), took place when the bride was fully mature and usually to the man of her choice, although her father and, especially, her mother had a veto. The presence and participation of the wife of the donor at the sacrifice was a requirement of the ritual. Daughters could, at a pinch, take the place of sons, women could inherit property and both sexes could make up for marital undesirability by a suitable addition of wealth. Widows were mentioned and even remarried; the contemporary evidence of the later custom of widow immolation is dubious at best.

Nevertheless, the purpose of marriage for women was the production of sons expected to perform funeral rites and sacrifices for their progenitors; wives were subordinate to their husbands, and women are often depicted as sexual temptresses, diverting men from their ascetic and moral duties. Nor was the standard litany of misogynist abuse entirely absent, even from the *Rigveda*: 'There can be no friendship with women, as they have the hearts of wolves or jackals.'[10] By the later vedic period, moreover, the rot had set in and the Brahmanas displayed both the curse of caste and the misogyny that was to increase, pervading and disfiguring Indian society up to the present. The Satapatha Brahmana identifies women with evil, and declares, 'The woman, the shudra, the dog and the crow are falsehood.'[11] The same text goes on to suggest that they should be excluded from meetings. The vilification of women had proceeded to such a point that, in the *Mahabharata* epic, the puzzled philosopher-king Yudhisthira was moved to ask, 'If women are wicked and vicious by their very nature, how could the dharmashastra [righteous conduct] writers enjoin that they should participate with their husbands in religious duties?'

POLITICAL AND RELIGIOUS DEVELOPMENTS

The polities that emerged late during the first millennium BCE were chiefdoms known as janapadas, and named after the land tracts they occupied. Their rulers were scions of the dominant clans of such communities, whose authority derived partly from the support of subordinate rajanyas (kshatriyas) and partly from the legitimation conferred by ritual experts. Political authority was complex; groups of kinsmen were deemed collective possessors of local power; territories were consecrated by one of several sacrifices performed by ritualists and sponsored by chieftains; in addition, there were several kinds of assemblies whose members shared with rajas the rights to tribute from the vaishyas and were accordingly called 'eaters of the vaishya' (*visamatta*).

From the largest of the chiefdoms emerged the first primitive monarchies, whose kings were made and made visible by royal sacrifices and by the attendance of courtiers as royal servants. The major royal sacrifices (*rajasuya*, *vajapeya* and *ashvamedha*) were known from before the time of the Buddha (fifth century BCE) and were occasionally revived and performed well into medieval times. The rajasuya was a royal consecration by which a new king was imbued with divine power, identified with the vedic Indra, with Prajapati, the Lord of Beings of the Purushashukta hymn, and finally with Vishnu – all the result of a year-long series of ceremonies. Once consecrated, the king's powers had occasionally to be refreshed with other ceremonies; one was the vajapeya, where, among other rituals, through drinking a highly charged ambrosia concocted by priests, a king's failing energy and strength were revived and his vigour was increased, enabling him to undertake new conquests.

THE ASHVAMEDHA

The horse sacrifice (ashvamedha) was the most famous of royal sacrifices, for it was associated with a king's conquests in every direction, his *digvijaya*. In this ritual, the king's horse was consecrated, and, accompanied by his kinsmen and other armed warriors, allowed to roam where it would for a year. Wherever the horse trod, there the sovereignty of its master was proclaimed and, if contested, defended by his soldiers. At the climax of the ceremonies, after the year had elapsed, the horse was slaughtered and the principal queen, known as the *Mahisi* (Great Female Buffalo), was required to copulate with the dead animal.

> As she lies there, she taunts the horse about his sexual performance, and she and the lesser wives of the king engage in obscene banter with the priests, while hundreds of female attendants of the queens, their hair half unbound, circle the horse and the unfortunate lady, singing, dancing, and slapping their thighs. The verbal part of the ceremony is extremely explicit, and in fact tested the limits of tolerance of our scholarly predecessors.[12]

Of course, only the very wealthiest of rulers could sponsor such ceremonies.

THE MAHAJANAPADAS AND THE EARLY KINGDOMS

The nature of political institutions and their relations with communities of the time is more clearly seen at this point, too. Between the period of composition of the Sanskrit hymns of the *Rigveda* – 1500 to 1000 BCE – and about 400 BCE, when the Sanskrit epics *Mahabharata* and *Ramayana* were composed, small monarchies were the loci of power and supra-local politics. These mahajanapada, which can be translated as 'great communities', first mentioned in post-vedic religious sources, had evolved from what are often referred to as 'tribal kingdoms'. Sixteen such 'great communities' existed in the basin of the Ganges river, which now contained the principal population of the subcontinent, leaving older settlements in the northwest in a backwater. These 'great communities' were distributed over the northern subcontinent from Gandhara in the northwest, with Taxila its capital, to Anga with its

Plate 3 Ashvamedha-yaga (Horse sacrifice ceremony). A cleaned-up version of the horse sacrifice in which the queen, who sits sedately by the chief priest, is the only female presence. The horse who prances before them is slaughtered in the upper left-hand corner. Watercolour by Sital Das, Locknow, c.1780 (IOL Johnson Album 5, No. 21, Neg. No. B. 7651, by permission of the British Library).

capital of Campa in the eastern Gangetic plain, south to Avanti and its core headquarters of Ujjaini. All of these places figured in the war around which the story of the *Mahabharata* was framed.

The mahajanapadas of the Gangetic plain were pre-state political formations; political leadership was vested in ruling clans which evolved into the ruling lineages of the monarchies founded around the sixth century BCE. Among the latter was the conquering kingdom of Magadha, whose authority was superseded and extended by the Mauryan kingdom over the whole of the Ganges valley, beginning around 300 BCE.

Another among the earliest states to emerge from the historic chiefdoms of the north Indian plain was Koshala, in a territory north of the Ganges watered by a tributary called the Ghaghara. The region around its capital at Ayodhya was able to sustain a rich agriculture owing to the plenitude of irrigation. Reliable crops of barley and rice were cultivated with ploughs using iron shares to increase the depth of tillage. Conflicts are recorded among local groups and settlements over the control of water courses and the labour required for the more intensive cultivation of wet rice and for the construction and maintenance of the dams needed to regulate water use and prevent floods. Buddhist documents of the time reported the taxes demanded by the kings of Koshala from land-holding households, the royal practice of taking cultivable fields by escheat from such households and the collection of customs duties from traders. Money was sought from all quarters to equip armies and defend royal perquisites from lesser Aryan magnates.

At about the same time, Magadha was emerging south of the Ganges, 250 miles from Ayodhya. Unlike the rulers of Koshala, who were from rajanya clans, Bimbisara, the founder of Magadha, was referred to as *srenika* (from *sreni*, meaning guild), which suggests that he came from the ranks of traders or artisans. Nevertheless, he ruled a kingdom said in the epic *Mahabharata* to contain 80,000 villages, and each of these irrigated settlements was under a headman who met with the others on occasion as a great assembly to attend the king and his son Ajatasatru. The Magadha kings built a powerful fortified capital at Rajagriha, set back from the river plain which it commanded from rocky heights.

Marriage links were forged between the Koshala and Magadha rulers, and in time the distant Koshala territory was incorporated by Magadha, as eventually were a number of other polities. Among the latter was the Vrijji confederation of clans, located about fifty miles north of the Ganges homeland of the Magadhas, and notable for maintaining an older style of rule through lineages and clan assemblies. The latter were designated by the term, *gana-sangha*, 'gana' for the lineage society composed of clans and 'sangha' for the collegiate principle of political organization.

The *Mahabharata* and the *Ramayana*

India's great epic poem, the *Mahabharata*, began to be compiled or composed around 400 BCE, but may have taken several centuries to reach its final form. Among its aims was the delineation of a type of monarchy: one section of the epic – the Santi Parvan – was devoted to setting out a theory of Aryan kingship, justifying and describing its elaborate royal sacrifices. In it, the human condition was conceived of as framed by recurring cycles of public morality, each beginning with an act of creation in accordance with the Rigvedic hymn of the primeval sacrifice that initiated an era (*yuga*) of perfect purity, the *kritayuga*. During this era, the inherent righteousness of the people made social and political institutions unnecessary. But progressive weakening of popular morality proceeded from age to age until the 'black' era, or *kaliyuga*, ensued. Then political institutions had to be introduced: kings to rule and to punish evil, and also to maintain *varnashramadharma*, proper behaviour – the duty (*dharma*) to follow caste and life-stage (*ashrama*) rules. Mankind was to be taught the path to follow, beginning with the appropriate relations of love (*kama*), progressing to the understanding and proper pursuit of interest and advantage (*artha*), and culminating in the higher order of general and personal morality implied in the notion of dharma. The eventual outcome of this moral trajectory was deliverance from life and the succession of rebirths by the attainment of salvation (*moksha*).

Proper rule required kings of talent and inspiration, and they were not always to be found among the highest rajanyas of the Aryan clans. Hence, the *Mahabharata* allowed that since competence and efficaciousness were critical criteria for kingship, and these were not always acquired with birth as a

1926-3-1-01

Plate 4 Rama, Sita and Lakshmana (Rama's brother) menaced by a demon host; from the *Ramayana*. Kangra-style painting from the Pahari hills. Early nineteenth century (BM OA. 1926. 3-1. 01, Courtesy of the Trustees of the British Museum).

kshatriya, morality and correct values could be achieved by able non-kshatriyas through the ritual transformation of the rajasuya and ashvamedha sacrifices and through the counsel of learned brahman spiritual advisers. Properly consecrated kings, of whatever origin, established an order in which the rule of aggression and injustice, of 'big fish that eat small ones', was curbed. Such an ordered world was pleasing to the presiding great god of the Aryans, Vishnu (who had himself been promoted from his earlier minor sungod status), and he would add his support for the maintenance of a good society by occasionally making an appearance in any of a variety of disguised forms, such as that of a great fish (*matsya*), who saved mankind from an earth-destroying flood, or as Rama, the model king, or, in yet another avatar, as the Buddha.

In addition to the *Mahabharata*, and composed at about the same time or perhaps a little later, the other great Indian epic, the *Ramayana*, told the story of Rama, purportedly the king of Koshala. Rama manifested the qualities that became paradigmatic for all subsequent state dynasts. His adversary, Ravanna, the chieftain of Sri Lanka and abductor of Rama's wife Sita, symbolized the disordered polity where there were no kings and where the demons reigned as tyrants who knew neither royalty, nor caste, nor gods.

Both of the epics celebrated the victory of monarchy over the much older institution of lineage rule through chiefs. If the *Ramayana* provided the model for the perfect king and the triumph of dharmic kings over demonic chiefs in universal terms, the *Mahabharata* depicted a great civil war in which monarchy triumphed over lineage chieftainship in the middle Gangetic heartland of the Aryans. It recounts, in some 100,000 verses, the marshalling of forces and the battle between two related families of Aryan kshatriyas of the mahajanapada of Kuru. The Kaurava clansmen dominated the upper reaches of the Ganges from their capital of Hastinapura, while the Pandavas held the upper portion of the Yamuna from their capital at Indraprastha, the future Delhi. When the crucial battle was finally fought in Kurukshetra, a field in Kuru, it sealed the fate of the ancient kshatriya chieftainship, a political form that had endured for nearly a millennium.

Although kshatriyas, as individuals or as lineages, could continue to exercise some local dominance, from the time of the *Mahabharata* nearly all kings were in practice drawn from shudra families, beginning with the founder of the Nanda kingdom, one Mahapadma, whom Jaina sources and puranas claim was born of a shudra woman. The Nandas ruled in the territory of the Magadha kingdom for around a century, before being displaced in turn by the new-rising Mauryan kings.

INDIA'S SECOND URBANIZATION

In addition to zones of irrigated agriculture and relatively dense population within a still very heavily forested landscape, there was also a good deal of commercial interaction around this time, judging from the references to trade centres in documents of the Jaina sect. Cities appear again in the archaeological and literary remains of iron age cultures found in the extensive and fertile Gangetic river basin between 1000 and 500 BCE. Once more, however, we are mystified by them, despite very intensive archaeological research in sites from Taxila near the Indus in the west to the delta of the Ganges in the east. The mystery of this 'second urbanization', as it is sometimes called, begins to recede with the composition of Buddhist texts. For the first time we hear the language of urban folk, in the Pali canon of around 500 BCE, a date marking the end of the pre-formation of the classical pattern of Indian civilization. Thereupon commenced a traceable thousand-year evolution that culminated in the Gupta classical age, around CE 500, which Indians of the post-Gupta era and modern scholars alike have considered 'golden'.

The significance that scholars have attached to the two early urban phases – that of the northwest between 2500 and 1500 BCE and that of the Gangetic plain between about 1000 and 500 BCE – has changed over time. Particular ecological conditions are now thought to be involved in the decline of the earlier urbanization; that is, cities were probably abandoned as a result of flood damage combined with environmental degradation caused by deforestation and overcultivation, rather than by Aryan invaders from central Asia. That several cities in what is now Gujarat preserved the early urban material culture and possibly other features for 500 years longer supports the hypothesis of ecological decline of the northwestern cities. The existence of later Harappan cities in Gujarat as well as in the Punjab and the eastern Gangetic plain has interesting implications. One is the suggestion that the end of the cities of the Indus in Sind did not mean the end of Harappan culture; there is now thought to have been a robust 'mature' Harappan cultural era up to around 1000 BCE. The picture in the Punjab is less clear, except that settlements are found there with the usual assemblage of pottery, domestic architecture and certain artistic productions like bull and bird figurines and beads; however, a shift in staple food production from the wheat of the west to the rice of the east is evident.

In addition to the notion of a 'Later Harappan' culture extended in time is that of a spatial extension to merge with the Gangetic, iron age culture to the east and the urban impulse that found expression there from between 1000 and 500 BCE. In those centuries, a string of urban centres – towns rather than cities – came into existence, ranging from the western settlement of Indraprastha (the future Delhi) over the whole of the plain to Kashi (the future Benares) in the eastern Ganges. This later development suggests that there might have been a single extended urban phase beginning around 2500 BCE that possessed stronger and weaker moments, but nevertheless one in which town life never ceased to be an important element within the general cultural configuration of ancient times.

Such a possibility contradicts notions long cherished by archaeologists and historians: that there was an early, elaborate and significantly indigenous urban culture of northwest India which somehow had nothing to do with the subsequent cultural development begun by the invasion of primitive Aryan horsemen whose Sanskrit hymns bore the seeds of the fully blown 'golden age' culture of the Gupta age. Without doubt, Aryan invaders contributed to the long pre-formation of the classical cultural pattern achieved by Gupta times – if only by the gift of the Sanskrit language. Still, there was much else to the golden age culture of Gupta times that was contributed by others, especially by descendants of the neolithic farming communities of the northwest, but also by immigrants from the Mediterranean region and from Southeast Asia, and even, later on, by migrants from the Central Asian homeland of the Aryans, such as Hunas (Huns). Other cultural traditions about which we remain largely ignorant may also have influenced the evolving classical pattern. Some led to the formation of the Dravidian languages and literatures of the south, others to agricultural and handicraft systems more advanced and productive than the simple pastoral practices of the Aryans.

RELIGION IN THE LATER VEDIC PERIOD

Buddhism and Jainism were atheistic, ascetic and ethical systems that came into existence and were structured in opposition to the practices and beliefs of the 'later vedic' period (between about 900 and 500 BCE), when a religion based upon sacrificial ritual was carried out by specialists called 'brahmans', financed by wealthy and pious donors, and set out in manuals appropriately called 'brahmanas'. It was against this sacrificial cult and its practices that the

Buddha and Mahavira defined their ethical teachings; these were then pre-served and transmitted through orders of monks who were recruited from many social groups, including brahmans. Yet in all of this the religious activities of ordinary people were probably not much altered. Then and later they centred on the propitiation of local tutelary deities whose protection was supplicated or whose wilful destructiveness (usually in the form of disease) was averted through humble offerings.

The Gupta culture of the classical period owes much to formative processes dating from around 500 BCE, a period usually assigned to the religious careers of the founders of Buddhism and Jainism (although recent re-evaluation of the evidence now assigns their activities to a date closer to the end of the fifth century). It was in the same period that the two great epics, the *Mahabharata* and *Ramayana*, were first composed. Religion and literature are among the central markers of the classical pattern, and, of course, major sources of historical evidence. Both define the Aryan culture, which by the middle of the first millennium BCE was certainly an autonomous tradition.

In addition to the epics and the Buddhist canon there was another corpus of religious and social theory that added to the ideological content of early Indian society. These were traditions known as *itihasa-purana*, the first term of which still denotes 'history', and the second 'ancient tale'. Most of them began as genealogical records of great families and were the work of bards who produced panegyrics for patrons who would be famous. Contemporary with the formation of both of the great epics, *Mahabharata* and *Ramayana* – that is, around 400 BCE or later – the puranas extolled the rule of the kings of Magadha in terms similar to those used in the *Ramayana* to tell the story of Rama. Other puranas provided sacred biographies of the major gods Shiva and Vishnu, delineating the distinctive attributes of each deity so strikingly as to make them resistant to being incorporated into a single godhead when this was attempted in later centuries. These epic and puranic religious traditions mingled with Buddhism, which rose to prominence along with the Magadha kings and was to achieve its greatest historic moment in India during the Mauryan dynasty.

BUDDHISM

Like the vedas, the earliest records of Buddhist tradition were orally transmit-ted for several centuries. The oldest surviving written records, known as 'the Pali canon', were preserved in the Pali language (a close relative of Sanskrit) and found written on palm leaves in Ceylon, although it is now thought that the original canonical language must have been the dialect spoken at Magadha. Analysis indicates that even the Pali canon contains material of varying antiquity, just as the Old Testament does. Hence it is tempting to believe that pronouncements and attitudes attributed to the Buddha that do not seem ideally kindly and compassionate are products of later interpolation by monkish copyists.

Be that as it may, the Pali canon consists of three major divisions (*pitaka*, or 'baskets'), concerned respectively with the rules of the monastic order, with the discourses of the Buddha and with metaphysics. Each pitaka consists of a number of divisions and subdivisions. The Jatakas, or life stories of the Buddha, constitute one of the subdivisions of the discourse, or sermon, basket. In addition, there are a number of non-canonical Pali works, including commentaries on the pitakas, early works in Sanskrit and later ones in Tibetan and Chinese.

Apart from its doctrine, Buddhism possessed the institutional means to propagate its teachings in ethics and morality through the Buddhist *sangha*. Buddhists had adopted this ancient Aryan collegiate form as their pattern of organization, especially for their monasteries, the characteristic loci of Buddhist activity, even though monastic life was foreign to orthodox Hinduism. These institutions created a large written record to document their proceedings, their rules, the substantial properties donated by devoted followers, the results of debates about doctrinal questions and the missionary activities in which the monks engaged. In addition, two other Buddhist texts offer us significant information about this era: the *Dipavamsa* and *Mahavamsa*, which preserve and recount much of the early history of Buddhism in the Magadha kingdom.

According to Buddhist cosmology, castes were created after kings: the brahmans, who lived in the forests and studied the vedas, the vis (*vessa* in Pali), who married and produced and traded goods, and the *sudda* (shudras), who worked for vessa masters and hunted in the forests. In addition to these there were ascetics (*sramana*), who might come from any caste. While Buddhists accepted the prevailing theory of moral degradation and the dangers to mankind during the kaliyuga, they attributed the decline to the passions and lusts of men. When the resulting disorder made kingship necessary, men decided to elect one of their number; accordingly, he was called 'the great chosen one'.

BRAHMANISM AND HETERODOXY

Buddhism and the contemporary Jainism shared much with the contemporary brahmanical sacrificial religion, since all sprang from mystical and philosophical notions explored in the Upanishads, which were still in composition at around 500 BCE when the theologies of Buddhism and Jainism were being formed. Differences nevertheless remained between brahmanical sects and their competitors, one example of which pertains to the concept of *karma*. Karma means work or act, and in the formulations of vedic ritual manuals, 'action' referred to ritual and ceremonial performances so meticulously executed as to compel the gods to act in obedience to them. For Buddhists and Jainas, however, karma referred to the acts of ordinary men and women, the sum of whose lifetime behaviour determined the body in which the soul (*atman*) would be reborn in the process of transmigration (*samsara*). Upon death, that is, souls were thought to pass from one to another body and associated social condition. The idea that every good action brought a measure of happiness and each bad action sorrow tended to suggest a mechanical moral process leading to fatalism in some ancient thinkers. However, it was also believed that each migrating soul ultimately reunited with the single world spirit and the karma account would be closed when the cycle of creation ended; that is, when the mahayuga was completed. The 'world spirit' was called Brahman in some Upanishadic works and taken to be an impersonal essence, though some later works treated it as a creator god, and thus set the stage for the worship of the previously minor Rigvedic god Shiva as divine creator.

THE HISTORICAL BUDDHA

The teachings of the Buddha are the best known development of Upanishadic concepts. The historic title, 'the Buddha', derives from the meaning of that word: enlightened or awakened. Siddhartha, which was his personal name, is now thought to have been born, in the fifth century BCE, a prince of the Sakya clan (which had also adopted the name Gautama). He was said to have renounced his family and the prospect of ruling a gana-sangha community of the Himalayan foothills in order to seek truths to share with his people and those in the kingdoms of Koshala and Magadha. Wandering the forests as an ascetic and mendicant, he pondered the reasons for the pervasive sorrow of the world. Although he found rigorous austerities unfruitful, protracted meditation was finally rewarded when enlightenment came after he sat under a pipal tree (*Ficus religiosa*), near the town of Gaya in Magadha for forty-nine days. Suddenly he began to grasp the full implications of the common observation that sorrow and disappointment spring from desire. After seven more weeks of meditation, he left the Tree of Wisdom and travelled to Kashi, where he commenced teaching in a place called the Deer Park of Sarnath. The tradition of his followers recalls this 'Sermon of the Turning of the Wheel', with its 'Four Noble Truths' and 'Noble Eightfold Path'.

The Buddha's sermons concerned the sources and relief of sorrow, which he held arises from birth, from age, from disease, from death and from life's disappointments. Most of all, it arises from desire, from the thirst for delight, passion and pleasure; quenching this thirst, this desire, is the sole way to conquer sorrow, and can be achieved by following a middle way between gratification and the denial of pleasure through the pain and hardship of harsh asceticism. The middle way was an eightfold path consisting of rightness in views, resolve, speech, conduct, livelihood, efforts, memories and meditation.

Buddhist moderation was framed against existing religious practices. Buddhists excoriated the brahmanical sacrifices because they involved the slaughter of animals and because of the large fees paid by men of property and commerce who were gaining importance in the newly founded towns of Koshala, Magadha and other Gangetic principalities. Other sects that criticized brahmans, such as Jainas and Ajivikas, were condemned by Buddhists for their extreme ascetic practices.

Moderation won adherents among the wealthiest class of merchants, among modest householders and among the poorest and most despised. The last included shudras (agriculturists, herdsmen and artisans) and slaves, as the term *dasasudda* suggests. By the time of the Buddha, 'dasa' had come to designate persons without legal standing or rights who could be held in bondage on account of their debts, their birth to parents in bondage or capture during wars. Even lower in status than the dasas were those now called *candala*, the sight of whom was regarded as polluting. Shudras and candalas were mentioned sympathetically in some the earliest Buddhist jatakas, which may have heightened the appeal of Buddhism for those classes.

The jatakas paint a picture of the society of the middle of the first millennium BCE in the central Gangetic valley, a social order significantly changed from the earlier 'Aryan' society of the western Ganges. It was a more complex and urbanized formation, with little of the older gana-sangha collective identity. Such a society was fertile ground for the new ideologies, in the form of Buddhist doctrines and those of Jaina and Ajivika sects, all of which were alike in their emphasis on ethics and pure conduct rather than the propitiation of capricious gods.

The gods of the brahmanical sacrificial cult were not rejected so much as ignored by Buddhists and their contemporaries in heterodoxy. All these, however, posited the importance of particular great men – usually the founding teachers – and all spoke as brahmanical sectarians did of karma and samsara, though each put a different meaning upon how such doctrines worked. While Buddhists and Jainas believed that the condition of each individual existence was determined by behaviour in previous incarnations, they supposed it could be altered by actions in the current life. The Ajivikas, however, insisted on a rigorously deterministic view of the universe, with regard to which only severe asceticism was a possible ameliorator.

HAGIOGRAPHY AND DOCTRINE

The tendency to see the founders as inspired figures that lent themselves to hagiographical extension and a more deeply emotional religious development balanced the austerity of the heterodoxies. The Ajivikas of southern India considered their founder, Gosala, a divine figure. Similarly, later Buddhists apotheosized their founder. Yet this was a development the Buddha had expressly rejected: according to early Pali scriptures, he had taught that the doctrine alone should guide his disciples after he died. Nevertheless, his followers shortly contradicted their master and also began to transform his original teachings in the direction of pervasive popular beliefs, which undoubtedly brought emotional comfort to those suffering the uncertainties of an increasingly complex agrarian and mercantile society.

By the second and first centuries BCE reliefs on the Buddhist stupas at Bharhut and Sanchi depicted crowds of adoring worshippers of the founder, who now figured as a saviour. And his followers had added two other 'jewels' to the original doctrine, or *damma*: one was the person of the Buddha, who was now credited with having promised heaven to his believers; the other was the monastic order (*sangha*), which was dedicated to the propagation of both doctrine and the commemoration of the founder.

In addition, there was a new sectarian development, called by Buddhists the 'Greater Vehicle' (*Mahayana*), a salvation creed centred upon saints (*bodhisattvas*) who deliberately postponed or curtailed their own salvation in order to assist that of others. According to the Pali canon, Prince Siddhartha had gained his wisdom and ultimately his enlightenment as a result of a series of lives through which his soul passed in the processes of karma and samsara. The figure of the bodhisattva stemmed from the proposition that, as there had been previous existences of the Buddha, so his death was not the end, but an opening to another future in which he (and possibly other noble souls) would return to guide and to aid the salvation of others. The Mahayana form of Buddhism came to predominate in parts of Asia to the north of India, such as Tibet, Nepal and China, while the *Hinayana* (Lesser Vehicle) form is prevalent in the southern regions, such as Sri Lanka and Myanmar.

In the Hinayana writings of the earliest Buddhist period, men, even inspired men like the Buddha, could offer only modest assistance to others through example and counsel. Now, according to the Mahayanists, the individual attainment of nirvana while others remained in darkness would have been rather selfish in a teacher as compassionate as the Buddha; thus, the Buddha and the bodhisattvas who imitated him were depicted as self-sacrificing saviours in terms that seem to anticipate Christian beliefs:

> all that burden of pain I take upon myself, I assume, I endure . . . I must set all free, I must save all the world from the wilderness of birth, of old age, of disease, of being born again, of all sins . . . Because it is better that I alone be in pain, than that all those creatures fall into the place of misfortune. There I must give myself in bondage, and all the world must be redeemed from the wilderness of hell, beast-birth, and Yama's [the god of death's] world.[13]

Such expressions have suggested to some that Christianity and later Buddhist doctrine both derived from a common source of saviour religions found in western Asia in the closing years of the first millennium (if the idea of the bodhisattva was not directly influenced by Christianity itself). For example, a bodhisattva named Maitreya was said to be the Buddha of the future, who would manifest himself in a second coming. Like Christian saints, bodhisattvas proliferated, each with his own functions and symbols.

Whether or not all bodhisattvas were necessarily male was a matter of controversy, but early in the development of the Great Vehicle, saviouresses appeared with all the redeeming powers of their male counterparts. Some devotees even believed in female divinities possessed of a superior power called *shakti* that energized the male bodhisattvas through sexual union. This magical sexual power was likened to a thunderbolt (*vajra*), from which the name, Vajrayana, of the doctrine was derived.

JAINISM

Jainism was even more essentially moralistic in its outlook than Buddhism, with an even greater emphasis on austerity and mendicant monasticism as the sole route to salvation (*moksha* or *nirvana*), despite its martial-sounding terms such as 'great hero' (*Mahavira*) and 'victor' (*jina*) (the latter presumably referring to spiritual conflict). The teachings of the founder Vardhamana, who was revered by his followers as Mahavira, found an audience similar to that of

Buddhism in the complex villages and towns. Like followers of the Buddha, the wealthy were encouraged to make investments in the commerce and productivity of the communities in which they lived as a religious duty that increased the welfare of all, high and low, whether kinsmen or not; they were further enjoined to honesty in commercial dealings and frugality was considered as a form of piety.

The Buddhist sangha and Jaina monastery drew their monks and lay supporters from all social ranks, and both institutions conscientiously maintained close links with the societies about them. In fact, one reason for the success of Jainism in remaining a vital Indian religion with a significant following among merchants and artisans was that the laity followed the practice of periodic retreats in the monasteries where they lived as monks. And the influence was reciprocal. Jaina sectarian polemics written by monks even used the metaphor of 'squandering invested capital merely to realize immediate profit' in criticizing each other's arguments.[14]

According to Jaina tradition, the origin and career of Mahavira seem to parallel those of the Buddha. He was born to a chief of an Aryan clan and educated to hold high office. He renounced his heritage and family to wander and meditate, sometimes in the company of Gosala, the founder of the Ajivikas, whom he met in the second year and broke with in the tenth (supposedly because the latter was not convinced of the necessity of chastity and total abstemiousness). After thirteen years, often as a naked ascetic, he attained enlightenment and thereafter taught his doctrine in the kingdoms of the Ganges region before succumbing to a ritual of slow starvation near the Magadhan capital of Rajagriha around 400 BCE. His followers carried his teachings into the Deccan, where monasteries were established with the support of the founder of the Mauryan kingdom, Chandragupta.

Unlike Buddhism, Mahavira's sect never spread beyond India, but it remains a living tradition there. The order formed by his followers split in post-Mauryan times, one faction insisting on remaining naked (*Digambaras*, or 'sky-clad') as their teacher had been, and the other clothing themselves in white robes (*Shvetambaras*). Both sub-sects formulated new doctrines, and it was essentially through the serious cultivation of literature in Sanskrit and other languages that Jaina ideas, especially in ethics, were transmitted by the monks, who alone were considered eligible for salvation.

WOMEN IN THE HETERODOXIES

While the ethical heterodoxies attacked caste and inequality as well as the violence of brahmanical sacrifices, they tended to accept – and sometimes carry to bizarre extremes – the views also found in developing Hinduism that women were inferior, inherently sinful and a source of contamination to men, along with an obsession with salvation as release from seemingly endless transmigration and rebirth. For example, the Buddha at first thought that women should stay at home, although he later agreed that they could become nuns and even become *arhat* (worthy) (while always being inferior to any monk).

The story of the Buddha's change of mind is a famous one, and appears in the *Vinaya* or 'Discipline Basket'. About five years after his enlightenment, he was approached by his aunt, who politely asked:

> Pray, Reverend Sir, let women retire from household life to the houseless [i.e. mendicant] one, under the Doctrine and Discipline announced by The Tathagata [the title by which the Buddha referred to himself].[15]

The Enlightened One told her rather brusquely to hold her peace. After two more attempts on her part and curt refusals on his, the old woman was reduced to tears, exciting the compassion of Ananda, his most chivalrous follower (who at this point was not yet enlightened, and sometimes described as rather dim). Ananda weathered several similar refusals, and then asked if women, under doctrine and discipline, could not attain release from rebirth. The Buddha admitted that they could, and, after being further reminded that his aunt had been his wet nurse, rather wearily agreed to her ordination, stipulating that she must accept eight additional harsh regulations applicable only to the female religious. They involved the complete subordination of nuns to monks. Although they were accepted with alacrity, the Buddha still opined, with undue pessimism, that the ordination of women would reduce the duration of Buddhism from a thousand years to five hundred.

Even these sour reflections were not enough for the Enlightened One (or his later misogynist copyists). In one of the books of the Sermon Basket, when asked why women are not accorded the same status and rights as men, he is reported to have explained that: 'Women, Ananda, are uncontrollable . . . envious . . . greedy . . . weak in wisdom . . . A woman's heart is haunted by stinginess . . . jealousy . . . sensuality.'[16]

Buddhist tradition also records that, after the Buddha's death, a council was convened at which the first two pitakas were recited by the unfortunate Ananda, so that the assembled monks would know what they were. The monks then cross-examined him, in the course of which he was forced to confess to a variety of faults, one of which lay in obtaining the admission of women to the sangha, and another in permitting the body of the late Lord to be viewed first by women, who soiled it with their tears.

FEMALE SALVATION

Yet more revealing, and systematically so, the two (or two and a half, for a group called Yapaniya that died out in the fifteenth century seemed to occupy a sort of intermediate position) sects of Jainas held a debate that ran for a millennium and a half (from the second century CE to the eighteenth) over the question of whether women could attain salvation. In the course of their polemics, the disputants expounded several striking theories in human biology and sexual psychology. The major points of controversy revolved around the question of whether it was necessary to abjure clothes (as did the Digambaras in imitation of the founder's practice) in order to attain moksha (which, in Jaina cosmology, was higher than the seventh heaven). The Shvetambaras considered nudity optional, or, indeed, inappropriate to the degenerate times in which they felt they lived. They even cast doubt on the notion that nudity demonstrated non-attachment to possessions.

But both sides agreed that female nudity was out of the question, whether because of women's inherent ugliness and blemishes, because of the difficulties caused by menstruation or because of their vulnerability to sexual harassment and assault. The word for woman, *stri*, itself derived from a root meaning 'to cover', and this need for cover constantly reminds women (or, more likely, men) of their sexual nature and the shame and fear it engenders, which distracts them from the concentration required to attain the necessary spiritual detachment. Moreover, said an early Digambara writer, not only do clothes breed lice, which are killed by the activities of the wearer, but women's bodies themselves are the breeding places for microorganisms called *aparyaptas* that proliferate in their armpits, navels, between the breasts and especially in their vaginas, where they cause a constant itching that can be relieved only through intercourse (a notion reminiscent of the speculations of Sigmund Freud that female masturbation is elicited by the itching of intestinal worms). But intercourse, as well as menstruation, kills large numbers of the hypothetical aparyaptas, and hence violates the injunction of non-violence:

> When a man and a woman unite sexually, these beings in the vagina are destroyed, just as if a red-hot iron were inserted into a hollow piece of bamboo [filled with sesame seeds].[17]

Both sides recognized that in addition to the three bodily sexual forms, male, female and hermaphrodite, each form could have sexual feelings more usual in one of the other forms. Thus, they acknowledged the existence of not only homosexuality, but lesbianism and bisexuality, and did so without the usual anathematizing of traditional religions. In fact, the Digambaras argued that scriptural evidence that might be taken to mean that women were eligible for nirvana without having first been reborn as male really referred to men with female sexual orientation, i.e. to homosexual men.

The Shvetambara position was that if men with homosexual orientation could attain nirvana after suitable detachment from all desire (just as was incumbent upon heterosexual men), then so could females of either orientation. The Digambaras held that it was the woman's ineluctable anatomy and physiology, not her sexual orientation, that was the impediment to salvation, regardless of the impurities or malfunctioning that the male body could occasionally be subject to – such as tapeworms or bleeding haemorrhoids. And both sides agreed that hermaphrodites were barred from salvation.

Another argument adduced by the Digambaras was that just as women could not be born in the lowest of the seven hells – perhaps because their inherent weakness of volition extended to evil as well as good – so they could not attain the highest heaven, let alone the realm above. The Shvetambaras rejected the argument from symmetry, but it is very reminiscent of more modern (and equally dubious) theories of human development which posit 'the greater variability of the male', i.e. that just as there are more subnormal boys, so there are more male geniuses as well.

Both sides agreed that women were inferior in society and in the order. In fact, the Digambaras opined that female religious were called nuns by courtesy only, and by extension cast doubt on the Shvetambara claim to monkhood as well. Real monks, after all, did not wear clothes.

Buddhist positions on female salvation reflected a split of opinion somewhat similar to that between the Jaina factions. The Hinayana position, like that of the Digambaras, was that rebirth as (or transformation into) a male was a necessary prerequisite; the Mahayana sects, like the Shvetambaras, were more inclusive and more inclined to accept the possibility of female Buddhahood. The most popular treatise on the *Tathagatagarbha* (Buddha nature) is 'The Sutra of Queen Srimala Who Had the Lion's Roar [i.e. eloquence]', which originated in India and told of a queen who became a Buddha without changing her sex. Nevertheless, the question remains unresolved, for none of the 547 past lives of the Buddha narrated in the Jatakas was lived as a female, not even the animal rebirths. And, of course, the actual position of women, both within the order and outside, reflected the shared beliefs of both orthodox and heterodox communities.

Many followers of both Buddhist and Jaina doctrines and monastic communities were people of wealth and property; the motive for supporting these anti-sacrificial faiths might have been the protection of their wealth from arbitrary appropriation and unproductive waste in sacrifices. Both heterodoxies – as they appear against the mainstream of Indian religious development – accorded a sacred status to the teachings of their revered founders, and to traditions centred upon the person of a single, great teacher whose wisdom was passed through devoted followers in monastic institutions. The language of these teachings was a version of Sanskrit set down by grammarians such as Panini of the fourth century BCE.

THE NATURE OF THE MAURYAN KINGDOM

In the early part of the twentieth century, it was believed that we knew a great deal about the Mauryan kingdom, the greatest state to emerge up to its time. A text called the *Arthashastra* was discovered then, purportedly dating from the time of the Mauryan founder, Chandragupta, and thought to be the work of his minister, Kautilya. Many scholars now doubt its reliability as a description of any actual state. Certainly, India knew of no other centralized and bureaucratic state like that of Kautilya's description through the whole of its ancient and medieval past.

What we know more certainly about the Mauryan period derives from the rich set of documents that were inscribed on prominent rock faces and pillars along major trade routes under the protection of the Mauryan king Ashoka, during his reign from 270 to 230 BCE. These royal edicts have been found over an enormous portion of the subcontinent and traced an extended trade network radiating from the eastern Gangetic heartland of the kingdom. The

Plate 5 Ashokan pillar edict. Lauriya Nandagarh, Bihar. *c.*1860 (IOL ASIM 27 by permission of the British Library).

information gleaned from these edicts includes aspects of the history of Buddhism, since Ashoka was a professed follower of its teachings and royal protector of its institutions. The link between trade and Buddhist institutions remained strong for the next several centuries because the sites where the Buddhist monks of the *sangha* (assembly) concentrated for part of each year attracted the pious from almost all strata of society, including traders to supply the wants of monks and laity alike. Sacred centres became urban places in which commercial people were prominent, and the ethics of Buddhism suited the conservative and profit-orientated biases of merchants. Brahman-mediated sacrifices seemed profligate to the thrifty accountant's mentality of early Buddhist critiques.

When in 320 BCE Chandragupta Maurya established his rule at Pataliputra, near where several large tributaries of the Ganges enter the main stream, and where previous kingdoms had already been centred, a new political era was confirmed. By then the system of state politics in the form of the mahajanapadas – first mentioned in the Buddhist Pali canon – had endured for hundreds of years across a wide swath of northern India. Sixteen mahajanapadas were mentioned in the *Mahabharata* and *Ramayana*, and formed the political context of both epics. The system of political relations of these societies was indigenously developed. The technological bases on which they depended consisted of irrigated agriculture and the iron tools and weapons capable of subjugating the minor Aryan and non-Aryan communities to the small set of dynasts who commanded the mahajanapadas.

By the time of the Buddha, one of these hegemonic states, Magadha, had surpassed all others by virtue of its situation in the riverine confluence zone of Pataliputra, which was also near the rich iron deposits south of the Ganges. Magadha's suzerainty over the whole of the northern plain was established by the defeat of the Avanti kings at Ujjain, but this did not lead to any sort of consolidation. Rather, as Buddhist sources recount, there was continuous turbulence among the Magadhan military commanders, ending with usurpation of the chieftaincy by a soldier known as Mahapadma. Around 360 BCE, he established a new kingdom called Nanda, with a capital still at Pataliputra, from there he launched a successful conquest of the whole of the Ganges delta, and the coastal extensions into the east coast kingdom of Kalinga. The conquests of Mahapadma broke the back of the earlier mahajanapada system; they also undermined the logic of Aryan clan dominance, for he was known to have had a shudra mother. However, his numerous sons proved incapable of holding their father's patrimony, and the Nandas were shortly to be replaced by Chandragupta Maurya.

THE INVASION OF ALEXANDER THE GREAT

It was upon the system of lineage polities and their increasing links by trade that Alexander the Great fell between 330 and 326 BCE. His dream of conquest of the Gangetic plain was shattered by a mutiny of his soldiers in 326, after all of the Indus region had been subjected and the plain laid open. The immediate consequence of the invasion was the end of the mahajanapada polities and their replacement by a powerful new monarchy, the Mauryans. A tradition connects Chandragupta, the founder of that kingdom, with Alexander, but even if that was apocryphal there can be little question that this foreign penetration was partly responsible for the replacement of lineage polities by the new form initiated by the Mauryans. Even more decisive in this political transformation than Alexander's military intervention were two indigenous conditions: first, the vigorous commerce that tied the mahajanapadas together and undermined the logic of clan control; second, the rise of the new ideologies of Buddhism and Jainism that captured the loyalty of commercial peoples. The conjuncture of these two indigenous developments was to manifest itself during the reign of Ashoka, probably 268–233 BCE.

The founding of the Mauryan kingdom constituted a distinct break with the past in the wake of the disruptive invasion of Alexander the Great in 327 BCE and the explosion of trade contacts between the subcontinent and its neighbours on every side. Both developments engendered fundamental changes in the societies and cultures that had taken root in all parts of the area we are entitled henceforward to call 'India': a distinctive land and people with enviable achievements and products. Regardless of which elements of this identifiable whole arose from within the evolving cultural ground of the subcontinent and which were introduced from without, the course of the evolving civilization of India demonstrated a bias towards an elaboration of the foundational elements of the civilization, an elaboration of ancient roots.

The large and experienced army that won the thriving agricultural zone of the Ganges valley for the first Maurya was soon threatened by the incursions of Alexander the Great. Buoyed by his conquests of the Persians, Alexander advanced across the Punjab in 326 BCE, until his army encountered stiffening opposition (in which Chandragupta may have been involved). At that point his soldiers refused to move beyond the Beas River, the easternmost Indus tributary, and he was forced to withdraw from India in 324. He died shortly thereafter in Babylon, ending for the time being the threat to native Indian rulers, but leaving a changed territory in his wake.

Apart from hastening the destruction of the mahajanapada state system and stimulating the consolidation of the state founded by Chandragupta Maurya, the Greek invasion initiated a period during which Hellenistic influences changed the shape of the north Indian artistic and scientific world. The resulting Indo-Greek influences were manifested in both the style of Gandharan stone carving, which had decidedly Greek elements, and an enrichment of astronomical knowledge. Before Alexander, the few foreigners who had penetrated the frontiers of the Indian subcontinent, including the Achaemenids Cyrus II and Darius I of Persia, had seized tracts on the peripheries of the Indus. But no newcomers after the arrival of the Indo-Aryan speakers and before Alexander had established themselves in the Punjab.

That his soldiers found the task of overwhelming their opponents increasingly difficult suggests that there was not a great deal that Indians needed to learn from Greeks about warfare, and this suspicion was confirmed by the events that followed Alexander's death in 323 BCE. In 305 one of his successors attempted a reinvasion but was so fiercely resisted that he was forced to conclude a treaty with Chandragupta that accepted the latter's sovereignty south of the Hindu Kush range, over a territory as great as that commanded by the Mughals two millennia later. The fame of Chandragupta was established for posterity by the Greek ambassador Megasthenes. Fragments of his account were preserved in quotations by classical authors who were impressed by his descriptions of caste-like social divisions and of Pataliputra as one of the great cities of the ancient world.

Plate 6 The Bodhisattva Vajrapani shown as Hercules wearing the skin of the Nemean lion. Gandhara stone carving. Second/third century CE (BM OA. 1970. 7-18. 1, Courtesy of the Trustees of the British Museum).

THE *ARTHASHASTRA*

Along with Megasthenes' account, another source that enjoyed high standing as a description of the early Mauryan state was the *Arthashastra*, a treatise on power discovered in the early twentieth century and thought to have been written by one of Chandragupta's ministers. Originally taken as a depiction of the actual conditions of Chandragupta's court by one in a position to know, the polity described actually bears a closer resemblance to the world of the mahajanapadas that had been superseded by the Magadha–Nanda–Mauryan succession of kingdoms; that is, it depicts a world of small territories whose rulers were caught up in incessant conflict and cynical scheming for advantage. Reminiscent of the later work of Niccolo Machiavelli, *The Prince*, the *Arthashastra* cunningly instructs a putative ruler in the tricks of the trade, including the use of spies and secret agents, and is now believed to be more of a theoretical treatise than a description of an actual court.

One reason for suspecting its veracity as a description of the Mauryan regime of Chandragupta is that the political world of his grandson Ashoka was so very different. Ashoka's regnal dates are undergoing revision, but may have extended from 268 to 233 BCE. In any case, his reign provides us with the first documents of certain date: the texts of his rock and pillar edicts. These moralistic placards were exhortations by a ruler who was both a confessed follower of Buddhism and the self-confessed 'beloved of the gods'. Such documents could scarcely be more at variance with the oppressive and controlling tone and instructions of the *Arthashastra*. Ashoka's edicts conveyed toleration for variety and conferred autonomy under the broad umbrella of his authority to the people of the south, far from his Gangetic capital, and to others as distant as King Antiochos in Syria.

ASHOKA'S EMPIRE

If the extent of the Mauryan realm is traced by the outermost of his edicts, it covered an astonishing 1500 miles from the minor rock edict at Lampaka in the northwest to the major edicts of Karnataka in the south, and about 1200 miles from the major rock edict at Girnar on the Arabian Sea to edicts in Orissa. In the past it was not uncommon for historians to conflate the vast space thus outlined with the oppressive realm described in the *Arthashastra* and to posit one of the earliest and certainly one of the largest totalitarian regimes in all of history. Such a picture is no longer considered believable; at present what is taken to be the realm of Ashoka is a discontinuous set of several core regions separated by very large areas occupied by relatively autonomous peoples.

Four core regions have been identified as belonging to Ashoka's time, in addition to the kingdom's heartland in the eastern Gangetic plain around Pataliputra; each of these was apparently under the authority of close kin or servants of Ashoka himself: Taxila in the foothills of the Hindu Kush; Ujjain on the Malwa plateau; Kalinga extending southward along the east coast from the Ganges delta; and Suvarnagiri, in modern Karnataka, in the centre of the lower Deccan Plateau. Knitting these regions together were important trade routes. The northern road (*uttarapatha*) extended from Bengal to Taxila; another branched from the Ganges near the juncture with the Yamuna, joined the Narmada basin and continued to the Arabian seaport of Bharukaccha (Broach). Yet another branched southward (*dakshinapatha*) from Ujjain to the regional capital of Suvarnagiri, a centre for the production of gold and iron. In the newer view, Ashoka's edicts trace out this spacious commercial domain as a gigantic zone of Ashoka's moral authority.

Ashoka had his Buddhist-inspired moralizing edicts inscribed on distinctive pillars or upon prominent rocks where people passed or congregated. They traced a set of trade routes along which commodities passed to and from the Mauryan heartland in the eastern Gangetic plain. This road network continued to be plied throughout the imperial epoch, enabling the flow of commodities produced in all parts of the subcontinent. Along these same roads went Ashoka. Having become a lay Buddhist, he embarked on a year-long pilgrimage to all the sacred sites of his new faith; moreover, he deputized officers, called *dhamma-mahamatra* (ministers of morality), to spread the Buddha's teachings on righteous conduct. The seaports along both coasts of the subcontinent already carried the goods which inspired the legend of India's dazzling wealth and material creativity; its international reputation was further enhanced by Ashoka's decision in 257 BCE to dispatch emissaries (*duta*) to the realms of western Asia to preach the Buddha's doctrine.

In the edicts that he had inscribed on prominent rocks and on pillars surmounted by a capital depicting a lion (which is now a symbol of the modern Indian republic) Ashoka exhorted his 'subjects' to avoid eating meat and to treat their neighbours with good will. He also recorded sending Buddhist missionaries to various Greek successors to Alexander in western Asia, and that his own son Mahinda was despatched to Sri Lanka to propagate the faith. The dhamma-mahamatra and other missionaries may have had an intelligence function as well. Yet other officials were posted to provincial towns to administer justice and collect tribute. But beyond the trade routes and away from the towns of the extensive heartland between Ujjain and Pataliputra, there is no evidence of Ashoka's authority or that of his servants.

Ashoka's successors clung to a diminishing state structure until, around 185 BCE, a brahman general seized power and established a new ruling dynasty called Shunga. He revived the horse-sacrifice in contravention of the ban on animal offerings that had been imposed by Ashoka. But stability eluded the new state, thanks to invasions from central Asia by remnants of Alexander's old army, now under independent satraps who sought to rule more powerful states and use the wealth of India for their purposes.

TOWARDS THE CLASSICAL PATTERN

The middle of the first millennium BCE proved a critical time in the development of Indian civilization. Different conceptions of community, economy and social structure confronted each other, and the resolution of conflict contributed to the distinctive qualities of the Gupta age. Gupta religion, when it arrived, was a restored version – but only a version – of the early vedic religion, with a few of the same sky gods enjoying importance, and two new major deities – Shiva and Vishnu – defined by a theology also intimated in Buddhism. In this development, salvation was not attained through the ritual action of the sacrifice, but in a variety of ways, including special knowledge (*jnana*), as in early Buddhism and Jainism. Later Buddhist theology, for its part, incorporated the devotionalism of the worshippers of Shiva and Vishnu. Buddhists came to worship a saviour (bodhisattva), in a fashion similar to the religious traditions then emerging in western Asia.

The now transformed theology became canonical during the evolution of the two Sanskrit epics, which reached their present form around 100 BCE. This was the point at which the famous *Bhagavad Gita*, which celebrated the god Krishna, was interpolated into the *Mahabharata*, an episodic tale of intralineage rivalry, covetousness and irresponsibility. The *Ramayana* (a version of which was to be included in the *Mahabharata*) celebrated the career of Rama, the perfect king; he, like Krishna, was incorporated into the Hindu godhead as one of several earthly manifestations (*avatars*) of the god Vishnu, a benefactor of mankind. In a later to be developed genre of Sanskrit literature, *purana* ('ancient story'), the sacred and divine 'lives' of Shiva and Vishnu were recounted, along with the lineages of some of their royal devotees.

DIVINE ROYALTY

In the puranas, sacredness surrounded kingship, in contrast to the *Arthashastra*, which depicted kings more as managers of bureaucratic tyrannies. Rama, the model king, was himself an avatar of a god. While both conceptions of kingship were conceits, the puranic version was closer to the actual view (if not behaviour) of the real kings of the era. Another template for the perfect ruler had been historically set by the career of the Ashoka, who became a devotee of Buddhism around 250 BCE; and a related version of royal morality was set out in the dharmashastras of the Gupta period. The earliest and best known of these texts on duty and correct conduct was that attributed to the third century BCE sage Manu, who propounded a doctrine of royal divinity recalling the ritual puissance of an earlier epoch:

> For, when these creatures, being without a king, through fear dispersed in all directions, the Lord created a king for the protection of this whole [creation].
>
> Taking [for that purpose] eternal particles of Indra, of the Wind, of Yama, of the Sun, of Fire, of Varuna, of the Moon, and of the Lord of wealth [Kubera].
>
> Because a king has been formed of particles of those lords of the gods, he therefore surpasses all created beings in lustre;
>
> And, like the sun, he burns eyes and hearts; nor can anybody on earth even gaze on him . . .
>
> Even an infant king must not be despised, [from an idea] that he is a [mere] mortal; for he is a great deity in human form.[18]

Curiously, Manu is also the name of the mythical first king, who was said in the *Arthashastra* to have been elected by men. The duty of kings – their *rajadharma* – in either case was to maintain correct relations among castes and within as well as among communities, partly as an adjudicator of conflict and partly as moral model. Protection and nurturance of social collectivities – communities – was the responsibility of kings; the reciprocal responsibility of their subjects was some portion of their productivity and a considerable measure of devotion.

The divinity that kings had about them was different from the divine right claimed by absolutist kings of a later Europe. For Buddhist and Jaina rulers, sacredness meant ruling through moral example. Expressions in the edicts of Ashoka, the Buddhist emperor, reflect this: the king was beloved of the gods and the turner of the wheel of righteousness (*chakravartin*).

Of actual imperial rulers from the Mauryans to the Guptas something is known from stone and metal inscriptions. In addition, a good deal about ancient kings and culture is known fragmentarily from literary works such as the report of Megasthenes, the ambassador to the court of Chandragupta Maurya from Seleucus Nicator, who succeeded to a part of Alexander the Great's realm. His report contains a description of a social stratification resembling caste, in that groups were ranked according to birth. Megasthenes' description of the Mauryan capital, Pataliputra, supports the picture of a bureaucratic regime found in Kautiliya's *Arthashastra*, though he says nothing beyond that.

Ashoka's claims to sovereignty can be traced accurately from the distribution of his rock and pillar edicts, a distance of over 1500 miles. No other ruler equalled his claims until the Mughal emperor Aurangzeb in the late seventeenth century, although King Samudragupta of the Gupta dynasty left inscriptions tracing conquests extending over a half century (from about 330 CE) that came close: from southern Afghanistan, on one side of the subcontinent and a thousand miles from his capital in Pataliputra, to the middle of the Tamil country along the eastern coast of the peninsula, equally far from his capital.

HIERARCHIES OF ROYALTY

The inscriptions of various kingdoms of Mauryan and post-Mauryan times imply an imperial suzerainty that was only formal when it extended beyond the core regions of royal power. That is, the actual rulers of the peripheral places, having been defeated or in some other way forced to recognize the overlordship of the dominant king, were usually reinstalled by the conquering overlord. Royal installation (*rajabhisehka*) was a rite of anointment which powerful rulers arranged for themselves, but which they also insisted on carrying out upon subordinate kings. One of the principal claims of any imperial overlord was that, in addition to being a chakravartin (i.e. the moral centre of the political world), he was a *maharajadhiraja*; that is, a great king over the other kings whom he had installed. Like the great king-of-kings, subordinate kings had mastery over a core territory, with a capital fortified and manned by close allies who were often kinsmen. They were fully kings, but ruled smaller realms than the overlord. In this hierarchy of lordships, differences were scalar in both degree and kind: the greater the lord, the more extensive, fertile and populous was his core tract, on the basis of which he could and did demand homage and some military service from those below him.

The depth of such hierarchies could be considerable, through great and small kings and lesser chiefs; but in the end superordinate–subordinate relations came to rest on small communities, a circle of villages with associated pasturages and perhaps a small town under the control of a small set of warrior kinsmen. Political relations were fluid and often conflict-ridden, so that all would-be rulers adhered to strategies of alliance-making with equals and protective subordination to the more powerful. Under these circumstances, states consisted of little more than the ruler and his kinsmen followers, who doubled as local administrators and royal warriors. A minor kingdom could spring to major imperial importance and then shrink back within the lifetime of one able warrior; the relative power of one state over another came down to the skill and good fortune of one imperial warrior against another – and the relative resources of their respective bases in the population and the wealth with which to sustain their armed followers. These political relations were rooted in the time of the sixteen mahajanapadas, between the eighth and sixth centuries BCE.

THE DEVELOPMENT OF CASTE

The first documentary evidence of caste was contained in the *Rigveda* hymn collections, and hence dates from about 1000 BCE. As we saw earlier, one of the hymns described the sacrifice of a primal man, from whose bodily parts came the appropriately associated four varnas. Nothing more is heard about these varnas for a millennium; then they appear once more in Manu's dharmashastra, where the proliferating lower occupational groups are explained as birth groups (jatis) consisting of the descendants of illicit marriages of various kinds among the original varnas:

> In all castes [varna] those [children] only which are begotten in the direct order [i.e. where the husband is older than his wife] on wedded wives, equal [in caste and married as] virgins, are to be considered as belonging to the same caste [as their fathers].[19]

Apart from ranked birth groups, there existed unranked groups, who accounted for their corporate status through descent from a common ancestor and habitation in a common place, i.e. clans. The full development of caste and clan institutions, however, came several centuries after Manu's time.

In addition to blood and birth, another principle of affinity was found in associations of individuals in pursuit of religious and commercial advantage for themselves. These were called *sreni*, which is sometimes translated as guilds. And last but not least were the ties that arose from the accidents and choices inherent in common residence. Where people chose to be or found themselves, in particular places or communities, bonds of affinity were recognized, and this was the basis of the janapadas (literally, where clans placed their feet).

The multiplicity of ways in which the people of the imperial age were encouraged to recognize their connections with others narrowed the scope of political integration. That is, while there might be claims to enormous realms, such as Ashoka's, they actually referred to very porous entities riddled with large, scattered autonomous zones, a situation that contributed to the ease with which outsiders were able to establish new 'states' by conquest, and, eventually, to the transformation of political formations after 500 CE, when the last of the imperial regimes, the Guptas, were driven from their northern domains.

By the time of Ashoka, around 250 BCE, archaeology and inscriptions combine to indicate that, scattered among iron-using communities of the peninsula, there were urban settlements, often with monumental buildings such as monasteries and stupas, whose remains are still extant. The ruins of larger, more specialized, settlements are found along routes that followed rivers. Roads connected a relatively dense network of settlements in which were found the remains of metal-working and other useful craft production which entered an extensive commodity system. Maski, in the centre of the Deccan plateau, contains an Ashokan rock edict and the physical indications of miners, smelters and traders in metal goods. Its metal products were carried to the distant core of the Mauryan state in the northeast.

Other centres had different distinguishing features. A few were major political centres; others had monasteries and were centres of advanced learning. Many of the sites of this Mauryan urban phase contain the ruins of a monumental past and confirmed literary references in an ever-enlarging written corpus. Most of the Buddhist and Jaina canonical texts yield knowledge about religious developments involving other sects as well; in addition, however, there are non-canonical texts and inscriptions which yield still more evidence. Important among these are the reports of foreign travellers to the subcontinent, beginning with Megasthenes in the time of Alexander the Great and continuing with the accounts of Chinese monks like Fa-hsien, who sojourned in India between 399 and 414 CE with the aim of obtaining Buddhist texts.

EARLY HINDUISM

It is useful to distinguish between Aryan Brahmanism and the Hinduism that took its form during the early centuries of the present era. At that time, the gods Vishnu and Shiva begin to be shaped by a theogonic transformation of two previously minor deities into towering godheads that defied all efforts to reduce them to a single monotheism. An interesting testimony to the process comes from the Besnagar column, dating from the second century BCE and discovered near modern Bhopal on the northern edge of the Deccan plateau. Its inscription states that a local Indian king received an ambassador named Heliodorus who had been sent by the Greek king of Taxila (in modern Afghanistan), who erected the column as an act of devotion to the god Vasudeva, possibly already taken as a manifestation of Vishnu.

That the Greek successors of Alexander the Great's invasion might behave as devotees in this way was previously anticipated in a Pali work entitled 'Questions of Milinda'. Milinda, or Menander as he was also called, ruled in northern Punjab; he was the most famous of the heirs of Alexander who tried their fortunes in India, and in due course adopted the religious practices of their new subjects. In Menander's case, this was Buddhism, concerning which he addressed a series of questions to monkish adepts. So, for Heliodorus, the local god was Vasudeva, then or shortly later identified with Vishnu.

THE ASSIMILATION OF THE GODS

Another equally obscure vedic god, Narayana, was also associated with Vishnu and connected with the pastoral and warrior god Krishna, who played a prominent part in the still evolving *Mahabharata* epic as it moved to its final form during the fifth century CE. During these centuries as well, Vishnu was otherwise elaborated by the assimilation of a range of god-figures, including a boar, whose primitive worship was popular in western India, and, at the other extreme, Rama, the perfect king of the *Ramayana*. The boar – the divine Varaha – and Rama joined other assimilated deities as avatars, the manifestations in which Vishnu came among mankind to save it from demons. The entire panoply then constituted a pantheon of gods whose worship was equivalent to devotion to Vishnu.

Shiva is thought to have risen from the status of minor fertility god – perhaps dating from Harappan times – through the vedic god Rudra, eventually to be worshipped in the form of a phallus (*lingam*). In the course of time, Shiva too came to be associated with other gods: the elephant-faced Ganesha and the popular warrior god Skanda. Two further developments also contributed to the evolution of Hinduism: the creation of new sacred ideas that were preserved in a variety of textual traditions and the founding of institutions, especially that of the temple, by which Hinduism was to be maintained as the central, evolving religion of the majority of people of the subcontinent.

New religious formulations displaced the centrality of the textual traditions of later vedic times – the Brahmanas and Upanishads – though this earlier knowledge was not forgotten; generation after generation of brahmans continued to commit these complex older texts to memory and to teach them to other brahmans deemed appropriate by virtue of their birth. But they had become minor traditions, completely overtaken by the scriptures called purana and dharmashastra, and by various poetic works, including the *Mahabharata* and *Ramayana*. Puranas, or 'ancient stories', consisted of legends and religious instruction. The legends included genealogies of gods, royal dynasties and ancient kshatriya clans, while the instructions pertained to the proper conduct of worship. Eighteen of the puranas are considered 'major', but even they cannot be dated before the advent of the Gupta era in the fourth century CE.

Ashoka's *dhamma* (Prakrit for *dharma*, rule of conduct) remained important for Buddhists, but by the turn of the present era, around 100 BCE, other dharma texts began to appear, beginning with that of the sage Manu. The dharmashastras are called 'law books', but are really more like codes of the conduct considered appropriate for each of the four varnas and for the stages of life through which human beings must pass. They shed much light on Indian societies of that time, in terms of both eternal codes of conduct, where Manu's injunctions were repeated, and variant codes, based on approved local customs. While extolling the virtues of kings as the protectors of dharma, these texts spoke of other ways in which people were bound together in addition to their roles as subjects of dharmic kings. One such affiliational principle was that of blood, and hence connections with kinsmen; associations formed by blood ties were called *kula*. Caste was one kind of blood connection, clan another.

A major difference between the worship offered to the earlier vedic gods and that offered to Vishnu and Shiva was the latter's devotional character, and poetry was an important medium through which devotion was expressed; hymns of praise were recited and sung as a central part of worship. The vedic gods had for the most part been invoked and induced to serve mankind through the powerful rites of expert priests; in contrast, Vishnu and Shiva were invoked by loving songs that begged the boons and salvation promised by the gods, according to theologians. The gods controlled and could no longer be controlled, but only beseeched.

Devotional worship had its roots in the Buddhist worship of bodhisattvas, and even the theology of devotion to Shiva and Vishnu was similar, although Buddhist and Jaina communities of worship were largely urban, drawing followers from among merchants and artisans, whereas Hinduism fitted itself to existing rural Tamil communities. During the seventh century, Jainas and Buddhists were sometimes ruthlessly displaced from the towns. Nevertheless, the earliest poets and theologians of the new devotional Hinduism came from the southern part of India. The Tamil praises addressed to Shiva by the poet Tiruvalluvar were composed in the fifth century, and his couplets were followed by collections of hymns written by sixty-three traditional teachers of Shiva worship (*nayanar*). The Tamil worshippers of Vishnu (*alvar*) also produced paeans, and soon afterwards poems were composed in other southern languages – Kannada and Telugu – and devoted to Shiva and Vishnu in the various guises in which they manifested themselves. That Hindu devotional practices took their initial form in the south of the subcontinent is a reminder that the impact of Buddhism was as great there as in the north, even though the communitarian base of Hinduism was different.

HINDU WORSHIP AND COMMUNITY

Hindu communities of worship tended to preserve the older forms of community and local religious practice. Ancient cults were thereby assimilated

Plate 7 Vishnu and his ten avatars. By a South Indian artist, *c.*1800 (IOL Add OR 25; neg. no. B 8236, by permission of the British Library).

to the worship of puranic deities, such as the pastoralists' adoption of the Vasudeva–Krishna motif as protector of herds. Some of the other avatars were already objects of serious worship when they became assimilated to Vishnu, but now Krishna, Rama and the Buddha in the puranic avatar stories were meant to illustrate the powerful interventions of Vishnu when called upon by men. Thus he was said to have appeared as the fish Matsya who rescued Manu, the progenitor of men, from a flood; as the tortoise Kurma who plunged to the ocean depths to retrieve all sorts of sacred treasure deposited there by floods (including the goddess Lakshmi, one of Vishnu's consorts); as the dwarf Vamana who tricked the powerful demon Bali into granting him dominion over as much of the earth as he could cover in three strides. (In those three strides, however, he covered all of the earth and heaven, leaving only the nether world for the demon.) But apart from the popularity of the Varaha boar avatar among western Indians, the remainder seem not to have gained a wide following.

THE EVOLUTION OF KRISHNA AND RAMA

In contrast, the stature of Krishna grew. He was given a place in the *Mahabharata* as friend and counsellor of the Pandavas; more significantly, he

1974 6-17 014 (17)

Plate 8 Arjuna, and Krishna as his charioteer. Perhaps from Maharashtra, *c.*1800 (BM OA. 1974. 6-17. 014(17), Courtesy of the Trustees of the British Museum).

was given the central role in the *Bhagavad Gita*, where, as chariot-driver for the Pandava hero Arjuna, he reveals himself before the onset of the great epic battle:

> I am the beginning, the middle and the very end of beings ... Of the Adityas I am Vishnu; of the lights, the radiant sun; ... of the stars I am the moon ... of the senses I am mind and of beings I am consciousness ... of mountain-peaks I am Meru ... of the lakes I am the ocean ... of the sciences, the science of the self; of those who debate I am the dialectic ... I am death, the all-devouring and the origin of things that are yet to be ... There is no end to my divine manifestations ... What has been declared by Me is only illustrative of My infinite glory.[20]

Despite the declaration of transcendence, the more important message of Krishna in the *Bhagavad Gita* was the socially conservative, caste-affirming one of karma, action, the careful performance of one's appropriate behaviour without concern for the result.

At the other extreme from the grandiose, omniscient and omnipotent deity depicted above, Krishna was worshipped as Govinda ('lord of the herdsmen', another of Vishnu's names), a handsome dark shepherd whose flute lures the milkmaids (*gopis*) into amorous dalliance. By contrast, Rama, the perfect king of Ayodhya, came to represent an attribute of Vishnu that differentiated him from both Krishna-Govinda and Shiva: protection of the social order, as instanced by his destruction of the demon Ravana. While Rama is also depicted as dark in colour, unlike Krishna he is not the promiscuous lover, but the devoted husband of Sita and a loyal brother.

THE CHARACTER OF SHIVA

Shiva, represented by the lingam, presents very different qualities of divine lordship. A primordial natural force whose representation as a phallus connects him with the earth and with generation, Shiva is also a great ascetic, a mystic of astonishing power and fearsome beauty. As Nataraja (king of the dance), he creates a devastating ring of fire that destroys the universe at the completion of its cosmic cycle. Attempts to adopt Shiva into the avatar pantheon never took hold, and the only concession to domestication made in his legendary corpus was his marriage to Parvati, daughter of the personification of mountains, Himalaya, who joined him in his mountain hermitage.

Puranas continued to be produced throughout the medieval age in India, well after the major ones were completed between the third and eighth century. In the later puranas, the universal gods Vishnu and Shiva acquired a myriad of particularistic, local forms, and it is these forms that became the real foci of worship. On rare occasions, Shiva might appear spontaneously as a special emanation in some village or town; more often, however, Shiva and Vishnu were introduced to the locality as bridegrooms of a local goddess. These divine weddings explained the practice of sheltering and caring for the gods in the temples that began to be built from the fifth century CE, and divine marriage reciprocally raised to a higher rank in the divine hierarchy the familiar neighbourhood goddess who might already have been propitiated in connection with disease and importuned to ward off death. Alternatively, local goddesses might have been more general guardian spirits, or fertility or 'mother' goddesses, in any combination.

Because these goddesses enjoyed a high standing in most local agrarian and pastoral communities, care was taken not to exclude them from the devotional forms of religion that came to be called Hinduism. In many temples nominally devoted to Vishnu or Shiva, the major object of devotion is the goddess consort, who, according to her worshippers, was the source of the shakti of the great god himself.

If the religious devotion offered to Shiva and Vishnu in the multiplicity of their manifestations reinforced community solidarity through the new ideology, it also provided the means for linking communities into ever-larger networks of affiliation. Politically, state formation contributed to the same outcome and culminated in the Gupta kingdom, which is considered India's golden age.

DEVELOPMENTS IN THE SOUTH

While these developments were occurring in the northern, or continental, part of the subcontinent, a different set of cultures, or, some would say, civilizations, were taking shape in the peninsular south. The earliest expressed itself in the Tamil language, which, unlike Sanskrit, is not an Indo-European language, but one of an independent linguistic family called Dravidian that now includes some 150 million speakers, about one-fifth of the contemporary population of India.

The origin of the Tamils and other Dravidian speakers is not known. They were either very ancient occupants of the southern peninsula, and inhabitants of the stone age communities that have been surveyed there, or later invaders and conquerors of the earlier settlers, perhaps migrants from the eastern Mediterranean basin, though that is still only speculative. Archaeological remains suggest that most of the peninsula was occupied from an early time. Some sites reveal assemblages of hunting-fishing-gathering modes of economy in close proximity to nomadic pastoralists or hoe agriculturists.

The evidence from even the earliest Tamil sangam poems and the earliest of the Dravidian lexicons and grammars, the Tamil *Tolkapiyam* (*c.*300 CE) reveals northern, i.e. Sanskritic, elements mixed with the Dravidian, indicating substantial and very ancient interaction between people of the southern peninsula and those of the Gangetic basin. Another example of the interpenetration of northern and southern forms in the peninsular societies of antiquity comes from the early Marathi (the language of modern Maharashtra) writings. The grammatical structure of this language of the northern peninsula was inflected by Dravidian forms, though in other respects it is an Indo-European language. Influences of this order, which were intensified by the so-called 'second urbanization of India', point to the considerable mobility of all sorts of people into the subcontinent and around it, a process associated with the spread of Buddhist and Jaina sects from the eastern Ganges, where they originated, to the opposite end of the subcontinent and, in the case of Buddhism, beyond the seas to Sri Lanka and Southeast Asia.

TAMIL SANGAM POETRY AND THE MUVENDAR

The earliest surviving Tamil writings date from the second century BCE and consist of brief inscriptions found in the caves that sheltered Jaina ascetics, and they record donations to the sect. The *Devanagari* script used was the same as that of many Ashokan inscriptions of a century earlier, attesting to contacts between the northern and southern parts of the subcontinent. Nevertheless, the Tamil language of these brief records achieved a flowering during the first centuries of the common era, culminating in the emergence of a poetic corpus of very high quality, but couched in a distinctive script derived from the earlier one. To this corpus the name '*sangam* poetry' was applied not long afterwards, because the heroic and love poems were anthologized by a literary academy called sangam in obvious reference to the Buddhist sangha or brotherhood of monks. The sangam referred to was said to have been convened by the Pandyan dynasty of Tamil kings, who are dimly known from the Ashokan edicts along with two other Dravidian lineages, the Chola and the Chera. These three dynasties have often been treated as somewhat backward and peripheral, what modern scholars would call 'tribal', but the martial poems of the sangam corpus reveal that the kings of these three royal traditions ruled different parts of the southern peninsula. The Cholas and Pandyas were to enjoy considerable prominence in medieval times, when Tamils still referred to all three kings, or *muvendar*, as their rightful rulers.

THE AGE OF THE EARLY EMPIRES

The six and a half centuries separating Chandragupta's founding of the Mauryan kingdom and another Chandragupta, the founder of the Gupta kingdom, may be called an age of empires. From about 320 BCE to 320 CE, various historical sources make it possible to identify five kingdoms to which the label imperial could be attached, in the sense that suzerainty was claimed and apparently conceded over a substantial territory – such as the whole of the Gangetic plain – at least during the reign of one or perhaps two of the kings. The name 'Chandragupta' offers little guidance to imperial qualities; it means 'moon-protected'. Nor could the imperial designation be justified on the basis of the often hyperbolical claims made in the inscriptions of kings then and later; the inscriptions were more a way of registering assertions of sovereignty than proclaiming accepted facts. Where a king claimed to rule and inscribed his claim for all to see – as did Ashoka – it was a challenge to any and all of the local rulers. (A similar claim and challenge was embodied in the *ashvamedha*, the ceremony in which the peregrination of the royal horse defined a realm.)

The Indo-Greeks, as they have come to be called, showed flexibility when they insinuated their control over indigenous Indians, as indicated by the

Heliodorus pillar to Vasudeva at Besnagar and the patronage of Buddhists by the most famous of the Indo-Greeks, Menander. Through their coins, Hellenistic artistic conventions came to be known and imitated in northern India.

Other races followed the Indo-Greeks in the quest for fortune and power in India as the millennium closed amidst a high degree of inner Asian turbulence and central and northern Asian peoples irrupted into the subcontinent. Referred to as Shakas in India, less is known of them in Europe than of their kinsmen the Scyths. The Shakas represented the end process of the massive shifting of peoples that accompanied the consolidation of the Han dynasty in China around 100 BCE. Shaka rulers in India made use of the Indo-Greek title 'king of kings' in either a Persian or Sanskrit form, and they also adopted the Sanskrit title 'great king' (*maharaja*). Notwithstanding these formidable titles, Shaka states were modest confederations of chieftains, soon to be subjugated by yet newer invaders. The most powerful and enduring of these were called Kushanas, and they were to prove the last of the series of central Asian invaders that included, in addition to Shakas, Scyths and Hunas, elements of the same horsemen of the Asian steppe that destroyed the Roman Empire to the west.

Kanishka was the best known king of the Kushanas; from 115 to 140 CE he laid claim to a realm probably as vast as Ashoka's, though further to the north: from the Oxus basin, north of the Hindu Kush mountains, to Benares in the eastern Ganges basin and south to Gujarat. Kanishka's fabled wealth came from duties exacted from the land and sea trade routes that connected India with the Roman world. So large was this trade that Rome felt moved to limit it so as to stem the drain of the coins that defrayed the Indian export surplus. The attempt proved fruitless, and hordes of Roman coins were later found throughout the subcontinent; in fact, the largest number were found in the peninsula, all the way to the far south. Buddhists list Kanishka among their other famous patrons, Ashoka and Menander, in recognition of a council of monks he convened from which the development of Mahayana Buddhism commenced. Even so, his coins, which were of very fine quality along Greek lines, depicted the deities of the Hindus, of the Persians (especially Mithras) and of the Greeks.

AFTER ASHOKA

The interval between the death of Ashoka around 233 BCE and the rise of the Guptas, around 300 CE, has usually been dismissed as a dark age. As so often with dark ages, and with golden ones as well, the characterizations are made by near contemporaries or by later historians and both groups have their own, often distinct, motivations for the labels. Thus, contemporaries of the Gupta age saw it as a time when a new vigorous form of brahmanical religion took root, springing from the polluted ashes of Buddhism and other false faiths. Modern historians have looked upon the Gupta age as golden, but for somewhat different reasons, among them that it was the last great moment of autochthonous Indian development before the political and cultural impact of Islam.

Nevertheless, during the five hundred years between the Mauryans and the Guptas, impressive political, economic and cultural developments grew out of the intensive involvement of Indians with other Asian peoples, to the mutual enrichment of all. Politically, the subcontinent was divided among large states; along with that of the Kushanas in the North there was the Satavahana kingdom that reached across the entire peninsula. From Satavahana ports a vigorous trade was maintained with Southeast Asia, while the Kushanas traded overland with the Roman world. A third polity, the Shakas in Gujarat and Malwa, differed from the other two in following a confederational form. Ruling over older communities of farmers and herders who were slow to recognize their legitimacy, the Shakas gained acceptance around the seventh century, when the elite domesticated themselves as 'ancient Aryan Rajputs', a claim also employed by indigenous chiefs of various stripes.

In religion, everywhere in these domains sects dedicated to Shiva and Vishnu joined with the older streams of Buddhist and Jaina worship to make the age one of innovation and expansion, both in the formation of institutions and in the creation of new texts. Other related intellectual processes were also at work, leading to new cultural forms. At about the same time that the *Bhagavad Gita* was being joined with the epic *Mahabharata*, between 100 BCE and 100 CE, the compendium of behavioural rules that was to constitute the textual tradition of the dharmashastras was being finalized by the 'law-giver', Manu, and this Manu (or Manava) Dharmashastra was to be the ur-text and model for a vast and variable progeny of codifications intended to provide guidance for kings and their ministers on proper public and private conduct for over two thousand years, until (almost) superseded by modern jurisprudence and legislation.

Despite the development and elaboration of the oppressive, rigidifying minutiae of the 'law books', during the inter-imperial period the world of Indian artistic production was transformed through influences from Persia and from the Graeco-Roman world. By the close of the Mauryan era, distinctive Indian schools of sculpture and architecture had emerged that reflected these influences, without being overwhelmed by them, and manifested themselves in the classical pattern of the Guptas.

THE STATUS OF WOMEN DECLINES

Darkness can be said to have pervaded one aspect of society during the inter-imperial centuries: the degradation of women. In Hinduism, the monastic tradition was not institutionalized as it was in the heterodoxies of Buddhism and Jainism, where it was considered the only true path to spiritual liberation. Instead, Hindu men, particularly those of the upper castes, passed through several stages of life: that of initiate, when those of the twice-born castes received the sacred thread; that of student, when the upper castes studied the vedas; that of the married man, when they became householders; that of forest hermit, when the elderly man retired to meditate, either accompanied by his wife or without her; and finally that of the solitary ascetic. Since the Hindu man was enjoined to take a wife at the appropriate period of life, the roles and nature of women presented some difficulty. Unlike the monastic ascetic, the Hindu man was exhorted to have sons, and could not altogether avoid either women or sexuality.

The medical texts of *ayurveda*, and even the Dharmashastra of Manu, treat the sexuality of women as positive, even auspicious, when properly channelled (towards her husband, of course) and exercised at the time most favourable for conception. Channelling and restriction were necessary for women because of their promiscuous and vicious nature:

> Women do not care for beauty, nor is their attention fixed on age; [thinking] '[It is enough that] he is a man,' they give themselves to the handsome and to the ugly.
>
> Through their passion for men, through their mutable temper, through their natural heartlessness, they become disloyal towards their husbands, however carefully they may be guarded in this [world].
>
> [When creating them] Manu allotted to women [a love of their] bed, [of their] seat and [of] ornament, impure desires, wrath, dishonesty, malice and bad conduct.[21]

Men were of course more fastidious:

> For if the wife is not radiant with beauty, she will not attract her husband; but if she has no attractions for him, no children will be born.[22]

To assure correct channelling, Manu laid down many rules, even including the kinds of names girls should be given: 'easy to pronounce, not imply anything dreadful, possess a plain meaning . . . end in long vowels';[23] most famously, he declared that a woman is always a dependant:

> By a girl, by a young woman, or even by an aged one, nothing must be done independently, even in her own house.
>
> In childhood a female must be subject to her father, in youth to her husband, [and] when her lord is dead to her sons; a woman must never be independent.[24]

Manu approved of child brides, considering a girl of eight suitable for a man of twenty-four, and one of twelve appropriate for a man of thirty. He then went on to list eight types of 'marriage'. The most prestigious, and hence suited to brahman couplings, is that in which the maiden's father, 'having adorned [presumably with jewels] and honoured [her]', presents her as a gift to a learned man. If there was no dowry, or if the groom's family paid that of the bride, the marriage was ranked lower. In this ranking lay the seeds of the curse of dowry that has become a major social problem in modern India, among all castes, classes and even religions.

The 'love marriage', where the couple choose each other out of mutual sexual attraction, ranked just above forcible abduction accompanied by looting and the murder of the bride's family (a form of marriage Manu permitted the violent kshatriya caste). The very lowest ranking was reserved for the rape of a sleeping or otherwise defenceless girl, but 'love marriage' – that is, self-chosen marriage – still has a bad name in India today.

Yet Manu (and the other shastra writers) still revealed a great deal of confusion and inconsistency with respect to women, for, in addition to the strictures against them, there are a number of verses stressing the importance of honouring one's female relations and keeping them happy:

> Where women are honoured, there the gods are pleased; but where they are not honoured, no sacred rites yield rewards.
> Where female relations live in grief, the family soon wholly perishes; but that family where they are not unhappy ever prospers.[25]

There was no uncertainty or vagueness about the lengths to which a wife must go to keep her husband happy, on the other hand:

> Though destitute of virtue, or seeking pleasure [elsewhere], or devoid of good qualities, [yet] a husband must be constantly worshipped as a god by a faithful wife . . . if a wife obeys her husband, she will for that [reason alone] be exalted in heaven.
> A faithful wife, who desires to dwell [after death] with her husband, must never do anything that might displease him who took her hand, whether he be alive or dead.
> In reward of such conduct, a female who controls her thoughts, speech and actions, gains in this [life] highest renown, and in the next [world] a place near her husband.[26]

But it is on the issue of women's right to own property that Manu is most inconsistent and confused. The seemingly forthright statement, 'A wife, a son, and a slave, these three are declared to have no property; the wealth which they earn is [acquired] for him to whom they belong',[27] is contradicted by:

> What [was given] before the [nuptial] fire [i.e. dowry before marriage], what [was given] on the bridal procession, what was given in token of love, and what was received from her brother, mother, or father, that is called the sixfold property of a woman.
> [Such property], as well as a gift subsequent and what was given [to her] by her affectionate husband, shall go to her offspring, [even] if she dies in the lifetime of her husband.[28]

In one respect, Manu was (somewhat) kinder than, for example, the eighteenth-century writer Tryambaka, whose manual for the orthodox wives of Tanjore (in south India) strongly recommended *sahagamana* (dying with husband). Manu felt that such customs might be appropriate for the roughneck kshatriyas, but as for a brahman widow:

> At her pleasure let her emaciate her body by [living on] pure flowers, roots, and fruit; but she must never mention the name of another man after her husband has died.
> Until her death let her be patient [of hardships], self-controlled, and chaste, and strive [to fulfil] that most excellent duty which [is prescribed] for wives who have one husband only.[29]

In practice, this meant the widow's head was shaved, she was expected to sleep on the ground, eat one meal a day, do the most menial tasks, wear only the plainest, meanest garments, and no ornaments. She was excluded from all festivals and celebrations, since she was considered inauspicious to all but her own children. This penitential life was enjoined because the widow could never quite escape the suspicion that she was in some way responsible for her husband's premature demise (premature because, in the nature of things, she should have died first); her sin was probably that of infidelity, in a previous life if not in the current one, though it might simply have been some shortcoming in attention, concern and devotion.

The positions taken and the practices discussed by Manu and the other commentators and writers of dharmashastra are not quaint relics of the distant past, but alive and recurrent in India today – as the attempts to revive the custom of *sati* (widow immolation) within the past decade has shown. Child marriage, forced marriage, dowry and the expectation of abject wifely subservience, too, have enjoyed lengthy duration and continuity and are proving very difficult to stamp out. On a happier note, in 1985 the Indian Supreme Court ruled that:

> all gifts made over to a woman at the time of her marriage remained her absolute private property till the end; and that her husband, or any other, had no right to them without her sanction . . . But the Supreme Court, in fact, was upholding the right of a woman to retain nuptial gifts as enshrined in the ancient concept of *stridhan* (woman's wealth) first mooted by the Vedic [*sic*] sage Manu.[30]

THE GUPTA CLASSICAL PATTERN

The kings with whom the Gupta golden age was to be identified arose from such modest origins that the founder of the ruling line appears to have adopted the name of the Mauryan founder, Chandragupta, when he began his own reign in 320 CE, and married a daughter of the ancient Licchavi clan. The Licchavi lands lay between the Ganges and the Nepal Terai, which is now part of modern Bihar, where the ancient clan structure endured longest. Yet these provincials must have enjoyed a status superior to any that Chandragupta could claim, since his illustrious warrior son, Samudragupta, featured his Licchavi connection on his coins to buttress his claim to be a *maharajadhiraja* (great king over other kings). However, in practice he justified the title by greatly extending the patrimony he received from his father (the Gangetic territory from Prayaga to Pataliputra). According to Samudragupta's famous declaration, brazenly inscribed on a pillar at Prayaga (modern Allahabad) that dated from Ashoka's time or even earlier, he had conquered the whole of the fertile plain west of Prayaga to Mathura and launched a spectacular raid through Kalinga into the south as far as the early Pallava capital at Kanchipuram. All of this was grandiosely celebrated by an attempt to restore royal rituals long denounced by Buddhists – particularly the horse sacrifice.

Nevertheless, the dynastic founder's legacy remained the core of the

Plate 9 Gold coin of Samudragupta (335–80 CE), commemorating the marriage of his parents, Chandragupta I and Kumaradevi. Obverse inscribed 'Chandragupta' (on right), 'Kumaradevi-shri' (on left). Reverse, the goddess Lakshmi on a lion couchant, holding a fillet and cornucopia, inscribed 'Licchavayah' (BM C&M BMC 28, Courtesy of the Trustees of the British Museum).

imperial state in Samudragupta's time and for long afterwards. According to the rich body of Gupta inscriptions, envoys were posted to clusters of small agrarian communities, though what they actually did there is obscure in these and other documents of the time; it is probable that royal officials interfered in these localities only to restore order, so that trade could proceed profitably, and to ensure that tribute was received from the abundant harvests of the fertile and populous riverine plain.

Another duty of local officials during the Gupta period was to establish and superintend the vast increase in land grants to brahmans, who were given immunity from revenue demands. This could not have been an onerous responsibility since gifts of income to learned brahmans and ritualists flowed freely from locally dominant groups and their leaders in exchange for the prestige that attached to such charities and for the practical benefits of having educational centres for their children. Something of the same light-handed administrative relationship must have existed with respect to the guilds. These *sreni* engaged in craft production and trade, and were made up of individuals from diverse castes. They enjoyed autonomy over their mercantile and industrial centres, and immunities similar to those of brahmans. In this way, many diverse communities enjoyed an impressive period of expansion and prosperity within the heartland of the Gupta polity, as well as in the border lands where Gupta authority was very limited.

GUPTA STATE AND COMMUNITY

The Gupta imperial formation of the fourth and fifth centuries CE pointed to two political features that characterized states of the medieval period and extended into the eighteenth century: states and communities existed in a balanced relationship and lesser states nested under the suzerainty of a dominant monarchy. The authority exercised by the kingly state over its agrarian localities was residual: judicial and police functions were left in the hands of landed groups of various sorts and guild-like institutions, to be implemented in accordance with local customs concerning production, occupation and residence. Kings maintained a closer watch over the organization and function of religious institutions, especially temples, for which they and other powerful people in society provided the land and paid for the structures that housed gods, priests and the servants who tended the needs of the religious specialists. Because temples often became large institutions that attracted popular pilgrimage, new towns came into being to add to existing commercial and administrative centres.

A royal presence pervaded all these contexts, but was never the sole authority. The duty of kings (*rajadharma*), we are told in civil, social and familial codes, was limited to adjudicating conflicts among institutions assumed to be capable of self-government and internal conflict resolution in accordance with custom. The dharma texts picture a society constituted of self-governing communities protected by kings. In exchange for protection, kings were to enjoy some of their subjects' wealth. When properly advised by men learned in dharma, the king endowed society with a moral tone, though one that was constantly threatened by the cosmic forces of the 'black age', or kaliyuga.

In the ring of territories that bounded the core, lesser kings had been vanquished by the Guptas and then restored to their thrones in a ritual of empowerment and anointment (*abhisheka*) that the Gupta king carried out with his own hands. This ritual signalled his own status as *chakravartin* (responsible for the wheel of law that rolled through the land), a title that had been claimed by the founding Gupta. Although ruling independently, the client kings paid the Guptas some annual tribute and attended their formal audiences. By indirect authority, Gupta political influence was extended to the Punjab and Malwa in the west and Nepal and Bengal in the east. In turn, the border kings were surrounded by other yet more independent states, including remnants of the lands of the Kushanas in the far-western Indus region, the Shakas and the Vakataka kings in parts of the west-central peninsula of the subcontinent and, very precariously, a powerful state carved from the forests south of the Ganges heartland. Beyond lay the wholly independent Pallavas on the southeastern coast of the subcontinent, who had survived Samudragupta's incursion. In the far north were other kingdoms, some of whose rulers were in origin Hunas, linked to the Attila who devastated the Roman Empire; they were to do the same to India during the early sixth century CE.

As with ruling dynasties in other times and places, the successful passage of power from kings who enjoyed long reigns to sons with experience assured the Guptas impressive longevity – around two centuries – and impressive stability by Indian dynastic standards. The son of Samudragupta, Chandragupta II, or Vikramaditya, ruled from 375 to 415, defeated the independent Shaka principalities in western India and assumed patronage over the independent Vakataka kings in central and western India through marriage. Other conquests carried the Gupta overlordship to its greatest extent: from the delta of the Ganges in Bengal to the Indus and to Malwa.

Gupta influence reached even beyond India to Southeast Asia. Gold coins bore the visages of Gupta kings and proclaimed the Guptas world-class rulers, a claim spread by Indian traders who plied the seas bearing splendid goods.

Fa Hsien, a Chinese pilgrim searching for Buddhist manuscripts to bring back to China, reported back in detail the lavish court of Chandragupta II at Pataliputra, his numerous salaried officials and the wealth of his courtiers.

All this opulence was extended through the long reign of Chandragupta's son, Kumaragupta, but beginning in the reign of Kumaragupta's son Skandagupta, who had led the armies of his father, signs of resistance to the Gupta hegemony began to be seen in two quarters. One was the challenge to Gupta dominance from forest people living in the hill and wooded country south of the Ganges. Invasions from that quarter required large-scale military campaigns to be put down. More distant but no less important were the incursions of central Asian horsemen under pressure from the expanding power of the Huns over the entire Eurasian steppe. Just as some central Asian hordes drove Germanic tribes into the Roman world, destroying much of Gaul and Italy, others seized large parts of northwestern India during the sixth century, including Rajasthan and the western Ganges valley.

THE FLOWERING OF DEVOTIONAL RELIGION

The cultural achievements of the fourth and fifth centuries CE are undeniable. A new religion was created under the leadership of the resuscitated brahman priesthood, who traced their ritual and scholarly credentials to vedic sources. However, what emerged was based upon devotion rather than ritual mastery; puranas, not manuals of sacrifice, were the real texts of the new worship of Shiva and Vishnu – the legends and practices that were to comprise the future dominant religion of India. Among these foundational texts were the Vishnu Purana and the Markandeya Purana, which raised goddess worship to the highest level through adoration of Durga, Shiva's consort. And there were other Sanskrit works that marked the Gupta apogee, ranging from the dramatic and poetic works of Kalidasa to the inscriptions on temples built by the worshippers of Shiva and Vishnu, as well as Jainas, throughout the great territory of the Gupta overlordship. Temples were the palaces of reigning gods under the new worship, and inscriptions recorded the benefactions of kings and lesser lords, who were anxious to make visible their piety, and accordingly built shrines and granted vast lands, often whole villages, to brahmans in recognition of the special role they once more played after centuries of competition from Buddhism. Nevertheless, even more than stories of gods in Sanskrit, what fashioned the new faith was poetry that sang the praises of Shiva and Vishnu in demotic languages, beginning with Tamil and launching others on a trajectory into a rich literary outpouring.

Such cultural achievements suggest that town life had not lost all its vigour, as historians have all too often supposed when comparing the Gupta dispensation with that of the Mauryans. Trade and industrial production threw up new groups of potential patrons for religious works, but also for other works of literature and drama. Patrons often consisted of corporate groups, guilds of merchants and artisans, the very groups that were also responsible for town administration. This was not new, but some landed groups also enjoyed a significant elevation of status, as manifested by religious patronage. The result was an altering of caste hierarchies in Gupta domains: groups previously banished to the low rank of shudra now claimed to be twice-born and were supported in their claims by the brahmans whose work they patronized. The elevation of hitherto inferior castes was as important as the new definition of monarchy, which associated the state with the enhancement of brahmans as the joint custodians of the religion of the puranas.

SOCIAL MOBILITY UNDER THE GUPTAS

Of all of the dynasties of the classical period only the Kushana kings claimed a rule derived directly from divine sources, and they may have been inspired by the style of the Chinese Emperors, for the Kushana title, *devaputra*, has the same meaning as the Chinese 'Son of Heaven'. Other rulers of the age relied on royal sacrifices, such as the ashvamedha, to establish an anointed authority, and for this the participation of brahman priests was imperative. In Gupta times and later, kings expected brahmans to validate their claims to rule on the basis of qualities stipulated in the dharmashastras of the time: kings must be capable and virtuous (the sign of the last being their gifts to brahmans), and they should also be of appropriate caste, which meant kshatriyas. Puranas such as the Vishnu Purana provided lists of, and genealogies for, ruling families that extended from mythological pasts to the sixth century. Other puranas referred to non-kshatriya ruling houses, such as the Nandas and Mauryas, and also to foreign ruling houses from among Indo-Greeks and Shakas, some of whom were assigned an indefinite sort of royal status. These works thus accorded with the later dharma texts that no longer insisted, as the Manu Dharmashastra had, that kings must be kshatriyas by birth; it was now the *de facto* rule of a territory that conferred royal authority upon a man, whatever his birth and whatever his means of attaining power. Kshatriya status was an achieved, not an ascribed, rank.

Brahmans and kshatriyas were not the only groups to enhance their relative standings through cooperation. Others began a social ascent as a result of the revalorizing of their occupations. Such upwardly mobile groups included merchants and some types of artisan, and also those, of whatever caste, who engaged in scribal activities. Scribes enjoyed a steady improvement in reputation and status, overcoming the stigma of low caste attributed by Manu to the progeny of the illicit unions between brahmans and shudras, which was their supposed origin. By the eleventh century, kayasthas were found growing in numbers and esteem in a number of high-status regional castes. Such gains in social standing reflected a growing demand for bureaucrats to serve the administrative requirements of temples and kings who needed record keepers and judicial officials in post-Gupta times.

But there were also those who sank in social standing, and some regions outside the Gupta heartland suffered a loss of status, too. Some parts of ancient Aryavarta of the Ganges–Yamuna region around Delhi descended into the despised category of *mleccha-desa*. This was a designation of irredeemable pollution that attached to certain groups, such as forest dwellers and foreigners, as well as to the lands in which they dwelt. Occupation by Indo-Greeks and later by the Huns of the western Ganges basin was deemed by the law-givers of the Gupta age and later to have nullified the pristine purity of the land. Its pollution would continue until the rulers adopted the conduct of proper castes and the worship of proper gods. The assiduity with which foreign conquerors often took the hint is strikingly evident in the metamorphosis of many of the central Asian rulers of small states in western Indian into Rajputs.

THE CLASSICAL PATTERN ELABORATED AND EXTENDED: THE SOUTH

While the golden age of the Gupta era still shone in the northern portion of the subcontinent during the fourth and fifth centuries CE, an important epoch of civilization was also taking form in the peninsular south. The northern boundary of peninsular India is conveniently (for students and geographers) marked by the Vindhya mountains and the Narmada River, but neither ever constituted an insurmountable barrier to the passage of people, products or ideas.

In contrast to the rich riverine plains formed by the Indus and Ganges–Yamuna systems, peninsular India had as its core an ancient geological formation called the Deccan Plateau. It stretches southward, high and dry, for a thousand miles from the Vindhya range to the cape called Kanyakumari or Cape Comorin, and it reaches, slightly tipping, west to east from the narrow coastal plain on the Arabian Sea to the somewhat wider plain on the Bay of Bengal, an average of around six hundred miles.

RECIPROCAL INFLUENCES OF NORTH AND SOUTH

These distances assured a measure of isolation between north and south, but it was never absolute. From the south came both people and influences which shaped northern society; for example, during prehistoric times, a number of migrants of Paleo-Mediterranean stock moved up from the peninsula to add to the mosaic of northern India. More recently, Arab Muslims began to reside and trade on the peninsular southwestern coast, intermarrying with local women long before the arrival, after 1000 CE, of Turkic Muslims. Culturally, the devotional form of Hindu religious practice originated in the south and was later carried by south Indians to the Ganges basin.

But perhaps the flow of influence from north to south was greater. The complex and prolonged process of 'Aryanization' (by now defined essentially as the spread of Sanskrit culture) was carried into the peninsula by brahmans from the Ganges Valley as well as by Buddhists and Jainas from eastern India. This began at so early a date that none of the Dravidian languages used by peninsular people is free of substantial Sanskritic influence, mostly lexical, but containing elements of morphology as well. Samples of the Tamil language – considered the oldest of the Dravidian languages – from the first few centuries of this era contain traces of Sanskrit, and even the richly imaginative and inventive early poems of the Tamils include words drawn from the *Mahabharata*. And finally, from Mauryan inscriptions and other remains, we have good evidence of trade contacts between the Ganges basin and the centre of the peninsula. Products of the hand and the mind, as well as the womb, moved in both directions.

Ports and seaboard commerce also found a place in the earliest surviving poetry of the southern states. The Tamil poetry of the early centuries of the present era was enriched by an imagery of landscape that tells us something about the way Tamils viewed their world. Five distinctive landscapes figure in these poems, ranging from the cosmopolitan port towns of the coast and the thriving royal cities of the river valleys to the forested hills of pastoralists and barren lands of fierce fighters and robbers. The fertile and populous valleys were the domains of warrior chiefs, of pious brahmans and of skilled cultivators; they were the precursors of a future to which Tamils and other southern peoples began to move more rapidly from about the fifth century CE. Then powerful kingdoms rose and began to contend against northern states for universal sovereignty in the subcontinent.

The steps to political consolidation, however, were faltering. The kings celebrated in Tamil poetry were really chieftains of the people who shared the same locality, and they were internally divided into clans. If they were at all influenced by the great Mauryan king Ashoka, whose inscriptions and officials reached the northern edge of Tamil country, the influence was slow to manifest itself. Nevertheless, two genuine kingdoms did emerge in the northern parts of the peninsula around the beginning of the present era. One was established by a Jaina called Kharavela, who left an inscription in a cave in modern Orissa, with a somewhat self-contradictory message proclaiming both a belief in non-violence (the Jaina doctrine of *ahimsa*) and the conquest of Magadha, by which he drove an Indo-Greek ruler from his territory in north-western India, as well as an invasion of the territory of a Satavahana king in a neighbouring portion of the northern peninsula.

Kharavela's spacious realm was mentioned by the Roman historian Pliny, as was the Satavahana kingdom of Satakarni I, whom Pliny identified by the term Andarae (Andhra), as part of the central Deccan is still called. Both were formidable military states and, though one was Jaina and the other Hindu, royal patronage was also given to Buddhist monasteries such as the one at the Satavahana capital of Nagarjunakonda, in the fertile delta formed by the Godavari and Krishna rivers.

Further south, during the first centuries of the present era, three chieftaincies ruled the Tamils, according to inscriptions and the corpus of Tamil poetry noted above. These were the Cholas, the Pandyas and the Cheras, and each was dominant in a different portion of the southern peninsula. The Cholas and Cheras were based on the productive agricultural lands of the eastern and western reaches of the Kaveri river respectively, and Pandyas in the Vaigai river valley near the southernmost tip of the peninsula. There, in the city of Madurai, a ruler was said to have convened an academy with the purpose of producing an anthology of extant Tamil poems. The academy took as its name sangam from the Pali word *sangha* of the Buddhist order, which suggests the influence of Buddhists and Jainas in the culture of these early Tamils. The poetic corpus that resulted is called 'sangam poetry'.

Buddhism figured in a political crisis that preceded the rise of the Pallava kingdom in eastern Tamil country during the sixth century CE, when the three Tamil ruling houses were overthrown by an irruption of warriors from the hills. Later brahman writers identified the invaders as Buddhists and labelled them evil usurpers of legitimate royal authority. When these Kalabhras, as they were called, were later driven from power, much was made of the importance of restoring the worship of Shiva and Vishnu, the puranic gods established by the Guptas and their successors in the north. Buddhists and Jainas were then persecuted, according to the boasts of the founders of the later Pandyan and Pallava kingdoms, whose legitimacy seemed to depend on this method of demonstrating religious correctness.

Another factor that contributed to the rise of new kingdoms in the south, as well as in the north, after the fourth century CE was the significant development that took place in trade and in agriculture, which provided the material bases for these new states and supported their ideological justification. Paradoxically, the importance achieved by Buddhism and Jainism there suggests that there was an expansion of commodity production in the southern peninsula at this time. As in northern India, these religions were associated with traders, artisans and other essentially urban groups. Yet a strong relationship was also forged between teachers of these heterodox religions and marginal and hill groups in the peninsula. Moreover, the rulers of several major later dynasties – the seventh-century Pallavas of Tamil country and eleventh-century Hoysalas of Karnataka – were professed Jainas who converted to the worship of Shiva or Vishnu. For example, the second king in the Pallava line, Mahendravarman, claimed that the Shiva 'saint' Appar (himself a convert from Jainism) converted him to the worship of Shiva and persuaded him to launch a persecution of Jainas. The linkage between changes in religious affiliation and changes in the economic base of southern India is not wholly transparent, but the evidence does point to some important economic changes in peninsular society.

COMMERCE BY SEA

Peninsular India may always have been in far better contact with the larger world than the north, to judge from biblical references to King Solomon's ships being sent to southern ports to obtain luxury items: gold, silver, ivory and exotic goods such as peacocks. The fabled wealth of the Pandyan kings derived from their control of the pearl fisheries at the tip of the subcontinent, and was reported by Megasthenes in the fourth century BCE as well as by ancient geographers such as Ptolemy, along with other details of the lands, ports and capitals of the southern kingdoms.

Roman reports on the significance of trade with south India continue the earlier biblical and Greek references. Between these two periods, moreover, the discovery of the monsoon by navigators had occurred. At certain times of the year, winds could carry ships directly across the Arabian Sea, freeing them from the dangers of skirting pirate-infested coasts and shortening the passage by a matter of weeks. The volume of trade between the eastern Mediterranean and India had increased as a result. The Roman geographer Strabo noted this effect during the reign of the Emperor Augustus, and the anonymous author of *The Periplus of the Erythraean Sea* (somewhat later in the first century) told us more about commerce along the west coast of India, where he visited. To this evidence was added the accounts of the later geographer Ptolemy concerning the eastern coast of the peninsula and the first report on the trade links with Southeast Asia.

These accounts provide us with lists of the commodities exchanged through the peninsula. From distant China came silks, some of which were exchanged for products from the Gangetic plain and some for precious stones from Sri Lanka and Southeast Asia. Roman ceramic goods were also a part of this trade, as we learned when British archaeologists uncovered the entrepôt of Arikamedu near modern Pondicherry. At this site, residential quarters, warehouses, fortifications and dockworks were found along with Roman amphora, fine ceramic wares and coins. Roman coin hoards were also discovered in several other places across the peninsula, tracing a route from Kaveripattinam on the eastern coast to the port on the western coast which the Romans knew as Muziris, but whose identity is now uncertain.

To evidence of the flourishing commerce centred on the southern peninsula by the early centuries of the present era we can add evidence of the rapid spread of irrigated field agriculture capable of supporting ever larger populations and more powerful states, among them the Pallavas of Kanchipuram. (The reign of the fifth-century Pallava king Simhavishnu in the south overlapped that of Skandagupta in the north.)

The agrarian setting was one of the five landscapes in which Tamils lived, according to their early poetry. With the coming of the Pallavas, agriculturists and their powerful kings came to dominate all the other environments and cultures of the southern peninsula. The dynasty had established itself in the central Tamil plain, rich with watercourses that fed large storage lakes from which fields were irrigated to produce two or more crops annually.

The Pallavas were the first of a series of southern kingdoms to exercise sovereignty over substantial portions of the Indian peninsula and, occasionally, to intrude themselves into the politics of northern India and Southeast Asia as well. Pallava kings form a part of what is usually called the early medieval history of India for two reasons: they were zealous worshippers of the puranic gods Shiva and Vishnu and they protected as well as benefited from the rich farming communities that were the foundation of early medieval society everywhere. The conjoining of religion and statecraft was not new; rather it is the violent displacement of the religion, politics and economy of one period by another during Pallava times that marks an end to the ancient history of south India.

THE DISPLACEMENT OF THE HETERODOXIES

In northern India, Jainas and Buddhists were peacefully assimilated or benignly ignored when brahmanical religion was revived by Shaivite and Vaishnavite devotees, but the founding of the southern kingdoms of the Pallavas of Kanchipuram and the Pandyans of Madurai was accompanied by the murderous repression of Jainas in particular. This was owing more to ideological differences than to doctrinal differences *per se*. In the formation of these kingdoms, agrarian societies achieved dominance over previously mixed economies in which commerce and merchant communities had enjoyed a special standing, which Jainism and Buddhism had particularly profited by. Embodied in both of these ethical traditions was an ideology of transactionalism, expressed in teachings that emphasized the social practices of moderation and conservatism congenial to merchants, who preferred pragmatic moral codes to the profligacy of ritual brahmanism and its practitioners. This preference was carried over from hostility to vedic sacrifices into hostility to the new religion of devotionalism, which was called *bhakti*.

THE GODS OF PLACE

The coalescence of the bhakti sects coincided with the establishment of the new kingdoms of the Pallavas and the resurgence of one of the old *muvendar* (the three crowned chieftaincies of the Tamils: Chera, Chola and Pandya), the Pandyans. Elaborate public devotion to Shiva was made a central ideological element in both of these kingdoms. Not only were its kings devotees and generous benefactors of temples and their brahman priests, they also claimed to have defeated evil royal rivals, who were supporters of heretical Jainism and Buddhism. In relation to state formation, their claims depicted kings of passionate piety, and at the same time expressed a new ideology of place, as revealed, for example, in the following Tamil hymn to Shiva:

> Ah, sinful, I have left the path of love and service pure! Now well I know the meaning of my sickness and my pain. I will to worship. Fool! how long can I so far remain from Him, my pearl, my diamond rare, the king of great Arur [in the vicinity of modern Madras city].[31]

In sum, then, Jainism and Buddhism were ideologies of transactions between people, while place and territoriality were the salient political elements of bhakti. The hymns were sung to particular manifestations of a god in specific places. In this there is a persuasive fit between the structuring of communities among Tamils and the form of religion they made their own after the sixth century CE. This and the related processes involving rural localities and commerce, as well as the formation of state regimes, set the foundations for early medieval state and society, where new configurations of community and state emerged.

PART III

Medieval and Early Modern India

CHRONOLOGY OF PART III

543–566 CE Pulakeshin I, Founder of the Chalukyas of Badami.
6th century CE Development of *bhakti* worship; rise of the Pallavas.
6th to 7th centuries CE Rise of multiple kingdoms.
606–647 CE Reign of Harsha of Kanauj.
609–642 CE Pulakeshin II of Badami.
630–643 CE Hsuan Tsang in India to collect and translate Buddhist scripture.
675–685 CE I Tsing arrives by sea via Sumatra and stays at Nalanda.
7th to 9th centuries CE Tamil poet-saints; displacement of Buddhism and Jainism.
Early 8th century CE Arabs conquer Sind, raid India.
788–820 CE Shankara reinvigorates Hindu thought, copies Buddhist organization.
Mid 8th century CE Founding of the Rashtrakuta dynasty; overthrow of Chalukyas.
871–907 CE Aditya I defeats the Pallavas, founds the Chola dynasty.
985–1016 CE Rajarajachola founds the Chola empire of South India.
1000–1025 CE Mahmud of Ghazni conducts seventeen raids on North India.
11th to 14th centuries CE Efflorescence of *dharma* texts.
1156 CE Turkic Muslims under Mahmud of Ghur destroy Ghazni.
1193 CE Mahmud of Ghur seizes Delhi.
1206 CE Qutbuddin Aibak founds the Delhi sultanate.
1206–1290 CE 'Slave' sultans.
1290–1320 CE Khalji sultans.
1320–1415 CE Tughluq sultans.
1292–1306 CE Mongol invasion attempts.
1327 CE Transfer of capital from Delhi to Daulatabad.
1334 CE Independent sultanate of Madurai.
1336 CE Separate sultanate of Bengal. Foundation of Vijayanagara kingdom.
1345 CE Foundation of Bahmani kingdom.
1451 CE Bahlul Lodi seizes the Delhi throne.
1489–1520 CE Bahmani sultanate disintegrates into five independent states.
Early 16th century Apogee of Vijayanagara kingdom.
1526 CE Babur defeats Ibrahim Lodi at Panipat, becomes first Mughal emperor.
1540–1555 CE Rule of the Surs between defeat of Humayan and his restoration.
1556–1560 CE Bairam Khan regent for Akbar.
1565 CE Downfall of the Vijayanagara kingdom.
1600 CE Charter of East India Company granted by Queen Elizabeth I.
1601 CE Revolt of Prince Salim initiates recurrent Mughal infighting.
1605 CE Accession of Jahangir.
1628 CE Accession of Shah Jahan.
1657–1659 CE Shah Jahan imprisoned and fraternal struggle for succession.
1658 CE Accession of Aurangzeb; period of religious orthodoxy begins.
1659 CE Shivaji the Maratha takes Bijapur sultanate.
1659–1707 CE Aurangzeb tries to regain control of the Deccan from Marathas.
1685 CE Blockade of Bombay by Sir Joshua Child's brother; English defeated.
1688 CE Shambuji captured by Aurangzeb; Rajiram escapes.
1707 CE Death of Auranzeb; decline of the Mughal empire.
1707–1726 CE Rule of Murshid Quli Khan in Bengal, Bihar and Orissa.
1720–1818 CE Peshwa bureaucracy of the Marathas.
1739 CE Nadir Shah of Persia sacks Delhi and acquires the Peacock Throne.
1770 CE Great Bengal famine.
1784 CE Establishment of Board of Control of East India Company.
1813 CE Abolition of East India Company monopoly over trade.
1824 CE Sepoy mutiny at Barrackpur.
1829 CE Abolition of sati.
1833 CE East India Company ceases to trade.
1837–1900 CE Succession of severe famines and epidemics.
1853 CE Beginning of work on railways.
1857–1859 CE Mutiny in North India.
1858 CE Company dissolved; Parliament takes direct control of British India. Last Mughal emperor deposed.

EXTENDED READING FOR PART III

Harbans Mukhia, *Perspectives on Medieval History*. New Delhi: Vikas, 1993. Collection of essays on a wide-ranging set of issues – social, religious, political and technological – covering both early and later medieval North India; includes historical background to current religious contention.

Brajadulal Chattopadhyaya, *The Making of Early Medieval India*. Delhi: Oxford University Press, 1994. A set of essays covering particular topics, such as irrigation in medieval Rajasthan, urban centres and the origin of the Rajputs, but from a comparative, theoretical and universalizing point of view.

Richard Eaton, *The Rise of Islam and the Bengal Frontier, 1204–1760*. Berkeley: University of California Press, 1993. Detailed study of one of the two areas of India where mass conversion to Islam occurred, and its integration into an expanding agrarian society.

Mattiebelle Gittinger, *Master Dyers to the World: Technique and Trade in Early Indian Dyed Cotton Textiles*. Washington, DC: The Textile Museum, 1982. The catalogue of an exhibition of Indian cotton textiles, painted, stamped and dyed, for both Indian and world markets. Superb on how cloth fragments are documented and decorated. A treat.

Richard M. Eaton, *Sufis of Bijapur, 1300–1700*. Princeton, NJ: Princeton University Press, 1978. Close look at Sufism in its social setting in India. Introduction contains a succint history of the stages of Sufism.

George Michell and Antonio Martinelli, *The Royal Palaces of India*. London: Thames and Hudson, 1994. Ravishing.

David Ludden, *Peasant History in South India*. Princeton: Princeton University Press, 1985. One thousand years of change in the region of Tamilnadu.

Burton Stein, *Vijayanagar*. Cambridge: Cambridge University Press, 1989.

Sanjay Subrahmanyam, *The Political Economy of Commerce: Southern India, 1500–1650*. Cambridge: Cambridge University Press, 1990.

Michael N. Pearson, *The Portuguese in India*. Cambridge: Cambridge University Press, 1987.

K. N. Chaudhuri, *The Trading world of India and the English East India Company, 1668–1768*. Cambridge: Cambridge University Press, 1978.

Sanjay Subrahmanyam, *Improvising Empire: Portuguese Trade and Empire in the Bay of Bengal, 1500–1700*. Cambridge: Cambridge University Press, 1990. Important discussions of the activities of the main European powers in India.

Taipan Raychaudhuri and Irfan Habib (eds), *The Cambridge Economic History of India*, 2 vols. Cambridge: Cambridge University Press, 1982. Comprehensive from around 1500.

John F. Richards, *The Mughal Empire*. Cambridge: Cambridge University Press, 1993. An outstanding modern account, with comprehensive bibliographical guidance.

A. S. Beveridge, trans. *Babur-Nama*. Reprinted Delhi, Oxford University Press, 1970. The memoirs of the founder of the Mughal dynasty.

Muzaffar Alam and Sanjay Subrahmanyam (eds), *The Mughal State, 1526–1750*. Delhi: Oxford University Press, 1998.

Stephen P. Blake, *Shahjahanabad: The Sovereign City in Mughal India. 1639–1739*. Cambridge: Cambridge University Press, 1991. An illuminating study of an imperial city in comparative perspective.

André Wink, *Land and Sovereignty in India: Agrarian Society and Politics under the Eighteenth-century Maratha Svarajya*. Cambridge: Cambridge University Press, 1988.

Muzaffar Alam, *The Crisis of Empire in Mughal North India*. Delhi: Oxford University Press. 1986. An important reassessment of the "decline" of the Mughal state.

C. A. Bayly, *Indian Society and the Making of the British Empire*. Cambridge: Cambridge University Press, 1988. A brilliant and provocative study of the impact of the British up to the Mutiny, with valuable bibliographical guidance.

Eric Stokes, *The Peasant and the Raj*. Cambridge: Cambridge University Press, 1978.

Eric Stokes, *The Peasant Armed*. Oxford: Clarendon Press, 1986. Penetrating accounts of the Mutiny and its antecedents.

Burton Stein, *Thomas Munro: the Origins of the Colonial State and His Vision of Empire*. Delhi: Oxford University Press, 1989. An intellectual biography, drawing for the first time on the newly released Munro papers, of the creator of the revenue and administrative systems of the Bombay and Madras Presidencies in the early British colonial days in India.

Indrani Chatterjee, *Slavery and the Household in Colonial Bengal, 1770–1880*. Delhi: Oxford University Press, 1997. The interactions between women, children, kinship, the family, the Raj and a key social and economic institution in India under Hinduism, Islam and British occupation.

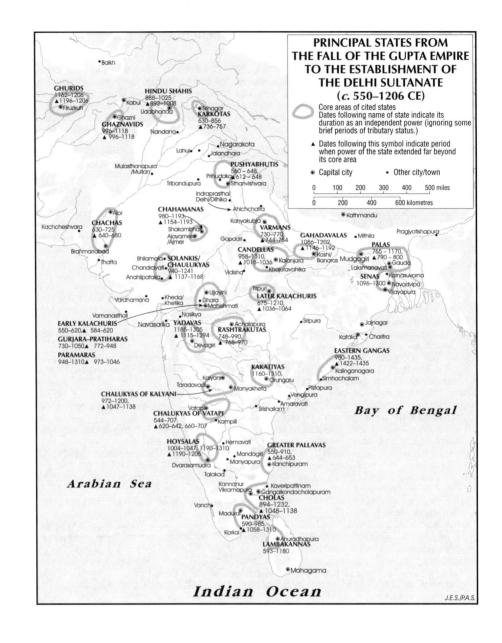

PRINCIPAL STATES FROM THE FALL OF THE GUPTA EMPIRE TO THE ESTABLISHMENT OF THE DELHI SULTANATE (*c.* 550–1206 CE)

Core areas of cited states
Dates following name of state indicate its duration as an independent power (ignoring some brief periods of tributary status.)

▲ Dates following this symbol indicate period when power of the state extended far beyond its core area

● Capital city   • Other city/town

0   100   200   300   400   500 miles
0   200   400   600 kilometres

• Balkh

GHURIDS
1162–1206
▲1196–1206
● Firuzkuh

HINDU SHAHIS
888–1025,
▲892–1008
● Kabul
Udabhanda •
Srinagar •
KARKOTAS
630–856
▲736–757
● Ghazni
GHAZNAVIDS
996–1118
▲996–1118
Nandana •
Lahur •
Nagarakota •
Jalandhara •
Mulasthanapura /Multan •
Tribandupura •
PUSHYABHUTIS
560–648,
▲612–648
Prithudaka ● Sthanvishvara •
Indraprastha/ Delhi/Dilhika •
Ahichchatra
• Kathmandu
Pragjyotishapura •
CHAHAMANAS
980–1193,
▲1154–1193
Shakambhari ●
Ajayameru /Ajmer
Kanyakubja ●
Gopadri •
VARMANS
730–770,
▲744–754
GAHADAVALAS
1086–1202,
▲1146–1192
• Mithila
• Kashi/ Bangras
Mudgagiri •
PALAS
765 – 1170,
▲790 – 800
● Gauda
Laksmanavati •
CHACHAS
630–725
▲640–680
Kachchheshvara •
• Brahmanabad
• Thatta
• Alor
Bhilamala •
Chandravati •
SOLANKIS/ CHAULUKYAS
940–1241
▲1137–1168
Anahilapataka ●
CANDELLAS
958–1310,
▲1018–1036
Kalanjara ●
Khajuravahika •
Vidisha •
SENAS
1096–1300
• Kamasuvarna
• Navadvipa
• Vijayapura
Vardhamana •
Kheda/ Khetika •
Dhara ●
Ujjayini ●
LATER KALACHURIS
675–1210,
▲1036–1064
Tripuri ●
Mahishmati ●
• Sripura
• Jajnagar
EARLY KALACHURIS
550–620, ▲584–620
GURJARA–PRATIHARAS
730–1050▲ 772–948
PARAMARAS
948–1310▲ 973–1046
Vamanasthali •
Navasarika •
Naslkya •
YADAVAS
1185–1305,
▲1115–1294
Devagiri ●
RASHTRAKUTAS
748–990,
▲768–970
Achalapura ●
Kataka ● • Charitra
EASTERN GANGAS
980–1435,
▲1422–1435
Kalinganagara •
Simhachalam •
CHALUKYAS OF KALYANI
972–1200,
▲1047–1138
Taradavadi •
Kalyani ●
Manyakheta ●
KAKATIYAS
1160–1310,
Orugallu ●
Pistapura •
Venglpura •
Amaravati •
Srishallam •
Bay of Bengal
CHALUKYAS OF VATAPI
544–707,
▲620–642, 660–707
Vatapi ●
• Kampili
HOYSALAS
1004–1047, 1190–1310,
▲1190–1205
Dvarasamudra ●
• Hemavati
Mandagiri •
Manyapura •
Talakad •
GREATER PALLAVAS
550–910,
▲644–653
● Kanchipuram
Arabian Sea
Kannanur Vikramapura •
• Kaveripattinam
● Gangaikondacholapuram
CHOLAS
894–1232,
▲1048–1138
Vanchi •
Madurai ●
PANDYAS
590–985,
▲1058–1310
Korkai •
• Anuradhapura
LAMBAKANNAS
593–1180
● Mahagama

Indian Ocean

J.E.S./P.A.S.

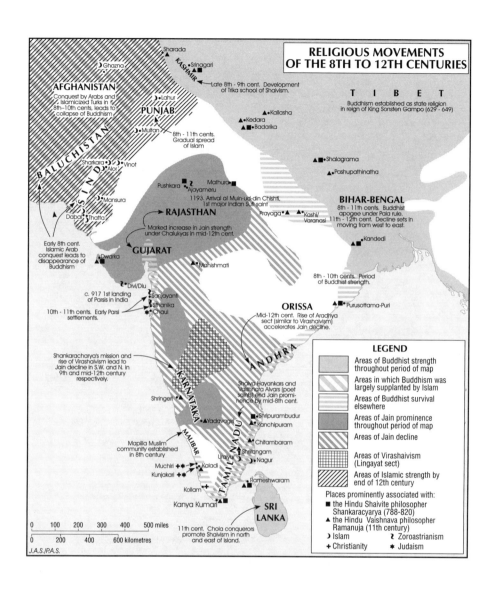

RELIGIOUS MOVEMENTS
OF THE 8TH TO 12TH CENTURIES

•Sharada

KASHMIR
)•Ghazna •Srinagari
Late 8th - 9th cent. Development
of Trika school of Shaivism.

TIBET

AFGHANISTAN
Conquest by Arabs and
Islamicized Turks in
8th–10th cents. leads to
collapse of Buddhism

•Lahur
PUNJAB

Buddhism established as state religion
in reign of King Sonsten Gampo (629 - 649)

▲•Kailasha
▲•Kedara
▲■•Badarika

)•Multan
8th - 11th cents.
Gradual spread
of Islam

S I N D

BALUCHISTAN

Sharkara)•Vinot
Alor
)•Mansura

▲■•Shalagrama

▲•Pashupathinatha

Pushkara ■z Mathura•
•Ajayameru

1193. Arrival of Muin-ud-din Chishti,
1st major Indian Sufi saint.

RAJASTHAN

Prayaga•▲ ▲•Kashi/
Varanasi

BIHAR-BENGAL
8th - 11th cents. Buddhist
apogee under Pala rule.
11th - 12th cent. Decline sets in
moving from west to east.

Dabal)Thatta
Marked increase in Jain strength
under Chalukyas in mid-12th cent.

GUJARAT

▲
Early 8th cent.
Islamic Arab
conquest leads to
disappearance of
Buddhism

)•Dwarka

•Kandedi

8th - 10th cents. Period
of Buddhist strength.

▲•Mahishmati

)Divi/Diu
c. 917 1st landing
of Parsis in India

z•Sanjayanti
z•Sthanika
✱•Chaul

ORISSA
Mid-12th cent. Rise of Aradhya
sect (similar to Virashaivism)
accelerates Jain decline.

▲■•Purusottama-Puri

10th - 11th cents. Early Parsi
settlements.

A N D H R A

Shankaracharya's mission and
rise of Virashaivism lead to
Jain decline in S.W. and N. in
9th and mid-12th century
respectively.

KARNATAKA

Shaiva Nayankars and
Vaishnava Alvars (poet
saints) end Jain promi-
hence by mid-8th cent.

Shringeri

▲•Yadavagiri
■•Shripurambudur
■•Kanchipuram

•Chitambaram

Mapilla Muslim
community established
in 8th century

MALIBAR

•Shrirangam

Uraiyur)•Nagur

Muchiri ✱✚ ✚•Koladi
Kunjakari ✚✱

TAMIL NADU

▲■•Rameshwaram

Kollam ✱✚

Kanya Kumari

SRI
LANKA

11th cent. Chola conquerors
promote Shaivism in north
and east of island.

0 100 200 300 400 500 miles
0 200 400 600 kilometres

J.A.S./P.A.S.

LEGEND

(light grey)	Areas of Buddhist strength throughout period of map
(diagonal hatch)	Areas in which Buddhism was largely supplanted by Islam
(horizontal lines)	Areas of Buddhist survival elsewhere
(dark grey)	Areas of Jain prominence throughout period of map
(vertical hatch)	Areas of Jain decline
(grid)	Areas of Virashaivism (Lingayat sect)
(diagonal hatch)	Areas of Islamic strength by end of 12th century

Places prominently associated with:
■ the Hindu Shaivite philosopher
  Shankaracyarya (788-820)
▲ the Hindu Vaishnava philosopher
  Ramanuja (11th century)
) Islam   z Zoroastrianism
✚ Christianity   ✱ Judaism

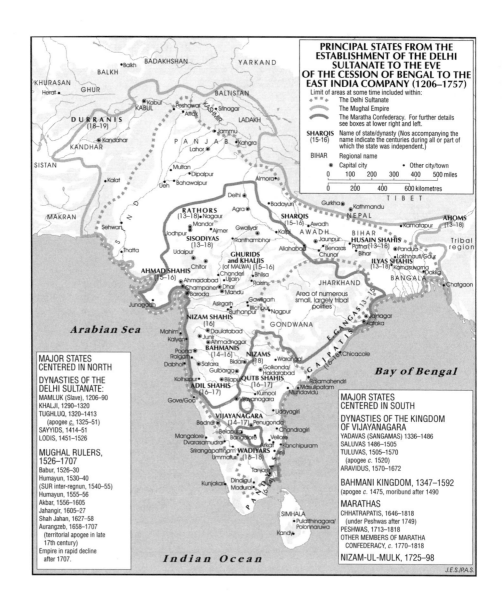

PRINCIPAL STATES FROM THE
ESTABLISHMENT OF THE DELHI
SULTANATE TO THE EVE
OF THE CESSION OF BENGAL TO THE
EAST INDIA COMPANY (1206–1757)

Limit of areas at some time included within:
- - - - The Delhi Sultanate
—— The Mughal Empire
—— The Maratha Confederacy. For further details
      see boxes at lower right and left.

SHARQIS   Name of state/dynasty (Nos accompanying the
(15-16)   name indicate the centuries during all or part of
           which the state was independent.)

BIHAR   Regional name
◉ Capital city   • Other city/town

0   100   200   300   400   500 miles
0   200   400   600 kilometres

MAJOR STATES CENTERED IN NORTH

DYNASTIES OF THE DELHI SULTANATE:
MAMLUK (Slave), 1206–90
KHALJI, 1290–1320
TUGHLUQ, 1320–1413
  (apogee c. 1325–51)
SAYYIDS, 1414–51
LODIS, 1451–1526

MUGHAL RULERS, 1526–1707
Babur, 1526–30
Humayun, 1530–40
(SUR inter-regnun, 1540–55)
Humayun, 1555–56
Akbar, 1556–1605
Jahangir, 1605–27
Shah Jahan, 1627–58
Aurangzeb, 1658–1707
  (territorial apogee in late
  17th century)
Empire in rapid decline
  after 1707.

MAJOR STATES CENTERED IN SOUTH

DYNASTIES OF THE KINGDOM OF VIJAYANAGARA
YADAVAS (SANGAMAS) 1336–1486
SALUVAS 1486–1505
TULUVAS, 1505–1570
  (apogee c. 1520)
ARAVIDUS, 1570–1672

BAHMANI KINGDOM, 1347–1592
(apogee c. 1475, moribund after 1490

MARATHAS
CHHATRAPATIS, 1646–1818
  (under Peshwas after 1749)
PESHWAS, 1713–1818
OTHER MEMBERS OF MARATHA
  CONFEDERACY, c. 1770–1818

NIZAM-UL-MULK, 1725–98

J.E.S./P.A.S.

[3] *MEDIEVAL INDIA*

INTRODUCTION

The Indian classical age spanned the Mauryan and Gupta eras, ending around 500 CE. Thus, it existed during approximately the same period as the classical empires of the west, and came to a close for some of the same reasons, which included destructive invasions from central Asia. Moreover, the historiographies of both Europe and India identify in the subsequent epoch precursors of the onset of modernity (around the sixteenth century in the west). Because of the workings of colonialism, Europe's modernity, after a lag, also became India's in a distorted form. But during Gupta times, different forms of monarchy, culture and economy had developed, and these persisted until the decline of the Mughals, the dynastic apogee of Indian Islamic rulers; thus, the historical epoch formed by these twelve centuries is called medieval for reasons that only partly stem from analogy with European history.

By the seventh century, 'India' was conceived both by the people of the subcontinent and by Chinese and other visitors as extending from the Himalayas to the southern tip of the Indian landmass. No longer was a distinction drawn between the northern, or continental, portion and the long peninsula that spread southward from the Gangetic heartland of the ancient Aryans. The integration was acknowledged in the dharma texts of post-Gupta times, which accepted that there were customs – the touchstone of the sacred law – that were different, but no less valid, in the south. For example, the strict prohibitions of consanguineous marriage in northern societies were not observed among most southerners, whose preferred form of marriage was actually between cousins. But Chinese Buddhist pilgrims sojourned in southern lands considering them part of the India where they might expect to find Buddhist texts and savants. By the seventh century, in fact, a single complex system of political, ideological, economic and cultural relations and institutions obtained over the whole of the subcontinent; southern peoples participated fully in the evolving history of India and it was in the south that many of the religious practices of the medieval age were first manifested.

THE QUESTION OF INDIAN FEUDALISM

Although the notion of an intermediate historical period has proven as legitimate and useful in India as in the Europe, there are still reasons to question the identification of shared detailed characteristics or common origin. The attempt to transfer 'feudalism' from Europe to India has been problematic principally because in Europe (or at least in some parts of Europe and at some times) it is a totalized system of political, social and economic institutions and ideas. That there was such a coherent system in India continues to be contested among historians. Furthermore, it is widely accepted that the integument of modern Europe, or at least that of western Europe, was formed by its medieval institutions, which thereby provided the foundations of both the national states and capitalist economic system that emerged between the fourteenth and the seventeenth centuries. Philosophically liberal historians see this as an ordered evolution that in Britain linked together the Magna Carta, the constitution of 1688, and the reforms of 1832; in economics, it linked the corporate features of medieval society to the mercantilist doctrines and practices of the fifteenth and sixteenth centuries, to the *laissez faire* practices of the eighteenth century and even to Keynesianism during the twentieth. Marxists see medieval institutions as containing the internal contradictions that generated revolutions, which in turn engendered the economic practices of capitalism and then the politics and cultures of bourgeois liberal societies.

No similarly coherent views exist concerning transformations, whether evolutionary or revolutionary, in the middle period in India. True, there is some acceptance of the notion of an 'Indian feudalism' for the period from the Guptas to the onset of Muslim territorial rule in the Gangetic basin; however, this is really more of a loose and uncritical analogy than a detailed correspondence. The analogy breaks down when attempts are made to attribute to 'Indian feudalism' a virtually point-by-point correspondence with the Anglo-French variety (itself usually based on an outdated and very general definition of European feudalism).

While there are good historical reasons for designating the post-Gupta, pre-sultanate age as distinctive, the same reasons make the label 'feudal' highly suspect. Everywhere in the subcontinent this was a dynamic age, in which peasant agriculture and large, agrarian communities came into being and laid the foundations for new kingdoms. These were not feudal states, however, because their rural communities consisted of peasant groups free to maintain their own corporate institutions and agrarian operations. For India, the term 'feudal' has no validity, except, perhaps, as a vague indicator of pre-capitalist/pre-modern societies.

The first practitioners of history in the nineteenth century had a good deal to say about ancient India. From surviving documents, imperial historians demarcated periods that were partly coded in the religious terms by which much of India, including its past, had come to be viewed by colonial eyes. Thus, there was supposedly a 'Hindu' period extending from about 300 CE to around 1200. It was followed by the 'Muslim' period that came to an end in the eighteenth century, to be superseded by a 'British' rather than a 'Christian' period. The idea of religiously defined epochs, at least before British times, continued to guide many historians who, meeting annually since 1940 as the Indian History Congress, formally adopted 1206 CE as the date when 'ancient India' ended and 'medieval India' began.

This formulation accorded well with the view that British imperial control was justified by the conquest of an old regime seen as Muslim, even if it was not wholly that. That old regime had to be shown as wicked, superstitious and violent in order to make that of the conquering East India Company seem morally superior: a blend of equal parts of business and Christianity, liberal rationality and a commitment to the rule of law. When the formal rule of the Company was replaced by the direct rule of the British Crown in 1858 (following the uprising of the Company's Indian soldiers), another generation of British historians were pleased and relieved to be able to attribute India's undeniable poverty to failures of Indian character combined with the corruption of the Company, now happily replaced by Queen Victoria's ministers.

Ironically, Indian nationalist opponents of imperialist historians, when they emerged in the late years of the nineteenth century, held similar views about the middle period of historical development. For them the last great moment for pre-colonial India was the Mughal kingdom of Akbar, who was the grandson of its founder. The greatness of Akbar's kingdom was deemed to have seeped away under his two successors and to have disappeared entirely during the bigoted reign of Aurangzeb.

A different perspective about the Indian medieval period is seen from the vantage point of the southern peninsula. If we were to say that the Muslim conquest and Islamic institutions, beginning around 1200 CE, define the medieval period, then what do we make of the fact that Islamic kingship and culture never became rooted in the south as it did in the north? Or should a characterization of the whole of the subcontinent based on a portion of the north be perpetuated?

And what are we to make of the nearly seven centuries between the fall of the Gupta emperors and the rise of Muslim sultans? Can the historical significance of the years following the classical Mauryan Gupta age be reduced to a preparation for five centuries of Muslim domination over northern India? To dismiss thus the centuries between 500 and 1200 as merely a degradation of classical Gupta culture and its political order suggests that India simply awaited the restored order of foreign sultans. Such a conception too conveniently implies the justifications of the later foreign rule of the British.

Rejecting such suspect instrumentalist formulations, medieval India will be defined here by the compact scaling of its politics and the gradual development of regional cultures and economies. This has a number of advantages. Smaller regional realms and social orders permit the treatment of Muslims and their kingdoms in the same manner as Hindus, and the southern peninsula in the same manner as the north. Smaller geographical scaling also avoids the implication that a whole subcontinent passively and presciently awaited its eventual conquest by Europeans.

Three general periods are taken up in this second part of the history of India: the post-Gupta, early medieval age in India and Southeast Asia, between 500 and 1200 CE; the incursions of Muslim power from 1000 CE, culminating with the establishment of a series of sultanates in the Gangetic plain from 1200 to 1500; and the conditions shaping the Mughal epoch of the seventeenth century.

The processes which define the transition from ancient to medieval Indian history are all-encompassing. One reason for positing a feudal epoch in India is a supposed decline of cities. Urban centres of commerce and of centralized state authority are thought to have declined from about the fourth century CE, leaving rural institutions in a dominant position during Gupta times, when agrarian production and therefore the power of landed interests became ascendant. De-urbanization suggests similarity with Europe, but the evidence for this thesis is somewhat thin.

What is clear, however, is the spread of field agriculture, and the dominance of agrarian over pastoral, if not over urban-based industrial and commercial, interests. Whether or not it resembled changes in Europe at about the same time, there is broad agreement that agricultural settlement spread more rapidly then ever before, from the scattered zones of secure riverine irrigation to ever larger areas. These enlarged agrarian zones consisted of mixed wet and dry cultivation and mixed agriculture and herding.

As landed communities proliferated and spread, the status enjoyed by brahmans increased. They were beneficiaries of income from donors whose gifts were recorded on stone and copper-plate inscriptions, which constitute a major historical source of medieval times and describe both the donors and recipients of the land grants made. The beneficiaries could be individuals or groups numbering up to a hundred or more households, who were settled in newly designated villages thenceforth to enjoy secure incomes and often exclusive residence. Although unarmed priests seem strange counterparts to European medieval knights, the rise to prominence of these brahman landed communities has been accepted as a marker of the Indian medieval age, if not a sign of Indian feudalism.

THE DEVELOPMENT OF CASTE

A second perceived process that demarcates the medieval from the ancient pertains to caste. As a system of hierarchical social and cultural relations among groups defined by birth, caste was a major preoccupation of the dharma texts from the early centuries of the present era onward. The dharmashastras took caste as a social totality and defined relations among persons according to their *varna*, a Sanskrit term literally meaning colour but substantively referring to a limited set of ranked social categories into which each actual birth group (*jati*) was fitted, with some anomalies. Ranking birth groups according to purity was one of the most ancient Indian preoccupations since it was first expressed in the vedic hymn of creation of the four varnas: brahmans, kshatriyas, vaishyas and shudras, or priests, warriors, commoners and servants. From ancient times the first three were considered purer than the fourth and were designated as 'twice-born' because males born into each underwent a ritual rebirth in a ceremony officiated by brahmans. This ritual of initiation, or investment with the sacred thread, was performed at different ages for each group: brahman males at the earliest age and vaishyas several years later, a reflection of the relative purity of the groups. By medieval times, if not before, groups who did not fit into the fourfold social and moral division – such as those whom British census officials later called tribal people, living in societies far removed from the agrarian settlements where the twice-born resided – were deemed even less pure than shudras; some were deemed so impure as to be untouchable.

Untouchable households within the medieval agrarian world and forest peoples who had never belonged to the life of peasant villages alike were excluded from the normative world of brahmans and were affected in two ways by the spread of settled agriculture in early medieval times. Individuals and groups could fall into the degradation of untouchability if they were or became landless and therefore were obliged to labour in the fields of others. The number of such households increased during the medieval age. As forests were felled to make way for cultivation and pastures, hunters and shifting cultivators of forested places were forced into dependency upon landed households of shudra and higher standing.

Why this dependence carried with it the degradation of untouchability is not obvious. It did not arise from cultivation as such, because all castes except brahmans were permitted to till the soil, and even brahmans could do so if life depended upon it. Rather, untouchability was explained in dharma texts as the result of practices considered polluting or else by generalization from captives taken in warfare, aliens without claims to the community protection enjoyed by others, who were reduced to such dependency. Persons and groups considered polluted for whatever reason were frequently prohibited from living in the main settlements of even shudra villages, and were excluded from participation in the ordinary communal religious life of such settlements, including worshipping the protective deities – usually goddesses – of agrarian localities.

Military service, however, was opened to previously forest and pastoral peoples, and many may have escaped the indignity of exclusion by becoming martial castes and claiming the title and name of 'Rajputs' (from *rajaputra*, son of a king or chief). The Rajput claims were recorded in Sanskrit inscriptions that constituted, as well as recorded, community charters in Rajasthan during the seventh century, when Rajput clans began to make themselves lords of various localities. These were relatively modest records, but called 'hero-stones', because the stones on which they were inscribed were planted in the chief villages of one or another of the traditional thirty-six Rajput clans to celebrate some hero who had defended the settlement from raiders. Just where these Rajputs had come from and who their enemies were, however, has been controversial, because while some historians have assumed their vedic antiquity as the first kshatriyas, others have insisted that they either emerged from below as tribal groups transformed themselves, or migrated from outside the subcontinent. Perhaps they even began as Hunas in Central Asia and were converted to Rajput status. Such transformations were common, and achieved by adopting titles and enlisting brahman ritualists and scribes for the purpose.

As in the south, the brahmans were rewarded with land for their services. From the processes of migration and the metamorphosis of lowly local groups into Rajputs, new communities were formed. Some of the clans – the Pratiharas, Guhilas and Chahamanas – succeeded in establishing identities as servants or sustainers of distant kings, assuming the title of 'great neighbour' (*mahasamanta*), which carried with it considerable political autonomy. By the ninth century, the Pratihara dynasty had progressed to referring to itself as sovereigns of Rajasthan and Kanauj too.

Sanskrit inscriptions assert the simultaneity of state and community formation, and provide new legitimacy to both. As in the south, the Sanskrit inscriptions frequently dealt with grants of land and with local politics. Sometimes, for example, Rajput grandees made grants to their subordinate kinsmen, thereby creating local hierarchies where none had existed among previously egalitarian pastoralists. Extending the new stratified communities yet further were marriages among the elites of different clans, which strengthened shared political interests and the process of Rajput state formation.

MEDIEVAL KINGDOMS

The early medieval age is also defined by new states and religious ideologies. Evidence of these political and religious changes dates from the time of the Gupta kings, beginning in the fourth century. That theirs was considered a classical age for near contemporaries is suggested by the practice of some succeeding dynasties of dating inscriptions in accordance with the Gupta era, but for many modern historians the Guptas were special because many practices and ideas that were to distinguish Indian society for the next thousand years are traced to the time of their age. Indeed, the medieval millennium can be demarcated by the widely separated reigns of two kings: Samudragupta, 335–75 CE, and Krishnadevaraya of Vijayanagara, 1509–29. Each represented a model in his own age and within his own dynastic tradition, as well as in the judgement of modern historians.

FROM THE GUPTAS TO HARSHA

Samudragupta's court poet, Harisena, declaimed the grandeur of his patron's conquests in a 360 CE inscription placed upon a pillar that already bore two of Ashoka's edicts. The use of the same advertising space as the original world-conqueror is as magnificent a gesture of self-glorification as the actual words of the later inscription. The text itself records that forty kings and kingdoms were conquered by Samudragupta: fourteen kingdoms were incorporated into the central portion of his own rapidly enlarging realm; another twelve defeated kings were reinstalled as his subordinates, and these included the Pallava kings of the southeastern coast of the subcontinent.

The destinies of two other classes of defeated sovereigns were also noted in the inscription. Some whose lands adjoined the Gupta capital at Pataliputra (modern Patna) were permitted to retain their positions subject to their attendance at Samudragupta's court. From those in more distant lands, such as Sri Lanka or the northwestern kingdom of the Kushanas, tribute was demanded and apparently received instead.

Samudragupta attributed his conquests to the divine favour he enjoyed, bringing to mind Ashoka, the Buddhist who claimed the title of 'beloved of the gods', and whose pillar he shared. Samudragupta, for his part, boasted of performing the royal horse sacrifice, which his panegyrist went so far as to assert made him the equal of Indra and other gods. This claim, recited in the Allahabad inscription, is mirrored in a contemporary dharma text, the *Naradasmriti*, as well. In one of the latest of the major dharmashastras, thought to have been created around 300 CE, its author, Narada, went beyond Manu's prototypic dharma text by speaking of the king as a god and denying that there was a difference between kings and brahmans: the protection that both conferred upon mankind, he said, stemmed from karma earned through austerities in prior lives. The conception of a kingship made sacred by legendary austerities, both in Samudragupta's Allahabad inscription and the Narada dharmashastra, harks anachronistically to a notion of ritual supremacy in the ancient brahmana period, a millennium before. In any case, claims of divine kingship were rarely made after Gupta times.

Samudragupta's vaulting pretensions masked another political story. Contemporaneous with the king and his successors were several kingdoms whose sovereignty endured as long or longer over a substantial part of the subcontinent. The Vakataka kings of the northern part of the Deccan plateau ruled independently from around 300 to 525 CE, although they seem never to have challenged Gupta hegemonic claims. Other kingdoms with similar autonomy for much of fourth to sixth centuries included the Hunas in the far north, the Shakas of the west and the Kadambas and Pallavas on the west and east coasts of the peninsula respectively. And it was not long before yet other dynasties arose, among them the Chalukyas and Cholas in the south, the Rashtrakutas in the west, and the house of Harshavardhana in the western Gangetic valley by the middle of the seventh century.

Between 500 and 1700 CE, several dozen kingdoms succeeded in extending their sovereignty for a time at least beyond their linguistic and cultural heartlands. We may call these 'imperial states'. As a rough measure of the regions they encompassed, the subcontinent can be divided into five historical macro-regions approximating the very large nineteenth-century provinces of British India. (The presidencies of Madras, Bombay and Bengal were three such historic regions, to which were added the combined United Provinces and Central India in the north-centre of the subcontinent and Punjab–Sind–Baluchistan in the north-west.)

Of these 'imperial states', two out of three were ruled by Hindu dynasts, but the most durable was the Muslim Mughal kingdom, which persisted from the middle of Akbar's reign, around 1580, to the reign of Muhammad Shah in 1730. Dominance in more than one cultural region by almost all of these states was usually the accomplishment of a single ruler, a great conquering warrior such as the sixth-century Huna invader Mihirikula, who established a large realm in the northwest. Other examples are Pulakeshin II, ruler of the seventh-century Chalukyan kingdom in the Deccan, and the mid-tenth-century Krishna III of the Rashtrakutas, also in the Deccan.

During those centuries, there was a steady, but small, migration of nomads, such as the Hunas, from the central Asian steppes. This trickle became more substantial and dangerous following conversion to Islam in the tenth century. Between 1000 and 1450 CE, there were other conquerors as well: Mahmud of Ghazni; Balban, the mamluk or 'slave' ruler of Delhi, and his two successors, the Khalji Sultan Alauddin and Muhammad the Tughluq, who subdued all of the Gangetic plain and much of the Deccan plateau.

In addition to these kingdoms, which for a time at least spanned two or more large regions of the subcontinent, there were numerous others, the scale of whose authority was far more limited but whose duration could nevertheless be considerable. Inscriptions from this early medieval period reveal over forty regional dynasties, and other literary sources confirm them. Among the latter were the chronicles of temples (*mahatmya* or *sthala purana*) and royal genealogical texts (*rajavamsavali*). In some cases oral traditions persist about some quite local and minor chiefly families who claimed royal status.

Though this multiplicity of rulers, with their dispersed sovereignties, testifies to a new state form which contributed to the dynamism of the early medieval period, there is little agreement among historians about the character of such states. Even those who have adopted the feudal conception for India have never specified the structure of the 'feudal state' that crowned the so-called feudal relations and institutions, except by implication in the example of the kingdom of Harshavardhana.

HARSHA AND HIS NEIGHBOURS: THE QUESTION OF CENTRALIZATION

Harsha, who was apparently offered the crown by the magnates of Kanauj (near modern Kanpur), came of a powerful chiefly family and ruled a realm nearly as large as the Gupta kingdom during the first half of the seventh century. His capital was in the fertile plain between the Ganges and Yamuna rivers. Apart from the rich agricultural potential and the valuable trade that entered the Gangetic plain at that point, the westward shift of the capital from Pataliputra in the eastern Gangetic basin offered improved defence of the entire plain from further despoliation at the hands of the Hunas who had preyed upon the last Gupta kings.

Harsha ruled from 606 to 647, and his capital became the focus of struggles among a succession of kingdoms until 1200, when Central Asian Muslims established their hegemony. And although he claimed a territory as great as that of the Guptas, Harsha's real sway did not extend beyond a compact territory in the richly watered lands between the Ganges and Yamuna rivers. We know this in part from a famous biography by the poet and playwright, Bana, to which was appended a description by the famous Chinese Buddhist monk Hsuan Tsang, who spent thirteen years (630–43 CE) in the vicinity while collecting sacred texts and relics to take back to China. His scriptural translations from the Sanskrit were accompanied by detailed discussions of the sacred places he visited.

A set of inscribed copper-plates of 632 CE tells us something about Harsha's kingdom. Characteristically, these inscriptions recorded a gift of land to two brahmans, and among the protectors of the gift were a set of political personages with state power. Some were mahasamantas, allied to the king but of a subordinate status; others were 'great kings' (maharajas), independent rulers who acknowledged Harsha's overlordship; and still others served the chakravartin, or emperor of the universe, as Harsha styled himself, in various capacities, including military. Lowest among the guarantors of the gift was the local community where the gifted lands were located. Donations to brahmans – and to Buddhists and Jainas before the time of Harsha – had usually come from a royal prince or a provincial governor. In these copper-plates, however, though the donor of the land was a soldier serving Harsha and the executor of the grant was an accountant in the king's service, the first of the dignitaries to be mentioned was the mahasamanta who ruled a territory adjoining the core tract of land around Kanauj.

It is tempting to compare the mahasamantas to the feudal vassals of medieval European kings. Like them, the mahasamantas were permitted to be virtually autonomous rulers of realms near the core tracts of their overlords, and may have paid them tribute as well as provided military service. But to argue that their lands were grants in lieu of salaries accorded by the rulers is to carry the analogy farther than the evidence warrants. In fact, the mahasamantas were territorial magnates in their own right, either by inheritance or conquest, whether or not they were given lands to support their official duties.

Against these dubious assumptions concerning the sudden and growing importance of samantas and mahasamantas it is possible to put forward a simpler explanation. Titles and the land grants were a means by which higher lords expressed ties to lesser rulers in an accretion of followerships that were constitutive of the great kingships of early medieval India. Rulers of this time spoke of their *samantachakra*, their circle of subordinates; the larger the circle, the more august the overlord. Both superior and inferior lords enhanced their security for a time, but while such arrangements can be reconciled with feudal relations, they cannot in themselves justify the appellation 'feudal'.

Whether Harsha's kingdom was actually less centralized than the Guptas' is uncertain. Most ancient historians agree that such centralized administration as may have existed – even under the powerful founder of the Guptas, Chandragupta, and his conquering successor Samudragupta – was restricted to the central part of the Gangetic plain between Pataliputra and Mathura. Beyond that zone, there was no centralized authority.

A more certain contrast between Harsha's polity and that of the Guptas may have been that the latter had few formidable opponents in northern India and, until quite late in their allotted time, no very formidable enemies beyond. When Harsha sought to extend his authority southward into the Deccan, however, he was humbled by King Pulakeshin II, the Chalukyan ruler of a Deccan kingdom from which inscriptions had begun to be issued in the sixth century. Inscriptions in Pulakeshin's capital, Badami, celebrated that victory by punning that his fighting elephants caused the mirth (*harsha*) of King Harsha to evaporate. Harsha's successor was summarily crushed by the king of Bengal.

Yet even the redoubtable Pulakeshin was not the absolute master of the southern peninsula, for during his long reign (610–42 CE) he was challenged by the Pallava kings, Mahendravarman and Narasimhavarman, who, for their part, faced opposition from lesser kings and reluctant subordinates, the Pandyan and Chola rulers of the far south of the peninsula. Incessant conflict followed in the next several centuries, centring on Kanauj and Harsha's rich patrimony there. During that time, warlords from every direction – Bengal, the Deccan, Rajasthan in the west and Kashmir in the north – strove to seize and hold Kanauj. The competition was terminated by the conquest of the entire Gangetic region by central Asian Muslims during the thirteenth century.

THE PENINSULAR KINGDOMS

Throughout most of India, even the feeble centralization of the Mauryan and Gupta regimes was absent. In the peninsula during early medieval times, a different state form took root in most of the extant kingdoms. The provenance and duration of the kingdoms of the Deccan and the far south can be traced by the distribution of inscriptions recovered during the past century of epigraphical collection in India. The kings of the Cholas and Pandyas, who are mentioned along with the distant kings of Syria, Macedonia, Epirus (on the Ionian coast) and Cyrene (in North Africa), were first noted in an edict of Ashoka that spoke of the kingdoms to which he sent Buddhist missionaries.

By the early centuries of the present era, mention of the ancient Cholas and Pandyas was joined by that of the Satavahana kings, whose domains reached across the entire Deccan plateau, and, on the northeast coast of modern Orissa, by the Chedi rulers of Kalinga. Scattered throughout the peninsula were minor dynasties of all sorts. Some of these were to attain very considerably greater sway by 500 CE, when the Guptas still ruled their core Gangetic territory. The Pallava and Kadamba kings ruled over eastern and western Deccan tracts, the Vakatakas over the central and northern Deccan, and a set of small kingdoms were found along the Orissan littoral. By the early seventh century, when Harsha's kingdom flourished in the central Ganges, the far south had come under the sway of the Pallava kings of Kanchipuram and much of the central and eastern Deccan was under the Chalukyas of Badami, Pulakeshin's line. These peninsular kingdoms did not evolve from within the Gupta political integument as the northern kingdoms supposedly did, but their existence reflected conditions of society which affected all early medieval kingdoms.

By the seventh century, then, a set of regional centres of power were well established, and it was to be characteristic of the medieval political system that there was no single imperial ruler, but many contenders striving for control over a small part of what they claimed. Each of a number of kingdoms was a loosely structured political system with sufficient resources of surplus food and population to support military formations capable of defence as well as predatory alliances with neighbours aimed at the conquest of distant others. Harsha's domains in the western Gangetic valley were subsequently overrun by a succession of contending kings, some from remote places. One of these was the Kashmiri Lalitaditya, whose place in history was made by defeating an Arab army that sought to invade the Ganges plain after having conquered Sind in 711 CE. Lalitaditya's campaigns against Kanauj were symptomatic of his recognition that the centre of geo-political gravity had shifted to the western Gangetic plain under threats to the area from beyond the northwestern mountain frontier. The danger from central Asia compounded threats to the Gangetic overlords from Kashmir and from the southern Deccan realm of the Rashtrakuta kings, who extended their rule to the Ganges region and to Kanauj around 1200.

REGIONALIZATION

A defining and central process of the early Indian medieval age was the consolidation of regional societies, in which process political forms were more important elements than hard territorial boundaries. The kingdoms of that age had fluid boundaries; they were states defined less by administration than by language, sectarian affiliations and temples. Political treatises continued an older rhetoric of pragmatic alliances among polities aimed at averting the violent swallowing of small states by larger ones. However, within the limited regions defined by royal claims, new political, linguistic, literary and social histories and boundaries were taking a shape that remains recognizable even in contemporary modern India.

At the core of this regionalizing process were two forces: one was socio-economic and had to do with the widespread displacement of pastoral by agrarian economies and less stratified societies by more hierarchical ones; the other was cultural, involving gods, temples, inspired poets and philosophers. But political forms mediated these directive influences of the post-classical world of India.

It is impossible to decide which of the components of the regionalizing process was the most important or determining: political, religious or cultural. It cannot be said that the emergence of smaller, more compact monarchies caused the religious, linguistic and literary developments of these centuries. At any rate, there is no evidence of any such intentions on the part of the new monarchs, and it seems that these kings were as much made by as makers of these developments. Possibly, the three aspects of regionalization were complexly related to other causal factors. Speculatively, it can be suggested that this was an age of rapid and generalized development of commodity production and also of town life, both of which contributed to India's reputation for fabulous wealth and elegance. Its products were sought by traders of the dynamic and expanding orders of the time in Tang China and the now Islamicized Arabian Peninsula. Traders from both areas found their ways to

Indian emporia or met Indian traders in other zones of commercial activity in the Middle East and Southeast Asia.

In addition to the production of goods, there was the explosion of Indian literary production, of Sanskrit productions of puranas and dramas, as well as a flowering of literatures in other languages. Both forms of production were attractive to people throughout and beyond the subcontinent. Where once Buddhist and Jaina ideologies flourished, in part by providing a moral justification for the pragmatic values of merchants and moneyed men, as well as by providing an institutional framework that linked Buddhist and Jaina monasteries with the high commerce of the age, these functions were now readily assumed by Hindu temples.

Buddhism and Jainism were displaced after Mauryan times, with considerable difficulty in some places. In Bengal, Buddhist institutions continued to enjoy supporters until Muslim iconoclasts destroyed many of their holy places in the twelfth century; a large proportion of Bengal's Buddhists converted to Islam; others were won to a form of regional devotional Vishnu worship. Far away in the Tamil cultural region, religion had long before become involved with both linguistic and political developments that moulded the regionalization process lying at the heart of medieval Indian historical change. And driving the Tamil cultural process was a deadly struggle between a new sort of brahmanical worship and the older religious hegemony of Buddhists and Jainas.

Sectarians of both sorts found political support from some Tamil rulers around the sixth century about whom little is known (and that mostly from hostile commentators who decried them as 'evil' rulers). They may have been hill chieftains who obtruded political control over the rich agricultural plains in which they found and patronized Buddhist and Jaina institutions and teachers. Even when these so-called usurpers of plains authority were driven off by kings such as the Pallavas, the victors continued to support Jainism until converted by teachers of the new devotional faith. Pallava Mahendravarman, for example, renounced his affiliation with Jainism, and turned against and persecuted its followers after becoming a Shiva worshipper. Other Tamil rulers followed suit as the Shiva cult armed itself with a powerful theology to compete against Buddhists and Jainas.

HINDU RESURGENCE AND LINGUISTIC FLUORESCENCE

A major formulator of the reinvigorated Hindu thought was Shankara, a brahman who combined philosophical adroitness with impressive organizational acumen. To oppose what he castigated as blasphemy, he returned to the ancient Upanishads (from which Buddhist doctrines had also evolved), and offered explanations of salvation as compelling as those of the hegemonic heterodoxies of his time and earlier. Besides incorporating and transcending Buddhist doctrines, he mimicked their institutions by establishing the monastery (*matha*) as a key institution in a number of sites. Four of these held special status as major missionary centres, each under a successor-teacher (*sankaracharya*).

The religious reforms were not wholly intellectual. In addition to borrowing and incorporating Buddhist and Jaina institutions, Shankara adopted a popular song form to compose praises to Shiva. These hymns of devotion became the foundation for the new and popular worship, one that has endured to the present throughout India under the name of Hinduism.

The religious devotionalism called *bhakti* which first took shape in Tamil country during the sixth century was anticipated earlier by the Krishna devotionalism found in the *Bhagavad Gita*, composed around the first century CE and incorporated into the *Mahabharata* around a century prior to Shankara's time. Further developments of the Tamil bhakti religion were the work of later poet devotees and theologians. According to tradition, between the sixth and tenth centuries, sixty-three Shiva- and twelve Vishnu-worshipping poets created a large corpus of Tamil devotional songs, and all are now revered as saints. Nor did theology lag far behind. Shankara's work in providing an intellectual base for popular worship of Shiva was also intended to maintain and strengthen brahman leadership, and this feature was imitated by the Vishnu cult as well.

Religious developments spurred the development of first Tamil and subsequently other languages between 1000 and 1300 CE. In the twelfth century, bhakti hymns were composed in Bengali by the saint Jayadev and in what is now called Hindi by Nimbarka of Mathura. Nimbarka was originally a south Indian brahman whose devotion to Krishna inspired him to a missionary vocation that helped to make Mathura the centre of the Krishna cult. In the same period, literary works, along with such technical auxiliaries as grammars and dictionaries, were written in Marathi, Bengali and several other languages.

Languages and literatures underwent a regionalization that made possible the spread and particularization of popular devotion to Vishnu, Shiva and the goddesses. Everywhere devotees imitated the Tamils, the first of the devotional worshippers to create a corpus of hymns in their own language. These compositions launched the development of all the modern languages of the subcontinent, those based on Sanskrit throughout the north, and others based upon a mix of Dravidian and Sanskrit words and grammatical forms in the south.

In addition to the bhakti songs, two other literary projects assumed special importance. One genre preserved or invented myths about the gods who were the divine objects of the songs and theology and were installed in temples devoted to their worship. These temples, along with the mathas, gave institutional focus to the religious reformation. The other stimulus to the literature of the early medieval age was the chronicles of ruling families of the time.

URBANIZATION AND THE COUNTRYSIDE

Temples and kings were crucial institutions of regional cultures during early medieval times, and both had the further effect of stimulating urbanization. Again, the Tamil country provides early examples. The major Shiva temples of Tanjavur and Madurai became the royal chapels of the Chola and Pandya kings respectively. Both ruling families lavished treasure on adorning and worshipping the deities enshrined, attracting a large permanent population of priestly officiants at each temple and throngs of pilgrims whose needs created the foundations for substantial urban centres.

We know all this from documents inscribed on the stone basements and walls of both temples and from the chronicles eulogizing the gods and demonstrating in the process that many of them were transformed local guardian spirits who were assimilated by stories to Shiva legends found in Sanskrit puranas or an even earlier time. This sort of 'Sanskritization', the assimilation of previous territorial spirits to the most august of gods, was also a necessary part of a process of 'regalization'. Would-be kings intent on converting their status from that of ambitious warriors and local chieftains into chakravartins aided in the metamorphosis of often minor, popular gods and goddesses into manifestations of Shiva or Vishnu, worthy of royal adoration.

In early medieval times, kings' temples were also palaces where royal business was conducted and royal rituals were enacted. Political capitals inevitably were or became temple centres, and many also became major urban centres. Royal worshippers and their gods attracted subjects and devotees in large numbers, and the servicing of both made each capital city an economic centre as well. In due course, lesser chiefs – grandees and magnates to whom the title 'Samanta' was applied and who maintained smaller courts in the scores of kingdoms of the early medieval age – began to imitate their superiors; we have another of India's moments of urbanization to mark.

The early medieval, commercial- and religious-led urbanization is one reason for scepticism regarding the notion of feudalism, which is conceptually related to deurbanization and decommercialization, to India. Nowhere is this clearer than in the manner in which the city of Kanauj in the western Gangetic plain became the focus of north Indian politics for several centuries, during which competing conquerors from the north, south, east and west strove to seize and hold it: the city had become the emblem of the chakravartin. But all over the subcontinent other cities were created as the centres of lordships; in most of them still survive the impressive monumental ruins that have made the archaeology of historical places a major intellectual enterprise in India. The pronounced urban character of the early medieval age accounts in part for the allure of India for the Turkic invaders from the steppes. For them, cities could be made to provide the means to sustain the new institutions of Islam and a new elite of Muslim fighters and rulers.

This was India's third urbanization, if we take the first to have been that of the Indus and the Indian northwest, and the second that of the Gangetic plain in pre-Mauryan times. In contrast to the first two moments of urban development, when towns were sparse and uniquely the sites of state-level authority, those of the early medieval age appeared in rich profusion, reflecting a wide dispersion of authority and close relations between political centres and the community base upon which the states were founded.

The relationship was variably manifested over the length and breadth of the subcontinent. In places relatively less well endowed by nature – such as Rajasthan in the northwest or Karnataka in the central peninsula – there appeared one sort of configuration of community and kingdom, while in the

Gangetic plain and the Coromandel plain in the south there was another. In Rajasthan and Karnataka, the caste culture of the medieval age was known, but the hierarchical practices of caste relations were attenuated by the principles of clan organization of the farming communities and their artisan and priestly clients that now characterized the countryside.

In the core zones of the early medieval age, Gangetic towns and communities from the sixth to the twelfth centuries, powerful landed groups had separated their identities from the older clan collectivities whence they emerged or whom they conquered. Thereupon, the older penates and vedic rituals of Aryan clansmen were shunned by the arriviste dominant peasantries of diverse clan origins. Instead, large holdings of land were granted to learned and priestly brahman adepts of the new bhakti faiths.

There is also evidence of the new enstructuration of communities in the other major medieval riverine loci of civilization in the subcontinent, the Palar and Kaveri basins in the south. Large rural settlements were created during the reigns of the Pallava and Chola kings of the seventh to thirteenth centuries, sometimes by the kings themselves, but more often by wealthy and powerful landed groups. The latter consisted of local communities of often hundreds of villages, who managed their economic, social and political affairs through their councils. For them, connections with brahmans conferred a status that others, such as artisans and merchants, could not hope to attain until several centuries later. Then, around the twelfth century, craftsmen and merchants organized an extensive oppositionary alliance and fought for a degree of parity with the landed. The southern communities provide rich documentation on the complex and competitive alignments of social groups of the early medieval age and also on the increasingly complex commercial world that was intruding upon medieval societies. Clan organization had no more importance here than in the Gangetic countryside.

THE MERCHANT GUILDS

Beginning in the ninth century, inscriptions drew attention to another kind of community whose function for many centuries was to provide trade links among agrarian communities in Karnataka and Tamil country with Sri Lanka and Southeast Asia. One group of traders called themselves the Five Hundred Lords of Ayyavolu (modern Aihole), a town that was formerly a subsidiary capital of the Chalukyas of Badami and a place with many temples and brahmans, some of whom seem to have become involved in the trading activities of the Five Hundred. But most of the Ayyavolu Lords were merchants, especially those who engaged in long-distance trade. Their inscriptions between the ninth and fourteenth centuries record their endowments to temples, and their gifts were often made in cooperation with the local merchant groups through whom the itinerant traders distributed their often exotic commodities.

In hundreds of stone inscriptions, partly in Sanskrit and partly in one of the southern languages, these prestigious itinerant traders who flourished until the fourteenth century harked back to the Chalukya kings, who, in the heyday of their rule over the Deccan in the seventh and eighth centuries, had capitals at several places in Karnataka, including Ayyavolu. The following passage was taken from a long inscription recorded by the guild of the Ayyavolu merchants in 1055 CE:

> Famed throughout the world, adorned with many good qualities, truth, purity, good conduct, policy, condescension, and prudence; protectors of the *vira-Bananju-dharma* [law of the heroic traders], having 32 *veloma*, 18 cities, 64 *yoga-pithas*, and *asramas* at the four points of the compass; born to be wanderers over many countries, the earth as their sack, . . . the serpent race as the cords, the betel pouch as a secret pocket, the horizon as their light;
> . . . by land routes and water routes penetrating into the regions of the six continents, with superior elephants, well-bred horses, large sapphires, moon-stones, pearls, rubies, diamonds . . . cardamoms, cloves, sandal, camphor musk, saffron and other perfumes and drugs; by selling which wholesale, or hawking about on their shoulders, preventing the loss by customs duties, they fill up the emperor's treasury of gold, his treasury of jewels, and his armoury of weapons; and from the rest they daily bestow gifts on pandits and munis; white umbrellas as their canopy, the mighty ocean as their moat, Indra as the hand-guard [of their swords], Varuna as the standard-bearer, Kubera as the treasurer, the nine planets as a belt . . . the sun and moon as the backers, the 33 gods as the spectators; like the elephant they attack and kill, like the cow they stand and kill, like the serpent, they kill with poison; like the lion they spring and kill . . . they make fun of the gone Mari [last epidemic] . . . clay they set fire to, of sand they make ropes; the thunderbolt they catch and exhibit; the sun and moon they draw down to earth;
> [T]hey converse about the frontal eye and four arms of Isvarabhattaraka, the loud laughter of Brahma, and the madness of Bhagavati. In the case of a sack which bursts from the contents collected from the four points of the compass, an ass which runs away [laden] with grain, a bar of gold that has been seized, a tax that has been evaded, a cry of looting, an assembly connected with caste customs, a bargain that has been made – they are not ones to fail.[1]

The obvious model for this inscription was the famous declaration of Krishna in the *Bhagavad Gita*, but it reveals that not only the entrepreneurial spirit but the culture and road wisdom of the backpacker were current a millennium ago.

Though the most flamboyant, the Five Hundred were not the only itinerant merchants who became a community because of their operations within a recognized if far-ranging zone. Another, called Manigramam, manifested their cosmopolitanism in the earliest of their epigraphs, which was inscribed on copper-plates still in the possession of the Syrian Christians of Kerala. Four languages figure in this inscription and as many scripts: early Tamil, Arabic, Hebrew and middle Persian. It sets out the conditions laid down for foreign traders at the port of Quilon by agreement with the local rulers. Members of both of these itinerant mercantile communities were found in ports and other commercial centres; they endowed temples, fed brahmans and contributed to the maintenance of irrigation works.

The traders' inscriptions dot the entire southern peninsula, tracing an inter-regional and international trade nexus of merchants of whom some were identified as *nanadeshi*, or of 'many countries', and others as local (*swadeshi*, 'own country'). These traders' groups provided one of the conduits for transporting Dravidian culture to Southeast Asia, an extension beyond the subcontinent of early medieval urbanization.

INDIAN INFLUENCES IN SOUTHEAST ASIA

For the medieval kingdoms, the sea provided opportunities for political, religious and commercial influence to reach beyond the subcontinent. In one direction lay western Asia and the energies of recently converted Muslim traders who penetrated the markets of the subcontinent during the eighth century, even as the Arab Muslim horsemen were turned away by Lalitaditya and other warriors. Trade with the eastern Mediterranean continued steadily after that. War horses and metal goods were imported; black pepper, sandalwood and textiles were exported; and Chinese silk and porcelain, obtained from Southeast Asia, were re-exported to the west. Hazardous individual voyages between western Asian and western Indian ports during the eighth and ninth centuries eventually gave way to a trade system among established emporia inhabited by cosmopolitan communities of Arabs, Jews and Armenians from western Asia. These provided convenient economic linkages across the Arabian Sea that enriched merchants on both sides.

Another ocean frontier opened to Southeast Asia. During the early centuries of the present era, three kingdoms emerged in the Indo-Chinese peninsula, covering parts of modern Thailand, Cambodia and Vietnam. Kings with Sanskritic names ruled these realms: Kaundinya and Jayavarman in the Funan kingdom between 400 and 500 CE, and, in the same period, Sruta Sreshta Varman of the Chenla kingdom, and Bhadravarman of Champa in the Indo-Chinese peninsula. These and lesser states that emerged before the seventh century in what is modern Malaysia and Java attest to a profound Indian impact upon its eastern neighbours.

The 'Indianization' of Southeast Asia was long thought to have been the result of military conquests which created what a generation of Indian nationalist historians called 'Greater India'. In more recent writings, these cultural and political influences are understood as both multifaceted and bilateral. Not only were merchants and especially religious scholars involved as well as soldiers, but exchanges took place at the behest of the Southeast Asians as well as for the profit of Indians. In religious matters the initiative is actually thought to have come more from Southeast Asians. They established extended connections with India and especially with south India during Pallava and Chola times, and, later, when Islam was introduced into Malaya, Java and Sumatra, it too was imported from south India.

True, Ashoka claimed to have sent missionaries to a number of places in Asia. But the religious instruction he initiated was broadened as knowledge of Sanskrit increased, opening the way into other forms of Indic learning, including the dharma texts on society and kingship. Inscriptions record that Southeast Asians sojourned in Indian seminaries in order to learn these religious innovations and translate them into their own tongues, and these learned men from various parts of insular and peninsular parts of Southeast Asia were certainly prime agents of cultural transfer. Having acquired Indian knowledge through Sanskrit and Prakrit, at first in order to learn the tenets of Buddhism, they soon found their way to the Sanskrit puranas that taught the still new form of bhakti worship, and, along with that, the dharmashastras containing models of social hierarchy and powerful monarchy. The devotional worship first devised in south India thus was carried to Southeast Asia as well as to the western and northern parts of the subcontinent.

At length the basics of the entire political and social system – a veritable manual that defined ancient India – were disseminated over all of Southeast Asia, stimulating the development of new societies and cultures there, as well as markets for Indian goods. Merchants from the southern coast of India provisioned these markets in return for gold and for the Chinese commodities that were valued imports in India.

Indian culture was changed in the transfer to Southeast Asia and one of the changes involved the nature of kingship. The notion of the god-king (*devaraya*) was developed in the Indo-Chinese peninsula by native monarchs, perhaps after they themselves had been introduced to the idea by the Naradasmriti. Claiming divinity for themselves, Khmer kings created vast and exquisite temple-palaces such as that at Angkor. Nevertheless, the idea was never adopted in India at that period; rather the converse. Medieval Indian kings were content to be only pious devotees, the first among the worshippers of the dominant deities of bhakti: Shiva, Vishnu and the Goddess, Devi or Durga, who were endowed with royal style. These deities had risen to prominence during the Gupta age, and they were to remain the most august of sovereigns, lavishly sheltered in the magnificent palaces which Indian temples after Gupta times became.

THE ROYALTY OF GODS AND THE DIVINITY OF KINGS

Though not gods themselves, Indian kings, like the kings of Southeast Asia, were conquerors, successful warriors capable of inspiring lesser chiefs and kings to ally with them in joint ventures undertaken as often for plunder and glory as for territory. Royal authority also depended on persuading lesser authorities – chiefly heads of peasant localities, small town markets and religious institutions – to accept their offers of protection in return for a portion of their subjects' wealth.

Early medieval Indian kingdoms were based in core territories over which the ruler and his household, and his kinsmen and associated households, exercised direct authority. There they adjudicated conflicts and collected revenue. The size of this core depended on how many soldiers – mounted and on foot – could be supported from its wealth, and on the relative strength of neighbouring lordships. But everywhere during the early medieval age, it was accepted that it was necessary to have a king, one who was close by if possible, but a distant king if not. Accordingly, over forty substantial royal lineages – kingdoms – left evidence of their authority between the seventh and eleventh centuries; each issued royal inscriptions in accordance with forms specified in the dharmic and puranic texts of the time. These records, in stone or on copper-plates, glorified the ruling family and the accomplishments of individual kings. They were placed on the walls of temples in order to make them widely known yet protected from vandals; building a royal temple was an obligation on any king who strove for greatness, according to the *Vishnudharmottarapurana* of Kashmir and other contemporary texts.

The principles of kingship from the seventh century on were stipulated in the same texts that provided the basis for the devotional worship of gods. The lot of mankind was vested in both divine and royal hands, and both kings and gods were given charismatic biographies. The puranas that recounted the careers and attributes of the Gupta-period gods were written between the fourth and the eight centuries, and served as manuals of worship as well. They were transmitted by learned sect leaders who associated closely with great and small kings and local chiefs. The credentials of even the most powerful rulers who supplied the resources to sustain sectarian institutions, were expressed in and justified by an ideology of religious devotion.

Kings and their divine patrons ruled large agrarian communities whose sedentary farming institutions and practices continued to expand during the medieval age. Pastoralists and forest people alike were drawn into agrarian society as their ancient hill and forest-covered homelands were converted to field agriculture and they themselves into field hands to meet the labour demands of more intensive cultivation. Surpluses of food and commodities such as cotton became increasingly available for ordinary as well as aristocratic households, and also for an explosion in cultural production.

THE ROLE OF THE SOUTHERN KINGDOMS

During the first two centuries of the present era, a dynasty of kings who called themselves Satavahanas exercised a sprawling sway over the land called Dakshinapatha, the Deccan plateau between the Narmada and Godavari river basins. They claimed universal dominion just as did their contemporaries in the north, the Kushana and Shaka kings, and all justified such claims by the conquest of minor rulers from whom homage was demanded, but very little else. Some of the minor principalities under Satavahana suzerainty were nothing more than chieftaincies, and these included the Chola, Pandya and Chera mentioned in Ashokan records.

Later, some of the minor principalities became more impressive. The Pallava kings ruled around the important trade centre of Kanchipuram on the southeast coast, which was known to Chinese merchants, as it had been to the Romans. However, it is likely that the Pallava kingdom owed its existence to the prosperous irrigation and dense agrarian settlement around Kanchipuram as well as to its trade. Along with the rise of the northern Tamil kingdom of the Pallavas, the Cholas and Pandyas in their respective river valley domains became more concentrated authorities, the smaller, more compact and wealthier monarchies that were the mark of the medieval era.

The Pallavas at their height ruled a region of 7000 square miles, the largest realm seen in the southeastern peninsula to date: they seem to have arisen from the northern fringes of Tamil-speakers. From the flourishing trade centre of Kanchipuram, they extended their sovereignty over all the Tamils during the seventh and eighth centuries. The core of their kingdom, however, was a region called Tondaimandalam, which had formerly been divided into twenty-four localities, each called a *kottam*, which had been dominated by two ancient chiefdoms before they were swept aside when the first Pallava proclaimed them as his realm in the late sixth century. Kottams were agrarian communities, prepared to share some of their wealth with the new line of Pallava kings and also to serve these kings as soldiers when, during the seventh century, Pallava sovereignty was extended far into the south, incorporating the domains of the Cholas.

Each kottam was a sub-region of pastoral and agrarian organization, inhabited by sets of village-based farmers, herdsmen and artisans who acted together to maintain the precious irrigation upon which cultivation depended. They constructed reservoirs resembling small lakes connected to the fields by channels. They also built small temples, among the earliest 'structural' temples in the subcontinent, to house the guardian spirits they propitiated against disease and other misfortune, and the chiefly families began to invite brahman families to settle among them and worship the puranic gods in return for livelihoods derived from the most productive lands. The peasantry of the kottams had earlier supported learned Jaina teachers in the same manner.

Pallava attempts to expand northward were thwarted by the rising power of the Rashtrakuta kings of Karnataka and Maharashtra. The latter conquered most of the southern peninsula during the eighth to tenth centuries, and at one point, under their king Krishna III in the middle of the tenth century, they joined the competition then in progress among the northern ruling families for control of Kanauj and the western Gangetic plain.

By the seventh century, and possibly earlier, Tamil-speaking people had not only internalized the ideas of royal sovereignty and legitimacy, but held that the previously unimpressive chieftaincies of the Cholas, the Pandyas and the Cheras – the last confined to the present Kerala region – had actually constituted three royal traditions of equal and legendary standing. The notion of the 'three kings' was expressed in Tamil poetry and inscriptions, and by the tenth century local magnates proudly claimed to be *muvendavelar*, the soldiers who by their valour sustained the three kingships.

Under the Pallavas and the Chola kings who succeeded them in the ninth century, royal authority was strongest in two widely separated zones: the countryside surrounding Kanchipuram in the basin of the Palar river, and the Tanjavur region, watered by the Kaveri River. The respective capitals of the Pallavas and Cholas were centred in zones defined by extensive irrigation systems, on which kings and their agents drew for support. In those core areas of their authority, temples were built and provision was made for large contingents of the priests and retainers whose role was to conduct the appropriate worship of the high gods Shiva and Vishnu. Accordingly, colonies of learned brahmans, supported by income from prosperous villages, were founded by kings and, in a process of imitation, by local chiefs who often referred to themselves as muvendavelar.

Most of the rest of the Tamil plain and its upland extensions were beyond the direct administration of the Pallava and Chola kings. There, minor kingdoms and chiefdoms were under the control of ruling lineages drawn from the dominant land-holding groups. Hundreds of territorial assemblies spoke for agrarian communities and were locally ruled by chiefs. These magnates also aped their betters by inscribing records of their grants to brahmans on the walls of their local temples, extending a kind of homage in the form of a largely symbolic subordination – and occasional service – to the Pallava and Chola kings.

An example of this kind of transaction was found in a set of copper-plates inscribed in 764, during the reign of Pallavamalla (Nandivarman II) in the village of Pullur, near modern Madras. Like other Pallava inscriptions it opens with the standard Sanskrit verses eulogizing the king, introducing a young chieftain and recording a gift to 108 'poor and pure' brahmans, for whom he sought the king's protection. The gift itself consisted of four riverine villages, including Pullur, that were to constitute a new settlement for the brahmans. Gifts of villages to brahmans (*brahmadeya*) conferred merit upon the chief and the king alike, for the latter was enjoined to protect it for all time. The Tamil language plates with which the inscription continued were presumably addressed to ordinary local people; these set out in detail the boundaries of the new settlement, which were to be demarcated in a public ceremony by the representative body of major local cultivators (*nattar*, people of the *nadu*, or agrarian locale) and recorded by accountants employed by the nattar. The grant ends by naming the brahman recipients of this prodigious grant of around 1000 acres of riverine land.

The record defined two communities. Each brahman beneficiary was punctiliously identified according to the sub-caste and the learned tradition (*sutra*) he was responsible for transmitting. The large number of brahman residents of the new villages enjoyed political autonomy from the surrounding villages of cultivators, pastoralists, traders and artisans. Their privileges and immunities were specified. For example, none save 'clean' castes could live within the village precincts, even though untouchables worked the fields that supported the brahman households. On the other hand, schools under brahman teachers were opened to shudras who might receive tuition in rhetoric, logic and warfare, among other subjects. (In the south, the kshatriya and vaishya varnas were largely missing, and these roles were often assumed by shudras.)

The young chief and his peasant subjects in many villages around Pullur were placed in a special relationship with the king. As a community, the villagers around Pullur gained status from their munificence, for it placed them in the prestigious position of patrons of brahman savants, along with the king whose protection was extended over their generous gift.

IDEOLOGY AND AUTHORITY IN SOUTH INDIA

In south India, royal authority was claimed both within the riverine cores of realms and sometimes also at considerable distances from the royal capitals. The Chola kings boasted of their overseas conquests, including the northern portion of the island of Sri Lanka, the Maldive Islands located to the west of India and the kingdom of Srivajaya in southern Sumatra. Rajarajachola boasted of the treasure taken from overseas and the more remote parts of the Indian peninsula, with which he built a magnificent royal temple in his capital Tanjavur. (The god of this shrine was Rajarajesvara, meaning the Shiva phallus worshipped by King Rajaraja.) His son Rajendrachola I claimed to have sent an army to conquer the Ganges, so that its sacred waters could be added to, and thus sanctify, the tank of his royal temple at Gangaikondacholapuram, on the north bank of the Kaveri river. Again, the name commemorated the conquest: it means 'the city of the Chola that seized the river Ganges'.

COMMUNITY AUTONOMY AND INSTITUTIONS

Despite these overweening claims, and apart from the immediate hinterlands of their royal precincts, the subjects of the Pallava, Chola and other southern kings between the seventh and the twelfth centuries managed their own affairs. Community institutions were the means of autonomy. Some were ancient institutions, such as the village and locality assemblies and chieftaincies; others, such as temples and the seminaries often attached to them, were more recent. In both the older and newer institutions, diverse customary arrangements were recognized and preserved, and most locales allocated a part of their wealth for the support of brahmans and the worship of both august puranic gods and humble, local guardian deities, who were principally goddesses.

An instance of the process of cultural generalization and elaboration was the incorporation by 'marriage' to Shiva of the autonomous goddess Minakshi. Marriage meant that Minakshi became assimilated to Shiva's consort-deity Parvati. The same example illustrates a second mechanism as well, for Minakshi's 'wedding' was first celebrated in a temple festival sumptuously sponsored by the kings whose capital, Madurai, was built around Minakshi's temple. This sort of synthesizing of religious, cultural and political elements was a central feature of regionalization and produced a diverse medieval cultural heritage that contrasts with the assumed unity of the classical Gupta age.

RELIGION IN SOUTHERN KINGSHIPS

Tamil devotees of Shiva had been the first to transform the stories of the gods in Sanskrit puranas by retelling them in ordinary Tamil beginning in the sixth century; by means of hymns in praise of Shiva, places and stories previously sacred to some tutelary deity were transformed into loci in which Shiva himself was manifested. One of the earliest of the Shiva hymnists was the poet Appar who, around 600 CE, had renounced the Jainism he had previously professed

Plate 10 The Minakshi-Sundareshvara (Shiva) temple at Madurai. By a South Indian artist, on European paper, watermarked 1820. Captioned in Telugu (BM OA. 1962. 12-31. 013(69), Courtesy of the Trustees of the British Museum).

and went on to persuade the Pallava king Mahendravarman I to abandon his Jaina teachers. Somewhat later, Sambandar, another Shiva hymnist, reputedly converted the Pandyan king in Madurai and persuaded him to rid his capital of the numerous Jaina teachers previously honoured and supported there by royal generosity. Sambandar may even have convinced the king to complete his conversion by impaling the heads of 8000 Jaina teachers, an event long celebrated at the major Shiva temple of Madurai.

The Chola kings were especially devout Shiva worshippers and may even have engaged in the rare religious persecution of the worshippers of Vishnu, who had meanwhile been carrying out a similar programme of hymn-making and theology. The traditions of Tamil Vishnu devotees refer to the desecration of some Vishnu temples by the late Chola king Kulottunga III. However, priestly and lay followers of Vishnu found other royal houses more sympathetic. One of the major theologians of Vishnu devotionalism, the Tamil brahman Ramanuja, succeeded in converting the king who was later known as Vishnuvardhana of the Hoysala dynasty of Karnataka, which was then engaged in displacing the Cholas in the far south. Nevertheless, Jainism – its doctrines and its shrines and seminaries – continued to enjoy support for a lengthy period in Karnataka, similar to the widespread support it enjoyed in Rajasthan owing to the patronage of the Solanki–Chaulukyan dynasty of the middle of the twelfth century.

Devotional worship became a major ideological element throughout early medieval India. Doctrinally, theism opposed itself to the ethical and atheistic traditions of Jainism and Buddhism, while at the same time incorporating elements of both. But there was a significant difference in practice: personal devotion was offered to gods whose daily life was celebrated as if they were kings, and this worship was conducted within buildings constructed to shelter the god as a palace sheltered a king. Devotions of this magnitude and the conspicuous support of devotee kings found favour in all parts of the subcontinent, as kings between the seventh to twelfth centuries sought ways to extend their sovereignty beyond the often narrowly circumscribed core territories of their realms. There was little evidence of awareness among most of the major kings of the subcontinent that a new and vigorous political force in the shape of Islam was establishing itself in northern India. Soon there would be a shift in historical developments substantial enough to warrant the designation of a new phase of medieval Indian history.

THE ADVENT OF ISLAM

India's west coast was acquainted with Arabs and other western Asians as part of the commercial expansion of the early medieval period, when a number of emporia were established in India. Arab and Jewish merchants not only sojourned on the Arabian Sea littoral of the subcontinent, but some were even granted special protection for the practice of their faiths and relieved of taxation. This is known from inscriptions, including one on copper-plates, dating from the ninth century, which made such a grant to the Jewish merchant-elder, Joseph Rabban, at the port of Cranganore, near Cochin.

In the eighth century, another sort of Arab presence appeared in the form of a Muslim army that conquered Sind. Between 711 and 725 CE, parts of Sind, the western Punjab, Rajasthan and Gujarat were occupied by Iraqi-Arab soldiers whose expansion was curtailed by the rajas of the Deccan and Gangetic plain. In this ancient heartland of the Indus civilization, and in parts of Punjab to the east, India's Islamic period might have begun then rather than in 1200 CE, but for the resistance shown to the invaders by the kings of Kanauj, among them one Yasovarman (c.736 CE), and by the later Rajput chiefs and kings who held Kanauj and most of northern India until the mid-tenth century.

Small advances were made from Sind into neighbouring Gujarat and the Kathiawar peninsula, where minor sultanates were established. These soon cut themselves off from Baghdad, and the sultans lived in peace with other rulers of Sind and western Punjab. For the time being, Islamic penetration of the subcontinent was concluded; the restless energies of certain Muslim leaders turned northward into Central Asia and began the conversion of the Turkic pastoralists in a process that joined another in changing the centre of Eurasia and ultimately the subcontinent.

Within its sphere of control in western India, the Arab-Islamic hegemony was governed from Baghdad by the Abbasid caliphs until the late ninth century, when Arab garrisons in India and elsewhere threw off caliphal control and began to rule as independent sultans. As far as the situation of their non-Muslim subjects was concerned, little was changed: most communities under Muslim control were permitted to govern themselves under their own chiefs as long as tribute was paid to their Muslim masters.

THE MAMLUK CONQUESTS

These arrangements were ended abruptly for Arab rulers and their subjects by the numerous pillaging incursions mounted by Mahmud of Ghazni between 1000 and 1025 CE. Mahmud's father was one of a new breed of warriors in Islamdom: a Turkish 'slave' soldier, or *mamluk*. They were either African or, more usually, central Asians bought as children and given military training for service against the Mongols, who were the great scourge of the time for Muslims as well as for the Chinese and Europeans. All of these older civilizations had to contend with the breakout of nomads from the Eurasian steppe, beginning with Scythians raids against southern Russian peasant communities and culminating with the Mongol devastation of ancient Eurasian states in the thirteenth century. At the time of his death in 1227 CE, Chingiz Khan, the most famous of the Mongol marauders, had formed a powerful confederation whose encampments were established on India's northern frontier, from which attacks as far into the interior as the Punjab were launched. Survival required skills and ruthlessness equal to those of the Mongol horsemen, and these began to develop in the Islamic world and elsewhere.

Mahmud's father had seized Ghazni, near modern Kabul, from the Persian governor of the Abbasid caliphs in a mutiny. Mahmud succeeded as sultan in 998 CE. He used his inheritance to begin a series of annual dry season campaigns deep into the western Gangetic plain and Gujarat. Notoriously, he destroyed the Shiva idol at the temple of Somnath in Kathiawar, carrying off a vast treasure of gold in 1025. With this he beautified his capital, making it in turn an attractive target for the depredations of later Turkic Muslims of the Ghur tribe, whose soldiers sacked and destroyed Ghazni in 1151.

Spectacular conquests such as Mahmud's were the result of the superior military might of Ghaznivid soldiers against both Muslim and non-Muslim enemies, and illustrate once more the significance of military developments. The prospect of loot for each victorious invading Muslim horseman assured that the casualties of this hazardous activity could easily be replaced by new recruits and their numbers increased by ambitious indigenous Indian converts of lowly status.

The ease with which Turk horsemen pillaged northern India during the eleventh century and then set about ruling the Gangetic plain during the next century has baffled many historians. Some have explained the success of these conquests by the audacity and ferocity of central Asian horsemen, combined with the military exhaustion of Indian kingdoms that had worm themselves out fighting for control of the western and central Gangetic plain around Kanauj. Yet these are scarcely credible explanations when one observes the succession of contending Indian states, each bringing new enthusiasm and military zeal to the enterprise of Gangetic dominion. Looting the capital and even the temples of an enemy was not unheard of among Indian rulers, either.

Yet the divisions and the accumulative wastage and cumulative waste of warfare among the largest Indian kingdoms who were then seeking to control the Gangetic plain and the difficulty of any ruler in successfully overcoming the independence and clannish preoccupations of Rajput soldiers may eventually have taken its toll. Muslim commentators not long after the original conquests may have come a little closer to the mark when they attributed their success to the failure of Indians to defend themselves and their territories, which they put down to arrogance. Indians, they said, viewed each other with distrust and the wider world with indifference, failing to notice the marvellous early conquests of Islam. Indeed, while Mahmud of Ghazni terrorized north-western India for seventeen successive years, the greatest contemporary Indian rulers, the Cholas, seemed blissfully unaware of these happenings.

Other factors too certainly contributed to the Muslim conquest. One was the career opportunities offered by the openness of central Asian fighting bands to any men who were willing to fight for wealth, honour and office. A second was that much of the Turkic central Asian homeland had been closed by Mongol expansion; the stranded Muslim invaders in India were forced to seek their fortunes there, and did so with the determination born of the absence of alternatives.

The Islamic rule now established for the first time in the centre of India was to remain in place until sovereignty was wrested from later Muslims, first by Maratha soldiers of western India in the eighteenth century, and finally by the British during the nineteenth century. In contrast to the British, who might have returned home and not become settled colonists, the Turkish 'slave warriors' had no choice because their way back to their central Asian homelands was blocked by the Mongols, and this remained the case until some of these Mongols were transformed into Muslim Mughals in the sixteenth century.

Apart from the immediate political consequences of introducing a new ruling stratum with a vigorous and alien religion into northern India, the new political elite was militarily superior to indigenous warrior-rulers. Among the few peoples and societies spared the devastations of the Mongol hordes were those Muslim steppe communities whose fighters determinedly matched Mongol skills on horses and general ferocity. These Turkic warriors may have saved India from the horrors that other Eurasians suffered at the hands of the Mongols.

Elsewhere, the small elite of Turkish warriors were too few to change the institutions, loyalties and faith of the myriad communities over which they lightly ruled. In fact, few among this warrior elite during the thirteenth century would have wished to change anything about these communities and the compliant way they offered tribute. Little is heard of uprisings against their rule; rather, it was the dispersed elite who were increasingly agitated by the growing ambition of their rulers in Delhi to assume royal prerogatives to match their titles as sultans.

This tendency was especially pronounced in the case of Balban, who ruled Delhi formally and informally for almost forty years, between 1249 and 1287. He was impatient with the idea of the sultan being merely a leader of a band of warriors who shared equal status and rights. Plainly too, he wanted a realm that extended beyond the Gangetic plain to include the rest of the subcontinent. But he was not alone; by the close of the thirteenth century, the drive to enlarge the kingdom became crystallized around two lineages of Delhi rulers: the Khalji sultans and the Tughluqs.

The Muslim resistance prevented deeper incursions, and in course of time a standing army under the rule and command of the Delhi sultanate stood watch against the Mongol terror. From its founding in 1206 by Qutubuddin Aibak, whoever commanded that toughened fighting force on the northern frontier was a generalissimo with a strong independent political position, a fact that conditioned the high politics of the subcontinent during the next several centuries. In that sense, the Mongol outbreak was as consequential for India as for their other adversaries, though with different consequences.

'SLAVE' SOLDIERS

The Muslim invaders of India after Mahmud of Ghazni are historically referred to as slaves because their ranks were composed of men, mostly of Turkic extraction, who had been sold as children into military service. Such men rose to high positions on the basis of skill, and from their ranks arose what is usually called the 'Slave Dynasty', who ruled from Delhi between 1206 and 1290. The longest to reign of the slave soldiers of Delhi was Sultan Iltutmish, who had served as a military commander of the founder of the Delhi sultanate, and, exceptionally, he was followed by his daughter Raziyya, who ruled ably and commanded an army for four years (1236–40), before being deposed and murdered by other, male, slave commanders.

The notion of slave-sultans becomes less strange when it is understood that at the time, throughout Eurasia, in Byzantine Christian as well as Islamic lands, strong male children were sold to be trained as warriors when their families considered they had enough sons to care for the flocks they owned. (A lucrative military career, after all, was the placement of choice for the younger sons of the British nobility and gentry though the nineteenth century as well.) Such calculations provided the pool upon which armies were built by conquering regimes such as the Ottomans of Anatolia and the Mamalukes of Egypt.

The rulers of Ghazni and of Ghur, as well as the later slave sultans of Delhi, would have received training in a form of cavalry warfare that depended on well drilled group formations and the volley-firing of arrows. The outcome of such training was a disciplined soldiery that swept their Indian opponents away, as they had others over the breadth of Eurasia. To be a slave attracted none of the disdain that attached to slaves in Indian society and other places, for Islam did not discriminate among the social origins of pious heroes (*ghazi*) who engaged in holy warfare (*jihad*) to protect and extend the 'Lands of the Faithful'.

To the egalitarian ideology that linked the ranks of the invaders was added the cultural bond of a common Turkic speech among warriors from different places; religion and language sustained the warriors for the Faith against their opponents, including Indians and Mongols, who were infidels in their eyes. When Mongol expansion collided with an Islam now borne by Turks rather than Arabs in the late twelfth century, conditions were in place for a major change in the structure of Indian politics. Under Mongol pressure, Muslim warrior bands were pushed from central Asia and pulled into the relatively less resistant world of India. Nevertheless, as long as the Mongols threatened the hold of the Delhi sultans over the Gangetic plain, a substantial army of Turkic fighters had to remain on the frontier with central Asia to oppose them. These were made up of the hardiest soldiers and, inevitably, the leaders among them soon sought to replace the hazards of frontier service with the pleasure and security of the cities of the Ganges. Thus, while it is true that India was spared the full onslaught of the Mongol depredations visited upon the Russian and Balkan peoples during the thirteenth century, the indirect consequences of successful defence was a steady stream of hardened Muslim horsemen who trickled into India and subdued the kingdoms of the Gangetic plain and the Deccan Plateau. Upon them, Muslim power advanced in the fourteenth century.

THE SECOND WAVE: ALAUDDIN KHALJI AND MUHAMMAD TUGHLUK

During the fourteenth century, Muslim authority and religion spread over the whole of the subcontinent. Two successors of the 'slave kings' ruled Delhi for nearly a century and deserve special notice for extending Muslim influence, and for their efforts to create more effective, centralized regimes in order to meet the mounting military costs of defending their hold over northern India from Mongol competitors. The first was Alauddin Khalji, whose full name included 'Sikander Sani', or 'second Alexander'. The range of his conquests was impressive: in the Punjab against the Mongols, in Rajasthan, in west-central India and even in the far south, where his soldiers toppled kingdoms in Karnataka and Andhra. The rapid extension of Delhi's authority, however, did little more than enlarge Alauddin's tributary region; most of his defeated adversaries were left in place, though not their treasuries.

Khalji authority in and around Delhi had been established by Alauddin's uncle and father-in-law. In 1295, Alauddin converted the territory his uncle gave him to administer as *amir* (notable) into a base from which he secretly launched raids into the Deccan; with the treasure seized, he persuaded important commanders to support his coup and the assassination of his uncle. Almost immediately afterwards, he was faced by a Mongol invasion led by a descendent of Chingiz Khan who had been attracted by the unsettled politics of the Gangetic region. Alauddin turned this invasion back in 1299, after the Mongols had succeeded in taking some parts of Delhi but failed to reduce his fortifications. A final Mongol attack was attempted in 1307–8, after which he experienced no further difficulties with Mongols. With his northern frontier secure, Alauddin and his chief lieutenant, Malik Kafur, who was not a Turk but a native convert, defeated rajas in Rajasthan and Gujarat before slashing into the southern peninsula, taking the distant centre of Madurai in 1310.

Alauddin's political and administrative reforms were as brilliant as his military exploits. Departing from the mode of governing which had been followed for a century, that of controlling a few cities as garrisoned places from which periodically to plunder the countryside, Alauddin undertook a survey of the agrarian resources around his capital, on the basis of which a standard revenue demand was fixed. This consisted of half the crop produced from arable land and a fixed tax on all animals reared by pastoralists. Revenue was henceforth to be collected by military officers of an enlarged standing army. In this way he increased his resources while reducing those of the erstwhile magnates of the countryside, the village and locality chiefs and petty rajas. Upon them he imposed sumptuary restrictions on clothing, horses and houses. More ambitious still, he established a system of forced procurement of food grains for Delhi and other garrison centres, wherein procurement prices were to be fixed and all grain collected as taxes was to be stored in state granaries. To ensure that these new regulations were followed, he set spies among his subjects who were responsible for reporting directly to him. Contemporary accounts speak of his having prohibited alcohol consumption in the vicinity of the capital. India had known nothing like this before. Alauddin died in 1316; perhaps the failure of his successors to retain power for more than a few years was a reaction to his harsh regime, and Alauddin's administrative changes proved transitory, especially compared with the measures of another fourteenth-century Delhi ruler, Muhammad Tughluq.

Tughluq was the son of a slave soldier in Alauddin's service who seized power from one of Alauddin's successors. Muhammad displaced his father in

Plate 11 The great citadel of Devagiri, Maharashtra, capital of the Yadavas in the eleventh to thirteenth centuries, later renamed Daulatabad (IOL Collection 430/6 (57); neg. no. B 26952, by permission of the British Library).

Delhi and ruled the central Gangetic plain from 1324 to 1351, much as Alauddin had displaced his uncle. Tughluq, however, dreamt of making the whole of the subcontinent his realm. Where Alauddin had conquered, looted, and left the old ruling families as his dependants, Muhammad sought extended sovereignty. To this end he shifted his capital from Delhi to the centre of the peninsula, changing the name of the former capital of the Yadava kings, Devagiri, to Daulatabad. This bold move produced chaos in both the former and new capitals, and in their hinterlands, especially when Muhammad himself decided that the move had been a mistake and ordered a return to Delhi – or what remained of it.

Muhammad Tughluq's twenty-six year reign has been treated harshly by historians, not only because of his capriciousness in relocating his capital. Another of his madcap innovations was his decision to change Alauddin Khalji's system of revenue collections in grain, which had been intended to assure food for his soldiers and also for the cities where his power resided. Muhammad decided that land revenue should henceforward be collected in money for the purpose of facilitating remittances from his now far-flung territories. When he discovered that the stock of coins and mintable silver was inadequate for so extensive a monetization, instead of abandoning his plan, Muhammad issued a token currency in copper, a notion of which Indians (and most of the rest of the world) had no experience. Counterfeiting soon became rife and the entire revenue system collapsed, and Tughluq's government soon followed as costly military adventures launched against Persia and central Asia failed to achieve their vague objectives.

The innovations of Alauddin Khalji and Muhammad Tughluq may be thought grandiose, and so they have been regarded. However, both were determined to end, or at least to contain, the spread of the pernicious *iqta* system, which the first Muslim rulers of Delhi had adopted. The iqtas were grants of income from a group of villages or a locality to officials, usually military, for their maintenance and that of their retinues. Such awards carried responsibility and power for collecting revenue on behalf of the state and maintaining order. Inevitably these service grants evolved into hereditary properties and entrenched local power. *Muqtis* (holders of iqta rights) became financially and politically independent of the sultan from whom the award originated.

On the whole, the Muslim rural elite, though far from the garrisons of the Delhi sultans, failed to link themselves in any substantial way to local peoples and their leaders, the chiefs whose authority derived from the dominant landed groups resident in and cultivating the fields. The Muslim warriors tended instead to be an alien presence on the north Indian countryside, terrorizing and plundering the agrarian population, objects of fear and loathing for their petty tyrannies.

Against the common modern indictments of Muhammad Tughluq as capricious and destructive, the chronicles of his time speak of his attempts to devise a polity to which his non-Muslim subjects could extend their allegiance. For example, he adopted some of the older Indian royal symbols, such as processions of richly caparisoned elephants on civic occasions, even though he was one of the few Delhi rulers who sought and obtained a document of investiture from the puppet Abbasid caliphs of Cairo.

MUSLIM HISTORIES

For the details of the cruelty and other aspects of the Khalji and Tughluq regimes, paradoxically we owe much to historical writings in Persian, often commissioned by Muslim rulers themselves. One of the earliest of the writers was Ziauddin Barni, whose mid-fourteenth-century account of the reign of Firuz Shah Tughluq showed a lively appreciation of the value of history, though perhaps not of the sort modern historians would admit to:

> After the science of Qur'anic commentary, of tradition [*Hadith*: sayings attributed to the Prophet, but not Koranic], of jurisprudence, and the mystic path of the Sufi shaikhs, I have not observed such advantage from any branch of learning as I have from history. History is the knowledge of the annals and traditions of prophets, caliphs, sultans, and of the great men of religion and of government . . . Low fellows, rascals, unfit and unworthy persons, inferior people, and those with base aspirations, people of unknown stock and mean natures, of no lineage and low lineage, loiterers and bazaar loafers – all these have no connection with history. It is not their trade and skill. A knowledge of history does not advantage

such people and profits them in no circumstance . . . Rather it is harmful to base and mean fellows for them to read and know history, not an advantage at all. What higher honor for history is it possible to conceive than that mean and low people have no desire or inclination for this rare form of knowledge, that it is of no profit to them in their low dealings and filthy morals, and that history is the only science of learning in any quarter from which they desire no benefit whatever?[2]

Some of these Persian-language chroniclers were born in India and others were migrants seeking their fortunes there. One of the migrant historians during Tughluq times was the famous Moroccan traveller, Ibn Battuta, while one of the native historians was Isami, grandson of one of the learned men who died when Muhammad Tughluq marched the population of Delhi to his distant new capital of Daulatabad. Isami duly chronicled his grandfather's martyrdom in his history of the Bahmani sultans who succeeded the Tughluqs and were a part of their undoing.

Other writers followed in increasing number, reflecting two important changes noticeable in the fourteenth century. One was the appearance of native-born Muslim intellectuals who, whether in the service of some sultan or not, wrote about their own times. These 'Hindustanis' or 'Deccanis' were differentiated by these labels from sojourners from other places. The term 'Hindustan' as a Muslim designation for the area of the Indo-Gangetic plain dates from roughly this time.

Muslims from Iran, Central Asia and East Africa were attracted to India by military service, but also by opportunities in commerce or professions such as teaching or law. Some became judges. These migrants, too, wrote contemporary accounts of their times and the events in the lives of illustrious rulers, accounts that have made it possible for historians to portray the Delhi sultanate with a vividness rarely possible before.

But it is not simply an artefact of contemporary accounts that rivets attention upon the biographies of Mahmud of Ghazni, Alauddin Khalji or Muhammad Tughluq. They were men of great energy and imagination as well as utterly ruthless – all qualities needed for the creation of a new state system, which for a time at least reached from the Himalayas to the southern shores of the Indian Ocean. In time, these regimes were transmuted from foreign despotisms that destroyed the existing ruling households and plundered their temples, into regimes that incorporated indigenous peoples, however much the likes of Maulana Muzaffar Shams Balkhi might inveigh against the practice. Turkic fighters intermarried with their non-Muslim subjects from the beginning, and this was one form of incorporation of, or perhaps by, indigenous groups; others were persuaded to accept the new conquerors and their religion because of the advantages that accompanied close association with the powerful, or swayed by the example and preaching of the Sufis or other Islamic schools.

The peripheral parts of Muhammad's realm soon made themselves independent. The process began in the far south, when Madurai was proclaimed a separate sultanate in 1334. It was followed in 1346 by Bengal. Not long after, most of the conquered territories around the new Daulatabad were declared an independent sultanate, called Bahmani after its founder, an Afghan or Turkish soldier formerly in Tughluq service.

THE INDIAN DEVELOPMENT OF ISLAM

By the twelfth century, the fundamental teachings of the Koran and the Sunna, traditions authoritatively attributed to the Prophet himself, formed the major elements of jurisprudence (*fiqh*, literally 'inquiry'), as codified in the *shariah* (law) and interpreted by several legal schools. One of the most important in western Asia was called Hanafite after its founder Abu Hanifa, who introduced the element of the personal judgement, or 'preferability', of the early masters as a legitimate supplementary principle, which added flexibility to theological interpretation.

This greater flexibility eased Muslim assimilation of the new conquests, thanks largely to the influence of al-Ghazzali, a Baghdadi scholar and adviser to the Turkic sultan of Iraq. His reputation subsequently grew in recognition of his part in averting a division among Muslims between pious followers of fiqh and *kalam* ('discussion') and the potentially disruptive mystics. The latter, who were a part of Islam from the beginning, claimed a direct affinity with the Prophet Muhammad and other early inspired formulators of the faith: they repudiated all dry legalisms. Al-Ghazzali is credited with having synthesized and shifted the philosophical ground of Islam away from its heavy emphasis on jurisprudence and formal theology to a balance between those formal elements and the unpredictable passions of the Sufis.

Sufism was expounded by poor wandering teachers – the term referred to the coarse wool garments they wore – who proclaimed that 'mystics learn from God, the *ulema* [learned men] from books', a sentiment seemingly echoed in al-Ghazzali's famous (though perhaps disingenuous) question: 'In what do discussions of divorce and on buying and selling prepare the believer for the beyond?' The mystical teachings of the Sufis converged with indigenous devotional forms of worship, making this form of Islam well adapted to the Indian condition.

From the earliest Muslim conquests, Jews and Christians had been permitted to practise their religions in recognition of the tradition shared with Islam, the possession of a holy book. As 'people of the book' and in recognition of the prophetic roles that had been played by Abraham and Jesus, Islam acknowledged that they too had been recipients of revelation (but had garbled or corrupted it, so the theory ran). Unlike pagans, polytheists and idolaters, they were not required to convert in order to live, but, in return for an always uncertain protection, a head tax (*jizya*) could be exacted from them. This was unproblematic for the conquerors when it concerned the small and isolated communities of Christians and Jews who made up parts of the diaspora merchant communities found in the seaports, but the extension of *dhimmi* (protected) status to the devotees of the vedic gods was potentially blasphemous.

EARLY ISLAMIC SOCIAL INFLUENCES

The Muslim conquerors of India may have been zealous, but they were practical men and, notwithstanding the pillaging of temples for their wealth, they gradually found it practical to extend to Hindus the protected dhimmi status. No serious attempt at mass conversion was ever made by any sultan or later Mughal emperor. Early in Islam's career in India it was recognized that the conversion of the vast and varied subject population to Islam, such as that which had occurred in the lands of sparse infidel or pagan populations conquered before, was not really feasible. So the toleration of Hindus was, from the point of view of the conquerors, a matter of expediency, and dhimmi status was the only category in which Islam could extend toleration to people of other religions. Moreover, from the point of view of the subject population, the accommodation was eased because the caste structure of Indian society, then as ever, flexibly adjusted to political vicissitudes of many sorts; outsiders like Muslims could be accepted as appropriate rulers providing that the autonomy of community institutions – among which caste was central – was not impaired.

If Muslim authority could not aspire to the domination of most of the north Indian countryside, it was soon evident that considerable direct Muslim control could be achieved in the towns and cities of the Gangetic plain and in parts of the Punjab and Bengal. These were placed under Muslim military and civilian officials as well as judges and other learned men who comprised the ulema. By the fourteenth century, while many urban artisans and merchants converted to Islam to be relieved of the jizya and other minor oppressions, most of the inhabitants of the countryside that surrounded the towns continued to enjoy their ancient autonomy, as did those parts of the Ganges basin most remote from Delhi, regardless of religion. In fact, an independent sultanate was proclaimed in Bengal, where, as in the Punjab, Muslims achieved considerable success in winning converts.

The reasons for the success of Islam in Bengal perhaps lie in the character of the religious institutions there. Bengal had been one of the few remaining places where Buddhist monasteries still functioned. There the sangha had enjoyed the patronage of Pala kings who achieved a brief hegemony over the Gangetic plain in the ninth century and ruled eastern India from Pataliputra until the early twelfth century, but was weakened by the conversion to Islam of merchants and artisans who had represented the mainstay of Buddhism from its earliest days. The records of the sultanate speak of massacres and Buddhism suffered a fatal decline.

Later, the mystics of Sufi orders preached a popular Islam which they combined with the expansion of agriculture in some still forested tracts of the eastern Gangetic delta, where the mass conversion to Islam of the peasantry that occurred in the days of Mughal rule had less to do with state policy than with class differences between the Bengali lords and the poor tenantry. The landlords had lately adopted devotional Vishnu-worship, but the tenantry proved more susceptible to Sufism. The Punjab, on the other hand, was special because it was a frontier between Mongols and Muslims, a place where

Mongol incursions caused fear and destruction, and where, as a result, Islam was popularly and gratefully associated with the defence of the land against Mongol predators.

The expansion of Muslim rule meant the diffusion of Muslim scholars and merchants. They had fled the thirteenth-century Mongol hegemony in central and western Asia for the relative safety of India. Some of the newcomers among the merchants joined the diasporic mercantile communities along both coasts of the peninsula; others accompanied the Turkic ghazis and settled down among non-Muslim merchant groups in the town and city bazaars of the Ganges region. As mosques were established for the worship of the faithful, new urban market places developed, offering expanded opportunities for trade and religious conversion. Artisan groups were not long in following the urban drift into Islam.

Conversion was not for opportunistic reasons alone, for Islamic savants and mystics also accompanied the new rule. The learned were responsible for teaching as well as implementing the injunctions of the shariah. The rules governing an ideal order were meant to be conveyed to rulers as well as to the ruled, either through formal instruction in a school (*madrassah*) or through the more informal instruction given by the ulema that gathered in the mosques for daily and Friday prayers. The ulema enjoyed careers and public respect; their influence was always important to the identity of Muslims, who were above all a religious communion.

In contrast, Sufi teachers, for whom poverty was ideological, were the purveyors of a mystic tradition which insisted on a personal bond between each believer and God, denying that either the institutions and offices of clerical interpreters or the laws of kings could replace it. Predictably, however, Sufis in India and elsewhere did form their own institutions to fortify the bond between teacher and devotee. Each Sufi order (*silsilah*) established a main centre in addition to several 'lodges' or 'retreats' where its version of the mystical way to God was transmitted. Two Sufi traditions which enjoyed particular success were the Suhravardi and Chishti silsilahs, both of which cultivated poetry, especially in Persian, to a high standard. Both of these orders had centres in fourteenth-century Delhi and, thanks to the patronage of the Khalji and Tughluq sultans, were able to establish satellite lodges through-out northern India and the Deccan. The Chishtis then and later were looked upon with special favour by Indian-born Muslims, because that order had declared its spiritual home to be India when others continued to look to homelands in central Asia or the Middle East. Since the major shrines of the Chishtis were in the subcontinent, as the Muslim rulers of the fifteenth century and later strove to justify their regimes in Indian as well as Muslim terms, the Chishtis received advantages of imperial patronage denied to other orders.

MUSLIM ARCHITECTURE IN INDIA

The processes of community formation in medieval India now included Muslim communities. In the cities, neighbourhoods were formed around the

Plate 12 The first Indian structure to be executed on Islamic principles of construction was the Alai Darwaza, the entrance pavilion to the Quwwat al-Islam at Delhi; it was built by the Khalji Sultan Alauddin in 1311 CE (IOL Photo 95/1, print 44, by permission of the British Library).

mansions of Muslim grandees, soldiers and officials, and also around the great mosques and madrassahs which architecturally dominated the locality. In these buildings, an architectural vocabulary was adopted consisting of what had become typical Islamic elements, such as the graceful decoration of doorways and walls with lines from the Koran written in the angular 'kufic' script. Beginning in the twelfth century, mosques in the imperial style were constructed by successive Muslim regimes centred on Delhi; but simultaneously, provincial styles emerged whose varied features were shaped by the availability of construction materials such as stone and the experience of local artisans, who were not necessarily Muslims and whose different traditions were imprinted on mosques found in Bengal, Kashmir or Gujarat. In Bengal, for example, the independent fourteenth-century sultans built their mosques in brick, the usual construction material for temples there, and had the brick work covered with plaster.

Modifications were made in the layout as well. From western Asia had come the template of the Arabian mosque with its pillared, domed roof and enclosed courtyard. The fully developed format actually covered three courtyards with three domes – the larger central dome flanked by smaller replicas on either side, but it too was altered by local building practices. Instead of an interior courtyard, Bengali rulers installed a grassy forecourt in which was dug a large tank for the ablutions of the faithful, and mounted a single dome upon a square building. In the Kashmiri capital, Srinagar, in 1395 Shah Hamadan built a wooden mosque with wooden walls enclosing a courtyard for prayer. Like the contemporary temples there, its two stories were supported by hundreds of decorated wooden pillars, and the whole was set on the masonry foundation of an ancient temple. Ahmadabad in Gujarat received its great congregational mosque in 1423, though it had been a province of Delhi since 1297. It was built by Ahmad Shah, a converted Rajput, who, when governor, declared the province an independent sultanate in 1411. His mosque was of stone, like the local temples, and its entry resembled the temple gateways of the region. The central prayer hall was of stone, with the sculpted pillars also found in contemporary temples.

SOCIAL CHANGES

Architectural eclecticism was matched by the cultural diversity of Muslim communities. Accepting Islam meant that converts were expected to alter their social and cultural practices to conform with those enunciated through their ulema or Sufi preceptors; these, however, were modified by regional norms. In practice, most Muslim converts continued to offer worship to the host of folk deities propitiated in the locality in which they lived, and most followed the rules of the castes into which they had been born. In this way Islamic practice itself was altered.

Because converts stubbornly maintained many of the caste practices of their Hindu origins, the unity of Muslims as a confessional community was compromised, customs associated with neighbourhood and region flourished, and the persistence of local and regional languages further defeated the development of an entirely unified Islamic community. But enough differences between Muslims and their Hindu co-residents of towns and cities remained to create a sort of different urban life, though one without the terrible interreligious conflicts that later developed; they were a manifestation of late colonial politics.

Some religious tension did arise in the Bengal countryside in the fifteenth century, when sheikhs of the Chishti and other Sufi orders castigated the sultan of Bengal for permitting non-Muslims to hold office and receive state honours. One of these, Maulana Muzaffar Shams Balkhi, wrote to the Bengal Sultan Ghayasuddin in about 1400:

> The vanquished unbelievers with heads hanging downward, exercise their power and authority and administer the lands which belong to them. But they have also been appointed [executive] officers over the Muslims, in the lands of Islam, and they impose their orders on them. Such things should not happen.[3]

Such criticisms mounted when a brahman named Raja Ganesh became the power behind the sultanate in Bengal. A threatened war within the province was averted when the Raja's son became a convert to Islam and in 1415 was proclaimed sultan with the Muslim name of Jalaludin Muhammad, under which he proceeded to issue coins. The Sufi leaders were furious at this, and pleaded with the sultan of Jaunpur in the Gangetic valley to drive the usurper away and restore proper Muslim authority. They failed, but Sultan Jalaludin took special pains to win over Chishti support and eventually succeeded by means of lavish patronage.

Islam also had indirect social influences. The Muslim conquests between the eleventh and fourteenth centuries removed royal protection from brahmanical institutions, but an efflorescence of dharma texts reinforced caste norms. Where the ancient kingships continued, the production of regional dharma texts was patronized by rulers such as Vikramaditya VI of the Kalyani Chalukyas, who commissioned a commentary on the law book of the ancient Videha sage Yajnavalkya. Ballalasena of Bengal, in the late twelfth century, sponsored the writing of five large dharma works; the Yadava king of Devagiri came to the aid of the code of Hemadri a century later; and the fourteenth-century Vijayanagara kings sponsored the *Parasara*, their minister Mahadeva's dharma commentary. Such were the acts of pious rajas, and the reasons for their support had as much to do with the appreciation of rajadharma found in these texts as with the reinvigoration of the brahmanical edge in caste relations.

The status of women declined, however, as they were placed under ever greater sequestration. The practice of purdah (from the Persian *parda*, veil or curtain), screening women from the gaze of non-family males, became more general in sultanate days only partly in imitation of Muslim practice. There had always been a lofty sense of personal and familial honour among kshatriyas, and notably among Rajputs, which was largely determined by the control of women. To bring dishonour upon a rival, his women were taken; hence men attempted to ensure their honour by restricting the sight of their female relatives to close kinsmen, and even, in case of threat, killing them before the enemy could dishonour them. An instance of this type occurred in 1568, when the Mughal Akbar was about to capture the Mewar fortress of Chitor; the Rajput defenders slew their women to prevent their falling into Muslim hands.

One way or another, India assimilated every new or foreign introduction and made it its own. Before the Delhi sultanate was crushed by a new central Asian conqueror, Timur (Tamerlane), Firuz Shah, a cousin of Muhammad Tughluq, had completed his relatively peaceful reign, during the course of which he had suspended military campaigns and made no attempts to win back the territories lost in the Deccan to the Bahmanis or in Bengal. Instead he consolidated a smaller north Indian realm, and there he built impressive mosques and fortresses and enriched the Gangetic countryside with irrigation works. A pious man, he bestowed presents on the ulema and also on converts, while also extending the jizya to brahmans who were previously exempt.

The sacking and massacre by Timur in Delhi in 1398 came a decade after Firuz Shah Tughluq died, and ended the first epoch of Muslim consolidation in north India that began with the slave sultans. A new period of Afghan and Mughal rule in north India commenced and endured until the early eighteenth

Plate 13 The burning of the Rajput women during the siege of Chitor, Rajesthan, 1568 (IS 2-1986 (69/117), Courtesy of the Victoria and Albert Museum).

Plate 14 Virupaksha temple, Vijayanagara, Karnataka. Elaborate large-scale religious monuments erected by medieval Hindu monarchs, such as this sixteenth-century temple complex, express the dependent relationship between the kings and their patron divinities (IOL Photo 965/1, plate 78, by permission of the British Library).

century, after the last great Mughal, Aurangzeb, conquered a set of southern sultanates deep in the peninsula, making the Mughals a subcontinental power for a brief time. His achievement was undermined by another: the rise of a Maratha regime in western India that replaced Mughal rule during the middle decades of the eighteenth century. It was they, rather than the Mughals, who ultimately yielded to the foreign rule of the English East India Company. But, before we consider that set of developments, attention must be given to the southern sultanates and to their Hindu competitors for hegemony over the peninsula, other aspects of the medieval period of India.

THE DECCAN AND THE SOUTH

When Muhammad Tughluq returned to Delhi, a former soldier in his employ, Zafar Khan, who seems to have been of Afghan or Turkic descent, seized Daulatabad and declared himself sultan under the title of Bahman Shah. This was in 1345 and two years later he shifted his capital further south to Gulbarga, in the rich river basin of northern Karnataka, from which the Rashtrakuta kings of the eighth to tenth centuries had earlier ruled not only the Deccan but parts of the far south and the Ganges plain as well. At almost exactly the same time, two new Hindu kingdoms were created that would stem the expansion of Muslim authority. Both states were built upon earlier polities that had fallen to the Muslim military onslaughts of the early fourteenth century; to a degree, these earlier defeats produced the later, more resistant kingdoms of Vijayanagara in southern Karnataka, and Gajapatis in Orissa.

From the outset, the measures adopted by Bahmani sultans, intended to strike fear in their neighbours, engendered opposition that with time became increasingly effective. The terror with which they are remembered is remarkable even for those brutal times, and the campaigns against the remnants of Muhammad Tughluq's armies were no less cruel than those against Hindu kings and chiefs in neighbouring Orissa and Andhra. Nevertheless, Bahman Shah and his successors found the consolidation of any sort of stable authority illusive, even around the Gulbarga area.

Perhaps for this reason Gulbarga was abandoned and a new capital established to the northwest, at Bidar, during the late fifteenth century. A Russian visitor in the 1470s described Bidar glowingly, and attributed much to the administrative and military reforms of the minister, Mahmud Gawan, a Persian official. Gawan had changed revenue practices and strengthened the central authority against Muslim grandees and Hindu chiefs alike. His reforming zeal brought about his assassination in 1481, which was followed by the disintegration of the sultanate into five smaller Muslim regimes, beginning with a declaration of independence by the Bahmani governor of Bijapur in 1489 and concluding with the separation of Golconda in 1519. These more compact Muslim kingdoms of the Deccan enjoyed nearly two centuries of independent rule before being taken in turn under the expanding sovereignty of the Mughal Aurangzeb. During that time, however, an important variant of Indo-Islamic culture was developed, including a common language, Urdu, which was destined to become the national language of Pakistan.

At the same time that the Bahmani sultanate was established, in southern Karnataka Vijayanagara, the 'City of Victory', was erected, tradition has it, on the instructions of the spiritual preceptor of its founders, Vidyaranya, head of the Shaivite Sringeri seminary in western Karnataka. This tradition lent the new kingdom an important ideological significance as protector of Hindu institutions against Muslims. Thus two new kingdoms – one Islamic and the other ostensibly Hindu – in the same cultural area conferred a prominence upon Karnataka it had not known for centuries.

In the event, Karnataka was not destined to hold both kingdoms for long. The Bahmanis shifted again to a more elevated site on the Deccan plateau where their new capital, Bidar, was constructed to rival the beauty of Gulbarga. On the eastern coast of the peninsula, in modern Orissa, yet another powerful state raised the stakes for Deccan hegemony. Its Gajapati rulers made their capital in the delta of the river Mahanadi and derived great wealth from the extensive zones of wet-rice cultivation and from the numerous ports and the rich trade carried on in the fifteenth century between the delta of the Ganges in Bengal and the deltas of the Godavari and Krishna rivers.

The high point of the Bahmani sultanate came when Mahmud Gawan became the chief minister in 1461. After serving several sultans for twenty years, he was assassinated by jealous courtiers, but during his brilliant ministership Bahmani power was established on both coasts by the seizure of Goa from the Vijayanagara kings. Mahmud Gawan improved the crude administration left by the Tughluqs in order to increase tax yields. Still, not even this masterly official could break the military stalemate with the Vijayanagara kings. Each time the Bahmani armies achieved a superior position and seemed poised to defeat their Hindu enemies, neighbouring sultanates on their northern frontier with Gujarat and Malwa would frustrate the design by threatening the Bahmanis and forcing a withdrawal from southern Karnataka. Thus, the Bahmani regime was prevented from benefiting from a superiority in military techniques that it and other Muslim regimes held over Vijayanagara for a time.

One of two Hindu regimes that weathered the brutal Bahmani times, the 'Gajapati' kingdom occupied a narrow coastal region in the northeastern peninsula. Orissa was a place of ancient historical importance; it was known as Kalinga when conquered by Ashoka around 250 BCE, and, after Gupta times, it boasted independent Ganga kings who proudly spoke of themselves as *gajapati*, or 'lords of [fighting] elephants'. This title may have been intended as a contrast with other medieval Hindu kings, such as the Tamil Cholas who used the appellation *narpati*, meaning 'lord of fighting men, or infantry forces', and the Vijayanagara kings of Karnataka who adopted the title of *ashvapati*, to celebrate their cavalry. It was not a modest age.

VIJAYANAGARA

Historians agree that the Vijayanagara kingdom was established in the 1340s by two brothers who were experienced soldiers, although they have disputed over whether the founders were Kannada-speakers who had soldiered for the Hoysala kings of Karnataka and succeeded to their domains or whether they were Telugus who had served the last Hindu kings of Warangal in Andhra and then joined the forces of Muhammad Tughluq. That debate aside, it is indisputable that the valour of the first two Vijayanagara kings, the brothers Harihara and Bukka, preserved the new and fragile kingdom from the superior forces of the Bahmani sultanate; more than that, they recovered Madurai from the short-lived sultanate that had been declared there when Muhammad Tughluq withdrew from the peninsula. When King Bukka had died in 1377, he passed a large realm to his son who ruled it as Harihara II until 1404.

Another element in the making of the image of the Vijayanagara kingdom was the close association of the founding brothers with the renowned Shaivite teacher and seminarian in Karnataka, Vidyaranya. According to one tradition, he persuaded the brothers to abandon their service to the Tughluqs and also to renounce the Islam that they are thought to have adopted when they entered that service. Vidyaranya allegedly charged the brothers to 'rescue' Shiva and the other gods from Muslim authority. Some inscriptions even suggest that the new kingdom was called Vidyanagara for a time in honour of the sage before it came to be called Vijayanagara, and that the guardian of all of its kings was Shiva in his manifestation as Virupaksha, to whom a major temple was built.

The name Vijayanagara means 'City of Victory', and during the last half of the fifteenth century, the kingdom fulfilled that boast by expanding from central Karnataka into most of the rest of the southern peninsula. Its kings adopted regal symbols dating from the seventh-century Chalukyan kings of Badami. In further mimicry, the capital was made a showplace of the temple architecture of all parts of their vast realm as the Vijayanagara kings incorporated the gods of those they subjugated. Their conquests entitled them to refer to themselves as 'great kings', though they still mostly called themselves 'kings of Karnataka', perhaps to resolve their questionable identification with that place and its people.

The piety and Hindu credentials of the Vijayanagara kings was shown by a set of exquisitely constructed temple complexes in their large, walled capital city, but their architectural investments did not prevent them from augmenting their military prowess by the adoption of handguns and cannon in their forces. Apart from the Delhi sultans of the fifteenth century, no Indian kingdom was as militarized as Vijayanagara. By the middle of the fifteenth century, its kings had learned from their experiences at the hands of the Muslim soldiery that superior cavalry had to be matched if they were to survive. It was the same lesson that had been taught by the Mongols, and had the same consequences. Soon Vijayanagara firearms were turned against the Bahmanis and those powerful newcomers to India, the Portuguese, who had ensconced themselves on the Karnataka coast.

Before long, Devaraya II of Vijayanagara started to recruit Muslim fighters to serve him and to train his soldiers in the new modes of warfare. He also permitted the construction of mosques in the capital city where Muslim soldiers were garrisoned. After Mahmud Gawan's death, the Bahmani regime began to collapse from internal contradictions, especially those within its army. Factional strife arose between indigenous Muslims and migrants from Arabia, Central Asia and Persia, and between Sunnis and Shi'ites, with the result that the sprawling Bahmani sultanate was divided by its governors into five independent sultanates between 1489 and 1520. These were Bijapur in Karnataka, Ahmadnagar and Berar in Maharashtra, and Bidar and Golconda in the Andhra country. After partition, conflict continued between the successors to the Bahmani sultans and the Vijayanagara kingdom, now transformed into a formidable fighting force and still recruiting Muslim soldiers.

On the wings of this primary conflict lurked the Gajapati rulers, who had inherited a royal tradition in their long, narrow coastal land from the founding of the Ganga kingdom in the Mahanadi delta during the twelfth century. Ganga kings built the famous temples of Jagannatha at Puri and the temple devoted to Surya, the sun god, at Konarak, north of Puri; they also blocked the expansion of Muslim power from Bengal, where an independent sultanate had long existed. In the late fifteenth century, some Ganga commanders seized power and established a new ruling dynasty, calling themselves the Suryavamshi dynasty, or descendants of the sun god, but more popularly, Gajapatis, lords of elephants. One of these new kings, Kapilendra, briefly won a territory extending from the delta of the Ganges in Bengal to the delta of the Kaveri, a coastal realm that was gradually absorbed by Vijayanagara kings seeking control of the trade coasts of the peninsula.

By the late sixteenth century the Gajapatis were overwhelmed by the expansion of a new Afghan regime in Bengal over the entire Orissan coast, but they left behind a royal ideology turning on an understanding of kingship that was rare in India: the belief that the true king was the god Jagannatha, and the human king was the son of that god on whose behalf he defended and governed the realm. The great temple at Puri was made to a scale and artistic elegance which rivalled the temple of the Cholas under Rajaraja at Tanjavur, though the god himself was represented by crude logs made sacred by the mantras of the priests, a feature conferring an importance on the priests of Jagannatha not enjoyed by others.

To support the expensive military habits and control the trade in cavalry mounts imported from the Persian Gulf, the Vijanagara kings required both money and administrative control. Vijayanagara governors were appointed to oversee the trade from both shores of the peninsula. These appointments had important economic and political implications: Vijayanagara's military modernization of the late fifteenth and sixteenth centuries transformed the kingdom from merely another medieval Indian state into a polity more powerful and centralized than any other non-Muslim regime.

Throughout the fifteenth century, wars were fought to maintain a fragile independence against the Bahmani sultans and the Gajapatis, at a high cost in casualties and in the increased power of the military commanders, one of whom finally usurped royal authority around 1500. His descendants were called the Tuluva dynasty because the founder came from the west coast territory of Tulunad. The greatest of the Tuluvas was Krishnadevaraya, who reigned from 1509 to 1529.

The five Muslim regimes that had succeeded to the territory of Bahmani sultans in the late fifteenth century strove to expand southward against Vijayanagara throughout the fifteenth and sixteenth centuries, but so evenly matched were the adversaries to become in cunning and military prowess that no stable ascendancy was achieved until King Krishnadevaraya brilliantly divided and then defeated the Deccani sultans in the first year of his reign. The first months of that reign tested the young king against several sultans who had succeeded to the Bahmani authority. When they joined together to invade Vijayanagara, Krishnadevaraya defeated them, and then, in a gesture of political grandeur, 'reinstated' each of them in his former realm, proclaiming, in the manner of a Samudragupta, that he had installed these 'foreigners' (*yavana*) on their thrones as a good overlord should.

His boundaries secure, Krishnadevaraya turned to two other political objectives. The first was to subdue the independent chieftains in the basin of the Tungabhadra river valley, and thereby take direct control of the kingdom's heartland of nearly 30,000 square miles. This was a first powerful step to a more centralized state than had been hitherto known in the south. A parallel move was on the ideological front: Krishnadevaraya's inscriptions announced that he had distributed the great treasure gained in his successful wars to all the major temples of southern India for the purpose of constructing towering temple gateways (*gopura*), called 'Rayagopurum' in his own honour. This munificence assured that his name and that of his dynasty would be famous among the Tamils, the nearby Telugus and the people of Karnataka.

The ascendancy he achieved might have held if those who followed him had continued his policy of suppression of territorial chiefdoms in pursuit of administrative and military centralization. As it was, his successors failed to sustain his 'reforms' in the shape of such costly state-building; many of the chiefly houses returned to their former prominence in the centre of the kingdom; factionalism among them intensified. Seizing their chance, the five sultans to the north who had earlier been humiliated now pounced upon the kingdom. The capital was taken in 1565, when some of the commanders in the Vijayanagara army changed sides and joined in sacking the city. The way was opened for a resumption of Islamic expansion. A new dynasty was forced to seek refuge elsewhere, spelling the end of the great kingdom. Nevertheless, even as they fled their enemies throughout the Tamil country over the next hundred years, the Vijayanagara kings held a shadowy authority and served as a model for a set of successor kingdoms that endured to the eighteenth century.

STATES AND COMMUNITIES

The brief moment of centralized authority achieved by Krishnadevaraya draws attention to the changing relationship between states and communities during the pre-Mughal medieval era of the thirteenth to sixteenth centuries. 'Centralization' pertains to closing the distance between states and communities, by reducing autonomy and by insinuating monarchical domination over the subjected civil societies. From the beginning of medieval times – in what was, indeed, a defining characteristic of that era – politics was constituted as relations between kings and a world of autonomous and autochthonous institutions organized as communities strongly identified with particular places and with unique histories. The balance between state and community in medieval times was ever a delicate one. In the pre-modern era generally, and in agrarian societies like India, communities consisted of villages and other sorts of localities. They contained castes and sects of considerable antiquity possessed of cherished traditions of self-regulation and customs that dharma texts proclaimed fundamental: not to be contested by kings in pursuit of their own 'rajadharma', but protected. Hence, centralization was likely to be long in coming and only imperfectly realized as well as vigorously contested. Even after states were accepted as a necessary condition for a good society in early medieval India, and even when the interests of many powerful people and groups found advance through association with state power and office, the pace of centralization in India was slow.

It was not until the sixteenth century that states participated significantly in economic development, and this was as a result of the demand for military modernization. Warfare, especially the spread of cavalry, the acquisition of firearms and the recruitment of men with the training and knowledge to shoot them, stimulated state efforts to penetrate previously autonomous socio-economic and political processes.

FIREARMS IN STATE FORMATION

During the sixteenth century, guns were very inaccurate and costly; nevertheless, they gave an edge to those possessing them, especially siege cannon capable of breaching fortifications. Krishnadevaraya's spectacular victories against his Muslim foes may have depended in part on the Portuguese gunners in his forces. At nearly the same time, in 1526, the founder of the Mughal regime in India, Babur, defeated an army of Sultan Ibrahim Lodi at Panipat with a relatively small force, and opened the Gangetic plain to Mughal ascendancy. His winning strategy involved the deployment of matchlockmen and mobile field guns against an enemy whose notions of military honour tended to spurn firearms.

As the use of firepower spread so did the effects upon the political system; chiefs as well as kings had to develop economic policies to provide for the purchase or manufacture of guns and to pay for soldiers adept in their use. Because the agrarian order of the subcontinent had continued the expansion begun during the early medieval period, this must be seen as an era of relative prosperity and population growth. State formation, while involving some destructive warfare, also stimulated production and trade. The exemplary policies of Firuz Shah in extending the irrigation system of the central Gangetic plain and shunning the militarist adventures of Muhammad Shah Tughluq have been noted. During the fifteenth century, similar investments in agrarian development were made in Vijayanagara.

ECONOMIC DEVELOPMENT

There it involved not the elaboration of riverine systems of irrigation, as in the Ganges area, but the construction of tanks set all around the kingdom. Tanks, or reservoirs for capturing rainwater and other drainage, were constructed by the relatively simple means of building bunds and sluice works to take advantage of existing topography and the two monsoons that annually visited the region. As in the north, tanks were sometimes ordered by rulers – kings or local magnates – for the purpose of increasing or securing agricultural production and therefore revenue to themselves. But irrigation was also a private investment activity of wealthy landed households, with the same motive: to increase the income or food stocks required to hold lesser households in a dependent relationships. Temples too undertook improvements on lands that were gifted to them, by investing money endowments in irrigation works and sharing the enhanced production with those who worked their lands.

Other manifestations of development around the sixteenth century were industrial and commercial. The Indian Ocean had become a major trade channel between China and the Middle East as early as the eighth century, when the Tang dynasty consolidated its power in China. Soon Chinese merchants were looking beyond Chinese sea and land frontiers for trade opportunities. Similarly, when Islam expanded from its Arabian homeland into the Fertile Crescent, and ultimately into central Asia, traders from the Islamic world sought markets and products to the east and south. During the eighth to the tenth centuries commercial voyages were undertaken at great risk to merchant entrepreneurs. By the year 1000, the hazards of this commerce had been reduced by a system of trade emporia stretching from one to the other end; merchants could now ply more safely between entrepôts. With the use of monsoon winds, which during the right season were capable of driving ships directly over the ocean between the Persian Gulf and China, the Indian Ocean trade was accomplished in dramatically shortened time and consisted of single voyages from one end to the other of this Eurasian system.

India was a central linking element in the system. This was not simply because it was at the geographical centre but because it produced valuable intermediate goods, notably textiles and spices. Trade centres were established on both of India's extensive coasts and these were under the administration of merchants, some local and others representing trade communities from many other places: Arabs, Jews, Armenians and others.

State regimes were attracted to these places, partly for the revenue that they could demand from traders, often little more than tribute or extortion, but also because, increasingly by the fifteenth century, these ports provided access to strategic commodities. For example, knowledge of the breeding of horses appropriate for heavy cavalry tactics was lacking in India at the time, and possibly the climatic conditions were lacking as well; hence Indian rulers had to devise other means for securing this essential war-good. Through the ports, war horses from Arabia could be imported by chiefs and kings in the Indian peninsula in the way that rulers in northern India had long obtained them overland from Central Asia. Guns were another strategic good that was obtained through the entrepôt commerce conducted by Muslims and, increasingly, by the Portuguese after they entered and to an extent dominated the trade in the late fifteenth and early sixteenth centuries with their superior firearms.

Autonomous bodies of traders controlled the emporia that made up the Indian sector of the international trade system, just as they did the interior market towns under authority delegated by local lords. The lords benefited from the trade centres as sources of revenue and bankers' loans for military and other expenditures; bankers also transferred land revenue and customs duties to treasuries by means of bills of exchange; and towns provided luxury goods for the elite consumption of chiefs and small rajas.

In addition to market towns there were towns strategically sited for defence, which were also often administrative centres, and still others that attained considerable size and permanence as pilgrimage centres. Urban communities, whether strategic and administrative, commercial or religious, nested in, but did not always reflect, the character of larger agrarian territories. In the extended plain from Gujarat to Bengal, where the Muslim overlordship was exercised from garrison towns, there was little shared ideologically with people of the countryside around, for few were Muslim except in Bengal and the

Punjab. But if shared religious affiliations was absent, class connections were not. By the sixteenth century, rural and urban domains were becoming closely interlinked by the increasing commonality of interests of dominant landed households, of whatever religious affiliation, and those holding state office and privileges.

Small market towns and a few large garrison cities grew in number throughout the Ganges basin during the consolidation of Muslim rule from the thirteenth to the sixteenth centuries. Towns were the prime loci of sultanate authority until the sixteenth century, when a growing number of sultanate officials had succeeded in establishing roots in the countryside. From at least Tughluq times, conditional service tenures over income from the land were in the process of conversion into hereditary holdings. Sixteenth-century muqtas joined other established landed families to provide thick links between countryside and town, where some continued to hold office and others to engage in trade. Enterprising muqtas could be found investing some of their personal wealth in agrarian development, either directly on lands that they had privatized or by offering others the incentive of reduced taxes on lands for which irrigation works had been constructed. In this way agrarian production and the private benefits of a few were enhanced. In addition, officials and local magnates sought to develop town markets (*qasba*) and rural market places (*ganj*) by deferring taxes on trade for several years.

Gangetic towns were garrisoned by the most dependable soldiers of the sultanate, where they could be kept ready for defence and from where campaigns against others were launched. The great congregational mosques (*jama masjid*) were monuments of Islamic rule and they, along with their ancillary institutions of Islamic tuition and the influential Sufi orders, formed a focus for the urban life of Muslims. No other riverine zone propagated the rich town-life found in the Ganges basin.

During much of the medieval period politics presented an ambiguity of perspective that became stronger over time. That is, viewed from the royal centre, all local authority was regarded as devolved from itself; previously (and still) autonomous magnates were perceived by central authorities as its officials, who were often given documents of appointment signifying their affiliation. From the viewpoint of the local lord, however, his power remained autochthonous, deriving from the standing and historical continuity of his household and kinsmen, and, precisely because of that standing, he was useful to sovereigns and rewarded by them. During the later medieval age, as states achieved increased powers to centralize – that is, to penetrate previously autonomous zones in their domains – this ambiguity persisted. The balance between magnates and kings shifted according to the strength of the royal centre, but tension remained and, with it, mutual antagonism. This balance was to be tested during the era of the Mughals.

In the century that followed, the Muslim expansion culminated in the conquests of the Mughal emperor Aurangzeb in the 1680s. Nevertheless, Islam never achieved the deep social penetration in southern India that followed the Muslim conquests in the northern heartland of Sanskritic culture, a failure many historians credit to the Vijayanagara kingdom. Hindu institutions and values were defended as an explicit element of Vijayanagara ideology. The kingdom's overlordship in the southern peninsula from the middle of the fourteenth to the middle of the sixteenth centuries provided the conditions for the further elaboration of distinctly south Indian cultures. Hence, not only was the massive political hegemony of Muslims delayed, but, as a result, the powerful Indo-Islamic culture that had come to maturity in northern India and parts of the northern Deccan failed to take root in the lower peninsula.

[4] *EARLY MODERN INDIA*

INTRODUCTION

Conquests within India by slave soldiers from central Asia were financed by iqtas, grants of the right to collect income from certain lands, intended as a substitute for a cash salary which was beyond the administrative capacities of primitive governments by conquest. Grants of landed income in return for services had long been common in India as a way of supporting religious teachers and institutions, but had rarely before been used for military purposes. In western Asia, where the slave soldiers had set up state regimes, these in time became bureaucratized; in India, however, although service landholding was important for the Muslim regimes, bureaucratization did not develop. In the sixteenth century, centralized administrative controls tightened, but, once made over to powerful soldiers and civil officials, land was easily assimilated into their individual patrimonies. Hence, the grants to government officials, which increased until they involved a vast proportion of the arable land in northern and parts of peninsular India, were lost to state control.

The relative weakness of centralized, bureaucratic institutions in India is somewhat unexpected when yet another element of the Indo-Islamic order is considered. That is the importance of Persian as a language of high culture and latterly of government. Ancient Persia's elaborate bureaucratic tradition had lasted until the time of the last pre-Muslim rulers, the Sassanids, who fell before the Arab Muslim armies around 640 CE, and some of it did reach India along with other Irano-Arabic ideas and institutions after the eleventh century. Balban, the longest-lived king of the 'Slave Dynasty' of Delhi, claimed to have retrieved the 'lustre of the Persian kings', but neither he nor his successors sought to replace the mamluk order with a Persianized bureaucratized structure of the sort adopted in Safavid Persia and Ottoman Turkey, notwithstanding the wealth of scribal talents available to them in India. Explaining this failure and other limitations of the transformation of India under the Islamic onslaught of later medieval times requires the recognition that, in the encounter with the Islamic world, the weight of tradition and historical inertia remained with Indian ways and their pre-Muslim course. Indeed, pre-Islamic values and institutions were not broken down by the encounter; instead, they hardened and formed even more conservative and rigid cysts, enclaves of pre-Islamic culture in the Muslim empire.

THE FORMATION OF AN INDO-ISLAMIC CULTURE

The military successes of the Muslim regimes that led to the subordination of much of the subcontinent by 1500 obscure a more historically significant development: the formation of a synthetic Indo-Islamic culture. This process began as early as the late tenth century, partly as an outcome of the changing shape of Islam. By then, certain original conditions had changed. Islam no longer belonged exclusively to the Arabs, and was no longer a unified confessional movement.

Less than twenty-five years after the death of the Prophet Muhammad, a split had occurred between the followers of his son-in-law Ali, who recognized only Ali and his descendants as the rightful heirs, and those who had supported other candidates for the caliphate, or leadership of the Islamic state. The rift hardened and deepened in the succeeding years, becoming doctrinal as well as political. The adherents of Ali and their successors became known as Shi'ites, and the others, the majority of Muslims in most Islamic countries, as Sunni.

During the tenth century the fission assumed serious political significance with the founding of the Shi'ite Fatimid caliphate centred on Cairo. The demise of the Abbasid (descended from the Prophet's uncle Abbas) caliphate and the rise of the Shi'ite Fatimids (descended from the Prophet's daughter Fatima) in North Africa was to prove momentous. There were now both an early or 'old' Islam anchored in an Arab cultural orientation and a new and evolving Shi'ite tradition. Paradoxically, Islamic expansionism was strengthened by the developing dual traditions. Beneath the new Persian-inflected high culture teamed a vast multiplicity of cultures and societies with diverse political, religious and social institutions. India was part of that mosaic, which attained something of a unity through a mobile intelligentsia consisting of learned and pious men who were lured from the older centres of learning in Cairo and Baghdad by far-flung Muslim rulers. By the beginning of the sixteenth century, the cultural fabric of Islam was a web of diverse languages, cuisines, domestic and community architectures, agricultural technologies and institutions of administration and law.

By the time Islam reached India, the exclusiveness of the first days of Arab expansionism, when Islam had conferred superior status upon Arab conquerors and was therefore a privilege to be guarded, was at an end. Islam had become more welcoming, and at times conversion was actively pursued. Those who did not convert could be protected as dhimmi. Yet the conferral of dhimmi status upon Hindus during the time of the Tughluqs must have seemed to many law-minded Muslims as an inappropriate extension of that doctrine. It had never been intended to apply to the presumably polytheistic worshippers of Shiva, Vishnu and a myriad of lesser deities.

On the other hand, even as tolerated non-believers, Hindus were subject to discriminatory tax demands, which in the case of commercial levies were several times the amounts paid by Muslims. Hindus were also denied access to lucrative administrative and military offices to which Muslims were entitled. And finally, for those who were town-based merchants and artisans, Hindus living under the fortresses of Muslim soldiers or plying roads controlled by Muslim horsemen found it tempting to add security as well as advantage to piety by converting. The inducements were even greater for those engaged in international trade, whose ships negotiated Muslim sea-lanes and ports in a great arc of commerce stretching from China to Spain, but especially through the Indian Ocean and Arabian Sea.

RELIGIOUS DIVERSITY UNDER THE MUSLIMS

The evolution of an Indo-Islamic tradition was complex. To begin with, there was no single Indian culture and body of practice to be modified; in addition to the majority faith, there were remnants of Buddhists, Jainas, Christians and Jews, and a large population of forest and hill people worshipping other sorts of divinities altogether.

But even within the mainstream of the two cultures of Islam and Hinduism, both sides in the encounter harboured heterodox devotionalisms, and every part of the subcontinent had a regional configuration of worship. Unlike the great splits which had riven Islam, however, the various regional forms of Shaivite and Vaishnavite devotionalism always followed the religious guidance of brahman priests, some of whom took part in the development of the devotional movements and were able to maintain their privileges and power in the new worship as well as the old.

By 1200 CE, the preservers of Muslim orthodoxy, the ulema, had come to accept reluctantly that a similar devotional current had made its home in Islam, in both the Islamic heartland and the conquered territories. Sufism, the mystic devotionalism of Islam, cut across the baffling indigenous sacred array of India. Mass piety among Hindus proved receptive to the sermons of Sufi masters (*pirs*); a number of them became their disciples and then went on to enter a seminary to imbibe the mystical way of the pir. The tenets of Hindu and Muslim mystics were similar enough that the ground was ripe for syncretic movements involving adherents of both religions. (Moreover, the passions of Hindu bhaktas had challenged law-minded brahman sectarian leaders in the same way that Sufis threatened the law-minded ulema.)

In matters of religion, neither Islam itself nor the various, supposedly more egalitarian, bhakti forms of devotionalism made much headway against the authority of the traditional priests. On the contrary, the devotional practices and theologies within Hinduism if anything strengthened hierarchical relations, as these became embedded in regional codes of conduct and preserved in texts as 'the custom of the region'. Notwithstanding the bhakti ideology that supposedly made all devotees equal, some remained clearly more equal than others, even within the 'pure' precincts of the shrine, and the distinction between polluting and pure castes was scrupulously preserved.

THE DECLINE OF TRADITIONAL KINGSHIP

Politically, Islam did not at first threaten the privileges of the subjugated kings, who complacently continued to measure their greatness by the number of lesser subjugated kings who offered them homage rather than by the territory they annexed. Thus kings could be 'conquered' but their territorial rights were not impaired, and centralization was thus impeded. But despite the political inertia of the traditional Hindu monarchies, they were eventually uprooted by the expansion of Muslim authority in later medieval times. Many communities were then separated from and thus deprived of the adjudicative and modest legislative transformations of which Hindu kings were capable. Bereft of kings, the north Indian communities fell under the petty tyrannies of priests and locality headmen, who were less willing than the kings had been to legitimate even small changes in the social orders under their rule. The situation was analogous to that of the *millat* in other Muslim lands, or ghetto societies in medieval Europe. In all of these, small communities of minority believers were permitted to practise their religions and govern themselves under the oversight of a Muslim or Christian governor. Such limited autonomy often produced authoritarian and sometimes tyrannical community leaders.

Medieval India was on vastly different scale from Europe when, after 1200, the whole of the core region of Sanskrit culture, the Gangetic plain, was brought under direct Muslim rule, yet a similar process can be discerned. The chain of authority between individual subjects, communities and kings was broken, leaving truncated polities of clan-based chiefs and very localized societies linked strongly neither horizontally to each other nor vertically to kings. The same effect spread beyond the Gangetic plain following the Muslim conquests in the Deccan, and, though non-Muslim elites often adopted certain of the superficial patterns of their conquerors, this produced no more change in their encysted condition than had the adoption of Muslim headgear or gowns by Christian millat leaders in Turkey.

The far south was spared the long domination of Muslim overlordship that deeply affected the north and the Deccan, yet it too manifested similar conservative reactions. The Vijayanagara kings had a keen sense of the danger posed by Islam to their power as well as their religion. As a result, archaic values were explicitly preserved, as the inscriptions make clear. Their claims to defend the dharma of their subjects – meaning the temple-based bhakti religion and proper caste relations – from the outrages of the sultanate regimes have all the earmarks of perceived threat. But while this concern may have served to justify the maintenance of militarist regimes, it cannot explain their aggressive wars of conquest against other Hindu rulers. Nor can it explain the failure to develop centralized polities during the sixteenth and seventeenth centuries, which left the subcontinent vulnerable to the colonial incursions that were to follow during the eighteenth century.

Deepening links between India and the Muslim international political economy undoubtedly set Indian society upon new pathways. Trade with India had long been crucial for the Islamic world, and it had also become increasingly important for Indians. Gold and silver coins came from western Asia as in earlier times precious metals had come from Rome to pay for Indian spices and manufactured goods; these coins provided the basis for currencies, if not the currencies themselves, that were used along the western coast from Sind to the far south and Sri Lanka.

THE MUGHAL EMPIRE

The Mughal, or Timurid, state that was founded by Babur between 1526 and 1530 was by the seventeenth century the largest and the most centralized state up to that time. Underlying it were the superior military capabilities of a generation of Central Asian soldiers, but it also owed much to anterior processes of political and economic consolidation. The Mughal state occupies an important place in the historiography of early modern India for another reason as well: it was the precursor for, and in a sense the cause of, the rise of the successor empire of the British colonialists, which endured for nearly the same amount of time; that is, around two centuries.

Formally, Mughal rule commenced in 1526, with Babur's victorious campaigns. He was a Chagathay Turk who claimed descent from both Timur (Tamerlane), the fourteenth-century scourge of Delhi, and, on his mother's side, the thirteenth-century Mongol marauder Chingiz Khan. Babur's descendants called themselves Timurids as well as Mughals (i.e. Mongols) in recognition of both origins. The vaunting of such progenitors pointed up the central character of the Mughal regime as a warrior state: it was born in war and it was sustained by war until the eighteenth century, when warfare destroyed it. Babur had been a cultured man driven from his patrimonial lands in Samarkand by invading Uzbekis, who were to give their names to the region. Despite assistance from Persia, Babur failed to regain his territory, and was forced to set out upon a conquest of his own. He adopted the military tactics of the Uzbek cavalry, which he cunningly combined with muskets and field artillery to make a force powerful enough in 1526 to wrest control from the Muslim masters of the Gangetic plain.

Another possible date for the beginning of the Mughal regime is 1600, when the institutions that defined the regime were set firmly in place and when the heartland of the empire was defined; both of these were the accomplishment of Babur's grandson Akbar. The realm so defined and governed was a vast territory of some 750,000 square miles, ranging from the frontier with Central Asia in northern Afghanistan to the northern uplands of the Deccan plateau, and from the Indus basin on the west to the Assamese highlands in the east.

The imperial career of the Mughal house is conventionally reckoned to have ended in 1707 when the emperor Aurangzeb, a fifth-generation descendant of Babur, died. His fifty-year reign began in 1658 with the Mughal state seeming as strong as ever or even stronger. But in Aurangzeb's later years the state was brought to the brink of destruction, over which it toppled within a decade and a half after his death; by 1720 imperial Mughal rule was largely finished and an epoch of two imperial centuries had closed.

THE AFGHAN EMPIRE

Before we enter into a detailed discussion of the Mughal 'New Age', it is important to take note of two previous dynasties to whose policies Mughal rule owed much. While there may be debate about whether Babur's military success over the Afghan and Rajput overlords of the Gangetic plain in 1526 was more definitive in launching the Mughal empire than Akbar's political achievements of 1600, there is no question about the importance of the administrative debt that the Mughals owed to their Afghan predecessors. Alone of the Muslim ruling class from 1200, the Afghan clan leaders persistently and successfully planted roots in the Indian communities to which their military offices took them, whether in the Gangetic plain or distant Andhra.

Bahlul Khan, the head of the Afghan Lodi clan, managed to seize the Delhi throne in 1451 and set about reasserting Delhi's authority after the chaos that had followed the death of Firuz Shah Tughluq a half-century before. Bahlul Lodi provided the foundation for Lodi dominance which his son Sikandar, who succeeded in 1489, brilliantly realized in a reign that lasted until 1517. Sikandar showed that it was possible to control the dangerous inter-tribal divisions among Afghan fighters that had proven fatal to previous regimes. However, his brother Ibrahim, who succeeded him, fell victim to Babur, who had been invited to overthrow him by one of his own disaffected nobles.

The Lodi clan was followed by the Suras, who were also of Afghan origin, and also fought and occasionally bested Babur and his son Humayun, the first two Mughal emperors. The greatest of the Sura rulers was Sher Khan, better known as Sher Shah. His grandfather had migrated from Afghanistan in pursuit of a military career for himself and his son, and took service under the revitalizing Lodis in the Punjab, where Sher Shah was born in 1472. Uncharacteristically for the son of a fighter, he left his Punjab home for Jaunpur in the Gangetic valley to study and became fluent in Persian. His abilities were more general, however, and he soon won an administrative office in Bihar, where he was recognized by Babur shortly after the latter's victory over Ibrahim at Panipat in 1526. Sher Shah soldiered under Babur during his campaign into the eastern Ganges, before joining the administration of an independent Afghan ruler of Bihar whom he replaced in the early 1530s.

Sher Shah had neither opposed nor supported Babur's son Humayun when the latter attempted to impose Mughal control over Bihar and Bengal, but when Humayun shifted his concerns to western India to defeat anti-Mughal forces in Gujarat, Sher Shah took Bengal and successfully defended this seizure against Humayun's army in 1539. He succeeded in driving the Mughals from the eastern and central Gangetic plain, making the Suras' realm suddenly enormous, in addition to being more efficiently managed than any previous state in the Ganges basin.

In the event, Sher Shah ruled northern India only briefly, from 1538 to 1545, when he died in battle. During his reign, however, he established a reputation for military genius as great as that of Babur and for administrative genius as great as that of Akbar. In 1545, the Sura empire extended from the five rivers of the Punjab to the eastern borders of the Ganges delta, including the town of Chittagong, and from the Narmada valley to the boundary with Kashmir in the north. This area exceeded that conquered by Babur and was only marginally smaller than that left by Akbar at his death in 1605; it also exceeded the territory dominated by the previously most successful Afghan ruler, Sikandar Lodi, whose administrative innovations Sher Shah did not hesitate to adopt.

THE LODI ADMINISTRATIVE LEGACY

Geographical divisions called *sarkar* by the Lodis were imposed over newly conquered tracts. This unit was later adopted by the Mughals and, after them, by the British, who termed it 'district', and eventually by the independent government of India. The meaning conveyed by the Persian word sarkar in the sixteenth century and later was 'government' or 'authority', and some twenty groupings of these districts, called provinces, were adopted by Babur and enumerated in his memoir, the *Babur Nama*. Within the sarkars were local territories, most commonly called *pargana*, that had long existed as historical communities rather than formal administrative tracts. The Mughal province, or *suba*, was imposed over the sarkars and parganas: in Akbar's time the suba of Bengal contained nineteen sarkars and over 600 parganas. The Delhi and Agra subas were smaller, containing eight and thirteen sarkars respectively, each with some 200 parganas.

It was at the sarkar level that the Lodi sultan's military and civil officials encountered and sought to dominate the countryside and towns. Consequently, it was sarkar officers who received the tribute that each local magnate agreed to pay when confronted by Sura authority and who were responsible for controlling the competition, often violent, among the locally powerful. Over each sarkar, Sher Shah placed a trusted officer whose tasks were essentially political and only secondarily fiscal.

On the frontiers of the realm, sarkars were joined together under the supervisory responsibility of an Afghan notable, who was a deputy of the sultan. In this way, attempts were made to contain the two levels of political authority that, on the one hand, provided the regime's principal income in tribute and was controlled by Afghan nobles, and, on the other hand, consisted of the core tracts of traditional political and economic integration – the parganas – which were the overseen by non-Afghans of various kinds.

The pargana was a level of political autonomy where fractious local dominance persisted throughout the sixteenth century; the number of them had increased greatly between the time of Sikandar Lodi and Sher Shah, when the area under Afghan control had doubled; one estimate speaks of over 100,000 parganas, each a sharply defined formation of local particularities, and all very resistant to overall control. Just as Sher Shah held absolute power to make policies for his state and executed these through individual subordinate military or civil officers, so his appointees at the sarkar level managed their often large tracts patrimonially through personal relations with other Afghans and with numerous village headmen and pargana chiefs. Even this modest administrative structure proved superior to that of the Khaljis and Tughluqs, and it was to provide the foundation for Akbar's system.

Sher Shah ruled from Agra. This city had become important during the sultanate period when the Delhi–Agra region formed a single political core centred on the converging fertile tract between the Yamuna and Ganges rivers. It was around Agra that he introduced a set of revenue reforms that he had perfected earlier in Bihar when he was a local administrator; the same reforms were to be further refined during Akbar's time. These involved the payment of land revenue in cash, collected from peasant producers on the basis of surveys of lands, crops, prices and yields. They also involved the participation of the state in enhancing productivity through reduced tax demands where land was reclaimed or irrigation improved.

THE ASCENT OF AKBAR

If Babur's superior military prowess provided one foundation for his Mughal successors, Akbar's wise political measures provided much of the rest. It was Akbar's work that laid the foundation for the good fortune of a series of long-lived and competent descendants.

Akbar's reign began shakily in 1556 with the accidental death in Delhi of his father, Humayun. Akbar's childhood was spent in Afghanistan, protected by trusted warriors. The twelve year old prince was crowned by a group of Humayun's principal officers led by the general Bairam Khan, who became regent and safeguarded the fragile regime from the Afghan followers of the Sur clan. It took several years before the Mughals became masters of the great fortress cities of Agra, Delhi, Lahore and Jaunpur, and this broad-based triangle-shaped territory defined their political and economic heartland.

Bairam Khan extended this zone of enormous agricultural productivity by conquests in Rajasthan and Malwa, but he now faced concerted opposition to his regency. Akbar showed his readiness to rule by joining a cabal against the regent made up of Sunni nobles of central Asian (Turanian) descent who opposed Bairam Khan's Shi'ite and Iranian connections, an anticipation of future divisions amongst great nobles later on. (Nobles, incidentally, were defined as those who had achieved 'khan' status, i.e. the recognition of their personal service to the Mughal ruler; besides Turanians and Iranians these included a few 'Hindustanis', a name applied to all those born in India.) Bairam Khan was dismissed and encouraged to undertake a pilgrimage to Mecca, but before be could leave India he was assassinated by a soldier with an old grievance.

Before Akbar could adopt and refine Sher Shah's system, he had first to secure his throne. He became an able soldier like his grandfather, but unlike the latter, was never educated and never learned to read. Soldiering and politics were more important talents in any case, given his situation, and he overcame both court factions and valiant enemies like the Rajputs to win back his Indian patrimony. Paradoxically, among his most valuable allies in this were Rajput clans, such as that at Jaipur, one of whose royal daughters he married.

Akbar's Hindu marriage established him as a Muslim ruler prepared to forge strong bonds with his Hindu subjects, and not only the aristocracy. His benevolence was confirmed by the abolition of the *jizya*, the poll tax levied on Hindu dhimmis. After brilliant and courageous conquests in Gujarat, in western Indian, and Bengal, in the east, Akbar stabilized his northern frontier by skilful diplomacy with both the Persians and their Uzbek enemies, gaining a powerful position at Kandahar in southern Afghanistan.

After some campaigns conducted personally against Afghans and Rajputs, which established his military reputation, Akbar initiated the first of his structural reforms, namely the creation of a new kind of nobility. The new system of Mughal nobility and appointments, along with his financial reforms, was the foundation of the system that Akbar devised between about 1560 and his death in 1605. He was determined to achieve a better balance among his following by countering the preponderant weight of the central Asian Turkic speakers, who had been his father's first supporters. To achieve this, and because he admired their culture, Akbar recruited Persians into his elite service.

He also introduced Indian-born fighters into his new nobility, turning to Rajputs and Indian-born Muslims of all sorts, except those of Afghan extraction, who remained suspect. Powerful lords of various parts of northern India were invited to submit to Mughal authority and share in the dignities and rewards of noble (*amir*) rank, including marriage into the imperial house. Those who did not submit, such as the senior Rajput house of Mewar, were ruthlessly extirpated. By 1580, Akbar had formed a corps of amirs numbering 200, with Iranian and Turanian amirs almost equally represented, while Rajputs and Hindustani Muslims constituted a minor sixth of their number.

The loyalty of his amirs was immediately challenged by an uprising involving some influential Muslim scholars who resisted Akbar's usual insistence that his name and titles be read during Friday mosque services; these clerics joined some of the Afghan nobility in a brief revolt. Though easily put down, it strengthened Akbar's resolve to exclude Afghans and take measures to depoliticize the ulema. His new nobles, on the other hand, had proven themselves worthy of the privileges of rank.

Collectively, their identity was defined through the word for 'dignity', *mansab*, representing an element of continuity with the great conquering Mongols from which Mughals claimed to come. A holder of noble rank was a *mansabdar*, and he was remunerated in one or two different ways. Each was invested with a personal rank by the emperor, which carried with it a money salary or an equivalent assignment of landed income. A second system of ranking was initiated in 1590, according to which a mansabdar could be entitled to payments calculated according to the number of mounted soldiers under his command. As this was a service nobility rather than an aristocracy, mansabdars could not pass their titles and ranks to their sons (in theory). The system was not a bureaucracy, however; mansabdars protected and extended the lands of the Mughal rulers but did little to make Mughal rule a centralized force capable of altering the structure of society significantly.

A more effective step in that direction was realized through Akbar's revenue reforms, with which the name of his minister Todar Mal is associated. He joined Akbar's service in 1561 and rose to the governorship of Bengal, the richest province in the empire. The resource base of Akbar's new order was land revenue, and here he wisely continued the administration of his Afghan predecessor, Sher Shah. This required an initially costly measurement of the cultivable land available, the value of which provided a known basis from which to calculate the revenue to be collected through intermediaries, such as tax farmers, or indirectly from lands assigned in lieu of salaries, the old iqta system, now renamed *jagir*. Either way, well over half of the output from the fields in his realm, after the costs of production had been met, is estimated to have been taken from the peasant producers by way of official taxes and unofficial exactions. Moreover, payments were exacted in money, and this required a well regulated silver currency.

The revenue intermediaries were dubiously called 'landholders' (*zamindars*). In fact, many zamindars were actually 'tax farmers', money men who contracted to pay Akbar's treasury an amount equal to the notional value of the revenue in some tract; in addition, zamindars collected taxes and maintained order with the help, if necessary, of Mughal officials and soldiers. Others who were also called zamindars were local magnates, even lesser kings, who transmitted tribute from their territory in return for the right to continue to rule, while sharing in the prestige of Mughal service. Thus, while Todar Mal's revenue organization vastly enriched Akbar, as a form of administration it left a great deal of autonomy to local social leaders who had dominated community life before the coming of the Mughals.

In time these magnates completed a development that was latent in the pre-Mughal sixteenth century by turning themselves into a hereditary gentry whose culture selectively imitated court Mughals, but whose interests remained resolutely local. The new gentry included not only the landed magnates, or zamindars, but merchants and minor government office-holders as well; as a class they were perhaps the chief beneficiaries of Mughal rule until the eighteenth century, when they withdrew their allegiance from the Mughals and contributed to their downfall.

To the scheme of taxation, Akbar added distinctive political features. He resumed lands that had been alienated by prior Muslim regimes and used their revenues to pay for military and civil services, most of which had become hereditary holdings. In their place, jagirs made up of carefully measured lands were used to pay for the services of all military and civil officials according to their rank. Each official held a rank carrying a salary; military officers received an additional entitlement to support the cavalry forces which they commanded.

The salary system was the keystone of the Mughal state to which Akbar added crucial innovations. One was ideological. He sought to neutralize, or, more accurately, to subordinate politically, the Muslim religious intelligentsia which consisted of jurists and mosque officials – the ulema – by boldly declaring his own primacy in matters of religion. Extending the royal prerogative to religion, and setting aside conservative Muslim theologians and jurists, encouraged his Hindu subjects to transfer their loyalty to his regime, and

Plate 15 Tomb of Shaikh Salim Chishti, Fatehpur Sikri, Uttar Pradesh. The tomb of this Muslim saint, who died in 1581, forms the centrepiece of the grandiose mosque erected by Akbar at his newly constructed palace city (IOL Collection 50a (46); neg. no. B 22073, by permission of the British Library).

certainly he was successful in winning the strategic cooperation of Rajput fighters. Their allegiance to him and his successors was remarkable and fully honoured by the series of able Mughal rulers that followed him.

AKBAR'S RELIGION

In Akbar's time, the ulema were an influential class, but an urban one. To many of the pious, Akbar seemed a supportive if not wholly zealous defender of the faith. Orthodox institutions flourished, as exemplified by the great mosque he constructed as part of Fatehpur Sikri, his new capital near Agra, which was founded at the site of the tomb of a great Chishti saint. The mosque dominated all other buildings in the city, and the emperor took a close and public interest in its affairs. His pious acts included sweeping the floors of the prayer hall and occasionally leading prayers. He also lent state sponsorship to pilgrimages to Mecca by maintaining a special *haj* ship which transported the devout at no cost and by making endowments in Mecca and Medina. Finally, he made regular visits to Ajmer in Rajasthan – some on foot – to the tomb of another of the famous Chishti sheikhs.

But he bitterly disappointed many of the pious scholars in his court. One of his critics was the Sunni historian Abdul Qadir Badauni, who left his observations of what went on in Fatehpur Sikri, especially in the Ibadat Khana, or house of prayers, which served Akbar as a place to conduct religious debates. These sometimes involved Sunni ulema and Sufi sheikhs of outspoken temperament and dubious orthodoxy – with the emperor as audience and participant:

> The controversies used to pass beyond the differences of Sunni and Shi'a, of Hanafi and Shafi'i [schools of shariah interpretation], of lawyer and divine, and they would attack the very bases of belief. And Makh-dum-ul-Mulk wrote a treatise to the effect that Sheikh 'Abd-al-Nabi had unjustly killed Khizr Khan Sarwani, who had been suspected of blaspheming the Prophet (peace be upon him!), and Mir Habsh, who had been suspected of being a Shi'a and saying that it was not right to repeat the prayers after him, because he was undutiful toward his father, and was himself afflicted with hemorrhoids. Sheikh 'Abd-al-Nabi replied to him that he was a fool and a heretic. Then the mullahs [Muslim theologians] became divided into two parties, and . . . became very Jews and Egyptians for hatred of each other. And persons of novel and whimsical opinions, in accordance with their pernicious ideas and vain doubts, coming out of ambush, decked the false in the garb of the true, and the wrong in the dress of right, and cast the emperor, who was possessed of an excellent disposition, and was an earnest searcher after truth, but very ignorant and a mere tyro . . . into perplexity, till doubt was heaped upon doubt, and he lost all definite aim, and the straight wall of the clear law . . . was broken down, so that after five or six years not a trace of Islam was left in him: and everything was turned topsy-turvy.

And if that was not enough, it appeared that the emperor also listened to the pundits of other religions – including Hindu pundits, Zoroastrians, Jainas and Catholic priests from Goa – with equal interest:

> Samanas [Hindu or Buddhist ascetics] and Brahmans . . . gained the advantage over every one in attaining the honor of interviews with His Majesty . . . And he made his courtiers listen to those revilings and attacks against our pure and easy, bright and holy faith . . .
>
> And at one time a Brahman, named Debi, who was one of the interpreters of the *Mahabharata*, was pulled up the wall of the castle sitting on a bedstead till he arrived near a balcony, which the emperor had made his bedchamber. Whilst thus suspended he instructed His Majesty in the secrets and legends of Hinduism, in the manner of worshipping idols, the fire, the sun and stars, and of revering the chief gods of these unbelievers . . . His Majesty, on hearing further how much the people of the country prized their institutions, began to look upon them with affection.[1]

The emperor was equally open to the purveyors of all faiths, it appeared. Where Hinduism was concerned, at least, this openness had a practical political rationale, which religious zealots could not accept. For the ruler of subjects who were overwhelmingly followers of their own gods and dharmic practices, a way of accommodation had to be devised, and here Akbar followed the pragmatic practices of previous sultans in northern and southern

India. To have attempted to place most of his subjects under continuous pressure to convert would have led to constant tension and possible rebellion.

Akbar's hostile attitude to the ulema, on the other hand, was deepened when inquiries into their wealth revealed that many of them possessed personal fortunes which were protected by charitable tax immunities fraudulently obtained. As a consequence, the lands of many of them were resumed, and Akbar conspicuously made new grants to non-Muslim divines.

Yet another area of conflict between Akbar and the ulema was shared by many of his subjects; this was his liking for Sufi teachers whom many of the legal-minded regarded as heretics. His Sufi sympathies caused special alarm when Akbar, in 1579, declared it his responsibility as ruler to judge religious disputes on issues where the shariah was not clear, citing 'the sound traditions':

> 'Surely the man who is dearest to God on the Day of Judgement is the just Imam [leader, king]. Whoever obeys the amir, obeys you and whoever rebels against him rebels against you' . . . The learned have given a decision that the status of a just king is greater before God than the status of an interpreter of the Law.[2]

Many of the pious-minded, including Badauni, who quoted this declaration, considered it a dangerous extension of his authority of interpretation into their sphere. They were even more deeply incensed by the articulation of what they considered a heretical 'Divine Faith', which was outlined in the writings of Akbar's friend and counsellor, Abul Fazl. The new dispensation dated from 1582; its doctrines were never fully elaborated, but glimpses afforded by contemporaries stressed the emperor's perfect wisdom, yet bore a strong imprint of Sufi mysticism, which stressed the direct link between individual and God. The reconciliation of these two principles was itself rather mystical:

> Know for certain that the perfect prophet and learned apostle, the possessor of fame, Akbar, that is the lord of wisdom, directs us to acknowledge that the self-existent being is the wisest teacher, and ordains the creatures with absolute power, so that the intelligent among them may be able to understand his [Akbar's] precepts; . . . therefore, according to the lights of our reason, let us investigate the mysteries of his [God's] creation.

The results of the investigation were clear:

> In the sequel it became evident to wise men that emancipation is to be obtained only by the knowledge of truth conformably with the precepts of the perfect prophet, the perfect lord of fame, Akbar, 'the Wise'; the practices enjoined by him are: renouncing and abandoning the world; refraining from lust, sensuality, entertainment, slaughter of what possesses life . . . purification of the soul by the yearning after God the all-just, and the union with the merciful Lord.[3]

In fact, Akbar changed the ideological basis of his state in relation to Islam early in his reign. In 1563, he abolished the tax upon pilgrims to Shiva, Vishnu and other temples, and, in the view of some of the ulema, explicitly contravened the shariah by permitting new shrines to be built. Later he abolished the tax to which all dhimmis were subject. The declaration of 1579 was the straw that broke the camel's back, and induced some high mosque officials that year to join a revolt of Afghan mansabdars. They issued religious edicts (*fatwas*) urging all Muslims to resist Akbar. Fatwas circulated widely in Bihar and Bengal and suppression of the revolt required Akbar to despatch an army over which Todar Mal was set.

POLITICAL IDEOLOGY UNDER AKBAR

Other components of the dominant ideological formation of the Mughal house were contained in the *Akbar-Nama* (*Book of Akbar*) and its appendix, the imperial gazetteer, *Ain-i-Akbari* (*Institutes of Akbar*), works which gave an account of the emperor's forty-seven year reign written by his trusty publicist Abul Fazl. The *Ain-i-Akbari* drums home the royal claims:

> No dignity is higher in the eyes of God than royalty and those who are wise drink from its auspicious fountain. A sufficient proof of this, for those who require one, is the fact that royalty is a remedy for the spirit of rebellion, and the reason why subjects obey. Even the meaning of the word *Padshah* [emperor] shows this, for *pad* signifies stability and possession.[4]

The overwhelming importance of Akbar was illustrated visually as well as described in print, for the benefit of his literate as well as his mostly illiterate subjects. Miniature paintings in the *Akbar Nama* embellish his imperial aura by depicting the emperor calmly controlling the chaotic world of men and animals (see cover). Fatehpur Sikri, the capital he built near Agra, reflected more of his radiance by incorporating the worship of the sun and moon, and the adoption of other practices of the majority of his subjects, so deplored by Badauni.

Topping the whole was Akbar's order of spiritual discipleship, which mimicked the relationship between the Sufi master and his devotees, and, conjoined with his earthly position, amounted to a near-deification of the person of the emperor. His 'disciples' included a majority of Mughal grandees, some of them the highest officers of the kingdom. These amirs shared the glory of Timurid military successes and its invincible territorial sway. In that way discipleship was an extension to courtiers of the older sultanate institution of the Ghazi, or 'holy warrior' who served God and was tied to the ruler by the same bond as Sufi disciple was to master.

To all these ingenious efforts to fix the loyalty of his subjects to himself and his house and to blunt divisions among Muslims and between them and the majority of his subjects, Akbar added other, more pragmatic, elements. The corps of mansabdars who carried out his military orders and commanded some 150,000 heavy cavalrymen were supported by grants of village income (jagir) which provided the salaries fixed by their rank, and were intended also to maintain the troops under their commands. These arrangements were maintained by masters of the mints as well as a minister of defence, since a high-quality currency was necessary to mediate all the complex relationships of Akbar's regime.

There was one obvious flaw in the scheme. Though the payment system was intended to individualize relations between Akbar and his commanders, and to establish quasi-feudal links between them, the lieutenants of the mansabdars were often men of the same ethnic identity as their commanders – Iranian, Turanian or Hindustani, as the case may be – and tied to their superiors by similar links of dependency. Faultlines of potential divisiveness were thereby reinforced. In fact, the appearance of very strong central authority was based largely on Akbar's own personality. Thus, patrimonial rather than bureaucratic, Akbar's regime lacked the means for its ordinances to be carried to a vast and fragmented people, where a massive weight of inertia assured that the little world of the pargana was scarcely touched, much less changed.

To be sure, by the end of his reign a new gentry was beginning to emerge from the pargana social world, reflecting connections with the central regime, and a similar new class emerged in the towns and cities of the empire, an urban class of men who enjoyed office or wealth, including tax-free landed income that came with religious offices. Though Akbar sought to limit the various tendencies of service-derived rights to become hereditary and self-perpetuating, he could not stem all the pressures leading to new class forms; these strengthened his system in the short term but laid grounds for later political weakness.

Both the charismatic and pragmatic elements of Akbar's system were endangered late in his reign through the revolt of his oldest son. Prince Salim's defiance of his father's authority culminated in his having his own name read out in the Friday services of Allahabad mosque in 1602, and he submitted to his father's indulgent authority in 1604 only because some of his supporters had shifted allegiance from him to his own son. Little time remained in which to bind the wounds of factional divisions among the military commanders and grandees of the empire who had chosen to side with Salim's revolt before Akbar died in 1605.

Both the revolt of a son and fratricide among the imperial princes were to become repeated features of the Mughal regime. Moreover, the effect was cumulative: each succession was more bitterly contested, until Aurangzeb surpassed all by defeating and killing two of his brothers and imprisoning his father, the emperor Shah Jahan. A cost that balanced the benefits of the remarkable sequence of competent heirs was that, with no rule of primogeniture, at the death of one ruler, and often before that, his sons would scheme and fight each other for the throne. The loyalty of powerful commanders and their soldiery was solicited and the resulting factions would throw themselves into violent wars before a succession was completed. Akbar's son Salim survived to rule as Jahangir, but those who supported him and their families were dealt with unmercifully.

AKBAR'S SUCCESSORS

Salim took the title of Jahangir and enjoyed a reign of twenty-two years, despite an inauspicious beginning with the revolt of his oldest son Khusrau. Jahangir was a less indulgent father than Akbar had been, and, after defeating Khusrau, had him blinded and kept in prison until he died in 1622. Moreover, because Khusrau had sought support from the Punjab sect of Sikhs and received the blessings of their spiritual head, the fifth Sikh Guru, Arjun, Jahangir had Arjun killed.

Sikhism is yet another Indian religion, like Buddhism and Jainism, developed partly from and partly in reaction to the evolving vedic tradition. It was founded by Guru Nanak in the religious revival of the fifteenth and sixteenth centuries. He preached a doctrine of universal toleration and seeking what was good and in common in all religion, and recruited followers among Hindus and Muslims. Sikhism was originally a peaceable and non-sectarian faith, opposed to caste and excessive asceticism, again like Buddhism, and also congenial to secular life.

When Nanak died, he nominated one of his disciples to succeed him, passing over his sons. Soon, however, the leadership became hereditary. Akbar was so impressed by the third Guru that he gave him a piece of land in Amritsar, on which the Golden Temple, the world headquarters of Sikhism, was built. The fifth Guru, Arjun, compiled the *Adi Granth*, the first Sikh sacred scripture, and put the sect on a secure financial basis by instituting a system of compulsory 'spiritual tribute' or tithes. His execution initiated a period of prolonged conflict with the Mughals. Arjun's son and heir began to organize a Sikh army; his successors increased the sect's militarization. The tenth and last Guru created a military fraternity and introduced the practices by which Sikh men are still distinguished: never cutting the hair or beard, wearing a turban and carrying a comb and a dagger.

Apart from his hostility to the Sikhs, Jahangir's was a reign of consolidation; in most matters he followed Akbar's tolerant religious policy. Akbar's order of imperial discipleship continued to bind selected nobles of the kingdom to the imperial family with a special, personal tie, and Jahangir maintained his father's reverence for certain mystical Sufis, exemplified by Sheikh Mu'inuddin Chishti, before whose tomb he prayed and won relief from 'fever and headache'.

Jahangir faithfully preserved his father's legacy of dedicating the Mughal kingdom to conquest and territorial expansion. Campaigns were launched against the forest peoples of Assam on the eastern frontier and against independent rajas in the Himalayan foothills from Kashmir to Bengal. He issued a challenge to the hegemony claimed by the Safavid rulers of Persia over Afghanistan, especially Kabul, Peshawar and Qandahar, which were important in the central Asian trade system of which northern India was part. Finally, a Mughal army was despatched to end the independent sultanates of the Deccan.

This last gave rise to an imperial crisis. After Jahangir's able son Khurram completed a brilliant conquest against the combined forces of the sultans of

Ahmednagar, Bijapur and Golconda, he too turned against his father. This was in 1622, and, as before, the uprising exacerbated court and army factionalism. Khurram's bid failed, but Jahangir forgave him on condition that the prince remain in the Deccan, far from the imperial court in Agra and its political temptations, and he had also to leave two of his sons as hostages for his good behaviour. Jahangir's death, late in 1627, was a signal for a last paroxysm of fighting among his sons and their supporters. These fratricidal conflicts were carried out with ruthlessness, and Khurram proved the most ruthless of all. He was crowned at Agra and his regnal name, Shah Jahan (originally given to him as a princely title), was read at the Jama Masjid there in January 1628.

An account of the early and middle years of Shah Jahan's reign, the *Padshah Nama* of 1647, is our main source of information on the growth of the imperial regime between the time of Akbar and that of his grandson. In the middle of Shah Jahan's reign, the Mughal imperial elite formed by Akbar as an instrument of his rule was composed as follows: the highest ranks consisted of 73 mansabdars, all Muslims (including four princes of the house), who commanded a total of 102,000 heavy cavalrymen; and 443 intermediate mansabdars, 80 per cent of whom were Muslims, including 126 Iranis, 103 Turanis, 26 Afghans and 65 Indian Muslims. The remaining 20 per cent were made up of 73 Rajput and 10 Maratha mansabdars.

Shah Jahan maintained an aggressive military pressure along the interior frontiers of the empire, as his predecessors had, but his lasting fame was not as a soldier. His artistic and architectural monuments have more than eclipsed his military exploits, beginning with the jewel-encrusted Peacock Throne and culminating in the Taj Mahal which entombed his beloved wife Mumtaz Mahal. His building programme was capped by the ambitious new capital in Delhi named for himself, Shahjahanabad. Here he erected a new fortress-palace, again in red stone, and nearby an enormous mosque, the Jama Masjid. All were surrounded by canals and traversed by broad avenues along which were the great mansions of his courtiers.

THE WARS OF THE MUGHAL SUCCESSION

Shahjahanabad was begun in 1639, at the crest of his reign. In 1657, an illness of the emperor's was a signal for his sons to open their campaigns for the succession. The empire was convulsed in a violent war among his four capable sons, a humiliating struggle for his authority while he was still alive. Closest to the emperor and to the throne was Dara Shukoh, an experienced soldier and administrator whom the seasoned army and bureaucratic elements favoured as most likely to continue Akbar's arrangements and his religious eclecticism. Dara Shukoh was a practising Sufi and an adept in Hindu theology, to whose mystical pantheism he was attracted; he even translated a number of the Upanishads into Persian. In his translations, composed around 1657, he wrote about himself as a religious mendicant and his work in the following way:

Plate 16 Dara Shukoh attending a debate. Drawing with touches of colour, *c.*1650 (IOL J. 4. 3; neg. no. B 4879, by permission of the British Library).

Muhammad Dara Shikoh in the year 1050 after Hijra [1640] went to Kashmir, the resemblance of paradise, and by the grace of God . . . he there obtained the auspicious opportunity of meeting the most perfect of sages, the flower of the gnostics [mystics] . . . Mullah Shah . . .

And whereas, he [Dara Shukoh] was impressed with a longing to behold the gnostics of every sect, and to hear the lofty expressions of monotheism, and had cast his eyes on many books of mysticism and had written a number of treatises thereon, and as the thirst of investigation for unity, which is a boundless ocean, became every moment increased, subtle doubts came into his mind for which he had no possibility of solution, except by the word of the Lord . . . And whereas the holy Qur'an is mostly allegorical, and at the present day, persons thoroughly conversant with the subtleties thereof are very rare, he became desirous of bringing in view all of the heavenly books, for the very words of God themselves are their own commentary . . . He had, therefore, cast his eyes on the Book of Moses, the Gospels, the Psalms and other scriptures, but the explanation of monotheism in them was compendious and enigmatical, and from the slovenly translations . . . their purport was not intelligible.

Thereafter he considered, as to why the discussion about monotheism is so conspicuous in India, and why Indian theologians and mystics of the ancient school do not disavow the Unity of God nor do they find any fault with the unitarians . . .

And the *summum bonum* of these four books [the four vedas], which contain all of the secrets of the Path and the contemplative exercises of pure monotheism, are called the *Upanekhats* [Upanishads] . . . And whereas this unsolicitous seeker after the Truth had in view the principle of the fundamental unity of the personality and not Arabic, Syriac, Hebrew and Sanskrit languages, he wanted to make without any worldly motive, in a clear style, an exact and literal translation of the *Upanekhat* into Persian . . . Thereby he also wanted to solve the mystery which underlies their efforts to conceal it from the Muslims.

And as at this period the city of Banares, which is the center of the sciences of this community, was in certain relations with this seeker of the Truth, he assembled together the pandits [Hindu scholars] and the sannyasis [Hindu ascetics], who were the most learned of the time and proficient in the *Upanekhat* . . . in the year 1067 after Hijra; and thus every difficulty and every sublime topic which he had desired or thought and had looked for and not found, he obtained.[5]

To his chief competitor, Aurangzeb, such liberal and syncretic views were anathema. An able soldier like Dara Shukoh, he was also a Muslim of great zeal. Around him was a powerful group of nobles and imperial soldiers, supported by Islamic theologians who urged a shift in state ideology in line with the injunctions of shariah and against previously tolerated pantheistic mysticism. The two other brothers, Murad and Shuja, and their supporters were ultimately caught in the manoeuvres of their elders, as were the Deccan sultans of Bijapur and Golconda.

Aurangzeb, who had been entrusted by Shah Jahan with advancing Mughal interests in the Deccan, demonstrated his enthusiasm for the task. He proposed that Golconda, with its flourishing international trade and its diamond mines, should be annexed to provide fresh resources for Mughal projects and to extend Mughal rule, a proposal to which his father objected. Shah Jahan was well disposed towards Abdullah Qutb Shah, the sultan of Golconda, the sultan having offered him protection during his revolt against Jahangir. Aurangzeb nevertheless went ahead with his plan, and enlisted a powerful ally in the person of the general Mohammad Sayyid Mir Jumla, a Persian adventurer and former diamond merchant. Together they concocted a plan for seizing power and executed it successfully in 1655 – only to be repudiated by

Shah Jahan at the urging of Dara Shukoh and forced to reinstate Qutb Shah. Shortly afterwards, Shah Jahan made Mir Jumla his chief minister in recognition of his talents, and soon agreed that the other large Deccan sultanate – Bijapur – should be conquered and incorporated into Mughal domains. In a campaign directed by Aurangzeb, Mir Jumla seized Bijapur in 1657, at the same moment that Shah Jahan was stricken and a war of succession commenced.

The first victim was Aurangzeb's brother Shuja, whose claim was supported by Mughal officials in Bengal, where he was governor. Shuja's army was met and defeated by Dara Shukoh as he advanced upon Agra. Another younger son of Shah Jahan, Murad, serving in Gujarat, also proclaimed himself emperor, seized the imperial treasure from the port of Surat and marched northward, where he joined his army with that of Aurangzeb, which was moving out of Bijapur; together they engaged and defeated an imperial army under the Rajput general Jaswant Singh Rathor which was loyal to the still living Shah Jahan. At Agra, Aurangzeb and Murad defeated Dara Shukoh, who fled Delhi to rally further support, leaving Agra and his father to his brothers. Shah Jahan surrendered in June 1658. Shortly after, Aurangzeb imprisoned him and assumed the throne under the title of Alamgir, 'seizer of the world'. The final stage of the war for the Peacock Throne went on for another year before Dara Shukoh was captured and killed in August 1659.

Aurangzeb's reign equalled that of Akbar in duration – from 1658 to 1707 – and possibly in significance for the Timurid house as well. He too sought a new ideological basis for the Mughal kingdom and lost no time in applying a different sort of Islam to fortify his rule. That was no easy task, since his incarceration of Shah Jahan explicitly violated the shariah as well as the sensibilities of many Mughal grandees and ordinary people. To counter criticism, Aurangzeb made a large gift to the authorities at Mecca, the acceptance of which was deemed to remove the opprobrium of his offence to sacred law.

Aurangzeb's deep religiosity was well known, as was his sense that the continuity of the Mughal state depended on the reassertion of a commitment to Islam, which set apart the Mughal regime from such contenders as the still powerful Rajputs in the north and the rising Marathas in the south. The state must be based on the shariah, and to that end he commissioned a group of jurists to draft a set of written opinions that would provide consistent guidance to Muslim judges on matters where the shariah was contradictory.

As to the religion of the vast majority of his subjects, he repudiated the tolerance of Akbar. Edicts were issued throughout the 1660s giving substance to the new religious ideology: construction of temples was severely restricted and in a few cases recently built shrines were destroyed; new taxes were imposed on temple pilgrimage and Hindu merchants, who paid twice the rate of Muslims; the jizya upon tolerated non-believers, dhimmis, was reimposed in 1679; and steps were taken to increase the proportion of Muslims in state employment.

SOCIAL AND ECONOMIC CONDITIONS
UNDER AURANGZEB

Despite his zeal for restructuring the benefits allowed to non-Muslims according to the demands of the ulema, Aurangzeb did not press for universal conversion. Such a policy would have generated fear and hostility among the mass of peasantry upon whose labours the state depended as much in 1690 as it had a century before, when Akbar was installing the Mughal institutions, and would threaten state revenues besides. Peasant flight was a serious practical concern and has been suggested as one of the reasons for the decline of the Mughals. Aurangzeb, like Shah Jahan, insisted that peasants were to be treated with consideration: if a poor farmer needed a plough, it should be provided by the zamindars; and if a farmer opened forested land to cultivation, he should be given a mark of honour such as a sash or turban. If any peasant household took flight, the reasons were to be ascertained and the causes removed. Behind this solicitude was an understanding that, given the relative plenitude of cultivable land, the beneficiaries of peasant flight would be other tax-receiving rulers.

In one place, an eastwardly passing political frontier of Mughal authority joined an agrarian frontier and a religious one, which was largely mediated through Sufi institutions, to open the prospect of settlement of a vast deltaic region formed by the shifting courses of the Ganges and Brahmaputra rivers in Bengal. Virgin forests were felled and the flood plain was planted with rice. The Mughal state actively supported the planting of Islamic institutions as well, and there, in eastern Bengal during the seventeenth century, hundreds of small rural mosques and saint-shrines provided the focus for agrarian development and the mass conversion of the peasantry. The Mughals granted land rights to both Hindu and Muslim groups, just as, some centuries before in Europe, Benedictine and Cistercian friars had been encouraged to open forested lands to the plough and reap the benefits as landlords.

In Bengal, it was principally Sufi masters who were attracted to the frontier, where neither state institutions nor powerful social ones – such as ancient landed castes – had any presence. There the *mullah*, the religious leader, became the authority in a locality which might consist of a few hundred households. These households were bound together as communities in a confessional body: by their celebration of the lifecycle rites of circumcision, marriage and mourning, and by participation in the festivals of the Islamic calendar and regular prayer at the congregational mosques they built. Land continued to be held by the descendants of the founding mullahs, or *pirs*, as they were respectfully called. The frontier conditions in Bengal during the seventeenth century helped it to become one of the two zones of dense Muslim occupation and conversion in the subcontinent, the other being the Punjab.

In the Punjab, meanwhile, relations with Sikhs worsened. Originally a quietistic sect whose teachings repudiated caste hierarchies, privilege and vested sect leaders, the Sikhs became militant in opposition to their Muslim oppressors. Under Aurangzeb the lash of oppression quickened: the Sikh guru

Tegh Bahadur was executed and new shrines (*gurdwara*) were prohibited. At the same time, the long-standing independence of Rajputs from interference in their successions was reversed and their access to high mansab posts curtailed.

FACTORS IN THE DECLINE OF THE MUGHAL STATE

Generations of Indian historians nurtured upon nationalist sentiments of Hindu–Muslim unity have considered these steps a form of political suicide, and there is little doubt that the effects of these enactments by Aurangzeb exacerbated tensions. However, there were other processes that did more to undermine the polity than religious bigotry. War took a heavy toll. The Timurid state had constantly expanded from the territory won by Babur, which reached from the Punjab in the west to the border with Bengal. Akbar added the Himalayan terai on the northern frontier; Rajasthan, Gujarat, Malwa and the northernmost Deccan sultanates (Berar and Khandesh) were added to the south and west and Bengal and Orissa in the east. Under Aurangzeb, the two remaining sultanates of Bijapur and Golconda fell, opening the entire southern peninsula to the Mughals. The successful use of firearms and the sheer size of their armies explains much of their success over other states until well into the seventeenth century. But the military lessons of the Mughals were learned, and the Rajputs and Marathas who served in their successful forces became adept in their methods.

As important as the spread of military capabilities in weakening the Mughal state was the crystallization of a new class of rural and urban families, a gentry, which relied less upon state employment and office than upon the property it had accumulated and local political domination through wealth and influence over local administrative officials. When gentry interests could no longer be sustained by the Mughals or, later, by the Marathas, and were even threatened by their regimes, gentry allegiance shifted to those who stood ready to protect property: Europeans. The shift was gradual and involved few threats to the existing substructure of local community life; at the level of the north Indian parganas, the rise of new rural and urban classes did not destroy as much as it modified a rural order which had gradually emerged beginning in the sixteenth century. Nevertheless, by the eighteenth century the gentry stood ready to protect its interests and those of rural peoples against the pressures of the state.

Given his personal beliefs, this situation was enough to have persuaded a vigorous and religious ruler like Aurangzeb to revitalize Mughal state ideology. An immediate effect of Aurangzeb's turn to state orthodoxy was austerity. Monumental and dramatic building programmes such as those sponsored by Akbar and Shah Jahan were now eschewed; support even for court musicians and painters who were then developing new mixed or Hindustani forms of expression all but ceased; wine and opium were banned. Aurangzeb's reformulations of the legal principles to be followed to defend Islam and Muslim society took the form of extensively codified norms collected as the *Fatawa-i-Alamgiri*. These instructions to Islamic judges were an indication of how far the ulema had retrieved the prominent place they had lost during Akbar's time.

Islamic orthodoxy was also involved in the alienation of the Rajputs upon whose loyalty and soldiers the Timurid house had depended from nearly the beginning. The Rajputs were incensed by the restoration of the jizya and other invidiously assessed taxes; more particularly, they suffered a decline in military employment and were stung by an unprecedented interference in Rajput-ruled polities. Suspicions were aroused when, in 1679, Aurangzeb delayed in approving the succession to the Marwar throne after the death of the famous general Maharaja Jaswant Singh. The right of the Mughal overlords to consent to Rajput successions had long before become perfunctory, and now the Marwar Rajputs rose in armed revolt. The revolt of Aurangzeb's son, Muhammad Akbar, and his alliance with some disaffected Rajputs, who saw the prince as a possible rallying focus, only complicated matters. The revolts were short-lived, but that of the prince highlighted yet another sort of problem, the growing menace of the Maratha kingdom, to which the prince in defeat turned for refuge.

ENTER THE MARATHAS

The Marathas had been a group of pastoralists and peasants of western India who had begun to form a state during the middle of the seventeenth century. Over a set of local chieftains who controlled the high and dry plateau lands under the hegemony of the Deccani sultans, a Maratha kingship was established by Shivaji Bhonsle, whose career was a colourful one even in his own bloody time. He was said to have engaged in Mafia-style diplomacy by going to negotiations with a Mughal general in concealed armour; when the bargaining bogged down, or the general tried to stab him, he disembowelled him with his steel-clawed gloves.

The Bhonsles were a chiefly household, similar to others that had acquired military experience in the service of the sultans of Ahmadnagar and Bijapur. Through this service they obtained superior land rights from both sultanates. In the 1650s, Shivaji began to build royal power. He reduced the ancient autonomy enjoyed by lesser Maratha chiefs in his own territory around Pune and thus added substantially to his patrimony. New territories were seized which gave him command of hill fortresses, from which he drove the soldiers of Bijapur and replaced them with his own commanders. Finally, he pounced upon the trade-rich sea coast below his domain on the high plateau.

These moves and the defeat of a Bijapur punitive expedition sent against him raised the concerns of Mughal officials, who were newly arrived in that part of the Deccan. When they took Pune to punish Shivaji for violating their protection of Bijapur, he brashly retook it and publicly humiliated the Mughal commander and his family. This was followed by an even more audacious action. In 1664 his soldiers plundered Surat, the major Mughal port on the Arabian Sea, removing a large treasure and holding Mecca-bound pilgrims to ransom.

Aurangzeb was stung into action. As the Rajputs remained important to Mughal rule, an army under the command of a Rajput general was ordered to destroy Shivaji and annex Bijapur. Shivaji finally sought peace, yielded the fortresses he had seized and accepted service as a mansabdar in the Mughal conquest of Bijapur that was to follow. He also consented to visit the imperial court at Agra, only to suffer humiliations there which persuaded him to escape, allegedly by hiding in a basket.

In 1666, he was again leading his Maratha soldiers in new conquests. Aurangzeb, determined to limit Maratha interference in his Deccan plans, attempted to patch up their differences, but these efforts failed and, in 1670, Shivaji again pillaged Surat and fought off another Mughal army. He followed this in 1674 by declaring himself an independent and expressly dharmic king, whose rule was to be in accordance with medieval dharmashastras. In the few years left to him, Shivaji sought to assure the continuity of his royal house by taming his turbulent son Shambuji and by attempting to persuade Aurangzeb to restore the wise and tolerant provisions of earlier Mughals; for example, by rescinding the jizya. When he died in 1680, Shivaji was succeeded by his son.

The rebellious Mughal prince, Muhammad Akbar, tested Maratha protection when he proclaimed himself emperor in 1681. Since he had obtained Shambuji's assent to his attempted usurpation, his move involved a resumption of warfare between Marathas and Mughals. Not simply the revolt of another royal son, dangerous as that was, Prince Akbar's action drew wide support from among Mughal officers who rejected Aurangzeb's bigotry and the alienation of most of his subjects, and who were worried about turning political allies such as the Rajputs into enemies. The dangers of a formidable anti-Mughal alliance forming around Prince Akbar seemed real enough, given the disaffected sultans of Golconda and Bijapur and the ever troublesome Marathas. Such a coalition could easily challenge Mughal authority in the Deccan and move northward into the imperial heartland, where other potential allies could be found, such as the Marwar and Mewar Rajputs.

Mansabdars with experience of the Marathas both as military allies and as enemies had learned that their light cavalry and guerrilla tactics were proof against the Mughal combination of massive if cumbersome military campaigns and diplomacy that had previously been so successful. The Marathas actually thrived on plundering Mughal armies and seemed also to have become confident about holding their own against Mughal diplomacy. Therefore, many Mughal grandees would have preferred to compromise with imperial enemies in the Deccan and return to their homes in the north. But Aurangzeb was implacable. His resolve was tested when, in 1681, Shivaji's son and successor led a Maratha army into Mughal territory, seized the commercial centre of Bahadurpur in Berar, plundered its wealth and humiliated the conquered Muslims in an orgy of rape. At this affront, Aurangzeb concluded a hasty peace with the Mewar Rajputs and led an army into the Deccan.

THE LAST ACT OF THE MUGHALS

The first steps taken by the emperor were against the sultanates of Bijapur and Golconda; both were annexed and thereby denied as Muslim allies to his rebellious son Akbar, still in the protection of the Marathas. His attack upon the sultanates could be justified to Muslim critics, if that were necessary, on the grounds that the ulema of these territories had appealed for protection from Maratha incursions and also that the Shi'a sultans of the two kingdoms had made common cause with these same infidels. Bijapur fortress was taken in 1685 after a siege of a year, and Mughal administrative institutions were installed. A governor, financial officer and military commander were appointed and all forts placed under trusted Mughal officers. The sultanate of Golconda took somewhat longer to subdue; its annexation was not proclaimed until 1687, after the strong Golconda fortress was compromised by the treachery of some of its defenders.

These tasks accomplished, Aurangzeb sent an army to find and punish Shambuji for his depredations in Khandesh. The Maratha king was discovered and captured in 1688 and brought to Aurangzeb for punishment, which was to be hacked to death and fed to dogs. Moreover, his son and heir was captured and taken to the Mughal court. Seeing his vital supporters thus sundered, Aurangzeb's son Akbar fled to the asylum of Safavid Persia. Thus, in 1689 Aurangzeb appeared to have accomplished all that was necessary in the Deccan. His vast empire was increased by two hundred thousand square miles and its authority pressed far into Tamil country in the south; four new provinces added one-quarter to the size of his kingdom and their revenues promised to augment its wealth by the same proportion, especially from the famous diamond mines of Golconda, which became an imperial monopoly.

But peace was not to be Aurangzeb's lot. Shambuji's death did not render the Marathas tractable because his younger brother Rajaram was now crowned and renewed resistance to the Mughals. The new challenge was launched in the middle of Tamil country, from the fortress of Jinji where Rajaram had found refuge after escaping his besieged capital at Raigarh. For many long, weary years the emperor was to track bands of Maratha soldiers across the Tamil country and Maharashtra; in the process his soldiers took hundreds of Maratha hill fortresses by storm or by bribery. Yet, even after the death of the inveterate escapist Rajaram in 1700, resistance continued under the leadership of his widow, Tara Bai.

On the eve of his death in 1707, Aurangzeb had to concede that the Marathas continued to hold many fortified places and had managed to undermine the imperial campaign in other ways. It became evident that secret understandings between the Marathas and local Mughal officials secured the coexistence of sovereignty of both contenders in many parts of peninsular India, an accommodation based upon the success of Maratha military tactics.

Avoiding set battles with the heavy cavalry and cannons of the Mughal armies, Maratha bands harassed and plundered them everywhere. In the eastern parts of the Deccan, the Mughals fared somewhat better. The Telugu-speaking locality headmen and accountants in what had been Golconda cooperated with them, and revenue flowed regularly into the Mughal treasury. In the west, Maratha leaders of rural communities and small towns continued to view the Bhonsle successors of Shivaji as the legitimate kings of their land. Temporary concessions might be arranged with Mughal commanders willing to accept less than full dominion, but in the end the Marathas insisted on being ruled by Shivaji's descendants.

Open warfare between Mughals and Marathas dragged on, owing to the resourcefulness of the Marathas in coping with Mughal pressures. In addition to entering into understandings with local Mughal officials so as to avoid direct confrontations, which the latter especially sought to avoid, Maratha chiefs collected tributary payments to sustain their military forces. One of these was the *chauth*, or quarter of the collected revenue supposedly owed to local lords in western India as payment for the protection they were deemed to provide; another was a 10 per cent share of the payment that superior local administrators were owed as regional headmen, or *sardeshmukhi*. In effect, the Marathas imposed a dual government over much of the Deccan, conceding formal sovereignty to the Mughals in fortified towns, but maintaining control over rural communities and taking from them about a third of the revenues collected.

The greatest strength of the Marathas continued to be the Bhonsle royal family. In the face of all efforts by Aurangzeb to extirpate them, they endured. Tara Bai, Rajaram's widow, acting as regent for an infant son, successfully negotiated with the Mughals to preserve Bhonsle authority and the very existence of the Bhonsle monarchy, while simultaneously maintaining military pressure against Mughal centres. In 1702, she launched an army of 50,000 horsemen and infantry against the former Golconda kingdom, now called Hyderabad. The capital was plundered, as was the major nearby port on which the Mughals depended, Machilipatnam (Masulipatnam); trade there was disrupted for years. However, after Aurangzeb's death, Shambuji's son Shahu, who had been taken hostage, was released in order to set the cat among the pigeons in the Maratha capital. This was successful, and a civil war between the followers of Shahu and those of Tara Bai ensued, from which Shahu eventually emerged victorious; but for a while the Marathas were distracted from their campaign against the faltering Mughal empire.

THE DECLINE OF MUGHAL MORALE

Aurangzeb's obsession with the Deccan bled resources of treasure and men, but just as importantly, it took another kind of toll that may have been more debilitating, in the loss of confidence and commitment within the imperial military elite. The elan of its fighters had been a fundamental strength of the regime created by Akbar. During the late seventeenth century, however, it was observed that military commanders no longer maintained the complement of fighters and horses stipulated by their rank, and for which they were nominally awarded income. This was at once a breakdown in the former inspection of armed contingents and the systematic diversion of military funds to private ends. Many officers from northern territories resented the favour shown by Aurangzeb to the new mansabdars and commanders recruited from the defeated sultanates as a diplomatic gesture. Indeed, the Deccani nobles soon constituted nearly half of the highest ranking officials. Other Mughal officials were increasingly distressed about the condition of their own jagirs and lands far away in the north.

On the other hand, officials stationed in the Deccan complained of being unable to maintain themselves on the slender incomes from lands they had been granted as jagirs in lieu of salaries. The inadequacy of their entitlements was a result of the retention by the imperial regime of a substantial proportion of conquered lands, which were needed to replenish the central treasury and meet the burgeoning costs of the Deccan wars. Consequently, both old and new officials in the Deccan tended to be less firmly bound to the Mughal regime than their counterparts in the north had been from the time of Akbar.

Even while Aurangzeb lived, the loftiest nobles of the Mughal regime began to urge compromise with the Marathas and an end to warfare. Much had been neglected in the north as a result of the Deccan wars: revenues and civil order were diminishing. Alone among the older territories of the Mughals, Bengal continued to remit a reliable treasure to Agra. Mughal officials in Bengal were held in special esteem by Aurangzeb, who freed them to operate in their own interests as long as the stream of revenue continued to flow up the Ganges.

An example of the growing autonomy of even loyal Bengal officials is offered by the career of Murshid Quli Khan, who served as a *diwan*, or head of revenue administration. He is said to have begun life as a poor brahman and been purchased as a slave by a Mughal official, reared in his household and trained for financial office. While still young, he showed such promise that Aurangzeb despatched him to Bengal, when revenues from there seemed to falter in 1701. He succeeded in restoring them by a combination of administrative efficiency and ruthless punishment of defaulters. For this service he was rewarded with promotion to the governorship by Aurangzeb's successors and permitted nearly autonomous control of Bengal, which lasted for twenty years, with some interruptions, until long after Aurangzeb's death, and included moving the capital from Dacca to 'Murshidabad'.

Elsewhere in the north, Mughal authority was openly contested. A revolt among the chieftains of the Jat pastoralists and peasants south of the imperial capital of Agra posed a dangerous challenge. The Jats were strategically placed to intercept and plunder the bullock trains of treasure and trade passing into the Gangetic basin from the Deccan, and harried them until that route was abandoned. Aurangzeb sent an army to open the road and was humiliated when it was set upon and defeated and, adding insult to injury, the Jats looted the tomb of Akbar near Agra. His subsequent campaigns against the Jats attracted allies to the rebels from alienated Rajput houses now determined to oppose the restoration of imperial control in the very heart of Mughal territory. At this critical juncture, in early 1707, Aurangzeb died in the Deccan, a worn out man of eighty-nine.

Once again this was the signal for a contest among the imperial sons. Three of these remained alive. The winner this time was Muazzam, who defeated

Plate 17 The emperor Aurangzeb in old age. Mughal painting, *c.*1700 (IOL J. 2. 2.; neg. no. B 3140, by permission of the British Library).

and killed his brothers Azam and Kam Bakhsh and assumed the throne with the title of Bahadur Shah. However, he was sixty-three at the time and destined to live only another five years. The empire was in crisis, politically, administratively and financially, and there was little he could do. Facing him were the problems of neglect owing to the long wars in the Deccan, exacerbated by the Jat and Rajput uprisings. Soon to be added was the rebellion of the Sikhs immediately to the north of the Agra–Delhi axis of Mughal power, while in the Deccan Maratha armies had steadily grown and changed by adopting more advanced weapons and tactics.

The Sikhs rose under the leadership of a charismatic pretender, who had assumed political if not spiritual leadership after the assassination of the tenth and last Guru. He succeeded in winning the allegiance and religious affiliation of the Jats, who were then in the process of transforming themselves from pastoralists into sedentary farmers. They sought enhanced political and social status, and Banda, the new Muslim-born Sikh leader, offered both and won widespread support throughout the Punjab. Several campaigns by Mughal armies were required before Banda was captured, and tortured to death. Organized opposition ended, but the vigour of Sikh resistance was a startling reminder of the growing military parity between imperial forces and their enemies by 1712, when Bahadur Shah's death precipitated yet another succession war, and, from then on, the pace of palace coups quickened.

MUGHAL FISCAL DECLINE

The power to govern that remained with the Mughals had become dangerously shallow. The loss of military supremacy terminated the record of victories which for a century had added new territories for exploitation and provided the means of rewarding new officials. By Aurangzeb's reign there was a clear shortage of developed lands suitable for new jagirs for soldiers and civil servants. At the same time, the losses inflicted on Mughal armies by Marathas, Sikhs and Jats, and the efficiency of the revenue system set up in Akbar's time – the zabt system of land tax assessment and collection – was diminishing. Provincial diwans and lesser financial officers resorted increasingly to the method of contracting or 'farming' revenue collection; that is, they privatized revenue collection by selling to bankers, merchants and big landlords the right to collect and transmit some agreed amount of revenue to the treasury in return for a commission and the local political powers supposedly to carry out their tasks.

Tax-farming frequently resulted in diminished tax receipts in official hands and inevitably paved the way for a new class of rural gentry to replace the influence of imperial officials in the countryside. Furthermore, Islamic functionaries holding special religious rights to lands now saw their interests better served in alliance with other local land-holders than with a distant and manifestly weakened state. The new class was perhaps the most important transforming element of all that led to the ultimate downfall of the Mughals and shaped the era that succeeded them.

Before that new historical epoch was recognized, however, a final series of political disasters befell the later Mughals. Between the time of Bahadur Shah's death in 1712 and 1720 four bitterly fought succession wars convulsed the nobility and the army, with none of the healing periods of the long reigns that had followed earlier succession wars. The famous Peacock Throne became merely a front for powerful political and military manipulators. Among the most enduring of these adventurers were two brothers called Sayyid who found service and achieved high office under Bahadur Shah. After the latter's death they made and unmade by deposition and execution no less than five emperors. Even before the deposition of the first of these, Farruksiyar, their machinations had engendered such opposition from the older nobility that they found it politic to enter an alliance with the Marathas in 1718. At a stroke, the Marathas assumed the position of protectors of the Mughal heartland. In return they were granted unfettered rule over Maharashtra as well as over the territories outside of Maharashtra where they exacted a tribute (as chauth and sardesmukhi) of over a third of all revenues collected. Such vast concessions to an old enemy brought widespread contempt upon the sore-pressed scions of the imperial family of Babur.

By 1720, a demoralized Mughal nobility began to sever links to the regime that had created and sustained them. Most began to convert their official powers into personal benefits and to contest what fictionally remained of imperial authority. Latent divisions within the elite shaped opposition to the weakened centre, as, for example, when an early imperial deserter, the central Asian amir Nizam-ul-Mulk, rallied other Turanian and Iranian amirs and managed to defeat the Sayyids in 1720, even though the latter had Maratha support. This military success set the stage for the establishment of a quasi-independent kingdom for Nizam-ul-Mulk in Hyderabad in 1724.

Dismemberment proceeded in the heart of the empire. The governor of the Punjab had little contact with and sent less tribute to Delhi after 1713; he passed his rich territory as a virtually independent state to his son in 1726. Awadh, in the central and eastern Ganges plain, saw its governor begin to consolidate his personal control by removing the mansabdars from their jagirs if they resisted his power; his rupture with the centre was confirmed when he repulsed an army from Delhi in 1726.

Now Rajput houses began to encroach upon neighbouring Mughal tracts, and Afghan chiefs around Delhi carved out an independent principality called Rohilkhand Farrukhabad in 1728, and then began expanding southward to challenge Jat control. Finally, in Bengal, Murshid Quli Khan, after long serving his masters in Agra with Bengal's rich tribute, made a bid to create a near-independent kingdom for himself, which he passed to his son-in-law in 1727.

Behind the disintegration of the Mughal empire during the first quarter of the eighteenth century loomed the Maratha state. It attained its great power under Balaji Viswanath, the first of the Maratha 'Chief Ministers' (*peshwa*).

THE MARATHA MOMENT

The Marathas had emerged from among the dominant peasant clans living in the western Indian territory where the Marathi language was spoken. During the sixteenth century the sultans of Bijapur and Ahmadnagar had recruited them to serve as light cavalry and balance the political ambitions of the

Muslim soldiers in their employ. Other Maharashtrians to benefit from the equal opportunity policies of the Muslim overlords were brahmans, who were divided into those who lived on the dry plateau above the sea and called Deshastas, and those from the lowlands along the Arabian Sea, the Konkan region, who were called Chitpavans. Though all were Marathi-speakers, they distinguished their statuses carefully from the peasant Marathas. The brahmans derived their high standing from administrative service to Muslim regimes and also from their participation in the bhakti or devotional cults of Maharashtra.

In addition to supplying soldiers and administrators to neighbouring states, Maharashtra attracted economic interest. Cotton was spun, cultivated and woven, contributing a valuable commodity to the trade of the port of Surat. A thriving inter-regional commerce connected the high plateau and the littoral. From the littoral came a variety of useful coconut products, fish, salt, timber and fruit, which were exchanged for upland products, sugar cane, cotton, tobacco and pulses, which complemented the rice diet of the coast.

A final feature of sixteenth- and seventeenth-century Maharashtra which helps to explain some of the synergistic expansionism of the eighteenth century was the structure of local authority. A few towns and cites showed influences from and maintained contact with the wider Deccan region and the Arabian Sea coast outside of Maharashtra – Ahmadnagar, Aurangabad, Nagpur, Nasik and Burhanpur – but the politics of the region were those of rural chiefs called *deshmukh* (literally, 'head of the land or place').

The territorial sway of the deshmukhs extended over between twenty and 100 villages, each of which had a powerful headman (*patil*), assisted by a keeper of records (*kulkarni*). Headmen were inevitably drawn from the Maratha peasant castes, while village accountants were almost always brahmans. In the absence of a powerful state apparatus within the country, these local community-level officials were the government. The role of external authorities such as the Deccan sultans, or, later, occasionally the Mughals, was minimal; all of them took an irregular share of the taxes collected from agriculture and trade and conferred legitimating documents of investiture, or revenue collection contracts, upon deshmukhs, patils and kulkarnis. A more elevated deshmukh office was that of *sardeshmukhi*, head of deshmukhs, recognized by the Mughals, as was that of chief accountant (*deshkulkarni*). The ambiguity of such offices was revealed in a seventeenth-century Marathi political treatise, the *Ajnapatra*:

> the deshmukhs and deshkulkarnis, the patils et cetera, they may be called 'office-holders', but this is only a term of convention. They are in fact small but self-sufficient chiefs. They are not strong on their own, but they succeed in keeping up their power by allying themselves with the 'lord of all land' [i.e. the king]. Yet it must not be thought that their interests coincide with that of the latter. These people are in reality the *co-sharers* (*dayada*) of the kingdom.[6]

The writer was a minister of the Maratha king Shivaji, who, like other rulers of the seventeenth century, sought greater control over the autonomous countryside. The word 'dayada' aptly characterizes the lightness with which the state bore down upon Marathi-speakers in the seventeenth and eighteenth centuries, but the heavily localized socio-political system could be galvanized from within under vigorous leadership, which happened in Maharashtra in the early eighteenth century as Mughal power waned.

Aurangzeb's determination to stifle the political and military challenge of the Marathas had begun with the intention of punishing Shivaji's successor Shambuji for offering shelter to the rebel prince Akbar. Subsequently the emperor found other reasons to try to rid the Deccan of Maratha predations, and he dedicated the Mughal house to this ultimately vain pursuit. Shambuji faced the onslaught with skill and cunning, though in the end he was captured and executed. At the same time he found himself threatened by the deshmukhs who resented his royal pretensions; some of them even approached Aurangzeb, offering to join with Mughals against Shambuji providing they were adequately rewarded. In return for serving the Mughals, they wanted confirmation that all the special rights their families had accumulated would remain hereditary, and some of them were granted valuable jagirs by the wily emperor. Shambuji dealt with their treason by burning their villages, not sparing some who were close to his own family by marriage.

Shambuji's successors faced the same wavering loyalty from deshmukh families. Switching between Mughal and Maratha service regularly occurred, each change of employment an occasion for a deshmukh to add to his family property and entitlements. In return, when a deshmukh defected he took with him the militia he commanded. By the time of Shambuji's grandson King Shahu – a name meaning 'honest', and originally a soubriquet accorded by Aurangzeb to contrast his character with that of Shivaji – who ruled from 1708 to 1749, Maratha fighting bands could combine in formidable armies which regularly raided and pillaged Mughal tracts along the northern frontier. Soon they were reaching towards Delhi itself, as well as continuing to prey upon parts of Karnataka and the Tamil country.

THE NEW ECONOMIC AND SOCIAL OPPORTUNITIES UNDER THE MARATHAS

Warfare opened opportunities for talented commanders among deshmukh families, but there were also increased opportunities for brahmans, and they too contributed to the vigorous expansion of Maratha power early in the eighteenth century. Notable among them was the ministerial lineage of Chitpavans, who held the office of peshwa under king Shahu and his successors.

Originating modestly as that of keeper of records, under the Peshwa Balaji Viswanath, the office was transformed into that of prime minister of the kingdom, and hereditary to boot. Viswanath's son Bajirao held the post from 1720 to 1740 and Bajirao's son Balaji Bajirao from then to 1761. Under the peshwas a new elite formed consisting partly of old deshmukh families to which were added other, self-made, men, leaders of military bands who might have held pedigrees no greater than that of village headman. New men and households displaced older families that failed to meet the standards of rapine and cunning of the new era politics in an emergent Maratha state.

Given the persistent independence and fickle affiliation of the chiefly deshmukhs and warrior leaders among the Marathas, such solidity as the Maratha state possessed must be attributed to the personalities of Shahu and his ministers, the peshwas. Consolidation of royal power during the first half of the eighteenth century was tenuously achieved, or bought, through the conferral of royal entitlements upon those who served Shahu or the peshwa. These were non-hereditary grants of privilege and property, supposedly conditional on state service. However, the fighting elite who were the usual recipients of such honours assiduously converted the conditionality of the grants into community-backed, hereditary privileges called *watan*, a term signifying the 'home' and the core rights of a family upon which wealth and status depended. Nevertheless, during Shahu's forty-year reign, even while a large set of landed households profited from state employment, a stronger, more centralized, state structure began to take form, thanks to the ageing king and his succession of ministers.

During most of Shahu's reign, there was a steady increase in the territory under Maratha sway, from which tribute was extracted; after his death in 1749, and until 1761, these conquests were at first continued under the peshwa Balaji Bajirao. Shahu's perspicacious choice of the twenty year old Bajirao to follow his father into the office of peshwa in 1720 had defied advice, but misgivings were stilled when Bajirao outlined his plans. He had decided to launch the major Maratha thrust against the Mughals, leaving for the future the possibility of advancing the Maratha hegemony into the south and against the realm of the Nizam of Hyderabad. He also decided that he himself should assume command of this northern expedition on behalf of Shahu, so as to assure that the king alone accrued the glory and wealth of humbling the Mughals that he was sure would follow. To finance this military campaign, he judged that the treasure it would yield would pay for both the war and the subsequent administration of Gujarat and Malwa. Even Delhi itself was not ruled out as an object of conquest and source of treasure.

Bajirao was astute in his choice of commanders for these undertakings. Passing over the established elite of the deshmukhs, commands were given to new men of the Gaikwad, Holkar and Shinde families, who had been loyal to Shahu and to his father and now to himself. Enhanced armies were formed, and when they were not deployed on the peshwa's conquests they served his interests by being hired out to lesser lords in some remote conflict.

The northern adventure proceeded. Malwa and Gujarat were freed of Mughal domination by the mid-1720s, after the dispirited Mughal commanders were defeated along with troops of the Nizam who intervened on behalf of the Mughals. Now it became necessary to deal with the Nizam, and this Bajirao did; in 1728 the main force of the Nizam was trapped by Maratha horsemen in the favourable guerrilla terrain around Aurangabad and forced to agree to terms. Bajirao demanded the recognition of Shahu as the king of Maharashtra and overlord of the rest of the Deccan, from which the tribute of chauth and sardeshmukhi could be legitimately collected by Maratha officials.

The way to a resumption of the northern conquests was open and during the 1730s Maratha forces – larger than ever – ranged northward to the Gangetic valley and finally raided Delhi in 1737. A ransom was collected from the humiliated Mughal emperor, and a year later the Marathas inflicted a crushing defeat on another Mughal army. A treaty agreed at Bhopal in 1739 formally ceded Malwa – from the Narmada to the Chambal river – to the Marathas. This placed their authority some fifty miles south of Agra, and the victorious Bajirao added a large tribute of treasure for presentation to Shahu.

Having conquered this vast territory, the peshwa lost no time in consolidating Maratha rule by appointing Maratha collectors of tribute in the courts of the larger zamindars. The conquest of Malwa became a model for other conquests. Maratha rule was first established in the countryside rather than cities, and at the outset no effort was made to displace local, rural magnates, merely to collect tribute from them.

The confidence with which Bajirao extended the power of the Marathas grew not so much from their military supremacy as from the weakness of their enemies, especially the Mughals. True, the Marathas mounted ever-larger forces. In the early eighteenth century, their armies consisted of no more than 5000 horsemen and no artillery; after 1720, the operating units doubled in size but even then they were not able to match the Mughals and their other enemies in artillery, which proved a serious limitation in wars against the Nizam in the middle 1730s. Eventually, however, the Mughal failure to maintain the efficiency of their gunnery after Aurangzeb's time became evident to all during the cataclysmic invasion of India by the Iranian king Nadir Shah.

Having driven the Mughals from Afghanistan with surprising ease, Nadir Shah was emboldened to press on into the Punjab and continue on to Delhi, where he defeated a demoralized Mughal army in 1739. As a final humiliation of the once great Mughals, the city was sacked and over 20,000 of its inhabitants were killed during the pillage. A vast treasure was looted, including the Peacock Throne itself. And one element in Nadir Shah's success was his improved artillery, especially horse-mounted guns for use against the Mughal cavalry.

MARATHA MONETARY MASTERY

The Maratha overlordship in the Deccan was based less upon its superior military might than upon the qualities of the Maratha elite that grew up under the peshwas and Shahu in the years before 1740. (At the same time, the former imperial Mughal ruling class was being scattered among provincial and minor courts.) Talented and ambitious peasant Marathas found openings to fortune even as those of the older elite of deshmukh families fell, and brahmans rose with the same tide. Their scribal abilities were at a premium as conquests were followed by the establishment of civil rule. The peshwa's Chitpavan kinsmen were the special recipients of honours and office, not merely as bureaucrats, but as soldiers in the manner of Bajirao himself. Other brahmans became bankers, joining those from traditional banking groups who were being drawn into state service. Financial knowledge and institutions were mobilized to realize the prompt transmission of tribute from an increasingly extensive empire, and Bajirao adopted the policy of centralizing all fiscal functions in Pune by 1740.

The northern frontiers of the Maratha state were rapidly pushed into Rajasthan, Delhi and the Punjab; to the east, the Marathas launched raids from Nagpur against Bihar, Bengal and Orissa; and the older area of Maratha influence to the south – Karnataka and the Tamil and Telugu areas eastwards – experienced a Maratha overlordship now invigorated by its subcontinental dominance. Between 1745 and 1751 plundering expeditions were launched yearly by the Maratha chieftain Raghuji Bhonsle and vigorously opposed by Alivardi Khan in Bengal, now more or less independent of Delhi. Raghuji nevertheless forced a settlement which placed Orissa under a governor chosen by the Marathas, making it a Maratha province in effect, and in addition a very large tribute was forthcoming from Bengal. The conflict between Marathas and the Nizam continued over Karnataka, on the southeastern frontier of the Marathas, becoming a stalemate in which Karnataka was shared between both.

Periodic raiding gave way to more permanent administrative milking by the 1750s, which saw a new element added to the complex politics of the Deccan when a French-led army of mercenaries acting for the Nizam fought against Maratha soldiers and provided impressive evidence of a newer European military technology. This was based upon well drilled infantry formations backed by rapid-firing, precision-cast artillery pieces, both of which diminished the advantages previously enjoyed by Maratha light cavalry.

Further to the north, in Rajasthan, Maratha influence took another form; there territorial aggrandizement was eschewed in favour of the enforcement of a tribute system over numerous large and small lordships. A lucrative sideline of the Rajasthan policy was the hiring out of Maratha squadrons to minor chiefs who were engaged in fighting each other for some territorial advantage. In time, the Maratha tributary regime extended itself to within fifty miles of Delhi, where, in a narrow tract, the remnant of the great Mughal empire gasped its last.

PESHWA BUREAUCRACY

Malwa and Gujarat, closer to the Maratha heartland, had greater wealth than Rajasthan and were treated in a different way. A system of revenue farming was introduced to provide a reliable stream of income to the peshwa without any costly reforms of the socio-economic and political structure of local society. The key Maratha official in this system was called the *kamavisdar*; he was appointed by the peshwa and empowered to maintain a small body of soldiers to police the administrative tract for which he had purchased the right to collect revenue. A small staff of clerks and minor servants, usually brahmans, were employed to maintain the accurate revenue records demanded by the peshwa. Tax-farming contracts were auctioned annually after the revenue for a particular place was first estimated by the peshwa's civil servants, usually on the basis of previous years' yields. An aspiring tax farmer who won the kamavisdar contract was expected to have a reputation for wealth and probity; he was required to pay a portion of the whole of the anticipated revenue – one-third to one-half – either out of his own wealth or from what he could borrow from bankers. Conscientious kamavisdars prepared detailed records of the localities they had bid for so that they might repeat the process in subsequent years. Most of them also invested in the cultivation and commerce of their allotted territories, expecting to add profits to the commissions they took from the revenue contract.

Record-keeping under the peshwas exceeded any previously known in India, judging from their *daftars*, which were ledgers of correspondence and account books. These have provided a rich resource for modern historians as well as a model for local administration, imitated by the British India in the next century. The Maratha regime at its zenith was headed by literate brahmans who made policies as well as account books. Other regimes of the time also employed scribes and some kinds of records were maintained, often by brahmans whose caste practices were not priestly, but secular, working in the world of politics and commerce just as the Chitpavans did. Hence, while the Chitpavans may have devised the most elaborate system of documentary control India had known up to that point, they were not the only ones to attempt it, in part at least because the problems of governance had become more complicated for all by the eighteenth century.

By then, if not before, bureaucratic management began to be as important to states as military and charismatic lordship. Accurate record-keeping had been introduced in numerous local settings and institutions, but not until the eighteenth century did the principle find expression at the apex of a political order, thanks to brahman managers who constructed a state form that matched the challenges of the age, yet accorded well with their traditional caste occupation.

Regimes like the peshwas' look distinctly modern in comparison with the Mughals', to whose fall they contributed militarily. But the seeds of the Mughal demise were not merely military, or administrative. Peasant restiveness and rebellions had stretched them beyond their already desperate condition in the Deccan. At the same time, a gentry nurtured within Mughal society saw its interests better served in opposition to the Timurid regime. The Maratha kingdom of the eighteenth century faced some of the same pressures of change, but devised ways of surmounting them, at least for a time.

The peshwas had to dominate a complex world of negotiation with the diverse local institutions that the Marathas encountered in such far-flung places as Malwa, Gujarat, Khandesh and their territories in the Kaveri basin and elsewhere in the south. Zamindars, or big landlords, village headmen representing powerful peasant castes, and deshmukhs, or regional chiefs, had to be either suppressed or integrated into increasingly centralized structures. That meant bending these historically autonomous magnates to the will and the ordinances of the rulers. As never before, resources had to be assessed accurately and in detail so that central demands could be accepted as legitimate by the traditional heads of communities who were still capable of effective and costly resistance.

Gradually, during the eighteenth century the proto-gentry of the sixteenth century emerged as a class. Its members were privileged in their political relations with states like the Maratha and the British who succeeded them, and they were involved in rural commodity production and in market towns. This elite also assumed roles as arbiters of local culture, as trustees of religious organizations, which had previously belonged to kings; from that sponsorship they acquired yet another increment of prestige in their social worlds.

Mirroring the processes of social mobility and class formation were new forms of production. The early eighteenth century was once more an epoch of building, most notably of mansions of wealthy families, whose imposing exterior walls enclosed sumptuous interiors with accessibility limited in accordance with the principles of purdah. A new market for luxury consumption of metal work, ornamental ivory, wood and silver work developed, and support for musicians and poets was made part of the quasi-court life of the elite. A new class of wealthy, powerful households had emerged which was to constitute the basis for a modern middle class during the twentieth century.

THE WARS OF MARATHA SUCCESSION

King Shahu's long reign ended in 1749. A confusion of succession struggles among factions of the royal family promptly ensued, until the peshwa Balaji Bajirao intervened to restore order. The leaders of the various contending factions were convened and forced to accept the conditions he set down, for by this time the peshwa was the true ruler in all but name. He decided that the capital of the kingdom would henceforward be Pune, not Satara, where Shahu had held court; certain offices, such as that of nominal head of the armies, which had been royal appointments, were abolished and along with them many royal rights. All power as well as authority was now concentrated in the peshwa's office, and he insisted that he would control the king in all things.

The usurpation of royal power by a brahman minister merely ratified a situation long in development. With a more centralized government structure had come other accretions of ministerial power. Balaji Bajirao now commanded an army of paid soldiers; no longer did Maratha soldiers retire from campaigns each year in order to cultivate their fields. The day of the Maratha peasant warrior band was over; most fighting men now served as paid soldiers, garrisoned in forts and towns far from home, and trained as infantrymen as well as horsemen. Artillery, however, remained marginally incorporated. The large guns were nominally under the command of Maratha officers; those who fired and maintained them were often foreigners – Portuguese, French and British – but the guns themselves were not up to the state of artillery art already known to Europeans and to a new, menacing force destined to extinguish the imperial moment of the Marathas at Panipat, near Delhi, in 1761.

Panipat brought the Marathas into fatal contact with the king of the Afghans, Ahmad Shah Abdali of the Durrani clan, who had already proved himself capable of halting the Maratha advance into the Punjab, which he invaded eight times before finally pressing on towards Delhi. The Marathas were now divided among several commanders who approached battle with widely differing tactics; some followed the old system utilizing light horse, others adopted the ponderous Mughal tactics and one Muslim commander modelled his force on the European lines of trained and coordinated infantry and artillery.

Artillery decided the battle in January, 1761: the light, mobile artillery of the Afghans proved lethal against both Maratha cavalry and infantry. Six months were to elapse before the shattered remnants of the Maratha armies that had gathered at Panipat found their way back to Maharashtra, and by then Maratha supremacy over the subcontinent had passed.

MARATHA DISINTEGRATION

During the next forty years, the polity briefly centralized by the peshwas dissolved into a set of states united in one objective: they would no longer brook the arrogant rule of Chitpavan ministers. Otherwise the major Maratha houses, all founded by members of the new military elite that had emerged under the peshwas, concentrated on making kingdoms of their own. The new kingdoms were at Baroda in Gujarat under the Gaikwad family, at Indore in Malwa and in the central Deccan tracts north of the Narmada under the Holkars. South of Delhi at Gwalior was the Shinde (or Sindhia) family; at Nagpur in western Maharashtra the Bhonsles endured; and, finally, in the Pune region, descendants of the peshwas retained a territorial sway made fragile by competing smaller houses in the heartland of the former state. It was this set of fissiparous Maratha states, fragments of the great expansion of the middle decades of the eighteenth century, that confronted a British power then in the process of territorial entrenchment in Bengal and the Carnatic, and poised to open the colonial era of Indian history.

THE SHADOW OF EUROPE

By the late seventeenth century, trade along both the Coromandel (east) and Malabar (west) coasts of the peninsula had grown vastly in volume and value in response to the demand for Indian textiles and spices by Europeans who were then organized into corporate trading companies: the East India Companies of the British, Dutch and French. So integral to the trade had these Europeans become that at one point Sir Josiah Child, a leading Director of the English Company, believed that he could wrest trading privileges from the Mughals. With a dozen warships obtained from King James II, his brother blockaded Bombay and other nearby ports and seized some ships that were under Mughal licence in 1685. By that point, Bombay island, occupied by the English, had begun slowly to jostle for place with Surat as the premier trading centre on the west coast; on the east coast, they traded from Madras from 1639, while to the south the French were ensconced at Pondicherry, and to the north the Dutch at Pulicat. Child demanded that the Mughals exclude from the trade all Europeans except the English Company and seized the ships of other Europeans and Indian traders. Aurangzeb angrily ordered the suspension of all English trade on the west coast and had Company goods confiscated there as well as in Bengal. Humiliated, the English sued for peace, pardon and the resumption of ordinary trade, and agreed to pay compensation.

But the gathering economic power of European traders was not long to be denied, for not only did their armed ships and capital reserves, consisting of silver imported from the New World, assure domination over India's international trade, but their autonomous centres, such as Fort St George at Madras, attracted wealthy Indian traders and bankers, who responded to the relative peace and protection of property in these places. European capital also began to find its way into the territorial governance of coastal societies through the institution of tax farming that was widely adopted in western and eastern India during the later seventeenth century.

Medieval ideas and institutions continued to evolve during this period, but the evolution was increasingly influenced by interaction with Europeans who were undergoing significant changes themselves. Thus there are two processes to consider, each with its own history, as well as the interaction between them.

Two centuries after the Portuguese opened contact, traders from Europe had become a great deal more numerous. English and Dutch merchants began regular trade with India in the early seventeenth century, by which time the Portuguese had been edged out. By the close of the century, the English had eliminated the Dutch East India Company from competition, leaving only the French as weak economic but dangerous political rivals by the middle of the eighteenth century.

India in 1700 presented a deceptive picture. Superficially, the Mughal kingdom was enormous, wealthy, powerful and stable. The temerity of the English East India Company in launching a war against the Mughals in 1686 was punished by Aurangzeb; the English had mistakenly thought to use their mastery of the seas around India to offset Mughal military power and gain commercial advantage. After their humiliation, they were fortunate to be permitted to resume their lucrative trade. The wealth of the empire's cities, the prized qualities of its manufactured goods, attracted a vigorous international trade, and the seeming capacity of Indian agriculture to sustain the land revenue upon which government operations and massive armies were based – all of these appeared set to continue. Little wonder then that many in the seventeenth century and since called it 'a New Age'.

THE FRAGILITY OF THE MUGHAL 'NEW AGE'

Against this assessment, and casting deep doubt upon it, is another which accounts for the abrupt decline of a great state within a short time of the passing of Aurangzeb in 1707. The so-called Mughal 'New Age' was foreshortened by the collapse of its administrative frame during the last half of

Aurangzeb's long reign. Akbar's system had grown massive and top heavy in taking the war to the Deccan against Marathas, and his campaigns had other consequences as well. Aurangzeb had followed Muhammad Tughluq to nearly the same place in the Deccan to make a new capital. Because he was determined to crush Shivaji and his Maratha successors, Aurangabad was established in Maratha country as his frontier capital. That it actually does contain Aurangzeb's modest tomb symbolizes the role of the Deccan in becoming the grave of the Mughal dynasty. By the last quarter of the seventeenth century, little cultivable land remained for assignment to new officials recruited to serve the emperor in the Deccan, and everywhere old and new Mughal retainers demanded more from peasant producers. The onerous demands partially account for the risings of the Sikh and Jat peasantries that took place in the very heart of Mughal India. These rebellions were also influenced by and centred upon community ideologies, or, appropriately, 'communalism', based upon ethnic and religious elements of identity and popular mobilizations of the sort that served as foci for the new political regimes which took shape during the eighteenth century.

An additional cumulative and weakening change during the Mughal age after Akbar was the spread of Babur's military innovation, consisting of light cavalry coordinated with mobile artillery, to every sort of ambitious warrior chief. Simultaneously and fatally, the Mughals abandoned that mode of warfare, and the change was telling. Akbar had made a bold cavalry dash of 400 miles to Gujarat with a small force and won that rich province by surprise and mobility; the Mughal armies of the seventeenth century had became massive and sluggish, if grand, processions of elephants, hordes of camp-followers and provisioners, and siege guns. The resulting slow-moving fortress-city was intimidating, but it was also vulnerable to more agile, gun-using horsemen, such as those of the Maratha chieftain Shivaji during the late seventeenth century. Aurangzeb paid a high price in attempting to contain the Maratha marauders during the late seventeenth century, so high that the horses of the Maratha Peshwas of the eighteenth century swept the entire Mughal military aside to seize its Gangetic heartland.

Arguably then, their sudden decline shows that the Mughals did not launch a 'New Age', and did not set a course for some future India. They were manifestly the culmination of India's medieval age, a period in which regimes of all sorts strove with limited success for a greater centralization capable of exploiting the state-building potentialities of urbanized money-economies and international trade. The Afghan regime of Sher Shah pushed centralization further and faster than others, and his innovations were incorporated into a Mughal regime with marginally more military might than the Afghans could muster. Mughal military dominance was not limited by clan organization, as the Afghans were, and able soldiers were freely recruited to Mughal service from far afield in Africa and Persia, as well as from among non-Muslims in the subcontinent. This and the administrative frame constructed by Akbar provided the means for the Mughal regime to remain powerful when other old regimes in the world were undergoing the 'seventeenth-century crises' which historians of Europe record (and assume too easily must have been world-wide). The Mughals perfected the institutions of the later medieval age and delayed India's next political, social and economic crises until the eighteenth century, when new solutions were contrived that endured until well into the colonial age.

[5] THE EAST INDIA COMPANY

INTRODUCTION

It was considered strange, even at the time, that a trading company should acquire an empire, and many attempts at explanation have been made in the intervening years. What needs explanation is both how and why it happened. The standard witticism on the subject is that it had happened in a fit of absence of mind, but, to the extent that this is true, it can be argued that the absence of mind was more on the part of the indigenous rulers of India than of their mercenary conquerors.

EXPLAINING EMPIRE

Many, even among nationalist historians, accepted the views of imperial historical defenders of British rule that the East India Company's conquest of India was necessitated by the chaos that allegedly followed Aurangzeb's death. After 1707, many imperialist and nationalist historians agree, an era of devastating wars commenced, causing economic decline and anarchy that was arrested only with the establishment of Company rule. Some in both the imperialist and nationalist camps held the further view that the Company – under farsighted men like Thomas Munro, Mountstuart Elphinstone, John Malcolm and Charles Metcalf – initiated promising developments during the early nineteenth century that were later subverted by Queen Victoria's ministers between 1858 and 1901.

Against these understandings of the transition to colonial domination over India, there is another which sets out a very different development. According to this newer argument, the political systems and economy prevailing after the death of Aurangzeb were more robust and orderly than previously supposed; this was so partly because the states created during the eighteenth century borrowed freely and improvised upon Mughal institutions and practices. For example, eighteenth-century regimes often succeeded by directly and constructively involving themselves in the promotion of agrarian production, as had the Mughals, by insisting, admittedly with uneven success, that those receiving lands to support their military, civil or religious offices should increase cultivation.

In more recent work it has emerged that sustained and substantial, if uneven, economic growth and political development was more characteristic of the post-Mughal eighteenth century. This has been well documented in monographs of the past fifteen years tracing the rise of compact, regional polities – such as those of the Marathas and Sikhs in western and northern India – and numerous other, smaller kingdoms.

But how did such relatively stable states emerge and, no less, why did so many of them fall prey to the East India Company by the end of the eighteenth century? The answers to both questions may lie in the same set of developments. As noted earlier, Aurangzeb's India witnessed the growth of mercantile commerce and the emergence of 'gentry' classes on the land. Previous interpretations have seen the mounting resistance to the demands of Mughal officials in the later seventeenth century as signs of 'peasant' revolt. However, the newer historiography has stressed that both the forces involved and the ambitions expressed went considerably beyond the conventional meaning of 'peasant'. While the mobilizations of the Marathas, Sikhs and other groups may have drawn on peasant support, they also involved a different range of social actors whose roles were enhanced as simple rebellion gave way to the processes of state formation.

Bankers and merchants were needed to supply finance; scribal groups to provide administrative skills; ideologues to legitimate new rulerships drawn from the humble ranks of imperial soldiers or erstwhile peasant chieftains. These adjuncts of the newly powerful included educated and often cultivated brahmins and Muslims, as well as scions of the Vaishya castes. Their influence within the new state order grew steadily, particularly in response to the need to finance wars. Classical Mughal taxation practices, which had centred on direct systems of collection, progressively gave way to forms of tax farming under which men of wealth – bankers and merchant magnates – bid for the right to collect revenues in a designated place, and added their own capital to the commissions they received for collections to make investments in the lands and commerce being taxed; they also used the police powers that went along with tax collecting to coerce the producers of commodities. Revenue-related commercial activities such as these, together with the robust domestic and foreign trade, hastened the development of an indigenous capitalist class in India well before the onset of formal colonial domination.

Another aspect of indigenous development during the eighteenth century was the increasing recruitment of the Muslim ruling elite from native stock instead of from often distant parts of Islamdom. Most of the new rulers were drawn from families of converts or groups long resident in India, such as the Afghans who founded the small Rohilla kingdom in the western Ganges plain. Similarly, the new rulers of Hindu states were less often scions of the medieval ruling Rajput clans of kshatriya lineage, and more often of dominant regional peasant stock, such as the Maratha Kunbis or the Sikh Jats. Where such locally recruited, 'sons-of-the-soil' (nativist) elites comprised an important part of the dominant landlord and ruling strata, the direct agrarian exploitation of the earlier Mughal age could no longer be practised. Even in the few larger kingdoms of the eighteenth century, and certainly in most others, older

Plate 18 The *haveli* of the Divetia family in Ahmedabad, Gujarat. Havelis, substantial timber structures, were both home and business headquarters of important trading families in a hierarchical mercantile community in the eighteenth and nineteenth centuries (courtesy of Vivek Nanda).

Mughal practices were replaced by economies more tuned to securing revenue from regional and international commerce, shifting the tax burden from the cultivators to commodity-producers and traders.

The socio-economic underpinnings of 'the state' in South Asia, then, were changing as state-building processes moved towards the creation of more unitary and centralized orders which displaced the segmented political forma-tions of the past. In this, Muslim and Hindu regimes shared much in common with their Ottoman and Safavid counterparts in contemporary west Asia, and, indeed, with post-medieval states in an earlier period of the European past. However, one factor obtruded into those processes in India to a greater degree than in west Asia and the comparable period in Europe. This was the presence of European traders themselves, who had already come to play a major role in India's sea-borne commerce and were penetrating progressively further inland as the new states of the eighteenth century were in formation. The bankers, scribes, gentries and even peasantries who constituted the backbones of these states also had interested connections with Europeans which could potentially put pressure on their loyalties.

THE PORTUGUESE IN ASIA

When the Anglo-Indian relationship began, Akbar's India was one of the largest and most powerful kingdoms of all of Eurasia, and the realm of Queen

Elizabeth one of its smallest, weakest and most peripheral. The European power that during the preceding century had had the most experience and success in exploring and dominating trade in the Indian Ocean was Portugal. The Portuguese had arrived in India in 1498 in three ships under the command of Vasco da Gama, who had sailed around the Cape of Good Hope and anchored on the Malabar coast. They soon entered into negotiations with the local ruler in an unsuccessful attempt to secure monopoly trading privileges to their own nation state.

At that point, the 'rights' to explore and lay claim to the hitherto unknown and unchristian parts of the world were divided (with the blessings of the Pope) between Spain and Portugal; while Spain had been awarded the New World (except for the easternmost part of South America, which projected out of the Spanish hemisphere), Asia had fallen to the adventurous Portuguese. Despite their inability at once to exclude the Arab infidels, trade with India increased and, by 1505, a viceroy was appointed who entered his office with empire aforethought, and they soon established trading posts at several places along the west coast.

The Indian Ocean trade, before the advent of the Portuguese, had been by and large free. In order to gain control of the system, the Portuguese had to go to the expense of equipping and maintaining armed forces. The trading posts became 'customs', or, rather extortion, stations, where 'letters of protection' were bought by merchants to 'protect' them from official Portuguese piracy on the high seas. The local rulers along the coast were willing enough to come to agreements which provided their territories with revenue and did not seem to impact upon their own powers. Arab and European traders were all one to them.

The really lucrative commodities at the time, however, were not Indian, but came directly or indirectly from the Spice Islands of Indonesia. The pepper that Vasco da Gama returned with was so profitable, the king made the pepper trade a royal monopoly, along with the African gold that explorers had previously returned with. The weakness in the system came from two sources which would also afflict later arrivals: Portugal was an even smaller and poorer state than England, and rapidly became dependent on an overseas trade that could be sustained only by force that would have to yield to stronger and better-armed competitors when they appeared; and kings were chronically short of cash with which to finance their territorial adventures and domestic extravagances.

To try to remedy the shortage of manpower with which to control the trade, as well as to further the cause of Christianizing the heathen, the Portuguese encouraged the marriage of sailors and servants to native women. To improve their cash flow situations, kings fell into the practice of franchising their monopolies in exchange for a steady assured income and the release from governmental risk and responsibility, as well as the sale of offices. Even so, they remained dependent on fluctuating trade conditions and regularly overspent their incomes and fell into bankruptcy. By the sixteenth century, two other powers appeared on the scene and Portuguese competition declined rapidly. These were the Dutch and the British, who both took advantage of the defeat of the Spanish Armada in 1588 to venture abroad in defiance of the Papal Bull.

THE DUTCH AND ENGLISH COMPETITION

In 1579, seven of the Netherlands provinces united in their prolonged struggle for independence from Spain, and eventually won a truce in 1609. Despite the desperate domestic preoccupations, private merchant vessels began voyages to the Indian Ocean at the same time as did the British. In 1597, the Dutch concluded a treaty with the king of Bantam in the East Indies, and by 1601 had sent a score of expeditions there and almost secured a monopoly of the spice trade. This inspired the merchants of London to club together and petition Queen Elizabeth for a charter granting them the monopoly of trade with the East, which of course was not hers to give away; nevertheless, she graciously conferred vast notional powers upon 'the Governor and Merchants of London merchants trading into the East Indies'. The charter bestowed upon the new East India Company a monopoly of all trade with India within Elizabeth's realm and, more presumptuously, a monopoly over all trade between India and Europe.

Not to be outdone, the Dutch created an East India company of their own a year later, in 1602, and granted it the same theoretical monopolistic privileges. Competition and often bloody conflict between British and Dutch merchants until late in the seventeenth century was assured. At that point, an accommodation was reached defining a sphere of commercial dominance for each: Java for the Dutch and India for the British. Monopolies are such standard features of mercantilist practice that it is easily forgotten that they are but particular manifestations of a general European programme, that of building strong states by means of unifying authority under central institutions – kings and national legislatures – and of increasing the resources available to these institutions for use against internal and external enemies.

The British at first tried to concentrate their trade efforts on the Spice Islands, but found, like the Dutch, that Indian calicoes were in great demand in Bantam and the Moluccas in exchange for spices. They therefore arrived in Surat in 1612, and, in the face of Portuguese objections, obtained permission from the Mughal emperor Jahangir to establish a trading post or 'factory' there. By 1620, the Portuguese had been defeated in battle often enough to neutralize any threat they posed, but the Dutch had proved insuperable in the Spice Islands, and the British concentrated more and more on the Indian trade, especially in textiles.

THE COMPANY RAMPANT

By the mid-seventeenth century, the Company had over a score of factories, including some on the Bay of Bengal as well as several in the interior. In 1640 they received permission from the representative of the faded Vijayanagara power to build a fort near a village that was to become the modern city of

Madras, and in 1668 King Charles II, following the practices of kings, in exchange for a large loan and a nominal rent transferred to the Company the city of Bombay, which had been part of the dowry of his Portuguese queen, Catherine of Braganza.

Indian rulers followed similar practices: a steady income or large loan in the hand was worth the bothersome responsibility for bits and pieces of peripheral territory. Little by little, the Company was granted permission to set up enclaves and other rights and privileges of trade. It was but a short step to interference in Indian political rivalries in search of yet more privileges and relief from customs duties.

Another European player in the Indian game that, like the Portuguese and Dutch, eventually lost out to the good fortune and tactics of the British was the French East India Company, which had been belatedly founded in 1664. Despite Dutch opposition, the French Company established a factory at Surat in 1668. In 1674, its employee François Martin founded Pondicherry on the Coromandel coast south of Madras, and in 1690 built a factory near Calcutta. Later the French became not only commercial but military rivals of the British in Europe, North America and Asia. In India, they had a tendency to back opposing factions of native political rivalries.

Indian participation in Company trade

Between 1600 and the early nineteenth century, the commerce of the East India Company and that of its officials, trading privately on their own accounts, involved the participation of Indian personnel and institutions. The success of a season of trade depended on Indian merchants to be responsible for all contracts with the suppliers of Indian commodities to the Company, as well as for the sale of goods imported on Company ships. Often, too, an Indian merchant mediated between the Company and the local political powers, and upon these diplomatic mediations depended financial success. The personal fortunes of Europeans, arising from private trading, which was not prohibited until the reforms of Lord Cornwallis (who was Governor-General in the closing years of the eighteenth century), were left largely in the hands of trusted Indian agents as well.

In any case, short- and medium-term credit was obtained from Indian bankers, to whom great fortunes also accrued. A part of the profit was regularly invested by Indian bankers and financiers in collateral economic fields of activity, such as in textile production. And, finally, the actual commodities that were exported to Europe, to Java and to China – spices and textiles at first, and later cotton, indigo and opium – were produced and collected for Company procurement by a mixed group of Indian entrepreneurs, including the leaders of groups of weavers or other artisans, and village headmen and local chiefs who controlled supplies of agrarian products, such as grain and cotton. All of these shared to a greater or lesser extent in the profits of Company trade, but they were not true partners; these were the holders of East India Company stock in London. For most of the seventeenth and eighteenth centuries, Indians were mere agents in the Company's growing network of operations set within the encompassing mercantilistic structure of Indian political regimes.

THE JOINT TRAJECTORY OF DEVELOPMENT

By the middle of the eighteenth century, the East India Company had become one of the great mercantilist enterprises in the world as well as the east, and, in asserting its dominance over ever-larger parts of the subcontinent, it thrust existing, weaker Indian mercantilist institutions on to higher levels of development. The relational web between India and Britain was woven quite early, well before actual British dominion was formalized.

Locking the structures of Britain and India into a common developing process from around 1700 altered the course of development of them both at strategic junctures. The notion of a common trajectory between India and Britain may appear arguable given the asymmetrical coercive power of colonial subjugation, but the long prehistory of that subjugation permitted a certain reciprocity between India and Britain from the seventeenth century on. There is no need at this point to examine the multifarious ways in which India was profoundly changed by its relationship with Britain, since that subject occupies a large part of this book. The reverse impact, however, that upon Britain, was manifested as well in several fundamental ways, mostly mediated by the Company, its operations and its patronage. The East India Company became one of the two great financial corporations and a core institution in Britain's eighteenth-century financial dominance, fiscal planning and international commerce. Company patronage – the lucrative places it offered both ordinary and exalted Britons – was so great that the British political establishment dared not bring it into ordinary politics until the middle of the nineteenth century. Company armies, along with Royal regiments maintained in and by British India, conquered and held much of the British eastern empire.

CLIVE'S CAREER

The death of Nizam-ul-Mulk in Hyderabad in 1748 set off the usual Mughal fraternal strife among his sons. In addition, a similar contest was pursued between the sons of the nawab of Arcot, another Mughal governor who had established a quasi-independent realm for himself at a level below that of Hyderabad. In both contests, the French and British forces backed opposing claimants, and, in the end, the French candidate won in Hyderabad, and the British-backed prince in Arcot. In 1751, Robert Clive, a captain in the Company army, along with some Indian 'sepoys' also in the Company employ, took Arcot and defended it against a larger enemy force.

In 1757, the hero of Arcot recaptured Calcutta, which had been taken by the nawab of Bengal. Clive had entered into an intrigue with the commander of the nawab's forces, Mir Jafar, who deserted his master on the battlefield and was rewarded by the English by being installed in his place. This battle, at Plassey, is often considered the true beginning of the British Empire in India,

Plate 19 'A European, probably Sir David Ochterlony, in Indian dress, smoking a hookah and watching a nautch in his house in Delhi. By a Delhi artist, *c.*1820.' Note portraits oddly placed above the doors (IOL Add OR2, neg. no. B710, by permission of the British Library).

since it resulted in enormous properties falling into Company ownership. Clive shortly went on to capture and destroy the nearby French settlement at Chandernagore, and to defeat the Dutch at Biderra, putting paid to the rivalry of both in Bengal. He himself was able to take personal control of an enormous provincial property. Leasing it to a succession of Indian nawabs for exorbitant tributes made such vast fortunes for Clive and his colleagues as to earn them the derisive title of 'Nabob' (a garbled form of nawab) from envious Englishmen of the time, and led to such criticisms of his rule that Bengal was taken under direct Company administration in 1765; the Company itself became the Dewan of Bengal. This was the basis of the 'double government' of the Company's acquisitions in Bengal, Bihar and Orissa, in which native rulers retained their styles and dignities and received a stipulated annual income, while the Company administered the government and collected the revenues through Indian officials.

Ironically, as an administrator, Clive was given the special brief of rooting out corruption among the Company officers, which, however, he found not only intractable but not even amenable to being systematized. On his return to England, he was both made Baron Clive of Plassey and condemned for illegally appropriating £234,000 of Company plunder. Brooding, he cut his own throat in 1774.

THE COMPANY TAKES POWER

The East India Company's turn to arms and overt militarization had an immediate impact on Indian politics, although one marked by complexity and ambiguity. Clive's victories, especially that at Plassey, had been achieved by the use of the new European techniques of infantry warfare. In the wake of his victories, too, the Company's grip on commerce (or at least that of its officials and merchants in their 'private' trading capacity) had greatly increased. Seeing this, many of India's new independent rulers paradoxically were drawn closer. The Company received a host of requests for officers to train infantry divisions from sultans and kings, and even for contingents of Company troops to support royal armies. So it soon added mercenary services to the many functions which it provided in its new dominions, and rapidly came to realize this method of advancing its influence at very little cost. A 'subsidiary alliance' system was conjured up, whereby the planting of Company soldiery on Indian states that paid their expenses became a prerequisite for doing further business. The further business in turn included a variety of commercial services which brought the treasuries of many states under effective Company control. When, towards the end of the century – and in the context of war with France – the British state committed itself to an imperial mission in India, pressing the Company to convert its influence into territory, conquest was achieved with remarkable ease.

With hindsight, the fatal attraction of so many new Indian regimes to the Company in the middle decades of the eighteenth century seems puzzling. Did the Muslim nawabs and Hindu kings not appreciate the risks they were running in becoming Company 'allies' and clients? Part of the answer may lie in the extent to which the Company concealed its character and ambitions as they developed behind two screens. On the one hand, it made no bid to establish itself as an independent source of state sovereignty. It did not behave as a sultan or king, with a display of royal symbols; nor did it evince formal claims to territorial expansion. Rather, it continued to recognize the sovereignty of the Mughal emperor, and presented itself as merely the supplier of a set of technical and commercial services for hire. On the other hand, knowledge of the Company's political position in England was freely available in India, and suggested that any imperial role would be against the interests and wishes of directors and Parliament. In such circumstances, Indian rulers were lulled into the belief that the services they bought would be without threat to themselves – certainly not in comparison to other, more immediate dangers on their doorsteps. Warfare between regional rulers was intense, and 'subsidiary alliance' bought protection against neighbourly invasion.

Yet there were a few native rulers who did sense the way the wind could blow. In Mysore, from the 1770s, Haidar Ali and his son Tipu Sultan set out to beat the Company at its own game; to this end Haidar concentrated on acquiring an independent army, free from Company influence, and on improving centralized control over his fiscal system. Driving westwards, father and son sought to capture the rich spice gardens of Malabar, on which they planned to build a mercantilist empire of their own with an entrepôt at Mangalore to rival anything in English possession. Haidar even considered developing a navy with which to take the sea back from European grasp.

Tipu dreamed on an even grander scale, penning plans for the promotion of state-owned industries and direct control of the revenue system down to the level of the individual peasant household. In the early 1780s, an expansive Mysore came close to ejecting the Company from its southern base of Madras. A little later, in the Punjab, the redoubtable Ranjit Singh began to build a kingdom capable of keeping the English at bay for another two generations. His particular advantage was his access to overland trade routes to west and central Asia, which maintained commercial flows outside the Company's reach. Belatedly, too, Baji Rao II, the last of the Peshwas of Pune, sought to make a final stand for the independence of his domains.

All these attempts to resist the rising power of the Company came to nought. In Mysore, at least part of the reason lay in the failure of other rulers to share Haidar's perspicacity and their greater fear of his growing strength. Following Haidar's death from cancer in 1782, Cornwallis's initial defeat of Tipu Sultan in 1792–3 was achieved with very few Company troops, supplemented by armies from most of Tipu's neighbours: the Marathas, Hyderabad and Travancore. In the case of the Punjab, the problem was internecine strife following Ranjit Singh's death in 1839; a bitter struggle for succession eventually opened the way for the Company's arms in 1846–8. But in both cases, and that of Baji Rao II as well, other forces were also at work.

In 1792–3 and again in 1799, when Seringapatam was finally captured and Tipu killed, the Company received substantial help from scribal, commercial and gentry groups inside Mysorean territory itself. Indeed, following Tipu's death and the restoration of the Hindu dynasty that Haidar had replaced, financial administration of the kingdom was left in the hands of Tipu's own dewan, the brahman Purniah, who shortly afterwards received the reward of a substantial jagir for his services to the English. Meanwhile, at Pune, Baji Rao II's call to arms had received no response even from his own inamdars and relatives, whose loyalty the Company had succeeded in buying with promises to recognize and enhance their commercial and landed privileges. In the Punjab, the Company's conquest was facilitated through connections with urban Hindu banking families whose commercial networks ran down the Ganges Valley into its own territories. Ultimately, the collapse of Indian resistance to Company power owed much to the 'subversion' of indigenous regimes by the dominant groups and 'capitalist' classes thrown up by the social processes of the previous century.

In retrospect at least this is not very surprising. Europe's grip on commercial wealth and military power was, by the last quarter of the eighteenth century, too firm to be dislodged. In a way, even Haidar and Tipu realized this when they sought to use the French rivalry with the English – especially at sea – to compensate for their own relative weakness. Yet replacing the dependency on one European power with that on another hardly amounts to the freedom they aspired to, and Mysore's allies were already standing on the trapdoor of history when they were called in. French naval incompetence had cost Haidar his chance to eject the British in 1782, and by the time his son accepted the honours of the French Revolution as 'Citoyen Tipu', the writing in southern India was already on the wall. Beneath the new rulers, alliance with Europeans (and increasingly with the British) represented an act of little more than prudence to those Indian social groups who enjoyed privilege and wealth in the new state systems.

Two other factors enhanced this tendency. The first was the economic and social tensions created by the shift to more centralized state forms. While state power now worked more directly to promote commercial prosperity, it was not entirely clear whose prosperity would be enhanced. Rulers in the eighteenth century sought to fill their own treasuries first. Pressed by the constant need for ready cash, usually for military campaigns, they had been known to squeeze local commercial groups until their eyes bulged; Tipu particularly favoured flogging recalcitrant amildars to make them disgorge their hoarded cash. Hence, the transition from Mughal overlordship to the newer, tighter state forms was not smooth but generated many potential internal (as well as external) conflicts. Moreover, certain recurrent forms of economic conflict carried implications for social and cultural strife as well; most notably, Muslim rulers who sought to increase taxation on or confiscate the substantial properties held in the name of Hindu temples or by high-caste groups risked facing resistance framed along religious lines.

Indian states were slow to generate secure property forms, those which demarcated unequivocally the rights of the ruler from those of 'private' subjects. On the other hand, at least until it gained state hegemony for itself – which was not until the second decade of the nineteenth century – the Company, as a company of merchants, held the rights of 'private' property to be essential to civilization as they knew it.

In addition to the Company's congenial economic stance, many British officials took a genuine scholarly and philosophical interest in India, which helped to shape the judicial view. Foremost among these was Sir William Jones, who served in Bengal as a judge of the Supreme Court from 1783 to his death in 1794 and was one of the earliest Englishmen to learn Sanskrit and translate some of its classics into English. Under his influence and that of other like-minded jurists, the Company's early judiciary was able to detect these rights in their antiquarian studies of ancient Hindu law, which tied them to distinctive religious privileges. A theory popular among Company officials in the late nineteenth century saw a highly sophisticated and commercial Hindu civilization brought to ruin by Islamic despotism, from which the English saw it as their duty to rescue India.

Whatever the truth of this convenient vision, its appeal to large numbers among the commercial, scribal and gentry classes was pronounced. The extension of Company power promised to secure commercial and revenue privileges as a form of private property, and to safeguard the wealth of religious institutions from the avarice or desperation of Indian rulers. The Company self-consciously set out to connect itself to the rising social groupings of the time, and they were not slow in responding.

THE COMPANY IN GOVERNMENT

As the Company began to acquire real political power in India, however, its character began to change and it faced new opposition, not least at home. The first governor-general, Warren Hastings, appointed under the first Parliamentary Regulating Act for India of 1773, took up his position with the view that the historical institutions already developed in India provided the best basis for British rule. Nevertheless, three years after his retirement in 1785, Hastings was impeached on twenty charges arising from his term in office. These included corruption and the violation of the rights of prominent Indians, whom he had vindictively harried and from whom he had illegally extorted large sums of money.

Hastings's prosecutor, Edmund Burke, who was later to win fame for his writings against the French Revolution, was already a leading public man. He possessed considerable knowledge of India through correspondence with kinsmen there, through his advocacy on behalf of Indian rulers and through his own diligent participation on parliamentary committees dealing with Indian affairs. The trial lasted many years, heaped much discredit upon the Company and was said to be the among the most popular of London's entertainments. In the end Hastings was acquitted of all the indictments against him, although he was bankrupted by legal costs and eventually died in penury.

The imaginations of Company merchants in India were slow to grasp the implications of assuming hegemonic power in the huge subcontinent; in London, many were totally opposed to such a conquest. Company share-holders objected to wars after Josiah Child's humiliating encounter with Aurangzeb. Subsequent military adventures were cautiously entered upon to safeguard trade against the Dutch in the seventeenth century and the French in the middle of the eighteenth. Wars, they knew, endangered dividends, which the shareholders of the Company insisted on receiving even when there were no operating profits to divide and they had to be borrowed in London's money market.

Company officials were appointed to India on the strict understanding with the directors in London that they would not wage war. But they violated their undertakings frequently. In 1786, for example, Lord Cornwallis, the British general who had been forced to surrender to the American revolutionary forces at Yorktown, accepted a no-war injunction when he took service as Governor-General. In order to ensure himself of greater independence than his predecessor Warren Hastings, however, he insisted on the command of the Company armies and also that his decisions should not be subject to the veto of his council in Calcutta. Consequently, when, shortly after arriving in India, he became convinced that Tipu Sultan threatened the British position in south India, he attacked so ruthlessly as to bring rare criticism on his long public career.

Cornwallis's 1793 reforms of the Company's operations in India were an outcome of Warren Hastings's impeachment. Nevertheless, few of his contemporaries were prepared for his 'Permanent Settlement' of the land revenues of Bengal and his legal and administrative changes, all of which set the government of Bengal on a deliberate course of modernization along European lines. This was not what Burke, who favoured nourishing Indian institutions, had had in mind. Indian institutions, practices and personnel were to form the basis upon which administration was founded in the other territories that the Company acquired up until 1830, but not in Bengal.

The most striking of Cornwallis's Bengal reforms was found in the collection of land revenues in the 150,000 square mile territory, which had been made up of the three older Mughal provinces of Bengal, Bihar and Orissa. What had previously been collected through large and small tax-farmers, who were called 'zamindars' following the Persian word for 'landholder', was henceforward to be collected from landlords, to whom full, permanent ownership rights were awarded on the condition that they punctiliously pay a fixed revenue demand. That is, in a single enactment, a small group of landowners – still called 'zamindars' – was created and the rights of other cultivators in the land that they tilled were abrogated. The zamindars, however, were expected to see that the agrarian resources they owned were maintained and improved, and were liable to dispossession if they defaulted in their revenue obligations. The Permanent Settlement of Bengal was presented as a pragmatic measure for dealing with the concrete difficulties of collecting land taxes from a peasant population impoverished and depleted by a famine in 1769–70, which, in Bengal as in many other parts of India, frequently moved about to better their situations, negotiating the best possible terms of land tenancy with new landlords.

The reforms initiated by Cornwallis set the development of the colonial state in British India for the next generation, whether it was in adopting his measures elsewhere, as happened in parts of Madras; or in devising alternative revenue schemes, such as the collection of revenue from a vast body of smallholders, in the form of the ryotwari system introduced in most of Madras and Bombay; or the village-based revenue operations adopted in northern India. All aspects of the Company's operations – the civil service, the judiciary and the Company's commerce – were now centred on land revenue administration. Of these, Company trade was the least changed; the mercantilist orientation of the Company and other eighteenth-century regimes continued, with existing monopolies over salt collections and sales and over opium maintained. Moreover, land revenue receipts – a form of tribute owed to the Company for its conquests – were utilized in part to buy some of the goods the Company exported from India.

The law reforms were meant to provide protection for the newly created landlords of Bengal from the arbitrary impositions of Company civil officials – the misdeeds of which Warren Hastings had been accused. Cornwallis replaced the judicial system originally followed by Hastings, which had been based on Islamic principles, with a hierarchy of civil and criminal courts. Notionally the new judiciary followed 'native' law in most matters that did not pertain to contractual matters; on the latter, English law prevailed. 'Customary practices' were to be applied by newly appointed English magistrates, and were codified according to the texts collected and translated by Sir William

Jones and his successors. The result was to make rigid what had been flexible practices, and to privilege some usages over others.

One further set of changes had to do with European civil servants of the East India Company. Henceforward they were prohibited from any commercial activities. This was to avoid conflicts of interest between personal gain and official responsibilities; to compensate for the opportunities for personal enrichment forfeited, salaries were substantially increased. The argument that better salaries would attract a better class of civil careerist was of course also brought forward.

THE MADRAS SYSTEM OF ADMINISTRATION

At nearly the same time that these changes were being introduced in Bengal, in Madras a system was constructed along different judicial and administrative principles, although the Madras system also took revenue collection as its fundamental concern. Called 'ryotwar', the system was predicated on direct collections from millions of individual small landholders, called in Persian *raayat*, meaning 'subject' or 'cultivator'. The 'ryot' under this system paid to the state a share of his crop calculated from the productive capacity of the fields that he engaged to cultivate each year. This entailed a different and more numerous civil service from that of Bengal, where most officials were judicial officers. In Madras, and later in Bombay, the key European administrator was called 'the Collector', and his task was to supervise land surveys and to issue an individual revenue agreement to each of tens of thousands of small cultivators in twenty revenue districts in his province. The Collectors were aided in this onerous task by thousands of Indian subordinates.

The chief spokesman for the Madras system, Thomas Munro, struggled for years to achieve an appropriate judiciary for this sort of arrangement. Munro finally succeeded in replacing the Cornwallis judiciary by one of his own design during his governorship, between 1819 and 1827. Under his judicial system, substantial judicial authority was vested in Indian local officials who, Munro argued, should rightly be involved in revenue and legal administration, in contrast to the situation that obtained in Bengal under Cornwallis.

Subsequent territorial additions to Company dominion produced further changes, but, in the main, the administration of most later acquisitions was set in accordance with the Madras pattern. This meant preserving more of the pre-colonial institutional fabric than was permitted under the expressly 'modernizing' policy of Bengal. In all of this, pragmatism, rather than doctrine, was the guide for those who made Company policy, certainly those who made it in India.

BRITISH IDEOLOGY

While French physiocratic notions were introduced into debates about the revenue settlement in Bengal or utilitarian doctrines into discussions of the Bombay arrangements, there is little evidence that they directly informed policy-making. The hope of James Mill that Benthamite doctrines could be

Plate 20 Sir Thomas Munro. Mezzotint engraving by Martin Shee, *c.*1828 (IOL P 1559; neg. no. B 18670, by permission of the British Library).

made to work in India and the desire of many evangelicals that Christianity might be promoted were the main direct manifestations of doctrinal preferences in Indian policy-making; such preferences appealed to sentiments in Britain, but were not much heeded by officials confronting problems in India. True, a growing number of European civil and military officials professed evangelical Christianity, and for some this coloured their official duties; none the less, the policy of the Company in the early phase of territorial rule was prudently neutral about religion. As a result, Christian critics in England complained about the financial and other support the Madras government gave to Hindu temples and the maintenance of privileges to individual Hindu and Muslim priests and teachers in continuation of the pre-colonial regimes, at the same time as Christian missionaries were banned. The caution of the

Madras government was vindicated to some extent when the mutiny of the Company's soldiers at its Vellore garrison in 1806 was found to have resulted in part from resentment on the part of the rank and file over the open proselytizing engaged in by their European officers. The situation ominously anticipated the Great Mutiny of fifty years later.

THE COMPANY PERPETUATES THE PAST

Company rule was resolutely practical, and, when the views of some of the founders, such as Munro and Mountstuart Elphinstone (who was Governor of Bombay from 1819 to 1827), are considered, the reasons for this non-doctrinaire pragmatism are obvious. These men and others of their time were impressed by the institutional framework which they discovered beneath the shell of the Indian regimes they defeated. The first generation of Company administrators found these institutions efficient and the elite strata of Indians who managed them capable, responsible and responsive to the political tasks of the Company.

Moreover, Indian men of wealth and property were attracted to the protection of their property and the opportunities presented by the Company to increase it; this tendency obviously applied to the zamindar beneficiaries of the Cornwallis land policy and to leaders of dominant peasant castes in the ryotwari system of Madras and Bombay to whom jobs and privileges were offered. It also characterized the heads of landed clans in the Gangetic area, where exclusive rights were conferred upon village communities and their landed 'brotherhoods'. In general, then, the ancient powers of local magnates over lower groups of tenants and landless labourers were reinforced, and new opportunities were offered to the older scribal groups who found secure and pensionable employment in Company or European business offices. For many Indian groups, the first half-century of European colonial dominance offered opportunities for good business and good careers; few threats were offered to the interests or standing of the majority who renounced military resistance to the Company. Company practices persisted along these lines until about 1830, refining the older mercantilist practices of eighteenth-century regimes, and bringing them to the highest point of their development; furthermore, the Company provided at least as much protection for cultural and religious institutions as had any of these older regimes.

SLAVERY IN INDIA

One indigenous institution that was controversially perpetuated by Company rule was slavery, whose history exemplifies the enmeshing of British and indigenous elite interests. When the East India Company charter came up for renewal in 1833, there was a good deal of pressure in Parliament to link it with the Emancipation Act, which was simultaneously being considered. In fact the Emancipation Act of 1833 was originally supposed to abolish slavery in all the British colonies, but in the end was amended to apply only to four areas:

the West Indies, Mauritius, Canada and the Cape of Good Hope. In British India, slavery continued to flourish on so large a scale that, it was protested, abolition would cause great economic hardship. The slaves set free in the colonies in 1834 were estimated at about one million; the numbers in North and South America at about four million. Several estimates of the numbers in India have been made, and run between eight million and double that amount. Even the lower figure means there were three times as many slaves in India as in the United States at that time, and more than in all the countries of the New World combined.

The general British policy was one of non-interference with the social and religious customs of the country. Nevertheless, the government did from time to time prohibit practices it considered particularly objectionable, such as sati, female infanticide and dacoity (*thagi*): the murder of travellers and theft of their valuables, including children, whose practitioners claimed for it the status of a caste occupation. But, unlike sati and infanticide, to interfere with slavery would interfere not only in the family but in property, which was even more sacred. Hence the abolition of slavery was slower in arriving. Its continuance in British India was justified by officials there in a number of ways. First, it was of immemorial antiquity, and inherited by the Europeans, not instituted by them as in the Americas. Moreover, it was not a matter of race, and only partly of caste.

It is certainly true that slavery was very ancient. The inveterate categorizer Manu recognized seven types, according to the terms under which the slave was acquired:

> There are slaves of seven kinds, [viz.] he who is made captive under a standard [i.e. a prisoner of war], he who serves for his daily food, he who is born in the house, he who is bought and he who is given, he who is inherited from ancestors, and he who is enslaved by way of punishment.[1]

Narada, in his dharmashastra, went further than Manu on this occasion too, subdividing and adding categories to bring the number up to fifteen, one of which apparently included a child whose adoption was defective in some way, while another resulted from a lost wager. In addition, bondage for debt and non-payment of taxes were added, if they did not exist in antiquity.

The nature of Indian slavery was extremely complex and cut across the categories of caste, kin, gender, religion and role. Although slaves were usually thought of as coming from the shudra castes, members of other varnas could be enslaved as well. In theory, slaves were supposed to be of lower caste than their masters, but we have already seen that the first Nizam of Murshidabad is reputed to have been a brahman boy sold into slavery, although by the rule brahmans were exempted from bondage.

Slavery was also part and parcel of Muslim traditions and institutions. We have seen that the founders of the Delhi sultanate were known as the 'Slave Dynasty' because they arose from a soldiery whose ranks were composed of men, mostly of Turkic extraction, who had been sold as children into military service. The emperor Akbar enrolled his slaves among his 'disciples', who also included some of the highest grandees in the land.

Thus slaves in India were not only acquired in different ways but played many different roles. In addition to agricultural and military slaves, domestic slavery was pervasive. While for plantation work strong adult males were the most desirable, for their many different roles and functions Indians preferred to acquire children of both sexes who could be trained up to the master's (or mistress's) requirements. They were trained in a great variety of skills to function as cooks, seamstresses, musicians, dancers, weavers, dyers, scribes, business agents, carpenters, ironmongers, surgeons, bricklayers and every other type of craft, as well as body servants and menials. Female slaves were if anything more useful, since, in addition to the various economic, entertainment and status-enhancing skills and roles they could perform, they were the producers of other slaves, and these were a valuable commodity. In general, the status of a child was held to follow that of its mother, though the master could decide otherwise.

A distinction is still sometimes made in the literature on the subject between slaves whose function was primarily to bring wealth to their owners through productive labour and those who provided comfort, entertainment and status – supposedly the Indian type. This is clearly a false distinction, not only because of the numerous useful economic activities in which Indian slaves engaged, and because domestic and entertainment activities themselves have economic value, but because Indian slavery did include agricultural labourers. The East India Company itself owned slaves who worked their estates in Malabar. However, unlike in the American system, slaves belonging to wealthy landowners often had land given to them either rent free or for a nominal rent, from which they were expected to support themselves. In return, they were required to render certain services to their masters. In parts of southern India, such as Malabar, Karnataka and the Tamil country, there were many such slaves.

Unlike in the American version, where slaves were of a different race from their masters, the line between the free and the unfree in the Indian household was not drawn with absolute clarity; in any case, the enormous powers possessed by the patriarchal heads of households meant that the control they exercised over their wives and children was not much different in either degree or kind from their control over their slaves. The great diversity and the tendency of many domestic slaves to be considered and treated as quasi-kin, secondary wives and children, on occasion even to inherit from or succeed their masters, gave some British officials the impression that Indian slavery was mild if not benign. It was often looked on as an alternative to death or other forms of punishment, such as imprisonment or transportation, so that the slave owner sometimes pictured himself in the role of saviour, providing the slave with home, family and employment. Sir William Jones, the Sanskrit scholar and judge of the Supreme Court, referred to his own child slaves as those he had 'rescued from death or misery' in almost the same breath as he deplored the sight of boatloads of children, most of them stolen from their parents, coming down the river to be sold in Calcutta.[2]

In times of famine, parents often sold their children, men their wives or sisters, and adults themselves in exchange for security and food, leading one of the Indian Law Commissioners investigating in 1840 to refer to slavery as 'the Indian poor law'. In fact, the high cost of alternative means of sustaining the destitute was an important consideration impeding abolition.

But there were certainly other aspects of the British involvement with slave-owning that were more difficult to extenuate. Among the British in eighteenth-century India, black slaves, who were called 'coffrees', were particularly fashionable (as they were in Europe, too – it was not until 1772 that a court case decided that slavery had no basis in law in England). The overseas trade in both directions was extensive and carried on very profitably, first by the Portuguese, then by the French and Dutch. Boys were often castrated in the Middle East before being shipped to India; the majority did not survive the journey. Those that did were in demand as keepers of the harems of wealthy Indians.

The British were actively engaged in the practice of slavery not only as individuals, but on an institutional level as well, since their administrators and courts were charged with supervision and enforcement: penalizing owners who employed excessively cruel punishments, deciding the disposition of runaways, and defining and regulating the conditions of servitude and the slave trade. This led to a number of paradoxical and inconsistent decisions. In 1772, for example, Warren Hastings decided that enslavement was an appropriate punishment for dacoity. Two years later he declared that the practice of stealing children from their parents in order to sell them had increased since the advent of British government; the remedy was the enforcement of the rule that no slave should be sold without a deed establishing the right of the seller (often the parent) to dispose of him.

In addition to the kidnapping of children, other aspects that English gentlemen found repugnant about slavery included the overseas trade which was so extensively carried out by their Dutch and French rivals and the sale of girl children to mistresses of dancing troupes, with all the implications of unchastity that surrounded dancing girls. The route chosen by reforming officials in India was that of mitigation and amelioration, with abolition as the eventual stated goal. After issuing his regulation forbidding the sale of slaves without certified documentation that they were already in a state of servitude, Hastings was asked by the provincial council at Dacca whether slave status, under his ruling, was to continue to be extended to the children of slaves born subsequently. The Council anxiously reminded him that 'it is an established Custom throughout the Dacca Districts to keep in Bondage all the offspring and descendants of persons who have once become slaves'.[3]

Instead of abolition, efforts were first made to suppress the export trade, which was carried on with particular vigour by the Company's Dutch and French competitors, but these were ineffectual. Even when slavery was finally abolished by the government of India in 1843, it was done in a somewhat indirect fashion by an act stating that government officers were no longer to sell slaves for rent or revenue, and the courts and judicial machinery would no longer enforce the rights of slave owners to their slaves. As one writer noted, the provisions aimed mainly at transforming the condition of agricultural slaves, difficult as it was for them even to know their new-found rights, let alone to enforce them. For domestic slaves it was even more difficult, and there are doubts about whether such slavery has even yet disappeared.

THE EMERGENCE OF A NEW ORDER

The symbiotic relationship between India's nascent capitalist and gentry classes and the East India Company started to come under new pressures during the first quarter of the nineteenth century and, by around 1830, can be seen to have given way to a new configuration of political forces, marked much more clearly by British ascendency and the trappings of 'colonialism'. Several factors lay behind this shift. First, India's terms of trade with the rest of the world economy had changed. Until the 1820s, the Company had broadly maintained and exploited the mercantilist system developed in concert with predecessor regimes. But then, the proportion of finished textiles exported from India was reduced and the amount of raw cotton to supply Britain's textile mills increased; second, the pattern of export booms and slumps became more marked. Both were consequences of the deepened penetration of the world economy in general and that of its European leader, Britain, in particular, along with an advancing integration of a national market and monetary system in India under colonial auspices. This historic reversal in India's trade with the rest of the world was the first sign of its financial subordination.

Napoleon's blockade of Europe from 1807 reduced the volume of imports of Indian textiles, which stimulated cloth production in Britain. Unlike the Indian, British cloth was now produced by factory methods, on the lines that had been stimulated by wartime needs for military uniforms and arms. With the defeat of revolutionary France, a reverse flow of textiles to India initiated a long-term partial deindustrialization of Indian cloth production. This reversal also negated the continued monopoly of the Company, which was increasingly under criticism as British merchant capital sought access to Indian markets. The Company's monopoly of trade with India was ended in 1813, and in 1833 all trade by the Company was terminated. The parliamentary charter renewed for the East India Company in that year suggested that the Company would not endure for much longer: the Crown was now prepared to assume direct rule.

From Roman times, export surpluses from India were balanced by imports of silver and gold. This changed after 1835, when the value of imports began to increase rapidly, reaching a peak around 1860, partly owing to the high costs of the industrial goods required for the construction of railways on the subcontinent. Another reversal of India's international economic relations had to do with the triangular trade that had long existed between Britain, India and China, in which Indian bankers and shippers played an important role. During the middle decades of the nineteenth century that trade was replaced by direct, bilateral, commercial links between a hegemonic imperial Britain and a Chinese empire enfeebled by the military humiliation inflicted by

Europeans. Trade concessions from a defeated China opened preferential access for British capital through the favoured form of the managing agency.

These shifts in the patterns of trade, together with the growing power of Britain's industrial monopoly, altered the character of the relations between British and Indian capital. The Company was dependent upon Indian capital from the very beginning of its operations in the early seventeenth century, and this reliance continued after the East India Company assumed territorial control in the later eighteenth century. Indian bankers and traders shifted their skills and resources to the mercantilist interests of the British masters of the country and served them with even greater zeal than they had served the old Indian mercantilist regimes, for under the British property and wealth proved more secure. In the countryside, this cooperation was to continue into the later nineteenth century, thanks to changes in the laws that assisted the development and maintenance of a wealthy and protected rural class of rentier and usurer interests.

In the cities and where international commodities were produced and gathered for export, however, Indian capitalists were destined to be frozen out by foreign capital. They were displaced from their earlier central and profitable role in ship-building and owning, and in banking and insurance, after the 1830s, when British managing agencies took over the most lucrative lines of the buoyant international commerce of the later nineteenth century, while Indian capital retreated into less profitable ventures. Competition between indigenous and foreign capitalists continued in this disadvantageous course for a further century. Managing agencies flourished as centres of western capital until the 1830s, when many collapsed as a consequence of a world depression in trade. The next economic crisis, that of 1846–7, finished off the first to have been undertaken by Indian capitalists, that of Dwarkanath Tagore, grandfather of another precedent-breaker, Rabindranath Tagore, the Bengali poet and Nobel laureate.

STATE INTERVENTION, SOCIAL REFORM, AND 'SATI'

The shift in relations between British and Indian capital and the transition to a new capitalist order in India was most closely associated with the governor-generalship of Lord William Cavendish Bentinck, which began in 1828. Under his administration, policies which had limited the ambitions of government to those inherited from predecessor regimes began to be abandoned and stronger, if by no means wholly committed, policies of 'reform' and 'improvement' were substituted in their stead. In the economic sphere, Bentinck invested in improved transport facilities, which enhanced the impact of British imports and opened the way for cheap, industrially produced cloth to displace Indian textiles and to deal a death-blow to the ancient commercial structure.

The overtly interventionist policies in social and economic matters marked a heightened confidence in the British rulers. Bentinck's modernizing reforms had the effect of favouring the interests of capitalists, especially those of Britain, against the older landed groups of India. Some interpretations of the

Indian Rebellion of 1857–9 – that greatest of challenges to British rule – insist that Bentinck's measures in the 1830s contributed to it. They represented an attempt to impose the social mores of metropolitan capitalists on to their erstwhile Indian collaborators, who were in the process of being moved steadily to a moral, as well as economic and political, periphery.

The most celebrated of Bentinck's interventions concerned the abolition of *sati* (or 'suttee', the immolation of Hindu widows in the cremation fires of their husbands), which, along with that of other 'odious practices', was pressed on the Company as an objective of reform by the increasing number of Christian missionaries and British business travellers present in India. The issue of sati abolition gave rise to great controversy. Most notably, it divided the generation of Indian intellectuals and commercial men who had grown up with the rise of British power and were now obliged to confront its fuller meaning for the future of their own society. On one side stood the likes of Ram Mohun Roy, who was strongly opposed to the practice. Roy not only brought to bear a variety of learned arguments to support his case, but showed deep sympathy over the cruelties and indignities women were forced to endure in everyday life; in his view sati was only the extreme logical extension of the general degradation that was the lot of Hindu females in his time, as for millennia in the past. Among his most passionate and eloquent denunciations of the treatment of women by his compatriots were two pamphlets, originally written in Bengali some dozen years before abolition and self-translated into English. In these pamphlets Roy simulated debates between an 'advocate' and an 'opponent' of sati. Of course, all the best lines went to the 'opponent', who was particularly incensed by the extra atrocity of tying the unfortunate widow to the funeral pile to make sure she did not escape. At the end of the 'second debate' the 'opponent' concluded:

> At marriage the wife is recognized as half of her husband, but in after-conduct they are treated worse than inferior animals. For the woman is employed to do the work of a slave in the house, such as, in her turn, to clean the place very early in the morning, whether cold or wet, to scour the dishes, to wash the floor, to cook night and day, to prepare and serve food for her husband, father[-in-law], mother-in-law, sisters-in-law, brothers-in-law, and friends and connections! . . . If in the preparation or serving up of the victuals they commit the smallest fault, what insult do they not receive from their husband, their mother-in-law, and the younger brothers of their husband? After all the male part of the family have satisfied themselves, the women content themselves with what may be left, whether sufficient in quantity or not . . . As long as the husband is poor, she suffers every kind of trouble, and when he becomes rich, she is altogether heart-broken . . . If unable to bear such cruel usage, a wife leaves her husband's house to live separately from him, then the influence of the husband with the magisterial authority is generally sufficient to place her again in his hands; when, in revenge for her quitting him, he seizes every pretext to torment her in various ways, and sometimes even puts her privately to death. These are facts occurring every day and not to be denied. What I lament is, that, seeing the women thus dependent and exposed to every misery, you feel for them no compassion, that might exempt them from being tied down and burnt to death.[4]

Plate 21 The fiery trial of Sita; Rama and Lakshmana salute her miraculous preservation which demonstrates that she had not been guilty of having been raped in captivity. When a widow burned on her husband's funeral pyre, that, too, was held to demonstrate her chastity and fidelity. The fact that Sita, the model of wifely virtue, was required to make this incendiary demonstration shows that the association was made in Indian tradition as early as the finalization of the *Ramayana*. Panel from a Bengal story-telling scroll, mid-nineteenth century (BM OA. 1955. 10-8. 096, Courtesy of the Trustees of the British Museum).

Some of Roy's contemporaries saw things differently and opposed the abolition regulation of 1829. Their own arguments were laid out in two petitions, both phrased in all the terms the writers felt might have weight with their peculiar conquerors, who talked of freedom and welfare but employed force and expropriation, and reflected a sensitivity to the use repeatedly made of women as objects in defining the limits of colonial intervention; more along those lines was to come later in the century.

What is curious is that, while the opponents of sati pictured the widow as weak, helpless and often drugged, the advocates presented her as strong, self-willed and heroic. The first petition, presented to Lord William Bentinck in opposition to his determination to abolish the practice, stated:

Under the sanction of immemorial usage as well as precept, Hindoo widows perform, of their own accord and pleasure, and for the benefit of their Husbands' souls and for their own, the sacrifice of self-immolation called Suttee – which is not merely a sacred *duty* but a high privilege to her who sincerely believes in the doctrines of her religion – and we humbly submit that any interference with a persuasion of so high and self-annihilating nature is not only an unjust and intolerant dictation into matters of conscience, but is likely wholly to fail in procuring the end proposed.[5]

When this petition wholly failed in procuring the end proposed, a second petition was sent to the Privy Council in London, the court of last appeal. In it, sati was defended on the grounds of ancient custom and 'our sacred books [which] we deny the right of our Rulers to judge'. It too argued that the Governor-General's regulation against sati violated the constitutional guarantees of Indian subjects to religious freedom, and went on to compare the Hindu population favourably with their Muslim compatriots with respect to loyalty, but ended with a veiled threat:

> For above a century the Hindoo population of British India has always been the most attached . . . of Your Majesty's native subjects . . . conciliated by the toleration and protection hitherto strictly observed and exercised towards their religion, caste, and habits, and not, like another class of their native fellow-subjects [i.e. Muslims], regretting a lost domination. On Hindoo allegiance and fidelity the local Government [i.e. the Bengal Presidency] have ever reposed with the most implicit and deserved confidence. Their solidarity composes by far the largest portion of a numerous and gallant army . . . The Hindoos compose nine-tenths of the population of British India, and of this Presidency by far the largest proportion of men of wealth, of intelligence, of enterprise, and of knowledge . . . who with one voice implore the abrogation of the first law which has given them serious reasons to dread that their own faith and their own laws will no longer be preserved to them inviolable.[6]

This petition failed as well, and sati was legally abolished. Yet sati, after all, affected only a small number of upper or aspiring castes, and, as Roy pointed out, the conditions of the generality of women during their lives remained wretched, regardless of whether sati was legal or not. During the entire sati debate, women themselves were never heard from, while for men it was not so much the issue itself, but control of social custom, that touched a nerve.

THE CONSOLIDATION OF BRITISH POWER

Behind the new confidence expressed by Bentinck's government also lay the harder fact that, by the late 1820s, the Company's arms had succeeded in establishing a seemingly unassailable dominance over the Indian polity that altered the nature of collaborative relationships not only with Indian commercial and banking groups in places like Calcutta, but with Indian society at large. The first generation of colonial rulers could not have installed British authority but for the collaboration of powerful landed groups, wealthy commercial interests and influential scribes. Collaborators such as these were protected by Company officials and were further strengthened by judicial and land tenure changes. Property relations and the legal and police protection given to individual wealth were important privileges which persuaded local elites to surrender their domination over minor administrative offices in favour of the secure status of landed proprietors. By the middle decades of the nineteenth century the leadership strata of rural and many urban communities had discovered that there were greater advantages for themselves and their families through a British connection than could be realized through the historical communities from which they had emerged.

During their early rule, the British anxiously sought allies in the country-side, and in the end it was the Indian sepoys of the Company who won India for them. Though some of these soldiers were recruited from the river plains first seized by the Company, most came from small landed households in the dry uplands, who had for long augmented household income and status with martial pursuits. These included major peasant groups like the Jats of the north, the Marathas of the west and the Reddis of the south; all had domin-ated their respective countrysides, not so much as a result of formal political offices or of any high caste standing they possessed, but because from their humble ranks came the mass of small and some large landlords, and they were the sort who prospered under early Company rule. Some of the more substan-tial ruling families, descended from military mercenary forebears, preserved a tenuous independence by entering into the subsidiary alliances that Lord Wellesley (the Governor-General from 1798 to 1805) had offered. It was an exchange of the security of their local authority and prerogatives in return for acceptance of the Company's suzerainty and some tribute.

These were the groups upon whom the Company's eighteenth-century operations had depended, but they began to be prised from their close alliance with the Company during Bentinck's time. In the parts of British India where the *ryotwari* system (in which land was settled on the cultivator by the govern-ment for a fixed period, while the government took half the produce) was established, many of the smaller rural magnates who had achieved new and secure wealth as minor officials in the Company's revenue operations found that they were being replaced by scribal specialists acting under the increas-ingly direct administrative management of European Company officers. Where revenue systems other than ryotwari operated, some landed household-ers found themselves eased from positions of wealth and local authority, although others actually improved their positions under the early nineteenth-century Company regime. Formerly great lords found matters more difficult and dangerous as the few remaining large Indian kingdoms suffered defeat at the hands of the Company. The Marathas were finally overcome in 1818; the first of a series of wars against the kingdom of Burma was launched in 1824; Sind was annexed in 1843; and the defeat of the Sikhs brought the Punjab under Company rule in 1849.

These victories consolidated the reputation of the Company's soldiery and reduced the need for subsidiary allies, princely or yeomanly. The relinquishing of the native allies had the added advantage of silencing criticism from the Company's enemies in Britain that such alliances simply perpetuated the tyrannical rule of Indian princes, who were easy in the assurance that any rising of their subjects would be put down by British-led Company troops.

The result was extension of direct Company rule over yet more of the territories previously under independent rulers – often in violation of existing treaties. Departures from earlier Company practice such as these loosed a deepening anxiety in the core of Indian civil society, which had included a very widespread constituency of Company supporters.

MUTINY AND REVOLT

Had the confidence of the British in Bentinck's time not been tinged with a heightening of racial arrogance, they might have paid more heed to this deepening anxiety. The precipitate advance of British power was accompanied by a growing restlessness in some key areas of the new state. Armed uprisings against the engulfing British overlordship became more frequent, although the Company was always able to restore order, thanks to the loyalty and efficiency of its sepoys. Therefore, any rebellion in the sepoy garrisons caused alarm. At Vellore, in the Madras Presidency, Muslim sepoys rose against their officers in 1806, supposedly agitated by Muslim sympathizers with the family of the defeated Tipu Sultan of Mysore. Moreover, Hindu soldiers were disaffected by the Christian evangelical activities of some British commanders. At Barrackpur, in Bengal, soldiers refused service in the second Burmese War in 1824 on the grounds that the perquisites of past service were not being offered. Both these insubordinations were put down with relative ease, and afterwards the commanders expressed renewed confidence in the loyalty of their troops. They failed to recognize the widespread unrest that had come into being by 1857, much of it concentrated in strategic Awadh in the central Gangetic plain, whose ruling family was dismissed for 'misrule' in 1856.

The great Indian Mutiny and Civil Rebellion of 1857 came as a shock that was to reverberate through all the relations of the British Indian empire for the next ninety years. Large numbers of sepoys in the Bengal army rose against British rule and set out to restore a variety of previous ruling dynasties. As their action threatened the military force which was the real basis of British power, so a widespread civil rebellion also emerged in which many of the newly installed institutions associated with the 'modernizing' imperatives of the empire – law courts, government offices, Christian missionaries – were singled out for attack. For a moment it appeared as if the century of British rule since the battle of Plassey was about to be wiped away from India's history.

But it was not to be. Once more Indian allies came to the rescue. During the months that rebellion raged in the north, large parts of British India remained peaceful and Company soldiers steadfast to their British officers. In several cases this was highly surprising. The Bombay army consisted of men recruited from the yeomanry of Maharashtra, whom the East India Company had required three wars to defeat less than half a century earlier, and the Sikh soldiers of the Company's Punjab army, who had been defeated by the British a mere eight years before 1857. Both joined in suppressing the mutinous soldiers of the Gangetic plain, and even in the heartland of the civil uprising against Company rule in 1857 there were many local magnates who refused to participate or to allow the mutineers to establish control in their localities.

The Mutiny was defeated; yet it taught a lesson which the British thereafter were not slow to learn. This was that Indian interest and opinion had to be consulted more closely in any 'modern' development under colonial rule. Too precipitate or rapid a move to impose 'Anglicist' conventions and mores ran the risk of alienating important collaborators and promoting disaffection. From then on, the Raj would advance with greater caution and, if its objectives still remained some species of 'modernization', they would have to be at least partly anchored in Indian society itself. The mission adopted in Bentinck's time, to convert Indians to Englishmen, was abandoned after 1857 in favour of a turning back to collaboration – although on terms in which the metropolitan power of Britain was firmly underscored.

LATE COMPANY RULE

There can be no account of the institutions and culture of the Indian subcontinent during the past 150 years that does not place colonial subjugation at the centre. Domination extended to all of the basic institutions – political, economic and cultural – but did not extend to replacing indigenous institutions with British ones. As colonial subjects, Indians were neither invited nor permitted to enjoy the rights of 'freeborn Englishmen'. Instead, British political and economic domination left many earlier institutions only partially transformed. The new social classes that took root were not those that might have been formed had India's modern capitalism evolved in other circumstances.

India's colonial capitalism replicated the class forms of capitalism anywhere, but with special imperialist markings. The Indian bourgeoisie was very slow to free itself from the tutelage of British business and the British state in India; Indian capitalists were slow to decide to risk their wealth by supporting nationalist forces, and only did so when many became convinced that national independence would be achieved and that their task was to guard against an independent regime that was hostile to Indian big business. Another major social segment of capitalist society – the middle class, or petty bourgeoisie – was very large and politically very important. Its evolution under colonial domination determined that it was never a national class in the sense that the high Indian bourgeoisie was. Instead, a highly fragmented lower-middle class emerged, one that maintained close connections with the diverse communitarian bases from which it complexly and slowly emerged after the sixteenth century. It carried with it, as its essential ideology, robust community orientations and values.

Social transformation in the territories under the English East India Company intensified around the first quarter of the nineteenth century. Politically, the colonial regime passed from the experienced officials of the East India Company in London and in India, mainly concerned with India and China, into the control of others more concerned with evolving imperial interests which the Raj was intended to serve. The determination of Indian policy passed from one set of institutions to another. Until 1858, policy had been set by the major stockholders of the East India Company, together with nominees of successive British ministries to a body commonly called 'The Board of Control', established in 1784 (as Parliamentary Commissioners for Affairs in India). After 1858, Indian policy was set by ministers of the Crown, a change that had been contemplated in charters granted by Parliament to the Company, the most recent in 1854.

PART IV

Contemporary South Asia

CHRONOLOGY OF PART IV

1877 CE Queen Victoria calls herself Empress of India.
1878 CE Indian Forest Act claims state ownership, denies traditional rights.
1861 CE Indian Councils Act gives Indians local electoral participation.
1885 CE First meeting of Indian National Congress.
1883 CE Famine Code; Ilbert Bill initiates local self-government.
1891 CE Age of Consent Bill.
1892 CE Indian Councils Act increases Indian participation in local government.
1893 CE Cow protection agitation Hindu–Muslim hostility.
1905 CE Partition of Bengal; boycott of imported cloth; swadeshi movement.
1906 CE Muslim League founded.
1907 CE Rise of 'extremist' nationalism challenges 'moderate' Congressmen.
1909 CE Morley–Minto reforms initiate communal representation in legislatures.
1912 CE Capital moved from Calcutta to New Delhi.
1914–1918 CE First World War.
1915 CE Gandhi returns to India from South Africa, enters politics.
1917 CE Rowlatt Acts threaten civil liberties.
1918 CE Montague–Chelmsford Report promising further political reforms.
1919 CE Amritsar massacre.
1920 CE Khilafat and non-cooperation movements; Gandhi reorganizes Congress.
1922 CE Gandhi suspends non-cooperation because of violence; Gandhi is jailed.
1924 CE Khilafat movement ends as Caliphate is abolished.
1924–1925 CE Vaikam satyagraha.
1927 CE Appointment of Simon Commission.
1929–1939 CE Great Depression.
1930 CE Gandhi marches to Dandi to protest the salt tax, is jailed.
1930–1932 CE Round Table Conference.
1930–1935 CE Civil Disobedience campaign.
1931 CE Gandhi–Irwin Pact; Gandhi attends Round Table Conference.
1932 CE Pune Pact giving reserved legislative places to the depressed classes.
1935 CE Government of India Act, later basis for the Indian constitution.
1939–1945 CE Second World War.
1940 CE Lahore Resolution. Muslim League calls for separate Muslim state.
1942 CE Bose goes to Japan, then recruits pro-Japanese Indian army. Cripps's mission offers move to dominion status; 'Quit India' movement.
1943 CE Man-made Bengal famine.
1947 CE Independence and partition of India and Pakistan; major violence ensues.
1948 CE Murder of Gandhi; death of Jinnah. Ceasefire in Indo-Pakistan war over Kashmir.
1949 CE Indian Constitution adopted.
1950 CE Patel dies.
1951 CE Beginning of the Farakka Barrage scheme.
1952 CE India adopts family planning to slow population growth.
1955 CE Bandung Conference; Hindu Marriage Act sets minimum marriage ages.
1956 CE Pakistan Constitution adopted; India reorganized on linguistic lines.
1958 CE Pakistan Constitution abrogated; Ayub Khan rules by military coup.
1959 CE Presidential rule imposed over Kerala.
1961 CE Dowry Prohibition Act; start of the Sardar Sarovar Project; Goa seized.
1962 CE War with China over remote Aksai Chin; India suffers defeat.
1964 CE Nehru dies.
Mid-1960s CE Green Revolution.
1971 CE Bangladesh (East Pakistan) becomes independent.

EXTENDED READING FOR PART IV

Kumkum Sangari and Sudesh Vaid (eds), *Recasting Women: Essays in Indian Colonial History*. New Brunswick, NJ: Rutgers University Press, 1990. Set of topics on women under British colonialism, feminist and nationalist.
Eleanor Zelliot, *From Untouchable to Dalit: Essays on the Ambedkar Movement*. New Delhi:

Manohar, 1992. Set of essays on the emergence of self-conscious identity and politics of India's oppressed castes, with emphasis on Ambedkar and the Mahars.

Michael Edwardes, *The Myth of the Mahatma: Gandhi, the British and the Raj*. London: Constable, 1986. Debunking view of the British as imperialists in India – and the opponent they found to their liking.

Emma Tarlo, *Clothing Matters: Dress and Identity in India*. London: Hurst and Company, 1996. Wide-ranging study of the social and political (as well as aesthetic) considerations that have gone into Indian national, caste and regional dress. Wonderful accounts of the nineteenth-century colonial influence and Gandhi's obsession with undyed homespun and handloomed wear.

Partha Mitter, *Art and Nationalism in Colonial India, 1850–1922 (Occidental Orientations)*. Cambridge: Cambridge University Press, 1994. A study of the impact of western art, social attitudes and politics on British India, mostly through the set of painters, printmakers and cartoonists who debated the extent to which European artistic styles and technology could be adapted to traditional Indian iconography on the one hand, and social and political satire on the other.

Kingsley Davis, *The Population of India and Pakistan*. New York: Russell & Russell, 1951. Argument by world's leading living demographer that the governments of the subcontinent should introduce population curbing policies; published just before India took the plunge. Shows how far contraceptive use has penetrated the population since, when it was essentially limited to the urban upper class.

Tim Dyson (ed.), *India's Historical Demography: Studies in Famine, Disease and Society*. London: Curzon Press, 1989. Collection of topical essays. Very technical, but enlightening on the interactions between famine and disease, between famine and fertility, and why the difference in male and female death rates increased as overall mortality decreased.

T. Richard Blurton, *Hindu Art*. London: British Museum Press, 1992. Beautifully illustrated and succinctly explicated survey covering painting, sculpture and religious architecture from the seals of Mohenjo-Daro to the folk figurines and posters of the present.

Amita Baviskar, *In the Belly of the River: Tribal Conflicts over Development in the Narmada Valley*. Delhi: Oxford University Press, 1995. Very interesting description and discussion of the background and history of the Narmada Valley controversy, from the point of view of a participant observer. Candid about intra-village politics.

Thomas Weber, *Hugging the Trees: the Story of the Chipko Movement*. New Delhi: Viking (Penguin), 1987. A sympathetic account of its Gandhian as well as historical roots, but includes all the controversies and myths about the movement (e.g. that it was a women's movement); now a bit dated.

Ramachandra Guha, *The Unquiet Woods: Ecological Change and Peasant Resistance in the Himalaya*. Berkeley: University of California Press, 1990. A background and history of the Chipko movement as the culmination of a century of peasant resistance to government and business appropriation of traditional rights and resources. Identifies three wings of the movement.

S. Theodore Baskaran, *The Message Bearers: the Nationalist Politics and the Entertainment Media in South India, 1880–1945*. Madras: Cre-A, 1981. The popular arts, drama, songs and cinema, particularly in regional languages, were difficult for the British to censor effectively, and became vehicles for the expression of nationalist aspirations.

Hermann Goetz, *India: Five Thousand Years of Indian Art*. London: Methuen, 1964. Unusually, includes dance in this wide-ranging survey of the visual arts.

Sumit Guha, *Environment, Ethnicity and Politics in India 1350–1991*. Cambridge: Cambridge University Press, forthcoming. A study of 'tribal communities' which argues that their apparent timeless isolation is an artefact of racial anthropology and colonial policy, and that they were previously major participants in the political and economic transactions that constituted regional polities in South Asia.

Sumit Guha (ed.), *Agricultural Productivity in British India: Growth, Stagnation or Decline?*. Delhi: Oxford University Press, 1992. Reviews the titular controversy and argues on the basis of substantial new material and research that agricultural output did in fact stagnate in India through the first half of the twentieth century.

Christopher Bayly, *Rulers, Townsmen and Bazaars; North Indian Society in the Age of British Expansion, 1770–1870*. Cambridge: Cambridge University Press, 1983. Argues against the prevailing view that chaos followed Aurangzeb's death in 1707. Says that the states created during the eighteenth century borrowed freely from and improvised upon Mughal institutions and practices, with the result that their political systems and economy were more robust and orderly than previously supposed.

Joyce Lebra-Chapman, *The Rani of Jhansi: a Study in Female Heroism in India*. Honolulu: University of Hawaii Press, 1986. An accounting and analysis of the legendary status of 'India's Joan of Arc', 'the best and bravest of the rebels' of the Mutiny of 1857.

IMPORTANT EVENTS IN THE INDEPENDENCE STRUGGLE 1879–1947

AFGHANISTAN

Sources of Khilafat Hijrah (migration) to Afghanistan, '20

SIND

Muslim movemnt to separate Sind from Bombay, '23-'26

Karachi

• Srinagar '31
▲ Kohat '24
Lahore Conspiracy case '28
• Jammu '31
A '27
W. & C. PUNJAB
Multan • '22 '46-'47

Amritsar Jallianwala Bagh massacre, '19

Delhi Coronation Durbar, '11 Capital moved from Calcutta '12

Court martials of India National Army officers, '45-'46

▲ Katarpur '18
Meerut Communist conspiracy trial, '29-'33

GURGAON DT. BHARATPUR & ALWAR
▲ '24, '47

Aligarh 1st nationalist university estd., '20; shifted to Delhi '25

Lucknow 1st Khilafat Conference, '11

Cawnpore ▲ '31
AGRA DT. '31 '47

Allahabad Nehru home becomes Congress HQ, '30

UNITED PROV. AND BIHAR

W. BIHAR 1893-94, '17

CHINA

RAE BARELI DT. Center of No-Rent Campaign, '30-'32

Chauri Chaura: mob violence leads Gandhi to halt non-cooperation campaign, '22

CHAMPARAN DT. Indigo tenants' campaign, '17

Bengal partition line '05-'12

NEPAL

B
B, C

C. BIHAR '46

1897, '26, '46

Dacca

Comilla

BHUTAN

C KAMRUP DT.

Muslim League estd., '08

Meirang Indian National Army hoists flag on Indian soil '43

KAIRA DT. No-tax campaign, '18

Ahmedabad ⊕ '16, '18
▲ Labor satyagraha, '18
B, C
INDIA

C Calcutta 1897, '26, '46

Salt March/ Ahmedabad to Dandi, '30
C
Dandi

Indian National Congress estd. by A. O Hume et al., 1885

Trials of B. G. Tilak, 1897, '08; mass demonstrations follow

Abortive rebellion of V. B. Phadke, 1879 Ganapati Festival estd. by B. G. Tilak, 1873; spreads throughout Maharashtra

Servants of India Soc. estd. by G. K. Gokhale, '06 Home Rule League estd. by B. G. Tilak, '16

Nagpur Rashtriya Swayamsevak Sangh (RSS) estd. '25
C
Wardha ⊕ '36
Flag satyagraha, '23

KHANDESH
Bombay ▲ 1893, '29, '32
Poona • Raigad Shivaji Festival estd. by B. G. Tilak, 1896; spreads throughout Maharashtra
C
Gulbarga • '24
B, C

CENTRAL INDIA

C

ORISSA

Utkal movement for separate Orissa, '03-'35

NOAKHALI and TIPPERA DTS., tour by Gandhi to restore harmony, '46-'47

KORAPUT DT.

BURMA

Separated from India in '37; indep. in '48.

SATARA DT.

DHARWAR DT.

Movement for separate Andhra province, '13 ff.

W. GODAVARI & GUNTUR DTS.

ANDAMAN ISLANDS

Penal settlement for prominent political activists

Port Blair

COIMBATORE DT.

MALABAR DT.
• Madras
Home Rule League established by Annie Besant, '46

Moplah Rebellion in support of Khilafat Movement '21-'22
C

Widespread liquor shop picketing in S. India, '31

J.E.S./P.A.S.

CEYLON
Indep. in '48.
▲ Mooloya Estate '40

LEGEND

⊕ Gandhian ashram with date of founding

⚲ Gandhian activity

▲ Major riot with political consequences

⚓ Chief sites of Royal Indian Navy mutiny, 1946

Areas of widespread disturbances and independence campaigns: A 1919, B 1920-22, C 1942

Areas of widespread communal riots, 1946-47

☐ Political/social movements (movements drawing support from wide areas are shown, with panels placed at headquarters of place of founding)

DATES: Years in the 19th century are noted in full, for years in the 20th century, the initial "19" is omited.

0   100   200   300   400   500 miles

0   200   400   600 kilometres

MILESTONES ON THE ROAD TO INDEPENDENCE

1885 - Founding of Indian National Congress (INC)

1905 - Bengal partition leads to Swadeshi movement, spreading to many parts of India, 1905-08

1906 - Founding of Muslim League

1909 - Indian Councils Act

1912 - Bengal partition annulled, capital shifted to Delhi

1919 - Government of India Act, leading to first elected legislature, 1921

1921 - INC calls for Swaraj (complete independence)

1935 - Goverment of India Act expands powers of legislatures and enlarges electorate.

1940 - Muslim League call for creation of Pakistan

1942 and 1946 Unsuccessful Cabinet Missions to negotiate terms of Indian independence

1947 - Independence and partition of India, independence of Pakistan.

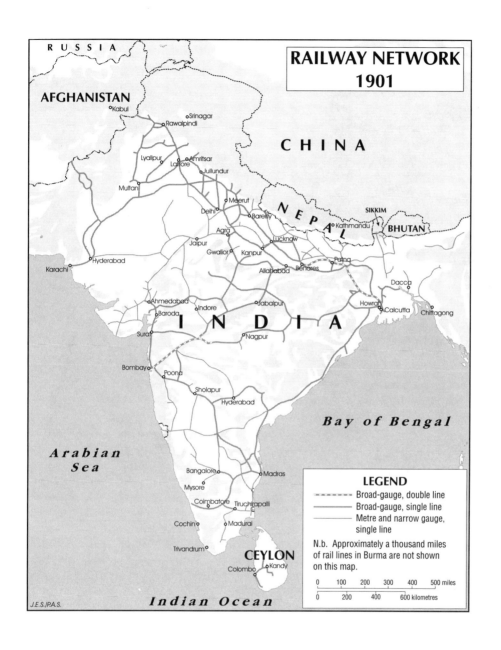

RAILWAY NETWORK 1901

RUSSIA

AFGHANISTAN

CHINA

Kabul

Srinagar
Rawalpindi

Lyalipur
Lahore
Amritsar
Jullundur

Multan

Meerut

Delhi

Barelly

NEPAL

SIKKIM

Kathmandu

BHUTAN

Agra
Jaipur
Gwalior
Kanpur

Lucknow

Patna

Karachi

Hyderabad

Allahabad
Benares

Dacca

Ahmedabad
Baroda
Indore
Jabalpur

Howrah
Calcutta

Chittagong

I N D I A

Surat
Nagpur

Bombay
Poona

Sholapur

Hyderabad

Bay of Bengal

Arabian
Sea

Bangalore
Madras
Mysore
Coimbatore
Tiruchirapalli
Cochin
Madurai

Trivandrum

CEYLON

Colombo
Kandy

Indian Ocean

LEGEND

Broad-gauge, double line
Broad-gauge, single line
Metre and narrow gauge,
single line

N.b. Approximately a thousand miles
of rail lines in Burma are not shown
on this map.

0   100   200   300   400   500 miles
0   200   400   600 kilometres

J.E.S./P.A.S.

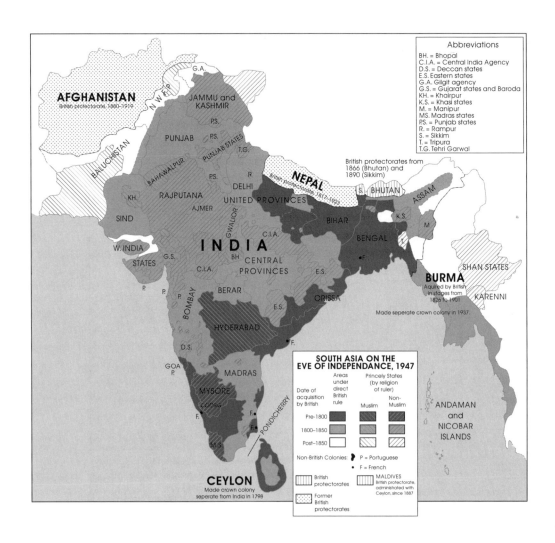

SOUTH ASIA ON THE EVE OF INDEPENDENCE, 1947

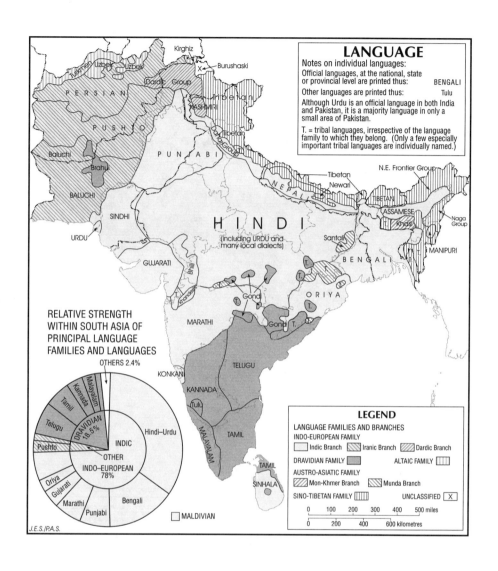

LANGUAGE

Notes on individual languages:

Official languages, at the national, state or provincial level are printed thus: **BENGALI**

Other languages are printed thus: Tulu

Although Urdu is an official language in both India and Pakistan, it is a majority language in only a small area of Pakistan.

T. = tribal languages, irrespective of the language family to which they belong. (Only a few especially important tribal languages are individually named.)

Kirghiz

Burushaski

Turkmen Uzbek Uzbek

Dardic Group

Tibetan

P E R S I A N

KASHMIRI

P U S H T O

Tibetan

Baluchi

Brahui

P U N J A B I

BALUCHI

Tibetan

Tibetan Group

Tibetan

N.E. Frontier Group

N E P A L I

Newari

SINDHI

H I N D I

TIBETAN

ASSAMESE

URDU

(including URDU and many local dialects)

Khasi

Naga Group

GUJARATI

Santali

MANIPURI

Bhili

T.

T.

B E N G A L I

RELATIVE STRENGTH WITHIN SOUTH ASIA OF PRINCIPAL LANGUAGE FAMILIES AND LANGUAGES

Gond

O R I Y A

T.

OTHERS 2.4%

Khandesh

T.

Gondi T.

MARATHI

KONKANI

TELUGU

Malayalam

Kannada

Tamil

DRAVIDIAN 19.5%

Telugu

INDIC

Hindi–Urdu

KANNADA

Pushto

Tulu

OTHER INDO–EUROPEAN 78%

TAMIL

Oriya

Gujarati

Marathi

Bengali

TAMIL

Punjabi

MALDIVIAN

MALAYALAM

SINHALA

LEGEND

LANGUAGE FAMILIES AND BRANCHES

INDO-EUROPEAN FAMILY

| | Indic Branch | | Iranic Branch | | Dardic Branch |

DRAVIDIAN FAMILY | ALTAIC FAMILY

AUSTRO-ASIATIC FAMILY

| Mon-Khmer Branch | | Munda Branch |

SINO-TIBETAN FAMILY | UNCLASSIFIED X

| 0 | 100 | 200 | 300 | 400 | 500 miles |

| 0 | 200 | 400 | 600 kilometres |

J.E.S./P.A.S.

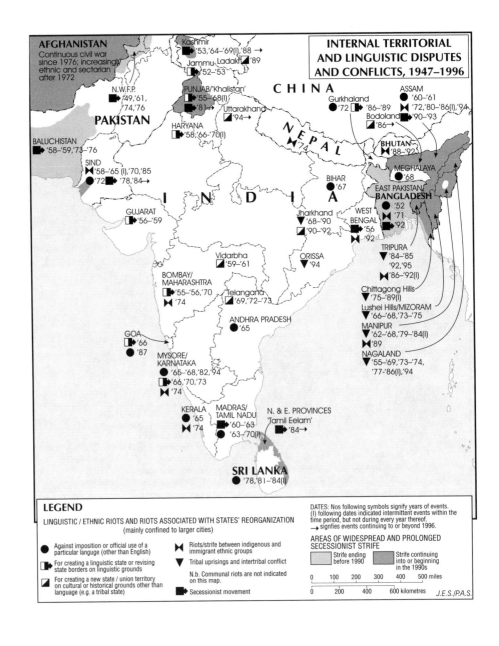

INTERNAL TERRITORIAL AND LINGUISTIC DISPUTES AND CONFLICTS, 1947–1996

AFGHANISTAN Continuous civil war since 1976; increasingly ethnic and sectarian after 1972

PAKISTAN

N.W.F.P. '49,'61, '74,'76

BALUCHISTAN '58–'59,'73–'76

SIND '58–'65 (I),'70,'85 '72 '78,'84→

GUJARAT '56–'59

Kashmir '53,'64–'69(I),'88 →
Jammu Ladakh '89
'52–'53

PUNJAB/'Khalistan' '55–'68(I) '81→ Uttarakhand '94

HARYANA '58,'66–'70(I)

C H I N A

N E P A L '74

BHUTAN '88–'92

Gurkhaland '72 '86–'89

ASSAM '60–'61 '72,'80–'86(I),'94
Bodoland '90–'93 '86→

MEGHALAYA '68

BIHAR '67

Jharkhand '68–'90 '90–'92

WEST BENGAL '56 '92

EAST PAKISTAN/ BANGLADESH '52 '71 '92

Vidarbha '59–'61

BOMBAY/ MAHARASHTRA '55–'56,'70 '74

Telangana '69,'72–'73

ORISSA '94

TRIPURA '84–'85 '92,'95 '86–'92(I)

Chittagong Hills '75–'89(I)
Lushei Hills/MIZORAM '66–'68,'73–'75
MANIPUR '62–'68,'79–'84(I) '89
NAGALAND '55–'69,'73–'74, '77–'86(I),'94

ANDHRA PRADESH '65

GOA '66 '87

MYSORE/ KARNATAKA '65–'68,'82,'94 '66,'70,'73 '74

KERALA '65 '74

MADRAS/ TAMIL NADU '60–'63 '63–'70(I)

N. & E. PROVINCES 'Tamil Eelam' '84→

SRI LANKA '78,'81–'84(I)

LEGEND

LINGUISTIC / ETHNIC RIOTS AND RIOTS ASSOCIATED WITH STATES' REORGANIZATION (mainly confined to larger cities)

● Against imposition or official use of a particular language (other than English)

▮▶ For creating a linguistic state or revising state borders on linguistic grounds

◪ For creating a new state / union territory on cultural or historical grounds other than language (e.g. a tribal state)

▶◀ Riots/strife between indigenous and immigrant ethnic groups

▼ Tribal uprisings and intertribal conflict

N.b. Communal riots are not indicated on this map.

◼▶ Secessionist movement

DATES: Nos following symbols signify years of events. (I) following dates indicated intermittent events within the time period, but not during every year thereof. → signifies events continuing to or beyond 1996.

AREAS OF WIDESPREAD AND PROLONGED SECESSIONIST STRIFE

☐ Strife ending before 1990   ▨ Strife continuing into or beginning in the 1990s

0 100 200 300 400 500 miles
0   200   400   600 kilometres

J.E.S./P.A.S.

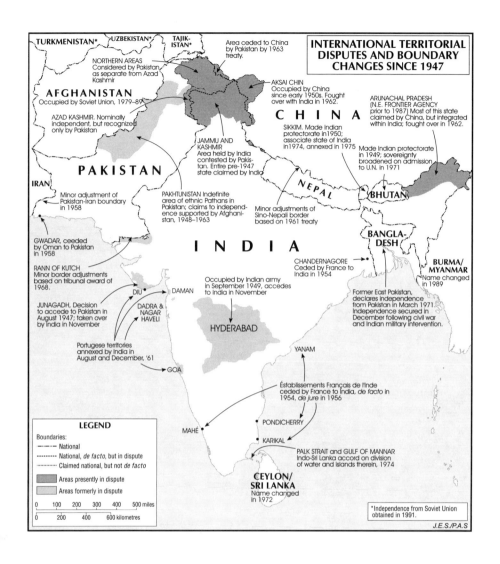

INTERNATIONAL TERRITORIAL DISPUTES AND BOUNDARY CHANGES SINCE 1947

TURKMENISTAN*   UZBEKISTAN*   TAJIK-ISTAN*

Area ceded to China by Pakistan by 1963 treaty.

NORTHERN AREAS Considered by Pakistan as separate from Azad Kashmir

AFGHANISTAN
Occupied by Soviet Union, 1979–89

AKSAI CHIN Occupied by China since early 1950s. Fought over with India in 1962.

C H I N A

AZAD KASHMIR. Nominally independent, but recognized only by Pakistan

ARUNACHAL PRADESH (N.E. FRONTIER AGENCY prior to 1987) Most of this state claimed by China, but integrated within India; fought over in 1962.

SIKKIM. Made Indian protectorate in1950; associate state of India in1974, annexed in 1975

JAMMU AND KASHMIR Area held by India contested by Pakistan. Entire pre-1947 state claimed by India

Made Indian protectorate in 1949; sovereignty broadened on admission to U.N. in 1971

PAKISTAN

N E P A L   **BHUTAN**

IRAN

Minor adjustment of Pakistan-Iran boundary in 1958

PAKHTUNISTAN Indefinite area of ethnic Pathans in Pakistan; claims to independence supported by Afghanistan, 1948–1963

Minor adjustments of Sino-Nepali border based on 1961 treaty

BANGLA-DESH

GWADAR, ceeded by Oman to Pakistan in 1958

I N D I A

CHANDERNAGORE Ceded by France to India in 1954

BURMA/ MYANMAR Name changed in 1989

RANN OF KUTCH Minor border adjustments based on tribunal award of 1968.

Occupied by Indian army in September 1949, accedes to India in November

DIU   DAMAN

JUNAGADH, Decision to accede to Pakistan in August 1947; taken over by India in November

DADRA & NAGAR HAVELI

Former East Pakistan, declares independence from Pakistan in March 1971. Independence secured in December following civil war and Indian military intervention.

HYDERABAD

Portugese territories annexed by India in August and December, '61

YANAM

GOA

Éstablissements Français de l'Inde ceded by France to India, de facto in 1954, de jure in 1956

MAHÉ

PONDICHERRY

KARIKAL

PALK STRAIT and GULF OF MANNAR Indo-Sri Lanka accord on division of water and islands therein, 1974

CEYLON/ SRI LANKA Name changed in 1972

LEGEND
Boundaries:
- ·—·—·— National
- -------- National, de facto, but in dispute
- ·········· Claimed national, but not de facto
- ▨ Areas presently in dispute
- ▨ Areas formerly in dispute

0   100   200   300   400   500 miles
0   200   400   600 kilometres

*Independence from Soviet Union obtained in 1991.

J.E.S./P.A.S

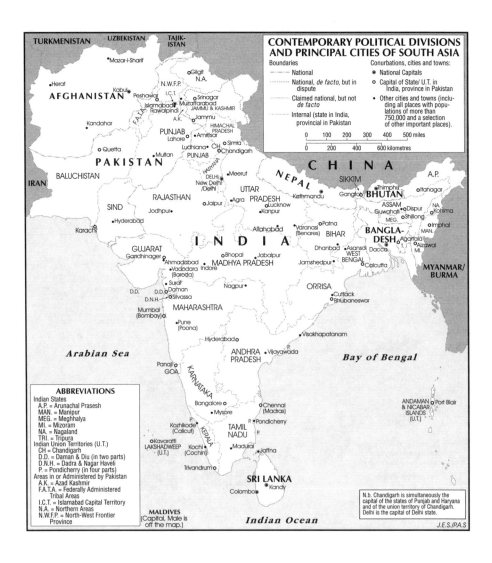

CONTEMPORARY POLITICAL DIVISIONS AND PRINCIPAL CITIES OF SOUTH ASIA

Boundaries

- - - - - National

- - - - - National, *de facto*, but in dispute

· · · · · Claimed national, but not *de facto*

— · — Internal (state in India, provincial in Pakistan)

Conurbations, cities and towns:

⊛ National Capitals

○ Capital of State/ U.T. in India, province in Pakistan

• Other cities and towns (including all places with populations of more than 750,000 and a selection of other important places).

```
0    100   200   300   400   500 miles
0      200      400      600 kilometres
```

ABBREVIATIONS

Indian States
A.P. = Arunachal Prasesh
MAN. = Manipur
MEG. = Meghhalya
MI. = Mizoram
NA. = Nagaland
TRI. = Tripura
Indian Union Territories (U.T.)
CH = Chandigarh
D.D. = Daman & Diu (in two parts)
D.N.H. = Dadra & Nagar Haveli
P. = Pondicherry (in four parts)
Areas in or Administered by Pakistan
A.K. = Azad Kashmir
F.A.T.A. = Federally Administered Tribal Areas
I.C.T. = Islamabad Capital Territory
N.A. = Northern Areas
N.W.F.P. = North-West Frontier Province

N.b. Chandigarh is simultaneously the capital of the states of Punjab and Haryana and of the union territory of Chandigarh. Delhi is the capital of Delhi state.

J.E.S./P.A.S

[6] THE CROWN REPLACES THE COMPANY

THE CONTEMPORARY STATE

In 1858, following the Mutiny and seemingly as a direct outcome, the East India Company was dismantled and its powers of government passed directly to the British Crown. In many ways, this was no more than a belated rationalization of a situation that had long been developing. Divested of its monopolistic economic powers in 1813, and all trade operations in 1833, the Company's political functions were hedged in by the supervision of Westminster, which was exercised through the Parliamentary Commissioners for the Affairs of India (popularly called 'the Board of Control'). By 1850 little remained of the once-mighty Honourable Company beyond a body of stockholders.

In other ways, the shift to Crown rule was significant. It visibly confirmed the fact, which had remained symbolically obscure, that India was actually ruled from Britain. Until 1858, the Company had taken part of its ruling title from the Mughal emperor (for many years a drug-addicted captive in Delhi), and, albeit less and less convincingly, had presented itself as an Indian state. Now the foreign character of British rule became incontestable and a focus for political response and organization. Furthermore, in transferring authority from a chartered mercantile company, the British also made it clear that their Indian territories constituted and were to be governed as a unitary state. They had established a power which could in the future be taken over en bloc by other bodies. Hence, although at first the change seemed to bring no dramatic changes on the ground in India, it marked the passage there from the modern to the contemporary state.

Modernity in India, as in Europe, began with the replacement of one social formation, usually called medieval, by another, in a process that started around the sixteenth century. In Europe the transition to modernity was very swiftly made in places like England and France, while India proceeded somewhat more slowly.

After 1500, pressures from a growth in population over the previous two centuries led to fragmented land-holding, to diminished productivity and finally to the emergence of capitalist production, either on large landed estates, as in England and Prussia, or on the holdings of small proprietors, as in France and elsewhere. This new economic power led to a political crisis as the result of a growth of trade, markets and capitalist relations within the weakening shell of a feudal order. There are also those who hold that feudalism was forced into crisis and ultimately destroyed by intensified conflict between landlords and agrarian workers, which, together with extended market relations, rendered serfdom an anomalous institution and opened the door to the emergence of capitalist agrarian relations.

Whatever the causes or combinations of causes, the principles of political economy are invariably invoked to complete the explanation of the transition to capitalism and modernity in Europe. Deliberate state-building policies were adopted, which we call 'mercantilism'. According to this doctrine, strong states were created by combining state institutions, such as the army and a bureaucracy empowered to levy taxes and tariffs, with the institutions of merchant capitalism and the creation of corporate mercantile bodies chartered to manage monopolies from which state treasuries benefited, and also to execute foreign policy tasks. The East India companies of England, France and Holland were created for such purposes. Thus India, or at least empire, was an integral part of mercantilist modernity in Europe. The economies of these two widely separated zones of Eurasia underwent similar changes, and henceforward the economies of western Europe and India became increasingly enmeshed.

India experienced no crisis of feudalism as such, but in post-Mughal times its medieval institutions were transformed in significant ways to create the conditions for the movement to capitalism and modernity. Akbar and his successors had achieved a higher degree of centralization of authority, state power and bureaucratic control in their extended Gangetic heartland than had previous states. Nevertheless, strong resistance to state rule continued even in the core territories around Delhi and Agra, and the structure of the paragana world of local socio-economic organization by dominant lineages and peasant castes was not fundamentally changed even after parganas were taken over by officials of the state. Centralization was very imperfect and older patrimonial forms of authority prevailed along with bureaucracy.

Beyond Mughal politics, deeper changes were proceeding. Small market towns multiplied and grain and credit markets proliferated, driven by commercial developments responding to expanding trade circuits that reached Europe. Indian exports, led by pepper and textiles, attracted European merchants who brought to international trade a sustained supply of silver from the New World with which to support the stable Mughal silver rupee.

On balance, Mughal society was an advance over previous medieval regimes and displayed indicators of a future where a set of political, economic and cultural transformations led to a new social order. In both Europe and India, imperial polities were displaced by smaller states, and these more modest states were better integrated politically as well as culturally. Some earlier classes lost privileges while others gained, and state-building projects benefited from the deliberate and systematic deployment of economic measures with which the terms 'mercantilism' and 'political economy' have since been associated.

The great influence of cultural changes in the definition of European modernity was not matched in India. Nothing in India corresponds to the liberating dynamism of the Renaissance in Europe, especially in the manner in which secular and scientific values were freed from the confines of Christian doctrine. India knew no such liberalization, but then, it can be said, it had also known little of the previous stultifying confinement of medieval Catholicism; Islam in India and elsewhere never closed itself off from science and diverse thought as had medieval Christianity.

If Europe and India entered modernity at about the same time and in some of the same ways, the two became more firmly linked at the onset of the contemporary period. Yet the multiplicity of the peoples of the subcontinent and the diversity of their cultures and experiences deny the possibility of a single view about when the foundation of today's India or Pakistan was laid. For the present purposes, then, 'contemporary history' began in India and for Indians around the middle of the nineteenth century, when a set of political, economic and cultural forms became evident which had been only partially glimpsed before. That is the time when the direct antecedents of the present can be identified as structures of causal importance, when the patterns of institutions and ideology by which the current generation shares a general and significant context took shape.

AFTER THE MUTINY

In the course of the past 150 years, communities of considerable antiquity have become ever more fractured by the combined pressures of conflict along class lines and the loss of their substantial historical autonomy. Wholly new relationships between states and communities appeared after 1830, and a shift to relatively greater exogenous influences upon social, cultural and economic development was notable. Even when a degree of ideological coherence has been preserved in the persistent evocation of caste and religious identities and loyalties, the social worlds to which these ideologies refer and from which they originated have been completely transformed. Neither caste nor religion nor place, the ancient determinants of affinity, has a meaning unchanged from that expressed in medieval dharmashastras. Perhaps such continuity was not to be expected, but the reduction of the ties binding people to particular places and to filaments of ideology, which are thus incapable of protecting ancient historical interests, is a striking characteristic of the contemporary age.

The uprising of the Company's sepoys in 1857 precipitated the supplanting of the Company in 1858. The suppression of the 'Great Mutiny' and the threat that it posed to any sort of British rule was the work of British soldiers aided by Indian allies, including the Sikhs, and the fear of other uprisings cast a shadow over the rest of the nineteenth century. But more important in the long run was the effect of the transference of power in locking Britain and India into a common trajectory. Together with Britain, India henceforward moved towards more sophisticated and bureaucratic governmental structures, with departments dedicated to technical functions and expected to contribute to market-driven economic development according to the liberal philosophy of the state and government. In addition, an increasingly central role was assigned to India in the expanding British Empire, particularly in providing and paying for the soldiers needed to secure imperial objectives. British and Indian soldiers fought in many parts of Asia, Africa and even Europe for these ends, their costs borne for the most part by India's agricultural producers; and its sons, especially those of the Punjab, supplied most of the soldiery.

Superficially, crown rule after the rebellion caused surprisingly few changes in the structure of authority within India. From the base administrative level of revenue (the judicial district) to the provincial capital, or 'Presidency' of Madras, Bombay or Calcutta, and between the governors in those provincial capitals and London, these levels of authority remained much as they had been under the Company during the previous half-century. Minor British aristocrats continued to be appointed to the executive offices of governor and governor-general; specialist recruitment filled the highest judicial posts; and most policies were set by councils manned by senior Indian Civil Service officers.

One major alteration had already been intimated in the Company era. This was the development of technical departments such as public works, concerned with roads and irrigation, forestry and police. These had been introduced at the provincial level and by the later nineteenth century each had become a bureaucracy that reached down into every district. The effect on district administration was significant, for this was the point where government most consistently connected with the governed. Changes here meant a departure from an earlier ideal formulated by the early nineteenth-century founders of Company administration. Men such as Mountstuart Elphinstone, John Malcolm and Thomas Munro had been all-powerful local executives, and such proconsular officials were considered responsible for holding the loyalty of Indians to the British cause during the Rebellion, especially in the Punjab.

THE RULERS AND THE RULED

The principle of personal local rule began to be attenuated before the rebellion, and when the Crown assumed direct control over India in its aftermath, local authority had become an oligarchy of European civil servants. By the later nineteenth century, European wives and families of district officials joined their men, and in some places other Europeans – teachers, planters, businessmen – constituted large enough colonies to form small and exclusive European enclaves within the vast Indian world. Provincial capitals partook of the same social patterns of encysted Europeans, with their clubs and playing fields, separated alike from the native aristocracy, from the emerging western educated Indian professionals who were forming a middle class, from the very numerous lower-middle-class families of merchants, bazaarmen, artisans and minor government officials, and, finally, from the urban poor.

District towns and provincial cities continued to be linked to rural hinterlands by a variety of complex ties. Connections often dating from medieval times deepened during the eighteenth century, when intensified commercialization combined with state-building to thicken the network of urban–rural relationships. Still, India remained an overwhelmingly rural society during the nineteenth century, and when the first provincial censuses began to be compiled around mid-century, urban places were modestly defined as anything with a population in excess of 5000. Population counts of India as a whole in 1872, 1881 and 1891 reported the proportion of persons living in towns (still defined as having 5000 or more inhabitants) as low: a mere 10 per cent urban residence was reached in 1901, when there were around 2100 towns with a total population of 21 million. At Independence, in 1947, urban residence had increased to 15 per cent of the population – nearly 50 million who lived in some 2700 urban places.

While the formation of classes in towns and cities has attracted attention owing to the bias of historical interpretation towards political and economic modernization, class relations also intensified throughout the countryside during the nineteenth century. That is, beneath the assumed preponderance of what is still taken to be traditional caste society, there were clusters of men of diverse caste origin whose superior wealth, housing and education distinguished them from others of similar traditional ranking. Whether western-educated professionals serving as minor government officials, or day-labourers, positions within the nexus of expanding capitalist relations created relations with others that inflected caste and religious orientations.

Bengal presented an extreme example of class formation. It contained Calcutta, 'City of Palaces' and capital of British India. This was the city with the earliest and most western-educated Indians, the first westernized intelligentsia and, before it was displaced by Bombay, the most advanced commercial centre of the subcontinent. While Bengal's urban population was among the smallest in all of the provinces of India, reaching only 5 per cent at the end of the nineteenth century, at the beginning of the nineteenth century the Bengal countryside was among the most commercialized in India, and this was reflected in the high proportion of the rural workforce – perhaps 80 per cent – who depended on wage labour for their survival.

Elsewhere, a different configuration of rural classes could be discerned. By the middle of the nineteenth century, it is possible to delineate broad classes of rural dwellers whose social, political and economic interests were distinctive and powerful enough to vie with, and at times to override, ancient sentiments of caste, sect and locality. Everywhere there existed a tripartite division of rural classes. The highest consisted of two landed categories, sometimes distinguished as separate classes. In many places there were landlords, a thin layer of proprietorial households with security of tenure over enough land to avoid the work of cultivation beyond supervising tenants or daily wage labourers, who augmented their agricultural incomes by money-lending. Beneath the holders of large and secure lands were rich farmers who both owned and cultivated land and, at times of peak need, because they had substantial holdings, would hire others as well. Rich farmers traded in grain and served as small-scale, local money-lenders to augment their money earnings.

For some scholars, the distinction drawn between landlords and rich farmers is meaningless, except perhaps in those parts of India where a large landlord class was created by revenue settlements, such as those in Cornwallis's Bengal and parts of Madras. In most of India what was more important than the relative size or security of the holdings of individual landlords was the manner in which those with substantial lands employed day labourers to cultivate them, engaged in grain trading and usury to fortify their economic and social dominance, and forged multiplex bonds with leading groups in the towns and cities. Often, what connected the countryside and towns was far more significant than what divided them.

Somewhat aloof from such relationships was the second and far more numerous agricultural stratum, consisting of middle farmers. Their land-holdings were barely sufficient to absorb all or most of their family labour and not large enough to require the hiring of others. Though middle farmers did not usually offer their own labour for sale, they were placed under great pressure to do so by the demands of tax collectors and the wish to avoid indebtedness to the money-lenders. The abiding fear of middling farmers, as they were sometimes called, was slipping into the ranks of the impoverished cultivating families who must work for others as tenants or day-labourers. These lowest of rural social groups consisted of families without enough land to absorb their labour or to generate the money they required for subsistence; they occasionally worked for others, usually neighbours. In places of high and irrigated production there was a rural proletariat, with neither land nor tools nor draft animals, who were obliged to hire themselves out as day-labourers, and were often tied to particular landed families by indebtedness that could be passed on through the generations.

Classes were a familiar feature of urban life at the same time. Benares was a city of 200,000 in 1827; two-thirds of its male workforce were divided occupationally into the following categories: craftsmen and textile workers, traders and bankers, transporters and those providing personal and professional services, such as barbers and washermen. There were also professionals, physicians and lawyers, and, of course, in Benares as in other pilgrimage towns, such as Allahabad and Gaya, a large number of priests. At the beginning of the nineteenth century, for example, over 40,000 brahmans lived on charity in Benares and comprised nearly a fifth of the population. The wealthiest urbanites consisted of two distinct groups. There were the grand households of rural magnates whose wealth derived from the rents they received as absentee rural landlords and from holdings of valuable urban land, as well as profits from usury and grain trading. The other patrician group consisted of bankers and big money-lenders with substantial rent and interest incomes, and wholesale merchants. This was the bourgeoisie proper. Beneath them was the usual population of towns and cities anywhere: lower middle-class artisan-traders, petty traders of the bazaars, commodity brokers and labour contractors, petty money-lenders and religious and governmental functionaries. At the bottom were the paupers driven from the hazards of rural exploitation to a similar life of chance and misery in towns. In northern India, a larger proportion of all urban classes were Muslim, a residue of the demographic shaping of earlier Muslim rule.

The urban population of India grew slowly during the nineteenth century, but it was not numbers alone that made urbanites significant in the modern epoch. From the early nineteenth century, urban classes were adjuncts of and agents for the colonial state whose institutions would transform India and make its modernity. While businessmen, including Europeans, played a part in this transformation, modern business progressed slowly. In 1815 Calcutta had but twenty-three European merchants, assisted by only a few more big Hindu merchants and bankers, and a scattering of Muslim firms; most of the trading was conducted by Bengali firms in old-fashioned ways. By mid-century the modern commercial sector in Calcutta included 173 European merchants and agents, around fifty big Indian banking firms (of whom eight were from Madras), thirty-five Muslim and 160 smaller Bengali firms.

These numbers were as nothing compared to the great landlords of Bengal, those created by the Cornwallis settlement of landed estates. Around 1870, 500 zamindars, as they were called, held estates exceeding 20,000 acres; another 16,000 held estates of 500 to 20,000 acres, while 138,000 landlords held properties of less than 500 acres. This was in a Bengal where most families were supported by a few irrigated acres. Against these large numbers, the urban-based capitalists of the age seem trifling, and so too do the educated.

In 1859, there were a mere thirteen government colleges with around 2000 students in all of British India. Another 30,000 students were in secondary government schools. Yet, from this modest base rose the Indian middle and lower middle classes that were to sweep Europeans from their hegemonic command of the subcontinent. This was achieved partly through the growing participation of Indians in official administration. Again, numbers are small to begin with. In 1850, Indians holding superior, local administrative posts amounted to around 3000. To find so few Indians in positions of localized authority would have been disappointing to someone like Thomas Munro, who, as governor of Madras in 1824, had advocated, in what was intended as his valedictorian statement of principle before departing India, the increased involvement of Indians in their own government:

> With what grace can we talk of our paternal government, if we exclude ... [Indians] from every important office and say ... that in a country of fifteen million of inhabitants, no man but a European shall be entrusted with so much authority as to order a single stroke of the rattan ...
>
> Our books alone will do little or nothing ... [to] improve the character of a nation. To produce this effect, it must be open to the road of wealth and honour, and public employment.[1]

But even these few opportunities for secure, pensionable government employment were an inducement for the widespread support of privately funded schools to augment those supported by missionary organizations and those receiving state aid. As a result of this combined investment in schools, matriculates from private and public secondary schools and colleges became numerous enough by 1857 to justify founding universities at the Presidency cities of Bombay, Calcutta and Madras.

The extension of western education, however, was not enough to assure the appropriate employment of all graduates. Thus, in the same year that the Company regime was pushed from power by the mutinous Indian soldiers of its northern army, the foundations were being laid for the development of a stratum of educated Indians whose economic and political frustrations fused into a nationalistic opposition in the late decades of the nineteenth century.

THE BEGINNINGS OF INDIAN POLITICAL PARTICIPATION

The gradual opening up of representative assemblies to participation by western-educated Indians was also an important political change. Town and district councils were created by the Indian Councils Act of 1861 and ultimately, through a series of similar enactments, membership in the Viceregal council was opened to an educated Indian elite. This very limited participation in government was deemed an appropriate reward to the middle class for their assent to and even occasional initiation of increased taxation.

These political concessions were seen as gains by many Indians, but there were some losses, principally economic ones, that marked the contemporary era and differentiated it from the preceding era of modern history. By the 1830s, a new balance had been struck between the interests and institutions of indigenous capitalists and those of foreign capitalists. For two centuries before then, Indian capitalists – including wholesale traders, bankers and textile industrialists – had enjoyed a large degree of state support in return for their contributions to the extant regimes. The term mercantilism has been applied to the policies of many pre-colonial regimes in recognition of the core of measures designed to promote state building. Strong regimes needed to finance military modernization based on firearms, which required measures for raising money revenues from commerce to augment land taxes. Accordingly, seventeenth- and eighteenth-century Indian states sought to develop their regional economies by encouraging commodity production so as to broaden the tax-base from which to finance the importation of military supplies and standing armies of trained soldiers to use these new weapons. All of this required the contributions of Indian capitalists. In return for their collaboration they received lucrative offices as tax-farmers and holders of monopolies. Rural communities throughout eighteenth-century India were thus drawn into a deeper web of commerce and finance as a result of the state-building of the post-Mughal era.

ECONOMIC POLICIES OF COMPANY AND CROWN

Before we turn to the emergence of these political developments, a more comprehensive assessment should be made of their material and cultural foundations. From its onset, East India Company rule in Bengal and Madras constituted an intensification of the mercantilist practices followed by states of the eighteenth century. Practices for enhancing state power were brought to a higher stage by the Company in increasing its control and command over the resources of its conquered subjects, and by encouraging petty commodity production and monetization through its demand for taxes in cash. In these ways, British rule was different in degree rather than kind, but in other ways it was a different kind of rule. As an international trading corporation with major interests in Europe and in China, the Company mobilized the products, skills and capital of Indians as never before. Until 1813, when its monopoly over trade with Europe was terminated, the Company's trade operations coupled with its function as a government assured that Indian textiles and agricultural commodities, such as cotton, sugar and opium, were at its own disposal; and its importation of opium into China – in violation of Chinese law – turned a British trade deficit with that country into a substantial surplus.

In the atmosphere of commercial and monetary intensification that these activities generated, it is hardly surprising that there should have been major changes in the relative advantages of various groups, depending on their relation to the productive forms of the Indian economy. At a general level, however, two transformative processes – deindustrialization and repeasantization – are often said to have been inflicted upon the most commercialized zones of the subcontinent, but neither of these processes was so destructive of older forms as to transform Indian society as profoundly as the term 'modernization' implies.

The accusation of India's 'deindustrialization' is predicated on the uncontested observation that, in comparison with other eighteenth-century Asian societies, except China, India was an industrial giant; it produced a wide range of goods of very high quality, sources of envy and wonder, as Hegel's paean confirms. Textiles and metal wares were leading industrial products, and there were impressive back-linkages to extensive cotton production in many parts of the country, as well as to mining and smelting of a high technical order. During most of the first century of East India Company tutelage, these productive forms remained in place, and there were even some efforts to improve older methods by selective modernization. One such was the adoption of the seeds and some of the techniques of the American cotton states to meet the growing demand for Indian textiles in Europe, via Britain, and in Southeast Asia, in exchange for the spices grown there.

However, by the 1840s the nature of exports changed, first slowly and then more rapidly, from finished Indian textiles to raw cotton for manufacture by the new steam-driven machinery of Britain. From then until the eve of the First World War, India – once the envy of the world for its cloth – imported almost half of the textiles exported from Britain. When that trade was interrupted by the First World War, tariff restrictions against Indian machine textile were relaxed, and modern factory production of textiles was permitted. Similarly, the heavy engineering works of pre-colonial India had produced good artillery pieces for Indian states. These works were now closed down, and British-made engineering products – not necessarily superior to or cheaper than the Indian versions – were substituted, damaging India's industrial potential, but fulfilling its role as an imperial market.

Economic changes after 1860 were driven by the consolidation of national and international markets for many old and some new Indian commodities.

Modern factory production of textiles led this development in India as it had in Europe, and, in a similar way, textile exports were followed by coal and finally iron and steel. These developments accelerated socio-economic changes of not only the occupations of many Indians but the social context in which many families and communities existed henceforward. Modern urban workers appeared in established commercial centres like Bombay, where old mercantile wealth in the hands of Indian capitalists was transformed into the industrial capital of modern textile mills. The interests of these Indian financiers spread across the subcontinent, where they merged with investors from Bengal. Bengali financiers opened coal and iron fields in Bihar and new cities appeared, like Jamshedpur, founded by the Parsi Tatas of Bombay.

Rural institutions were no less affected by these transformations, though the consequence was not development but what is now known as underdevelopment. During the early decades of the nineteenth century, prices for agrarian commodities declined at a time when the demand for cash for taxes and rents in many parts of the subcontinent increased, bringing hardship to lower agrarian and pastoral groups. Yet when prices began to rise after 1860, it was again the wealthy farmers and money-lenders who benefited, leading to substantial concentrations of resources in their hands. But there was also hostility between the gainers, as the riots of substantial Maratha farmers against Marwari money-lenders in 1875 around Pune show.

INCREASING IMPORTS FROM BRITAIN; INCREASING DEARTH IN INDIA

British capital and consumer goods increased their penetration with the development of railways that began in 1854. Railways were constructed in accord with the logic of imperial benefit, with British capital under a guarantee of a fixed return to foreign investors, another way in which British capitalism was strengthened by the colonial connection. What was called the 'free trade era' before 1914 was little other than a system that favoured the importation of British manufactures through a variety of formal and informal methods; it anticipated what, in the depression of 1930s, was to be called imperial preference, and it resulted in the degradation of previous Indian manufacturing and transport industries. The redundant workers were then pressed into agricultural pursuits, and repeasantized.

These processes are reflected in Indian censuses carried out in 1881 and 1931, where workers in agriculture reportedly increased by 28 per cent, while those in non-agricultural occupations declined by 8 per cent. The trends observed in these censuses may have been even greater in the four previous decades, those between 1840 and 1880 (before regular censuses were taken). During the eighteenth and early nineteenth centuries, less than half of the workforce may have been engaged in cultivation and activities ancillary to it, whereas by the late nineteenth century the agriculturally dependent had risen to 75 per cent, an enormous additional weight borne by an Indian agriculture already well behind that of Europe in its productivity and its technology. Under such increased dependence upon agricultural work, social relations in the countryside were bound to become more hazardous for the poor, and so they did. Some of the changes were gradual at first, but the increasing pace of change in the later nineteenth century must have contributed to the ferocity of the devastating famines that ensued.

Famine and disease were the more lethal consequences of change during the century of British imperial dominance that began in 1840, but chronically inadequate nutrition and consequent morbidity revealed a degradation of the socio-cultural fabric of the entire subcontinent. In the vast countryside this was both cause and symptom of the weakening of communities. As wealth became concentrated in a few households and as the political means for local cooperation were lost in bureaucratic divisions of responsibility on functional lines, communities lost their historic ability to maintain institutions capable of responding to crises within a locality. Caste relations which contributed to community cooperation, as, for example, between client and patron castes, were profoundly changed by the propensity of British law and census operations to confer new meanings and functions, lifting local groups out of historical contexts and responsibilities.

Along with sects and communities, caste relations had always responded to changing historical circumstances. How else could the essences and traditions of some supposed antiquity have been maintained in the face of such changes as the enormous expansion of agrarian over pastoral economies, the Muslim domination of northern India or the imposition of European dominance? From being parts of communities and of kingdoms, Indians were now subject to new ruling frameworks. Once, local religious and political authorities, as well as distant kings, had maintained what they could of customary relations and reciprocal entitlements under flexible, locally sensitive rules; now law courts under British justices set new terms. British judicial and civil officials would not preserve the entitlements and perquisites of this group or that when, according to their own principles of property, there were no reasons to do so. Censuses and other modern control measures tended to homogenize some diverse local privileges and responsibilities and to discard other claims to distinctive rights and traditions as irrelevant or inconvenient.

THE SOCIAL FABRIC IS RENT

In this way were lost local rural social relations and practices, which were the results of communitarian struggles against military lordships that came and went; hard-won rights were set aside, and communal integrity was subject to legal and police assaults in the interests of some local groups against others. Those who won these local struggles often did so through their privileged relations with colonial officials who could determine who lost old prerogatives and who gained new ones. Gainers tended to be those who were deemed owners of property and payers of taxes in cash, or practitioners of professions thought useful – scribes, lawyers, landlords – while losers included some of previously high station such as minor rulers and most of the smaller cultivating families. Thus were rural communities over the whole of the subcontinent transformed.

This is not to suggest that colonial domination in India replaced an idyllic world of custom and fairness with the individualist and pluralist ethic of western society and culture. Pre-colonial India had its full measure of stratification, of exploitation, of oppression and of misery. Moreover, there were European values that genuinely attracted Indians, since many sought and sacrificed to acquire English or another European language, western education and western goods. These made profound changes in the lifestyles of Indians, at least of Indian men; older institutional and cultural forms yielded to new institutions and ideologies as they groped for a modernity that might be theirs or, alternatively, sought to protect some of their older privileges and immunities. But from the mid-nineteenth century assimilation into political, social and cultural identities that cut across older community boundaries and through communal institutions was unprecedented. The authoritative centres of these newer formations and ideologies always lay elsewhere, far from the cores of historical localities, in the towns and cities; they were under the control of professionals – party politicians, bureaucrats, populist godmen and industrial tycoons – with interests often distant from or only tangentially related to older communities.

THE RULE OF THE RAJ

Crown rule in India had begun promisingly. In November 1858, Queen Victoria issued a proclamation 'to the Princes, Chiefs and People of India', reassuring the first two that their dignities and privileges would be maintained along with extant treaties with the East India Company. To the non-aristocratic Indian public, of all religions and races, government employment was promised in accordance with their 'education, ability, and integrity'. The generosity of her words was meant to mend the breach that had been opened between government and people by the uprising of the year before.

Her proclamation was followed shortly by the Government of India Act of 1858, which set out other priorities. A Secretary of State for India was appointed and made a member of the Westminster Cabinet; his office and staff, however, were funded from Indian revenues. The Parliamentary Commissioners were replaced by the Council of India, most of whose fifteen members were to be nominated from among retiring directors of the East India Company; the remainder were to have served for ten years in India. This arrangement implied very substantial continuity of personnel and thus of policies between the Company regime and its imperial successors, but it also meant that authority had become more centralized by diluting the influence of Company directors.

Victoria's promise of Indian participation in high office was so slow to be realized that by 1880 there were a mere sixteen Indians among the 900 members of the Indian Civil Service (ICS). The 1858 Act confirmed the arrangement made a few years earlier to recruit the elite administrative corps by competitive examinations held in England. In the years following, the conditions which candidates had to meet became increasingly stringent: the

Plate 22 'The Viceroy's elephants. When the Governor-General, Lord Dalhousie, tried to replace his state howdah "of wood painted like a street cab" with a grander one of silver, he was accused of reckless extravagance. The Lieutenant-Governors of the Punjab continued to use elephants for touring outlying districts long after the Viceroys had resigned themselves to travelling by train. One unfortunate Lieutenant-Governor, Sir Henry Durand, lost his life in 1871 when his elephant's howdah was crushed under an archway' (IOL, Ray Desmond, *Victorian India in Focus*. London: HMSO, 1982, p. 82, plate 61, by permission of the British Library).

maximum age was lowered from 23 to 21 years, and in the 1870s to 19 years, with the additional requirement of a probationary period of two years at an English university. Thus the nearly one thousand civil servants constituting the professional highly paid administrators of British India were overwhelmingly Britons who had passed rigorous examinations in English. This outcome was seen by many to violate the expressed commitment in the East India Company charter of 1833 to open senior offices to Indians, a promise that had been reiterated by the Queen in 1858.

But the proclamation had been meant only to allay Indian apprehensions about the Crown regime that replaced the Company, and British cynicism prevailed. Indian recruitment to senior offices was resisted even as it became clear that able candidates were emerging from the new universities established in Calcutta, Madras and Bombay in 1857, and all agreed on the need for more high officials. Moreover, it had occurred to those ever-parsimonious custodians of power in India, that, besides considerations of justice and feasibility, senior Indian civil servants would cost less in salaries and pensions, and that the same examinations could be held simultaneously in Britain and India.

Yet the senior officials in India and their allies in Britain could not bring themselves to trust Indians with significant authority. The Viceroy, Lord Lytton, wrote confidentially in 1879 that commitments to substantial Indian access to high office would never be fulfilled and that it remained only to decide whether to repudiate the promise or continue in the regrettable course of deception. Others, less arrogant or less honest than Lytton, thought that the safer way forward was to create a second tier of administrators: young, educated Indians from 'good families and social positions' should hold up to a sixth of the superior offices. Such a scheme was introduced in 1880, designated the Statutory Civil Service, but it stilled none of the demand for simultaneous examinations. Proposals in the 1890s to offer such examinations were rejected on new grounds: the domination of Hindus in higher education meant that Muslims and Sikhs with long experience and traditions of ruling in India would be unfairly disadvantaged.

The reluctance in London and Calcutta to open offices to Indians stemmed, in addition to the universal unwillingness ever to renounce power voluntarily, from current social-Darwinist theories of racial superiority. Having even a few trusted Indians participate in policy discussions about how Indian resources could be allocated to ease poverty was especially distasteful to British officials of the late nineteenth century. To their embarrassment the voices most critical on the subject of Indian poverty were other Englishmen, including some of their colleagues in the very highest posts, rather than the educated middle-class Indians whom Lord Lytton feared. In fact, middle-class Indians for the most part cherished *laissez-faire* attitudes not much different from those of their British contemporaries and masters.

From the 1870s until the turn of the century, Dadabhai Naoroji, a Bombay Parsi businessman who succeeded in winning a seat in Parliament, issued a set of papers, speeches and letters condemning the deployment of Indian resources for the benefit of the British. In 1901, his collected writings were published as a book entitled *Poverty and Un-British Rule in India*, which was to focus public discussion on the economic issues. In the same year, a similar indictment appeared in William Digby's ironically titled *'Prosperous' British India*. Digby was the honorary secretary of the Indian Famine Relief Fund, and already known as a critic of the Madras government for its passivity in the terrible famine of the 1870s. In 1888 he had begun to lobby for more effective welfare measures by drawing attention to the deepening poverty of India revealed in confidential investigations carried out by the Raj.

These studies had themselves been forced on the imperial government by other criticisms from the highly placed civil official W. W. Hunter, respected for his numerous statistical, linguistic and rural studies, as well as for his editorship of the twenty-three volume *Imperial Gazetteer of India*, published between 1881 and 1887. In 1881 he published a small book claiming that a fifth of the Indian people went through life without sufficient food. In addition to inspiring the studies which Digby exploited for his 1901 castigation of imperial policies and the mass poverty they entailed, Hunter's 1881 indictment also prompted provincial publications that attempted to counter the poverty charge. One adroit work of policy defence was by an early and trusted Indian bureaucrat, Srinivasa Raghavaiyangar; in 1893 the Madras authorities published his *Memorandum of the Progress of the Madras Presidency during the Last Forty Years of British Administration*. Nevertheless, even its 650 pages failed to refute Hunter's brief and bleak charges.

Openings for Indians in the officer corps of the Indian army were also excruciatingly slow to appear, even though heavy responsibilities continued to be placed upon the Indian army by the imperial activities of the later nineteenth century: in Egypt in 1882, leading to the quasi-colonial subjugation of that kingdom; in Sudan in 1885–6 and 1896; in China against the Boxers in 1900. Nor were Indian appointments increased under Lord Curzon, when a massive 52 per cent of the Indian budget in 1904–5 was committed to the military.

The lessons drawn from the mutiny of Company sepoys in 1857 enforced the concentration of Europeans in the high ranks of British-Indian regiments. Fears of mutiny lingered and justified a one-third ratio of European troops strategically garrisoned throughout British India, and their domination over artillery units as well as the superior commands. Strengthening British control of the army was costly and explains why military expenditures remained the largest category in Indian budgets well into the twentieth century.

Next to the army, the continuation of an older colonial pattern depended upon civil administrators. Appointments to serve as Company merchants, soldiers, judges or civil officials in India had long been the gift of Company directors. The directors, who were among the most important men of affairs in seventeenth- and eighteenth-century London, conferred political patronage upon their young clients, each appointing his protégés to the one of the three Company presidencies – Bombay, Calcutta, Madras – in which he had particular interests and influence. This was one cause of the differences in the style of administration among the presidencies, which lingered long after the Company itself lost direct governmental responsibility. Distinctive provincial patterns in their administrative, revenue and judicial practices resulted in a variability which reduced the degree of centralized administrative authority that could be achieved over all of British India.

LIBERALISM AT HOME, BUREAUCRACY ABROAD

While this European administrative elite struggled to become a more powerful instrument on the subcontinent, in Britain government influence over civil society diminished in accordance with liberal principles. Courts and contracts governed public transactions, including the freedom of workers to contract as individuals with employers, but not to combine in unions. Administrators in India marched to a different drum: their policies were to fix, not to free, labour and resources, and to offer privileges to those who served as intermediaries between imperial authority and a massive and poor population.

The Indian Civil Service, consisting of around a thousand officers, administered the whole of British India in 1872, when the population enumerated by the first general census was 185.5 million. The rest of India's 240 millions were ruled by some six hundred Indian princes, who themselves were clients of the British and permitted limited self-rule. To look after their interests, a smaller Indian Political Service was created. After 1854, when officials began to be selected by competitive examination, principally from among graduates of major British universities, a new stratum of British society was brought into contact with India. Increasingly, whole middle-class families began living in segregated residential neighbourhoods, in elegant 'bungalows' with numerous servants, enjoying restricted clubs and playing fields, setting themselves rigorously apart from those whom they ruled. New social and political attitudes inevitably resulted and contributed to the political awakening of western-educated Indians by the turn of the twentieth century.

More immediate was the change in the character of Indian administration itself. Bureaucracy intensified in British Indian provinces as well as in the domains of India's princes after 1860. The undivided local authority and powers of the individual official of the late eighteenth and early nineteenth centuries – whether the collector of revenue in Madras and Bombay, the magistrate in Bengal or the commissioner in the Northwest Provinces – were replaced by those of several officials, each with specific functions. In addition to revenue collectors there were autonomous judicial, police and technical officers who dealt with irrigation and public works or forestry. Some of these technical officers were introduced late in the Company era, but their numbers increased under government rule.

Far more numerous than European officials, Indian subordinate administrators also had a history of practices and privileges gained under the rule of the Company and of the Indian princes during the early nineteenth century. Most of the established ways continued under Crown rule, even when recruitment changed. Dominant landed groups had earlier been the source of subordinate officers, who joined in the expectation that their local standing would increase their effectiveness. The landed men were gradually replaced by recruitment from scribal groups, often outsiders. Literate brahmans or kayasthas with record-keeping skills were found more useful and politically safer servants in the increasingly bureaucratized structure of the later nineteenth century. As for the magnates who were displaced from office, the interests of the more powerful among them were often preserved and even enhanced by legal changes that conferred secure land-holding rights. This was one aspect of class formation that was accelerated by changes in the economy of the late nineteenth century.

Another significant change that became evident by the middle of the 1850s was the rise of an Indian public opinion, capable of and wanting increased participation in the administration of India. The founding of the British Indian Association of Bengal in 1851 was a manifestation of this new public sense; it was followed by similar organizations in Bombay and Madras. From these new association petitions were directed to the British Parliament as that body considered what all knew would be the last charter for the East India Company in 1854.

Other opportunities began to be offered to educated Indians. Elective councils had come into being in 1861, extending modest local self-government and shifting responsibility for education and other amenities to the self-imposed taxation of an enlarging Indian middle class. Political concessions of this sort were gradually and teasingly increased to assist moderate Indian politicians to confront more radical challengers. Notwithstanding this emerging political division among educated Indians during the late nineteenth century, they agreed in their hostility to that other middle class in India: resident Britons, referred to as 'Anglo-Indians', and sometimes as a 'middle-class aristocracy'. Between the two middle classes there could be only growing suspicion and resentment, and occasional open confrontation as Indians joined the professions of law, education and journalism. Indian professionals particularly resented attempts to control the Indian-language press or to deny Indians the right to possess firearms.

The imperial Raj, along with other states in the nineteenth century, sought limited ends: to fix its external borders, often after a military action, to set out new rules or laws for the conduct of public business and to engage in the great game with other imperial powers. It was to take a considerable time for a view of India as a whole to emerge. Thus Richard Wellesley, Governor-General from 1798 to 1805, saw India as a vital centre for opposition to Napoleon's plans to expand into the Middle East.

By the middle of the nineteenth century, the frontiers of British India were fixed favourably against a weakened imperial China as well as against clientized smaller states on the northern fringes of the subcontinent from Persia to Burma. Domestically, the prevailing conceptions of limited government would have discouraged interventions by the state beyond the occasional ban of some 'odious practices', such the abolition of dacoity, which was a response to complaints from commercial travellers. Even the ban on sati was a capitulation to criticism of Company rule by Christian missionaries.

REFORM MOVEMENTS

Social, religious and finally political reform bodies proliferated in the two thousand or so smaller towns of British India towards the close of the century. 'District towns' in Bengal had branches of the Brahmo Samaj, and, to a lesser extent, small towns of the Bombay Presidency had branches of the Prarthana Samaj, a movement similar to the Brahmo Samaj, but founded in Bombay in 1867. More overtly political were the nominally religious reform associations which were formed by educated men in the provincial cities. In the Punjab and elsewhere in the western Gangetic plain, the Arya Samaj, founded in 1875, won adherents in smaller towns to an ideology that condemned caste and superstition. In the eastern Ganges area, in contrast, various explicitly Hindu-affirming reform bodies, adopting names such as Hindu Samaj, came into existence. Similar reform activities began among Parsis in western India and among Muslims, with the eventual establishment of the Aligarh Anglo-Muhammadan College in 1875, by Sayyid Ahmad Khan. Inevitably, such explicitly religious reform bodies, brought into being to meet and to refute the allegations of Christian missionaries as well as to advance the process of western education, took on political purposes and began to elaborate public ideologies.

The principle of 'limited government' and the doctrine of *laissez-faire* should have discouraged the East India Company and inhibited the imperial Raj from intervening in Indian society unless they had been goaded by missionaries and other well placed critics. However, on even so important a matter as the unfettered workings of markets and contracts, the Company contravened its liberal principles where state income was concerned, by imposing monopolies over the trade of opium and salt which were maintained until late in the nineteenth century. Taxes on land production and trade remained high, whether justified by utilitarian doctrines or inherited orientalist attitudes.

An expansion of state functions in British and in princely India occurred as a result of the terrible famines of the later nineteenth century, which caused the same embarrassment as the earlier issue of sati, and undermined the belief that the imperial presence was beneficial to imperial subjects. A reluctant regime decided that state resources had to be deployed and that anti-famine measures were best managed through technical experts. This decision hastened the development of modern bureaucracy in India. Officials trained in forest management, irrigation or public works were posted to carry out development schemes in every province. Civil service technicians recruited in Britain were shifted from district to district to supervise the projects. Together with European police and medical specialists – the one to fill the jails and the other to supervise the health of inmates – these technicians made up one of the largest and best-qualified administrations in the nineteenth-century world. The culture of bureaucracy and technique reached its apotheosis under Lord Curzon, who proudly announced: 'Efficiency has been our gospel, the keynote of our administration.'

ZAMINDARS AND RYOTWARS: REVENUE AND EXPENSES

Even after Crown rule had completed nearly half of its allotted historical time of a century, the bureaucratic virtue of which Curzon spoke was difficult to discover in the several provinces, with their distinctive administrative methods and styles. Provincial variation reflected the different history and resource endowments. Bengal, the most advanced commercial zone of British India and of all of the Company dominions, was the most lightly administered. The Permanent Settlement of 1793 had vested property in a landlord class created by Lord Cornwallis with the hope of forming a set of improving rural capitalists out of what he construed as an indigenous gentry. In reality, these new Indian squires derived from other, less genteel, sources. While a few were of ancient local chiefly families, most were tax farmers recently appointed by the nawabs who had succeeded Mughal governors earlier in the eighteenth century. Few of Cornwallis's new zamindars had any inclination to become rural capitalists. Before long most of them had lost their estates to entrepreneurs from Calcutta – city men with few interests in the countryside apart from the profits to be made. In Bengal, Company and later imperial local administrators were almost exclusively magistrates whose principal task it was to protect the new landed property and enforce contractual obligations. But even these judicial officials were few, and fewer still were those who had any detailed understanding of the tracts they ministered.

The presidencies of Madras and Bombay were for the most part poorer places. Land was considered state property partly because there was so much of it and it was of such inferior quality that few wanted to own it. Instead, small peasant producers farmed lands for an annual rental from the Company's landlord state. Fields were measured and assessed so as to determine the rent (or revenue – the British could not decide what to call their claim to a share of production) to be demanded from each of the hundreds of thousands of small cultivators to whom written agreements were issued. This method of revenue collection was called *ryotwari*, or 'peasant-based payment', in contrast to *zamindari*, or 'landlord-based payment', and obtained almost everywhere in Bombay and Madras; its operation required an enormous staff of minor Indian officials working under British 'collectors'.

During the first fifteen years after Crown rule began in 1858, half, or nearly half, of all revenue was raised from the land; the balance came from taxes on opium sold in the country and abroad, on salt and, in small measure, from income taxes, stamps and so forth. Over half of the expenditures between 1860 and 1870 were on the army and on administration (33 and 22 per cent respectively, the latter largely comprising the cost of revenue collection); a further 12 per cent of total costs went to the payment of debts; the remaining one-third or so consisted of small expenditures including public works, such as irrigation.

Budgets increased after 1900, but the pattern of both revenue collection and expenditure was slow to change. Taxes on land yielded half of the revenues collected until 1918, after which they fell first to a third and then to a quarter in 1930; during the same time, customs and income taxes gradually increased to replace declining land taxes, and the salt tax – perhaps the most regressive form of imperial taxation – fell from around 15 per cent in 1872 to 10 per cent in 1918 and 5 per cent in 1930.

The revenues collected usually met state expenses and, except for a few years, yielded a surplus that was passed to Britain in the form of 'Home Charges'. These were justified as obligations deemed to arise in India and therefore to be met by transferring a portion of the revenue collected in India to the United Kingdom; these 'obligations' included the fixed dividends that had been awarded to the Company's shareholders when its governing powers were lost in 1858. The Home Charges were raised principally from Indian land taxes, and, not long after 1860, Indian nationalists began to refer to them as 'the Drain', the cost to Indians of maintaining imperial institutions.

Around 1860 government expenditures in Bengal, Northwestern Provinces, Punjab, Madras and Bombay exceeded the revenues collected, because of the high residual costs of suppressing the Mutiny and civil uprisings. Then, until 1872, there was a return to annual surpluses averaging 70.6 million rupees(about £7 million), which rose to over £20 million by the end of the century. But the total net transfer of resources from India to Britain was actually twice that amount, for by the end of the nineteenth century Britain had achieved a favourable annual balance of trade with India in about the same amount, some £25 million in 1880. The double withdrawal of treasure and commodities from an impoverished India was used to balance Britain's trade deficit with the USA and Europe.

THE POLITICAL ECONOMY OF THE LATE NINETEENTH CENTURY

After 1860, the imperial Raj seldom saw fit to justify itself, as the East India Company had been required to do during parliamentary investigations and discussions when its charter was renewed in 1813, 1833 and 1854. If Indian affairs attracted scant interest during the early nineteenth century, later almost total public indifference prevailed at home. Even when the Secretary of State for India was called upon to explain some Indian problem or policy to colleagues in the Cabinet or Parliament, he could scarcely be held to a higher standard of concern for ordinary Indians than his ministry had for ordinary Britons. Victorian statesmen were concerned about imperial defence, the conditions for profitable trade and the maintenance of a steady stream of tribute from the colonies (as the more honest would admit). Twentieth-century British politicians were equally limited in their concerns about India, though they had come to appreciate that some participation in policy formulation was a necessary cost of nurturing a moderate Indian political public to offset the radicals.

For their part, most Indian politicians proved content with a small part in the governance of their land, and shared with the British the notion that the market economy properly allocated the benefits in which they partook; the more radical, including wealthy professionals, demanded comprehensive and timely social, economic and political reforms as a matter of principle. The tempo of politics during the twentieth century was set by the interplay of these two tendencies within the Indian National Congress and grudging reforms from Britain when expedient.

During most of the nineteenth century, revenue demands were so high as to depress incomes and deter productive investment, and heavy indirect taxes were levied on consumption staples of the poorest. This punishing extractive regime eased slightly later in the century, but the scale of state-sponsored development remained nugatory: a great deal was taken from the people of India and precious little returned.

Those who governed India during the later nineteenth century were certain that markets would set prices, determine supplies and distribute benefits. They were certain too that there was little for the state to do; even the provision of education was left to Indians themselves and to missionary bodies. As in Britain, railways and transport canals were initially constructed by private enterprise, but whereas the risks of such enterprises in Britain were borne by British investors, in India it was Indian cultivators, the principal tax-payers, who bore the risks, though not the gains. Guaranteed returns were offered to British railway- and canal-makers in order to attract them to India from profitable construction works in Europe. Besides guarantees, loans from revenue collections made in India were offered to European companies at low or no interest to carry out private development schemes; one was the East India Irrigation and Canal Company, launched in 1867 for works to be carried out in the eastern province of Orissa. So vigorous was the search for investments in essential services – roads, schools, hospitals – that the British authorities granted considerable local self-government as early as 1819 in Bengal and elsewhere in 1861 and 1882, so that Indians could levy taxes for local amenities.

TECHNOLOGY AND COMMUNICATIONS

The increased interlocking of the economies of Britain and India, so profitable to the former, was partly a function of technological change, which speeded up noticeably after the 1850s and dramatically closed the distances between the British metropole and its premier colonial possession. Major political and economic consequences followed upon the improvement of communications between Europe and Asia through telegraphy and steamships: London and Calcutta were connected by telegraph in 1870 and Calcutta with other capitals in India from 1854; the Suez Canal, completed by de Lesseps in 1869, reduced the journey between Europe and India by some 4000 miles. Consequently it became possible for closer policy control to be exerted by London upon Calcutta and later New Delhi and also for the penetration of world economic forces to be intensified.

By 1910, India had the fourth largest railway system in the world, construction having began in India in 1853, as early as anywhere in the world. British capitalists were induced to undertake railway development by government guarantees of a fixed return on their investments, a project that by contrast cost Indians £50 million. By 1869, provincial and even local governments as well as princely states joined in the construction of lines, and out of this vast enterprise came a transportation system that made British India a national commodity market. There were military advantages as well: the new railways provided a means for speedily transporting soldiers wherever in India or the world they might be needed.

The high costs of rail development were criticized then and later, especially for the lack of benefit to the natives. In contrast to national railway developments elsewhere, the Indian people achieved few of the ancillary advantages of the new technology. Apart from employment as unskilled labourers, Indians gained neither money nor experience in modern engineering from the building of locomotives and rolling stock, for these came from Britain and benefited owners and workers there. Very few advanced technical skills were imparted, since Indians held a mere 10 per cent of superior posts in the railways by 1921, and only 700 locomotives were made in India over the century before independence.

Roads, canals and railways all hastened the tempo of commercialization in British India, and a burst of export expansion during the 1860s led to prosperity, especially where cotton could be grown. In the early 1860s, cotton acreage quickly expanded in response to a fivefold increase in cotton prices as stocks curtailed by the American Civil War were replaced. When that war ended, the price for cotton retreated, as did prices for export wheat from northern India, as a result of competition from United States, Canada, Australia and Argentina, where mechanization of wheat production had begun. By the 1890s railways were carrying a large proportion of hardy and cheap food grains to distant markets, and producers were caught up in credit pressures previously unknown. With the ending of the isolation of their local markets, small farmers had to finance their debts in the risky export trade or lose their land. Partly because the Indian authorities steadfastly refused to protect small producers, there were major losses of productive resources to money lenders, while food exports to distant markets constituted a different sort of 'drain' and contributed to the terrible series of famines to which the imperial regime was slow to respond.

FAMINE AND FAMINE MEASURES

Famines were and remain complex events, with political, social and cultural determinants. The scarcity of food supplies, the usual condition in many parts of India, and, as in other poor places of the world, well-tried practices for coping with food scarcity existed, such as temporary migration to places thought or known to be better endowed, or consumption of 'famine foods' available in the forests. But dearths can become famines that kill the most vulnerable sections of a population: the ill, the very young and the old. These events are remembered in India as elsewhere by special names, marking moments of absolute time by which other, lesser events are dated; thus, after a devastating famine in Gujarat in 1899, people dated events as so many weeks, months, years before or after the famine, just as they did with the Bengal famine of 1943.

The British knew about Indian famines well before the East India Company assumed political responsibility for India. Peter Mundy, an early seventeenth-century Company agent, reported a devastating series of bad harvests and food shortages in Gujarat and elsewhere in western India which drove cultivators and artisans to migrate, some making their way a thousand miles to the southern tip of India, where they continue to live. Mundy described the responses of the Mughal governor of the province, including the punishment of profiteers and those who adulterated foods, and he noted with appreciation the free food distributions ordered by the Emperor Shah Jahan, who also bade officials to remit a fraction of land taxes and to provide charity from government treasuries.

All of this must have seemed wildly generous to the first British officials of Bengal, where famine in 1769–70 led to the deaths of an estimated third of a population of thirty million. Notwithstanding the risk of severe food shortages, nineteenth-century officials remained doggedly attached to principles of free trade and non-interference with markets. Bureaucratic cowardice also entered. Fearing for their careers, most officials were reluctant to recommend

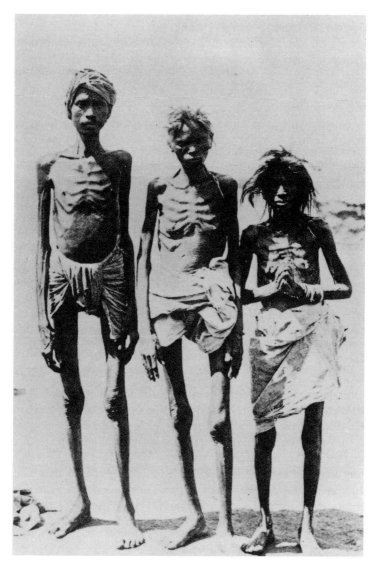

Plate 23 Victims of a nineteenth-century famine (no other identification), presumably taken by a European, probably an employee of the Raj (IOL Ray Desmond, *Victorian India in Focus*. London: HMSO, 1982, p. 3, by permission of the British Library).

that the revenues of the country be reduced to deal with dearth or that investments be made in public projects, such as irrigation works, which once provided a money income to otherwise destitute rural families and served to avert such events in future.

These ideological and career barriers to positive official efforts to reduce the mortality caused by famine proved to be as difficult to overcome in India as in Ireland somewhat earlier, and the reasons were not different. For in addition to doctrinaire political-economy pieties about non-interference with markets, there was an element of racialism that contributed to official inertia about alleviating Irish and Indian famine deaths. But neither doctrinal rectitude nor racism should be exaggerated; the record of Britain's rulers with the English poor – their poor laws and poor houses – was also deplorable.

Widespread and intense dearth began in 1866–7, though localized famines leading to higher than usual death-rates had occurred in many places even during the first half of the nineteenth century. The famine which struck in 1866–7 is usually called the Orissa famine, but in reality mortality extended well into the Gangetic Valley, far down the eastern coast of the Madras Presidency and across the peninsula to parts of the Hyderabad and Mysore principalities. Three million people were affected and deaths of 800,000 in excess of normal were recorded. Almost immediately afterwards, from 1868 to 1870, famines affecting around 21 million struck Rajasthan, the western Ganges region and parts of central India and the northern Deccan, causing excess deaths of around 400,000. During the last thirty years of the century the dreadful toll increased: 1873–4 in Bengal and eastern India, affecting a quarter of a million; 1876–8, involving 36 million in parts of the Ganges again and also Madras, Bombay, Mysore and Hyderabad, with deaths of 3.5 million. The century ended with two other massive outbreaks of famine and disease nearly everywhere in the subcontinent, with more fearsome death counts: 1896–7, affecting 96 million and causing the excess deaths of over 5 million, and again in 1899–1900, with 60 million affected and another 5 million dying prematurely.

These periods of high morbidity and mortality are still sometimes erroneously dismissed as a patch of bad luck with the monsoon. The full causes of the tragic loss of life were more historically significant, and they were multiple. From the time of the Governor-General William Bentinck, wider market networks for food commodities had emerged as a result of improved road and river transport; railways added to this trend by mid-century. Forward grain contracting logically extended market relations, so that in places where food was usually in surplus and exported, exports continued even when shortages occurred, prices soared and starvation deaths were reported. The government was slow to interfere with the effects of market and contractual relations, but was finally forced to intervene by criticisms in Britain as the toll of deaths became known there.

Inertia was finally surmounted in India when the viceroy Lord Lytton overcame his scruples to declare that when the grain markets failed to supply shortages in some places the imperial state must intervene through the provision of additional income to meet food purchases. Under his successor Lord Ripon in 1880, a Famine Code was promulgated for official guidance in how to know when famine conditions threatened and what to do about it. The code wisely declared a preference for helping the destitute in their own villages rather than resorting to camps, where it had been discovered that poor sanitation brought widespread death through disease.

That most of the deaths were not directly from starvation, but from disease swept along by the transport improvements to become the pandemics of the later nineteenth century, merely deepened the embarrassment of the imperial regime before its critics at home, and, increasingly as the century closed, in India. The consequence for the Indian countryside of several decades of mounting commercialization was the weakening and in some cases the destruction of older structures of social insurance and entitlement without any alternative protection until after the onset of the twentieth century. Then, at last, food-relief measures and public heath programmes blunted some of the fury of nineteenth-century famines.

The theory that the scourge of nearly half a century was caused by poor monsoons – acts of nature for which neither the state nor any human agency was responsible – was believed for a time. However, the virtual elimination of mass famine deaths for most of the twentieth century, when recorded climate data have not been different, makes such a fatalistic explanation unacceptable. The terrible recurrences of sustained food scarcity resulted in part from the rapid commercialization of the agrarian economy beginning in the 1860s. Contributions to the disasters came from the cotton 'boom', the development of a national market linked through the railways and the more exacting contractual arrangements for moving food and other commodities regardless of social costs. The impact of these changes on a large and very poor rural population meant that even minor dislocations in food supply could lead to severe mortality unless interventions were made.

Though the Famine Code was an important commitment by the imperial state, Victorian imperial officials only grudgingly matched this responsibility with programmes that might alleviate poverty and change a backward agriculture. Between 1891 and 1935, the single largest budgetary expenditure continued to be what it had been for a century: military, on which about 25 per cent of the budget was spent. Other large spending was related: police, law and justice increased from about 8 per cent of the total in 1891 to 10 per cent in 1935. Education and public health measures that began in the 1890s comprised a trivial 1 per cent and rose to 9 per cent by 1935. Agriculture rose to a derisory 1 per cent of total outlays in 1935, while spending on public works was held at a modest 4 per cent in 1891. These were pathetic outlays for that sector of the economy which had long generated most of the revenues, and still contributed 44 per cent in the 1890s.

Prior to the era of colonial rule, many communal forms of social insurance – entitlements to shares of communal resources – had served to spread risk widely over any region stricken by failure of the rains. Along with a high degree of economic isolation between communities, these entitlements limited the severity and scale of most naturally occurring shortages. During colonial times, however, community institutions were weakened by more sharply marked class relationships, and the railways combined with greater commodification of agricultural production to effect shortages of even the coarser types of grains. In contrast to the poor, wealthy landholders, farmers and merchants held their own and might even have gained in absolute terms. They could command prices for the grain they received by way of rent and in forced sales, especially when it could be transported by rail to distant urban markets. Class relations were thus deeply etched into the history of the later nineteenth century. From being an object of admiration by much of the world for its wealth and products during the fifteenth to the eighteenth centuries, India slid into deeper poverty partly as a result of its modernization and especially its railways.

POVERTY AND POPULATION

Cumulative poverty certainly contributed to the terrible famine mortality of the later nineteenth century. This was a disturbing conclusion reached by some of the highest placed British officials, and some of these aired their views in publications, to the annoyance of the government. Reliable censuses are a fairly recent development, but between 1750 and 1900 the population of the subcontinent is thought to have increased from around 190 to 285 million; this was an annual rate of 0.3 per cent, somewhat below the estimated increase of world population and well below that of Asia in general, let alone that of a rapidly developing country like the United States, which experienced annual increases of 1.5 per cent.

Demographic patterns did not begin to change from modest levels until the 1920s. The census of 1911 showed a modest increase to 303 million from the 285 million enumerated in 1901; in 1921 the population had grown to a mere 306 million. Poverty in those decades cannot have been caused by increased population, as we have become accustomed to suppose in the late twentieth century; causality moved the opposite way. Poverty was a brake upon population increases and was caused, like famine, by many factors.

CULTURAL CHANGE, EDUCATION AND NEW CLASSES

Brief as it was in India's long history, the colonial epoch left a legacy of cultural changes equal to and even surpassing those of other periods. Despite the deep changes wrought by Islam after 1200 in transforming the subcontinent into the largest Muslim society in the world, and in laying the foundation for two of the most populous Islamic states of our time, the impact of Europe had even greater effects: in addition to the expansion through state patronage of another world religion, Christianity, European world domination ushered in the industrial and western intellectual revolutions.

Indian speakers of the English language appeared very early in the colonial encounter; they were called *dubashis* (literally, those with two languages) in the seventeenth- and eighteenth-century world of small European trade centres, and had successively learned Portuguese, Dutch, French and English as before them others had learned Persian in order to serve Mughals. The East India Company in Madras, and later in Calcutta and Bombay, employed them as intermediaries to link Company officials with the markets that they sought to control. To the dubashis were later added a larger group of English speakers who served in the first of the territories which the Company acquired by purchase in Bengal and Madras. Formal schooling played little part in the acquisition of English and other European languages; instruction was obtained from family elders who often had menial jobs with the Europeans. Indeed, the numerous clerks of the East India Company's commercial, and later legal and political, offices learned their jobs by sitting with relatives who were employed by the Company. They learned to write and keep the records without pay until they were proficient enough to be employed themselves. English-medium schools came later, and enrolments there increased rapidly during the later nineteenth century.

THE EDUCATION DEBATE

These educational developments are usually referred to as 'western', meaning schooling based upon the curricula of upper schools, colleges and professional (e.g. law) schools in Britain, with English the medium of instruction. Very few young Indians found their way to Europe for education, and little was spent to support western schools in India. Nevertheless, the relative prosperity achieved by the turn of the nineteenth century in the Presidency cities of Calcutta, Bombay and Madras made for the flourishing condition of European education there, which had little to do with official support. Indeed, one of the most frequently cited examples of cultural arrogance and neglect at this time is the report of Thomas B. Macaulay on the deliberations over whether the paltry funds for education earmarked in the 1813 charter of the Company should be spent on western or on Indian learning and languages. New to India, where he was appointed in 1834 by British political patrons to repair his financial fortune and to assist in codification of Indian law, Macaulay unhesitatingly chose the 'Anglicist' option, opposing the preference of orientalists (the word then meant simply scholars of eastern cultures) for classical and demotic Indian learning in indigenous languages. The orientalist viewpoint had been eloquently put by Sir William Jones, who died in 1794 after a brilliant career of learning and the launching of what later became the Asiatic Society of Bengal. Those of a similar persuasion later argued that the modest government provision for schooling should be used to preserve and transmit Indian ancient knowledge because it was a heritage and because it was knowledge worthy of preservation by any standards.

In his famous 'Minute on education', Macaulay disparaged that opinion with a bland confidence unencumbered by any knowledge of classical or contemporary texts and languages, asserting:

> All parties seem to be agreed on one point, that the dialects commonly spoken among the natives of this part of India contain neither literary nor scientific information, and are, moreover, so poor and rude that, until they are enriched from some other quarter, it will not be possible to translate any valuable work into them . . .
>
> I have no knowledge of either Sanscrit or Arabic. But . . . I have read translations of the most celebrated Arabic and Sanscrit works. I have conversed . . . with men distinguished in the Eastern tongues. I am quite ready to take the Oriental learning at the valuation of the Orientalists themselves. I have never found one among them who would deny that a single shelf of a good European

Plate 24 Raja Ram Mohun Roy. Watercolour, *c.*1832 (IOL WD 1288; B 989, by permission of the British Library).

> library was worth the whole native literature of India and Arabia. The intrinsic superiority of the Western literature is, indeed, fully admitted by those members of the committee who support the Oriental plan of education . . .

Then he got to the nub of his case. The rulers needed interpreters:

> We must at present do our best to form a class who may be interpreters between us and the million whom we govern; a class of persons Indian in blood and colour, but English in taste, in opinions, in morals and in intellect.[2]

He then went on to argue that knowledge of English would actually benefit the native literatures, just as knowledge of Greek and Latin had enriched English learning.

Ram Mohun Roy, in an 1823 letter to the then Governor-General Lord Amherst, had been even more vehement in arguing for the Anglicist form of education, but in a style that could not have contrasted more with that of Macaulay. Roy had learnt Persian, Arabic and Sanskrit at a tender age, and began the study of English when he was twenty-two. He also had a sense of humour:

> Humbly reluctant as the natives of India are to obtrude upon the notice of government the sentiments they entertain on any public measure, there are circumstances when silence would be carrying this respectful feeling to culpable excess. The present rulers of India, coming from a distance of many thousand miles to govern a people whose language, literature, manners, customs, and ideas, are almost entirely new and strange to them . . . We should therefore be guilty of a gross dereliction of duty to ourselves and afford our rulers just grounds of complaint at our apathy did we omit, on occasions of importance like the present.
>
> The establishment of a new Sanscrit School in Calcutta evinces the laudable desire of government to improve the natives of India by education – a blessing for which they must ever be grateful, and every well-wisher of the human race must be desirous that the efforts made to promote it should be guided by the most enlightened principles, so that the stream of intelligence may flow in the most useful channels.
>
> When this seminary of learning was proposed . . . we were filled with sanguine hopes that this sum would be laid out in employing European gentlemen of talent and education to instruct the natives of India in mathematics, natural philosophy, chemistry, anatomy and other useful sciences.

Instead, he was dashed to learn that what was proposed was something similar to what already existed in India in abundance. He then went into an analysis of the niceties of Sanskrit and vedic learning, which he compared to medieval scholastic learning, as to both intricacy and practical uselessness, except, he hinted, for its past function in confining learning to a small elite of exalted rank:

> If it had been intended to keep the British nation in ignorance of real knowledge, the Baconian philosophy would not have been allowed to displace the system of the schoolmen which was the best calculated to perpetuate ignorance. In the same manner the Sanscrit system of education would be the best calculated to keep this country in darkness, if such had been the policy of the British legislature.[3]

By 1850, there were 22,000 students in British Indian state-funded schools. There were colleges in Benares, Agra, Calcutta, Pune, Bombay and Madras. Eight out of ten students were Hindus and the remainder divided about equally between Muslims and others. In 1857, a number of the colleges in Calcutta, Bombay and Madras were combined and became universities. Enrolments climbed. By the middle of the 1880s, students of English alone numbered 98,000, rising to over 500,000 in 1907. The largest number of degrees awarded between 1864 and 1873 were from Calcutta University, with over 12,000, followed by Madras University with 5500 and Bombay University with 2700. By the middle of the 1870s, the differences between Hindu and Muslim college students were marked: in Bengal, where Muslims constituted a majority of the population, the number of Hindus passing the University of Calcutta entrance examination was nearly 1200, the number of Muslims only 66, a mere 5 per cent. By 1886, 1230 Hindus had successfully entered the university, but only 91 Muslims, still a nugatory 7 per cent. Successful candidates for the BA degree were in about the same proportion. During the 1870s, the 6800 scholars registered at the University of Madras showed a similar skewed distribution: 66 per cent of the graduates consisted of brahmans, who were a mere 3 per cent of the population of the province according to the 1891 census. Between 1873 and 1893, state funds available for higher education were reduced in the knowledge that alternative funding would be forthcoming from Indians. Brahmans of course had always required that their young men be educated as a condition of carrying out their hereditary ritual and scribal occupations.

EDUCATING SITA

Rural and women's education lagged badly behind throughout the nineteenth century. Special efforts were required by those living in small towns to set up schools and also to pay the living expenses of their children at the major collegiate centres. The urban bias in education and in the occupational pursuits that followed shaped the sort of cultural change that occurred in the later nineteenth century. Substantial family resources had to be set aside for education, and a great many young men (and it remained men) during the later nineteenth and early twentieth centuries had several years' experience of living away from their parents in the largest cities while attending schools and colleges.

Female education was the prerogative of a few wealthy families during the Company period, when most girls and women were tutored at home. Certainly, no provision for the education of women was made in educational policy. Nevertheless, some schools did come into existence, supported by private efforts. A survey of Madras found over 5000 girls enrolled in Indian language schools, as against 179,000 boys. As the Company refused to assist girls' schools and families of respectable middling status were unwilling to have their daughters attend mission schools, such schools were supported by private subscription. Sometimes these private efforts received helpful endorsements from famous public men, such as Ram Mohun Roy in Bengal, and later organizations dedicated to purposes other than education also became involved. The Gujarat Vernacular Society, which was established to encourage the publication of books in the Gujarati language, opened a school for girls at Ahmadnagar in 1849; another was started in Agra.

By mid-century places for girls began to increase more rapidly, but they still represented only a small fraction of those for boys. In the cities voluntary organizations like those of the Parsis, the Prarthana Samaj and the Deccan Educational Society in Bombay opened girls' schools. The Brahmo Samaj did the same in Calcutta, and the Arya Samaj in several Punjab cities. As a result, Madras had 256 girls' schools, with an enrolment of 7000 day students and another thousand boarders, Calcutta had 288 schools with 7000 pupils, while Bombay, with only 65 schools, taught 6500 female students. But this was a large-city phenomenon; elsewhere there were many fewer schools. In the whole of the Northwest Provinces in the Gangetic valley there were but 17 schools and 386 female pupils.

At the close of the century there were 82,000 pupils in girls' schools in British India, and an additional 42,000 attended mixed schools. A few teacher's colleges had been founded for women, but an Education Commission of 1881 admitted that there were no more than 2 per cent of school-age girls actually in school, and even fewer (1 per cent) who could read and write.

THE PRESS IN THE NINETEENTH CENTURY

During the nineteenth century groups other than brahmans sought literacy as well as numeracy in order to achieve better careers in administrative office or commerce. A further spur to reading was the development of an indigenous publishing industry. In 1853, forty-six presses in Bengal produced over 250 books and pamphlets in Bengali, with print runs of 418,000; in addition, there were nineteen Bengali-language newspapers producing 8000 issues, many daily. Concern about this proliferation of Indian-owned newspapers led officials to shift their censorious attention from the English-language press. Since the 1820s they had sought to control English periodicals because of the criticisms of official policy, but now the focus fell upon publications in Indian languages. The Vernacular Press Act of 1878 provided for bonds to be posted by publishers of Indian-language newspapers and for the confiscation of equipment in cases of repeated incitement of disaffection against the government or for racial or religious defamation.

The first Indian-owned presses were established in Calcutta and were journalistically sophisticated as well as critical because that city had the largest intelligentsia and because it was the capital of British India. Other large cities soon followed suit, however. In Bombay an Indian press which was started in 1861 received news by telegraph about Britain and the rest of the world through Reuters news service in London and English newspapers. Similar ventures were begun by Indian entrepreneurs in Madras, where the first evening paper, the *Madras Mail*, was launched in 1868, and in Allahabad and in Lahore also in the 1860s and 1870s.

The content of the Indian press was increasingly political and nationalistic. Bengali papers began to suggest that admiration for British culture and institutions was unnatural for a conquered people and offered as alternatives the lives of European revolutionaries such as the Italian Mazzini. Most Indian newspapers, whether in English or Indian languages, covered administrative news, often criticizing the actions of individual officials and giving full reports on debates in the town and district assemblies created by the Indian Councils Act of 1861. Another focus of the Indian-language press was in countering

Christian propaganda. Tamil journals disputed the views presented by missionary publications as well as producing light literature in Tamil for entertainment. Like the northern Indian languages at the time, Tamil and other southern languages developed the new prose and poetic capabilities that characterize these languages today.

Growing literacy in English and Indian languages was stimulated and abetted by the establishment of literary associations. The middle-class intellectuals of Calcutta again took the lead with the Calcutta Book Society, where discussions were regularly conducted in English, even when the subject concerned a Bengali work. Not long afterwards, in 1874, the Society for the Improvement of Bengali Language and Literature was founded in a self-conscious effort to modernize popular literature. By the late nineteenth century, those with the money to purchase literacy could also enjoy some of the fruits of the modernity that the press and language developments were promulgating.

VOLUNTARY ASSOCIATIONS AND CHARITIES

Another form of new public association emerged from the famines of the 1870s. One of these was organized by William Digby, already mentioned above as the author of a bitingly critical book on British policies and Indian poverty which appeared in 1901. In the 1870s, while editing a daily newspaper, he served as secretary of the Madras Famine Relief Committee. Digby, who was European like the other members of the Famine Relief Fund, also called upon his middle-class Indian friends to organize effective bodies for lobbying; these, he thought, should be modelled on the Pune Saravajanik Sabha, a voluntary association formed in 1870 expressly to act as a bridge between the Bombay government and the people of the province. The famine which stalked the Deccan soon afterwards provided the occasion for the Pune Sabha to press for improved measures for dealing with food scarcity.

To an extent Digby's call was realized in the 1877 revival of the Madras Native Association, founded over twenty years before, along with similar organizations in Calcutta and Bombay, for the purpose of petitioning the parliamentary committee hearing evidence on the renewal of the East India Charter in 1854. Unlike the Calcutta and Bombay petitions at that time, which called for more offices to be available to Indians, the demands of the Madras group turned on more pragmatic matters: greater expenditure on roads and other commercially related improvements. Now, in the 1870s, the Madras Native Association adopted the pattern of the Pune Sarvajanik Sabha to form an information bridge between the mass of people and the state, by gathering information about popular needs and by organizing meetings to discuss government proposals. Lord Ripon's proposal to extend elective self-government to municipalities and rural boards was explained and endorsed, and evidence was presented on whether it was feasible for government funds to be reduced or withdrawn from higher education, which measures the Association opposed.

Voluntary associations such as those in Pune and Madras and the Indian

Association established by Surendranath Banerji in 1876 differed from associations formed to promote the interests of particular regional caste groups – usually wealthy landed or commercial castes – and from sectarian associations of Hindus, Muslims or Sikhs. Not limited by ascriptive principles of birth or family religious preferences, the new organizations appealed to individual men of education, whether in the professions, in business or in government, and the core agenda was political reform, along the lines being widely discussed in the English-language Indian press, whose circulation had reached around 276,000 in 1905. These modern men formed the basis of the nationalist politics that was to emerge in the early years of the twentieth century, expanded from the narrow preserve of a handful of western-educated professionals to a broader class base.

THE INDIAN CLASS SYSTEM

Professional and business employment often required educated Indians to leave their home provinces to become members of communities in which English was the *lingua franca*. The same mobility that made English a valuable asset also constituted an information grid about conditions in the rest of the subcontinent, and thus laid the groundwork for a national consciousness. Bengalis, the first modern intellectuals and professionals in India, had become so distant from the interests of businessmen by the twentieth century that they were surprised to learn that in Bombay and Madras the English publications most sought after were those that pertained to trade and business. Bengali intellectuals were also surprised that these other educated Indians complained less about the opportunities for government careers than about the need for improved transportation and commercial development. In still other places the English-educated middle classes were formed from landed households that had been connected with the old Mughal or Maratha regimes as revenue contractors; for example, in nineteenth-century Maharashtra, Bal Gangaghar Tilak and Gopal Krishna Gokhale.

A sizable wealthy commercial class was slower to adopt western ways. Prominent among them were Gujaratis in Bombay and Marwaris in Bombay and Calcutta. These families retained strong links to a past that they were loath to see weakened; their businesses continued to depend upon family networks. Most also continued their affiliations with older religious and cultural institutions and lagged behind Parsis and Maratha and Bengali brahmans in adopting western education, dress, furnishings or houses. Few Gujarati or Marwari monied men sent their children to the new schools or themselves joined the socially pluralistic public associations until the twentieth century. In these and in other ways they had not freed themselves from the community structures of eighteenth-century India, from the complex and contradictory older relations between the mercantilist economies and state, on the one hand, and the still robust communitarian institutions, on the other.

At the other end of the class system of the later nineteenth century, a large underclass of families barely survived upon money wages or upon small loans they were compelled to take, keeping them in a constant state of indebtedness.

Estimating the size of this underclass is difficult; however, the charge made by the senior imperial official W. W. Hunter in 1881 that forty million, a fifth of the population of British India, lacked sufficient food was never refuted. As cities grew during the century so did the large urban pauper population of street vendors and craftsmen with paltry stocks and tools, carters and casual labourers; they could be as volatile and riotous as they were during the eighteenth century.

Between the urban educated middle class and paupers of town and country was a lower middle class that emerged from small towns and their rural hinterlands of the eighteenth century and later. In addition to merchants, money-lenders and artisan-traders, there were others directly linked by economic activities in urban markets of all sorts: labour, credit and commodities. Along with small town groups and linked economically and in other ways, small-holding, rich and middle peasants can also be included in this petty bourgeoisie, since they were clearly differentiated from the landless agrarian workers who made up a large underclass of wage-dependent labourers.

Rooted in the ancient community structures of India, but with numerous branches in the proliferating towns of the past two centuries, this lower middle class were major supporters of local institutions and their concomitant ideologies. Included in this were religious institutions, which continued to possess privileges and entitlements, such as tax-free land holdings, derived from past regimes and now protected by local institutions. By the late nineteenth century, and often with the assistance of more westernized professionals, lower middle-class men initiated religious reform movements that mimicked the voluntarism of higher-class and caste men. In addition, with the aim of removing the obloquy to which they were subjected by the high-caste Indians upon whom government officers depended for their understanding of caste practices and positions, the middle-ranking castes formed associations both to represent their interests to government and to enforce new norms.

THE ILBERT BILL AND THE ORIGINS OF NATIONALISM

The religious and social reform movements of the later nineteenth century reflected and reinforced the growing self-esteem of the Indian middle classes. This class confidence soon collided with the social arrogance of that 'other middle class' of Britons and ignited the first act of embryonic Indian nationalism, the Ilbert Bill agitation of 1883.

Sir Courtney Persegrime Ilbert was a Law Member of the viceregal council of Lord Ripon, the most popular of the nineteenth-century viceroys. Both were intent on ending some of the rankling judicial privileges of Europeans, including their right to choose not to be tried before Indian justices. Ilbert's proposal to end that immunity created an inevitable furore among Europeans. Defence associations were organized throughout British India, with funds to publicize opposition to the measure, and mobilization duly produced a counter movement by Indians in support of Ilbert's legislation. Nevertheless, the government capitulated to European opposition and substituted a weaker enactment that specified that some Europeans' cases might be heard by Indian judges, but permitted the defendant to insist on a jury trial, where half the jurors were European. Moreover, the discrimination that the revised bill perpetuated was extended to Presidency towns where the Criminal Procedure Code of 1873 had permitted trial of Europeans by Indian magistrates and judges.

The Ilbert agitation had multiple significance. One was ideological. The Anglo-Indian position was that the Raj was built upon the unchallengeable superiority of Europeans and that to suggest the equality of Indian ability and character, as Ilbert did, must diminish 'European character' and with it British security and power. This open manifestation of social Darwinism signalled to educated Indians that a new and difficult era was at hand. Another outcome of the Ilbert confrontation was the glaring demonstration that far from being encouraged to share the rule of their land, as had been implied in Victoria's 1858 proclamation, Indians were despised. Just as important were the practical and organizational lessons learnt. The remedy for the racist offence was to imitate the successful tactics of the Anglo-Indian middle class.

In the same year, 1883, an Indian National Conference was convened in Calcutta to focus upon a set of Indian grievances and seek their redress. The leadership was taken by Surendranath Banerji, one of those able young Indians who had overcome all impediments to win a place in the Indian Civil Service by examination. Having passed, Banerji was driven to litigation to sustain his candidacy, and, once appointed, he was dismissed on what many believed were inadequate grounds. Hence Banerji had personal as well as philosophical reasons for his form of nationalism.

THE POLITICIZATION OF CLASS, CASTE AND GENDER

The complex and interrelated set of social forces which gathered during the last quarter of the nineteenth century produced a new social alternative to that based fragmentarily on caste and sect institutions set in regional and local settings. The forces of the contemporary world pressed towards the formation of national classes, and the social transformation that began during the pre-colonial eighteenth century was hastened and shaped by the colonial policies of the next century. Yet Indian institutions were constantly subject to imperial demands that left some ancient oppressive practices unreformed and even strengthened. Thus, at the same time that an urban bourgeoisie arose partly out of opportunities to serve the administrative and commercial needs of the new rulers – and eventually constituted perhaps a tenth of the population – there remained a large underclass of mostly rural families for whom each day posed a threat to their slender resources. Between these two strata was a thick layer of lower middle-class households – rural and urban – striving for some of the security of the more wealthy but in grim fear of falling into the abyss of the underclass.

The western-educated middle class was the most relentlessly observed segment of contemporary Indian society. During much of the twentieth century, they were under surveillance from the police and political officers of the Raj; later they were the subjects of study by political scientists and historians. What this class thought of itself and its world was not kept secret either, for its members' self-perceptions received wide publicity in their newspapers, pamphlets and manifestos.

Middle-class consciousness expressed itself in diverse ways. Middle-class Indians were keen about educating their children, so they supported schools and served on the governing bodies of colleges and universities. Most also signed petitions for more and better government employment, the removal of commercial disincentives and improvements in business opportunities. But most generally and significantly, middle-class Indians dedicated themselves individually and collectively to religious reform and revival – class consciousness was expressed through redefinition of traditions and values. Hence religion remained at the core of nationalist sentiments, and communal struggles remind us of this ideologically centring fact.

LATE NINETEENTH-CENTURY SOCIAL REFORMERS

The model for reform and revival came from Bengal during the early decades of the nineteenth century. While the abolition of sati and thugi by Lord Bentinck was meant to assuage British critics of the Raj, these actions often won the approval and also the participation of Indians like Ram Mohun Roy. But in the last part of the century the reform impulse had all but passed from Bengal, whose heirs of the early movement fell to quarrelling with each other. The torch had been picked up by the western-educated in other parts of the country.

Madhav Govinda Ranade was a celebrated social reformer during the last forty years of the century in Maharashtra, in part because he enjoyed the prestige of being a judge of the Bombay High Court. Himself a brahman, he was an early advocate of lifting the restrictions on high caste women. He founded both the Widow Re-marriage Association in 1861, which sought to implement an act permitting widows to marry that had been passed in 1856, and the Deccan Education Society, which was concerned in part to increase facilities for the education of girls and young women. In addition, he joined others in pressing for legislation to raise the age at which marriages could be consummated, which eventuated in the Age of Consent Bill of 1890.

Religious liberals like Ranade debated furiously with conservative pundits over the interpretation of dharma texts on such questions; on the other hand, political liberals like the scholar R. G. Bhandarakar argued against radicals such as B. G. Tilak over whether state law or voluntary changes in social norms should prevail. In this debate, as in others, the nominal subjects were neither consulted nor permitted a voice; they were pawns in debates about other issues having to do with how much social change, and what sort, was to accompany the political reforms close to the hearts of men of the Indian National Congress (which in 1885 had succeeded the Indian National Conference).

The calls for reform in the later nineteenth century created tension between the desire to change political institutions by opening them to more Indian participation and the desire to leave social practices fundamentally unaltered. A sign of this tension was that the most zealous reformers continued to observe older marriage customs in their families, including betrothal of children, while they pressed for laws raising the legal age of marriage. Ranade himself married a child of eleven after his wife died. To deal with such apparent hypocrisy or contradiction required arguments that could appeal to a widening Indian middle class in the professions and commerce, but also to the British regime from whom new laws and offices had to be sought. The construction of social attitudes and ends within changing political frameworks occurred in India as in Europe as the work of the same kind of modern ideologues.

Less moderate voices were beginning to be heard. Among them was that of a woman, the first Indian feminist to address other women directly about emancipation. Ramabai was the daughter of a Maharashtrian brahman of particularly exalted caste, which also happened to be that of the reformer Ranade. Her father had turned from the impersonal and mystical *advaita* doctrine to bhakti devotionalism. Furthermore, as an educational experiment he took his child bride to a forest hut so remote that tigers prowled around it at night, in order to tutor her in Sanskrit. His daughter was born in that hut, and in turn taught Sanskrit by her mother.

Ramabai's father (despite his own example) also took a stand against the early marriage of women, so that, after his death, which was shortly followed by that of her mother and the rest of her family, she remained unmarried at the almost unheard of age of twenty-two. By this time she and her brother had made their way to Calcutta, where she impressed many assembled pundits with her astonishing memory and knowledge of Sanskrit, to the point where they awarded her the title 'Sarasvati' after the goddess of wisdom. From that occasion she was called 'pundita', even though both she and her brother had abandoned the Hindu faith. When her brother died, she married his friend, who was a lawyer but a member of a shudra caste. For a woman to marry down in the caste system was considered a particularly heinous sin.

After only nineteen months, her husband too died, leaving her with a baby daughter. She went to Pune intending to learn English, and was befriended by Ranade, but was subjected to vicious gossip by the orthodox. This criticism focused her attention on the social evils afflicting the lives of Indian women, and she gave evidence before Sir W. W. Hunter's Education Commission in 1883.

In the same year, she travelled to England and became converted to Christianity. During a trip to the United States, she wrote and published the indictment of the condition of Indian women for which she is best known. As to the situation of widows of the traditionally high (and increasingly aspiring) castes, her condemnation reached the hyperbolic, though, unlike right-thinking males, whether Indian or European, contemporary reformers or later historians, she realized that marriage was not necessarily the universal panacea for the afflictions of women:

Re-marriage, therefore, is not available, nor would it be at all times desirable as a mitigation of the sufferer's lot. So the poor, helpless high-caste widow with the one chance of ending her miseries in the Suttee rite taken away from her, remains as in past ages with none to help her.[4]

Returning to India, and supported by her American Christian friends, Ramabai opened a school for high-caste girls, hoping to attract a large proportion of child widows and infused with a missionary spirit that became progressively more open. As a result, she became the subject of a number of hagiographic biographies which added 'saint' to her titles, but also lost the support of liberal Indian male reformers, and was the special target of criticism by B. G. Tilak. Nothing daunted, she used the occasion of the terrible famine and plague afflicting Maharashtra and Gujarat in the 1890s to expand her refuge to include the rescue and education of its female victims, regardless of caste (although the 'Rescue Home' for 'fallen women' was kept carefully separate from the high-caste school). Around her figure, then, were played out the debates and conflicts of the politics of caste, class, religion and gender that suffused the reform and proto-nationalist movements of the late nineteenth century.

Some men too were demanding more vigorous reform from the imperial regime. Behramji Malabari, a member of the Parsi community of Bombay, organized a campaign for legislation against the practice of child marriage, a project which captured the interest of intellectuals elsewhere and ultimately received such attention in Britain itself as to bring forth a law prohibiting child marriage in 1891. By that time, however, yet more extreme voices were raised against moderate reformers who merely importuned, as Ranade did, or gently pressured, as Malabari did.

B. G. Tilak was one of these new spokesmen who combined social reform with an increasingly patriotic and political set. Tilak had impressive credentials as an educational reformer and was the editor of an English-language newspaper in Pune near Bombay. He opposed British legislation to change social and religious customs, because, he said, Indians themselves must change those practices which they found offensive, and not depend on the laws of foreign rulers. He not only preached opposition to reform legislation, but also opposed anti-plague measures on the grounds that fumigation of houses by low caste health employees was a deliberate provocation to high caste Hindus like himself.

Tilak was a successful publicist for and organizer of public happenings during the later 1890s, an example of which was his festival of the seventeenth-century Maratha king Shivaji, whom he celebrated as a fighter for freedom against the Mughals, the earlier colonists. He also introduced the public worship of Ganapati, the elephant-faced son of the god Shiva, a deity as popular among Maharashtrians as the goddess Durga (or Kali) was in Bengal. For some of these striking tactics, Tilak was convicted of sedition and exiled for some years to Burma. However, the multifaceted activities of Tilak were not matched by other ideologues of his day, who concentrated on ever-evocative religious symbols and arguments to express their national consciousness and patriotism.

One of these was the Bengali socio-religious publicist Swami Vivekananda, who became famous for his addresses on Hindu devotional philosophy at the 1893 World Congress of Religions in Chicago. Despite his fame, he was condemned by orthodox Hindus for suggesting that the lower castes should be allowed to engage in the Hindu rituals from which they were traditionally excluded. This was necessary, he said, in order to save them from the blandishments of missionaries or, worse, from socialists and anarchists, his demons of the day. Vivekananda's activist ideology rekindled the desire for political change among many western-educated young Bengalis, which proved an important preparation for the action to which they would be called during the nationalist upsurge of 1907.

An anonymous movement began in the Gangetic region to promote a ban on the slaughter of cows, which won wide public support among orthodox Hindus in the lower echelons of the middle class. Though nominally an expression of piety by Hindus, for whom cows were sacred, the issue was publicized in explicitly anti-Muslim terms, for they were eaters of cow flesh. The movement, however, was not a new departure into political mobilization on a communal basis; an earlier example was the founding of the Arya Samaj in 1875 by Dayananda Saraswati.

After a spell as a wandering ascetic in the western Gangetic plain, Dayananda settled in the Punjab to preach a new social gospel. Practices such as child marriage, the prohibition of widow remarriage and the alleged polluting effects of foreign travel were condemned as arbitrarily imposed by 'ignorant brahmans' without scriptural sanction. He advocated going 'back to the vedas'. This was reminiscent of Ram Mohun Roy's criticisms early in the century, as were the positive principles Dayananda enunciated: a strict monotheism, condemnation of idolatry and rejection of brahman domination of ritual and social practices. He insisted that a purified Hinduism was superior to Islam and Sikhism in the Punjab and to Christianity everywhere. He founded the Arya Samaj in 1875, an organization which still retains its militant character. Young educated Punjabis were stirred by his teachings, which seemed more congenial to their parochial tastes than those of the Bengali professionals and government servants, who carried with them the odium of carpetbaggers.

The Arya Samaj suffered a division that was becoming general in reform movements, over whether to concentrate on achieving better educational and economic opportunities or to engage in muscular forms of religious contestation. One wing of Samajists advocated English-medium colleges and tolerance for meat eating, while others advocated a militant programme of counter-conversion (*shuddi*) directed at Muslims and Christians, and laws for cow protection, including the outlawing of commercial slaughterhouses that dealt in beef. This more explicit and confrontational Hindu consciousness of the early twentieth century anticipated the openly anti-Muslim ideology of later movements usually labelled communalist.

MUSLIM MOVEMENTS

In all of this heightened political awareness, Muslims were less active. In the late eighteenth century there had been a movement in the east of Bengal called the Shariat Ullah which intended to strengthen knowledge of Islamic law among ordinary people to offset Christian propaganda. A century later, two major reform movements arose among Muslims, of which one was within the small but growing middle class that included men of the modern professions as well as members of older landlord families of the Gangetic plain. Among them was Sayyid Ahmad Khan, a rationalist who turned to a public career on behalf of his co-religionists after retiring from the judicial service of the Raj. A British loyalist, he founded the first centre of western higher education specifically for Muslims, the Anglo-Oriental College at Aligarh.

The other Muslim movement of this time differed in its class appeal and programme. Founded by two soldiers who had risen against their British officers in 1857, Muhammad Qasim Nanawtawi and Rashid Ahmed Gangohi, this anti-British movement centred upon the Deoband seminary, established in 1867. By the late decades of the century, Deobandis, as they were called, were inveighing against both British rule and the anti-cow slaughter and counter-conversion movements, which they believed enjoyed the covert support of British officialdom.

These Muslim mobilizations differed from each other in another way, besides their attitude to British rule. The college at Aligarh was meant to attract the support and the sons of wealthy Muslim landowners, whereas the Deoband seminary attracted a lower stratum of middle-class Muslims: petty landlords, small town traders, religious leaders and teachers (*mullahs*), minor government officials and artisans.

For the Aligarh constituency, there was a programme of western studies to make wealthy young Muslims into British gentlemen while yet preserving their Islam. This aim was pronounced in the influential writings by Sir Sayyid, who assured his British friends that an Islamic orientation need not be hostile towards Christianity. Deobandis, by contrast, were schooled in the teachings of the Middle Eastern Wahhabi movement, intent on purifying and defending Islam against the onslaughts of European political and cultural dominance. Wahhabis gathered in Peshawar, on the frontier with Afghanistan, from where their agents spread as far away as Bengal to mobilize Indian Muslim support against Britain's military activities on India's northwestern frontier. Not surprisingly, the Deobandis attracted British surveillance and ultimately many were imprisoned on the grounds that they were under the influence of the pan-Islamic mentor Jamal al-Din al-Afghani, who resided in Calcutta and Hyderabad for several years around 1880 and preached a seditious line of cooperation between Muslims and Hindus to oppose British imperialism. While British authorities maintained a careful watch over the Deobandis and pan-Islamicists, they nurtured Sir Sayyid's Aligarh experiment with westernization and collaboration.

The government administrators of the later nineteenth century had come to accept that Muslims were overrepresented in the public services of northern

India and that a better balance should be struck between them and Hindus in public employment. After having enjoyed centuries of patronage and privileges under Muslim rulers, former grandees, subordinate officials and religious leaders were resentful as jobs and perquisites passed from them to Hindus. The employment of Muslims slipped from a high of 64 per cent of public offices in 1857 to 35 per cent in the early twentieth century, though this was still higher than their proportion of the Gangetic population. Resentment flared against the Hindu scribal and commercial groups who succeeded them, and turned to rage as anti-Muslim calls for cow protection accompanied provocatively noisy processions of Hindus near mosques during services.

Even before the turn of the twentieth century the growing divisions within the Indian lower-middle class led to a raising crescendo of religious rioting in northern India. Where Muslims formed a substantial portion of the population, in the towns of the central and eastern United Provinces, rioting broke out in 1892–3 and reached other cities as far away as Rangoon before the decade ended. The police attributed these affrays to cow protection agitation and the harassment of Muslim worshippers, but along with religious confrontation there were economic conflicts. Violence occurred between Hindu peasants and Muslim landlords and petty officials in the central Ganges region, and between small Muslim artisan and trading groups and exploitative Hindu bankers and big merchants in Gangetic towns; in eastern Bengal and the Punjab, Muslim peasants lashed out against Hindu money-lenders and traders or Hindu landlords.

Along the Malabar coast, there were other outbreaks of rural violence by Muslim tenants and small cultivators against Hindu landlords and money-lenders. Muslim farmers, who were called Moplahs, developed a high degree of self-conscious identification as the descendants of the sixteenth-century soldiers who had fought holy wars against the enemies of Islam: Hindus and Christian Portuguese. They recreated their roles as militant religious martyrs during the middle decades of the nineteenth century and again in risings between 1882 and 1896. They courted death at the hands of the police in the belief that they would be immediately spirited to paradise.

But behind the religious fervour there were worldly causes, in this case the indebtedness of Muslim farmers to landlords; debt collection was enforced by the courts and led to large-scale evictions. The Moplah actions against Hindu landlords destroyed property, including temples, and their violence continued into the 1920s. While the active fighters never numbered more than a few hundred, they enjoyed the sympathy and support of other Malabar Muslims.

INDUSTRIAL WORKERS AND FOREST FOLK

Two other socio-economic groupings that found particular niches and manifested political consciousness were the industrial working class, emerging in the jute and cotton textile factories of Calcutta and Bombay, and the hill and forest peoples. Factory workers had became numerous enough by 1881 to justify the promulgation of a factory act by the government. Like laws passed in Britain ostensibly to limit child and female labour, this rare extension of

British welfare legislation to India had the latent purpose of reducing the price advantage enjoyed by factory-made goods, in this case by provisions insisting on costly safety provisions. British manufacturers were glad of measures to offset the lower wages that made Indian textiles more competitive in the Indian market than imported British cloth. More laws on factory employment appeared in 1891 and 1911, but did nothing to improve poor working conditions or to avert strikes among the first Indian industrial workers, who were as yet a minuscule part of the Indian workforce. They were certainly too few to contest the main ground with middle-class professionals, managers and bureaucrats who spoke for India as the Indian National Congress from 1885 to 1907.

The relatively small population living in India's forest and hill tracts who acquired a new self- and political-consciousness during the later nineteenth century were called 'tribals' in official language. Ostensibly they differed from most peasant people in not being divided into castes. By the late nineteenth century, they may have accounted for about 10 per cent of the population and were always among the poorest. Censuses starting in 1872 employed the terminology of 'tribal' as one of their categories for a particular reason. If the forest and hill people were organized 'tribally', they were deemed to have no historic rights in the lands they had long exploited for hunting and gathering and some shifting cultivation. Rights to landed property were conceded to field agriculturists only; that is, to peasant householders organized into castes.

Regulations enacted from 1898 on sought to restrict the use of the forest, and were justified on the grounds of reducing the soil erosion that lowered agricultural production and generating revenue from commercial forestry. Protests by the forest folk against the regulations were followed by a series of uprisings in which bow-and-arrow armies faced firearms. Inspired tribal leaders arose to demand the restoration of their rights to use freely the products of the forest and to practise small-scale shifting cultivation. Official and sociological assumptions were defied when the presumably backward, fragmented forest groups formed alliances and presented challenges, not merely by their crude but effective militarization, but also by inspired arguments which were mobilized as bases for revitalization movements.

The rebellions of the Santhal and other 'Kheroal' (egg-born) people of 1855 and 1870 in northeastern and northwestern India respectively, and the millenarianist rebellion in Gujarat by the Naikda forest people in 1868, were examples of such movements. These were (and are) called *adivasi* or 'tribals', and all borrowed from Hinduism or Christianity and mixed pre-existing beliefs in magic and myth into an ideology of mobilization. All attributed special sanctity to the forest, and identified their own well-being, or even existence, with it. (See Plate 1.) Resistance culminated in the 1899 uprising of the Munda peoples of the forested hills around Ranchi, in eastern India. Their older system of communal land-holding had been destroyed by foreclosures by money-lenders, government-appointed landlords and labour contractors licensed and protected by British authorities. All attempts at intervention by missionaries working among Mundas were ignored by officialdom. Finally, the

Mundas found a charismatic leader, the son of a sharecropper and a Christian with a smattering of missionary education, who prophesied a new era and led attacks upon police stations around Ranchi. The movement was violently suppressed but remained a lively and treasured tradition to be resurrected in the later Jharkhkand movement that formed part of the nationalist agitations of the 1920s and 1930s.

In other parts of the subcontinent, forest people continued to organize against the assaults on their traditional way of life; their protests, though suppressed, continued to erupt throughout the early decades of the twentieth century, merging into the larger framework of popular nationalist struggles when illiterate 'tribals' joined peasant neighbours to oppose British rule.

PEASANT PROTEST

The politicization of India's vast agricultural population may have been as significant as the later middle-class urban opposition to Curzon's 'efficiency' reforms in Bengal. In the last quarter of the nineteenth century, major landholders began to resort to force to protect their economic interests. The Deccan riots in 1875, when wealthy farmers in the Pune and Ahmadnagar districts of Bombay Presidency attacked Marwari money-lenders from Rajasthan, demonstrated this new determination. The repayment of debts contracted by these farmers to increase production during the cotton boom of the previous decades had proved impossible when cotton prices collapsed after the US Civil War. Court proceedings led to the loss of much land through foreclosures, which prompted rich farmers to burn debt-bonds and loot grain stores. They were often led in these activities by village headmen or major landholders, and local Maratha money-lenders were usually spared. The British appear to have recognized the justice of some of these violent actions of 1875 by passing a debt relief act a few years later to protect against land loss as a result of debt.

Pune was also the scene of even more violent actions under the leadership of a brahman intellectual named Phadke in 1879. Seemingly influenced by the rioting of 1875, as well as by the earliest writings on the 'Drain', and spurred as well by religious revivalism in the local colleges, Phadke led a secret group of bandits who raised money by robbery to finance their programme of sabotaging communications.

In Pabna, Bengal, a prosperous zone of multi-cropped rice production and jute, protests were organized by mass meetings and funds were raised for litigation against landlords when cultivators found their occupancy rights under the tenancy laws of 1859 being violated. In such protests, politics became confused, since the British were often looked upon as protectors against the machinations of Indian oppressors; indeed, protesters frequently cried the virtues of British rule and appealed for the intervention of the empress of India. Such sentiments won the sympathy of British officials and encouraged them to strengthen tenancy regulations against landlord oppression.

Most of the rural agitations of the late nineteenth century had some basis in class conflict, and most were peaceful and legalistic. As the century closed, however, calls began to be heard for the non-payment of revenue or rents unless the violations of regulations and agreements ceased. Rent and revenue strikes did occur sporadically; for example, in Assam in 1893–4 and in Bombay in 1896–7, where B. G. Tilak justified the looting of food stores because of famine conditions and for the same reason demanded rent and revenue remissions and an end to judicial distraints of farmers' property for debt repayment.

To these and other rural crises the government offered feeble remedies. One ameliorative measure was to restore tenancy rights lost as a result of the zamindari revenue settlements in Bengal and elsewhere. Still, new levels of entrenched power were attained by rural magnates such as the great Avadh landlords of the central Gangetic plain, who were converted from major revenue contractors into holders of large, private landed estates and dominators of local governments and markets. Elsewhere landlords held places of influence by shifting their roles from rent receivers to rural creditors and joining merchants and money-lenders in controlling the credit and commodity markets used by smallholding peasants. Rural class tensions intensified during the late nineteenth century, giving rise to powerful tenant movements in provinces like Bengal.

CASTE CHANGES

The class character of the growing political protest was accompanied by a reinforcement of caste consciousness. Caste solidarity served as an important mobilizing force, at a time when the operations of government censuses acted to strengthen caste culture and organization. Older sociological notions of caste have always supposed a virtually unchanging ancient institution. This was the view of high-caste advisers to the British, who stood to gain most from it. Now it is recognized that during the nineteenth century, as throughout history, caste relations were continuously redefined to meet changing circumstances and conditions. For example, during the late eighteenth century, when Mughals ruled western India, some Maharashtrian brahmans are known to have adopted the Islamic title of mullah, meaning one learned in holy law, in the hope of being spared the poll tax to which non-Muslims were subject. European colonialism, for its part, imposed obvious pressures and opportunities that could hardly be met by unchanging usages and beliefs from some past age.

The East India Company officials had no thought of altering the various systems of caste they encountered in different parts of India when they converted from a trading company into a state. Nevertheless, they did change a great deal and inflected caste with a different political edge. Brahman 'experts' often proposed arbitrarily defined rigid rules for what had been flexible and variable usages, and these were further hardened by codification and publication for use by magistrates and judges whose decisions created legal precedents. Printed legal and social codes were meant to reduce the dependence of the British upon Indian subordinates, always suspected of harbouring interests of their own, but codes and judicial decisions constituted new knowledge categories, replacing those contained in dharmashastras. To these recent conceptions were added other knowledge; for instance, the findings of linguistic and ethnographic surveys, which were also meant to assist officials in their work, but had wider effects.

In response to the ordering of what the British took to be current social and cultural practice, Indian groups often petitioned to change the way in which they were ranked with respect to others. Groups enumerated as belonging to the shudras would protest that they were formerly kings or priests and thus deserved to be registered as kshatriyas or brahmans. To support such pleading, lobbying organizations were formed, usually called by the ancient Sanskrit word for assembly, *sabha*, to press their claims. To make these claims convincing, caste associations would often call for changes in the conduct of their members; for example, for the adoption of teetotalism or vegetarianism, which were markers of higher caste status accepted by the British. In addition, caste sabhas hired publicists to write pamphlets and even books supporting their claims. It is hardly surprising that the leaders of such social movements were in excellent positions to assume significant political roles as nationalist activities intensified after 1907, first in Bengal and then more widely, bringing political and social movements into the same public orbit.

[7]   *TOWARDS FREEDOM*

TWO TYPES OF NATIONALISM

Indian politics in the first half of the twentieth century was dominated by attempts to 'recover' the nation from the British; in the second half, the political mission was to 'fulfil' the destiny that had been imputed to that nation. Yet both projects suffered from contradictions inherent in the idea of nationalism itself. On the one hand, the idea draws on the intellectual heritage of secularism and liberalism, and has as its goal the establishment of a polity based on self-determination regardless of colour, creed or class. Such a pluralist vision of 'civic' nationalism marked some of the efforts of the Indian National Congress from the days of the early 'moderates' to the stronger, socialist ambitions of Jawaharlal Nehru and to the founding of the post-independence, constitutionally based Indian state.

On the other hand, the idea also draws on a different, and no less well entrenched, system of political meanings associated with the symbols of 'community' as they shade into the political processes of 'communalism'. Whether these symbols elicit participation on the basis of religious appeals, or those of caste or language, the salient element of this process is the idiom of 'community'. The term implies that a perceived or claimed commonality, however vaguely defined, could transform a disparate people into a single collective body, as if they lived together in a small village or urban neighbourhood.

Both a secular and a communal nationalism began at the same time, around 1880, and ran parallel with each other. Even as independence achieved under the Indian National Congress was followed for some thirty years by the pluralist, secular politics practised under Jawaharlal Nehru's Congress Party, there existed another, equally well established political process based upon communal mobilization, throughout the same period, with an alternative claim to nationhood based upon the Hindu majority religion of India.

Labels such as nationalism, communalism, extremism and moderation are problematic. In Indian usage, 'communalism' usually refers to political mobilizations and alignments based upon differences between Hindus and Muslims; as discussed above, the term can also include contestations among caste and language groupings. In any case, there is a general notion among social scientists that communalism is anti-nationalist, but that is inaccurate.

There is a communalist conception of nation that is primarily based on Hindu–Muslim differences, but it also includes language, and this form was launched at the same time as secular nationalism.

'Hindu nationalism' has been a vehicle for political action in the Gangetic plain, the historic Indian heartland, since the 1880s. Then and subsequently, contention between Hindus and Muslims arose from genuine and significant differences, such as the revulsion of many Hindus against the butchering of cattle for the food of Muslims (and Christians), and Muslim resentment about noisy processions, some religious, some not, in the precincts of mosques where they disturbed prayer. But religious conflict from an early time inevitably involved other tensions. There were challenges of older elites by new in the changing order of nineteenth-century India. An example of this is the loss of wealth and standing of Muslim and Hindu landed households when they were deprived of their status as zamindars and leaders of local society. When these fallen households were Muslim and when the counter-elites were formed around Hindu merchants and professionals, civil violence on religious lines was sometimes resorted to in order to maintain older privileges.

At the other end of the class structure was the economic hardship that resulted when hand-woven textiles were displaced by machine-made cloth in small shops and stalls of urban markets. When, as often in Gangetic towns, the weavers were Muslim and the sellers of factory goods were Hindu, the two groups contended on religious grounds. Still another example in the Gangetic region, with its relatively high Muslim population (about 20 per cent in some places), derives from the depression period of the 1920s and 1930s, when competition for lowly jobs in market towns intensified. Then Hindu artisans and low-caste workers turned against Muslims and untouchables, using religion in a militant form to mobilize and protect their economic interests.

Again, ostensibly religious reasons for mobilization and violence masked other objectives of political action. Colonial authorities fomented some of this discord to weaken the solidarity of politicized groups in the 1930s, attempting to divide and immobilize them. The failure of the politics of independent India to ameliorate the colonial record in this respect is widely acknowledged: religion, caste and language have all been deployed by major political parties, and contending nationalisms continue to be a crucial element of politics throughout the subcontinent as a result.

Studies of nationalism in India delineate phases in the idiom and practices of nationalists. 'Extremist' nationalism is considered to be rooted in communal sentiment and hatreds, as 'moderate' nationalism is supposedly based in secular, constitutional forms of politics. The first period of the Indian National Congress from 1885 is often designated its 'moderate' phase, in that founders of the Congress were Indian and British professional men. The earliest meetings even enjoyed the official patronage of the viceroy. They met as loyal subjects mildly stating their modest objectives, and did so during the Christmas holidays when the courts or government offices where many worked were closed. Their petitions gently reminded the Viceregal Council and the Secretary of State for India in the British cabinet of Victoria's 1858 offer of fuller participation of Indians in their governance. Between annual meetings even these mild chidings by the Congress ceased, because the Congress had no elected officials and no continuing executive to act between the meetings.

The presidents of the annual meetings included Europeans like Allan Octavian Hume, a retired member of the Indian Civil Service, who won sympathetic encouragement for the Congress from the Earl of Dufferin, viceroy from 1884 to 1888. Neither he nor others chosen by the local arrangements committees of the cities that hosted the Congresses were likely to transgress the bounds of courtesy by stridency. Certainly, for some time there was no tolerance of or platform for those who demanded that British rule must be more determinedly opposed. Even so, official patronage lasted only a few years before being overtaken by disdain for the courteously couched demands that issued from each Congress meeting.

An era of 'extremism' is deemed to have dated from 1907, according to the conventional chronology of Indian nationalism, because an 'extremist' challenge to 'moderate' congressmen and to the Raj set into motion an oscillation between the two tendencies that was pulsed by frustrations over the slow progress of constitutionalist and petitioning Indian politicians. This led to brief outbreaks of violent nationalist opposition and suppression, followed by a return to moderate tactics. The cycle was broken in 1920 by Mahatma Gandhi. Nationalist campaigns henceforward were to be disciplined and non-violent.

COW PROTECTION

A few years after the first meeting of the 'moderate' founders of the Congress in Bombay in 1885, serious riots erupted between Hindus and Muslims around Patna in Bihar, in eastern India. These 1893 disorders, which led to Muslim deaths, ostensibly grew out of the Hindu passion for rescuing cows from Muslim slaughterhouses. 'Cow protection' had become a stirring issue in the Ganges region and a frequent cause of civil disorders. The 1893 rioting occurred in one of the most densely populated districts in India, and less than a decade after the propagandists of the Hindu-nationalist Arya Samaj began their activities there. Thus both peaceful *and* violent methods as well as secular *and* communal objectives occupied the same historical moment, and both nationalisms henceforward represented alternative political trajectories for different Indian groups or for the same groups at different times.

From the late nineteenth century, communalists were concerned with the internal make-up of the Indian people: they were concerned over the question of which groups were properly 'Indian'. It was left to others – political pluralists and secularists – to determine how the different peoples of the subcontinent were to fit into some as yet undefined socio-political whole, an *Indian* nation.

Divisions were undeniable by the early twentieth century, which witnessed the crystallization of two conflicting conceptions about appropriate political activity. For western-educated professionals the idea was to achieve the type of nation state that was enjoyed by men of their class in western Europe and North America. This conception identified India's nationalist elite, including

Motilal Nehru, a successful lawyer of Allahabad and father of Jawaharlal Nehru. He sought to bring all of India's religions and traditions into a single secular political movement aimed at increasing self-government in the pattern of the 'White Dominions' of the British Empire. Against this goal, there was another which motivated popular organizations that identified with Hindu revival. One such was the Prayag Hindu Samaj; 'Prayag' was the ancient name of the place that the Muslims and the British after them called Allahabad, Motilal Nehru's city. This Samaj, or society, was established in 1880, five years before the National Congress, but then met concurrently with the Congress at its annual meetings until both organizations agreed that their projects and agendas had become too divergent. By the early 1890s the Prayag Hindu Samaj along with other organizations in northern India had adopted programmes that included cow protection and script reform: replacing the Arabic script for writing the Hindi language with Devanagari, which was the script used for Sanskrit. Thus both religious and linguistic concerns separated them.

EARLY CONGRESS AND ITS ADVERSARIES

The first generation of Congressmen took pride in the moderation of their programmes and the elite character of their leadership; they had no desire to make the reform of British rule a popular cause, even when a younger set of westernized political leaders began to voice their dismay. One young critic was Aurobindo Ghosh, who had been educated in England. After his application for the Indian Civil Service (ICS) failed because of a deficiency of horsemanship, he began teaching in Baroda (in western India) and publishing criticisms of Congress leaders which won him a following among other younger western-educated men. Two of these – Lala Lajpat Rai in the Punjab and Tilak in the Bombay Presidency – joined Ghosh in advocating the formation of secret societies to oppose the partition of Bengal, which was then being proposed.

By 1902, Ghosh was teaching in his native Bengal and had become active in promoting a boycott of British imports. For this, Ghosh, along with Lajpat Rai and Tilak, received the extremist label; all contributed to the first moment of mass politics in modern India – the anti-partition agitation that lasted from 1905 to 1908. The young reformers would probably not have shifted the direction and style of politics simply by condemning what they called 'Congress mendicancy'. Their demands for tactical change succeeded because dissension already existed among Congressmen during the 1890s. In Bengal, the Punjab and Madras, the Congress was riven by factions which frequently turned on personalities, as usual in politics, but also on differences of emphasis and interest.

Madras presents an interesting and complex example. There, western-educated Tamil brahmans, a tiny proportion of the total population, dominated public life: the law, the press and the highest ranks of official employment opened to Indians. One group of this Madras elite was identified by the part of the city called Mylapore, where they and many other brahmans lived. Opposing them was a faction consisting mostly of other Tamil brahmans with alliances extending to subordinate political centres, some in the northern, Telugu-speaking part of the Madras Presidency and others in the far south. The tiny Mylapore clique dominated the Congress organization until 1905, when their equally few opponents seized the opportunity to replace them by adopting the radical colours of men like Ghosh and Tilak and moving the Madras Congress into alliance with the Bengal Congress during the 1905 agitations.

THE BENGAL PARTITION

By then there was a change in both the style and the substance of the Raj, just as there was in Congress. At the turn of the twentieth century, the imperial government of India looked as indomitable as it believed itself to be. In 1899, Lord Curzon of Kedleston had assumed the viceregal office as if it were a throne, full of confidence about British power in Asia and not a little impatient with the cautious way of senior members of the ICS who constituted his council. George Nathaniel Curzon was well prepared for his powerful office and vigorous role in defining policies by virtue of his travels in many parts of Asia and by the backing he enjoyed from other leaders of the Conservative Party at home. To these advantages he added great energy and the determination to give India a prominence in British policy formation. Paradoxically, the policies of financial and administrative autonomy in India received a powerful advocate in him.

Curzon's self-confidence was not greatly different from that of most of the ICS, the elite administrative corps. By the late years of the nineteenth century, the tentativeness of even the most enthusiastic of utilitarian-minded officials had changed into an authoritarianism brooking neither advice from that small British public concerned about India nor dissent from Indians. Nevertheless, in addition to the complaints about the neglect of the problem of poverty voiced by a few respected civil servants such as Sir W. W. Hunter, there were Indian critics as well: Dadabhai Naoroji, the British-based Parsi businessman and MP, and the retired government officer, R. C. Dutt, who achieved one of the highest positions open to Indians in the ICS. To meet these sundry criticisms, books were commissioned from the provincial governments to refute their accusations. Neither famine nor poverty was going to be permitted to blight the deep contentment of the Raj with its superb management of the great gem in Victoria's crown.

Nevertheless, the new viceroy showed dangerous hubris in rejecting the opposition of his council (consisting of experienced civil servants) to the way he planned to partition Bengal in order to improve the management of that very large and populous province. For this and other measures, Curzon was soon being compared unfavourably with Lord Ripon by Indian public opinion. Whereas Ripon was seen to be sincerely committed to a gradual extension of their participation at all levels of government, Curzon was not; his dismissal of warnings from senior British advisers contributed to the radicalization of the Indian National Congress.

There was a strong case for dividing the province of Bengal. It was the

শ্রীচণ্ডমণ্ডা - *Terribly Sympathetic*

Plate 25 'Terribly Sympathetic'. Lithograph after a water-colour by Gagenendranath Tagore, modern Bengal school, *c.*1917 (IS77 – 1979, Courtesy of the Victoria and Albert Museum).

largest in British India, with 78.5 million people, of whom nearly a third were Muslims. Of the two provinces into which it was divided, 'East Bengal and Assam' was predominantly Muslim, with a population of 38 million made up by adding the mostly non-Muslim Assamese from the hill country that had been won from Burma in three wars between 1826 and 1886. The other part was the western province called 'Bengal', now reduced to about 55 million, of whom 16 per cent were Muslims. Bengali-speakers became a minority as a result of adding to the truncated western portion of what was formerly Bengal the old provinces of Bihar, with its Hindi-speakers, and Orissa, where Oriya was spoken.

However insistent Curzon and his advisers were about the purely administrative reasons for partition, other motives soon transpired. A leading Curzon adviser noted that opposition to British rule would certainly increase within a united Bengal. On the other hand, in 1904 Curzon promised the Muslims of Dacca, in the proposed eastern Bengal, that partition in the following year would create a Muslim unity unknown since Mughal times. With government encouragement, Muslim landlords in Bengal formed the Muslim League in 1906 with support from Muslim businessmen involved in the sale of British imports and opposed to the boycott that was organized in protest against partition.

In the half-year before partition was to take effect, Congress organized numerous large meetings in Calcutta at which petitions against partition were gathered and presented to indifferent officials. The ineffectuality of petitions was admitted by the old Congress leader Surendranath Banerji, and, as the day of partition approached, he acknowledged that sterner measures, such as the refusal to buy British goods, were justified. He and others preferred to call this by the term *swadeshi* ('own country') rather than boycott, but agreed that the ban should go beyond British goods to include other targets. Government schools began to be shunned and shops and schools were picketed on Partition Day, 16 October 1905.

Police and army units were sent to clear the pickets, and violent encounters ensued. As these increased so did the trepidations of older Congress leaders, who persuaded their militant younger colleagues to lift the school boycott. Banerji and others, including G. K. Gokhale, then president of the Congress, withdrew their support for the boycott on learning of the appointment of John Morley, a Gladstonian in a newly elected Liberal government, as Secretary of State for India. They placed their trust in him, thinking he would be sympathetic to the Indian middle class, and hoped the partition would be rescinded through his intervention.

RESISTANCE AND REFORM

Over the following three years, as the tempo of political resistance increased, those expecting changes from London were bitterly disappointed and humiliated. When Curzon's partition went ahead, neither Gokhale's now-tattered reputation nor that of the elder statesman Dadabhai Naoroji could still the demand for more strenuous opposition to the British, even though Morley made it clear that he would tolerate neither boycott nor terrorism. Privately, however, he began to frame an Indian constitutional reform package to woo the Congress away from its increasingly radical leaders.

Calcutta was not only the seat of British authority for Bengal and India, it was also the economic, social and cultural centre of 'respectable' Bengalis, the *bhadralok* ('higher people'). With its colleges and its government offices and courts, it was a place known personally and affectionately to generations of professional men throughout eastern India. Political radicalism, so-called extremism, was more than simply a political alternative to the constitutional politics favoured by men like Gokhale. The radicalism of some high-caste Bengalis and Maharashtrians at the turn of the twentieth century manifested the anxiety of declining elite groups in both provinces. Brahmans and other Bengalis of high caste, the first Indians to be westernized, despaired to see their positions challenged by members of merchant and scribal castes in Calcutta and by new spokesmen for the Muslim tenantry of eastern Bengal.

Like the Bengal bhadralok, Maratha brahmans of Bombay province found their elite standing contested by lower-caste businessmen who were preparing Bombay to replace Calcutta as the commercial centre of India. Class standing and changing political conditions interacted to reduce the status of some as others' fortunes rose and to encourage the adoption by losers of new strategies in the more competitive practice of Indian nationalist politics.

Many mercantile groups were delighted by the success of the boycott. From 1906 to 1908, as militancy passed from Calcutta to smaller towns throughout Bengal, committees directed the boycott in imitation of Calcutta, with the same impressive results. By 1906 imported cotton thread and fabric had fallen by 25 and 40 per cent respectively, producing complaints from British manufacturers. As the Indians' share of the market in textiles increased proportionally, so did their profits, partly because they raised prices despite protests from swadeshi leaders in Bengal. Sales of handloom products also increased, possibly as a reaction to the greed of Bombay textile manufacturers. But another reason was the encouragement from swadeshi committees who were aware of the political advantages of assisting family-based artisanal production and thus anticipated Gandhi's later campaign for the use of *khadi* (handspun and handloom cloth) as a political tactic.

The agitation against the Bengal partition from 1905 to 1907 marked a strengthening of radical and at times violent propensities among those committed to the Indian national cause. Tilak's work in Pune during the 1890s had anticipated this, but now new methods appeared, and violence spread. Bombs were occasionally deployed by the revolutionary groups that began to be formed under leaders such as Aurobindo Ghosh. Attempts were made to assassinate high British officials, and armed robberies were committed to finance terrorist activities and publications. Street violence also mounted in connection with strikes organized among office workers in European firms, among tram drivers, in railway shops and in jute factories, where workers' demands were mixed with swadeshi propaganda.

Not all of India was caught up in this agitation. In the United Provinces, which extended over much of the Gangetic valley, moderate leaders of the Congress movement stifled radicalism and continued to cooperate with British officials. There and elsewhere in northern India the 'Bengal cause' was rejected because Bengalis were resented for their predominance in white-collar employment and commercial services, as well as in the professions. In some of those places popular movements were more likely to be mounted for Hindi to be granted equal status with English as an official language, so as to offset the advantage which Bengalis enjoyed by their facility in English. Another reason for the diminished radicalism of the Gangetic region was that Muslims became suspicious of the nationalist cause when it took on a Hindu religious fervour.

DISCONTENT IN THE PUNJAB

Nevertheless, in many parts of the Punjab, Madras and Bombay, the tempo of resistance to British policies quickened under stimulation from the Bengal swadeshi movement. In the Punjab, for example, there was a form of swadeshi based on the activities of business groups who had begun to establish banks, insurance companies and schools during the late years of the nineteenth century. The school projects in particular reflected the strong desire of merchant and scribal groups to educate their sons in order to improve their employment prospects.

Another reason for the growth of swadeshi sentiment among Punjabis was the increasing tension between Muslims (who were half the population in that province) and both Hindus and Sikhs. And unique to the Punjab and nearby tracts were other determinants of heightened political consciousness, such as the Arya Samaj, which promised to create colleges like that of Aligarh for Muslims, free of Christian missionary influence.

The tension between Muslims and non-Muslims in the Punjab predated the Bengal partition agitation, as did the anger at the British in the canal-irrigated colonies they constructed on the Punjabi rivers. The degree of regimentation thought necessary to repay the investments in riverine works and make these schemes profitable for the Raj was a particular cause of resentment. Higher water rates and arbitrary controls added other grievances, as did an outbreak of plague and increased prices for the food on which farm workers depended. For all these reasons, the Punjab was the scene of political mobilization equal to that of Bengal, and subjected to even firmer repression out of fear that anti-British sentiments could infect the army, in which Punjabis were still heavily represented.

The boiling discontent among Punjabis provided radicals, among them Lala Lajpat Rai, with a popular following and a rare opportunity to discomfit both Punjabi political opponents and the British by demonstrations in 1907. For these activities Lajpat Rai was exiled from the province and all political meetings and strikes were banned; at the same time, however, the regimentation in canal colonies was eased and water rates were reduced.

Agitation in Madras

The heightened political atmosphere of the Punjab around 1907 was affected by factional struggles of the sort that afflicted the Madras scene and contributed to the weakening of moderate politics there as well. While Madras city remained in the hands of the Mylapore oligarchy, other Congressmen in the city and elsewhere in the Presidency were agitating for stronger measures to be taken in support of the Bengal movement. To embarrass the Mylapore leadership, politicians in the Telugu-speaking districts of northern Madras Presidency (destined to be called Andhra) introduced the singing of the banned Bengali song, *Bande Mataram* ('Hail the Mother [India]') by the writer Bankim Chandra Chatterjee. This anthem was widely sung by schoolchildren in defiance of the police ban. Soon afterwards, around 1910, the Andhra Mahasahbha was formed to campaign for a province in India for Telugu-speaking people, a goal that required nearly fifty years to be realized. Others in Madras took more direct steps by founding the Swadeshi Steam Navigation Company, which was intended to compete with a British firm plying the route from south India to Colombo in Ceylon (as it was then known).

Some activists in Madras moved quickly from boycott to terrorist activities, including the murder of a British magistrate. And there also, in 1905, activists celebrated the revolution in Russia as a blow against autocracy and European imperialism. The same sentiment was repeated later by the Tamil poet Subrahmanya Bharati when he celebrated the Russian revolution of 1917.

A somewhat different type of utopianism inspired Aurobindo Ghosh, who in 1909 retired from terrorism and politics to settle in the southern town of Pondicherry (then under French control). There, safe from British threats and surveillance, he founded the now world famous ashram of Auroville, a sort of idealistic cooperative that still produces the best French bread in India.

Swadeshi in Bombay

The influence of the swadeshi movement led to the launching of India's first steel works by the Tata family in Bombay. The Tatas were among the loyalist Parsi business elite of Bombay, whose new steel enterprise was looked upon sympathetically by officialdom because it did not injure British commercial interests, but instead affected Indian imports of Belgian steel products.

On the other hand, attempts by swadeshi leaders to organize textile factory workers into unions were opposed by Indian no less vigorously than by European factory managers. They too attempted to lengthen the working day so as to take advantage of the opportunities for exploitation inherent in the introduction of electric lighting, which caused Bombay textile workers to launch a strike in 1905. The textile manufacturers were pleased with the profits that had come their way as a result of the swadeshi movement, but refused to lower their prices on the most humble bits of cloth consumed by the very poor, since, they said, such a move would constitute an unwarranted interference with the free market; they saw no irony or contradiction in their stance.

Outside of commercialized Bombay, Tilak remained a beacon for radical tactics in western India from 1905, as he had for over a decade. Pune, the intellectual centre of Maharashtra and Tilak's base, saw the revival of some of his earlier religio-patriotic events centred on Shivaji and the elephant god Ganapati. To these street events was added a campaign of mass picketing of liquor shops, another element that was to become a part of Gandhi's movement. The divide between city and countryside was narrowed when Bombay workmen laid down their tools and took to the streets protesting against the Tilak's trial for his articles on Bengal terrorism in his newspaper, *Kesari*. When he was sentenced to six years' imprisonment in 1908, a general strike was called in which sixteen people were killed by the police and army.

When moderates had been challenged during the 1906 annual Congress at Calcutta by the threatened election of the radical leaders Tilak or Lajpat Rai, they called upon the revered Dadabhai Naoroji to calm and counsel greater caution. Even then, the radical programme carried the session, with resolutions in favour of boycott, swadeshi, *swaraj* (self-rule) and a nationalist reform of education. Naoroji himself spoke of swaraj as the goal of the Congress. The stage was therefore set for another, more decisive encounter between the older leadership and their challengers at the 1907 annual meeting in Surat, on the western coast. As was customary, the local organizing committee selected the president for the proceedings, choosing a well known Bengali moderate. Rumours circulated that the resolutions of the year before would be repudiated. Clashes among delegates, some violent, broke out and led to a walkout by the moderates; subsequent efforts by Tilak and the Bengal radicals to repair the breach failed, but by 1908 the concessions promised by the Morley–Minto reforms were known, and the pro-British tendency of the Congress was successful. Or so it seemed.

REPRESSION AND COMPROMISE: DIVIDED ELECTORATES

The repression of swadeshi leaders after 1905 was a new tactic for the British, one that they entered upon reluctantly, for now the targets of police violence and judicial harassment were those western-educated middle-class men hitherto thought the bulwark of British rule. Civil rights were abrogated in order to suppress the political activities of students from middle-class families; many were arrested simply for singing the swadeshi anthem *Bande Mataram*, and their parents were prevented from assembling in meetings considered by police (but not courts) to be seditious. Ultimately swadeshi committees were outlawed, a cause for despair among some of the British, including the Secretary of State, John Morley, since this was a troubling sign of a loss of the moral superiority upon which he and others depended to legitimate their rule.

Resistance to the partition of Bengal was countered by violence. In the end, the radical leadership in Bengal and Maharashtra was broken by imprisonment, and meetings and picketing were subjected to police attacks. But following violent repression came concessions. Constitutionalists of the Congress were given a boost by the grant of modest political reforms in a parliamentary enactment in 1909. Known as Morley–Minto Reform Act (after

Morley and the viceroy, the Earl of Minto), this act slightly increased the number of Indians who could be elected to legislative bodies according to the 1861 Indian Councils Act, and also permitted them to discuss budgets and to move resolutions for the first time. It was therefore an indirect consequence of the decision to partition Bengal. There had been intimations of the Morley–Minto reforms as early as the middle of 1906, yet it took another three years before these emerged as the Indian Councils Act of 1909. Announcing the enactment in Calcutta was supposed to strengthen the viceregal hand by giving the impression that the reforms actually originated in India.

The events of the years 1907–9 tended to recur in the evolving politics of the freedom struggle. Concessions from the regime were brandished before moderates to split them from radical Congressmen, upon whom repression was visited. The Bengal partition produced a new set of radical nationalist activists in this process; it also sparked the organization of a Muslim political orientation that sometimes merged with the Indian National Congress but for the most part remained separate and eventually achieved the separate nation of Pakistan for its efforts. By promulgating the 1909 reform acts, the government intended to win over the more moderate elements within the nationalist movement of the country. Each play of the reform card in subsequent years meant the extension of more rights and roused more expectations of additional rights. This tactic carried considerable hazards for continued British dominion, but that was for the future.

Indian members of councils at all levels were allowed to question budgets and other matters, but they were hobbled by the way the elective seats were apportioned. The number and allocation of elected seats below the imperial council were left to each province to work out, and administrative adjustments could prevent damaging combinations against British power. Yet more of an obstacle was the principle of separate electorates, which meant that coalitions among different groups of electors were difficult to form in lower councils and impossible in the imperial and provincial legislative councils, where the number of elected members was a minority. Voters were supposed to select council members according to which of several diverse electorates they belonged to: professionals, landholders, Muslims, European or Indian businessmen. Even government officials constituted a separate electorate for local councils! In addition, income requirements restricted the eligibility of the voters, assuring that the most disadvantaged were denied the political means of ameliorating their positions, though this condition was selectively applied. Muslims of a certain income, for example, were entitled to vote, while Hindus with the same income were deemed too poor to qualify.

Arguably the most important political consequence of the Bengal partition was the founding of the Muslim League late in 1906. This was the triumph of a political elite based in Aligarh, where they enjoyed considerable and open support from British officials. The successors of Sayyid Ahmed Khan's educational movement at Aligarh would occasionally lobby the government, claiming to be the authoritative voice of India's Muslims. Other educated Muslims disagreed. A resolution passed by Aligarh students in 1906, for example, advocated Hindu–Muslim political cooperation in the swadeshi cause and condemned the slavish loyalty of their leaders to a regime that offered nothing to Muslims. The resolution embarrassed the Muslim leadership and alerted their British supporters, including the then principal of the Anglo-Muhammadan College in Aligarh, to the need to deflect the youthful Muslim radicals. Before the year ended the League was formed; it was intended as an alternative to the radical swadeshi leaders and also a lobby for the greater participation of Muslims in the public life of British India.

British official support was obvious: a meeting between the Aligarh Muslim leaders and the viceroy, Lord Minto, was arranged late in 1906 to make the case for a separate Muslim electorate. Though Minto admitted privately to Morley in London that the large share of seats finally allocated to Muslims under the 1909 scheme could scarcely be justified, the convenience to the government of the continued goodwill of Muslims outweighed scruples of this sort.

The fickleness of the British position on India's Muslims was revealed only later, when the province of East Bengal and Assam, created in 1905, was peremptorily dissolved and Bengal was reunited in 1911. The relocation of the capital of British India to New Delhi in 1912 was accompanied by the suggestion that the move recalled the great Mughal past, a suggestion that failed to consider that what Muslims remembered more recently about Delhi was the humiliation of the dismissal of the last Mughal, old and blind, after the Mutiny.

The removal of the capital from Bengal and its rambunctious educated Calcutta citizenry was another consequence of the Bengal partition agitation. Calcutta remained the provincial capital of a reunited Bengal, but a new capital deemed worthy of the majesty of the imperial Raj was constructed and called New Delhi. That, together with the onset of the World War of 1914, heralded a new though disquieting political and social age for India on top of the residues of the previous decade of turmoil. Terrorism persisted in Bengal, where there were swadeshi-inspired armed robberies, while in the Punjab assassinations were still attempted, most spectacularly a bomb attack in which the viceroy, Lord Harding, was wounded on his official entry into the new capital in December 1912.

Meanwhile, young revolutionaries began a diaspora to London, the European continent and North America. When an India Office official was murdered in London in 1909, that city was made a hazardous place for Indian nationalists, while France and increasingly Germany seemed to offer asylum as European diplomatic tensions mounted before 1914. Farther afield, in British Columbia and in several of the western states of the USA, Sikh immigrants became businessmen and skilled workers and found new homes in the face of considerable racism. From among these 15,000 or so migrants to North America a movement calling itself *Ghadr* ('revolution') was formed in 1913, and published a newspaper by that name in several Indian languages. Inevitably, alliances among these migrant Indian communities of political refugees and various left political movements were formed. Har Dayal, a founder of the Ghadr movement, was a paid agent of the anarcho-syndicalist International Workers of the World, which was headquartered in San

Francisco, and some expatriate Indians became Communists following the 1917 October Revolution.

WAR, SACRIFICE AND MASS POLITICAL MOBILIZATION

India was declared to be in a state of war with Germany and its allies in 1914 without any sounding of Indian opinion. In fact, the expectation by imperial officials of Indian approval and participation, however grudging, proved correct; British soldiers and many Indian regiments were confidently transferred from India to various theatres of war. At one point a mere 15,000 British soldiers remained in India, even though the war was waged against the Ottoman regime of Turkey, whose ruler was regarded by India's Sunni Muslims as the successor (*khalifa*, Caliph) of the prophet Muhammad.

The stripping of troops from India did not go altogether unexploited. Bengal's revolutionaries intensified their armed robberies ('dacoity'), and conspired with German agents to obtain arms and explosives in order to disrupt rail communications. These adventures were thwarted by police infiltration, and ordinary Indians cared little about these schemes or others planned by Punjabi revolutionaries. Minor disaffections were fomented among Punjabi troops in Indian garrisons, but these were also uncovered and quashed.

More spectacular were the efforts of the Ghadrs of North America to organize a return to India and to support revolutionary activities against British rule. Their ship reached Calcutta, where they were met by armed police. Twenty-two Ghadrs were killed and another 8000 were subsequently jailed. Berlin too was a centre for the planning and funding of many of these activities, which gave the British authorities an excuse – if that were needed – to take heavy repressive measures against Indian terrorists.

The sacrifices of these young revolutionaries, who were engaged, as they saw it, in the liberation of their country, were numerically dwarfed by the deaths of Indians serving the Crown on battlefields in Europe and the Near East. To support an Indian Army, now expanded to over two million men, and their campaigns in Europe and Mesopotamia, the drain of resources from India was intensified. For Indians this truly was a 'world' war to which, in addition to men and *matériel*, the poor of India, without their assent, contributed to a £100 million gift to the British government. War taxes and loans stripped the accumulated assets of the country and necessitated additional taxes to meet burgeoning expenditures. Price levels rose as imported goods were shunted to military needs, and the provision of fodder crops for military animals led to a sharp rise in animal feeds when these could be obtained at all. War 'loans' were often confiscatory, income taxes quintupled and customs duties collected nearly doubled pre-war collections, adding to the price inflation. All of this directly affected farmers as well as business groups.

Somewhat surprisingly, B. G. Tilak and others raised money and recruited soldiers for the British cause. This was done in the expectation that support for

Britain in that time of travail would be rewarded after the war ended. Radicals like Tilak were at this point also attempting to repair the division that had opened between them and the moderate leaders in 1907. In fact, politicians of all persuasions sought a renewed unity during the war; Tilak and his followers, who had been driven from the Congress after the chaos of the Surat session in 1907, were invited to rejoin and help to devise new political approaches to the British when the war ended. To Mahatma Gandhi too, the war offered a prospect of a unified movement for freedom, but one which continued and carried all ethnic divisions before it. Encouraged, he supported the war aims of the allies.

Tilak had become the most respected elder statesmen of the nationalist cause. Former adversaries, like Gokhale, were dead, and the old radical leader was cautiously welcomed back and accorded new prestige when his imprisonment ended in 1914. Soon he was joined by new political figures destined to play large roles in the coming years. Among these was Mrs Annie Besant. She had drifted through a career of political dissent in Britain (where she gained notoriety as an advocate of birth control) before becoming associated with, and then in 1907 presiding over, the Theosophical Society at its world headquarters in Madras. Her Irish and socialist hostility to British rule led to contact with the more radical elements of the Congress, and with them she founded the Indian Home Rule League, the first of her many contributions to India's nationalist struggles. Tilak followed her example by establishing a Home Rule branch in Maharashtra, and from these two bodies there issued forth a stream of pamphlets in English and other languages through a network of hundreds of Home Rule League branches with over 30,000 members.

THE RISE OF MUSLIM NATIONALISM

Adherents were won in the highest echelons of Indian professions, including the prominent Bombay lawyer Mohammed Ali Jinnah, destined to become founder of Pakistan. He had been born in Karachi and had built a highly successful practice as a barrister in Bombay. He originally entered politics in alignment with moderate Congress leaders, such as Naoroji and Gokhale, but in 1913 joined the Muslim League and soon became its president. Jinnah and other Muslim professionals were determined to change the Muslim League to meet the need for new and modern leadership for India's Muslims.

The issue of moment for Muslims was the British action against the Ottoman regime of Turkey. As German allies, the Ottomans were driven by the British from Arab territories that had long been part of their empire. Now the last shred of Ottoman prestige, the Caliphate (*khilafat*), the successorship to the authority of the prophet Muhammad, was threatened. World Islamic interests served to bring Jinnah and the Muslim League together with Tilak and the Congress in 1916, and their joint meetings charted actions against the British.

This unity came at a crucial time when the two great centres of agitation, Bengal and the Punjab, had been reduced to sullen inactivity through police repression. Home rule appealed to middle-class men and awakened their participation, first in Madras and Maharashtra and then in the United Provinces and Gujarat. With the approaching end of the war, Home Rule invigorated the Congress session of 1917, which met under the presidency of Annie Besant. The British had briefly and imprudently imprisoned her, thereby assuring that her cause would hold centre stage.

Almost immediately nationalist unity was shattered thanks to the promulgation of constitutional reform, which was to be popularly named after the Secretary of State for India, Edwin Montagu, and the viceroy, Lord Chelmsford. The reform was announced to a startled House of Commons on 20 August 1917 by Montagu, who declared that 'responsible government' or a form of limited representative democracy was the aim of British policy for India, and promised substantial further steps towards that end, including a new India Act in 1919.

The effect of this announcement was instant and predictable. Suddenly moderate politicians had second thoughts about embracing a possibly reformed Tilak and were shaken by Montagu's threats to repress antigovernment activities vigorously. Even Mrs Besant and some of her European and Indian Theosophist colleagues deserted radical causes as a result of Montagu's reform announcement. Soon afterwards, Tilak departed the Indian political battlefield to prosecute a libel case in England. Then a government announcement that new police were being introduced to curb imagined seditious schemes restored the divided Congress to its previous unity. And finally, a new sort of leader emerged in Mohandas Karamchand Gandhi.

IMPERIALISM'S PARADOXICAL ENEMY

Gandhi was the leading genius of the later, and ultimately successful, campaign for India's independence. His innovative techniques created an aura of almost mystical reverence not only for his followers but for the global audience he acquired thanks in large part to fortuitous and new developments in communications, most notably the cinema newsreel. His martyr's death completed the conditions for his canonization. As a result, two aspects of his role have tended to be masked or discounted. The first was the idiosyncratic authoritarianism of his style of leadership, which often disconcerted his most loyal followers and admirers. The second, paradoxically, was his comforting (to adversaries and beneficiaries) refusal to disturb the status quo of the Indian social and economic hierarchy, which was screened by his patronizing concern for the victims of the curse of untouchability and his insistence on unity across class and caste. While his ideal of a nation consisting of autonomous villages whose inhabitants lived in Spartan simplicity was consigned to the realm of utopian fantasy, he successfully prevented other, more radical forms of social and economic idealism from being realized. He bitterly disappointed the leader of the untouchables, Dr Bhimrao Ramji Ambedkar, and his implacable opposition to contraception may in the end have amplified the misery of those for whom he professed concern, women and the poor, as well as the severe problems of sustainability that India faces even now.

The son of a minister of one of the smallest of India's numerous princely states, Gandhi completed his education by obtaining a law degree in London. His career as a lawyer in Bombay failed to prosper, so he undertook a commission to do some legal work for Indian merchants in South Africa. There, after having experienced humiliating discrimination himself, he became involved in a civil rights struggle against racial laws and practices. It was in the course of his South African involvement that he devised a method of non-violent resistance, which he called *satyagraha* (truth force), that won concessions for Indians there, the admiration of Gandhi's enemies and the applause of many in India when he returned there in 1915.

During the next several years he became involved in a variety of rural movements among farmers and also in an agitation on behalf of textile workers in Ahmedabad. These activities brought him followers among the more active and radical of Congress leaders in western as well as eastern India, and also provided him with a sense of the way India was changing under the conditions of the war in Europe. At work in India then were processes that would become the foundations for Gandhi's later campaigns. Among the most important of these were industrial and demographic changes and an intensified form of ethnicized politics. Ironically, they were inimical to the sort of India that Gandhi wanted to see and strove to produce.

Although he held no office, he was able not only to mesmerize India's vast urban and rural millions, but to take absolute control of Congress, with its educated, sophisticated and often cynical membership. He did this by careful and almost obsessive attention to the symbols – sometimes of his own creation – which he imputed to 'the nation', such as the flag and the Gandhian cap, which he designed with care for all its aspects of production and ease of maintenance. Foremost and most visible among the symbols he adopted was his own dress – the loincloth and shawl – which he deliberately chose, after much reflection, as a protest against India's grinding poverty, and which eventually became seen all over the world as a rebuke to the pretensions of the imperialists.

Because Gandhi's character and personality were so influential in determining the crucial phases of the birth of the Indian nation, and because, more than any other politician, he insisted on making his own life and preoccupations into political instruments, it is important to discuss them here at least briefly. Indefatigable, unwavering in his views and personally courageous in effecting them, he was, paradoxically, so quixotic and unpredictable at times that his closest associates often despaired, then and later, of understanding his behaviour. Yet his overlapping obsessions with 'purity' and sex, which have subsequently made him such a treat for psychoanalytically inclined writers, were not only defined by Hindu tradition (as set forth, for example, in the code of Manu), but perfectly in accord with pervasive nineteenth-century preoccupations. It was in his selective use and insouciant violation of traditional practices that his originality lay. The result was that his campaigns on behalf of untouchables, which have attained mythic status, were couched in ways that were insensitive and demeaning even as he claimed to uplift, while, despite his large female following and many female associates, his influence on women, both personally and politically, was largely malign.

His stress on *ahimsa* (non-violence) was marred by his yet greater emphasis on suffering and endurance, which, since he exemplified it in his own 'fasts unto death', points to a strong sado-masochistic streak in his character. In manifesting his attitudes to both untouchables and women he was completely unembarrassable; he perfected the technique of protesting the innocence, and even nobility, of his pronouncements and actions so confidently as to imply that any impurity of thought lay in the mind of his challenger. A number of instances of this appear in his newsletter, which he ostentatiously named *Harijan* (children of God, his own ambiguous term for untouchables). For example, there was an exchange between him and a visiting Christian evange-list, in which he welcomed Christian prayer but not proselytising:

> *Gandhiji:* If Christians want to associate themselves with the reform movement they should do so without any idea of conversion.
> *Dr Mott:* . . . should they not preach the Gospel with reference to its acceptance?
> *Gandhiji:* Would you, Dr Mott, preach the Gospel to a cow? Well, some of the untouchables are worse than cows in understanding.[1]

When Jagjivan Ram, an untouchable politician in the Congress, objected to this slur against his caste's intelligence, Gandhi neatly skirted the point by claiming that no offence was intended: the cow was the exemplar of gentleness and patient suffering.[2]

Unlike untouchables, women in early twentieth-century India were still unable to debate collectively and protest against the assumptions and condi-tions under which they lived. Moreover, an analysis of social and political satirical cartoons of the period in Bengal revealed the obsessional fears even educated men felt that, once emancipated, women would neglect both hus-band and housework.[3] Nevertheless, Gandhi's treatment of his own wife is notorious, even in the circumstances in which it occurred, largely because he wrote about it in detail. He revealed that his attitude to sex, even within marriage, early became one of disgust at a shameful indulgence. He held the common nineteenth-century belief in a sort of 'spermatic economy', in which the expenditure of semen drained a man's energies and left him at least temporarily weakened. This conceit was no harmless foible, either in India or elsewhere. In Gandhi's case, he was able to make it an issue of public policy which wasted many valuable years in which India's burgeoning population could have been more effectively addressed. In answer to a query about a fledgling birth control movement in 1936, he responded: birth control is 'a movement which must result in the vitality of the whole race being drained'.[4] Instead, he endorsed 'self-control'. Until he himself attained 'self-control', he alone determined not only when sexual intercourse was to take place, regardless of any other consideration, but also when to trumpet his victory in achieving permanent celibacy. For any woman, in almost any society, but particularly in those more prudish times and in that extremely prudish culture, to be publicly discussed in any kind of sexual context was and is humiliating.

Gandhi humiliated both his wife and other women in many contexts. Much to her distress, he forced his high-caste wife to attend to the bedpans of guests who did not choose to look after their own. And, celibate or not, his thoughts and actions continued to be permeated by sex. In the ashram (a sort of commune) he founded in South Africa, he gathered a number of adolescents about him, whom he required to bathe naked together, an occasion he liked to witness, and to sleep close together. When, inevitably, one of the boys taunted a couple of girls, and the girls complained, he insisted on cutting off the girls' hair, which is the sign of the (sexually) sinful, penitent woman in India as elsewhere. The action was explained in typical Gandhian fashion as giving security to the girls and 'steriliz[ing] the sinner's eye'.[5]

Not infrequently, Gandhi managed to combine his preoccupations with sex and untouchability. In addition to urging the sort of change of heart that had been so unsuccessful in abolishing slavery in the west in the previous century, he espoused the copulative approach to the elimination of prejudice, at one point musing: 'If I had my way I would persuade all caste Hindu girls coming under my influence to select Harijan husbands.'[6] Of course, Hindu girls at that time and since, as he very well knew, were not free to select their husbands, with or without his influence.

ENTER THE MAHATMA

From the time of his return to India in 1915, there was public interest in speculating on the political role that Gandhi would assume. Would he join the moderate followers of Gokhale, whom he was known to respect, or the more radical Indian Congressmen? Gokhale had counselled Gandhi not to rush to a decision but to travel the country and see the conditions. This he did, discovering that he shared almost none of the constitutionalist views and political timidity of Gokhale's followers. Gandhi signalled his decision by launching himself into campaigns for social justice. Two of these were rural, one in Champaran, Bihar, among indigo producers, the other in Kheda, Gujarat, where small-holding farmers faced the loss of their lands for debt. He further became involved in the labour disputes of millhands in Ahmedabad, also in his native Gujarat.

The rural conflicts into which Gandhi was drawn began long before his return from South Africa. The resistance of peasants in Bihar to the exploitative measures taken by indigo planters, with official support, had led to violent confrontations before the war. Similar mobilizations had taken place among Gujarati farmers who had lost land to money-lenders as a result of foreclosures issued by courts and enforced by police. The end of the war revealed to Gandhi and to other observers a rising tide of conflict that jeopardized nationalist unity. Factory workers such as those in Allahabad, belatedly seeking to share some of the wartime profits of the textile manufacturers, went on strike, raising the prospect of widespread industrial confrontation.

At the same time, Gandhi was aware of the increased rioting between

Hindus and Muslims in cities from Calcutta to Allahabad, which threatened the new-found amity between the largely Hindu Congress and the Muslim League. In the Madras and Bombay Presidencies, another old division became sharper: the growing public conflict between brahmans and middle-caste non-brahmans over the domination of official and professional employment by brahmans. Elsewhere in British India and also in the larger, more advanced princely states such as Mysore, a similar brahman hold over official employment was the cause of rancour among educated non-brahmans.

Intensifying these various conflicts and posing additional potential threats to national aspirations were subnational demands for linguistic homelands. Telugu-speakers in the northern districts of the Madras Presidency began annual conferences (later called the Andhra Mahasabha) to focus their demands for more public jobs and the use of Telugu in schools where it was the mother-tongue. In 1918, the Madras provincial Congress allowed a separate Andhra caucus within the Congress. Only slightly behind the Telugus were Malayalam-speakers from the southwest coast in the princely state of Travancore and the Malabar district of Madras. In both of these agitations, the principal adversary was the Tamil-speaking brahman; thus caste and language combined to form new subnationalisms even as the Congress was moving towards another phase of mass activity as the war in Europe ended.

The reforms announced in 1917 were promulgated as the Government of India Act of 1919, which began the promised evolution towards self-government within the British Empire. According to its central constitutional principle, which was called 'dyarchy', some areas (education, health, agriculture) were made the responsibility of provincial legislatures under ministers elected by the separate electorates of the 1909 India Act, while more important matters (law and order and revenue) were reserved for a central authority, the Viceroy's Council of State and Imperial Legislature. Elected majorities could not override a viceregal veto on proposed legislation.

Behind the 1919 Act was the desire to achieve two imperial objectives. One was to continue to devolve financial responsibility upon Indian bodies, especially for funding health and education. This freed British authorities from the odium incurred by increasing taxes or curtailing services. Second, the Montagu–Chelmsford scheme was intended to broaden the strata of Indians willing to collaborate with imperial authority. And candidates were not wanting; many who had profited from the war wanted no change in their fortunate circumstances.

ECONOMIC OPPORTUNITIES, CIVIL UNREST

The war had produced opportunities for Indian capitalists and a growing alertness to their class interests, as Gandhi learned in his rediscovery of India. Windfall profits from military contracting were enjoyed by textile manufacturers supplying uniforms and engineering firms supplying machine-made goods for the final production of small arms and ammunition as well as field guns. The huge profits made by British owners of jute mills who supplied fabric for sandbags and tents attracted Indian capitalists, especially Marwari bankers from Rajasthan, to take up lucrative businesses in Calcutta. These money men had flourished under the wartime command economy and now possessed the capital for major investment in jute production, the first by Indians in that industry. Marwaris also joined older Parsi and Gujarati capitalists in the production of cotton textiles to replace British imports, which did not resume for some time after the war. Markets and profits gained by Indian manufacturers as a result of the wartime interruptions of imports were the foundation for other advances; the new industrialists began to look to the Congress to sustain their wartime advantages with appropriate measures, and they stood ready to support the Congress by their financial contributions for the purpose.

Indian industrialists also looked to the Congress to ease their troubles with their workers. Trade unionism was in its infancy and led by middle-class nationalists. Growing labour discontent was fuelled by rising prices and growing unemployment, especially in places like the Punjab where many soldiers recruited over the previous four years were suddenly demobilized. The militancy of urban workers resulted in more violence in 1918–19, in addition to food riots in Bombay, Madras and Bengal and numerous smaller towns, and violent disturbances aimed at Marwari money-lenders by Muslim debtors in Calcutta. The fear of influenza, which was then a worldwide epidemic, contributed an undercurrent of anxiety to the general unease springing from economic sources.

Hopes for an orderly and peaceful progress to a more representative system were dashed by the promulgation of judicial regulations intended to provide the government with additional powers against seditious behaviour, and these regulations, named after Justice Rowlatt, who headed the judicial committee that framed them, turned hope into suspicion of the government's post-war intentions. Suspicion became outrage after the war when a peaceful demonstration against the Rowlatt Acts and against deteriorating economic conditions in Amritsar in the Punjab resulted in the killing of 379 and wounding of 1200 unarmed demonstrators by an army unit under the commanded of General Dyer. When, shortly afterwards, General Dyer was officially commended, Gandhi still urged that only a determined non-violent campaign against the British regime could abort the gathering violence of protest against the Punjab massacre, the rage of Muslims over the violation of the Caliphal institution, a massive textile workers' strike in Bombay involving 125,000 and numerous smaller strikes elsewhere.

All these factors fed into civil strife originating from the political movements of the time, of which the most prominent were anti-Rowlatt demonstrations and a resurgence of revolutionary fervour not seen since the Bengal partition days. For many politicized intellectuals, their politics were borne on a tide of world changes signalled by the Bolshevik Revolution of 1917 and the welcome renunciation of Russia's Asian empire by Lenin and Trotsky, who vowed to struggle alongside the world's subject people against the tyranny of imperialism. It was into this ferment that Gandhi strode to seize the nationalist movement and to redirect its energies and purposes fundamentally.

THE FIRST CAMPAIGNS

At fifty, Gandhi was a seasoned politician with credentials for courage and imagination won against the racist Boers and British officials in South Africa. Nevertheless, he appeared an ill-fitting candidate for the leadership that was to become his, all his, within a few years of the end of the Great War. He had no formal standing within any Congress clique, and he presented a strange programme of non-violent opposition. His 'satyagraha' was a technique for confronting the state by challenging its moral authority and legality with peaceful demonstrations, occasional pickets and strikes (*hartals*, the closing of shops and businesses and the withdrawal of labour as political protests), and finally by courting arrest for the violation of specific unjust laws. Gandhi had devised his strategies of non-violence in South Africa, and described them in his book *Hind Swaraj* (*Indian Self-rule*) in 1909. In India he added other ideas that sometimes seemed quirky to many Indians, such as sexual self-restraint and a preference for simple rural styles of living and forms of production over industrial society. Yet he was an adaptive fighter, as he had proven by supporting the war through recruitment and other means.

The Amritsar massacre fixed national political attention upon a campaign in which Gandhi had already become involved; he had announced in February 1919 that the Rowlatt bills must be resisted and that he would deploy satyagraha for the first time in India. There were ordinances limiting the widespread, though peaceful, meetings against the Rowlatt police bills of 1919, which were used to justify the state violence. Gandhi's plan was for volunteers (*satyagrahins*) to court arrest by violating a law prohibiting the sale of literature that approved of hartals. A sign of the moderation of his approach is that, in fixing the date for national 'strike', Gandhi chose a Sunday, when few people were at work anyway, and even those who were were instructed not to participate without permission from their employers!

Gandhi believed his non-violent programme could not only avert violence but also promote an alliance for political action among many different groups, including Home Rule Leaguers and Muslims offended by the humiliating terms being forced upon the Turks by the victors in the Great War. Hartals were launched in the Punjab, the scene of the massacre, and also in Delhi, Bombay and Calcutta. But the deaths at Jullianwallabagh on 13 April led to more violent demonstrations and some sabotage of government buildings and telegraph lines. The police repressed these and charged perpetrators under the Rowlatt regulations, punishing many by flogging. Particularly vigorous demonstrations were staged on the streets of New Delhi, where strong amity and cooperation between Hindus and Muslims was evident. This demonstration of unity panicked the government into arresting Gandhi in an act that brought a fresh round of confrontations, in places that had previously been quiet and in others which had become quiet under police repression. For Gandhi the lesson of this event was that the control of violence in the face of police brutality required that participants be adequately prepared for the violence they would receive. Satyagrahins should be constituted of a smaller, more select and disciplined core.

Chastened by repression, the Congress met as usual at Christmas in 1919 in Amritsar to plan their next moves, this time presided by Motilal Nehru, an early member. At Amritsar, a moderate line was adopted. Gandhi and Jinnah joined in applauding the constitutional reforms that had been announced, and condemnation of the actions of Dyer's troops was withheld pending the outcome of an inquiry into the event. Such urgency as was evident at that session came from Muslims, led by Jinnah, for the protection of the Caliphate. They called for a Congress campaign aimed at retaining the Ottoman sultan as the protector of Muslim holy places and sought to press Britain into the restoration of Ottoman rule over Arab territories, a somewhat embarrassingly imperialist demand.

The Congress was divided over how to pursue these objectives. Among those closest to Gandhi were businessmen like those who had invited him to South Africa years before; many were involved in the sale of European textiles and were thus least receptive to the swadeshi message. Others who sought more vigorous forms of political activity included Muslim clerics and Muslim journalists; the first group had great influence over Muslims in small towns and villages, while the second were both urban and more disposed to strong steps, including resistance to Rowlatt.

Gandhi urged 'non-cooperation' to these differing groups. His proposal received general assent from a special meeting of the Congress convened in 1920 to consider the findings of the commission that had investigated the events in Amritsar the year before. The report was castigated as a whitewash by Gandhi, who announced steps to remedy the errors that had failed to anticipate violence in his earlier campaign, steps by which he recreated the Congress as a mass movement.

Gandhi's organizational reform of 1920 was the most significant event in the history of Congress since its founding in 1885. It was transformed into a disciplined, mass organization capable of executing his non-violent strategy. A decisive first step was taken at another special meeting in September 1920, where the boycott of schools, courts, councils and foreign goods was approved as an appropriate response to the exoneration and official approbation of General Dyer. Nationalist schools and arbitration bodies were to replace government schools and courts, while Indian-made – and in the case of textiles, preferably hand-made – goods were to be substituted for British imports. These broad objectives would be achieved by a wholly new organization of the Indian National Congress, approved at the December meeting at Nagpur later in 1920.

Two sweeping changes were at once announced. Gandhi declared the goal of attaining 'swaraj within one year' through non-violent means. What this swaraj meant precisely and what non-violent means were to be deployed were left unspecified, and left to Gandhi to decide. Second, Congress became a genuine mass political party, with dues-paying members and a hierarchy of committees reaching from the village level upwards through town, district and provincial committees, to all-India committees. Very significantly, the provincial (*pradesh*) divisions of the new Congress were not the existing British ones but a new set based on linguistic regions covering the entire subcontinent, including the princely domains. The operating logic was that mass political work should be conducted within meaningful cultural regions, not the arbitrary and (it was thought) deliberately divisive administrative areas created by the British. A crucial concession was added at Gandhi's insistence: a provincial committee for Telugu-speakers. At the apex of all of this was a small Congress Working Committee, the executive authority of the movement, which was prepared now, as never before, to channel the forces for change building within the country.

He and other leaders tested these changes by organizing successful demonstrations during the visit of the Prince of Wales to India in 1921, but less than a year later, he abruptly and unilaterally ended the campaign when violence erupted. While his action was a stunning demonstration of his singular personal control over the national campaign, in the view of many his authority seemed arbitrary and even whimsical. His Muslim and more radical followers were especially critical. A large number of them withdrew from the Congress campaign as a result of Gandhi's decision.

Despite any whimsy in implementation, the clarity of Gandhi's political vision and the skill with which he carried the reforms in 1920 provided the foundation for what was to follow: twenty-five years of stewardship over the freedom movement. He knew the hazards to be negotiated. The British must be brought to a point where they would abdicate their rule without terrible destruction, thus assuring that freedom was not an empty achievement. To accomplish this he had to devise means of a moral sort, able to inspire the disciplined participation of millions of Indians, and equal to compelling the British to grant freedom, if not willingly, at least with resignation.

Gandhi found his means in non-violent satyagraha. He insisted that it was not a cowardly form of resistance; rather, it required the most determined kind of courage. He depended on the personal bravery of his followers, not only to win the British over but, most importantly, to contain the violent elements within Indian society that were struggling to find expression in the difficult years following the war.

GANDHI AND ISLAM

Gandhi continued to work closely with Muslim leaders who were caught up in the khilafat movement, protesting the abolition of the Ottoman Caliphate. This he did partly for the principled reason that India's Muslims comprised a quarter of that larger body politic which must free itself from British domination, and therefore deserved the support of all Indians, but he also hoped to prevent their being used again as a prop for British power, as had happened during most of the nineteenth century. In 1920 the khilafat cause became transformed from the protection of a remote and archaic Turkish monarch into a mobilization against the more proximate and dangerous British enemy.

Apart from an aroused Muslim public, there was the post-war militancy of industrial workers to deal with. Strikes were launched in 1919 against Indian firms forced to retrench as wartime demand slackened in all Indian industrial centres, which had led to unemployment or reduced wages for hundreds of thousands of workers. By 1921, nearly seven million work days were lost through strikes, in most cases spontaneous stoppages, not the result of trade union decisions. Unions were few, but in this period of labour militancy their numbers increased. Usually these were led by middle-class men whose backgrounds and outlooks differed in no essential ways from the loyalist employers with whom they engaged in collective bargaining; but there were other, more radical trade unions in Bengal, Madras and Bombay that opposed the collaborationist philosophy of partnerships between employers and workers. These radical trade unionists refused to join Congress unionists and their All India Trades Union Congress, which affiliated with the Indian National Congress in 1920.

Pressures upon Gandhi and the Congress for more radical politics came from India's vast agrarian poor as well. This was signalled by the enthusiasm with which non-cooperation was taken up. Even in backward places like Bihar, the village court (*panchayat*) proved a popular substitute for government courts, and an anti-liquor campaign, meant partly to deprive the government of excise taxes and partly to discourage drunkenness among the poorest workers, was a success. Cooperation between Hindus and Muslims prevailed in the countryside for a considerable time. Perhaps most impressive of all was the prominence given to Gandhi's demand for the inclusion of untouchables in all local political programmes. Upper-caste Congressmen detested untouchable involvement, but such was their respect for Gandhi, they did not dare oppose him when he insisted on it.

In other ways, Gandhi's agrarian leadership was frequently challenged from below; for example, when he opposed the withholding of rent from oppressive landlords on the grounds that this would divide landlords from tenants and so weaken the struggle against British rule. He urged similar restraint upon labour leaders lest Indian capitalists be pushed into the arms of imperialists by workers' demands. As a result certain actions were vetoed; for instance, the idea of refusing to pay taxes was rejected because it could easily become a rent strike. In some areas Gandhi's leadership was questioned: Maharashtrian politicians who succeeded to leadership after the death of Tilak in 1920 expressed doubts that Gandhi's non-violence would restrain the radicalized industrial workers in Bombay.

NON-COOPERATION

Despite these limitations, non-cooperation was vigorously pursued in many parts of the country, most successfully where experienced nationalist leaders existed, such as in the Punjab, Bengal and Madras. New zones of political activity opened, as in Gujarat, where a militant non-cooperation campaign was launched in a single sub-district, Bardoli, to demonstrate its wider applicability. Also new was mass activity in some princely states, such as Rajasthan, where peasant and hill groups organized against the oppressive policies of their rulers. Madras was the scene of a very successful anti-liquor campaign that cost the government a fifth of its liquor excise in 1920. In the Telugu-speaking parts of Madras non-cooperation was pressed more radically. Despite Gandhi's attempt to discourage it, taxes were withheld.

Possibly the most impressive non-cooperation campaign was in the central Gangetic valley, an area of political quiescence under conservative social and political elites. In 1920 and 1921 its cities and towns saw demonstrations against the British, as did the countryside, in a militancy headed by new leaders who were to guide the Congress for an entire generation. Among them was Jawaharlal Nehru, Motilal's son, who, after returning from schooling in England, had spent some time investigating agrarian conditions among India's vast rural poor. He and his colleagues made contact with the network of hundreds of peasant (*kisan*) committees established some years before by Home Rule League advocates; these bodies had forced changes in the practices of landlords and police by demonstrations against the capriciousness and violence of both. To the younger Nehru, the justice and militancy of small and middle farmers in the central Gangetic plain were as inspiring as actions of the ordinary people in cities who boycotted and marred the 1921 visit of the Prince of Wales to India. Consequently, young Nehru was particularly resentful of Gandhi's suspension of the non-cooperation campaign owing to the violence of villagers in Bihar against local police, which had led to the deaths of seventeen policeman and the retaliatory killing of 172 farmers in February 1922.

The name of that village, Chauri-Chaura, came to signify Gandhi's iron hold on politics during the 1920s and 1930s. The incident itself resulted from police provocation and violence against non-cooperation volunteers, who had been picketing liquor sales and protesting against the high price of food. Gandhi's suspension of a national campaign because of incidents in one village produced shock and resentment: shock because no one had taken his threats to suspend seriously, and resentment that such a momentous decision about a political force that was growing greater each week could be taken by Gandhi alone. Nehru later recalled his anger and that of other younger leaders at the time; others, such as Jinnah, concluded with disgust that the success of the khilafat movement could not be left in the hands of someone so quixotic. Against their criticisms, it must be pointed out that Gandhi had insisted throughout that non-cooperation would lose its compelling moral efficacy if it became violent. And when satyagraha recommenced during the 1930s there can be no doubt that the millions involved were impressed that if they lost their disciplined self-control and struck back against police violence, Gandhi would again suspend action, a conviction that accounted for the bravery and steadfastness of countless ordinary Indians under dire provocation.

For the moment, however, all political action had ceased. Having jailed numerous Congress leaders during the campaign, the British, who had not dared to do so before, brought Gandhi to trial in March 1922 and sentenced him to six years' imprisonment. This ushered in another period of disorder that led to new political and socio-economic conditions and eventually to new British concessions around 1930.

BETWEEN CAMPAIGNS

From prison, Gandhi continued to provide guidance through his contributions to his journal *Young India*. In its pages he launched the Indian Khadi Board to coordinate hand spinning, which was paradoxically recommended for everyone as the core of what his followers called 'the constructive programme' to alleviate the plight of the poorest. When this programme was barely passed by a sceptical Working Committee of Congress, Gandhi concluded that many Congressmen – possibly a majority – did not favour his kind of politics and actually pined to re-enter the councils from which they had resigned in the early time of non-cooperation. He was right, and those seeking the modest reforms possible within these bodies organized a party to contest the council elections due in 1923. Proclaiming theirs the Swaraj Party, they argued that they were as true as any to his spirit.

During Gandhi's incarceration, protests against a police ban on flying the Congress flag attracted volunteers for arrest from all over. Other Gandhian-style actions included intervention through satyagraha in support of a group of Sikhs who sought to wrest control of their *gurdwara* shrines from corrupt religious figures who were accused of working closely with the British. Two other satyagrahas were launched against increased taxes in Gujarat and restrictions on entering temples by low caste people in Travancore State. None of these actions concluded unambiguously, for all involved compromises. Still, they offer evidence of the widening adoption of Gandhian methods and participation, a training ground for struggles to come in the 1930s.

Meanwhile the more constitutionally minded majority of Congress leaders contrived to discomfit the British in other ways. Having won very strongly in the 1923 elections for several provincial legislatures, the first under the provisions of the 1919 India Act, they proceeded to demonstrate that the Act had no real power in Indian eyes. Repeatedly Congress councillors manoeuvred provincial governors into arbitrary enactments by skilful procrastination. The tactics were calculated to convince both Indians and the British public that far greater concessions were necessary to make the constitutional route one that commanded a following in India over the methods of Gandhi or, worse, the violence of communalists or the revolutionary politics of communists.

THE RESUMPTION OF HINDU–MUSLIM HOSTILITY

The khilafat movement which had united Congress and the League between 1918 and 1924 collapsed following the abolition of the khilafat by Turks themselves after the overthrow of the Ottoman sultanate in 1924. Strife between Hindus and Muslims turned deadly during the later 1920s, after the unprecedented unity of the khilafat movement. It became evident that unity had merely interrupted a process of intensified communal conflict that began in the late nineteenth century; once again during the middle and later 1920s cow-slaughter riots erupted in small towns and cities all the way from the frontier of British India with Afghanistan to the eastern boundary of Bengal with Burma. Muslim competition for jobs, whether relatively prestigious in government or lowly, intensified the hostility of lower middle-class Hindus.

Behind much of this lay a generalized crisis in certain lines of employment, such as the declining market for the handloom products of Muslim weavers who were displaced by the output of textiles from mills owned by Hindus. Kanpur in the United Provinces was the site of large-scale rioting between Muslims and Hindus in 1931 on this account. Older causes for suspicion and conflict continued in places where landlords and tenants were of different religions, as in eastern Bengal, or where followers of the Hindu Mahasabha, formed in 1915, pressed their programme for the 'reconversion' of Muslims. That Congress leaders and even Gandhi himself did not explicitly repudiate such inflammatory religious campaigns, and often maintained close personal relations with their leaders, was not lost on Muslims.

COMMUNISTS, NEHRU AND THE LEFT

A communist movement emerged in the 1920s to add to the political woes of the mainstream nationalists of the Congress. Some Indians had become communists while in exile in Europe, escaping persecution for terrorist activities during the war. One such, M. N. Roy, had made his way to Russia after the Bolshevik revolution and became active in the Communist International Bureau (Comintern). Others became communists while in India, often achieving prominent places in the non-cooperation and khilafat campaigns. Following Comintern policy, they opposed the organization of a separate Communist Party and advocated working within existing organizations instead. Notwithstanding the minuscule numbers of communists, the police maintained close surveillance and subjected them to judicial harassment. Nevertheless, some succeeded in ensconcing themselves in the major textile unions, where they offered alternative strategies to those of Congress union leaders.

Another locus of communist, or at least left, political interest was among some of the younger leaders of the Congress itself. Jawaharlal Nehru admired and followed Gandhi, but had occasional qualms about the older man's mysticism, religiosity and arbitrariness. As Nehru and Subhas Chandra Bose developed their political views, it was inevitable that they would explore communism and even participate in communist-led actions. This Nehru did while in Europe, becoming involved in anti-colonial organizations and declaring himself a socialist. Together with his father, he visited and was impressed by the Soviet Union as a bastion against imperialism and as a model for the kind of socio-economic change he thought appropriate for India if it was to escape its massive poverty.

THE DEVELOPMENT OF INDIAN INDUSTRY

At the same time that Britain and the other warring nations of Europe learned that they could not pursue nineteenth-century political goals except at the high level of slaughter exacted by twentieth-century military technology, India was making impressive strides in adopting that technology. During the First World War, India's industrial output increased to meet imperial military requirements in Asia and to replace imports of civilian goods from Britain as well as Germany. The basis for modernizing Indian industrial technology had been laid in the 1850s, before the end of the East India Company. At that time, three modern industries were started. Jute mills were established in Bengal that, by 1911, employed around 330,000. Cotton mills were started in Bombay in 1856, and their number rose from 47 in 1875 to 271 in 1914. Employment in that industry, which remained concentrated in western India, rose to 3.2 million between 1911 and 1951. Iron and steel came last, with the Tata Iron and Steel Company started in 1907 as a joint-stock company subscribed by Parsi and Hindu investors. While the war barred European imports of industrial goods, US and Japanese imports rose, so that the scope for rapid advances in capacity was limited. Not so profits, whose buoyancy encouraged new investments in modern tools. Wartime conditions also offered an opportunity for more technical training of Indians, including those with investment or technical and managerial experience. In short, the emergence of a modern bourgeoisie as well as an enlarged industrial workforce was encouraged, and both cherished the expectation of benefiting from the politics of the twentieth century.

POVERTY AND POPULATION

Other factors were developing as well. India's population for the past century is known from decennial censuses of increasing accuracy. Census-taking began in 1871, when the population, as adjusted later, stood at about 255 million, rising to around 390 million in 1941. Though this was a modest average annual increase of 0.6 per cent, the base of the population was so large that even small annual increases pressed upon the output of food and other goods. Competition for resources and benefits mounted and, with competition, distress and political unrest. Both became sharper between 1921 and 1941, when the average increase in population had more than doubled over that of the best estimates for the nineteenth century.

Growth was uneven: the sharpest increases in population between 1921 and 1941 were in eastern and central India, while the south lagged well behind at less than 1 per cent per annum. The lower rate reflected the famine mortality of the late nineteenth century and the greater incidence of morbidity from cholera, malaria, smallpox and dysentery. Illness and death would have been even higher during the late nineteenth and early twentieth centuries except for the development of drought-resistant crops and better agrarian techniques, as well as advances in public health, notably the widespread inoculation programmes.

Poor health and poverty went together with inadequate development funding. Southern India received a smaller proportion of public investment in railways, roads, power and irrigation than other parts of British India. With a

Plate 26 'Embroiderers. Embroidery in India has close links with folk art and its skills are handed down from generation to generation' (IOL Ray Desmond, *Victorian India in Focus*. London: HMSO, 1982, p. 44, plate 33, by permission of the British Library).

smaller population than Madras province, the Punjab and parts of north-western India received nearly a fifth more in public investment until 1914; Bombay Presidency received substantially more, too. Most of the southern peninsula remained at the same level of poverty as Bihar and Orissa.

In all regions, certain occupations suffered disproportionately during the inter-war years. The income of artisans steadily declined, and these included not only producers of handicraft goods who were disadvantaged by industrially produced textiles but all who depended for some of their livelihood on part-time employment making cheap furniture or processing commercial products like tea. Nevertheless, such was the general level of poverty that for many part-time producers of low-value goods and services India's vast poor comprised a market. Economic recession continued through the rest of the 1920s and India slid, along with those parts of the world for whom the 1920s had been prosperous years, into the prolonged and desperate depression of the 1930s. Then the link between politics and poverty became a great deal more direct.

The depression that began in 1929 caused the value of agricultural commodities, which had been declining slowly from the mid-1920s, to plummet: prices for raw cotton, rice and jute were nearly halved between 1929 and 1931, and wholesale prices generally fell by about the same proportion. Most affected by these declining commodity prices were relatively substantial producers – the rural middle class – with surpluses to sell and heavy obligations in rent, revenue and interest to pay. This was a constituency which the Congress and peasant organizations could mobilize with slogans demanding a reduction or moratorium on taxes, rents and debts; but the Congress was ever concerned not to lose the support of landlords, and even some rich peasants, if too much advocacy went to poorer farmers.

As it happened, wealthier rural families resorted to distress sales of their gold hoardings, and the freeing of gold was all that made it possible to maintain the level of Home Charges, the flow of taxation from India to London, during the depression. Calls for a devaluation of the rupee so as to ease the losses to Indian producers went unheard because a cheaper rupee would diminish the value of the Home Charges, which nationalists termed 'the Drain'. Remittances from India during the economically troubled 1920s and 1930s eased Britain's depression. As much as a sixth of the earnings from financial services in London for capital investments, insurance, freight charges and royalties originated in India; and this was in addition to the flow of pension payments to retired officials. London would tolerate no diminution of these transfers because of Indian distress.

PROTECTING INDUSTRY, NEGLECTING WORKERS

As India's exports fell, so of course did her imports, which affected the British economy in places like Manchester, whence machine-made cotton goods went to India; between 1929 and 1932 British exports fell by about three-quarters. Though the government of Great Britain was now a coalition including the Labour Party, no greater efforts were made to protect Lancashire workers in this depressed time than were offered to Indian agricultural export producers. There was one difference, however. While London would not consent to shelter the rupee as it did its own sterling currency through devaluation, India was permitted to raise protective duties on cotton, paper and sugar, thus achieving a degree of economic independence not known earlier. Given this protection, many of the principal British industrial exporters to India decided to create Indian subsidiaries as a means of holding the markets they had long dominated. The resulting increased industrial employment, coupled with the training of Indian technicians, hastened industrial development in the subcontinent, even though these gains were offset by the strengthening of financial controls which kept the rupee on a gold standard.

Thus, one effect of the depression was to enlarge the share of Indian-based manufacturing in the home market. Textiles produced in mills overtook those from England; the same was true for sugar products, cement and paper. Tata's steel production and competitive costs were robust enough by the middle 1930s to permit an end to tariff protection, and Indian-owned industries spread from Bombay and Ahmedabad and to eastern, central and southern India as industrial investment displaced older forms of commercial, real estate and money-lending operations. Indian money men responded to this increasingly national economy with a keener interest in and attempts to influence nationalist politics, a tilt that distressed government officials because it weakened yet another defence against nationalism. From a different point of view, however, the same shift caused problems for some Congress leaders. While many were pleased by the money that was made available for their causes from the highest commercial groups, others bridled at the effect of their new, rich allies in causing the Congress support for industrial workers, which had never been strong, to weaken.

Workers in the expanding Indian-owned industries suffered the usual bad working conditions of early industrialization, to which were added the recessionary wage cuts of the 1920s; both worsened during the 1930s. The subsequent strikes against wage cuts and for improved working conditions were met with lockouts and repression. An example of the last was a series of trials of union officials staged in Meerut between 1929 and 1933, ostensibly against communists.

In the end, however, it was the spectre of rural poverty and distress that the depression years from 1929 on imprinted upon the country – and beyond, as cinema news began to create a world culture. Audiences in the industrialized countries became accustomed to the sight of throngs of impoverished Indians. These images truly reflected an expanding population on an agrarian base that had not kept up: Indian per capita income remained static between the end of the First World War and the Second. Against this scissoring effect of a rapidly increasing population and relatively static resources, the mild interventions of the Raj, still wedded to liberal policies, were feeble. So, once again, in what had become the way of politics in India, popular protests were met by a combination of police and judicial repression followed by political concessions, with a major concern of the government being to win back some of the Indian middle-class support it had lost. Once again, there was a confused response from the Indian side.

THE SIMON COMMISSION AND ITS CONSEQUENCES

The political concessions began unpromisingly. When it was announced in November 1927 that a commission under Sir John Simon would visit India to take evidence on the workings of the 1919 constitution with a view to reform, there was at first a rare, unified Indian reaction: one of general disgust that the Simon Commission was to have no Indian members. This 'all white' group was resentfully dismissed by Congress as well as the Muslim League. They declared their intention to boycott the Commission and to cooperate instead on devising a constitution embodying the principle of 'dominion status', inspired by the self-rule that had been conceded to the white dominions of the British Empire by the Statute of Westminster of 1926.

The constitutionalists' leader was Motilal Nehru, and a report largely of his making came out in early 1928, reflecting the views of older politicians in and out of the Congress. Younger Congressmen, including Jawaharlal Nehru, were unimpressed by the report, mostly because they thought that constitution-making, whether by the British with their Commission or by moderate politicians like the elder Nehru, was not the way to achieve the fundamental changes in society that were needed.

Another avenue of opposition appeared in the street demonstrations and strikes that were launched against the Simon Commission and the renewal of the boycott of British goods. Clashes with the police in 1928 led to fatalities, notably that of the old Punjab leader Lajpat Rai. Students were another centre of opposition to the direction that Motilal Nehru and other constitutionalists were taking; many were caught up in new organizations such as the Socialist Youth Congress presided over by Jawaharlal Nehru. While his father called for dominion status, the younger Nehru and Subhas Bose rallied a group within Congress to repudiate the goal of an India within the Commonwealth and to declare for an independent republic. Further still from the moderate constitutionalism of the older Nehru were terrorists and communists. Terrorists resurfaced in the late 1920s in Bengal and the Punjab, and appeared for the first time in the United Provinces.

Unity for the constitutional project floundered as a result of opposition from Hindu nationalists. Specifically, they opposed an agreement of late 1927 for cooperation between the Muslim League and Congress, according to which the League renounced the separate electorates granted under the 1909 India Act, and Congress in return agreed to accept a fixed minority representation of Muslims in the legislative bodies. The Hindu Mahasabha attacked this compromise as a godless capitulation to Islam, a position that was supported by Congress representatives in a meeting of several parties in 1928. Thus encouraged, the religious nationalists demanded that Congress support a programme of 'reconversion' of non-Hindus.

Confronted with this rejection, many followers of an embarrassed Jinnah abandoned the Congress alliance to cooperate with Simon and his colleagues. At the same time, the radicals in the Congress, meeting in Lahore, stiffened their opposition to the Simon Commission by demanding complete independence from Britain and the immediate introduction of socialist measures to remedy the poverty of the country. This oscillation between a powerful conservative religious bloc and a radical socialist one within the Congress could have inspired little confidence among either Muslims or Congressmen, while it also weakened the front presented against British proposals for constitutional reform during the late 1920s.

The annual Congress session of 1928 in Calcutta sought vainly to recapture the earlier unity. Once again Jinnah pleaded for opposing the British on the basis of guaranteed minority representation for Muslims; once again this was rejected by a Congress leadership fearful of losing the support of Hindu conservatives. Jinnah then joined other Muslims to gain what they could from the Simon Commission through councils based upon a continuation of separate electorates. This break between Hindus and Muslims was squarely the responsibility of Hindu zealots in the Congress and the pusillanimity of many Congress leaders who not only broke a united Indian front during the Simon Commission's travels around the country but also assured that Muslims would remain aloof during the next period of mass politics in 1930, again led by Gandhi and called the Civil Disobedience campaign. As before, and as it was to be in the future, religion placed a barrier before progressive nationalist aspirations.

CONDITIONS FOR A NEW POLITICS

During the late 1920s, the nationalist initiative passed to the constitutionalist Swarajya Party with the blessing of Gandhi. He himself was jailed for two years after calling off his campaign, and appeared to be a spent political force as more conventional politicians reasserted an old dominance in the Swarajya Party, and as younger Congressmen came into prominence, the latter including the future first prime minister of an Indian republic, Jawaharlal Nehru.

Though apparently a failure, the non-cooperation campaign that followed the First World War actually laid the foundations for the agitations of the 1930s. Mobilizations were again mounted by the new linguistically organized Congress, with appeals to regional traditions in the language of the people, and by regional leaders. Once again, control was concentrated in Gandhi's hands through the network of his personal relations with leaders of the regional pradesh committees.

Nationalist critics of British imperialism, including some historians, long ago pointed to the many ways in which the imperial regime divided Indian groups from each other and practised ethnic politics in order the better to dominate all of them. However, it is true that ethnic identities and bondings were already present and significant in the later medieval and early modern polities, when various 'sons-of-the-soil' (populist agrarian) movements became strong. Examples include those of the Telugu leaders of major cultivating groups who dominated sixteenth- and seventeenth-century Vijayanagara and post-Vijayanagara 'nayaka' regimes, and, later, the Maratha and Sikh regimes of the seventeenth to nineteenth centuries, which were led by ruling lineages of landed clans of essentially peasant peoples. An example of the conventionally more important form of political-ethnicity was represented by Muslim ruling groups, where the lines of filiation were based not so much on place, as were Maratha and Sikh identities, but on sectarian distinctions, such as the Sunni–Shia split, or on distinctions of cultural origin: Arabo-Persian, Central Asian or indigenous Indian. The sons-of-the-soil and Islamic variants of ethnicity persisted into the twentieth century, and formed part of the warp on which Gandhi's political career was woven.

In the early twentieth century the nationalist movement changed dramatically. From being compliant participants in empty legislative debates in 1909, nationalists succeeded in winning a large measure of provincial political authority, which has since continued to order much of the Indian political world. In the course of that transformation, patriotic Indians devised new political practices and ideas, and these were to affect the larger world during the twentieth century.

The final constitutional step was taken with the promulgation of the

Government of India Act of 1935, designed as a federation of autonomous provinces of the Raj and balanced by a set of Indian princely states; in addition, an elected central political structure was foreshadowed with the seemingly unlikely condition that half of India's princes agreed to join the federal system. This was largely the constitution that was adopted by the present independent states of the Indian subcontinent.

[8] GANDHI'S TRIUMPH

GANDHI opposed both the politics of class and the industrialization of India; both could only destroy what for him was the double foundation of Indian society and nationhood: a moral structure of community relations that included a caste system purged of the exploitation of untouchables and a socio-economic base consisting of a localized agrarian order freed from domination by big government and big business. The India that must replace that of British domination, for Gandhi, was one to be viewed as a myriad of communities, loosely and voluntarily joined by bonds of shared culture, co-sharers in the historical traditions on which India was constituted, whose principles were constructed around caste interrelations and mutual tolerance of religious differences. It was not the small rural world of nineteenth-century British administrators who spoke of tiny, autonomous political communities – 'village republics' – that they presumed had always existed, or that of a hierarchical and technical order of mutual interrelations among specialized castes (which has been called the 'jajmani system'). Neither politics nor economically ordered divisions of labour underpinned community for Gandhi, but a shared morality and tolerance, together with simple and austere lifestyles.

Gandhi was an ethical absolutist, but one whose vision seemed at times paradoxical. Though there was no place in his scheme for modern capitalism, he refused to call for the expropriation of the wealth of India's capitalists; rather, he argued, those with great wealth, including those who funded the work of the Congress, must be persuaded, non-violently, to regard their wealth as a trust to be used for the betterment of the most vulnerable in society. On the same basis he opposed compulsory land reform, saying that those with landed wealth must learn that they too were trustees of community resources to be justly shared. He seemed to see no contradiction between his refusal to view society in class terms and his reliance on moral suasion to distribute wealth more equitably.

CIVIL DISOBEDIENCE

A new period of national agitation arose in the early 1930s, which was to prove the most massive of all, forcing another major constitutional concession from the British and laying the groundwork for the final struggles for freedom during the 1940s. But it too revealed both strengths and weaknesses. During most of the 1920s, Swarajya Party men made nationalist politics, holding to a call for constitutional reform leading to greater self-government and cooperation with the British. They were guided by the emergent 'Commonwealth' philosophy and by the example of 'dominion status' then being realized in the white parts of the Empire. After his release from prison, Gandhi conducted a programme parallel and sympathetic to that of the Swarajya Party, by beginning a mass movement for the spinning and weaving of handloomed clothing. It was a continuation of the boycott principle, but one that did not threaten the interests of the Indian capitalists who gave financial support to the Swarajists.

When concessions of greater self-government were denied by the viceroy Lord Irwin in 1929, the Congress, at its annual meeting in December that year, boldly declared that India's independence would take effect in January 1930. The Congress was then under the presidency of the young Jawaharlal Nehru, elected with Gandhi's support as the younger leader most likely to heed his authority. This proved a valid expectation, for Nehru looked to Gandhi to devise a programme to achieve independence. Once more the emphasis would be on civil disobedience, a non-violent mass movement like that of a decade before; but now Indians were aware that should violence occur, Gandhi would call the campaign off.

The Civil Disobedience campaign opened in 1930 and lasted, with some interruptions, until 1935. Indians and Britons alike were impressed by the sacrifices and discipline of so many ordinary people committed to non-violent resistance. Civil disobedience now was also more politically and socially complex than in previous campaigns, reflected changes in the country during the 1920s and presaged the issues and fissures of the post-independence era.

There were certain weaknesses acknowledged in the campaign of the early 1930s. The principal one was the alienation of Muslims. They shared less directly in most regional traditions and were less moved, and often threatened, by appeals to such traditions. For instance, in many parts of the Gangetic plain, legislation was demanded to end the slaughter of cows. For Muslims, and the far fewer Indian Christians, beef was a preferred as well as a cheap food, and not easily given up. Moreover, Muslims were overrepresented in the towns and cities; two-thirds of the Muslims of the United Provinces in the Gangetic plain were of urban residence, and many engaged in small retail businesses that depended on the distribution of British goods. Hence Muslims tended to be marginal to the dominant rural cultural values and their economic interests were opposed to those of Indian capitalists who owned or had interests in textile mills, and who profited from the boycott of imported cloth.

URBAN AND RURAL UNREST

Depressed economic conditions had led to wage cuts and strikes in the railways and in such major industries as cotton, textiles and jute. Attempts to keep trade unionist and worker militancy off the Congress agenda were momentarily defeated when the Congress meeting of December 1929 was invaded by a group of Calcutta workers demanding the passage of a raft of radical resolutions, including full independence. Meanwhile, textile workers in Bombay, led by communists who had displaced Congress unionists, countered wage cuts by massive and peaceful picketing between April and October 1928. The strikes failed when Pathan strikebreakers were brought from northwestern India and police attacked picket lines. Not surprisingly, the strikes were followed by riots between Pathan and non-Pathan workers in early 1929. Other textile strikes were abandoned after Congress unionists persuaded the low-caste union members to wrest leadership from mostly brahman communist leaders.

Official repression was capped in 1929 by the trial of some thirty labour leaders in Meerut in the United Provinces on charges of criminal conspiracy; many were communists and three were English. British anti-unionism achieved its objective simply by lengthening the proceedings, for the accused were imprisoned on remand and therefore out of action for the four-year duration of the trial, after which stiff sentences were imposed. Some Congressmen took advantage of the British tactics to displace the left-wing union leadership. Despite being under combined attack, labour militancy continued in the metal industry and in government railway shops. It would have continued longer and spread over more industries except for Gandhi's constant disapproval.

The situation in rural India was no less agitated. Militancy among the rural poor – caused by the prolongation of the depressed economic conditions of the late 1920s – did not lag much behind that of industrial workers during the uneasy prelude to civil disobedience. Congress leaders, even radicals in Bengal and Punjab, followed Gandhi's aversion to being involved in conflicts between agricultural labourers, share-croppers and landlords, or even to taking positions on agrarian class questions. Their restraint had usually to do with fears that entering into these conflicts would alienate the propertied groups and drive them into the arms of the British.

The most acute rural class conflicts occurred where the permanent settlement with zamindars had established a substantial landlord class; but even there Congress strategists shrank from attempting to improve the lot of poorer agrarian workers, whether labourers or share-croppers. This was illustrated in Bihar during the late 1920s. Congressmen there, not previously known for their militancy, supported the vigorous Bihar Provincial Kisan (peasant) Sabha, founded by a religious leader, Swami Sahajananda Saraswati, in 1929. He had been active in the earlier non-cooperation campaign, and was now organizing small zamindars and rich peasants against big zamindar landlords, but offering little to landless labourers.

Deciding not to become involved in rural strife from which no immediate political advantage could be realized led to some serious Congress losses. For example, when in 1926 Congressmen avoided partisanship in the violent clashes between Hindu landlords and Muslim share-croppers in Pabna, central Bengal, Muslim politicians seized the opportunity to form a separate Praja (people's) Party, opposed to Hindu as well as Muslim landlords. Similarly, in the Punjab, the Congress, this time in alliance with the Hindu Mahasabha, eschewed struggles between cultivators and their money-lending creditors because in some places the former were Sikhs and the latter Hindus. This left rich political pickings for the Sikh Akali movement, which now added to its principal purpose of taking over shrines from corrupt officiants the leadership of militant farmers against Hindu money-lenders and oppressive landlords. Such losses to the Congress were not easily repaired.

Elsewhere in British India this anti-Congress opportunism was less evident. Madras and Bombay, where the 'ryotwari' revenue settlement was between the state and individual small-holders, experienced hostility against the government rather than private landlords. There the Congress organized protests opposing revenue increases. When, in 1927, the Madras authorities sought a 20 per cent revenue increase from Andhra districts, reflecting the appreciation of land values there, a storm of popular opposition arose among the rich and middle peasants who had been the main beneficiaries of the enhanced land values. Kisan organizations were led by Congressmen who had participated in Gandhi's non-cooperation campaign and remained Gandhian in allegiance and in their non-violence.

Gandhian methods were also deployed and further refined in the Gujarat countryside, where Gandhi was able to demonstrate that his form of political action served to empower the rural poor without creating alarm that his interventions would lead to violence. In Gujarat, rich farmers called Patidars ruthlessly exploited low-caste labourers on their lands. From 1922 to 1928 Gandhi's followers, many belonging to the Patidar caste themselves, struggled to improve the lot of the underclass by moral appeals, but without much success.

Hoping to take advantage of the divided rural society, the British felt free to impose revenue increases of over 20 per cent, which prompted Congress to react with a successful and non-violent campaign. At the same time, Congress cadres won the support of the victimized labourers by skilfully publicizing a Gandhian ideology that repudiated class differences and insisted that money-lender, landlord and field worker had a common purpose in joining together to resist the exorbitant demands of the government. The outcome was that in 1929 the Bombay authorities postponed the land tax increases, ostensibly to permit further investigation. Actually, according to documents of the time, they were surprised by the level of general support for the movement throughout Gujarat and also feared the prospect of a general strike, which workers in Bombay threatened if force was used against the tax defaulters in the countryside.

POOR LOSERS, RICH NATIONALISTS

The strike threat was a success for Gandhi, a demonstration of how an unpopular and autocratic government could be resisted by the joint efforts of rural people and urban workers; it also vindicated the technique of non-violence and promoted a unifying ideological approach, though to the disadvantage of the poorest in the community. The refusal by Congress leaders to consider programmes to improve the lot of the very poor could not be disguised; indeed, it was upon that basis that the moderates in Congress and Gandhi were supported by the captains of India's industry and the middle class in the late 1920s prelude to civil disobedience.

Some leading Bombay businessmen had earlier supported the boycott of the Simon Commission because they opposed the government's financial policies, which included an overvalued rupee and refusal to instigate tariffs to protect Indian manufactures. In other cities a few big businessmen had earned nationalist credentials by their participation in non-cooperation. In Bengal, for instance, some were angered when their efforts to enter the profitable jute industry were frustrated by the refusal of European banks to provide loans. But others, like the Tatas of Bombay, distrusted the whole of the nationalist cause, especially its trade unionists, and urged other capitalists to join them in funding a separate political party to oppose the Congress.

Between the two extremes of capitalists – non-cooperators on the one hand and opponents like Tata on the other – was a larger, more politically astute stratum led by G. D. Birla, the Marwari industrialist. He became a close friend of Gandhi, and it was in the garden of his Delhi mansion that Gandhi was assassinated in 1948. During the 1920s Birla expressed the viewpoint of an emerging national bourgeoisie by arguing that the best way forward for Indian capital was to support moderates in the Congress – the swarajists led by Motilal Nehru – who sought constitutional reform and orderly economic relations. In this way Birla and those who followed him registered their Indian patriotism while protecting their national class interest.

The conservatism of Birla and other capitalists appealed to Gandhi. In the late 1920s he was concerned to stave off the growing demands of younger Congressmen for a renewal of more vigorous action to achieve full independence. To throttle these demands while appearing to continue resistance to the British, Gandhi proposed what he called constructive work in villages and other goals, such as the uplift of 'untouchables', khadi production and liquor prohibition. He also agreed to an expansion of the boycott of British goods and the public burning of foreign cloth. These were activities which Gandhi felt confident he could control, whereas aroused urban workers, the educated young and the rural poor were not such pliant followers. He went as far as to state that he would head no movement that did not accept his definition of ends and means and his ultimate authority.

Moreover, he doubted that the Congress was ready for another mass campaign; its membership was not large enough in most places. Therefore he worked to forestall any impetuous Congress action by supporting Jawaharlal Nehru for the Congress presidency in 1929. This seeming paradox shows Gandhi's astuteness, for in choosing the young Nehru over older candidates, Gandhi selected an agent capable of reining in Congress radicals, among whom Nehru was counted, but one who would also be compliant with his own wishes.

At the same moment, a newly elected British Labour government came to the aid of Gandhi by offering a consideration of dominion status, with terms to be discussed at a Round Table conference in London in 1930, when the recommendations of the Simon Commission would also be considered.

Controversy immediately rent the Congress, with some doubting the sincerity of the viceroy Lord Irwin's offer, others demanding that Congress should be awarded a majority of seats at the London conference. When that was refused, the stage was once again set for confrontation, which was signalled by Nehru's presidential speech at the Lahore Congress in December 1929. He produced a stirring vision of a republican and socialist India, which explicitly repudiated Gandhi's class-blind policies. His colleague Subhas Chandra Bose promptly urged a socialist strategy of non-payment of taxes and a general strike, but this was deemed too radical for the assembly. The contending factions finally struck a compromise, leaving the executive working committee to determine the specific actions to be undertaken. As Gandhi was asked to join them, it seemed likely that it would be his programme that would lead India to what was now the official goal of the Congress: *Purna Swaraj*, full independence.

THE SALT TAX

When Gandhi announced that the Congress would mount a satyagraha against the salt tax even Nehru was appalled. Yet within a short time, his disparagers, among them Lord Irwin, were forced to express admiration for Gandhi's selection of a cause that unified all opinion and provided an arena for genuinely massive disobedience. The more comprehensive left programme of Nehru and Bose would doubtless have alienated landlords, fearful of a no-rent movement, and businessmen worried about a renewal of strikes, but because the salt tax was the most regressive in India, it was a perfect symbol of imperialist exploitation of mankind's neediest.

Dramatically, Gandhi announced that he would march with some of his followers from his rural headquarters, or ashram, in mid-Gujarat to the Arabian Sea at Dandi, and violate the state monopoly by collecting sea salt for their own use. The salt march began in March 1930, reached the sea a month later and was watched throughout the world thanks to the medium of cinematic news. Gandhi was filmed holding the salt he had scooped up and announcing that such defiance would be undertaken by Indians everywhere, along with boycotts of foreign cloth and liquor. Again, he cautioned that there must be no violence whatever the provocation, and soon afterwards, other actions commenced: there were no-tax campaigns in Gujarat (but non-payment of rent was still eschewed) and a renewal of non-violent infractions of laws that restricted access to and the use of forest products was initiated in parts of Central India. But violence erupted in Bengal and in Bombay and the instigators were Indians, not the British police or military. Textile workers burnt liquor shops and attacked police and government buildings when they learned in May that Gandhi had been arrested for breaking the salt laws. Martial law restored order there and also in Chittagong, on the other side of the subcontinent, where Bengali terrorists seized an armoury and proclaimed themselves the 'Indian Republican Army'. A gun battle was required to subdue them.

Inconsistently, Gandhi dismissed these and other breaches of non-violence as minor aberrations, mere details in a general campaign of disciplined satyagraha; he pointed to the jails filling with those who had announced they would break the law and were prepared to serve sentences. Jailed resisters in 1930 were twice as numerous as in 1921–2, and most of them were from the Gangetic plain, which had not previously been involved in non-cooperation.

The Pathans of the Northwest Frontier Province were new entrants to nationalist politics under Abdul Gaffar Khan. A Muslim reformer turned Gandhian in order to end the blood feuds that kept Pathan society divided and easily ruled, he organized satyagrahas involving all the clans and classes in demonstrations around the provincial capital of Peshawar. However, when these peaceful demonstrators were fired on by police in April 1930 and over two hundred protesters were killed, the province erupted into violence. The army was called in to quell this new disorder, but some Hindu soldiers showed sympathy and refused to fire upon the Muslim demonstrators. In more remote parts of the province, the rising of hill Muslims in solidarity with other Pathans was answered by bombardments from British aircraft. This action preceded the bombing of Ethiopians by Italian fascists, and was perpetrated by a liberal western democracy.

Political actions during 1930 involved new forces which emerged to replace the diminished participation of students and industrial workers. Many more lower-middle-class clerks, traders and shop assistants joined demonstrations. And while Bombay's workers, still nursing wounds from the attacks visited upon them the previous year, remained quiet, they were replaced by increased participation from the countryside, a sign that by 1930 Gandhians had become firmly rooted in many places and their actions were sustained, massive and highly disciplined. To areas in coastal Andhra, Bihar and parts of the United Provinces were added new zones of Gandhian activism: the Pathans of the northwest and farmers from Karnataka and Maharashtra. Generally, too, as the first line of leadership were jailed and their places taken by less experienced and often more radical activists, there was a drift towards more radical anti-government action likely to lead to no-rent strikes and violent confrontations.

Jawaharlal Nehru applied himself to his home region of the United Provinces, working closely with villagers until his arrest in October 1930. By the time of his incarceration, Nehru had begun to remark on a slowing of political action and a general weariness among the majority of his followers, and simultaneously, an increasing radicalization among others. Noting that fewer middle-class urban professionals or Muslims were engaged than a decade before, Nehru rejoiced at the new and eager involvement of cultivators. The broad middle stratum of farmers of the Jat caste, who formed the backbone of aroused countrymen, could hardly be restrained from such radical measures as denying the state its land taxes. (Collections had already become difficult for the government, since one manifestation of rural satyagraha was the resignation from office of village headmen and accountants, key revenue officers.)

Some ugly communal conflicts marred the campaigns in towns and cities, where Congressmen picketed Muslim shops that sold imported goods or failed to observe hartals to mark certain nationalist events. But the mass urban mobilization was beginning to ebb when Nehru and others began to look at what might be achieved from the second session of the London Round Table meetings that had been called to consider the constitutional proposals of the Simon Commission.

Congress had boycotted the first Round Table, leaving it to others to present their views: various Muslim groups, nationalists of the Hindu Mahasabha, Sikhs, a set of secular politicians calling themselves Liberals and a large contingent of Indian princes. Dominion status, deemed premature by the Simon Commission, was not to be considered, which mattered little to the Indians who were there. Some interest in a weak federal assembly to which the viceroy might submit legislative proposals was evinced by representatives from large principalities like Hyderabad and Mysore. The British were also cheered by the divisions among Hindus, Muslims and Sikhs as they failed utterly to agree about a formula for allocating of seats in provincial legislatures.

It is little wonder that some of the more liberal participants in the first Round Table sessions returned from London early in 1931 to urge Congress to attend the second session and join with them in working for a viable constitution under an Indian majority. The Labour Prime Minister Ramsay MacDonald had offered something like this as the first session of the Round Table adjourned, though he reserved the areas of defence, external affairs and finance. By February 1931, Gandhi and other Congress members were ready to revert to negotiations on those terms, and the viceroy, Lord Irwin, agreed to meet with them.

The Gandhi–Irwin Pact of March 1931, by which Congress agreed to end the Civil Disobedience movement and send Gandhi to London as its only representative, provided very little in return for suspending what had been declared to be an all-out fight against British rule. Gandhi's capitulation – and it was in the end his decision – is as difficult to understand now as it was then. Nehru recalled that by early 1931 there was widespread exhaustion and despair, but it has alternatively been suggested that the reason Gandhi closed the campaign was actually pressure from business backers of Congress, who saw few of their interests being advanced and who therefore threatened to abandon the Congress. In London, Gandhi was unable to accept the idea of separate communal electorates which was favoured by the British, the Muslims and even the representatives of the Hindu depressed classes; he began a 'fast unto death'.

In January 1932, civil disobedience was resumed in response to popular pressure from below. This followed the Karachi session of the Congress at the end of 1931, whose dispirited resolutions failed to address the crucial issues of rural poverty and indebtedness, to the disappointment of many in the Gujarat and Andhra provincial Congresses. Dismay among Congress followers was further manifested in the declining membership of some of the most historically active Congress bodies in the country.

Pressure for a return to battle came from the impoverished countryside. With prices for their commodities continuing to fall, even the better-off farmers were unable or unwilling to pay their revenues, rents or debts. Those who could not resist the honours and perquisites of minor village offices were ostracized by others, often to the extent of being excluded from marriage

Plate 27 Gandhi at the second Round Table Conference, St James's Palace, London, September 1931 (IOL Photo 13 (1); neg. no. B1132, by permission of the British Library).

networks by fellow caste members. In Gujarat, Gandhi intervened to persuade officials there to ease tax demands on farmers, and also relaxed his strictures against rent and tax strikes by permitting cultivators to pay only a portion of what they owed, a gesture interpreted by radical local leaders as permission to withhold both completely.

Rural militancy raged throughout the United Provinces, almost always in the face of cautious Congress leaders, including Nehru, who were also slow to take up an increasingly popular demand for an end to zamindari rights to land ownership and a transfer of titles to those with tenant rights. Agrarian radicalism was found everywhere, from the princely state of Kashmir, far in the north, to Andhra and Travancore in the south. Not all popular agitations were against tax collectors and landlords, however; in the south there were demands for Congress to support campaigns to permit the lower castes to enter temples, from which they had been historically excluded.

While Congress leaders struggled to control a countryside aflame with demands for action against the government, the latter were coping with a conservative tide from the home government. The feeble liberalism of Lord Irwin was under criticism by the Tories, including Winston Churchill. Irwin's viceregal successor, Lord Willingdon, held a view that was popular among some imperial bureaucrats that it had been an error to enhance Gandhi's leadership by negotiating with him as an equal, and Willingdon's harder attitude was supported by the coalition government under the Labour Party's

Ramsay MacDonald. Several promises that Irwin had given for fiscal reforms and for protective duties on some Indian exports were repudiated, with the pretext of compensating for land revenue and income taxes lost as a result of the depression.

Faced with this intransigence and convinced that the resumed Round Table conference was unlikely to yield concessions, Gandhi determined on a two-pronged strategy. To win Muslim agreement to join the Congress in a demand for immediate swaraj he agreed to all Muslim claims to representation; to win the British public over to India's cause he travelled to London to explain it directly. The first stratagem failed because of continued suspicions of the Congress on the part of Muslims; the second was successful. Among the enduring benefits of the publicity that the press and newsreels around the world gave to his London visit was the public sympathy for Indian national aspirations generated in the United States; it was reflected after the Second World War in Franklin Roosevelt's warning to Churchill against the reassertion of British rule.

CIVIL DISOBEDIENCE RESUMES

For the moment it was urgent to deal with a new attack from the imperial bureaucracy. Reminiscent of the Rowlatt bills after the First World War, police regulations in January 1932 banned certain Congress bodies and activities and allowed arbitrary arrest of leaders and confiscation of their property. Gandhi himself was arrested. This declaration of war against Indian nationalism was followed by a resumption of civil disobedience, which was to continue for another eighteen bitter and futile months.

The return to civil disobedience, however, forestalled further spontaneous and uncontrolled demonstrations, and Gandhi hoped that it would ease demands on him for more vigorous actions. In addition to relaxing some earlier strictures, such as those against withholding rents, he sanctioned the defiance of ordinances banning political assembly and flying the Congress flag. In the course of the next year, the prisons filled with 120,000 civil disobedience volunteers, the highest proportion of whom were shop assistants, office workers and, for the first time, women.

Although women had been admitted to the Indian National Congress from its founding as individuals, self-conscious feminism was remarkably late in arriving, and for a long time regarded with suspicion as an alien import. The involvement of women in politics, although it included a demand made as early as 1917 for women to vote on the same basis as men, was envisaged entirely in service to nationalism. The benefits pressed for in terms of health, welfare and education were demanded in the name of the contributions they would assist women to make to their families or to the nation at large. Gandhi identified in women those qualities he felt were most suited to the carrying out of his programmes, and took special delight in bringing women out of purdah so that he could see, touch and enrol them in a women's corps called 'servants of the nation' (*desh sevika*). Under his influence, large numbers of middle-class women emerged from seclusion in order, at his direction and with the

Plate 28 European ladies at the wedding of a maharaja's daughter, 1932 (Harald Lechenperg).

peculiarly Indian emphasis on housework that has characterized all discussions of the role of women, to engage in menial tasks in the service of men of lower caste, as well as to court arrest and imprisonment for picketing shops and engaging in other forms of civil disobedience.

Other groups fell away. Muslims were absent from the ranks of resisters between 1932 and 1934, while industrial workers participated, though both groups engaged in the rioting which occurred in Bombay between Hindus and Muslims in May and July of 1932. In addition, many middle and rich farmers withdrew the support they had given to Congress during the earlier non-cooperation movement of the 1920s: they could no longer risk losing their land for non-payment of land taxes. Finally, some Indian businessmen began quietly to retreat from their former supportive positions. The pressures of the depression and shrinking profits dictated some sort of accommodation with the government.

THE EFFECTS OF THE DEPRESSION

As nothing had before, the depression of the 1930s made manifest the costs of Indian colonial dependency. In more advanced contemporary states, public spending blunted the social and hence the political effects of the Great Depression. In Britain, expenditures for social welfare trebled between 1928 and 1936, and in the USA, the defence and police budgets were slashed in order to fund poor relief schemes. Other parts of the British Empire – Canada and Australia, for example – also had altered patterns of expenditure during the 1920s and 1930s. Canada allocated 5 per cent of its central funds to augment provincial expenditures to assist the poor in 1936, whereas Australia reduced its military expenditures from nearly half of total public costs in 1928 to less than a quarter, while expanding social welfare payments from nearly nothing to 15 per cent by 1936.

While these adjustments were being made by other nations, including two dominions of the Empire, India's military absorbed increased proportions of its budgetary allocations, moving from an average of 25 per cent to 45 per cent in 1928 and holding at over 40 per cent in 1936–7, while public health spending to rose to a mere 1 per cent. Critics also pointed out that Indians suffered greater hardship than the poor of other countries, including Britain, where job-creating public investments were undertaken as anti-depression measures, some of which protected its manufactures at the expense of firms and workers in India, who continued to struggle for external markets with a rupee pegged at a punishing deflationary and uncompetitive rate.

THE UNTOUCHABLE ISSUE

Given the staggering array of problems facing Indians, it is not difficult to understand how stunned and disappointed many were with Gandhi's decision to make the uplift of untouchables a key element of the Congress programme. It was construed as if British imperialism was no longer to be the main adversary, but high-caste Hindus! While admirable in moral terms and certainly consistent with Gandhi's long commitment to the improvement of life for the depressed castes, his political judgement was again questioned. Although Congress had been founded in 1885 in the midst of the social reform movements of the nineteenth century, most of its members considered it best to concentrate on political rather than social issues to avoid divisiveness. At its founding, in any case, the burning social issues seemed to revolve around the inhumane treatment of women. Despite his celebrated book, *Poverty and Un-British Rule in India*, the desire to avoid social upheaval was explicitly stated by Dadabhai Naoroji, the wealthy Parsi who was to be twice Congress president and the first Indian to be elected a member of the House of Commons in England. The Congress, he said, was a political organization 'to represent to our rulers our political aspirations, not to discuss social reforms'.

However, by 1917, two years after Gandhi's return to India, Congress had achieved sufficient unity between extremists and moderates and even enough harmony with the Muslim League to turn its consideration to the fact that untouchables constituted a sizable proportion of the population, variously estimated between one-seventh and one-quarter, that could add political weight to congenial organizations. Some of them were already aligned with the non-brahman movement in Madras, which was opposed to the Congress.

At its annual meeting that year, the National Congress passed a resolution recognizing the necessity of removing the disabilities of untouchability, which included prohibitions on admission to schools, hospitals, courts, public offices, public water supplies, temples and so forth. There had been a meeting of the 'depressed classes' in Bombay the year before, which had called for such a resolution in exchange for support of the Congress–Muslim League position on constitutional change, and helped to concentrate minds.

Then began an argument about the best approach. Gandhi achieved an iron rule over the Congress leadership the following year, when Mrs Besant, who had been elected president in 1917 but had proved moderate beyond expectations, was swept aside. As usual, he considered untouchability a religious and moral problem, not a legal or economic one. But if it was a religious issue in Hinduism, the origins of untouchability seemed relevant because of the prevalent belief that one's status in life was 'deserved'; that is, a result of behaviour in previous lives. As believers in rebirth, the elimination of untouchability required that this view on the part of high caste Hindus be addressed.

Gandhi and some other high-caste reformers held that there was no scriptural basis for a fifth caste, that they should really be included among shudras. His general view of caste was that it was occupationally based, and that members of a caste, whether viewed as varna or jati, should engage in their traditional types of work for the harmonious functioning of all society. Although the work of shudras was that of serving the other castes, it did not make them less worthy of respect, or prevent them from engaging in other pursuits in their spare time. (Curiously enough, his own caste was originally that of merchants, but his forebears had been state government officials for some generations; furthermore, when he himself broke with tradition and went abroad to study, he was expelled from his caste.)

His prototypical untouchable was the Bhangi, whose work was scavenging and cleaning toilets. His idea was that, since all work should be considered equally honourable, Bhangis would have the same status as brahmans, but go on cleaning toilets. To achieve the necessary change in attitude, he himself did and encouraged his followers to do all kinds of 'polluting' things, such as touching untouchables. But it proved one thing to get his followers to do symbolic and temporary 'sanitary work' (cleaning latrines), and quite another to get untouchable children admitted to national schools. In contrast, the younger Nehru, as a secularist and socialist, believed that secular nationalism would solve the problem automatically.

Among untouchables themselves, there were several theories about how their castes came upon their depressed status. Some claimed to have been descendants of kshatriyas, warriors who owed their humiliation to having been defeated in battle; others that they were descendants of the original inhabitants of the Indian subcontinent, the remnants of a people conquered by the Aryan invaders; still others that they were descendants of Buddhists who were the victims of the earlier persecutions that had accompanied Hindu revivalism.

THE UNTOUCHABLE LEADER

The most important leader of the untouchables in the first half of the twentieth century, Dr Bhimrao Ramji Ambedkar, was born into the Mahar caste in Maharashtra, a large group who constituted one-tenth of the population of that state. Their traditional village occupation was sweeping, carrying messages, hauling away dead cattle and other such menial work (but not latrine cleaning or hauling 'night soil', which was considered even more polluting). During the nineteenth and early twentieth centuries many had left the villages to became workers in the new industries and railways, or domestic servants to the British. Those who managed to obtain an education sometimes went into primary school teaching. The acquisition of education inevitably led to social mobility and more militant caste leadership. Some, including Ambedkar's father and grandfather, served in the army and picked up some education there, although the army stopped recruiting Mahars about 1892, the year of Ambedkar's birth, when the British rejected the community's petition claiming to be of warrior descent.

Ambedkar never claimed this, nor did he claim that they had been the original pre-Aryan settlers. That is, he rejected any attempt at ethnic distinction and insisted that the disadvantages were social, not racial, in origin. Later, when he leaned towards Buddhism, to which he formally converted shortly before his death, he did entertain the theory that untouchables were descendants of persecuted Buddhists. For a long time, however, he tried to reform Hinduism. In addition to participation in temple entry campaigns, he put forth such suggestions as that priests should be chosen by examination. In 1927 he burned the *Manusmriti* (Code of Manu) publicly, and in 1956 he converted to Buddhism (eventually others followed him, and there are now about three million Buddhists in India).

As a promising youth, he was given scholarships by the Gaekwad of Baroda to go to college and eventually to go abroad, where he earned a PhD from Columbia University in New York, a DSc from the University of London and a law degree. He returned to India in 1923 to organize his fellow untouchables, and was encouraged by some of the caste Hindus with whom he became associated (he himself married a brahman doctor). He started schools, newspapers and political parties. Along with other Maharashtrian reformers, he rejected Gandhi's patronizing and outdated ideology and programmes from the start. However, as he put it, 'when one is spurned by everyone, even the sympathy shown by Mahatma Gandhi is of no little importance'.

Ambedkar was realistic enough to know that he needed to work with reformers of all stripes. Although he rejected all socially defined hierarchical distinctions, he wished to make untouchables aware of their unjustly debased condition and to gain political power for them in any way possible, including separatism, i.e. constituting untouchables as a 'community'. To this end, as well as because of the discrimination against them in housing, he established hostels for untouchable students. But he did not try to glorify certain 'traditional' practices associated with untouchable status, such as drinking alcohol and eating carrion beef; instead, he urged his followers to abandon them and take on 'high-caste' behaviour – which, in the case of women, included wearing high-caste dress, such as the 'long' sari – all as a sign of inner self-respect, and outward assertion.

Eventually, however, he denounced Hinduism as unreformable, and, after publicly burning a copy of the code of Manu, determined that his community must rise through the acquisition of political power. For Gandhi, the preser-

Plate 29 Dr Bhimrao Ramji Ambedkar. New Delhi, 1946 (IOL Photo 134/1 Print 37; neg. no. B/W 17207, by permission of the British Library).

vation of the *Hindu* community intact took precedence even over the uplift of the untouchables. He and Ambedkar were on a collision course. It was a collision course between two centuries as well as two men: Gandhi's views were quintessentially Victorian while Ambedkar had espoused a twentieth-century belief in modernization and progress for all, as well as universal human rights.

Ambedkar first publicly analysed the differences between them in the context of the Vaikam satyagraha of 1924–5. In Kerala, discrimination against the untouchable castes was so extreme that some were not even permitted to use roadways passing near to temples, let alone enter and worship in them. A satyagraha, conducted according to Gandhian principles, was begun at the Kerala Vaikam temple by members of one of the 'depressed castes' along with some caste Hindus and a Syrian Christian. Gandhi visited the site during the second year of the demonstration and attempted to debate with the brahman temple priest, but without success. He then apparently decided that such interventions were not worth the bitterness and divisiveness they cost, and (surprisingly for one so concerned with religion) never took an active role in further temple entry campaigns. The official Congress position was that no coercion should be used.

In a speech delivered during the Vaikam satyagraha, Ambedkar pointed out that Gandhi did not lay as great a stress on the removal of untouchability as, for example, on the wearing of homespun cotton clothing or on Hindu–Muslim unity. The rejection of untouchability was not a condition for entrance to or voting in the Congress. But the real crisis between them came in 1931.

Ambedkar was named as one of two 'depressed class' delegates to the Round Table Conference in London to discuss the future political representation of Indians in their own legislatures. Muslims, Sikhs, Anglo-Indians and Christians all wanted separate electorates; that is, to be able to elect their own representatives. Consequently, Ambedkar demanded that untouchables should constitute a separate electorate as well. The British agreed, and Gandhi decided to 'fast unto death' in protest. Eventually, Ambedkar gave in, fearful of the consequences of being blamed for Gandhi's death, but not before he won 148 reserved seats in the provincial legislatures (rather than the 78 he would have had under a separate electorate that the government had offered) in what was known as the 'Poona [Pune] pact'.

Gandhi had begun to call untouchables Harijans, 'children of God', a move that offended both orthodox Hindus and politically aware untouchables themselves. Ambedkar pointed out that a new name and even Gandhi's sincere efforts had not diminished the prejudices against or the oppression of low-caste peoples by high-caste Hindus. There was nothing for untouchables to turn to except what might be got through such political power as he was offered in London. Gandhi's fast was a form of blackmail of Ambedkar, not the British. Later he said his 'fast unto death' was only against separate electorates, which would make untouchable 'hooligans' ally with Muslim 'hooligans' to kill caste Hindus.

At the second session of the Round Table Conference, at which he was at liberty to participate, Gandhi questioned Ambedkar's qualifications to represent untouchables, asserting that he himself represented the vast majority of them. In 1932, he organized a society aimed at the removal of the stigma of untouchability, which he called the 'Servants of the Harijans Society' (*Harijan*

Sevak Sangh). Ambedkar and several other prominent untouchables were on the board, but shortly left when the society refused to press for civic and economic rights. Gandhi characteristically explained the absence of untouchable leadership by saying that it was an organization of penitents whose purpose was the expiation of guilt.

When Congress won power in provincial legislatures before independence, it was weak in dealing with the untouchable question. In 1942, Ambedkar became labour minister in the viceroy's cabinet, and tried once more to establish a separate electorate, but without success. However, he did manage to establish affirmative action in government service, and, in 1944, scholarships for untouchables in higher education. In 1945, he published *What Congress and Gandhi Have Done to the Untouchables*, a scathing attack on the lack of compulsion on the issue of untouchability. In it, he called the Harijan Sevak Sangh a political charity, intended simply to co-opt the untouchable movement into Congress. The book ended, 'Good God! Is this man Gandhi our saviour?' In due course, it was answered (by C. Rajagopalachari), without irony, to the effect that progress in India 'does not compare ill with what has been done in America for Negroes, or in the South African Republic for the natives of Africa, or for the Jews in civilized Europe'.[1]

Despite his rancour, Ambedkar was included in the first cabinet formed after independence (as Law Minister). He chaired the drafting committee for the constitution, in which untouchability was declared abolished, and heard Gandhi's name cheered as the liberator and source of these constitutional provisions when they were read out. In the actual transfer of power, however, the British had given scant regard to the untouchables, making provision for no special rights or privileges beyond what had originally been allotted in reserved seats in the legislatures. Subsequent attempts to extend affirmative action have met with stiff high caste opposition; moreover, many castes have claimed 'untouchable', 'scheduled', 'tribal' or, the favourite, 'other backward caste' (OBC) status in order to get whatever privileges or money may be on offer, whether or not they are actually poor and deprived, either individually or collectively, and preferably with as little stigma as possible in the labelling attached.

Gandhi's quixotic but highly principled diversion from the imperialist enemy to the problem of untouchables brought criticism from two opposite sides of the Indian political spectrum within the Congress. From orthodox Hindu elements there was resentment that he should squander his attention and political capital on those whom they despised. Secularists and socialists within the Congress felt that Gandhi's fixation upon untouchables was a disastrous dissipation of nationalist energies at a time when British repressions had never been greater. Despite both criticisms, Gandhi's concern for untouchables persisted. After his release from jail, he continued his efforts through his weekly newsletter, which he renamed *Harijan*, to improve the status of the seventh part of India's population that was condemned to social ostracism. All the while, however, he tried to minimize class divisions by steadfastly refusing to link the depressed state of Harijans with their position as exploited agricultural labourers.

THE LEFT IN POLITICS

Jawaharlal Nehru and Subhas Bose were among those who, impatient with Gandhi's programmes and methods, looked upon socialism as an alternative source for nationalist policies capable of meeting the country's economic and social needs, as well as a link to potential international support. Both were aware that industrialists in India, both British and Indian, sought to ease the squeeze on their profits during the prolonged depression by repressing trade unions and curtailing workers' benefits. Jute and cotton manufacturers imposed wage cuts of 17 per cent in 1933, and unions, badly weakened by police and judicial oppression, were powerless to prevent it. Further weakness came from political squabbles among small groups of the left. The situation improved, however, after Indian communists came into line with communist parties elsewhere following the Seventh Congress of the Communist International, where it was decided in 1935 to forge 'united fronts' against the right. Unity of the Indian left was also encouraged by labour militancy, as strikers doubled in number from around 128,000 in 1932 to 220,000 in 1934.

Socialism opened a space in the Indian political scene, first appealing to trade unionists of all sorts, then to farmers' organizations and the many individuals who found they could no longer support a Gandhian programme that refused to deal with oppressive economic conditions. To frustrate this left unity, the government banned the Communist Party of India in 1934 under a law of sedition dating from earlier in the century, but communists easily found an alternative locus in a newly formed affiliate of the Congress, the Congress Socialist Party. Soon after, socialists and communists made inroads into another centre of popular mobilization in the countryside, the Kisan Sabhas, which now adopted stronger tactics against oppressive landlords.

THE GOVERNMENT OF INDIA ACT OF 1935

This consolidation of a politics of the left was a cue for the British to return to constitutional reform. A new Government of India Act was promised for 1935, which was to be the last by the British Parliament and the most lasting, for its provisions endured through the remainder of the era of colonial subjugation and were carried over to operate as the fundamental constitutional framework for the post-independence Indian Republic.

The proposed new legislation underwent an extended gestation. The viceroy, Lord Irwin, had promised a major constitutional reform in 1929, and he had added that dominion status would be discussed when he negotiated with Gandhi in 1931. In fact, Indians contributed little to the 1935 Act. While the final Round Table session in late 1932 included Indian representatives, there was no detailed discussion of the proposed enactment. That was reserved for parliamentary debates in which a small band of members sympathetic to the Indian cause pitted themselves against a vindicative majority led by Winston Churchill. The exclusion of Indian opinion meant that no group in India had anything good to say about the Act when it was finally promulgated. Most denounced the increased centralization of government through powers conferred upon executive offices. Provincial governors were to have the 'discretionary power' to call the legislature, to refuse to assent to their bills and, most undemocratic of all, to take control of a province from its elected majority ministry for reasons of public order. Nevertheless, substantial powers were vested in elective provincial governments, and the electorate was increased fivefold to 30 million voters.

The federal state envisaged by the 1935 Act could come into effect only when half of the princes of India agreed to join it. In the meantime, the central government, free of democratically elected participants, was extremely powerful. Foreign affairs and defence remained the responsibility of the viceroy, as did central finances, the railways and all matters touching on the civil service, money and debts.

That the 1935 Act did not actually introduce a federal system, or make that likely, suited many in India as it suited the British political establishment. Muslims had no wish for a strong, democratic central government, since this would be dominated by a large Hindu majority; Indian princes, reassured by the ebbing tide of nationalist militancy in the 1930s, were content to leave their relationship with the British unchanged. This was the sort of constitution that socialist critics had said would emerge if their moderate colleagues in the Congress had their way. In fact, a large majority in the Congress continued to believe that the way forward to a free India was the slow path of incremental constitutional change that preserved order and property against the chaos they felt socialism threatened.

NEHRU UNDER GANDHI

The persisting political weight of the Indian right during the 1930s has been obscured by the apparent surge of the Congress left under the leadership of Nehru. It was a leadership made brilliant by its unwavering exhortations to the Indian people to achieve a just and modern India, a socialist India; so dazzling was the man that it is easy to miss how often the movement at whose head he marched for thirty years took quite other directions. Although at once tuned to and able passionately to express demands for social and economic justice, Nehru continued to accept the tutelage of Gandhi and to resist many commitments to action stemming from leftist ideology. It is both difficult and essential to appreciate this subordination of Nehru to Gandhi and of the Congress left to the right when examining the several years leading to the Second World War and the final act of the freedom struggle.

INFIGHTING IN CONGRESS

Presiding over the Congress at Lucknow in 1936, Jawaharlal Nehru proclaimed his commitment to scientific socialism and his opposition not only to imperialism but also to fascism and thus his solidarity with the people of Spain, Abyssinia and China. The generous identification of a beleaguered Indian freedom struggle with other struggles against oppression abroad was a mark of Nehru's capacious vision of India's place in the world. As to matters closer at hand, he told his colleagues that the provincial elections, scheduled for the following year in accordance with the 1935 Act, would be fought on a radical socio-economic programme, which he confidently expected to carry the country.

The depression drove nationalist politics to the left, a trend marked by the founding of the Congress Socialist Party within the Congress itself and its mass organization of industrial workers, students and women. Eventually, some of its members drifted under communist leadership, which prompted Gandhi to intervene for fear that class politics would compete with nationalist ones. As before, when left-leaning politics surged among Congress-followers, Gandhi urged the election of Jawaharlal Nehru to the presidency of the Congress. Although himself a leading light of the left faction of the Congress, Nehru was so securely under the tutelage of Gandhi that the latter was confident that Nehru's high standing with radicals could be used to diffuse the full impact of class politics upon India's freedom movement, which Gandhi found distasteful for its divisiveness and uncongeniality to his own notions about India's future.

Once again, Gandhi's confidence was vindicated. However, Nehru devised a curious strategy: Congress members were to stand for provincial office under the arrangements of the 1935 Act, but refuse to take any seats. In the elections that took place in 1937, Congress did indeed win majorities everywhere except the Punjab and Bengal. But even in these provinces, regional parties won with massive support from newly enfranchised independent farmers and tenants who were suffering from depression-deflated prices. Thus, there was pressure on all sides to take office and introduce economically ameliorative legislation, an action that had been a demand of the Congress left. Under pressure, an awkward compromise was effected: Congress winners of constituency seats were permitted to accept office, while the Congress pradesh committees in the provinces were to maintain hostility to the ministries thus formed.

The untenability of the compromise led to a direct challenge from the Congress left in support of the candidacy of Subhas Chandra Bose for the presidency of the Congress, expressly against the preferences of Gandhi. Bose won but found himself unable to execute his office in the face of the intractable opposition of the majority of the working committee, who were Gandhi partisans. In April 1939, he resigned; it was a victory for Gandhi but a dangerous alienation of the popular Bose, who commenced a course of violent opposition as the Second World War began.

Other socialists were brought into the working committee to help Nehru to frame a campaign for agrarian change, one that followed the programme of the All India Kisan Sabha: reduced land revenue and rent demands, an end to forced labour, restoration of forest rights and recognition of agrarian trade unions. It was with this radical programme that Nehru and his colleagues overwhelmed the Muslim League and other parties in the 1937 provincial elections; the League gained but a quarter of seats reserved for Muslims, while the rest went to Congress candidates. It seemed a spectacular demonstration of the power of a secular, socialist and internationalist Congress over any of the narrowly defined alternatives, including the Gandhian programme.

All acknowledged the highly successful electoral attraction of Nehru. In addition to the mobilization of the rural vote in most provinces, thanks to the Kisan Sabhas, the organized labour vote was handily corralled by the newly unified federation of unions, the All India Congress of Trade Unions under communist leadership. Other mass organizations – of students, writers and women – took active parts in canvassing votes in urban constituencies. The results seemed to be a victory for the Congress left. In actuality, the 1937 elections were as much a victory for the Congress right. Together with their capitalist allies, the Congress right-wing succeeded in maintaining its dominance over the Congress movement as a whole.

The private correspondence of leading Congress rightists and their moneyed allies at the time oozed a cynical confidence that the rhetoric of Nehru and the Congress left was mere talk and that in the end Gandhi would restrain Nehru's socialism: 'Bolshevik propaganda will find fertile soil in India [but] Mahatma Gandhi's movement [has] diverted the people from adapting [sic] violent methods to his non-violent methods', wrote Lalji Naranji to Purshotamadas Thakurdas.[2]

They were also confident that the right-wing majority in the Congress working committee, together with Gandhi's judicious interventions, would offset the militancy of the election manifesto under which Nehru won, and that, with a secure Congress win, pressure to take office would grow and further divert the Nehru-led left. This proved another correct prediction when the Congress was found to have won majorities in five out of eleven provinces (Bihar, Central Provinces, Madras, Orissa, and the United Provinces) and was only a few votes short in Bombay. Moreover, Congress won not only most of the seats reserved for Muslims, but also most of the reserved untouchable seats, except in Bombay, where a party formed by Dr Ambedkar was successful. Official backing for some of the loyalist parties of landlords in the United Provinces or the Justice Party, an anti-brahman Madras party, failed to diminish the extent of the Congress victory.

It was immediately obvious that the gesture of refusing office could not be sustained. The right-wing majority of the Congress executive committee defeated a motion from the left to stand by the manifesto promise of declining office, and instead the right carried a motion to accept office on condition that, in each province where a majority had been won, the Congress leaders were satisfied that the (non-elected) governor would refrain from using his 'discretionary power', which rendered elective office meaningless in cases of strong disagreement. How this could be ascertained was unclear, and so Congress took office. G. D. Birla was among those who considered this decision a reassuring sign of the strength of the right, and he noted the ease with which Nehru capitulated, with a little persuasion from Gandhi. There was a second important result of the 1937 elections that would have pleased Birla and other money men. Contesting for legislative assembly seats was shown to require finance beyond anything the Congress possessed, but that wealthy business-men and some mass organizations, like the farmers, did have. It was a sobering discovery for many would-be seekers of elective office.

Ministries were formed in six provinces, and the Congress and mass organizations saw their memberships rocket with expectations of vast changes. These were dashed as left supporters angrily watched the new Congress ministers resort to police measures to deal with old tensions between communities and classes in their provinces, a confirmation of the latent political conservatism of most elected Congressmen. Nevertheless, the rhetoric of the left continued to resound in legislatures and in the streets even as the Congress moved un-waveringly rightwards. Cordial relations were established between Congress ministers and upper echelon bureaucrats.

An early and vexing issue on which a compromise was reached pertained to the release of political prisoners. Most of the governors accepted that this had to be arranged but managed to deflect the demand for a general amnesty by insisting that each case must be reviewed. There was agreement that the repressive laws of 1932 would have to be repealed; however, it became a matter of embarrassment when, soon after they were withdrawn, many Congress ministers spoke of reimposing them in order to put down communal rioting and strikes fomented by an increasingly frustrated left. To the delight, if not the sincere admiration, of many British observers, the Congress Working Committee agreed that the 1932 laws were necessary to defend life and property.

OTHER POLITICAL ACTORS

The election campaign had encouraged cooperation between the Congress and the Muslim League in the United Provinces, mainly for the purpose of denying victory to an officially backed landlord party there, but also because League members were as disappointed as the Congress that the 1935 Constitution made the imperial centre stronger than ever. A return to the amity between the Congress and the League following their Lucknow Pact of 1916 seemed possible, except for the sheer size of the Congress majority. Seeing no need to settle for anything less than maximum advantage, Congress leaders spurned a League proposal for a coalition in the United Provinces and even indulged in the fantasy of absorbing into the Congress those Leaguers who had won seats. This tactic was not unrealistic for the right to consider, since the League there was made up of zamindars and other large landholders, as well as military and civil officers unlikely to support the overtly left-wing aims of the United Provinces ministry – Nehru's home base. Inevitably, the United Provinces Congress did dilute its demands as a result of the dominant weight of its own right wing, but the rebuffed Muslim League thenceforward determined to build its own mass base in order to stand more successfully in future elections; the sole means for accomplishing that was an intensification of its ideological differences with Congress; that is, playing on the religious fears of Muslims. Thus, soon after the formation of Congress ministries, communal strife intensified in the heartland of northern India.

Bengal, with its large Muslim population, had a similar problem and outcome. Muslim politicians, more radical there, had long advocated abolition of zamindars without compensation; in 1937 they called for reduced rents and compulsory primary education. Militant demands such as these caused uneasy relations between Bengali Muslims and the League under Jinnah. But to ally with the Congress in Bengal was even more fraught with risk. Not only were most zamindars Hindus there, but Gandhi continued to reject attacks upon landlordism. With few of their co-religionists in jail but an enormous number of poor tenant farmers, Bengali Muslims considered tenancy relief more important than the release of political prisoners, which had been the first aim of the Congress ministry. In the end it proved simpler for Bengal's Muslim leaders to trim some of their radical demands than to forsake their constituency, so they uneasily entered the Muslim League.

All attempts to achieve coalition between Congress and League politicians in provinces with numerous Muslims were bedevilled by deepening communal tension. Ominously, Hindu and Muslim organizations had begun to form paramilitaries such as the Rashtriya Swayamsavak Sangh (RSS, the National Cultural Association), which was started in Maharashtra by followers of the Hindu Mahasabha in the 1920s. By the early 1930s the RSS had spread into the United Provinces and Punjab, and boasted a membership of 100,000 trained and disciplined fighters for Hindu causes. They were matched by similar Muslim groups, such as the one in Punjab formed as a check against Hindu and Sikh bullies. Mounting lethal hatreds were to occupy socialists like Nehru and Gandhians alike during the late 1930s.

By that time other major political and class alignments had taken shape and were to persist through the last phase of the freedom movement and the early years of independence. Particularly significant was the right-leaning parochial politics found in the diverse social and cultural settings of the lower middle class, which was empowered as never before by Gandhi's organizational reform of Congress. The centre of political gravity in the late 1930s had shifted downwards to the popular but fragmented base of society.

Unlike Nehru, most Congressmen were not internationalist in outlook. Freedom was defined as a release from British rule, a *freedom from*; but there also was a growing realization of a need for *freedom to* give lasting political form to a sentiment constituted by the ethnic markers of language, religion and common residence. The wariness about internationalism was to a degree dictated by Congress's adversaries: on one side was the Muslim League and its justification in being part of worldwide Islam, but on the other were the ethnically fractured, subnationalist movements of Sikhs in the north, and of Telugu-, Tamil- and Marathi-speakers in south and central India. In addition, the majority of Tamils and Maharashtrians partly defined themselves in political opposition to brahmans, who enjoyed a high profile in the Congress, especially among its leaders. Fragmentation of this sort put pressure on the leadership to counter with an Indian identity that offered places to Muslims and the host of others in whose names and for whose futures the Congress wanted to speak. Most Congressmen knew that to fail to take cognizance of the diverse religious, linguistic or other cultural elements would be to pass advantages to other politicians and parties. Congress dared not to trifle with these identities as it did with the poor.

Congressmen knew and feared the political attractions of V. D. Savarkar's Hindu Mahasabha and the RSS. Sarvarkar was an early twentieth-century Tilak follower and terrorist who spoke of a Hindu India in his 1923 pamphlet entitled *Hindutva* ('the essence of Hinduism'). This he saw as a religio-cultural and political category, which he claimed could be made compelling for all who lived in the subcontinent, considered themselves descended from a common Aryan racial stock and cherished and kept alive a common tradition. When Savarkar attempted to be more specific about the attributes of this 'hindutva', what he had in mind resembled nothing so much as a Maharashtrian brahman of the Chitpavan sub-caste to which he belonged, as Tilak before him and Nathuram Godse, who was to be Gandhi's assassin, after.

Against this tendency towards fragmentary parochialism, with leanings towards intolerance and political conservatism, was the influence of big businessmen. They supported a genuinely pluralist and internationalist Congress, and they had diverse social origins: middle- to high-caste Hindus from all the regions from western Gujarat to eastern Bengal, and from northern Rajasthan to southern Madras; Muslims from an equally dispersed provenance; and a scattering of Parsis and Jews. Not surprisingly, these capitalists found it difficult to persuade many in the Congress of the 1930s that they were as patriotic as any other section of society, that their opposition to the British was something other than a self-interested concern to gain advantages over their British counterparts operating in the country. Hardest to persuade were those of the left who were doctrinally certain that Indian capitalists must be anti-nationalist collaborators in alliance with the imperialist capitalists; leftists were reinforced in that persuasion by Indian business's suppression of workers' demands for better conditions and pay during the long depression years.

The European war had thrust industrial development forward through the provision of military equipment and the substitution of Indian-made goods for those previously imported. By 1939, the eve of the Second World War, industrial self-sufficiency had been attained, and a major part of Indian output issued from Indian-owned factories. Another shift from older patterns was that the capital for this transition came from India itself, including remnants of a pre-capitalist time – its wealthy princes, who joined the ranks of industrial capitalists in the production of jute and textiles. Indian capital was also becoming prominent in shipping, insurance and banking, coal and tea, and was taking the lead in the formation of new industries such as cement and heavy chemicals.

India's tycoons skilfully lobbied for their interests through the Federation of Indian Chambers of Commerce and Industry (FICCI) from 1927 on. Soon the FICCI was accepted as representing Indian capital by the British, and Birla, whose money-lending ancestors had spread from their Rajasthan homeland throughout northern India, persuaded more of his capitalist colleagues that the best way forward in the turbulent 1920s and 1930s was to support the moderate elements within the Congress. Those who followed him into the

Congress added the weight of wealth to the political right to oppose the socialists, aping the strategy of the British in attempting to isolate the left from the nationalist mainstream.

Nevertheless, their political purposes differed from those of the government as much as their economic interests. Birla and men like him had discovered that there was good business to be made as nationalists. Independence, when it came – and Birla was certain that it would – would provide even better opportunities for Indian capitalism as long as anti-imperialism did not come to mean anti-capitalism and the left was denied hegemony in the freedom movement. Had the left of Congress achieved that sort of position, India's capitalists would have been as imperialist as any Briton of the time.

The Congress high command in the working committee during the 1930s always included those who had begun their political careers as Gandhians but had withdrawn from active involvement in village and Harijan uplift. They nevertheless remained personally close to Gandhi and regularly did his bidding to keep the left at bay. Among the ex-Gandhians were such future greats as C. Rajagopalachari, who became governor-general of independent India in 1948, Vallabhbhai Patel, Nehru's future deputy prime minister, and Rajendra Prasad, India's first president. Each appreciated the reliance of the Congress on the financial contributions from Indian businessmen to meet organization and election costs; hence all were close to Indian capitalists, who could expect a sympathetic viewing of their patriotic credentials.

THE RIGHT PREVAILS

While it is true that Congress became more ideologically vocal during the late 1930s, the views and purposes of rightists prevailed over socialists. On several key issues there was no serious conflict between the two sides. Both envisioned an Indian economy based upon a modern industrial foundation with a large, state-planned public sector, a strong, unified state capable of executing complex tasks of technological development and a society being transformed from particularistic and hierarchical caste relations to the modernity of equality and merit. On the other hand, Gandhians and the mass of India's people continued to inhabit a world of caste, of localism and of small property; they were distrustful of the modernist position, whether capitalist or socialist.

Gandhi held out a very different future from Nehru and his colleagues, one that fitted the expectations of India's lower middle class, the source of his enormous and continuing authority. His political constituency was certainly not the businessmen who paid him court and paid the bills he and others incurred to strengthen the Congress. True, his view of the role of capitalists was reassuring, just as his often expressed view of an Indian future based upon its villages might have been disturbing. India's rich held wealth as a trust, he said; it should not be taken from them but (voluntarily) deployed by them for the betterment of all. How this was to be accomplished – other than by supporting his causes – was for the wealthy themselves to decide; it must be left to their compassion and patriotism. His notions of trusteeship, non-violence, and consensual politics and his repudiation of class struggle did not go down so well with industrial workers. At the end of the 1930s they were a class toughened by two decades of strikes and confrontations with strikebreakers, the police and the army; they were also well led, by communists among others.

Between India's capitalists and proletarians were two other political classes. One was the not very numerous but nevertheless influential class of professionals and intellectuals, especially the western-educated, who, along with trade unionists, provided much of the support the socialists enjoyed. The other political class were Gandhi's people, the large Indian social stratum of the Indian lower-middle class found in thousands of small towns, a few larger cities and throughout the countryside. Between 1920 and 1930, while the overall population of the subcontinent increased by 11 per cent, the urban population rose by 18 per cent; at its core were city and small-town bazaar people, artisans, teachers and other lower public employees. These townsmen were linked to the other major constituents of the lower-middle class, the independent farmers and other rural small property holders. Their social objectives were to acquire and hold enough resources to preserve themselves from the humiliation of poverty and extreme economic dependency and, if possible, to become the patrons of others.

It was to members of this class, with their distrust and envy of those with secure wealth and their loathing for those below themselves, that Gandhi had passed the control of Congress organizations by means of his reforms from the 1920s, in the belief that he could manage their fears and shape their aspirations. Under his organizational reforms, which laid the groundwork for his mass satyagrahas, Congress was structured in three tiers, at the base of which were spokesmen for the lower-middle class of locally dominant castes and petty commodity producers. Middle-ranking castes – such as the Jats of the Punjab and western United Provinces, the Patidars of Gujarat, the Yadavas and Kumris of Bihar, the Marathas of Maharashtra-Bombay, the Kammas and Reddis of Telugu-speaking (Andhra) Madras and the Pallis of Tamil-speaking Madras – represented the Congress locally. Most of them had achieved greater literacy and some financial security during the 1920s and 1930s, and they were to benefit from two later significant changes: the abolition of the zamindari settlement of the 1950s, which shifted land from absentee landlords to smaller resident agrarian entrepreneurs like themselves; and the Green Revolution of the mid-1960s on, which substantially increased their wealth. Even in the 1920s, however, leaders of these middling caste/lower middle-class rural and small-town groupings had begun to insert themselves into the second tier of the Congress, the provincial level, which had been created in 1920 for mass mobilization. Under Gandhi's guidance and through his labours, the myriad local village and town sections of the Congress became linked at this level.

Gandhi's personal political network was sustained by a routine of correspondence with thousands of people and reinforced by personal contact as he incessantly travelled, usually in third-class railway cars emptied of their poor occupants so that he could conduct his important work. (His associate, the poet Sarojini Naidu, once commented that no one would ever know what it cost his followers to keep Mr Gandhi poor.) Gandhi's most impressive and least recognized accomplishment was this network, an achievement chronicled in a remarkable collection of over eighty thick volumes of letters and other writings, together with a detailed calendar of his engagements.

To followers in every part of the subcontinent, he provided the national political viewpoints they required, or he wished them to have, through his visits, his letters and the multilingual publications *Young India* and *Harijan*. And, when he needed them, he marshalled his battalions. During his mass campaigns, his highly publicized visits brought out hundreds of thousands to hear him and be exhorted to participate in his programmes of village and 'Harijan' uplift and khadi spinning. These programmes were low cost, co-operative endeavours, easily sustained by the resources available to rural societies, and promoting them enlarged the reputations of his immediate clients, his 'nationalist subcontractors', with scores of thousands of their own local clients. His diffuse following gave Gandhi the enormous power he enjoyed from the late 1920s until the time of the death.

He had retired from the Congress in 1934, ostensibly to devote all his time to 'village work', but it was as much to distance himself from the burgeoning left-led mass Congress organizations with whom he carried little influence. By the middle of the 1930s, Gandhi had added what he called basic education to his programme of khadi and the uplift of untouchables. His aim was to raise the status of manual work through literacy in the regional languages of the country. As in his organizational reforms of 1921, the commonly spoken regional languages became the media of instruction and of public communication. Also under his urging, Congress ministries in Bombay and Madras imposed prohibition, thereby denying the provincial governments lucrative revenues from the licensing of liquor shops. Nevertheless, both left and untouchable activists considered his campaigns during the 1930s irrelevant, either to the achievement of freedom or to the amelioration of social evils.

Before Gandhi's time, communalist politicians had sought to mobilize others on the basis of shared traditional values, but did this less successfully than Gandhi. Unlike other Congress leaders, he did not spurn rural traditions as backward or as barriers to progress. Rather he said they were the true foundation for India's future; the others were spurious and repugnant. He offered to defend these values and institutions on condition that his political clients adopted a minimal set of his principles – non-violence, Harijan uplift and khadi promotion – and eschewed class conflicts that might weaken the freedom struggle, even though this meant a variety of social injustices would remain as unaddressed as they had always been.

The non-agrarian sections of Gandhi's followers joined in tilting India's nationalist politics away from the collective means and ends of the socialist modernizers. They consisted of town and city occupational groups: bazaar traders; self-employed craftsmen who combined the production of goods with their sale locally and, through transport agents, in distant markets; assorted economic brokers, agents of big grain merchants who also engaged in petty money-lending; labour recruiters and contractors of piece-work production, who were thus linked downwards to an underclass of casual labourers and upwards to the major recruiters of labour among commercial and contractor groups; rent collectors; petty office holders and minor contractors of government services; and a host of minor religious functionaries. All these urban groups were linked to villages comprising the hinterland of any town by economic ties, often by political bonds, and always through marriage and religious relationships.

Gandhi provided a way for these often fragmented social elements of India to participate in nationalism by supporting programmes ostensibly opposed to big capitalism as well as to a socialism which threatened petty privileges. Leading this constituency, Gandhi faced and defeated the strongest bid for hegemony over the Congress by the left during the late 1930s. This proved one of the most impressive intervals in Gandhi's long political career, and from his victory he emerged with uncontested leadership for the final phase of the struggle for freedom.

INDIANS AND FOREIGNERS IN COMPETITION

On the other hand, businessmen appreciated the continuing Congress boycott of imported goods, which expanded their share of the market, and its tariff barriers against foreign (including British) imports. A growing concern among Indian capitalists was competition from subsidiaries of international firms beginning to operate in India. Most of these were largely financed by British capital and challenged the market share attained by Indian manufacturers of soap, rubber and tobacco products and chemicals and machines, whose demands for protection were unheeded. Commercial pressures like those of the late 1930s stimulated the first discussions of economic planning as a joint concern of Congress and business leaders. In 1938, Subhas Bose proposed a National Planning Committee of the Congress to be convened by Jawaharlal Nehru. This plan was met with enthusiasm and serious participation by Indian business tycoons, showing that Indian capital was effectively working with both sides of the Congress – the Gandhian right as well as the left of Bose and Nehru – to gain its ends.

The Congress ministry in Bombay pushed through anti-union laws in a nervous response to vague threats from some British and Indian capitalists to transfer their investments from Bombay to Bengal, Punjab or, better still, princely states bereft of labour legislation. The compliant Bombay law of November 1938 imposed compulsory arbitration of workplace disputes and jail sentences for illegal strikes, as well as increasing the difficulty for unions to win legal recognition. Opposition to this repressive law came from the Muslim League, from Ambedkar's untouchables and from some other non-Congress groups, who rallied in large meetings in Bombay and launched a brief, but effective, general strike throughout the province. The Congress regime in Bombay was more deeply discredited in the following year for using the police regulations imposed with the commencement of the war in Europe to repress a strike against a British-owned oil company. Neither Nehru nor Bose publicly opposed the Bombay ministers, fearing to upset Gandhi and the Congress right.

Gandhi remained aloof from formal Congress affairs in the late 1930s, but his hand was never far from the major levers of political action, as was perhaps most evident in the tentativeness of its agrarian policies. The Indian countryside contained a natural constituency for the Congress, and this was reflected in its large rural membership. Grievances of the mass of middle and small Indian farmers were many, though not as great as the plight of pauperized landless labourers – the detritus of a decade of depression. Indebtedness and heavy and rising rents punished the poorest most harshly, yet Congress regimes everywhere consistently failed the mass of their rural followers and, to the amazement of the British, actually offered relief to landlords. Thus was mocked the election manifesto promise, agreed at the Faizpur session in 1937, to abolish landlordism. Bihar presented the ultimate irony when zamindars actually threatened civil disobedience against some cautious changes in their privileges. Elsewhere, capitulations were numerous as Congress ministries proved no more sympathetic to agrarian distress than the landlord party of Unionists in Punjab.

AGITATIONS OF THE 1930S

It is little wonder that the countryside seethed. Membership in Kisan Sabhas increased and attained massive numbers by 1938, rising to a spectacular 250,000 members in Bihar. In addition, strong actions were organized in scattered localities: in Bengal for lower irrigation rates and rents; in Bihar for the restoration of lands from which tenants had been evicted; in the Punjab for lower land revenue and irrigation rates. Anti-zamindari demonstrations occurred in those parts of Andhra where a zamindari settlement had been imposed in 1802. The duly elected authorities met these actions with repression. Plainly, Congress governments had no patience with the militancy of agriculturists and other rural organizations in which leftists had achieved leading roles. In 1938 and 1939, agrarian militancy was actually condemned by the Congress leadership, including Nehru and Bose, who complained about the 'class war' in the countryside that pitched India's farmers against 'their' governments. Here was seen the firm Gandhian hand of restraint, not only against the unpatriotic demands being placed upon Congress regimes but also against attempts of poor tenants to force concessions from landlords. However, in none of this rural unrest were the problems of the most deprived of rural groups addressed. The landless and most penurious, who were almost always untouchables, were supposedly under the protection of Gandhi's Harijan movement.

Another political upheaval of the late 1930s where Gandhi's stilling hand was applied involved what he regarded as diversionary democratic movements. Within several princely states movements were stirring to gain the same civil rights enjoyed in British India. Gandhi mandated that Congress should not interfere with the political rights (or wrongs) of Indians living under princes, and he was quick to criticize the working committee when it responded sympathetically to pleas from farmers' leaders in princely Mysore for organizational support. The Congress session of 1938 ratified the policy of offering only moral support and sympathy to democratic demands in princely domains, specifically endorsing Gandhi's position that princes should increase civil liberties and reduce their own privileges, but only voluntarily. Still, lower-class pressure continued to grow, soon matching that of British India, and Gandhi grudgingly approved a satyagraha, but restricted it to a single small state in Gujarat where he enjoyed unusual support. He undertook a fast there that failed to achieve anything, and soon more assertive demonstrations demanding democratic rights began in a number of the major princely states.

Conditions were especially oppressive in Hyderabad, the largest princedom, where a Muslim ruler and a small elite controlled 90 per cent of government jobs. Urdu was the official language in a population overwhelmingly Hindu, half of whom spoke Telugu and the rest Marathi and Kannada. Hyderabadi speakers of Telugu and Marathi established cultural associations to promote their languages and to lobby for modest political reforms. By 1938, the Andhra movement of Telugu-speakers had organized successful non-violent oppositional activities, which Gandhi ordered stopped because they pitted Hindu subjects against a Muslim ruler.

But it was the unquenchable militancy of class politics pressing from below that brought the most serious crisis to the Congress during the 1930s. This came from the Congress left, which, with mass organizations, opposed the conservative drift of Congress ministries.

The All India Trades Union Congress, formed in 1920 by middle-class nationalists, had come under the growing influence of communists. Following the Meerut trials and the purge of communists from Congress unions, trade unionists of the left formed a separate federation of unions which was disbanded when the Comintern mandated a united front against fascism. Accordingly, the members rejoined the Trades Union Congress, where they remained an influential caucus along with members of the Congress Socialist Party. Another mass organization in which communists and other leftists involved themselves was the All India Kisan Sabha, from its first meeting in 1936. They formed one of the two major tendencies within the Kisan movement, insisting that its major problem was the struggle against landlords and debt.

The left drift extended to students as well. The All India Student Conference (to be called Federation later) was inaugurated by Jawaharlal Nehru and presided over by Muhammad Ali Jinnah in 1936, which suggested that its goals were moderate. Soon after its founding, however, spokesmen of left student provincial organizations demanded a radicalization of Congress policies and expressed admiration for the Soviet Union's efforts to organize anti-fascist fronts in Europe and China. Nehru visited Spain in 1938 to convey the solidarity of the Congress with the Republic against Franco, and he and Subhas Bose were consistently to speak for the Congress left in this regard.

Adding to the crescendo of radical demands was a move to re-elect Bose for a second consecutive term when the Congress met in Tripuri (Jabalpur), in the

Central Provinces. Nehru had been honoured by a second term the previous year, but his close relationship with Gandhi made him acceptable to most centrist Congressmen, in ways that the more independent Bose was not. The Tripuri 'crisis' arose when Bose's left-supported candidacy prevailed in January 1939, and Gandhi declared that the Bose victory was his personal defeat. A majority of members of the working committee thereupon resigned, and the Congress right denounced Bose's proposed election manifesto, which had set a time limit for a British response to the call of swaraj, and threatened a resumption of mass civil disobedience. An alternative resolution replacing the Bose demand was passed because Gandhi had put himself and his prestige behind it. Bose resigned the presidency, attempted to mobilize a resumption of civil disobedience and was banned for indiscipline from holding any Congress office for three years, including his presidency of the Bengal provincial Congress.

Internal conflict persisted over the continued repression by some ministries of labour and farmer movements, but it was prevented from becoming even more prolonged and intense by the British declaration of war in September 1939. India had become a belligerent against the Axis powers without even token consultation with state ministries or political leaders. This provided a perfect excuse for Congress to resign from its frustrating trial of ruling some of the provinces of India.

WAR AND THE LAST ACT BEGINS

When Britain declared war against the Axis powers, Indians were brought into the hostilities without consultation. Accordingly, Congress leaders announced that they would not cooperate with the war effort, took peaceful steps to impede it and were imprisoned. This left a generation of younger Congressmen to devise actions of their own. That these men were beyond Gandhi's personal control became clear as they launched increasingly violent anti-government actions which reached a crescendo of sabotage in August 1942. At this point, Gandhi reasserted his authority with a call for individual acts of non-violent protest (satyagraha) against the British.

During the Second World War, however, it was not Bose, Gandhi or Nehru who set the pace and programmes of politics, but Mohammad Ali Jinnah, head of the Muslim League and leader of a movement for an independent Pakistan that took definite shape in the 1940s. His was a conception of nation and community different from that of Gandhi or Nehru, in that he rejected an India consisting of diverse social and religious collectivities, whether under a secular commitment to a modernizing social democracy of Nehru's design or under a Gandhian vision of numerous autonomous communities. Instead, he posited that Islam constituted a sufficient basis for separate nationhood, that the India under Britain actually comprised two separate nations whose destinies could not be attained except as independent of both Britain and each other. It was a brutally simple notion that was to command the politics of the 1940s.

Jinnah shared with Gandhi certain social attributes that favoured his rise to leadership. Like Gandhi, Jinnah was born into the somewhat politically marginal merchant class. Hence, he did not belong to the traditionally educated classes; nor did he spring from martial or landed families. Jinnah, like Gandhi, was a lawyer, which provided him with spatial as well as social mobility, though, in contrast to Gandhi, Jinnah was a brilliant early success. Again, each began his political activities as secularist and moderate, but each made religion the centre of his personal politics, even though neither was conventionally religious.

After a period of intense involvement in the khilafat movement of the 1920s, Jinnah withdrew from politics and built a great fortune as a lawyer, much of it in England, where he participated in the Round Table conferences on the constitutional future of India, where Gandhi nominally represented the Congress. Jinnah was cool to the idea of a separate nation for Indian Muslims, called Pakistan (an acronym constructed from the letters of the provinces of British India in which Muslims constituted the bulk of the population), when it was first formulated in the early 1930s. Possibly he believed that a major role awaited him under the new political scheme provided by the 1935 constitution. However, when the Congress leadership refused to consider electoral accommodations that would allow Muslim ministries to emerge from the dominantly Muslim provinces and provide a political base and role for himself and his co-religionists, Jinnah warmed to the separatist view, and flung himself energetically into its attainment at the 1940 session of the Muslim League at Lahore in the Punjab.

However vague it might have been, the Lahore resolution did mark a starting point for the emergence of Pakistan. The year 1940 was also the moment when Jinnah commenced his mission as 'Great Leader' (*Qaid-i-Azam*). Above all, the task then was to counter the Congress claim that it alone spoke for the political aspirations of all Indians. By this point it had become clear that Congress leaders, and Nehru in particular, would not agree to Jinnah's demand for cooperation with the Muslim League as equals in the attainment of freedom. Consequently, Jinnah offered the British wartime cooperation in return for a commitment to treat the League on a par with the Congress, which was made easier after Congress resigned its provincial ministries in 1939 and suspended all negotiations with the government.

More difficult for Jinnah were his strained relations with other Muslim politicians. He had constantly to guard against losing what soft support he had from other Muslim political leaders in the Punjab and Bengal. Politicians there looked suspiciously upon any arrangements under which they and their populous provinces might lose importance to some abstract 'Pakistan'. Given this anxiety, Jinnah prudently said little about specific political arrangements; that is, the kind of state Indian Muslims might seek to achieve. Instead he concentrated on the ideological encompassment of Muslims in an all-embracing Islam. 'Pakistan' did not at first mean a nation state, an entity with fixed boundaries and a centre, but an ambiguous embodiment of religious sentiment, an extensive confessional community. It was a formulation that recalled the *mahajanapada* political formation of the first millennium BCE, when the community *was* the state.

Throughout the complex and indeterminate wartime negotiations with the Congress and imperial officials, Jinnah's difficulties with provincial leaders in the Punjab and Bengal spread to those of Sind and the Northwest Frontier Province. Personal disagreements and suspicions deepened among all these leaders, and each province was riven by factional divisions. All agreed on one crucial point, however: Jinnah was the 'Great Leader', free to speak for the 'nation', and he would remain that as long as he did not interfere in the provincial politics of his followers.

Though he was not a Punjabi, Jinnah was accepted as the leading spokesman for the large Muslim majority of that province, whose landlords feared the implementation of radical land reform if Congress succeeded. In the course of the war, Jinnah's independence and prestige continually rose as he skilfully avoided the domination of the Congress movement while wringing from Gandhi an acceptance of the idea of a 'Pakistan' in a confederated arrangement of some sort. As the war neared its end, the British looked again at changes in the Indian constitution, but Jinnah refused to ease their passage by insisting that his League was the sole representative of all the Muslims of the subcontinent. His stance was deliberately intended to challenge the Congress's secular principles and the position of Muslims within the Congress as well. When a Labour government was formed in Britain in 1945, all discussions of constitutions were reduced to the single question of how to transfer government power to India. With the final dramatic events at hand, Jinnah would be an undisputed key player.

INDIA IN THE WAR

That India would be a major staging base for the war became inevitable when German and Japanese policies were coordinated. Fearing that the nationalists would use the disruptions of the war to advance their cause, the British modified the 1935 Constitution to permit a take-over of provincial administrations and a restriction of civil liberties. This action received approval from Westminster in May 1940 when the government passed into Winston Churchill's hands, as Hitler's panzers were sweeping over the Low Countries and France. Churchill's imperialism remained obdurate as Japanese victories in Southeast Asia brought India closer to the war. Famously, he had proclaimed that he would not 'preside over the liquidation of the British Empire', however expedient for winning Indian support of the war. Nevertheless, he adopted an ostensibly compliant attitude, agreeing that Stafford Cripps, a Labourite minister in his national coalition government, should have political talks with the Congress and others in the spring of 1942.

The viceroy, Lord Linlithgow, rejected an offer from the Congress to support the war effort in return for post-war political concessions. Gandhi had apparently agreed with the offer and other proposals for cooperation by the Congress at the time. Two years later he was to reverse himself and, incidentally, repudiate the support he gave Britain during the First World War.

Rejection of the Congress offer came from imperial bureaucrats who were anxious to confront nationalists and to regain the dominance lost by the concessions of the 1935 Act and the period of Congress rule from 1937 to late 1939.

Some years before, when Nehru and Krishna Menon were visiting Europe, Cripps had told them that the Labour Party was committed to the transfer of power in India to a constituent assembly elected on universal suffrage providing that British interests were protected for a transitional period. Cripps's mission on behalf of the British cabinet in early 1942 acknowledged increasing pressures for change that arose from several sources. First, there were Labour members like Cripps and Clement Attlee in the cabinet who personally believed that Indian freedom was a right; their belief was reinforced by sympathizers in Britain who pressured the war cabinet for a more liberalized policy. Then there was the US president, Franklin Roosevelt, who was eager to support the British war effort but was mindful of the historical American resentment of the British. Roosevelt had told Churchill, when they met to synchronize policies after Pearl Harbor, that there was considerable American sympathy for the Indian nationalist cause. The Chinese leader Chiang Kai-shek also announced China's support for Indian freedom. Though Churchill was forced into a more public concessionary position, he yielded none of his private and effective opposition to Indian nationalism.

For several years the National Congress offered little challenge to the wartime British. The dominant right wing and Gandhi continued to regard the Congress left as its major problem. Left-wing Congressmen demanded opposition to Britain's war, and they managed to extract a commitment at the 1940 annual session that civil disobedience would resume should the conditional offer of Congress's wartime cooperation be rejected. At the same time, Gandhi was given exclusive responsibility for the timing and prosecution of such resumption.

Aware that the government yearned for a pretext to unleash its formidable new powers against the Congress, he authorized a few trusted followers to court arrest by making anti-war speeches. They included Nehru and a Gandhian of long standing, Vinoba Bhave, who was later to be considered Gandhi's spiritual heir. Others followed, and by late 1941, 20,000 designated volunteers were jailed. While communists supported the war after the Soviet Union was invaded by Germany, Congress and non-Congress socialists denounced the war and also Gandhi's ineffectual opposition. Those who tried to mount alternative anti-war actions were usually picked off by an alert and powerful police force, though there were exceptions. A courageous and effective civil disobedience was launched by Subhas Bose, won wide support among Muslims and farmers in remote parts of Bengal and spread to Mysore and Kerala, because it was directed against landlords and their police allies as well as against the war.

The improving economic conditions in 1940 may explain why there was not more militancy in India. As elsewhere in the world, state spending in anticipation of the war had stimulated an economy battered by two decades of depression. Agricultural prices began a slow and steady upward movement with the first mobilizations, and, as during the European war of 1914–18, industrial employment rose with the production of war-goods. As the war curtailed European and Japanese imports, a wider section of the domestic market was opened for Indian-produced goods. Between 1939 and 1942 factory employment increased by a third. Even more than mere import substitution was involved in this surge, for by 1941 India was making automobiles, ships and even aircraft.

For Muslims the early war years were a time of political consolidation. Jinnah insisted that the Muslim League was the sole representative of Muslim interests and had a veto over all proposed constitutional arrangements. Among politicians there was a growing sentiment favouring a separate Muslim homeland. The idea was broached in pamphlets written by Punjabi Muslim students at Cambridge University in 1933 and 1935, which dubbed the future nation 'Pakistan'. The word was formed by combining the initials of Punjab, Afghanistan, Kashmir and Sind, and the suffix of Baluchistan; the resulting acronym meant 'land of the pure' in Urdu. Oddly, Bengal, with the largest concentration of Muslims, was not included. Suggestions for a separate, Muslim homeland won the cynical sympathy of British officials, who were always interested in seeing divisions among political groupings in the subcontinent. With the fall of Burma, war suddenly came to India's borders in March 1942; at the same time the German invasion of the Soviet Union led India's communists to support what was now a 'people's' war. The proximity of war closed nationalist ranks and intensified demands for strong mass resistance to the British, a mood that grew with the news of British defeats. Opposition to the war effort now united Gandhians and socialists in and out of the Congress, and brought a large patriotic following to Subhas Bose. Managing to elude imprisonment as the Congress's most radical leader, Bose had fled to Germany, determined to take what assistance he could in his struggle for India's freedom. From there he was taken to Japan by submarine and finally to Japanese-held Singapore, where he proclaimed that an Indian Independence Army would free India by military means. The army he recruited consisted of 20,000 Indian prisoners of war in Japanese camps, soldiers who had been surrendered by their commanders in Malaya. The subsequent campaign through the jungles of Burma at the side of Japanese soldiers was cheered by Indian nationalists.

THE CRIPPS MISSION

British vulnerability and the continued pressure from their American and Chinese allies forced a changed attitude towards Indian reform. Churchill now proposed dominion status, with the additional right of a free India to leave the Commonwealth should this be the decision of a constituent assembly. In return, Indians were to agree to participate in the prosecution of the war under continued British authority. Sir Stafford Cripps was sent to India in March 1942 to explain provisions of this offer to Indians, leaving Churchill to soothe the viceroy, Linlithgow, who was outraged by his exclusion from the decision. Churchill explained that, if properly handled, the American critics would become convinced that any failure to reach agreement arose from the intransigence of the Indians.

Cripps actually left for India still unclear about what could be offered to Indian leaders, and what his cabinet colleagues would agree to. For their part, the Indians gave Cripps a somewhat confused response. Gandhi declined to be involved in discussions, leaving it to the designated Congress negotiators, Nehru and the Maulana Azad. They concentrated on settling the role of Indians in the central executive of the proposed government of India and interpreted Cripps's offer to be nothing less than complete Congress control of a cabinet, with the viceroy reduced to a figurehead. This was an arrangement which had not been imagined in London. The resulting muddle, some deliberately sown by Churchill, persuaded his cabinet colleagues to recall Cripps and declare the talks a failure owing to Indian opposition. The dashed hopes of the Cripps mission and the widespread Indian suspicion of British insincerity stoked a new militancy, with Gandhi initiating the 'Quit India' movement that extended from the summer of 1942 to the end of the war in 1945.

QUIT INDIA

Two wars were conducted on Indian soil for several years: one against Japan and the other against the imperial regime. The 'Quit India' campaign proclaimed by the Congress Working Committee on 8 August 1942 was a declaration of war. Non-violence was to be maintained as in the past, but the tight discipline of former campaigns was relaxed. Congress leaders knew that they faced immediate arrest and detention, so Gandhi announced that Indians must conduct the righteous war as best they could. He also extended the rules of engagement beyond courting jail to include a general strike, which he had long banned. The reasons for this new militancy on his part have long been debated. Nehru thought the reason for the change of tactics was his conviction that the British would crumble under the combined assault of Germany and Japan, and therefore British promises of post-war concessions were worthless. But another possible contributing reason might have been the pressure from below of long frustrations no longer containable through moderate measures. The massive spontaneous demonstrations that broke out when Congress leaders were arrested on 9 August, as they expected they would be, lend credence to this latter explanation.

The swiftness and strength of the British reaction confirmed that the imperial apparatus had been poised for this eventuality since 1939, when the war began. The military reverses in Asia had engendered panic among British military and bureaucratic officials who envisaged the imminent loss of Assam and Bengal to the combined Japanese and Indian National Army forces advancing through Burma; boats were sequestered and destroyed in Bengal lest they fall to the invader.

The consequent disruption of riverine transport contributed to the terrible Bengal famine of the following year. As the war continued, officials were dismayed when Indian businessmen withdrew their support. Fat profits had been realized early in the war from legitimate commerce as well as black-market operations, but some businessmen had suffered loses in Malaya and Burma, where they had followed the British flag, and, in any case, they resented the new taxes that were meant to soak up excess wartime profits. Of the many who believed that the day of the Raj was now over, some even thought that the interest of India as a whole would be advanced by joining the Japanese Co-prosperity Sphere. By late 1942, however, the Japanese seemed to have stalled on the Assam border, and the more normal cooperative relationship between Indian business and the British resumed, encouraged by the violence with which strikes were suppressed by British police.

Work stoppages opened the Quit India campaign in August. Trade unionists joined students to face the massed police and soldiers in several cities in northern and western India, and later in the month anti-government demonstrations were launched in the adjacent countryside, with students once again active as mobilizers. Communications facilities and military installations were attacked by rural guerrillas in parts of Bengal, Orissa, Bombay and Karnataka. While these activities did little to impede the prosecution of the war, by the end of 1943 some colonial officials were expressing concern at the pitch of civilian hostility to their rule. Retaliations escalated from police shootings to the destruction of whole villages, public flogging and even machine-gunning by aircraft in eastern India. Between August 1942 and December 1943, hundreds of occasions when unarmed demonstrators were fired upon were recorded. Fully a third of these occurred in Bombay, resulting in nearly 2000 casualties; in addition, some 2500 persons were sentenced to whipping.

In the revolutionary atmosphere of 1942 and 1943 the major actors were students. Official claims that urban and rural disorder was the work of criminals and hooligans were shown to be hollow, as widespread arrests and even deaths of middle- and even upper-caste students became public, and the police admitted that there were relatively few attacks against property. Zamindars and landlords who were considered unpatriotic were denied their rents, but these were few thanks to the increasing conviction that the British could well lose the war.

As usual, militancy was greater in some places than others. One previous hotbed of nationalist activity, the Punjab, saw little anti-British action between 1942 and 1945 because the lines of tripartite communal conflict among Muslims, Sikhs and Hindus had so hardened as to make resistance to the Raj secondary. In addition, the economic prosperity resulting from war purchases and remittances from Punjabi soldiers damped down patriotism. Madras too was quiet; the Congress there was led by Chakravarti Rajagopalachari, who preferred continued negotiation to strife. His moderation was reinforced in the Telugu-speaking districts of Madras and in Kerala where, because of significant communist influence, the war was supported.

Though anti-government actions were met with severity to prevent disruption of the war, the ultimate victory went to the nationalists largely because of defeatism and demoralization among the British leaders. General Archibald Wavell, on becoming viceroy in late 1943, told Churchill that the repressive force necessary to hold India after the war ended would exceed Britain's means, even if world opinion permitted such an effort.

Paradoxically, too, police repression and imprisonment restored the reputation of Congress soiled by the regressive state ministries it had led between 1937 and 1939. British prisons also sheltered Congress leaders from difficult decisions they would otherwise have faced: whether to welcome or to condemn a Japanese victory, and whether to support Subhas Bose's 'Azad Hind' (Free India) movement and Indian National Army. To many, Bose's programme resembled that of the Japanese fascists, who were in the process of losing their gamble to achieve Asian ascendancy through war. Nevertheless, the success of his soldiers in Burma had stirred as much patriotic sentiment among Indians as the sacrifices of imprisoned Congress leaders.

THE ECONOMY IN WAR

Deepening social distress as the war drew to a close benefited the Congress cause. During the war, an inflated currency chased limited commodities, including foodstuffs, and flourishing black markets easily evaded the feeble food rationing schemes. Shortages turned into dearth in many places and into a terrible famine in Bengal in 1943, where, during the summer and autumn, the coastal zones were without food because the boats had been removed to thwart the possible Japanese invasion in 1942. Starving refugees from the coastal areas thronged the roads to Calcutta, and three million people are reckoned to have perished.

While disaster haunted the poor in places like Bengal, great wealth was accumulated by others. Some windfall profits were taken partly from Bengal's misfortune, but far more from the wartime economy. Indeed, the Indian economy was transformed from being a debtor, whose service charges augmented the Home Charges, into a major holder of British debt as a result of forced loans and the deferred-payment purchase of war-goods. In the course of the war, Indian producers added a range of new industrial goods to their output, including aircraft, and Indian capitalists began to participate in planning discussions with Congress leaders to assure that the momentum of technical development gained during the war did not slacken. G. D. Birla and J. R. D. Tata initiated technical agreements and collaborations with UK and US firms, and devised a scheme for licensed technology transfers in 1944, called the 'Bombay Plan'. A doubling of India's per capita income through an intensive industrial drive over fifteen years was ambitiously prophesied. (The model for this was the Soviet industrialization of the 1930s, which had been forced by Stalin, but the Indian case differed in achieving industrial development by a mix of state and private sectors.)

JINNAH'S CHOICE

Optimistic prospects such as these assumed that independence could be negotiated peacefully with the British after the war. No account was taken of, or allowance made for, a possibly violent partition that could accompany the call for a separate Muslim homeland in the subcontinent. The Muslim League, along with the Communist Party, prospered during hostilities. When Congress withdrew from government in Madras, United Provinces, Bihar, Central Provinces and Orissa at the beginning of the war, the League improved its position in those places as well as in Assam, Sind, Bengal and the Northwest Frontier. In addition, the League strengthened itself tactically by organizing paramilitary adjuncts to defend Muslims and their neighbourhoods, and by addressing class interests in several ways. In Bengal and Punjab, the League adopted radical social policies as it strove to replace the leftist leadership of Muslim tenant farmers who struggled against Hindu zamindars, landlords and moneylenders. In other contexts, the League persuaded Muslim businessmen that they could enlarge their share of trade and manufacture if they had more political advantages. These and other arguments were widely publicized through the newspapers devoted to the League's causes in many parts of northern India.

As the war drew to a close, all minds were freer to refocus on the struggle for independence. In May 1946, when another British cabinet mission convened Indian politicians at Simla, Jinnah seemed vulnerable, even though he was the sole spokesman for the League. He enjoyed little support within the Punjab provincial assembly or among the Muslim-led ministry of that important state. His standing with the British remained high, however, for even though they no more agreed with the idea of a separate Muslim state than the Congress did, government officials appreciated the simplicity of a single negotiating voice for all of India's Muslims. This circumstance reinforced Jinnah's preference for stressing Islamic ideological claims rather than entering interminable arguments with his suspicious and divided followers over the concrete structure of government to succeed the Raj. The emphasis upon a religiously defined conception of nationhood rewarded the League, for it won three-quarters of the Muslim vote in the 1946 elections for provincial assemblies, a popular mandate that it had failed to achieve in 1937.

This was a triumph for Jinnah, who hastened to interpret the vote as a popular demand for a subcontinental homeland, and he encouraged his followers to celebrate the communal victory that the elections had delivered. Tensions heightened between Muslims and Hindus and Sikhs in the Punjab and elsewhere in north India, for, notwithstanding the League's success in 1946, it was unable to establish provincial ministries anywhere except in Sind, because Congress negotiated coalition ministries to exclude the League in several other provinces. Most galling was the situation in the Punjab, where Congress allied with Sikhs to form a ministry.

At this point important decisions from London changed the terms of play. The Attlee government announced that power was to be transferred 'to responsible Indian hands' sooner than had been expected, and that Jinnah's demand for League control over the whole of the Punjab and Bengal, with their large Hindu and Sikh minorities, was rejected.

Jinnah now faced a disagreeable choice. Muslims could remain in a weakly federated Indian union under the domination of Congress, or a partitioning of the subcontinent could be accepted that consisted of the 'mutilated' western districts of Punjab and the eastern districts of Bengal, minus Calcutta. It was hard to see how such a divided state could be governed, much less how it could offer any protection to the millions of Muslims who chose to remain in the Indian Republic. With little prospect of instantly creating a strong central authority and political institutions, Jinnah was again compelled to make Islamic ideology the poor substitute for a state that would lack both adequate resources and institutions. Upon a religiously legitimated centre was placed the heavy burden of overcoming the subnational patriotism and interests of Punjab and Bengal. A Muslim polity had to be constructed from the unpromising materials of a territorially and politically fractured people and a religious ideology with no obvious relevance to modern statehood.

The contrast with India could hardly have been greater; its secular ideology had been inherited from the British along with a viable institutional and constitutional framework of federalism with an already strong centre. Congress leaders, especially Sardar Patel, moved rapidly to increase central power by playing off competing provincial sentiments and interests, much as the British had when they held the centre under the 1935 act.

An astute politician, Jinnah appreciated that replacing the Raj at the centre of Pakistan could not occur with the same ease; it was for this reason that he took on the first post-independence governor-generalship. If there was to be a viable centre, the most rapid way was for Jinnah himself to become that.

At the end of the war, the communists for their part had to overcome the double opprobrium of having supported the war against the Axis powers and having upheld Jinnah's demands for a separate Muslim homeland (in accordance with Lenin's doctrine of self-determination for ethnic nationalities in the Soviet Union). Restored to legality during the war after having been outlawed in 1934, the communists used their freedom to organize, and party membership rose from 4000 in 1942 to over 100,000 in 1948, and many times that number were enrolled in trade unions and kisan and student mass organizations that were led by communists. Work with farmers in many parts of the country provided the Communist Party with a large 'vote bank' upon which it could call in elections when the war ended; it stood third after the Congress and League. One consequence of this prominence was the capture of intellectuals in many parts of India, but especially in Calcutta. Communists were well poised for the final act of the freedom movement that commenced in 1945.

THE BITTER VICTORY OF PARTITION

Frustratingly slow and discontinuous negotiations brought freedom at long last, but freedom entailed death on a scale remarkable even in a world that had been at war for a decade. Both negotiation and violence were perpetrated by the same parties: Hindus, Muslims and Sikhs.

Negotiations between the Congress and the League briefly recommenced in the last days of the war. In the late summer of 1944, Gandhi and Jinnah discussed the idea of a Muslim homeland following the anticipated British transfer of power. Rejecting proposals for plebiscites to determine if separation was desired, Jinnah put forth a demand for a Pakistan territory comprised of all provinces with a majority of Muslims, namely the Punjab, Sind, Baluchistan, the Northwest Frontier, Bengal and Assam. Any possible agreement was complicated by the certitude of the League leaders that once the war ended Congress would reassert the provincial power it had given up in 1939, and would in all likelihood win back the provinces where the League had installed ministries. The failure of the discussions shifted attention to new proposals from London.

Churchill instructed the viceroy to free the Congress leaders imprisoned during the war so that they might participate in a conference to discuss the next steps. Held at Simla, the viceregal summer headquarters in the Himalayas, the conference was doomed because from the first Congress was assumed by Lord Wavell to represent caste Hindus only, in the same way that the League was supposed to represent Muslims. Congress protested that among its members and its leaders were low-caste Indians and Muslims as well; not only was the Muslim Maulana Abul Kalam Azad the leader of the Congress delegation to Simla, he had been Congress president in 1940. Jinnah, for his part, insisted that the League must speak for all Muslims as a condition of further participation in the conference. This scuttled the conference and, in effect, validated Jinnah's claim that the League could veto any constitutional arrangements that the British sought to impose.

DECOLONIZING ASIA

Conditions overseas no longer permitted a stalemate. In July 1945 the Labour Party swept Churchill's Tories from office on a wave of national political change which included an end to imperialism. The demands of the Vietnamese and Indonesians for independence from their respective French and Dutch rulers, and the onset of their armed resistance to the restoration of European rule, added to the anti-imperialist post-war climate. It was thus an irony that British-led Indian troops who had been involved in the Japanese surrender in Indochina and Indonesia were charged with handing the territories back to French and Dutch officials.

In the new post-war situation, the call by the new Labour Prime Minister, Clement Attlee, for Indian elections – the first since 1937 – was only to be expected. So was another government decision: to try several hundred Indian soldiers who had served as officers in Bose's army. When the first trial, in which a Hindu, a Muslim and a Sikh were charged, was staged at the Red Fort in Delhi in November 1945 there was an outcry from the Muslim League and Congress, as well as dangerous grumbling in the Indian army in the Punjab. The loyalty of Indian soldiers serving in Indochina and Indonesia was now in question. It transpired that Wavell had expressed anxiety about committing Indians troops there for that very reason, but had been overruled by the wartime commander in Asia, Viscount Mountbatten, who was soon to begin a brief but significant career in India.

Wavell's problems in 1945 were not confined to the loyalty of Indian soldiers. Post-war unemployment exacerbated the distress caused by poor harvests in the usually food-surplus provinces of Bombay and Bengal, which sharply reduced rations. Then, in November 1945, students took to the streets of Calcutta to demand an end of the Indian National Army trials and were met by police gunfire which killed two of them – a Hindu and a Muslim, so that the unity across religion was symbolically important. Calcutta was restored to order only after yet more shooting.

Although both Gandhi and Nehru defended them, many Congress leaders condemned these police actions. The protests were a signal to the British of the deep public outrage against the trials, and all the remaining defendants were freed, except those against whom murder and brutality could be proven. But not even this was enough to still public anger, for when, in February 1946, one Abdul Rashid was sentenced to seven years' rigorous imprisonment, Calcutta was again convulsed by demonstrations, and a general strike during which over eighty persons were killed. And the spiral of violence and counter-violence expanded beyond Calcutta. Railway and postal workers resolved to take national strike actions partly as a response to repressions in Calcutta but also to protest rising prices for basic foods.

To all this was added what for the British was surely the most dangerous of events: a mutiny of naval personnel in Bombay. In February 1946 protests began against the falling standards of food in the Royal Navy, against pay differentials between Indian and European seamen, and against racial insults by white officers. Sailors too had identified with the soldiers being tried in Delhi and with those who objected to holding Indonesia for the returning Dutch colonists. The naval ratings at first resorted to peaceful hunger strikes, but soon violence erupted and escalated to the point where stations on the shore were bombarded from the ships. Bombay civilians began supporting the strike in July by breaching the siege lines around shore stations to provide the strikers with food. As word spread to naval units elsewhere, more strikes were declared, so that by early 1947 commanders of nearly eighty ships and twenty shore stations were coping with mutineers and attempting to break the strikes with force. This inspired students and workers in many places to back the mutineers by attacking police and soldiers. In all, over 200 civilians were killed.

For Indian nationalist leaders, these were no less difficult times. Sardar Patel (who was Home Member of the 'interim government') and Gandhi condemned the mutiny, Patel because a free India would also have need of a disciplined army and navy, and Gandhi because the sailors were setting such a bad example. Behind the deprecations of both lurked a frustrated inability to check the tide of violence. Outbreaks could now occur uncontrollably in all parts of India, and there was something new about the mood of unarmed protesters – more and more often of middle-class background – who stood their ground against firearms. Much of the militancy reflected the central position that the communists had attained in the years of their 'treachery', during which, operating quite legally, they had built massive followings capable of disciplined street fighting. Patel and other nationalist politicians bleakly saw their preferred strategy of non-violent resistance coupled with negotiations losing out to an entirely different kind of politics. Accordingly, a British call for general elections was hailed by Congress leaders who hoped to divert the energies presently driving protests in the streets.

The elections of December 1945 and January 1946 returned comfortable majorities for the Congress in constituencies with small Muslim populations; small majorities were achieved in the central assembly and in most provinces except Bengal, Sind and Punjab. The Muslim League performed as well as the Congress in other constituencies, winning four-fifths of the seats reserved for Muslims under the rules of the 1935 Constitution, though failing to win enough seats to form governments in Punjab and losing to the Congress in two of the provinces Jinnah had claimed for Pakistan at Simla: Assam and the Northwest Frontier. Nevertheless, the real winner in this election was Jinnah and the League, for the voting had been on religious lines, and though it was not explicitly a vote for Pakistan, Jinnah was able to draw that implication and insist on it in the troubled period that followed.

March 1946 saw another British cabinet mission to India. This time Stafford Cripps and two of his colleagues were empowered by Clement Attlee to investigate the possibilities for an interim government capable of drafting a constitution acceptable to British authorities. Freedom was no longer at issue, only when and under what circumstances. The British and the Congress both sought to forestall further protest, but a constant simmering disorder persisted – rail, postal and even police strikes. There was also talk of a general strike by leftist Congressmen and the communists. Despair over existing and threatened violence hastened an agreement between the members of the cabinet mission and the Congress that won little public approval.

What the cabinet mission finally came up with was a fudge so skilful that it was accepted by Congress and the League under opposite misapprehensions. The whole of India, including the princely states, was to be divided into three regional groups of provinces: one in the northwest, one in the northeast and the rest, which would form a weak federation. The central authority would handle defence, foreign affairs, currency and so forth. Jinnah and the League were under the impression that, in essence, the plan implied a separate Pakistan, with a constituent assembly for each group. The Congress, on the other hand, took the proposed central authority to imply a rejection of the Pakistan demand.

Efforts to arrange a constituent assembly election, however, were frustrated by questions about whom each party spoke for: Congress claimed to speak for everyone, while the League insisted that it alone represented Muslims. In the end, Jinnah withdrew from all discussions, stating ominously that the League would launch 'direct action' beginning on 16 August 1946 in order to achieve an independent Pakistan. For Wavell nothing remained except to propose an interim government without the League, and accordingly, in September, a Congress-dominated government was inaugurated with Nehru at its head. By this time, Jinnah's threat had been realized and bloody violence began, which involved not only the Muslim League against the Congress throughout northern India, but poor peasants against the landlords and their police and judicial allies. The chaos that the British and Congress leaders had feared now descended on the hapless people of India. A torrent of blood was to wash over the north for a year.

It began in Calcutta on 16 August 1946, as Jinnah had ordered. Attacks by Muslims were launched with the complicity of the Muslim chief minister of Bengal, who promised that there would be no interference from police or army. Three days of such attacks, followed by counter-attacks by Sikhs and Hindus, resulted in the deaths of 4000 and injury of over twice that number, mostly Muslims. Bombay's substantial Muslim population now struck out against Hindus, though not on so vast a scale. Violence then switched back to Bengal, this time the countryside of eastern Bengal where the large population of Muslim tenants set upon Hindu landlords, traders and money-lenders. Once again, the police stood by to permit 300 deaths and the destruction of property. By October, Bihar saw the first of similar attacks by Hindu peasants, which led to 7000 deaths.

Bad as these outbreaks were, and numbed as many became to the loss of life, religious mayhem in the Punjab paled all other instances. Beginning in August 1947, some 5000 Sikh and Hindu merchants and money-lenders were massacred in the predominantly Muslim west of the Punjab, between Amritsar and Multan, and the bloodletting escalated until millions of Hindus and Sikhs fled eastwards while Muslims flowed westwards. By 1948, the dead in the Punjab had reached 180,000, of whom two-thirds were Muslims. Six million Muslims had lost their homes and become refugees, while 4.5 million Hindus and Sikhs came there seeking refuge.

Nehru and his government could only watch the horror of this massive communal hatred in 1946, because the soldiers promised by the British never materialized. Eventually, the long-held secular commitment of the Congress weakened and partition of the subcontinent on religious grounds had to be accepted. Even then, the political frontiers failed to safeguard Muslims, Sikhs and Hindus from mutual slaughter. Millions of refugees were unable to find peace except in death as crowded trains moved to and from the Punjab or Bengal and arrived at their destinations laden with corpses.

GANDHI IS MURDERED AND THE VIOLENCE MOUNTS

Gandhi himself became a victim of religious hatred at the end of January 1948, when he was murdered in Delhi by a Maharashtrian Hindu extremist, Nathuram Godse. Gandhi's life ended at a moment of renewed greatness that few would have thought possible a few years before. After he removed himself from the frustrating negotiations for British withdrawal, his occasional inter- ventions into active politics seemed merely to confirm that he was past his time. Many of his colleagues had been persuaded of this when he proposed to the viceroy Viscount Mountbatten that Jinnah should be appointed prime minister of a unified India and that the British should remain for a while in order to protect the Hindu majority!

When communal killings flared in August 1946, Gandhi plunged into the worst of it in Bengal and Bihar. There he persuaded, cajoled and threatened with his fasts, in order to bring an end to the strife; successful in one place, he would be called elsewhere to repeat his miracles. As if by magic, but really through the power of his name, reputation and personal following, he checked communal killings in Calcutta when that city exploded again in late August 1947. In January 1948 he was in Delhi attempting to defuse the vengeance being exacted by Hindus and Sikhs upon Muslims for the deaths of co-religionists in the Punjab. There he undertook a fast not only to restrain those bent on communal reprisal, but also to influence the powerful Home Minister, Sardar Patel, who was refusing to share out the assets of the former imperial treasury with Pakistan, as had been agreed. Gandhi's insistence on justice for Pakistan now that the partition was a fact, and his repeated and personally dangerous meetings with Muslim groups in order to calm their hatred and fear, had prompted Godse's fanatical action.

Gandhi's death did not end wide-scale communal strife; that came only with exhaustion, and Indian politics began to resume its more normal course: Calcutta students took to the streets to oppose the use of Calcutta airfield by the French to resupply their soldiers in Vietnam, and purely economic strikes were launched by urban workers there and elsewhere in the Gangetic valley. Public disorder now emerged in the south of the subcontinent, which had been free from serious religious discord. There, and increasingly in the north, political focus shifted to the countryside, where a powerful class struggle was occurring.

Agrarian unrest had grown with rural poverty. In late 1946, the conditions of tenancy in northern Bengal had become so oppressive that a government commission recommended that share-croppers should receive two-thirds of the crop they produced, well above prevailing rates. Farmers there, through the Kisan Sabha of Bengal, undertook to implement this change, and communist students from Bengal's towns and cities were enlisted to organize local campaigns against unrepentant and powerful landlords. When the recommended two-thirds shares were seized from the threshing floors after harvests by those who had grown the crops, their action was legitimated by a new law in the Muslim-led provincial legislature; most of the tenantry were Muslims and the landlords Hindus.

At the opposite end of India, however, a political crisis arose with attacks against big landlords led by communists. They had built a strong regional rural movement there, involving workers who made ropes out of coir (coconut husk fibres), tappers of palm trees for the sap that was made into country liquor, fishermen and, finally, landless labourers. In 1946 the maharaja of the state and a minister cherished an ambition to maintain an independent Travancore when the British withdrew. An ostensibly 'democratic' reform of the state assembly, which actually masked the attrition of ancient local autonomy, led to a general strike against the maharaja's plan in October of that year. To this the state responded with martial law that resulted in the killing of 800 demonstrators, an incident remembered after the Republic of India was established in 1947, when Travancore was made part of the newly constituted state of Kerala in the Indian Union. An even more serious instance of rural unrest occurred in the Telugu-speaking part of Madras State known as Telangana. It lasted for five years and involved prolonged demands for agrarian reform by armed farmers in an area extending over 16,000 square miles and containing 3000 villages.

Despite their seriousness, these outbreaks were too scattered to affect the final stages of the transfer of power from the British to successors in the subcontinent, but the movements underscored a potential for an extension of the violence engendered by inter-religious hatred. The British government was persuaded by its officials in India to fix an early deadline for departure: June 1948. By then all arrangements were to be completed for handing authority to whatever political agents were deemed to control the various parts of the subcontinent, along with sovereignty over the princely states. Under the threat of a possible balkanization, all Indian political minds became concentrated upon the detailed proposals of Lord Mountbatten, who had been given full decision-making powers.

Mountbatten had proposed freedom with partition, a plan which the Congress accepted in late 1946, although it was dubbed, ominously, 'Plan Balkan'. In addition, the viceroy insisted on increasing the pace of the transition, with the result that power was to be passed from the British less than six months from the time that Clement Attlee designated Mountbatten as Wavell's successor in February. The promulgation of the India Independence Act by Parliament on 18 July 1947 would stipulate implementation on 15 August 1947. But the proposal was rejected by Nehru. He refused to accept that power was to be passed from the Crown to several elected bodies in British-Indian provinces, with the understanding that assemblies of two of the provinces – Bengal and Punjab – could make a further decision for internal partitions and that the six hundred or so princely states could choose to join either Pakistan or India or remain independent. Besides being a reversion to the earlier cabinet mission proposals, this was unacceptable to Nehru and other Congress leaders, because it was an invitation to create so many new states that their existence would depend upon continued subjugation to Britain or to the United States, which was replacing British and other European supremacy in Asia following the defeat of Japan.

Congress leaders therefore pressed Mountbatten to assent to the simple and straightforward proposal of dividing the subcontinent between two successor states, India and Pakistan. Along with independence, India should be granted dominion status, with a right to leave the Commonwealth if that was desired. Congress members rejected the need for constituent assemblies to establish the bases of these states; theirs was a plan that could be achieved quickly and could possibly avert further violence. Mountbatten agreed, but the bloody partition of the Punjab was not to be averted. Moreover, the convenience of a two-state solution spelled the violation of other nationalist ambitions. Some Bengalis had worked for an independent Bengal under the united rule of a Muslim majority but with minority rights to Hindus. Likewise, many followers of Abdul Ghaffar Khan, 'the Frontier Gandhi' of the Northwest Frontier Province and a constant supporter of secular democracy, wanted to set up a Pathan state. But neither the Congress nor the League leadership would be diverted from their determination to integrate rapidly the diverse political elements of India into one or the other of only two states.

The time for that heroic task was brief and the impediments seemed immense. For example, some of Mountbatten's officials believed that the princes of India, especially those of great states like Hyderabad, Mysore and Travancore in the south, and Bhopal and Kashmir in the north, which had historically been strong supporters of the Raj, should be rewarded by independent statehood. There were also demands for new states, such as for a Telugu-speaking Andhra. Mountbatten overrode the pressures from his subordinates on behalf of their client princes and lent his weight to Congress in managing the integration process. To those princes who signed the accession agreements by which their territories were incorporated into the Indian Union, the viceroy offered handsome payments from the revenue (the so-called 'privy purses') for the maintenance of princely styles, and some princes were even appointed governors of Indian states. As to the demands for new, culturally defined states within India, these were delayed until the middle 1950s on the strength of promises from the chief Congress negotiators, V. P. Menon and Sardar Patel, to whom credit for the swift assimilation of the Indian states is rightly given. They were assisted by the enthusiastic acceptance of the idea of partition by all parties. Now, even more than Muslims, Hindu and Sikh leaders saw partition as necessary to pave the way to a viable new state in which they would have important places.

POWER PASSES AT LONG LAST

As the Labour government of Britain sought a formula for the transfer of power, opposition between the League and Congress hardened and grounds for compromise in the proposed structure of the post-colonial government narrowed. In August 1946, Jinnah had incited Muslim rioting in Calcutta, which in turn led to Hindu violence against Muslims in Bihar, and the prospect of yet more to come elsewhere. Failing to see a way out of the escalating conflict that continued through early 1947, the British simply declared that they would leave India in June 1948, and appointed Lord Mountbatten as viceroy, charged to complete Britain's withdrawal. Mountbatten bluntly stated the terms of departure in a broadcast to all of India in June 1947: a separate dominion of Indian Muslims to include those territories in which they were a majority; partition of the Punjab and Bengal; a Parliamentary act conferring dominion status upon India and the provision of referendums to ascertain which of the two dominions certain disputed parts of the country would join. Bengal and the Punjab were duly partitioned by mutual agreement between the Congress and the League, and Parliament passed an act transferring British authority to Pakistan and India on 14 and 15 August 1947, respectively. India's independence was declared by a Constituent Assembly convened in Delhi, and Lord Mountbatten was appointed the first governor-general of this newest dominion of the Commonwealth. Pakistan was proclaimed then as well, but Mohammad Ali Jinnah was declared its governor-general and charged to convene an Assembly to prepare a Constitution for the new nation.

And so, as the announced date for the transfer of power approached, all was hastily put in place for the creation of the successors to the Raj. All in all, there seemed nothing to diminish the splendour of the midnight speech of Jawaharlal Nehru on 15 August proclaiming the new Indian nation.

[9]   NEW STATES, OLD NATIONS

Two violent events soon shattered the splendid moment of independence and were ominous for what was to follow: the terrible toll of death that attended the shift of peoples across the Punjab, followed by the outbreak of war between India and Pakistan over Kashmir. Both events conditioned much that was to come during the next fifteen years.

Violence came to the Punjab partly as a result of the way in which the frontier between India and Pakistan had been fixed by Mountbatten's officials. Boundaries were delineated secretly during the last months before independence so as to avoid public quarrels. The cession of western Punjab to Pakistan sundered tracts long inhabited by Sikhs, the third people of the Punjab, whose outrage led to vengeful attacks on hapless Muslim refugees. Fear of reprisal brought Sikh and Hindu refugees from the western districts of the Punjab allotted to Pakistan. Immediate and mutual hatred arose on both sides of the new Punjab frontier at the moment when the Kashmir issue, which also turned critically on the Punjab, exploded.

TERRITORIAL PASSAGE

The agreed principles for the affiliation of princely territories with either Pakistan or India were the religion of the inhabitants and the territorial propinquity to one or the other of the new states. In all but a handful of cases, the transfer of territory was uncontested, since generous terms were offered to the assorted princes by the successors to British overlordship. But two cases, involving large kingdoms, proved especially difficult: Hyderabad in the south and Kashmir in the north. In both there was a mismatch between the religious affiliations of the dominant population and the rulers; the Muslim Nizam of Hyderabad ruled Hindus, and the Hindu Maharaja of Kashmir ruled over Muslims. The outcomes of these two situations differed.

In Hyderabad, an aggressive Islamic party formed to oppose forcibly the expected union with India. Indian troops were committed in a 'police action' that quickly disarmed the opposition and bent them to a negotiated settlement. Hyderabad joined the Indian Union in 1950 and was soon merged with the first of a new generation of states, Andhra Pradesh, formed by splitting the former Madras Presidency along linguistic lines.

Kashmir was neither as large nor as old an independent realm as Hyderabad; it had been created rather off-handedly by the British after the first defeat of the Sikhs in 1846, as a reward to a Sikh grandee and former official who had sided with the British. This Himalayan kingdom was connected to India through a district of the Punjab, but its population was 77 per cent Muslim and it shared a boundary with Pakistan. Hence, it was anticipated that the maharaja would accede to Pakistan when the British paramountcy ended on 14–15 August. When he hesitated to do this, Pakistan launched a guerrilla onslaught meant to frighten its ruler into submission. Instead, the maharaja appealed to Mountbatten for assistance, and the governor-general agreed on condition that the ruler accede to India. Indian soldiers entered Kashmir and drove the Pakistan-sponsored irregulars from all but a small section of the state. The United Nations was then invited to mediate the quarrel. The UN mission insisted that the opinion of Kashmiris must be ascertained, while India insisted that no referendum could occur until all of the state had been cleared of irregulars.

In the last days of 1948, a ceasefire was agreed under the United Nations pending a referendum to determine the views of the people. Because that plebiscite was never conducted, relations were soured and wars fought by the two inheritors of British authority; their foreign policies and conduct from the onset of their existence as independent states have been shaped by the Kashmir dispute. There the deadlock has remained since 1947, a constant reminder of the difficulties that marked the births of the new states.

THE PROMISES OF INDEPENDENCE

Aside from the violence of partition, when independence came at last to the subcontinent it seemed that all the necessary conditions were in place for a course of steady development in the successors to the Raj: a highly centralized state system with an efficient bureaucracy and a military with traditions of obedience to civilian rule; an advanced judiciary; flourishing universities and scientific establishments; and partly industrialized economies. India presented just such a structure at the time of independence, but other conditions were also in evidence. A strong state system stood ready to complete the modernization of the country; outstanding British debts incurred during the war constituted a capital fund for starting that modernization, and it was soon to be augmented by the offer of capital transfers on favourable terms from the US-led 'aid to India club', which seemed to encourage Indian aims of national economic development along the lines of mixed socialist and capitalist principles.

Sympathetic assistance from the United States was partly motivated by the American strategic aim of thwarting the expansion of communism into so populous and promising a nation. Even before there was a 'Cold War', however, the cause of Indian independence had been advanced by the pressure which Franklin Roosevelt, the American wartime president, exerted upon Winston Churchill. American sympathy, abetted by anti-Soviet diplomacy, deepened with the apparent successes of the new Indian democracy. Reassuring too was the easy transformation of the Indian National Congress into a Congress Party in the form of a broad, centrist political alliance of diverse interests that resembled the dominant national parties in the USA, similarly constituted to maintain rather than to change existing social and economic patterns.

The political structure within which goals were formulated and means devised for their attainment in an independent India was the joint legacy of Jawaharlal Nehru and Sarder Vallabhbhai Patel. Each represented a focus for conflicting divisions around the centre of the Congress movement during the final struggle for freedom, which continued in the Congress Party after independence. Gandhi had not wanted the Congress to become a conventional party, preferring instead that the politics of the new nation find expression in factions representing different interests and programmes, including a Gandhian one. In his view, the Congress would wither away or become a non-partisan arena for discussing the nation's problems.

Within a short time it became clear from national elections in 1952 and 1957 that the Congress Party would dominate the politics of the states as well as the centre against challenges from rightist parties such as the Swatantra Party, which opposed public sector control of the economy, or those based on Hindu sectarianism, such as the Bharatiya Jana Sangh (People's Party of India), which had fascist-like fringes. The Congress Party also stood against the advances of the Communist Party of India, dreaded by the USA and Nehru alike.

Forging the Congress into a broad centrist, electioneering tool was the result of Nehru's somewhat leftist hammer beating upon Patel's rightist anvil. Had each of these successors to Gandhi sought to implement programmes appropriate to their ideological and class-linked political allies, two parties could have emerged, competing for power and, in the nature of two-party systems, alternating periods of power. As a single nationwide party with a base in urban as well as rural sections of India, and with the charisma of having attained freedom, the Congress proved a vehicle in which both men could see adequate scope for pursuing their respective political careers.

India's constitution: promises on paper

Designing the Constitution that was promulgated on 26 January 1950 was largely the work of Patel, who died at the end of that year. Successfully thwarting Nehru's desire that the constitution should be the work of a popularly elected body, Patel presided over a far less representative constituent assembly, one that was proposed previously by Lord Wavell on the basis of a limited franchise. It is therefore not surprising that the new constitution turned out to be an amended version of the Government of India Act of 1935. Democratic amendments that might have been anticipated, and that many demanded, did not find space in the new constitution. For example, the proposal that the governors of the new Indian states be elected by universal suffrage rather than appointed was dropped, because the war with Pakistan over Kashmir seemed to justify a stronger central regime.

A more democratic federalism was also resisted by maintaining the provision from the 1935 Act that state governments could be replaced by administration from the centre. This so-called President's Rule provided that the President of India, like the British viceroy before him, could proclaim an emergency and assume control of any state in the Indian republic, providing that parliamentary assent was obtained within two months of such an imposition and that new elections occurred within six months. As long as the Congress Party held the centre and governed most of the states, this emergency power had little effect. But the power to withdraw the mandate to rule from elected ministries for as much as six months was a potentially powerful threat to a genuinely multiparty federalism. This was revealed in 1959 when Nehru bowed to the demands of rightist cabinet colleagues and dismissed the elected communist government of Kerala, imposing presidential rule after a radical land reform programme was begun there.

Elsewhere in the 270-page constitution, a section of 'fundamental rights' was included. Most of these had been proposed by the Indian National Congress in the 1920s, in criticism of the feeble British protection of individual rights. The new constitution guaranteed freedom of speech, religion and association; rights to property, education and the preservation of minority cultures. These rights could be enforced in court. Other individual, economic and social rights mentioned included employment, a living wage, worker participation in the management of firms, access to legal representation and the protection of the environment. These latter rights were designated 'directive principles', intended to guide the legislatures and administrations as they conducted their business, but, unlike the former group, they were not enforceable in court.

Judicial reforms were also undertaken, and these were given over to the supervision of Dr Ambedkar, but Nehru took part in the deliberations as well. He agreed that private property should be protected from state appropriation by the provision of compensation for measures like land reform, a provision his colleagues had demanded in order to make any seriously redistributive land reform too expensive to be implemented. Neither Nehru nor Ambedkar was able to oppose successfully another strong rightist demand put forward by Patel: that no general personal law should be substituted for the separate codes for Hindus and for Muslims that had been devised by colonial lawyers; Patel and his followers feared that such a change would lend support to untouchables' and women's quests for equal benefits under the law. Ambedkar resigned from the Law Commission on this issue, while Nehru countered Patel's conservatism by introducing a large measure of reform through legislative enactments rather than changes in the constitution.

THE CENTRE AND THE STATES

The 1950 constitution called India 'Bharat', an ancient appellation, and described it as a 'Union of States' consisting of territories of various kinds, all derived from the colonial past: former provinces of the Raj, former princely states and both old and new centrally administered regions, such as Delhi. The demand that states be constituted according to language and cultural affinities had been anticipated by Gandhi's reforms of the organization of Congress in 1920, which encouraged the Telugu-speakers in Madras province to form the Andhra Pradesh Committee. Nehru conceded the legitimacy of the idea of basing states on cultural criteria, but he also regarded the reorganization of territories as dangerous, for it could lead to the 'balkanization' that had been previously predicted.

There was real danger that the political system would become so fragmented as to prevent a powerful centre from determining the Indian profile in the world at large. He and his colleagues therefore delayed action in the reorganization of the states until a leader of the Andhra movement died as a result of a fast in 1953, forcing a capitulation to the now emotional demand for linguistically based states. Four were created in the South: Tamil Nadu, Andhra Pradesh, Mysore (to become Karnataka, defined by the distribution of the Kannada language) and Kerala, which joined together Malayalam-speakers from the princely states of Travancore and Cochin and parts of old Madras districts.

The Indian constitution was amended in 1956, when the states of the Indian Union were reorganized. Originally, the Union had been composed of the former British provinces and the former princely states. These elements were superseded in 1956 by the creation of fourteen states based upon language and six so-called Union Territories, the latter consisting of Delhi and certain peripheral tracts. The amended structure was resisted by Nehru and others because of the latent dangers of encouraging a subnationalism in the country, even though it was precisely along such lines that the National Congress had organized its mobilizations since 1920. Localistic loyalties were as powerful in the 1950s as in the 1920s, which is why the same principles were demanded in the formation of the states of a free India. The state reforms of 1956 were an abdication of the principles of secularism and resource efficiency to the alternative principles of communalism.

In 1957, elections were conducted for the new linguistically defined electoral constituencies, and their outcome proved a triumph for explicitly 'sons-of-the-soil' interests in most of the provincial Congress parties. Everywhere these interests were centred on the rich farming class of the countryside and the lower middle-class townspeople. A variety of consequences ensued. First, fundamental reform of land-holding was now precluded: beyond the abolition of zamindars – the British-created estate holders in Bengal and a few other scattered places – the politically empowered richer farmers would permit no laws that reduced the command over wealth and over men afforded by possession of land. Second, western-educated, high-caste people in many places – brahmans in most cases – were displaced from their prominent places in the state-level Congress organizations by those who represented the lower middle classes in the villages and towns with political programmes that were less national in orientation and more narrowly devised to meet the demands of the wealthier members of regional political cultures.

By the mid-1950s, then, the political structure was fractured. On one side were language- and culture-bound state and local politics and politicians. On the other side was the old educated elite, which staffed the central bureaucracy of the Indian Administrative Service and world-class scientific establishments based in new national institutes. Both elites, administrative and scientific, worked in combination with and often at the service of a national bourgeoisie. The division between the mass of small-holders of urban and rural properties and the thin layer of owners of big capital and their professional and administrative allies was masked by Nehru and his colleagues and by their successors.

BROKEN PROMISES ON POVERTY

Unlike many of his Congress colleagues, Nehru was frustrated by his failure to ameliorate the poverty of India's massive rural poor. His impatience boiled over in 1955 when he pressed the Congress to proclaim as its purpose, and that of the Indian government, 'a socialistic pattern of society'. He explained that this goal was to be achieved through national ownership and control of the means of production. Fear instantly struck the party as farm leaders and industrialists worried that more than a political gesture might be involved. Leading an opposing force was the former Gandhian and Indian governor-general, Chakravarti Rajagopalachari. He went on to found the Swatantra Party, which aimed at winning the support of rich farmers in Madras, his own power base. His pretext was a decision taken at the 1955 meeting of the Congress Party at Avadi in Tamil Nadu to eradicate rural poverty by collectivizing agriculture. Though the Constitution had carefully stated as a 'fundamental right' that no compulsory expropriation of property was legal without adequate compensation, the socialist rhetoric of the new regime still inspired fear.

The defection of the right immediately forced a shift in Nehru's rhetoric from the 'socialistic pattern', with which he had sought to challenge the appeal of the communists, to more centrist utterances, so as to counter the attractions of Swatantra. Thus, hardly had he taken a socialist stand than he retreated once more to the reassuring centre which the Congress had long occupied. Centrist politics had been the way to accommodate the passions, if not always the interests, of the diverse political broad church that made up the Congress.

Despite his moderation, open conflict between Nehru and the Congress right erupted at times. In 1950, when attempts were made to consolidate the rightist domination of the Party, Nehru abandoned his usual neutrality by personally opposing the election of a candidate for Congress president supported by Patel and the right. Instead, Nehru threw his support to the presidential candidate of the Gandhians and socialists. After Patel's death in

December 1950, Nehru was freer to check his conservative opponents, and he even broke precedent by becoming president of the party in order to curb criticisms of his modernization programmes.

Nehru and the Congress both ostensibly remained committed to reducing poverty by the planned modernization of the economy and welfare measures. Nevertheless, deep disparities of income and benefit stubbornly persisted and may even have intensified during the 1950s, though this was obfuscated by the language of the two 'Five Year Plans' promulgated during that decade. These plans were modelled on the draft fifteen-year 'Bombay Plan' that had been adopted by the Congress in 1938. Effective planning for the economy unofficially ceased after the second plan ended at the close of the 1950s; since then such modest planned productive growth and welfare improvements as were stated as plan objectives have not been seriously pursued. Planning contributed to the ideology of social equality, but not to its actual attainment.

From his joint position of influence as prime minister and president of the Congress, between 1950 and 1954 Nehru forced through legislation abolishing zamindari rights in northern and eastern India as well as in some minor tracts in the south. British tenancy laws had already curtailed some of the arbitrary powers of the big landlords and landed intermediaries that had been created by Lord Cornwallis in 1793; thus the laws of the 1950s which limited the permitted size of individual land-holdings were not revolutionary, and generous compensation was paid for the loss of the remaining powers. Moreover, old landlords were often left with large 'home farms' consisting of the best of their old lands, and they easily circumvented the prohibitions on subletting by various subterfuges, such as calling share-croppers 'partners'. Wealthy farmers who bought parts of the old estates were the chief beneficiaries of the division of zamindari lands, and, when new laws were imposed to set ceilings on the amount of land that could be held, they too proved easily evaded by that powerful rural class whose collective vote sustained the Congress Party. While statuses and benefits were somewhat altered in India during Nehru's prime ministership, the rural poor remained as vulnerable as ever.

CONFRONTATION IN KERALA

The victory of the Communist Party in Kerala in 1957 came as a disagreeable surprise to the Congress. Not only did the Kerala communists launch an exemplary land reform programme, but they also devoted relatively large expenditures to basic education and health care, making that state the most egalitarian, best-educated and healthiest in the Indian union, though it remained among the poorest. In the general elections of 1952 and 1957 the Congress Party won majorities everywhere except in Kerala. Where they did win, the victories were the work of coalitions among wealthy peasant groups who dominated the twenty-one provincial, or pradesh, organizations. The Congress was no longer led by urban men and interests, but by small-town and rural men, and electoral success had been delivered essentially by powerful and wealthy farmers, the same ones who resisted Nehru's attempts to impose effective land reform. It was this stratum of rich farmers that mobilized the vote using the levers of caste loyalty and faction. As before independence, big-city money men and industrialists played a significant part in Congress Party electoral campaigns by paying for the full-time party workers, advertisements and motor vehicles required; just as before, funds were forthcoming on the understanding that class conflict would remain as muted after Gandhi's time as it was during his life.

It is hardly surprising, therefore, that there should have been pressure upon Nehru to rid the political scene of 'red subversion' in Kerala. Nehru and the leaders of Congress state regimes were moved by more than embarrassment to breach democratic process; they feared that the Indian bourgeoisie might shift its support from the Congress Party to the new political parties that were emerging to challenge the Congress with alternatives to Nehru's gamble on an economic transformation of India through planning and a mix of private and public development. When anti-communist students took to the streets, Nehru seized the pretext to violate his previously unimpeachable democratic principles and dismiss the elected communist government. The resultant 'disorders' were then used to justify the imposition of presidential rule over Kerala in 1959. The solution proved short-lived, however, for the communists again out-polled the Congress in elections of 1960, with around 45 per cent of the Kerala vote.

POLITICS RULES

When Nehru's Congress vacated the left-of-centre position it had momentarily sought to occupy, the parties of India's left moved to fill the gap. The Socialist Party, which had 10 per cent of the seats in the lower house of parliament, anticipated an increase in its representation. This was a reasonable expectation. It had been a prominent part of the Congress Party from the mid-1930s until Sardar Patel forced it out in 1948, claiming that it had been taken over by communists. Subsequent splits had weakened the Socialist Party challenge to both the Congress and the Communist Party of India. But communists themselves enjoyed consistent electoral success only in Bengal and Kerala, where they actually formed governments.

Forming on the political right of the free-enterprise Swatantra Party during the late 1950s was a consolidation of the fragmented Hindu nationalist movements that began to contest elections as a national party called the Bharata Jana Sangh (Indian People's Association). Its core symbols were Hinduism and Hindi – a national 'faith' and national language – and its social base consisted of small town bazaar people in northern India, merchants, money-lenders and small-scale commodity and labour brokers. Bitter Punjabi refugees from western Pakistan added a major component to this religious party. Whereas the Swatantra Party bid for the support of the wealthy within Congress, the Jana Sangh competed instead for the allegiance of a large lower middle class by stressing its difference from the nominally secularist Congress. Its populist religious propensities appealed in the countryside to small property-holders neglected by the big property supporters of Swatantra and repudiated by the communist enemies of property. The Jana Sangh commandeered the historical anti-Muslim cow-protection rhetoric of the late nineteenth century; from the more recent past, it ominously identified with the Rashtriya Swayam Sevak Sangh (RSS, or National Self-help Association). Because an RSS member had murdered Gandhi, some on the political right who revered Gandhi as the father of the nation withheld their allegiance, however attracted they might have been by the Jana Sangh claim to be the 'Indian' alternative to Congress and the egalitarian economic and social programmes policies of Nehru.

Planning was Nehru's chosen instrument for building the wealth of the country and the welfare of its poor. From 1938, he headed the Congress Planning Committee, whose purpose was to formulate a development programme for the future free India. During the Second World War, his plans were abetted by leading Bombay industrialists. G. D. Birla and J. R. D. Tata had devised a national plan for the first years after freedom. This 'Bombay Plan' outlined a mixed economy managed by a strong state responsible for the necessary infrastructure investment that was beyond the capacity of private investors. The public sector was to include the heavy industrial developments of steel, chemicals and engineering, where profits would be low for a long period, leaving to smaller investors and firms the supply of basic consumer needs. It was this strategy that Nehru adopted for the National Planning Commission in 1950.

Under his chairmanship, the Planning Commission adopted some features of Soviet strategy. Two 'five year plans' were carried out from 1950 to the time of Nehru's death, with large investments in agriculture and community development, irrigation and power, industry and mining, transport and communications, and social services. The first five year plan concentrated on rural poverty, especially on remedying backward practices in farming and animal husbandry and the restricted access so many peasants had to credit. Some 15 per cent of the total of development spending was deployed for these purposes and an equal proportion was devoted to irrigation and rural electrification projects. Industrial and mining development received about half as much funding as agriculture, while transport, especially railways, and social services (health, education, housing and welfare schemes) received less. The major thrust of the first plan was to achieve self-sufficiency in food, the supply of which had remained deficient some years after the war.

POPULATION PLANNING

Success proved illusory when the results of the first national census conducted in 1951 were analysed and revealed that inadequate account had been taken of the rapid increase of the population; impressive gains in food production resulted in no gain in per capita food availability. In 1952 India became the first country in the world to pursue a policy of attempting to limit the natural increase in its population. As a result, its progress on this front has been studied, directed, discussed and criticized to such an extent that, paradoxically, India has become a by-word for overpopulation.

There had been warnings of trouble ahead in the report of the Bengal

Famine Commission of 1945. Unfortunately, however, upon independence in 1947 the Health Ministry was placed in the hands of Rajkumari Amrit Kaur, a princess turned social worker, who, as a loyal Gandhian, set her face against all contraceptive devices. Yet India's population problem was a development of the mid-twentieth century. Between the censuses of 1911 and 1921, there was actually a decline of 0.3 per cent (thanks to the influenza pandemic of 1918–20). The 1931 census showed an increase of 1.1 per cent, and the rates continued to rise thereafter until they reached 2 per cent per year by 1961.

The programme begun in 1952, which focused on the 'rhythm method', had input from the World Health Organization (WHO), a foreign consultant and a budget of $31,000. The budget was increased sharply in every five year plan, but was still rather tentative throughout the 1950s. In fact, as late as November 1959, Nehru said in a television interview: 'Food must be a top priority. Some people imagine that we will solve India's problems by family planning. I do not agree.'

Nevertheless, in the same year there had been a shift to the promotion of sterilization, which, because it was a permanent method, meant a change from an emphasis on child spacing – beneficial to the health and welfare of both mothers and children – to total family size limitation, an emphasis which has remained until very recently. The result was that many women bore their children too early and too rapidly. Shortly after the shift to sterilization, cash incentives were introduced. Although in theory the programme was voluntary, the class bias in such a measure is obvious. Nor was 'family planning' free of other internal contradictions. Without a serious attempt to redistribute wealth, the ceiling placed on individual land-holding actually encouraged large families among property-holders.

In addition, demographic competition between castes, states and religious communities militated against the leaders of these groupings becoming enthusiastic about limiting the numbers of their constituents. Hindus and Muslims eyed each other and worried about the numerical advantage of their 'vote banks'. And it was not until 1976 that considerations of the allocation of central funds and parliamentary seats were applied in such a way as not to punish the states with greater family planning success.

The 1961 census brought home the shocking realization that the annual rate of population growth had actually risen in the 1950s (and fertility did not peak until 1974). The planners then set the goal of reducing the annual birth rate of 41 per thousand people to 25 by the year 1973. In fact, the goal has still not been reached, but the words 'goals' and 'targets' have been excised from family planning discussions and replaced by talk of maternal and child health schemes instead. In 1971, abortion was legalized and the minimum marriage age was raised from 15 to 18 for women, and from 18 to 21 for men, although the average marriage age for girls is still below the legal minimum.

Most of the funding for India's family planning schemes has been supplied by the central government, but from the start there was also input from the individual states and from a number of foreign agencies, including USAID, the Ford and Rockefeller Foundations, the Population Council and several

UN agencies, as well as bilateral help from countries including Sweden and Japan. Such help has not always been offered with sensitivity on the one side, or received with unmixed gratitude on the other. In 1966, for example, a group of visiting dignitaries representing the American aid agency USAID demanded, over the protests of the Indian Health Minister, that other aid projects be halted and the funding transferred to population control. In 1973 the Indian government closed the USAID office in Delhi in anger at the American bias towards Pakistan during the Indo-Pakistan war of 1971. Furthermore, while the WHO and UNICEF supported Indian family planning schemes, the Soviet Union, Switzerland, Belgium, the Philippines and several other countries voted against giving India UN family planning support, alleging that its programmes were coercive.

The actual period of coercion in India's birth control policy occurred for less than a year starting in April 1976. The year before, the High Court in Allahabad had found Mrs Indira Gandhi guilty of electoral irregularities; her response was to declare an 'emergency' in June 1975 and rule by fiat until January 1977. During this period, civil rights were abrogated, newspapers censored, many organizations banned and many thousands jailed for political reasons.

The National Population Policy, which was promulgated in April 1976 and never rescinded, included provisions for health care, nutrition and more stress on education for girls. The goal was an eventual average family size of two children. Cash incentives were offered for sterilizations. Though no central government compulsory sterilization legislation was planned, the states were permitted to pass their own laws. The implementation of the population policy was largely in the hands of Mrs Gandhi's son Sanjay, who pushed for sterilizations *en masse*, particularly around the Delhi area. Men were bribed or coerced into vasectomy booths, regardless of age, medical or marital status, or the number of children they already had, just to fulfil the quotas set for the 'recruiters'. As a result, hundreds of people died, either of post-operative infections or in the riots that the campaign provoked. These procedures were later credited with losing the election for Mrs Gandhi after she ended the Emergency in 1977.

The numbers of vasectomies plummeted the following year; the population control policy was not revoked, but only soft-pedalled. The drive for sterilizations has since focused on women, perhaps a less politically sensitive target. Curiously, some of the methods, such as vasectomy camps, that proved so unpopular in Delhi during the emergency had been first tried out in Kerala and pronounced a great success.

Unlike in the other states, women in Kerala have for many centuries enjoyed a relatively high status. Their sex ratio is almost 'normal', their life expectancy five years greater than that of the men and their literacy rate almost equal. The Kerala population has very good medical services compared to those of the rest of India, and its fertility rate is currently below replacement. It was the first state to negotiate the 'demographic transition' (from high birth and death rates to low ones), though other southern states, especially the neighbouring one of Tamil Nadu, are beginning to follow suit.

INDUSTRIAL DEVELOPMENT

Even before the end of the first plan, investments began to be shifted to industrial development, anticipating the thrust of the second five year plan. Despite the magnitude of the problems presented by rural poverty and a swelling population, the emphasis of the second, from 1956 to 1961, was maintained. Accordingly, the second plan saw outlays in steel production and heavy engineering more than doubled, with correspondingly less invested in agriculture and social services. Funds for the latter purposes began to be supplied from foreign sources, notably the USA; nevertheless, the premature shift from agricultural to industrial development left a legacy of a weak and dependent agrarian system to retard total development.

Estimates of the costs of the first plan had had to be raised continually, partly as a result of inexperience, the inadequate information available to the planners and the rising costs of goods that were required. By 1956, India had exhausted all the wartime sterling balances it had accumulated in Britain at the time of the transfer of power. The maintenance of its large planning and development initiative seemed doomed unless assistance came from abroad. Chinese methods of collectivized and cooperative production were not considered suitable for India, with its commitment to small-scale rural capitalism, and foreign donors like the USA, watching China with Cold War eyes, were apprehensive at attempts to displace the mixed state and private capital approach of India with its model of collectivist development. Nehru and his colleagues in planning nevertheless believed that one sustained push during the second plan could reduce poverty and backwardness, so a brief period of foreign support was seen as a tolerable necessity. It was envisaged that, having freed itself from the roots of its backwardness, the country would soon afterwards enter a prolonged era of self-sustaining economic and social growth in which living standards would rise to the point where India's rural poor could purchase the goods produced by the new industries. Eventually, one-sixth of the finance for the second plan came from a group of western countries on which India was forced to depend, and the balance of needed capital was raised through internal borrowing.

PAKISTAN IN PARALLEL

Pakistan's development was different from and even more problematic than that of its sister state of the subcontinent. In one view, Pakistan emerged from a historical process that began around 1000 CE, when Muslim Turks broke into the Punjab to establish Islamic rule over the populous Gangetic plain. Alternatively, the origin of the state lay in the Lahore Resolution of the Muslim League in 1940, which demanded a Muslim homeland in the subcontinent.

The commitment to a homeland for India's Muslims in 1940 was vague. The League's resolution in that year made no mention of 'Pakistan', the name coined by Chaudhri Rahmat Ali as a Cambridge student in the 1930s, nor was anything specific stipulated about the way in which a homeland was to be constituted. The Lahore resolution merely asserted that any future constitutional arrangements must accept the claim that the Muslims of India were a 'nation'. It was envisaged that in the northwest and northeast provinces where they were a majority, Muslims should have autonomy and sovereignty. Of Muslims elsewhere in British India, where they were minorities, little could be or was said.

While the formative stage of the Indian Republic arguably ended with the death of Nehru in 1964, a similar moment is more difficult to define for Pakistan. Was it when the army under its commander General Ayub Khan seized control in October 1958, thereby establishing the ascendancy of the nation's army and senior bureaucrats over its politicians and religious leaders? Or was the formative phase of Pakistan's history completed by the severance of the Bengal wing of the nation in 1971? Did not this later 'mutilation' and the creation of an independent Bangladesh in eastern Bengal actually resolve Jinnah's nightmare by leaving a more coherent Pakistani territory, one on which a new and different history was bound to be inscribed?

Again, opinion is divided, for while a smaller, more compact state was left in the northwest of the subcontinent, the prolonged conflict between the centre and provincial parts of what had formerly been called 'West Pakistan' was no less intense. The contest there continued between the dominant Punjabis – the mainstay and beneficiaries of military and bureaucratic preferment – and the regionally numerous Sindhis, Baluchis and Pathans.

NATION-BUILDING IN PAKISTAN

In any case, the northwestern and northeastern wings of the Indian subcontinent became Pakistan on 14 August 1947, a day before the Indian republic was proclaimed, but the sense of Pakistani nationhood was derivative, having been invented in response to the secular nationalism of the Congress Party, and for many years it remained uncertain. The first task was to choose or build a capital. India had inherited the vast imperial pile designed in New Delhi by the architect Edward Luytens and built on the historic site of Mughal authority for occupation by the British in 1911. Only the Sind port city of Karachi approached Delhi in size and cosmopolitanism, and it was therefore designated the new capital. A mere 200 former Indian Civil Service officers had opted for Pakistan, plus another thirty-six British officials who consented to serve the new state, and they had to be installed in temporary sheds. However, the police and local government officers were in place in the old provincial regimes, and the way was eased when a share of the treasure left by the British in New Delhi (which Gandhi had to force Patel to yield up) was finally obtained.

Splitting the armed forces between the new nations was more difficult. The Indian army in 1947 had grown to 410,000 as a result of wartime expansion, and consisted of a mixed force of Hindus, Muslims and Sikhs; no military units consisted of Muslims alone. Disposing of military material was also complicated by the fact that all weapons production was concentrated in what was now India, and it was there that most of the stores of arms and munitions were kept. Decisions about the sharing out of military resources, as well as all other aspects of the partition, took place during the post-partition communal bloodshed in the Punjab, which added to the difficulties. Yet, notwithstanding the hatred engendered between Sikhs and Muslims, the division of forces was finally carried out. Pakistan agreed to accept 30 per cent of the army personnel, 40 per cent of naval forces and 20 per cent of the air force.

LAW AND ORDER

The result left Pakistan denuded of defenders by the removal of nearly half of the battalions that had been stationed there (including the Hindu, Sikh and British forces). The need for a large army seemed acute, not only because of the felt threat from India, but because large parts of the country were in disarray. Criminal gangs murdered and looted in the border villages of the Punjab; elsewhere, as in the Northwest Frontier, the flight of British troops and the movements of non-Muslims towards India offered opportunities for more mayhem on the part of Pathan tribesmen. Moreover, the Pathans in Afghanistan, on Pakistan's northern frontier, began to seize border territories that had been lost to the British during the late nineteenth and twentieth centuries. On top of all this was added the infuriating decision by the maharaja of Kashmir to join India. Jinnah's impulse was to commit his slender military forces to reversing the Kashmir decision, but he was warned by the British commander-in-chief Auchinleck that this action would be viewed as an invasion of India; instead, a force of irregulars was deployed, who proved no match for the Indian troops that were loosed against them.

All these conditions left Pakistan with an anxious concern for defence that dictated its foreign policy and had other implications. Strengthening the military required the cooperation of the fledgling bureaucracy and led to such close military and administrative collaboration as to constitute an alliance capable of wresting political control from competing politicians and religious leaders.

PAKISTAN'S CONSTITUTION

Pakistan lost Jinnah within the first year of its independence, and his associate, the powerful leader of the Muslims of Uttar Pradesh, Liaquat Ali Khan, was assassinated in 1951 by an Afghan for reasons never discovered. Khan had managed the troubled political processes of the first years in his capacity as prime minister acting under the authority of the constituent assembly, which continued the struggle to devise a constitution until January 1956. Like India's 1950 constitution, it was a long document framed on the lines of the Government of India Act of 1935 in order to continue the centralized power of the Raj. The nine years required to agree upon and ratify it reflected the implacable differences among the politicians of the Muslim League and other parties, on the one hand, and between religious and political leaders, on the other.

Politicians in Pakistan, like their counterparts in the Congress, assumed that a modern administration and politico-legal framework should be created;

however, unlike in India, religious spokesmen had immense privileges, and they insisted on setting into place an Islamic regime. For those who sought a modern state, the major serious aim was that of creating a federal system that balanced established provincial and central interests. This was a relatively simple objective compared with the demands of diverse Islamic interests. Given these large differences, the absence of a dominant figure like Jinnah was sorely felt, for, had he lived, he might have reconciled the conflicting aims and foreshortened the constitution-making process. As it was, the prolonged controversy between political modernizers and their religious rivals discredited both sides and prepared the way for bureaucrats and soldiers to advance other interests.

The geographical division was but one cause of the extended delay. The agreement of the dominant Punjabi leadership to share power with neighbouring Sindhis, Baluchistanis and the Pathans of the northwest was difficult to arrive at. To this difficulty were added the demands of religious leaders that any constitution (if one were necessary at all to supplement that laid down by the Prophet Muhammad for governing Medina) must be based on Islamic principles, about which there was no general agreement. To many Pakistani religious leaders, the idea of a constituent assembly was blasphemy. Abdul Ala Maududi, the charismatic head of the Punjab-based Islam organization of mullahs, the Jamat-i-Islami, insisted that Islam needed no western constitution. A sacred constitution had been provided to all Muslims for all times by the Prophet and transmitted in shariah, Islamic canon law. Hence, for Maududi and other clerics, the Muslim League was engaging in a form of apostasy, a deviance from correct Islamic practices. Specifically, the prominent public place given to women in political discussions was excoriated. The accusation against the League of un-Islamic behaviour ended by opening the political arena to other forms of opposition as well, in particular to senior soldiers and administrators.

AMERICAN ECONOMIC INVOLVEMENT

The early development of Pakistan was also influenced by the special relationship that obtained with the United States. In October 1947, a few months after its independence began, Pakistan approached Washington with urgent requests for US$2 billion in aid to meet emergency administrative and defence costs. In return for aid the government was willing to align its foreign relations and defence polices with those of the USA. The overt client relationship that was sought contrasts sharply with India's principled non-alignment, both then and later, but warfare over Kashmir sharpened the desperation of the Pakistanis; the dispute had revealed military weakness and heightened the anxiety for external financial and diplomatic support.

The humiliating position of mendicancy eased when the USA decided to extend its world reach by creating the Southeast Asia Treaty Organization (SEATO) in 1954, conferring a partnership (albeit a weak and junior one) upon Pakistan for the purpose of containing Asian communism. The partnership included modest additional resources for building military strength and

enhanced the standing of the army in the political system. The central bureaucracy grew as a result of the conditions laid down by the Americans for the
receipt of aid. Over the twenty-five years from the creation of SEATO until the
USA-led opposition to the Soviet invasion of Afghanistan in 1979, the flow of
American arms served to intensify the martialization of the government, its
bureaucracy and, at length, the important business circles into which senior
members of the officer corps and civil administration had begun to insinuate
themselves. Whatever the domestic forces and external pressures from India in
determining national policy, dependency upon the United States was preponderant from the beginning.

Unlike the Congress Party in India after Independence, the Muslim League
lost its primacy in Pakistan politics after Jinnah's death in September 1948; it
fragmented into regional parties, each more concerned with building their
subnational constituencies than with the solution of Pakistan's national problems. The Pakistani army represented the strongest national institution, and
seized the major task of state-building. While not possessing better 'Islamic
qualifications', soldiers had the reputation for greater virtue and patriotism
than politicians, who, with few exceptions, acquired reputations as corrupt
self-seekers. A full-blown military dictatorship was preceded and facilitated
by the intrusion of the Cold War into the subcontinent, when the United
States invited Pakistan to join its Middle East Treaty Organization in
1955. The American connection provided a source of external support for
the military modernizers when they decided to set aside the constitution and
take formal control of the country, which happened in late 1958. Under
the direction of Ayub Khan, the military junta set aside the quarrelling
subnational parties and the squabbling religious leaders to launch a programme of agrarian and industrial modernization intended to create a national
capitalist economy controlled by an alliance of Punjabi soldiers and Sindhi
industrialists.

POLITICAL AND SOCIAL FRAGMENTATION

The Muslim League soon found that it had competitors. The most important
of these was the Awami League, which was particularly powerful in Bengal
and represented the special interests and problems of that teeming and impoverished province. Now renamed East Pakistan, it consisted of around one-
sixth of the territory, but contained nearly 10 million more people (42 million
Bengalis as against the 33 million in the west) than West Pakistan. The main
supporters of the Muslim League in East, as in West, Pakistan were Muslim
refugees from the United Provinces of British India.

Provincial elections in West Pakistan in 1951 gave the Muslim League an
overwhelming majority of seats, about three-quarters of the total. At the same
time, in Bengal the League lost its hold on voters because of resentment there
at the proportion of high posts held by Punjabis and because of the imposition
of Urdu as the official language. Issues such as these opened the way for the
Awami League to combine with some old Congress partisans to oppose the
League in the ballot box and elsewhere. General strikes were launched in

support of a radical programme of socio-economic measures and the retention of Bengali as the state language. These demonstrations continued in 1952 and were put down by military violence in the East Bengali provincial capital of Dacca. All remaining support for the Muslim League evaporated.

In West Pakistan, especially in the army and the bureaucracy, it was feared in the 1950s that the Awami League might fall under the influence of Bengal's active communist movement, an anxiety that fit well with the Cold War fixations and strategies of the USA. American strategic planners, despairing of recruiting Nehru's India to an anti-communist bloc in southern Asia, welcomed Pakistan's Punjabi elite to their crusade.

Soon Pakistan's industrialists, concentrated around the capital of Karachi, joined the alliance of soldiers and officials in clamouring for credits to import American machines for the production of consumer goods. They were also attracted to this alliance by gratitude to the police and army for maintaining order and discouraging strikes. In Bengal, too, jute producers and other industrialists were increasingly grateful for the repression of strikes by the police and army, which pushed politicians who strove to maintain something distinctively Bengali to more radical measures. Widespread popular opposition to the military pact with the USA resulted in demonstrations in Bengal when the formal treaty was signed, in March 1954. To still these anti-government rallies, governor's rule was imposed over an East Pakistan assembly dominated by an alliance of left parties.

At the root of Bengali opposition was outrage at the widening disparity of opportunity for non-Punjabis. Even as late as 1956, no Bengali had reached the upper echelons of the central civil service, and of the over 700 posts of the next tier of officials in East Pakistan, 90 per cent were staffed by Punjabis or by *muhajir* (literally 'refugees'); that is, Urdu-speaking migrants from the old United Provinces of British India. Bengalis and Pathans were permitted to take up some inferior offices, but qualified applicants from Sind and Baluchistan remained frozen out of the state employment that spelled decent salaries and the provision of pensions. By the late 1950s, opposition had spread in all the provinces – in the west as well as Bengal – against the Punjabis and their muhajir allies.

Though non-Punjabis in Pakistan were to a degree drawn together by the shared inequalities they suffered, there were complex cultural and also class differences that separated them. In India the same sort of complexity and competition was successfully mediated by the Congress Party, the prestige of whose victory over the British might have been wearing thin by the late 1950s, but still commanded respect under Nehru. His achievements in the world, in the Asian region and in the subcontinent, too, could not be matched by any Pakistani politicians. Without either a national party or leader to blunt the divisions in Pakistan, the glue of religious ideology grew ever more important. A common faith smoothed some of the fierce edges of linguistic, cultural and economic competition, and in the predominantly agrarian society of Pakistan during the 1950s, extended families provided the main locus of social coherence, while connections with other institutions were sustained by patronage relations between dominant local households and their clients.

Around 1950, national surveys revealed that about three-quarters of Pakistan's population of around 75 million were directly engaged in agriculture, from which around 60 per cent of total national income was generated. Owing to the advanced development of irrigation by the British in the riverine colonies of the Punjab, there was food enough for export, which supplied the currency to buy the manufactured goods that Pakistan did not produce. Because the existing pattern of rural production was deemed adequate, almost nothing was done to improve agriculture or to alter extant class relations. Landed lineages or extended landed 'brotherhoods' controlled all local economic, social and political relations, and continued in place together with traditional religious and social deference.

RELIGION AND MODERNIZATION

Islam – that is to say, the little world around the local mosque and Muslim schools – remained as it was, particularly after Jinnah and his Muslim League colleagues abandoned attempts at religious reform because efforts to introduce more uniform practices and beliefs had generated fierce resentment among the rural elite. As long as he and his successors spoke generally about Islam and did not interfere with the highly varied local practices and associated social structures, the countryside cared little about the controversies over religion in the cities.

There the Muslim League and other political parties fought continuously to defend their modernization policies against the excoriations of fundamentalists such as Maududi and his Jamat-i-Islami associates, who fulminated that any changes were Indian-inspired and 'un-Islamic'. To appease the mullahs, a ban on alcohol consumption was imposed, except in Karachi, the capital and largest commercial centre. The public impression, however, was that prohibition had been enacted less for reasons of piety than for the politically corrupt to profit from illegal production. Attempts to enforce specific, uniform religious observances during Ramazan led to violent opposition from Pathans, who heaped further discredit upon political leaders. Policy failures and scandals inspired politicians to yet more cynical recourse to religion; protection of the Faith became a substitute for effective state policies. Military and bureaucratic modernizers and political critics soon become impatient with incessant appeals to religion, and were joined during the 1950s and 1960s by a national bourgeoisie that had come into existence under the protection of the senior military and bureaucratic officials.

As in India, planning was the instrument of choice. Five year plans were instituted in 1954 with the aim of grafting an urban, industrial element upon an overwhelmingly agrarian society. The designated agents of planned development (and its first beneficiaries) were a commercial middle class, many of whom had migrated to the country from India at the time of partition and gathered in the new capital, where they joined older Sindhi merchants and bankers.

A major objective of directed economic change was repairing the economic dislocation caused by partition. Pre-partition trade had involved wheat from the northwestern and rice from the northeastern wings of the subcontinent, which were exchanged for the manufactured goods of northern India and elsewhere in the world. During the first years of independence, despite the bitterness of the Kashmir issue, an estimated 70 per cent of food exports still went across the frontier to India for this purpose. To reduce its dependency on foreign manufactures, state-directed expenditure for development was carried out between 1949 and 1954, and followed up in the first five year plan. The success of these measures was registered in a shift between 1949, when jute and raw cotton comprised 90 per cent of exports, and 1960, when those two commodities were reduced to about 50 per cent of exports and manufactured jute and cotton goods comprised about a quarter. In the same period, imports also changed, reflecting a restructured economy. Thus, in 1949 the country was self-sufficient in food, but cotton yarn, cloth and machinery were imported, while in 1960, food grains accounted for about 15 per cent of imports and machinery to support manufacturing in the country had risen to one-third of all imports.

There was a strong urban bias in development, with industry and mining, together with housing and urban infrastructure, accounting for about one-half of total developmental expenditure. Irrigation, power, transport and communications received around 10 per cent each of total development spending, and agriculture less than 5 per cent. No investments were recorded for education, health and other areas of social development in the earliest plan period. By 1960, development spending had increased fivefold, yet for all of this public and private investment there was virtually no change in per capita income: the population rose from around 79 million in 1949 to 99 million in 1960, an annual increase of nearly 3 per cent.

Like India during those first decades of independence, Pakistan depended upon foreign aid to bridge the gap between investment from domestic savings and its large public expenditures on modernization. During the 1960s, foreign aid rose to over 7 per cent of all the goods and services produced in the country, and most of this aid was deployed in non-agricultural expenditure. Thus, the country's farmers bore the brunt of sacrifice for economic development. Not only was agriculture denied the investment needed to increase output and rural incomes, but, because industrial development to substitute for imported commodities was protected by import controls, the cost of imported agricultural inputs such as fertilizer was added to the peasants' burdens.

Again like India, high military spending diminished the resources that might otherwise have been deployed to increase productivity and incomes. The result, in both nations, was the persistence of mass poverty, illiteracy and backwardness, with the slender advances in the economy consumed by population growth on a scale that cast a spectre of mass starvation over the entire subcontinent, as well as the other parts of the planet called 'the Third World', during the 1960s.

Jinnah was proven doubly wrong about the two-nation claim that lay behind the demand for Pakistan, and his error adumbrates what is perhaps the most significant aftermath of the nationalist era that formally ended in August

Plate 30 Nehru and Jinnah in the garden of Jinnah's house, May 1946 (IOL Photo 134/2 Print 28; neg. no. B 5135, by permission of the British Library).

1947. His invitation to India's Muslims to take up residence in the Pakistan homeland was not heeded by fully one-third of them, with the result that India, post-partition, remains one of the major Muslim nations in the world. The verdict against the two-nation claim was underlined by the movement of

Bengali Muslims for their own nation state, Bangladesh, in 1971. If there could be two nations, why not three? And disaffected groups in other provinces of the subcontinent have continued and still continue to pursue the logic of communalist separatism. The defection of east Bengal also demonstrated Jinnah's second, related, error, which was to suppose that Islam could overcome all prior subnational identities in what became Pakistan. Shortly after his death, quarrelling among the several major ethno-linguistic divisions of the western part of the divided nation reached a pitch that prevented promulgation of a constitution and laid the foundations for a military coup in 1958.

THE GREEN REVOLUTION: PROMISE OF PLENTY

The full consequences of widespread famine were averted – or perhaps merely delayed – in India, Pakistan and, since 1972, Bangladesh by the 'Green Revolution'. That transformation of agriculture in the subcontinent began during the 1960s with the introduction of a package of improvements in rice and wheat cultivation consisting of a combination of new high-yield seed varieties, chemical fertilizers and pesticides and irrigation based upon tube-wells, electric pumpsets and widespread electrification. The result was a quantum leap in grain production.

However, while the food shortages feared in the early 1960s were averted, Green Revolution technology exacerbated social tensions everywhere in the subcontinent. The inputs required were expensive, so the improved yields were realized only by those who were already in a position to pay for them. Rich farmers became richer everywhere, and farm families who had rarely engaged in wage labour now found themselves drawn into the paid work for others that intensive cultivation of the land made possible and necessary. Class differences were deepened and whatever remained of the older forms of community organization that had survived the age of high imperialism and the first decades of independent nationhood was now dissolved. The disadvantages of women working on the land were exacerbated, and there have been other unforeseen social and economic consequences as well. The high-yielding grain varieties have increased both harvests and crop instability. The result is that, thanks to relief programmes, dependent farm labourers are sometimes better off during 'abnormal' years, while independent peasants and shepherds fare worse.

Moreover, the success of the Green Revolution, which for a while turned India from a food-importing to a food-exporting nation, encouraged a mood of hubris. The environmental consequences of modern agriculture, the impact of fertilizers that washed into rivers, of pesticides that bred resistant strains of insects and disease, of the increased use of water on an increasingly water-stressed terrain, were ignored. Even when yields began to decrease, believers in the technological fix had faith that science could again and again produce miracles that would more than offset any adverse conditions.

ENVIRONMENTAL PROBLEMS, OLD AND NEW

India is and has been prone to all the environmental problems of both industrialized and poor countries: urban sprawl, noise, pollution, deforestation, desertification, silting, floods and droughts. But it is of special interest in several connections, particularly since it has given rise to some of the strongest and most innovative environmental movements among underdeveloped countries. Sometimes these have even involved members of the ruling Nehru dynasty, as when Jawaharlal Nehru turned some former princely hunting reserves into permanent wildlife reserves; when his daughter, Indira Gandhi, set out to save the tiger; or when her daughter-in-law served as Minister of the Environment.

DAM SCHEMES

On the other hand, the Indian government has often opposed 'bottom-up' environmental movements. Since independence, for a number of reasons, India has been notably enthusiastic about large-scale hydro-projects, even as 'Third World' countries go, and is now the site of more than half the world's large dams. It has also been the scene of several epic battles against the perceived ecological threats of such schemes, which are often aimed primarily at providing the relatively wealthy cities with water and electricity but uproot long-standing communities in the process. Of the many millions that have been displaced, only a small fraction have been resettled, not always to their satisfaction. (According to what has been termed a conservative estimate, some 14 million people have been displaced from their homes by big dam projects in India in the past 40 years, but only 3.5 million have been resettled by the state. The others have mostly landed up in the slums of big cities.)

One large dam scheme, that of Silent Valley in Kerala, was scrapped by the intervention of Mrs Gandhi, who capitulated to well publicized protests; but a more recent campaign, against a proposed river basin development scheme in the Narmada valley in Gujarat, Maharashtra and Madhya Pradesh, found the government of her heirs implacably determined to proceed in the face of widespread domestic as well as foreign opposition. The scheme was supposed to supply irrigation, drinking water and power, and in all envisaged thirty major dams, ten on the Narmada and the rest on tributaries, as well as 135 medium and 3000 minor ones. The Sardar Sarovar Project is the second largest in terms of area submerged and population displaced. Construction started in 1961, but proceeded slowly until the World Bank agreed to provide credit and loans for US$450 million in 1985, then 18 per cent of dam construction costs and 30 per cent of the water delivery project. It will cover 37,000 hectares and directly displace 27,000 families (152,000 people), but the total adversely affected will be more than a million. Those with no title to land will get no compensation. Those who are officially 'project-affected' or 'oustees' may not get anything either.

The protests eventually succeeded in forcing the World Bank to review its support for the project on the basis of deficiencies in the plans to rehabilitate the villages, but the Indian government preferred to go it alone, rejecting a proffered £200 million loan in April 1993 on the grounds that the Bank's conditions undermined the country's 'self-respect'.

FLOOD MANAGEMENT

Large dams have been criticized for environmental as well as social reasons: far from preventing floods, they have been accused of contributing to them. An increasingly respectable view of flood-prone regions, not only in India, is that where flooding is inherent, all attempts to contain large amounts of water have failed and eventually must fail. Embankments intended to control the rivers disrupt the natural drainage systems; the narrowing of the channel increases silting and the raising of the river beds, with worse consequences when they overflow, as eventually they do.

The Himalayas in particular are very new, active mountains, with violent storms and heavy rainfall. They are, moreover, subject to earthquakes, which have caused the bulk of soil movement and landslides. Consequently, the rivers are inherently given to flashing; records show there were many floods in the plains below even before the deforestation of the past couple of centuries. Flooding in Assam, for example, is mainly geologically and seismically caused. Earthquakes produce landslides and silting, which blocks and backs up rivers temporarily; when these natural dams burst, the floods are particularly devastating. (Even man-made dams must be allowed to discharge large amounts of water in stressful circumstances to prevent collapse.)

In a relentlessly growing population, it is most difficult to prevent people from encroaching on naturally flood-prone areas. An alternative strategy that has been suggested is for human populations to learn to live with and within the environment, rather than attempting to drain the wetlands, alter natural drainage patterns and even move rivers. So far, too many of the major attempts to reshape the environment have had unforeseen or uncontrollable consequences, whether economic, social or political.

One striking example of the political repercussions of attempts at environmental control may be found in the long-running dispute between India and East Pakistan (later called Bangladesh) over the diversion of the waters of the Ganges river, which runs through both countries. Its flow is subject to large seasonal variations. During the monsoon it often causes devastating floods, but in the dry season it is inadequate for the needs of the densely populated Bengal region. Starting in 1951, India planned the construction of a barrage at Farakka, near where the river enters Bangladesh, aimed at diverting enough water into the Hughli branch to flush out the port of Calcutta which lies downstream and was rapidly silting up. Despite the protests of Pakistan, and later Bangladesh, India proceeded with the construction unilaterally, and, since 1975, has diverted enough water to cause environmental damage that affects some 35 million Bangladeshis, not only by disrupting irrigation schemes, but, paradoxically, by worsening flood damage, owing to the increased silting that raised the river bed and caused the flood waters to spread further over the land.

The social results of the barrage included the displacement of some two million people from the affected area. A large number of these have migrated into India, which has given rise to ethnic conflicts in the Indian state of Assam, and has assisted right-wing fundamentalist Hindu groups, affiliated with the Bharata Janata Party (BJP), to mobilize anti-Muslim feeling among Hindus in the areas receiving the bulk of the migrants.

FIGHTING OVER THE FORESTS

Arguments have also been made that the state of deforestation in the mountains does not much affect the amounts of water released into the plains. Transpiration from leaves and deflection of rainfall mean that trees give off as well as absorb the water, especially when the rains are heavy. Nevertheless, the restoration of the forest cover is urgent for other reasons, including the well-being of the mountain dwellers themselves. As in other tropical and largely agrarian countries, forests play a particularly important role in maintaining the environmental balance needed to sustain plant and animal, and therefore human, life. The recommended proportion of forest cover, according to the Indian National Commission on Agriculture, is 33 per cent, yet at present only a minority of the regions of India still retain this much, and these are mostly in the northeastern hill states. In Jammu and Kashmir, however, the proportion is only 3 per cent, and overall the average is only about 10 per cent. The shortage of wood is so severe over many parts of India that animal dung is most commonly used for fuel, which in turn restricts its availability as fertilizer, and thus affects the productivity of the poorest farmers.

The politics of alienating forests from local control has frequently had a deleterious effect. Consequently, attempts to blame the hill people, who are often tribal and traditionally practised either hunting and gathering or shifting agriculture, for the disastrous floods that increasingly afflict the settled peasantry in the plains below the Himalayas have been generally unjust and arguably politically motivated, although sometimes protests by *dalits* ('the oppressed') against alienation of rights and deprivation of traditional livelihood have taken the form of deliberate destruction – which in turn has been used as a rationale for even more determined alienation.

The world-famous 'Chipko' (meaning 'hug' in Hindi) forest conservation movement has as one of its roots the traditions of special forest significance. In fact, prominent in the well stocked Chipko cultural armoury is a legendary incident involving the members of the Bishnoi sect of Rajasthan, which was founded in 1485. Among its rules was a prohibition against the cutting of green trees. In the eighteenth century, the maharaja of Jodhpur sent some men into a Bishnoi village to fetch wood to fire the lime kilns for a new palace. A villager named Amrita Devi set an example by hugging the first tree that had been marked for felling. Both she and the tree were cut down, and others followed suit until 364 villagers had been butchered. Only then did the maharaja have a change of heart.

But it was the British who brought in really systematic logging over large areas, shifting interest in particular types of trees at different times, according to the needs and profitability of the moment. Since independence, the transference of ownership of the forests, which were preserved, to the government has been followed by yearly allotments marked for felling being auctioned off, with industry as the favoured bidder, or by new species replacing the indigenous ones, according to varying policy decisions.

STRUGGLE OVER SPECIES: THE SURVIVAL OF THE FITTEST TREES

In the early nineteenth century, and following its defeat of the Marathas, the East India Company razed to the ground teak plantations belonging to the Maratha Kanhoji Angre. The Napoleonic Wars, however, stimulated a heavy demand for teak to build ships with. When railways were constructed, large numbers of trees were felled to provide sleepers, but so wastefully that many felled trees were left to rot. Before coal mines were in operation, wood was needed to power the locomotives. The twisted *chir* pine was unsuitable for sleepers, but later it came into demand for its resin which was used to make turpentine. The native Himalayan oak (*banj*), whose leaves provided fodder and whose branches provided fuel for the local people, was then cleared away to make room for stands of chir. (The irony is that the oak, which was for a long time thought otherwise useless, is now known to make good badminton rackets.) In the early twentieth century, there was a similar shift in attitude to bamboo, from a policy of eradication to prohibiting the natives from taking it freely for handicraft use. Post-colonial policy has taken these trends even further, substituting the exotic eucalyptus, which is less labour-intensive to raise and mainly valued for the pulpwood industries.

Beginning in 1865, laws were enacted to facilitate the acquisition of forest areas earmarked for railway supplies. The Indian Forest Act of 1878 claimed that original ownership of the forests was with the state, aiming to reduce local rights to privileges granted at the discretion of the state. Wastelands and fallow areas were included as 'forests'. This left only a little fuel for the local inhabitants and opened up the way for commercial exploitation, which was then emphasized at the expense of the 'minor forest produce' (MFP) that had traditionally been the prerogative of the indigenous people and included everything except timber: resin (used in the production of turpentine and shellac), oils, seeds, nuts, medicinal herbs, fruit, ivory, honey and wild silk (tussah), which tribal people used to trade with settled groups for their grain.

During the World Wars India was the sole source of timber for the Middle East. Following the example of the British, native rulers began to exploit their forests commercially as well. Because of the commercial value of timber, agriculture and forestry were considered opposed, not integrated, so the shifting agriculture of the mountains was deemed a sort of nuisance to be done away with, and its practitioners were reduced to wage labourers or plough farmers.

THE GANDHIAN CONNECTION

Another root of the Chipko movement lies in the teachings and methods of Gandhian satyagraha. (Gandhi's own vision, centred on his ideal of simple-living, self-supporting villages, is often considered as much ecological as spiritual.) The two most prominent spokesmen for the movement were closely connected with Gandhian disciples who were working in the Himalayas to improve health and sanitation and to develop artisanal industries for the hill people. The methods used are Gandhian in nature, centring on tree-hugging (in which the activist offers his own life rather than attacking his opponent) and the *padayatra* ('footmarch'), with educational intent.

Demonstrations in protest against the usurpation of traditional rights and livelihood, peaceful and violent, have a long history in the Indian forests, but resentment reached new heights with the passage of the Forest Act of 1927. In consequence, a number of 'forest satyagrahas' were organized, in which villagers asserted their rights in symbolic but peaceable fashion. Eventually partially successful, these demonstrations were violently suppressed, with the loss of many lives.

Following independence, the Congress Party, which had previously encouraged and supported forest protests, took over the powers and policies the imperialists had vacated, pushing them even further in its eagerness to modernize the Indian state. The continuance of colonial policy in the post-colonial era saw the emergence of a more formal phase of the forest movement in 1973, when a Gandhian-organized cooperative industry that made farm implements was denied the right to cut ash wood in a nearby forest; instead the trees were allotted to a sporting goods manufacturer from Allahabad. The local 'Self-rule Society' (DGSS) organized protests in which villagers assembled around the trees marked for felling, and persuaded or confused the lumberjacks into retreat.

In the decades since, the movement itself spread to other parts of India, taking the name *Appiko* ('hug' in Kannada) in the southern state of Karnataka. It also deepened from a dispute over rights to exploit local resources, developing a more explicitly philosophical and ecological stance, which linked it to similar movements well beyond Indian borders, and made two of its spokesmen world famous.

A third root lies in shallower and shakier ground. The Chipko movement is widely reported to be a women's movement. The globe-trotting Sunderlal Bahuguna has called himself 'a messenger of women', and public relations prominence has been given to the leadership of individual women, such as Amrita Devi and Gaura Devi, who led twenty-seven women in an action that saved the Reni forest in 1974 when the men had been tricked into leaving the area. But the campaign itself had been the decision of Chandi Prasad Bhatt, one of the male leaders, and, in general, the role of women has been, like their classic role, to be the arms rather than brains.

Nevertheless, one effect of the struggle, like other 'grassroots' movements, has been to bring the classic roles into question. In 1980, there was a confrontation between women and their male relatives, when the men were willing to close with a government offer to exchange a community forest for a package of village improvements, but the women realized that the loss of the trees meant more weary hiking in search of their daily necessities. Women's involvement inevitably challenges their traditional place in village society, which is found in the Chipko movement itself.

Environmental degradation bears particularly heavily on women, who have generally had the responsibility for providing their families with fuel, water and regular meals. When asked which trees were wanted, men say fruit (which can be sold for cash); women want fuel and fodder trees. There is thus a distinction (which has been found in Africa as well) between 'men's trees', often those suited to the production of cash crops, and 'women's trees', which directly provide the materials necessary to carry out their day-to-day responsibilities, and, indirectly in the form of milk and fertilizer, nutrition and other necessities for their families. Money, too, when placed in women's hands, is usually used to improve family health and welfare, but when given to or appropriated by men, frequently goes to purchase drink, tobacco or other male pleasures.

In addition to gathering fuel and fodder, women have traditionally harvested a host of 'minor forest products', including fibre for rope and baskets, fruit, medicines and seeds. The poor particularly depend on the gathering of MFP (as well as other common rights) for cash and direct consumption, which can come to 55 per cent of income in households with fewer than five acres. Nationalization has meant that MFP can legally be sold only to the government, which deals with the gatherers with great capriciousness, especially with women, or illegally sold for even less money. In any case, the gatherers get only a small fraction of the market price.

THE SPLINTERING OF ENVIRONMENTAL DISCOURSE

The Chipko movement has received a high international profile, and successfully adapted and contributed to the increasingly environmentally aware terms of discourse – if not of action – now used even by governments and major international institutions such as the World Bank. But it has been, like Gandhi himself, less successful in halting the inexorable march of 'development'. State ownership of resources is inevitably accompanied by a separation between professional 'science' and local, traditional and female lore – often well in advance of any truly scientific understanding of the phenomena involved – as well as between local and national 'needs', or at least interests.

In the case of forest policy, state ownership and control has meant the increase of monocultures, such as eucalyptus and tropical pine for industrial pulp, and teak rosewood for furniture. It has also resulted in the subsidizing of forest products to benefit industrialists. Even so-called 'social forestry' programmes, supposedly meant for the benefit of local communities, often stress cash crops, and in fact the major success of social forestry has been the raising of industrial softwoods on agricultural land. Eucalyptus displaces farm labour and food crops, while private farmers get free seedlings and state help. The major failure has been in supplying biomass for rural needs. The rural poor can often get control of land only by cutting trees and ploughing, which reduces even their stake in forest preservation.

Moreover, the Chipko movement itself was riven internally. Of its two major spokesmen, Chandi Prasad Bhatt believes that forests must be preserved and protected for the use and welfare of people, which means he is not averse to economic growth as long as it is controlled by and profits local people. Sunderlal Bahuguna, on the other hand, inclines more to 'deep ecology', stressing the place of human beings within the larger web of nature. (A third branch of the forest movement is more traditionally left wing, and stresses economic development and social transformation.)

POPULATION PRESSURE

India's recent concern with environmental issues takes on increasing urgency in light of the demographic pressure which the country faces. A persistent problem is that of maintaining a level of food production adequate to sustain a growing population. From around 1921 to 1981 the subcontinent's population increased at a steadily accelerating pace. Despite this alarming trend, substantial expansion in the area under irrigation and/or double cropping and – since the 1960s – the diffusion of the technology of the 'Green Revolution' enabled food production to outpace the rate of population growth, though at a social and environmental price which is still being exacted even as the increased yields are levelling off. It is not clear whether this 'quantum leap' can be repeated, let alone indefinitely, to keep pace with the still increasing population. Indeed, it is not clear whether the natural resources, so long taken for granted as free goods, can sustain even the present population.

Slowly falling birth rates have since led to some slackening in the rate of demographic growth, which nevertheless will continue for at least another half-century, because of the relative youth of the population thanks to earlier high birth rates. The absolute annual increase (now roughly 20 million in India and more than 25 million in South Asia as a whole) remains a major cause for concern. Moreover, the problem is exacerbated by rising levels of consumption among India's burgeoning middle class (now thought to number as many as 300 million), on the one hand, and, on the other hand, by steady deterioration of the limited resource base, the paucity of new land on to which to expand cultivation and a looming global shortage of grain reserves. No technological fix to this situation presently appears on India's horizon, and one cannot therefore feel confident that a new period of acute scarcity will not bring about, as has happened repeatedly in India's past, major and unforeseeable social and political changes.

Finally, the Indian tiger is once more under threat of extinction from newly rich Chinese willing to pay exorbitant prices for the tiger's bodily material used in traditional medicines.

THE CONDITION OF WOMEN:
BROKEN PROMISES

The early nineteenth century had been the period of some social reforms, when female infanticide and sati were made illegal by the foreign invader. The debate then moved on to the question of what to do about widows (though not unwanted girls), who were considered by all to constitute a social problem. While, strictly speaking, enforced widowhood was supposedly reserved to the higher castes because it was a generally accepted marker of caste 'purity', castes that wished to rise in status often imposed restrictions on the marriage of widows as a first step in that direction.

The first census, that of 1881, showed that one-fifth of the women of all castes were widows. All male observers, both Indian and British, and well into the second half of the twentieth century, accepted that 'young widows', defined as those whose marriages had not yet been consummated, were, in Gandhi's own words, 'a source of corruption and dangerous infection to society'.[1] The first remedy seemed obvious – get them married – although even Gandhi held the contradictory view that if her marriage had been consummated, a widow should never remarry.

In any case, the attempt by high caste reformers to encourage men to marry widows (who, like other women, had no say in the matter) was a dismal failure. The reformers then turned their attention to raising the age of consent; that is, the age at which sexual relations with girls, even within marriage, was legal. This, of course, did not tackle the problem of 'young widows'. In 1860, the age of consent was set at ten years. (It should be noted that it was only twelve in England at the time.) In the 1880s, women themselves began to agitate on this matter, and a petition urging the raising of the age of consent to twelve years was signed by two thousand and forwarded to Queen Victoria. The Bill was passed in 1891.

It was not until 1929 that the age of marriage itself was fixed at fourteen for girls, and eighteen for boys. The Hindu Marriage Act of 1955 set the minimum age for the marriage of Hindu girls at eighteen, which is still almost two years above the slowly rising average age. For the most part, however, such matters are determined by each religious community for itself.

Another avenue for improving the condition of widows that received attention from reformers was education. An educated girl, it was thought, was likely to be married later. Education would be even more beneficial to widows, since once a woman marries, she ceases to be the responsibility of her natal family, and once she is widowed she is often repudiated or mistreated by her in-laws. Hence many girls' schools were opened by social reformers in the nineteenth and early twentieth centuries.

The mean female age of marriage rose steadily in the twentieth century. In 1901 it was thirteen years; by 1961 it had risen to sixteen. However, female literacy remained low. In 1901, when around 10 per cent of males were judged literate, only 1 per cent of females were; in 1951, male literacy had risen to 25 per cent, while the overall female rate stood at 8 per cent. Though 13 per cent

Plate 31 Three voters queue outside a polling booth in Tamil Nadu, 1996 (two appear to be widows)(Courtesy of K. Gajendran and Frontline).

of females could read a decade later, this was still inadequate for altering the status of women in most parts of India. (At present the female literacy rate is still only 27 per cent, half that of the male.) Moreover, the figures vary widely with the regions, and are much lower in rural than in urban places.

Many other forms of discrimination suffered by women were not remedied, and some were institutionalized. The Hindu Marriage Act of 1955, which permitted divorce on the initiative of women as well as men, failed to accord the same standing to women's claims to 'reasonable grounds' for divorce as to men's. Moreover, husbands by right could demand that their wives resign from jobs they deemed inconvenient or inappropriate.

Other evils have actually increased. Dowry, like sati, was originally a marker of high-caste Hindu status. It has gradually been adopted by almost all segments of the population, since payment to bridegrooms and their families to enhance the value of 'the gift of a virgin' (*kanya dana*) was considered a more prestigious practice than payment to the bride's family ('bride-price'), which had long been the custom among middle-ranking castes (and Muslims). The Dowry Prohibition Act of 1961 (which excluded Muslims and the state of Kashmir) was never seriously implemented, so that women's families continue to be subjected to pressures from in-laws to add to the dowry paid at the time of marriage, pressures that include the harassment and abuse of hapless wives. Such practices sometimes culminate in suicide or murder, and since the number of castes following the practice of dowry increased during the twentieth century, more and more women were placed in jeopardy, and the amounts demanded have continued to increase.

From the first census, in 1881, the number of males counted in the population exceeded that of females, whereas, given equal nutrition and care, the ratio should show a preponderance of women, reflecting greater natural female longevity. The ratio of men to women in the Indian population continued to shift against women throughout the twentieth century: in 1901 there were 972 females to every thousand males; in 1951 the ratio had diminished to 946; and in 1961 to 942. This overall average varied regionally. Some states – Kerala, Orissa and Tamil Nadu – consistently showed a higher (though still depressed) ratio, while in others – such as Kashmir, Punjab and Rajasthan – it has always been much lower (and it is even lower in Pakistan). It is not known to what extent the census returns are distorted by the underenumeration of girls and women, who still lead relatively secluded lives; moreover, the ratio is subnormal throughout Asia (and even in parts of Africa, although in others families contrive to have fewer boy children). Nevertheless, in India, as in some other countries, it is certain that deliberate attempts are made to dispose of unwanted females through the practices of female infanticide, or, more usually, differential care (where girl children – and women – are given less, and less nutritious, food, and often deprived of medical treatment). Since it is now possible to determine foetal sex, the practice of aborting large numbers of unwanted female foetuses has been increasing as well. Although in India this practice is linked by the perpetrators to the ruinous costs of dowry and the marriage of daughters, it is found as well where marriage costs are borne by the groom's family, and, in any case, the prospective expenses of raising and settling sons are generally contemplated with equanimity.

WOMEN IN AGRICULTURE

Despite some advances in the professions and business, Indian women have been as fixed occupationally in agricultural and menial pursuits as ever they have been, and this means in work that paid the lowest wages. In 1911, three-quarters of working women were cultivators or agricultural workers; in 1961, when women in the workforce had nearly doubled in number, the proportion was marginally greater, and by 1991 it was over 80 per cent. Nearly 70 per cent of the population as a whole derives its livelihood from land resources, and women contribute an estimated 55–66 per cent of the total labour involved in farm production.

Even as agricultural workers, the position of women has deteriorated. Between 1951 and 1991, the proportion employed as labourers increased from 31 to 44 per cent, while those who worked as tenant cultivators decreased from 45 to 35 per cent. Until the beginning of the twentieth century, 80 per cent of India's natural resources were common property; at present 55 per cent is privately owned and 28 per cent under the control of the government. What common resources remain, of which women are heavy users, are badly managed and have deteriorated, since they are now mainly used by the poor. In general, the privatized titles have been given to men, and the government employees who manage what is government controlled are mostly male. Agricultural extension work, too, has been focused on male farmers.

The Green Revolution has meant a mechanization of operations such as irrigation and milling, which have been taken over by men, leaving women, who used to do the threshing, less in control of the grain raised by family labour, which is now taken directly from the land to the mill. Cash receipts are usually given to men. Moreover, the high-yielding grain varieties were bred to have shorter stalks, and, since they do not lodge as easily, leave less for gleaning. The shorter, stiffer stalks are less suited to animal fodder, the provision of which is still often the women's responsibility. The outcome of the lessening of women's control over food production and income has been a relative loss of status and an increase in wife battering.

THE WOMEN'S MOVEMENT IN INDIA

While Nehru opposed those of his colleagues who wished to see no changes in the relations between men and women or in the class structure, he was no sexual revolutionary. Although he did speak in support of the Dowry Prohibition Bill of 1961 when it was debated in a joint sitting of Parliament, he urged its passage as a family relief measure, referring with horror to the numbers of Indian girls who killed themselves out of shame because their families did not have the means to arrange suitable marriages for them.

The credit for launching the idea of women's suffrage in India has been claimed by Margaret Cousins, like Annie Besant an Irish woman who became an Indian reformer. In 1917, Cousins addressed a memorandum to the viceroy which was presented by a deputation of women led by Sarojini Naidu, and demanded better facilities for the health and education of women, and the removal of female disqualification in the spheres of administration and local government. It also, since the viceroy was concerned with the expansion of Indian rights to self-government, demanded the franchise on the same basis as that given to men. Although at first dismissed, women's suffrage was eventually achieved in India with far less opposition than it had met in the west.

In 1926, Cousins founded the All India Women's Conference, which later became the main forum for concern with social and educational reforms. Nevertheless, until the 1970s, women's rights and welfare continued to be asserted in the name of child, family or national betterment. In that decade, however, a movement that had been anxiously concerned with preserving femininity and reassuring the public that the activity of cooking would be maintained began to address a set of urgent issues that affected women of all classes and castes. These included child marriage, dowry, sexual harassment, rape and domestic violence, and the extreme overwork, exploitation, undernourishment and excessive childbearing that particularly afflicted poorer women. Since then, Indian feminism has rivalled or surpassed the western brands in activism, influence and sophistication, despite the enormous hurdles that still remain.

COMMUNAL POLITICS: SHATTERED PLURALISM

'Communal' politics in South Asia, expressed in terms of language, territory, religion and distinctive socio-cultural forms, including caste, flared repeatedly during the past century. For example, language conflict in the late nineteenth century was reflected in demands to replace the Arabic script which had been adopted for Urdu with the 'indigenous' Devanagari script of Sanskrit and Hindi. Another instance was the demand during the 1920s of Telugu-speakers in Madras Presidency for a separately administered territory within Madras and, eventually, a separate state. By the time that demand was acceded to, the notion that the Muslims of India were a separate nation by virtue of their religion had been realized by the creation of Pakistan.

By the middle of the 1960s, the politics of state systems and constituent communities had changed in dangerous ways in both India and Pakistan, although it differed markedly in the two countries in the first decades of statehood. The form of communal politics practised in Pakistan was ethnic, centred on the opposition of Bengalis, Sindhis, Pathans and Baluchis to the hegemony of Punjabis in the military and bureaucracy and increasingly in big business as well. Overwhelming, Punjabi privilege focused the politics of non-Punjabis and shaped it into a demand for territorial zones in which they could maximize opportunities for themselves or at least balance the accumulated advantages of Punjabis throughout the country. In India it focused on religion, caste and language in the competition for jobs and perceived privileges in the changing social and economic climate.

PUNJABI HEGEMONY IN PAKISTAN

Groups whose supra-local power in the Republic of India derived from their numbers and economic dominance were widely dispersed, in contrast with the political hegemony enjoyed by Punjabis alone in Pakistan. As a result of that singular Punjabi focus, ethnic politics focused on the opposition of regional parties and factions to the centre, whose bureaucracy and army were the special preserve of Punjabis. Another advantage enjoyed by Punjabis was the wealth they had derived by virtue of the endowment of canal irrigation from British times. Protection of that colonial inheritance was assured during the bloody birth throes of Pakistan, when millions of Muslims fled from eastern

Plate 32 'City for Sale' by Gulam Shaikh. Oil on canvas, 1981–4, 306 cm high, 204.5 cm wide. The painting ironically juxtaposes communal riots in Baroda with the cinema showing of *Silsila* (chain or pedigree) which took place at the same time. The painter commented, 'The two events constituted heights of vulgarity and violence: shameless profiteering from the public display of privacy and collective carnage.' A further intended irony is found in the group of three men to the right and a woman selling vegetables to the left: life proceeding as normal in the midst of a riot (IS15–1986, Courtesy of the Victoria and Albert Museum).

Punjab and other places to avoid massacres by Sikhs and Hindus. The authorities then limited the permanent settlement of refugees in the Punjab to other Punjabis. Urdu-speaking refugees from the Gangetic valley and elsewhere were settled in Sind, a relatively poor agricultural area. As for the largely Hindu urban populations of Karachi and other Sind cities, contrived attacks against them broke out in January 1948, inducing them to flee to India, whereupon their houses and businesses were taken over by Urdu-speaking refugees from India.

Bengalis, Pathans, Sindhis and Baluchis in their various regional homelands had differential success against the Punjabi-controlled centre. In Bengal and the Northwest Province there were homogeneous populations of Bengali- and Pushto-speakers with histories of political mobilization; for the Bengalis, activism began with the agitation against the Bengal partition of 1905, while for the Pushtos, it commenced with Abdul Ghaffar Khan's successful unification of Pathan clans to support Gandhi's satyagrahas in the 1920s. Extended conflict between Bengal and the Punjabi-dominated centre under a series of military dictators turned on the imposition of Urdu, the national language of Pakistan, on Bengalis and the denial of high civil service posts to them. Large and threatening Bengali demonstrations through the 1960s provoked violent repression by Punjabi soldiers until the short, bloody civil war ensued in which India intervened on behalf of the breakaway Bangladesh in 1971.

CASTE, RELIGION AND LANGUAGE IN INDIA

Communal politics is inevitably about claims to 'justice', including the demands of oppressed people for special benefits to compensate for past injustices or the 'natural justice' demanded by people of a historic territory for special access to opportunities there, as 'sons of the soil'. In India nothing approximating the hegemony of Punjabis in Pakistan existed in the 1960s. Rather, demands for employment and educational quotas arose from many sorts of groups, beginning with the lower castes. Known legally as 'scheduled castes', these were the untouchables of old, Gandhi's 'Harijans', whose new designation derived from a section of India's 1950 constitution which listed historically oppressed groups entitled to receive positive discrimination to compensate for ancient disabilities. Another designation used widely since the 1970s is *dalit* (literally, 'oppressed'). Demands by dalits for preference in employment or education quotas were met by opposition from others – including relatively well off sons of the soil – who considered that they deserved similar protection even though they were not untouchables.

Some manifestations of communal consciousness and politics in India did resemble the subnational politics of Pakistan. In 1947, on the eve of partition, some Bengalis belonging to the Muslim League joined others belonging to the Indian National Congress in proposing a separate state of Bengal, with the implication that differences between Muslims and Hindus were not as divisive as their shared language and culture was unifying. Jinnah supported the idea, but Congress leaders rejected it, partly because they saw this as a move toward the dreaded balkanization of the subcontinent and partly because business leaders in the Congress were loath to see Calcutta's resources lost to nationally controlled capitalism.

Another manifestation of subnationalist sentiment came from the part of the Punjab included in the Indian Union after independence, where an agitation began for a state called Khalistan to be a homeland for Sikhs. Here a religious and a linguistic national identity were combined, for the Punjabi language was written in the Sikh scripture (*Adi Granth*).

THE POWER OF THE PETTY BOURGEOISIE

It is easily assumed that the affinities of people for the places of their birth and residence, their language, their religion and their caste are primordial, entailing unconditional loyalty. Without denying that the ascriptive component of identity – for instance, the 'mother tongue' – is important, social class, particular practices and historical circumstances inflect and amend that inheritance.

The lower-middle class seems to be critically connected with communal politics. One explanation is that in this section of the middle class, in the subcontinent as elsewhere, there is particularly intense competition for employment considered socially prestigious, yet just within reach, such as urban white-collar jobs in government and business. During the twentieth century clerical workers have represented an expanding social category relative to the older classes in the subcontinent, such as the landowners, industrial workers and independent agriculturists. As a differentiated class segment, they emerged during the late eighteenth century as a manifestation of larger historical changes. Clerical employment burgeoned with the East India Company, as opportunities opened, primarily in government service, but also in managing agencies and other European-style firms. In the twentieth century there has been increasing competition for the regular salaries, pensions and prestige of government employment. Those with English educations and government jobs expected their sons to succeed them, and sought to exclude potential competitors. Some older groups lost their dominance. The decline of Muslim employment in the civil service of the United Provinces was well known: from having held around two-thirds of the high posts in 1857, Muslims in 1913 held but one-third, a fact that would have been noted as much by those who filled the jobs as by those who were excluded.

Another example of ethnic competition for employment was the Dravidian movement mounted by non-brahman Tamil-speakers against the Tamil brahman monopoly in coveted government employment in the Madras Presidency. Following the mood of the time, the logical outcome of non-brahman self-assertion was a call for the creation of 'Dravidistan' – a separate homeland for all non-brahman speakers of Dravidian languages. It was a demand by Tamil sons of the soil that neatly turned against the brahmans their ancient claim to have been migrants from the Aryan north, and denied them their genuine roots in the place of their birth. It also spawned a religious reform movement, termed 'Self-respect', which called for all non-brahmans to repudiate brahman priestly claims and so modify ritual and social practices accordingly. Out of this movement came the Justice Party, which won office under the 1919 constitution.

Non-brahman intellectuals of the first two decades of the twentieth century importuned the British authorities to increase the availability of government education and employment for lower castes. This demand was met in 1921 on the initiative of the Justice Party ministry in Madras. The Dravidistan project failed, however, because non-Tamils resented the hegemonic ambitions of Tamil politicians. All the same, the ground was prepared for emergence of the Tamil Dravida Munnetra Kazhagam (DMK), which displaced the Congress as the governing party in Tamil Nadu state in the 1960s.

THE BACKWARD CLASSES

More numerous than ethno-religious parties were the movements for the preferential advance of regional castes in the provinces where they were preponderant and influential. Gandhi's reforms of the Congress facilitated these movements, and the style of his politics through the 1930s encouraged spokesmen for the numerically significant landed castes to take control of local and provincial Congress offices. In 1953, these regionally dominant and politicized lower middle-class and caste groupings succeeded in pressing a reluctant central government to provide the same measure of positive educational and employment discrimination for them as for untouchable castes, or dalits. There were about 2400 of these so-called 'backward classes', who received entitlements similar to those of the 'scheduled castes' defined in the Constitution, an estimated one-third of India's population. The rural and small-town 'backward classes' were separately defined by each of the states, which also devised remedies for their 'backwardness'.

'Backward classes' are disproportionately constituted of middle and rich farmers. They have increased their wealth and with that their local power as a result of both the reforms which made land available for them to purchase or use and the improvements in agricultural production associated with the Green Revolution. Their claims to positive discrimination included quotas for assisted educational places and employment in government service for their sons. This not only diminished the scarce opportunities for dalits in the same state, but explicitly excluded from competition qualified candidates from other states. One of the most virulent examples of such a nativist movement was the Siva Sena (God's army) based in Bombay, which came into being in the mid-1960s with the object of harassing and intimidating south Indians who worked in the city. Their violent tactics were later extended to Maharashtrian Muslims as well.

Hostility between groups competing for scarce jobs and education was intensified by the prolonged economic depression of the 1920s and 1930s. It was especially vicious among the lowest class of workers in small towns and cities, where there was a constant struggle for lowly work, such as portering in markets or carrying materials on construction sites. Competition for such humble employment was constantly fed in the depression decades by migrants from the countryside in search of work. When competing groups were easily marked by religious or linguistic differences, the basis for communal mobilizations and violent confrontations was at hand. When to this incendiary combination were added the fears of established regional business groups about the invasive pressure upon their markets from large national and international firms, the organization of and funding for managed communal strife multiplied.

INDIA AND THE WORLD

External factors were just as important as the domestic situation for Nehru and India during the 1950s, and in ways additional to the reliance on the United States and its allies for development funds. Indeed, it was in the field of foreign relations that Nehru's achievements appeared to be most impressive. Domestically he was pulled from one side to the other of the Indian political spectrum in an effort to balance the communist-led left and the communalist right, and his secularizing and anti-poverty programmes were compromised, but the world agreed that he was one of its great statesmen.

The world into which the Indian republic was born in 1947 was a dangerously divided one, but one in which a new, large nation was bound to find a role. In the Cold War competition between the superpowers, which was the context in which India's foreign policies were defined by Nehru, India and China were both glittering prizes because of the sheer mass of their territories and peoples.

It was not surprising that anti-imperialism should have shaped a large part of his response. In foreign relations, there was no one in India with a standing to compare with that of Nehru, except perhaps V. K. Krishna Menon, Nehru's long-time friend, his delegate at the United Nations and perhaps his leftist conscience. In any case, both saw anti-imperialism as the foundation for India's alliances and antagonisms. And between the superpowers, Nehru considered the Americans the more dangerous. In his estimation, the Americans had inherited the British imperial interests along with its world-dominating capitalism, whereas the Soviets had renounced empire at the time of the Russian Revolution, and was excused its European expansion after the Second World War. The perceived danger of the United States was deepened by the clienthood into which Pakistan placed itself in service of the American aim of 'containing' Soviet influence in Asia.

The war over Kashmir had convinced Pakistan in 1948 that Indian military power in the subcontinent was greater than any it could mount; therefore it needed outside allies. The conflict over Kashmir had also persuaded both India and Pakistan that no reliance could be placed upon the United Nations, which had been unable to resolve the matter to the satisfaction of either country. Nevertheless, Nehru offered considerable assistance to the UN during the Korean War, which ultimately pitted the Americans against India's Chinese friends. India helped to negotiate the repatriation of Korean prisoners of war, an intervention appreciated on all sides. Again, India scored a foreign policy success by using its good offices in ending the war between France and the Vietminh nationalists, after the latter had frustrated post-war French attempts to re-establish their colonial regime. Indian assistance was seen as important in the Geneva Conference of 1954, which ended French control in Indochina.

BANDUNG AND NON-ALIGNMENT

When Pakistan joined the USA-sponsored Southeast Asian Treaty Organization, Nehru and Krishna Menon condemned what they saw as creeping American hegemony over Asia, acting through surrogates like Pakistan. In opposition, India took the initiative of organizing a highly successful meeting of the previously colonized nations of Asia and Africa in the Indonesian city of Bandung in 1955. A major event at the meeting was Nehru's enunciation of the doctrine of non-alignment: a refusal to join either of the blocs being constructed by the superpowers, while reserving the right to take a position on international issues according to the merits of each case.

Under his leadership, pressure from the two superpowers to align with one or the other was rejected; the issues in the struggle between the Cold War giants of the capitalist 'First' and socialist 'Second' worlds were to be treated as they arose and impacted on the 'Third World' of post-colonial, developing societies. Nehru also formulated a set of principles to govern relations among the 'Third World' powers: territorial integrity, non-aggression, non-interference, equality with mutual benefit and peaceful coexistence. Another of Nehru's achievements was in bringing the Chinese communists, in the person of Chou Enlai, into world affairs after an extended ostracism inspired largely by the United States. Concluding a treaty with the Chinese, in which China's incorporation of Tibet was recognized, in the year before the Bandung Conference, paved the way for achieving anti-imperialist unity.

The Bandung Conference earned India world respect and was crowned by a visit to India in 1955 of several important Soviet leaders, including Secretary of the Communist Party Khrushchev and President Bulganin, to cement a closer Indo-Soviet relationship. All in all, Nehru's diplomacy seemed a glorious confirmation of India's international importance, and it was surely Nehru's greatest moment. The second five year plan had been launched with the expectation that it would make India, already one of the most industrialized nations of the world, a truly modern state. The Congress Party seemed invincible to political foes and was enjoying vast prestige and affection throughout the country. The accomplishment of great diplomatic successes seemed to crown his achievements. It was but a moment, however, and signs of trouble soon emerged.

The world press began to raise awkward questions about the claim of non-alignment and impartiality in Cold War conflicts. Why, it was asked, when the British and Israelis invaded Nasser's Egypt in 1956, was Indian condemnation swift, whereas when the Soviet Union invaded Hungary disapprobation was withheld? And did not the dependence of the country on development credits and loans from the United States impair the impartiality needed for a truly non-aligned stance? Most distressing in every way, however, was the breakdown in Indo-Chinese relations. In October 1962, Nehru actually went to war with another non-aligned nation in defence of boundaries which India itself admitted had been unjustly drawn by British colonialism.

BANDUNG MISALIGNED

It was on the southern border of Tibet, high in the barren Himalayas, that the Chinese crisis arose not merely to embarrass Nehru but to deal a blow to his political standing from which he never recovered. Plainly, the resiliency that had carried him indomitably through the travails of establishing the new India was spent by the early 1960s. It was galling enough to suffer military defeat from a nation so like India in its antiquity and so close in its recent relations; it was worse that conflict with China made Indian policy seemingly revert to imperialist principles and precedents, making a mockery of the anti-imperialist stance at Bandung.

In 1950, China occupied Tibet, claiming that it was a part of China proper, long ruled by imperial Chinese authority and its republican successors. The Dalai Lama, who was both the religious and political ruler of the Tibetan people, fled to the Chinese border, but was persuaded to return by Chinese promises and one faction of his own court. The Indian government took the view that Tibet was part of China, though it had historically enjoyed a considerable degree of autonomy from Chinese rule. Nehru ordered that the military outposts inherited from the British on its Tibetan frontier be vacated, for to do otherwise would be to prolong arrangements imposed by British imperialism. This generous gesture was sealed in 1954 by a treaty between India and China which confirmed Indian trade rights in Tibet conducted via specified mountain passes, but left the actual frontier unresolved. Additionally, the treaty reiterated the principles which were to obtain in political relations between the two. There were to be five principles of peaceful coexistence, which the Indians called by the Sanskrit term *panchashila*, including mutual respect for the sovereignty and territory of each country, non-interference and non-aggression. These principles were restated at Bandung in the following year, a rhetorical flourish marking the high point of Indo-Chinese fraternity.

In 1955–6, revolts in Tibet and the threat of Chinese reprisals caused the Dalai Lama once more to flee to India; once more he was persuaded to return by Mao Zedong's promise not to implement any changes for six years – and by the intervention of Nehru himself. However, in 1959 a more general uprising triggered a third flight, murkily assisted by the American Central Intelligence Agency (CIA). Since then, the Dalai Lama has made his headquarters in northern India, and the continued harbouring and assistance given to him, and his subjects who accompanied and followed him, by the Indian government helped to feed the rising tension between the Chinese and Indian governments.

The Chinese government decided that its hold over Tibet and parts of its Central Asian territories required an all-weather military road, but, owing to the difficult mountain terrain, the project could not be completed without impinging on a tract that was designated Indian on existing maps. Because this barren plateau, Aksai Chin, was essential to Chinese plans, they decided to build the road through it quietly, supposing that so remote a place was not likely to be disputed. However, they also decided to pre-empt any objections that might arise by lodging some minor territorial claims in another sector of the frontier (which had been arbitrarily set by a British boundary commission in 1914). The plan was to finesse the Aksai Chin as part of a new boundary convention with India, and thus hold on to the new road.

Nehru sought to persuade the Chinese through secret negotiations to abandon the Aksai Chin road, but criticism began to mount from political enemies who could find little else to attack him about. Meanwhile, the Chinese grew impatient for the settlement of a matter they considered extremely important to their security, and began advancing small patrols closer to the strategic Karakoram Pass, nearly 19,000 feet over the eastern part of Kashmir. At this, India sent in troops and fighting broke out in October 1962. A division of Chinese troops pushed well into Assam without the slightest resistance from Indian military forces, and then, remarkably, withdrew; it had been a feint to cover a move on the Karakoram Pass, which lay about 100 miles north of Leh, the capital of Ladakh and part of Indian Kashmir. The Chinese seized and continued to hold the pass as well as a few hundred square miles of territory in what India insisted was a part of Kashmir. Chinese control over the high Aksai Chin plateau was assured, and both Nehru and the Indian army were defeated.

For Nehru there was to be no recovery of his previous standing, even though other foreign policy successes somewhat offset the failure with the Chinese. In 1960, he had replayed his leadership role among non-aligned nations at a conference in Belgrade, and then sought to use his prestige to persuade the Soviet leader Khrushchev to cease nuclear testing. Then, in 1961, he startled the world by abandoning his patient attempts to persuade the Portuguese dictator, Antonio de Oliviera Salazar, to give up Goa and other territories still held in India. An Indian army was sent in and seized Goa. Though this was a departure from the non-aggression that he would have preferred, most of the world sympathized with this use of force after long and fruitless diplomacy had failed. In the case of China, however, Nehru had shown himself to be self-deluded; he had failed to appreciate that vital Chinese interests involving Tibet might lead to the use of force despite his search for a peaceful resolution. Worse, he had placed himself in the position of defending and even entering into war over boundaries he admitted had been drawn by British imperialists. Yet in the end it was goading from his internal political opponents that had brought disaster. Disappointed and wasted by illness over the next two years, he died in May 1964.

PROMISES KEPT, PROMISES BROKEN

Independence had opened a new phase of historical development in India whose course became manifest within a very few years. Under Nehru, there were major achievements, which included: a democratic constitution based upon universal suffrage and incorporating secular and egalitarian principles; the displacement of some strata of encrusted privilege, such as princes and zamindars; the introduction of new patterns of land-holding in the still dominantly agrarian society of India; and the recognition of and attempts, however flawed, to restrain the runaway growth of the Indian population, which undermined measures to improve the general health of the people, and the status of women. The state was dedicated to a programme of rapid modernization of the industrial base inherited from the colonial period, while, at the same time, local control over the social base of agricultural production was strengthened. In foreign policy, Nehru also shaped a distinctive geo-politics based upon the concept of non-alignment with either Cold War superpower, but in concert with other nations of the post-colonial world. His triumph had seemed most complete in relation to the recently victorious communist regime of China, which Nehru took special pains to bring into the family of non-aligned states. His anti-imperialist credentials were crowned in 1961 when he seized the Portuguese colony of Goa on India's west coast following the persistent refusal of the Portuguese dictatorship to join in a diplomatic solution of that last bit of European imperialism in the subcontinent.

But the last years before he died were disappointing after the glorious decade of the 1950s. In nothing perhaps was this truer than in his failure and that of his Congress colleagues to establish a basis for Indian nationhood free from the imperilling residue of the historic communalism that had evolved in a complex and diverse subcontinent. Gandhi's vaguely articulated dream of rediscovering actual communities and making them the basis for a revitalized, moral and free India could not have been realized in a century when capitalism and socialism pointed Indians, along with most of world, to the means for effecting better lives for themselves and their children through industrial development. Nehru understood the imperfections of both of these compelling contemporary forces, and he believed that paths could be found or devised between the worst aspects of both alternatives. Now we are able to say that his judgement was flawed, however much we appreciate his hope for a better India. At the end of his life he seemed aware that the country had not been placed on the path to social justice and equality. Despite real achievements in its democratic institutions and in its science and technology, India was moving towards a future not different from or better than most of the world's societies, but among the poorest.

GLOSSARY OF NON-ENGLISH TERMS

abhisheka	coronation, annointment
ahimsa	non-violence
alvar	instructors of Vishnu worship
amir	general; prince
aparyapta	micro-organism
arhat	great soul, worthy one
artha	achieving one's ends
ashrama	rules
ashvamedha	horse sacrifice
ashvapati	cavalry
atman	soul
avatar	any of Vishnu's manifestations
ayurveda	traditional Indian medical system
banj	species of Himalayan oak
bhadralok	top people
bhakti	devotional worship
bodhisattva	Buddhist saint
brahmadeya	village gifted to a brahman group
brahman	member of a priestly caste
candala	untouchable caste
chakravartin	one who keeps the wheel turning
chauth	tribute paid to Maratha chiefs
chir	species of Himalayan pine
daftars	ledgers
dakshinapatha	southern road
dalit	oppressed
damma	righteousness, doctrine
dasa	slave
dasara	royal festival
dasasudda	slave
dayada	co-sharers
desh	country
deshmukh	rural chief
devaputra	son of god

devaraya	god-king
dhamma-mahamatra	ministers of morality
dharma	righteousness, doctrine
dharmashastra	code of behaviour
dhimmi	'protected' non-Muslims
Digambara	'sky clad' (naked) Jaina sect
digvijaya	royal conquests
diwan	government bureau or its chief officer
doab	land at confluence of two rivers
dubashi	bilingual
durbar	celebratory royal ceremony, court or levee
duta	emissaries
dvija	twice-born
fatwa	decision by an expert in shariah
fiqh	jurisprudence
gahapati	householder
gajapati	lord of fighting elephants
gana	clan
gana-sangha	clan assembly
ganj	rural market
ghadr	revolution
ghazi	warrior for the faith
gopi	milk maid, follower of Krishna
gopura	temple gateway
grihapati	householder
gurdwara	Sikh shrine
guru	teacher
haj	pilgrimage to Mecca
harijan	'children of god'; Gandhi's name for untouchables
hartal	strike, including closing shops and businesses
Hinayana	'Lesser Vehicle' Buddhist sect
hindutva	Hinduness
ignis	fire
inam	'gift', especially of rent-free land
iqta	assignment of grant of land by government to an individual
itihasa-purana	history tales
jagir	land given to pay for services to the crown
jama masjid	Friday (services) mosque
jana	clan
janapada	clan territory
jatakas	tales of the Buddha's lives
jati	occupational caste group
jihad	holy war
jina	victor
jizya	poll tax levied on non-Muslims

jnana	esoteric knowledge
kalam	discussion; Muslim scholasticism
kaliyuga	the age of chaos and evil
kama	love
kamavisdar	local tax farmer with police powers
kanya dana	gift of a virgin
karma	actions, behaviour
khadi	handspun and handloom cloth, particularly cotton
khalifa	Caliph; spiritual successor to the Prophet Muhammad
khilafat	caliphate; spiritual succession
kisan	peasant
kottam	small southern agrarian community
kritayuga	the pure first age
kshatra	power
kshatriya	member of warrior and ruler varna
kula	association on the basis of blood ties
kulkarni	record keeper
lingam	phallus, the symbol of Shiva
madrassah	Muslim college
mahajanapada	'great community'
mahanavami	great nine-day royal festival of South India
maharaja	great king
maharajadhiraja	great king over other kings
mahasamanta	'great neighbour'
mahatmya	temple chronicle
Mahayana	'Great Vehicle' Buddhist sect
mahayuga	entire cycle of yugas
Mahisi	chief vedic queen
mamluk	'slave' soldier
mansabdar	nobleman of Akbar's new order
matha	seminary, monastery
matsya	Vishnu as a fish
millat	minority religious enclave
mleccha	foreigner, barbarian
moksha	salvation
muhajir	Muslim migrants from India to Pakistan
muqti	recipient of an iqta
muvendavelar	soldiers of the three early Tamil royal dynasties
muventar	the three royal lineages of the Tamils
nadu	South Indian local community
nadu	local community
nanadeshi	foreign
narpati	lord of fighting men
nattar	dominant cultivators of the nadu
nayanar	instructors of Shiva worship

nirvana	salvation
padayatra	'foot march'; a form of demonstration
padshah	emperor
panchashila	five principles (of peaceful coexistence)
panchayat	village council
parda	Persian for purdah, the seclusion of women
pargana	local district, smaller than a sarkar
patil	village headman
peshwa	Maratha chief minister
pir	Sufi master
pitaka	basket, division of Buddhist scripture
pradesh	province
praja	'children'; subject people
purana	'ancient tale'; sacred narrative
purusha	primal man; person
qasba	urban market
raja	king; chief
rajabhisehka	coronation, annointment
rajadharma	king's duty
rajanya	warrior
rajaputra	king's son
rajasuya	coronation
rajavamsavali	genealogical text
rishi	sage
ryotwari	revenue system in which land is settled in return for produce
sabha	council of elders
sahagamana	immolation of the widow with her husband's corpse
samana	festive gathering
samantachakra	circle of subordinates
samiti	general assembly
samsara	transmigration
sangha	Buddhist assembly; monastic order
sankaracharya	abbot, bishop
sardeshmukh	local headman
sarkar	territorial district
sati	widow sacrifice; widow immolation
satyagraha	'truth force'; non-violent protest
satyagrahin	person engaging in satyagraha
sevika	servants
shakti	energy, life force
shariah	code of Muslim conduct
shuddi	reconversion to Hinduism
shudra	'servant'; labourer
Shvetambara	'white clad' Jaina sect
silsilah	'chain'; spiritual succession of Sufi masters

soma	intoxicating drink
sramana	ascetic
sreni	guild
srenika	guild member
sthala purana	temple chronicle
stri	woman
stridhan	women's property
suba	Mughal province
sudda	servant
sutra	portion of scripture
swadeshi	indigenous, 'own country'
swaraj	independence
thagi	dacoity; professional criminality
ulema	learned Muslim men
upanayana	initiation ceremony of the twice-born
uttarapatha	northern road
vajapeya	ceremony of royal reinvigouration
vajra	thunderbolt
varna	caste
varnashramadharma	proper caste behaviour
ventar	crowned king
vessa	commoner
vidatha	meeting
vis	commoners, farmers, traders
visamatta	receivers of tribute from vaishyas
watan	hereditary privileges
yaga	ritual, ceremony
yavana	Greek; 'foreigner'
yuga	age, eon
zamindar	landholder

PERSONS

r = regnal dates; (no office specified) = ruler; d = died; p = peshwa

Abu Hanifa (Muslim legist) ⟨d 767 CE⟩
Aditya I (Chola) ⟨871–907 CE⟩
Akbar (Mughal) ⟨r 1556–1605 CE⟩
al-Ghazzali (Muslim scholar) ⟨d 1111 CE⟩
Alauddin (Khalji) ⟨r 1296–1316 CE⟩
Alexander (the Great, king of Macedonia) ⟨356–323 BCE⟩
Ambedkar, Dr Bhimrao Ramji ('Untouchable' leader) ⟨1892–1956 CE⟩
Appar (Tamil Shaivite 'saint') ⟨c.7th century CE⟩
Arjun (Fifth Sikh Guru) ⟨1581–1606 CE⟩
Ashoka (Maurya) ⟨c.272–232 BCE⟩
Attlee, Clement (Labour Prime Minister of Britain) ⟨1883–1967 CE⟩
Augustus (Roman Emperor) ⟨c.23 CE⟩
Aurangzeb (Mughal) ⟨r 1658–1707 CE⟩
Azad, Maulana (Prominent Indian Muslim Congressman)
Babur (Mughal) ⟨1483–1530 CE⟩
Bahadur Shah (Sultan of Gujarat) ⟨r 1526–1537 CE⟩
Bahlul Lodi ⟨r 1451–1489 CE⟩
Bahuguna, Sunderlal (Chipko leader)
Bajirao (Peshwa of the Marathas) ⟨p 1720–1740 CE⟩
Balaji Bajirao (Peshwa of the Marathas) ⟨p 1740–1761 CE⟩
Balaji Viswanath (first Peshwa of the Marathas) ⟨p 1713–1720 CE⟩
Balban ('Slave') ⟨r 1266–1287 CE⟩
Banerji, Sir Surendranath (Nationalist) ⟨1848–1925 CE⟩
Bentinck, Lord William (Governor-general, Bengal and India) ⟨1828–1835 CE⟩
Besant, Mrs Annie (Theosophist; social reformer; nationalist) ⟨1847–1933 CE⟩
Bhatt, Chandi Prasad (Chipko leader)
Birla, G. D. (Indian industrialist)
Bose, Subhas Chandra (Nationalist politician) ⟨1897–1945 CE⟩
Bukka (Vijayanagara) ⟨d 1377 CE⟩
Burke, Edmund (British writer, philosopher, politician) ⟨1729–1797 CE⟩
Chandragupta (Gupta) ⟨r 320 CE⟩
Chandragupta (Maurya) ⟨c.322–298 BCE⟩
Child, Sir Joshua (Chairman of the East India Company) ⟨late 17th century CE⟩

Chingiz Khan (Mongol) ⟨d 1227 CE⟩

Churchill, Sir Winston (Conservative British Prime Minister 1940–1945, 1951–1955) ⟨1874–1965 CE⟩

Clive, Robert, Lord (Governor of Bengal, 1765–1767) ⟨1725–1774 CE⟩

Cornwallis, Charles, Lord (Governor-general, 1786–1793; 1805) ⟨1738–1805 CE⟩

Cripps, Sir Stafford (British negotiator with India) ⟨1889–1952 CE⟩

Curzon, George Nathaniel, Lord (Viceroy, 1899–1905) ⟨1859–1925 CE⟩

Dadabhai Naoroji (Indian nationalist; MP in England) ⟨1825–1917 CE⟩

Dara Shukoh (Mughal prince; son of Shah Jehan) ⟨1615–1659 CE⟩

Dayananda Saraswati, Swami (Religious reformer) ⟨1824–1883 CE⟩

Devaraya II (Vijayanagara) ⟨r 1424–1446 CE⟩

Digby, Sir William (Social reformer) ⟨1849–1904 CE⟩

Dyer, William (General, ordered the massacre of Amritsar, April 1919)

Elphinstone, Mountstuart (Governor of Bombay, 1819–1827) ⟨1779–1859 CE⟩

Firuz Shah (Tughluq) ⟨r 1351–87 CE⟩

Gaffar Khan, Abdul (Gandhian Pathan leader; the 'Frontier Gandhi')

Gandhi, Indira (Indian Prime Minister) ⟨1917–1982 CE⟩

Gandhi, Mohandas Karamchand ⟨1869–1948 CE⟩

Ghosh, Aurobindo (Nationalist and founder of Auroville) ⟨1872–1950 CE⟩

Gokhale, Gopal Krishna (Nationalist) ⟨1866–1915 CE⟩

Guru Nanak (Sikh leader) ⟨1469–1538 CE⟩

Harihara II (Vijayanagara) ⟨d 1404 CE⟩

Harshavardhana [Harsha] (Kanauj) ⟨r 606–647 CE⟩

Hastings, Warren (Governor-general of Bengal) ⟨1732–1818 CE⟩

Humayun (Mughal) ⟨r 1530–1540, 1555–1556 CE⟩

Hume, Allan Octavian (Organizer of the Indian National Congress) ⟨1829–1912 CE⟩

Hunter, Sir William Wilson (Writer, educator, social reformer) ⟨1840–1900 CE⟩

Ibrahim Lodi (Delhi) ⟨r 1517–1526 CE⟩

Iltutmish ('Slave') ⟨r 1211–1236 CE⟩

Irwin, Edward, Lord (Viceroy 1925–1931) ⟨1881–1946 CE⟩

Jahangir (Mughal) ⟨r 1605–1627 CE⟩

Jinnah, Mohammed Ali (Nationalist politician; founder of Pakistan) ⟨1876–1948 CE⟩

Jones, Sir William (Legist, Orientalist) ⟨1746–1794 CE⟩

Kanishka (Kushana) ⟨r 115–140 CE⟩

Kapilendra (Gajapati) ⟨r 1435–1467 CE⟩

Krishnadevaraya (Tuluva) ⟨r 1509–1529 CE⟩

Kumaragupta ⟨r 415–455 CE⟩

Lala Lajpat Rai (Prominent Congressman and nationalist) ⟨1856–1859 CE⟩

Lalitaditya (Kashmir) ⟨r 724–760 CE⟩

Macaulay, Thomas B., Lord (Historian) ⟨1800–1859 CE⟩

MacDonald, Ramsay (Labour British Prime Minister 1924, 1929–1935) ⟨1866–1937 CE⟩

Mahendravarman (Pallava) ⟨d 630 CE⟩

Malabari, Behramji (Social reformer) ⟨1853–1912 CE⟩

Malcolm, Sir John (Governor of Bombay 1827–1830) ⟨1769–1833 CE⟩
Mill, James (Philosopher) ⟨1773–1836 CE⟩
Minto, Lord (II; Viceroy 1905–1910) ⟨1845–1914 CE⟩
Montagu, Edwin Samuel (Secretary of State for India 1917–1922) ⟨1879–1924 CE⟩
Morley, John, Lord (Secretary of State for India 1905–1910) ⟨1838–1923 CE⟩
Mountbatten, Lord Louis (Last Viceroy of India) ⟨1900–1979 CE⟩
Muhammad (Muslim prophet) ⟨d 632 CE⟩
Muhammad Tughluq ⟨1325–1351 CE⟩
Munro, Sir Thomas (Governor of Madras, 1820–1827) ⟨1761–1827 CE⟩
Murshid Quli Khan (Nizam of Bengal) ⟨r 1707–1726 CE⟩
Nanak, Guru (Sikh leader) ⟨1469–1538 CE⟩
Naoroji, Dadabhai (Indian nationalist; MP in England) ⟨1825–1917 CE⟩
Nehru, Jawaharlal ⟨1889–1964 CE⟩
Nehru, Motilal (Lawyer; nationalist; 'non-cooperator') ⟨1861–1931 CE⟩
Ochterlony, Sir David (General, East India Company) ⟨1758–1825 CE⟩
Patel, Sardar Vallabhbhai (Nationalist; Deputy Prime Minister) ⟨1875–1950 CE⟩
Pliny (Roman writer) ⟨d 73 CE⟩
Pulakeshin I (Badami Chalukya) ⟨mid-6th CENTURY CE⟩
Pulukeshin II (Badami Chalukya) ⟨609–642 CE⟩
Qutbuddin Aibak ('Slave') ⟨r 1206–1210 CE⟩
Rajagopalichari, Chakravarti (Congressman, Gandhian and Swatantra founder)
Rajarajachola ⟨r 985–1016 CE⟩
Rajendrachola I ⟨r 1012–1044 CE⟩
Ram Mohun Roy (Hindu social reformer) ⟨1772–1833 CE⟩
Ramabai, Pandita (Sanskrit scholar; educator of women) ⟨1858–1922 CE⟩
Ramanuja (Vaishnava philosopher) ⟨d 1137 CE⟩
Ranade, Madhav Govinda (Social reformer) ⟨1852–1904 CE⟩
Ripon, Lord George (Governor-general of India 1880–1884) ⟨1827–1909 CE⟩
Samudragupta ⟨r 335–375 CE⟩
Sayyid Ahmad Khan, Sir (Muslim leader and separatist) ⟨1815–1898 CE⟩
Shah Jahan (Mughal) ⟨r 1628–1658 CE⟩
Shahu (Maratha) ⟨r 1708–1749 CE⟩
Shambuji (Maratha) ⟨r 1680–1689 CE⟩
Shankara (Hindu theologian) ⟨788–820 CE⟩
Sher Shah (Sur) ⟨r 1539–1545 CE⟩
Shivaji Bhonsle (Maratha) ⟨1620–1680 CE⟩
Sikandar Lodi ⟨r 1489–1517 CE⟩
Tara Bai (Maratha) ⟨regent 1700–1707 CE⟩
Tilak, Bal Gangaghar (Nationalist; scholar) ⟨1857–1920 CE⟩
Timur [Tamerlane] (Mughal) ⟨d 1405 CE⟩
Tipu Sultan (Mysore) ⟨r 1783–1799 CE⟩
Vikramaditya VI (Kalyani Chalukya) ⟨r 1076–1127 CE⟩
Vishnuvardhana (Hoysala) ⟨d 1152 CE⟩
Wavell, Archibald, Lord (Governor-general 1943–1947) ⟨1883–1950 CE⟩
Wellesley, Richard, Lord (Governor-general, 1798-1805 CE) ⟨1760–1842⟩

NOTES

CHAPTER 1: INTRODUCTION

1 Satapatha-Brahmana, I Kanda, 4 Adhyaya, 1 Brahmana, verses 14–15, according to the text of the Madhyandina School, translated by Julius Eggeling. Oxford, 1882.

2 'Motupalli Pillar-Inscription of Ganapatideva: AD 1244–5', edited by E. Hultzsch, in *Epigraphica Indica*, 12, 1913–14, pp. 188ff.

3 G. W. F. Hegel, *The Philosophy of History*, translated by J. Sibree. Buffalo, NY: Prometheus Press, 1991.

CHAPTER 2: ANCIENT DAYS

1 RV, I, 1; translated by R. N. Dandekar, in W. Theodore de Bary (ed.), *Sources of Indian Tradition*. New York: Columbia University Press, 1958, p. 9.

2 RV, X, 129, 3, 6, 7; translated by Wendy Doniger, *The Rigveda*. Harmondsworth: Penguin, 1981, p. 25.

3 RV, X, 90, 6, 12; translated by R. T. H. Griffith, Benares, 1896–7.

4 RV X, 27, 11.

5 RV I, 117, 8.

6 Isha Upanishad, 8; translated by F. Max Muller, *Sacred Books of the East*, Part 1, Vol. I. Oxford: Oxford University Press, 1879–82, p. 312.

7 Shvetashvatara Upanishad, Adhayaya III, 2, 11, in F. Max Muller, *Sacred Books of the East*, Vol. XV. Oxford: Clarendon Press, 1884, pp. 244, 246.

8 RV III, 55, 16.

9 RV X, 85, 26.

10 RV X, 95, 15.

11 RV III, 2, 23.

12 Stephanie Jamison, *Sacrificed Wife/Sacrificer's Wife: Women, Ritual and Hospitality in Ancient India*, Oxford: Oxford University Press, 1996.

13 Vajradhvaja Sutra, *Shiksha-samuccaya*, compiled by Shantideva, chiefly from earlier Mahayana Sutras; translated by Cecil Bendall and W. H. D. Rouse. London: John Murray, 1922, p. 256.

14 Tarkarahasyadipikvrtti of Acarya Gunaratna and Yuktiprabodha of Upadhyaya Meghavijaya, both in Padmanabh S. Jaini, *Gender and Salvation*. Berkeley: University of California Press, 1991, pp. 153, no. 21, and 167, no. 17.

15 Culla-Vagga X, 1, in Henry Clarke Warren, *Buddhism in Translations*. Cambridge: Harvard University Press, 1922, p. 441.

16 Anguttara-Nikaya, IV, 8, 10; quoted from Cornelia D. Church, 'Temptress, wife,

nun: women's role in early Buddhism', *Anima: an Experiential Journal*, 1(2), 1975, p. 55, and cited by Rita Gross, *Buddhism after Patriarchy*. Albany: State University of New York Press, 1993, p. 42; see also Albert Schweitzer, *Indian Thought and Its Development*. Boston: The Beacon Press, 1936, p. 95.

17 Yuktiprabodha, in Padmanabh S. Jaini, *Gender and Salvation*. Berkeley: University of California Press, 1991, p. 179.

18 *The Laws of Manu*, VII, 3–6, 8; translated by Georg Buhler, Vol. XXV, *The Sacred Books of the East*. Oxford: Clarendon Press, 1886.

19 Ibid., X, 5.

20 *Bhagavad Gita*, X, 20–41; translated by S. Radhakrishnan, in Sarvepalli Radhakrishnan and Charles A. Moore, *A Source Book in Indian Philosophy*. Bombay: Oxford University Press, 1957, pp. 136–8.

21 *The Laws of Manu*, IX, 14, 15, 17.

22 Ibid., III, 61.

23 Ibid., I, 33.

24 Ibid., V, 147, 148; IX, 3.

25 Ibid., III, 56, 57.

26 Ibid., V, 154, 155, 156, 166.

27 Ibid., VIII, 416.

28 Ibid., IX, 194, 195.

29 Ibid., V, 157, 158.

30 Sunil Sethi, *India Today*, April 1985, p. 57; quoted in I. Julia Leslie, *The Perfect Wife*. Delhi: Oxford University Press, 1989, p. 279.

31 Sundaramurti Swami, 68, in F. Kingsbury and G. E. Phillips, *Hymns of the Tamil Shaivite Saints*. London: Oxford University Press, 1921, p. 75.

CHAPTER 3: MEDIEVAL INDIA

1 Quoted in Hermann Kulke and Dietmar Rothermund, *A History of India*. London: Croom Helm, 1986, p. 126; translated by K. A. Nilakanta Sastri, 'A Tamil merchant guild in Sumatra', *Tijdschrift voor Indische Taal-, Land- en Volkenkunde*, 72, 1932, pp. 321–5; see also K. A. Nilakanta Sastri, *A History of South India from Prehistoric Times to the Fall of Vijayanagar*. Indian Branch: Oxford University Press, 1932, pp. 321–2.

2 Ziauddin Barni, *Tarikh-i-Firuz Shahi*; translated in William Theodore de Bary et al. (compilers), *Sources of Indian Tradition*. New York: Columbia University Press, 1958, pp. 521–2.

3 S. H. Askari (trans.), 'The correspondence of two fourteenth century Sufi saints of Bihar with the contemporary sovereigns of Delhi and Bengal', *Journal of the Bihar Research Society*, 42, 1956, p. 187.

CHAPTER 4: EARLY MODERN INDIA

1 'Abd ul-Qadir Badauni, *Muntakhab ut-Tawarikh*, II; translated in William Theodore de Bary et al. (compilers), *Sources of Indian Tradition*. New York: Columbia University Press, 1958, pp. 439–40.

2 Declaration of Akbar's status as judge. Ibid., pp. 507–8.

3 Muhsin-i-Fani, *Dabistan-i-Mazahib*; 443.

4 Abul Fazl, *Ain-i-Akbari*; 505.

5 From Hasrat, *Dara Shikoh*; translated in William Theodore de Bary et al., op. cit., n. 1, pp. 446–8.

6 N. Banhatti (ed.), *Ajnapatra*. Poona, 1974; translated in Andre Wink, *Land and Sovereignty in India*. Cambridge: Cambridge University Press, 1986, p. 186.

CHAPTER 5: THE EAST INDIA COMPANY

1   *The Laws of Manu*, VIII, 415; translated by Georg Buhler, Vol. XXV, *The Sacred Books of the East*. Oxford: Clarendon Press, 1886.
2   Extract from the charge, Parliamentary Papers, 1828, Vol. 24, pp. 9–10.
3   20 June 1774, Bengal Revenue Consultations Legislative Report No. 351.
4   Raja Rammohun Roy, 'A second conference between an advocate for, and an opponent of, the practice of burning widows alive', in *English Works, Part III* (ed. Kalidas Nag and Debajyoti Burman). Calcutta: Sadharan Brahmo Samaj, 1945, pp. 26–7.
5   Petition to Lord William Bentinck against Regulation XVII of 1929, printed in A. F. Salahuddin Ahmed, *Social Ideas and Social Change in Bengal, 1818–1835*. Leiden: E. J. Brill, 1965, p. 176.
6   London, Public Record Office, Privy Council Registers (PC 2), 7 July 1832.

CHAPTER 6: THE CROWN REPLACES THE COMPANY

1   From *Madras Secret Proceedings*, 25 August 1825, vol. 103, pp. 305–408. Quoted in Burton Stein, *Thomas Munro*. Delhi: Oxford University Press, 1989, pp. 290–1.
2   In W. Theodore de Bary (ed.), *Sources of Indian Tradition, Vol. II*. New York: Columbia University Press, 1958, pp. 44–5.
3   Raja Rammohun Roy, 'A letter on English education', in *English Works*, Part IV (ed. Kalidas Nag and Debajyoti Burman). Calcutta: Sadharan Brahmo Samaj, 1945, pp. 33–6.
4   Pundita Ramabai Sarasvati, *The High-caste Hindu Woman*. London: George Bell, 1888, p. 52.

CHAPTER 7: TOWARDS FREEDOM

1   *Harijan*, 19 December 1936.
2   Nalin Vilochan Sharma, 'A biography of Jagjivan Ram', *The Working Man*. Patna: Jagjivan Ram Abinandan Granth Committee, 1957, p. 83.
3   Partha Mitter, *Art and Nationalism in Colonial India, 1850–1922*. Cambridge: Cambridge University Press, 1994, p. 170.
4   *Harijan*, 12 December 1936.
5   M. K. Gandhi, *Satyagraha in South Africa*. Ahmedabad: Navajivan Publishing House, 1928, p. 245; translated by Valji Govind Desai.
6   *Harijan*, 7 July 1946.

CHAPTER 8: GANDHI'S TRIUMPH

1   C. Ragagopalachari, *Ambedkar Refuted*. Bombay: Hind Kitab, 1946, p. 14.
2   28 March 1930, Thakurdas Papers, Nehru Memorial Museum Library, Delhi. Quoted in A. D. D. Gordon, *Businessmen and Politics*. Canberra, 1978, p. 202.

CHAPTER 9: NEW STATES, OLD NATIONS

1   *Young India*, 26 August 1926.

BURTON STEIN (1 AUGUST 1926 TO 26 APRIL 1996)

Burton Stein wrote in his introduction to this book that it was intended to be:

> taken not as a recording of events as they sequentially unfolded in real time but rather as an accounting. In the first instance, it is an account of how that part of humankind that has inhabited the Indian subcontinent devised ways of coping with the variable habitats of its landform, of the ideas and institutions they invented to give shape and continuity to their societies, and how they exploited opportunities and coped with threats from beyond their land, often by incorporating threatening outsiders.
>
> But there is another accounting to be made as well: my own view of that long, complex history. That is the outcome of a complex of knowledge, experience, and sentiments that have shaped my present attitudes and understanding of the history of the Indian subcontinent and influenced my evaluation of older historical views of events and processes as well as the newer interpretations that have not yet received much attention.

Burt did not live to complete his accounting, and it was left to others to prepare this work for publication. In particular, a concluding chapter was never written, and we can only guess what it might have contained from the book itself and various published and unpublished papers and talks he delivered during its preparation. But, in addition, we have the impressions of a number of his colleagues who have followed his writings with interest, with whom he engaged in so many informal debates and discussions over the decades of his working life, and who have themselves influenced his thinking.

On 17 September 1996, a workshop was held at the School of Oriental and African Studies in London, where several of his colleagues presented papers in the course of which they reflected on the evolution of his historical approach and on his own influence on the field of Indian studies. The following are excerpts from several of the papers presented there.

From David Washbrook (Centre for Indian Studies, St Antony's College, Oxford University):

However it was exactly formulated, the notion that colonialism fundamentally broke the pattern of the Indian past was virtually axiomatic. This was an axiom which, at many different levels, Burt's work was concerned to challenge. Not, of course, that he didn't consider colonialism to represent a significant intervention which changed the contours of Indian history, but rather that his research trajectory from medieval times gave him a sense that it was an intervention into something that was already going on, possessed its own dynamics and energies and wasn't going to be stopped by a handful of white men in funny hats. Rather, although re-contextualized, South India's historical past continued to inform and, in many ways, to direct the possibilities of change in the colonial period itself. South Indian society in the nineteenth and twentieth centuries owed at least as much to its own local inheritances as to whatever was imposed upon it by Britain and 'the West'.

Burt's perspectives on South India over the '*longue durée*', of course, derived from a research focus which was as broad in time as it was narrow in space. There can be very few historians whose work spans fifteen centuries and yet remains engaged, the whole time, with one relatively small geographical area. Burt knew his South India 'longitudinally' like few historians have ever known any other place.

He was, it should be said, helped by a rich tradition of prior scholarship, which, perhaps because of the unique nature of its source materials, created possibilities for a depth of study rarely found elsewhere. The great heritage of South Indian epigraphy opens up visions on a past containing not only kings, emperors and gods, but also castes, peoples and, above all, communities. However, to engage the latter from these sources also requires a rare kind of genius.

In this context, I think, Burt's own genius was distinctively 'modernist' in inspiration – which is what separated him from most of his peers working in the medieval period. He refused to accept the then-prevailing conventions (which today might be associated with Orientalism) that the medieval past was 'made' by the prescriptive force of depersonalized systems of 'civilization', 'culture' and religious belief. He insisted that it should be shown – as was more conventional in 'modern' history – being made by self-conscious people themselves, through their interactions first with nature and then with each other.

The inadequacies of much received Marxist historiography – based on a social process of capitalism which is supposed to lead to a deepening polarization between 'capitalists' and 'proletarians' – are obvious enough and, of themselves, no doubt account for the abandonment of the paradigm by most historians today. But this abandonment has also involved virtually vacating the entire ground which Marxist history sought to occupy and giving up the very attempt to explain and theorize about just what – if not this – capitalism might mean for, and do to, the relations and structures of society. Burt, in his last years, was, I think, trying to reinstate some of these 'big' questions once again.

In particular, his work on South India drew attention to the extent to which the 'petty bourgeoisie' – the residual class in Marxist theory – actually were, if not the dominant, then the most general class under colonial and post-colonial conditions of capitalism. In the nineteenth and twentieth centuries South India's experience has been that of the proliferation – not contraction – of 'small property'.

Burt's last original research project was very much concerned to explore and explain how this happened – and what it might mean for the social relations both of India and of the global capital which produced it. He did not get all that far with his project, certainly not as far as he would have wanted, but he was moving, I think, in some very interesting directions, which it seems to me several other scholars are now starting to follow as they take back from post-modernism the challenge to which it aspired but failed to meet, namely that of providing a more coherent understanding of our own times.

Burt's work on the petty bourgeoisie also figured in his own response and counter to post-modernism in another way. Besides vacating thinking about the historical specificities of capitalism, post-modernism also vacated thinking about the connections between the material and cultural universes, which Burt also regarded as critical and wished to reinstate. His own work on the petty bourgeoisie was related to locating, among other things, the material bases of Indian 'communalism' and 'populist' political culture. In a society based upon the concrete individualisms of 'small property', how might one conjure up any sense of 'community' and even of 'society'?

What Burt was ultimately going to make of all this, we shall never know. But here, as in so many other parts of his work, it was not where his ideas ultimately went that was so important, but rather it was where they began and what, in all sorts of ways, they sparked off.

From Christopher J. Fuller (Department of Anthropology, London School of Economics and Political Science):

Stein warned his students that historians should not become 'retrospective anthropologists' and he saw anthropology, like, for example, economics, as a source of different ideas for doing history. The principal specific example of such an idea is the concept of the 'segmentary state', adopted in the mid-1970s and used in *Peasant State and Society*. This was a sophisticated borrowing from the rather sophisticated political anthropology of Africa developed by British social anthropology; social anthropology was apparently more congenial to Stein than American cultural anthropology at that time. In more general terms, Stein was influenced by and knowledgeable about anthropology and ethnography because his model of the south Indian state depended on an analysis of local society (hence of caste, kinship, village economy and politics) and of religion and ritual symbolism; none of these issues preoccupied macro-political historians, who were mostly ignorant of anthropological evidence. Anthropology gave Stein some weapons to attack such historians.

In his work on temples and *inams*, Stein's interest in cultural anthropology became more explicit, though it was obviously present throughout *Peasant State and Society*. In 1983, Stein (with Tony Good and myself) organized a South Asian Anthropologists' Group conference on history and anthropology: Stein's paper, 'Does culture make practice perfect?', referred to the modern persistence of medieval values and ideologies, and to cultural understandings as deeply inflected by earlier meanings; 'culture' was described as an active ideological framing from the past. Stein was using the language of modern cultural anthropology even if he treated cultural meanings as 'ideology'.

I think that by the late 1980s Stein's sympathy for anthropology had declined. However, I am sure that in his continual engagement with anthropology, Stein was much more critically aware than most scholars of the pitfalls of interdisciplinary work. Stein owed quite a lot to anthropology, but he remained fully a historian.

From Christopher A. Bayly (St Catharine's College, Cambridge University):

Burt wrote explicitly in the introduction to his *Thomas Munro* that his early south Indian intellectual interests were aroused by issues of village-level development. The 'wet zone' and 'dry zone', with their appropriate 'wet' and 'dry' types of peasant which appear in his *Peasant State and Society*, were shaped out of his early fieldwork experience. In his historical work he tended to emphasize the small scale: local systems of power and influence, dominant lineages and peasant *nadus*. These were clearly the real social contexts for the long-term mobilization of productive processes in Indian rural society.

Like that of most American academics of the 1950s and 1960s, Burt's work was covertly anti-neo-colonial and overtly anti-colonial in spirit. Burt adopted a Marxist politics which sometimes sat rather uneasily with his emphasis on objectified 'culture'. Much of his earlier theoretical work arose, then, from the attempt to get behind colonial categories of society to discover what were the real unities, the real political and social structures which might have fostered or impeded development. Chola and post-Chola kingship in Burt's work is a structure of legitimacy governed mainly by extended kinship and ritual. The great novelty of Burt's south Indian work was to adapt models which had been used to describe tribal and unsettled societies to peasant societies and ones with literate cultural specialists. Of course, the dominant warrior castes of the north and the Mughal royal centre had no absolute analogies in the south.

One of Burt's outstanding qualities was his tenacity in following up the issue of pre-colonial change and trying to characterize in detail the new order introduced into India by colonialism. This was, paradoxically, because he was always interested in the origin of the present. His concern was with the question: when, why and how did a particular version of the modern state and a particular version of capitalism become established in south Asia?

Thus the long unchanging ages of south Indian *nadus* and peasant states in Burt's early work themselves buckled and took on new form in his later writings. In time, he began to give a picture of significant change in state structures, commerce and rural society. This gradual shift of perspective had by last year given him a clear contextual history of south Asia which stretched from the Cholas and their north Indian equivalents to the present day.

The story would have gone something like this. Society in the five hundred years after the decline of the Cholas was unchanging for a number of interrelated reasons. As far as the economy of everyday life was concerned, a probable slow increase in population, expanding settlement patterns, the creeping expansion of wet zone agriculture into the uplands and plains, gradually created a peasant elite which was able to invest, trade and determine the form of the loose state structures which were emerging contemporaneously. Later, after about 1500, the expansion of external commerce and the inflow of precious metals into some centres consolidated the development of an integrated merchant order throughout south and central India. Corporate forms of holding and storing wealth vitiated the control of even the most powerful lineages. The continuing importance of ritual prestige, particularly in relation to temples, shot through class relations with different and divisive assumptions.

The second motor behind these changes was the extractive polity, and this became clearer as Burt began to try to account for Vijayanagara and the Nayakas. At first he had been unwilling to place too much importance on the phenomenon of state centralization. He saw the emphasis on 'Muhammadan invasion' as a hangover from the old imperialist and, worse, Hindu nationalist historiography. But by the later 1980s, the 'sultanist state' had become a major actor in his work. While this entity probably remained 'segmentary' in some respects, and certainly continued to include people across the lines of caste, language and religion, it did have horses and sophisticated weapons. Moreover, its rituals of state incorporation through *durbars*, the giving and taking of silver and gold, feeding brahmins and symbolic city-building were very expensive. For Burt, by the time that he wrote his *Vijayanagara* for the New Cambridge History series, Vijayanagar and the Nayakas had become economically constituted states, with fiscal policies and strategies of conquest. Previously, in *Peasant State*, they had seemed more like the slowly moving avatars of the Chola *nadus*.

Burt, as I said at the beginning, was always concerned to account for the present, and his problematique had taken him from the village-level development of the 1960s, through the ryotwari settlement of *Munro* back to the tenth century. In his last years he made that historical pilgrimage in the opposite direction. Just as the pressure of the northern sultanates had galvanized the segmentary states of the south into the economic, if not yet the political, base for military fiscalism, so the appearance of an even more intrusive and revenue-hungry state in the form of the East India Company forced one further pre-colonial adaptation. At least in the case of the Mysore sultans, Burt thought, south India had spawned a military-fiscal state where revenue extraction was implanted through a body of centrally controlled officials. Of course, this effort foundered on the contradiction between the fiscal demands of the centre and the need to generate resources in the lineage-dominated segments of the periphery. But the effort did decisively shape large parts of south Indian society and provided some of the tools with which the British were to hammer into shape a new and yet more intrusive state power.

Ultimately, the most striking thing about Burt, a quality that he displayed more than any other recent historian, was his ability to move easily from the cultural detail of regional societies to the broader framework of world history. His intellectual and social concerns will continue to inform our field well beyond our present generation, and the international upsurge of ethnic conflict and the social consequences of economic neo-liberalism will continue to return us again and again to the questions underlying Burton Stein's work.

Books by Burton Stein referred to above:

Peasant State and Society in Medieval South India. Delhi: Oxford University Press, 1980.

Thomas Munro, the Origins of the Colonial State and his Vision of Empire. Delhi: Oxford University Press, 1989.

The New Cambridge History of India, Volume I.2: Vijayanagara. Cambridge: Cambridge University Press, 1989.

INDEX

Note: This index should be used in conjunction with other tables in this volume: contents, persons, glossary, chronologies. Thus, full names will be found in persons. Items listed in the contents are generally not indexed for the sections listed. Thus, 'India' is not indexed; 'Gandhi' is not indexed for Chapter 8; (English) East India Company is not indexed for Chapter 5. (That's the theory.) Plurals (names usually ending in 's') indicate families (e.g. Guptas), castes (brahmans), other national or subnational groupings (e.g. Aryans) or institutions (e.g. dharmashastras, iqtas, janapadas). Languages (often ending in 'i') indicate either the language itself or its speakers.